ALCOHOLISM
Interdisciplinary Approaches to an Enduring Problem

ALCOHOLISM

Interdisciplinary Approaches to an Enduring Problem

Edited by

RALPH E. TARTER and A. ARTHUR SUGERMAN

Carrier Clinic Foundation, Belle Mead, New Jersey
Rutgers Medical School
Graduate School of Applied and Professional Psychology,
Rutgers University, Piscataway, New Jersey

1976

Addison-Wesley Publishing Company
Advanced Book Program
Reading, Massachusetts
London · Amsterdam · Don Mills, Ontario · Sydney · Tokyo

Library of Congress Cataloging in Publication Data
Main entry under title:

Alcoholism : interdisciplinary approaches to an enduring problem.

Includes index.
1. Alcoholism--Addresses, essays, lectures. 2. Alcohol--Physiological effect--Addresses, essays, lectures. 3. Alcoholism--Treatment--Addresses, essays, lectures. I. Tarter, Ralph E. II. Sugerman, A. Arthur.
HV5035.A47 362.2'92 76-12551
ISBN 0-201-08146-6
ISBN 0-201-08145-8 pbk.

Reproduced by Addison-Wesley Publishing Company, Inc., Advanced Book Program, Reading, Massachusetts, from camera-ready copy prepared by the office of the editors.

Manufactured in the United States of America

ABCDEFGHIJ-HA-79876

Contents

PART II

PROCESSES IN ALCOHOLISM

List of Contributors

Remi J. Cadoret, M.D. Professor of Psychiatry, The University of Iowa Hospitals and Clinics, Iowa City, Iowa.

Don Cahalan, Ph.D. Professor of Behavioral Sciences in Residence, School of Public Health, University of California, Berkeley, California.

Ira H. Cisin, Ph.D. Professor of Sociology, The George Washington University, Washington, D.C.

Jonathan Cole, M.D. McLean Hospital, Belmont Massachusetts.

David L. Davies, D.M. Medical Director, Alcohol Education Center, Maudsley Hospital, London, England. Formerly, Dean of the Institute of Psychiatry, University of London.

George P. Dominick, B.D. Inpatient Unit Director, Alcohol and Drug Specialty Unit, Georgia Mental Health Institute, Atlanta, Georgia.

Douglas H. Fehr, Ph.D. Associate Professor, Department of Psychiatry and Behavioral Sciences, The University of Oklahoma Health Sciences Center, Oklahoma City, Oklahoma.

Gerhard Freund, M.D. Chief, Endocrinology Section, Veteran's Administration Hospital; Professor of Medicine, University of Florida College of Medicine, Gainesville, Florida.

Edith S. Gomberg, Ph.D. Professor, School of Social Work, University of Michigan, Ann Arbor, Michigan.

Donald W. Goodwin, M.D. Professor of Psychiatry, Washington University, School of Medicine, St. Louis, Missouri.

Milton M. Gross, M.D. Professor of Psychiatry; Director, Division of Alcoholism, Department of Psychiatry, State University of New York, Downstate Medical Center, Brooklyn, New York.

John M. Hastey, M.S. Co-Director, Sleep Laboratory, Department of Psychiatry, Downstate Medical Center, Brooklyn, New York.

Helmut Hoffman, Ph.D. Director, Alcohol and Drug Unit, and Director of Research, Willmar State Hospital, Willmar, Minnesota.

Ben M. Jones, Ph.D. Assistant Professor of Psychiatry and Behavioral Sciences, University of Oklahoma Health Sciences Center; Associate Director, Oklahoma Center for Alcohol and Drug related Studies, Oklahoma City, Oklahoma.

Mark A. Korsten, M.D. Investigator, Alcohol Research Laboratory, Bronx Veteran's Administration Hospital; Instructor of Medicine, Mt. Sinai School of Medicine, City University of New York, Bronx, New York.

Charles S. Lieber, M.D. Chief, Alcohol Research Laboratory, Bronx Veteran's Administration Hospital; Professor of Medicine, Mt. Sinai School of Medicine, City University of New York, Bronx, New York.

Stephen A. Lisman, Ph.D. Assistant Professor, Department of Psychology, State University of New York at Binghamton, Binghamton, New York.

Donald E. Meeks, D.S.W. Associate Director, Clinical Institute Alcoholism and Drug Addiction Foundation of Ontario; Professor of Social Work, Faculty of Social Work, University of Toronto, Toronto, Canada.

Peter M. Miller, Ph.D. Associate Professor and Director, Psychology Training Program, Department of Psychiatry and Human Behavior University of Mississippi Medical Center, Jackson, Mississippi.

Peter E. Nathan, Ph.D. Professor and Director, Alcohol Behavior Research Laboratory, Rutgers University, New Brunswick, New Jersey.

John L. Norris, M.D. Chairman, Board of Trustees, Alcoholics Anonymous, New London, New Hampshire.

Alfonso Paredes, M.D. Professor of Psychiatry and Behavioral Sciences; Director, Oklahoma Center for Alcohol and Drug Related Studies, University of Oklahoma Health Sciences Center, Oklahoma City, Oklahoma.

Oscar A. Parsons, Ph.D. Professor of Psychiatry and Behavioral Sciences, University of Oklahoma Health Sciences Center, Oklahoma City, Oklahoma.

Orvis H. Rundell, Ph.D. Adjunct Assistant Professor of Psychiatry and Behavioral Sciences, University of Oklahoma Health Sciences Center, Oklahoma City, Oklahoma.

Ralph S. Ryback, M.D. Director of Alcohol and Drug Abuse Services, McLean Hospital, Belmont, Massachusetts, and Assistant Professor of Psychiatry, Harvard Medical School.

Dorothea U. Schneider, B.A. University of Wisconsin-Milwaukee, Milwaukee, Wisconsin.

Richard Stivers, Ph.D. Assistant Professor of Sociology, Illinois State University, Normal, Illinois.

A. Arthur Sugerman, M.D.,Med.D.Sc. Director of Research, Carrier Clinic Foundation, Belle Mead, New Jersey, and Clinical Associate Professor of Psychiatry, Rutgers Medical School; Contributing Faculty, Graduate School of Applied and Professional Psychology, Rutgers University, Piscataway, New Jersey.

Ralph E. Tarter, Ph.D. Carrier Clinic Foundation, Belle Mead, New Jersey Clinical Assistant Professor of Psychiatry Rutgers Medical School; Contributing Faculty, Graduate School of Applied and Professional Psychology, Rutgers University, Piscataway, N.J.

Archer Tongue, M.D. Director, International Council on Alcohol and Addictions, Lausanne, Switzerland.

Preface

In recent years alcoholism has become a field of great interest to science, government, industry, and the helping professions. Society has become aware of the tremendous cost and burden of suffering which has followed so many years of neglect and indifference to the problem of alcoholism.

Research has proceeded on many fronts and involved many disciplines. Not only has there been a concerted effort in the biomedical and social sciences, but direct action is being taken in such disparate areas as management, criminology, and the legislature to implement treatment for the afflicted. Striking advances in basic research, particularly in such disciplines as genetics, metabolism, behavioral analysis, and epidemiology have helped to dispel commonly-held assumptions about this complex disorder.

We have attempted to make available in a single volume the present state of knowledge of the causes, processes, and treatment of alcoholism. Our approach has been eclectic, and we have not tried to reconcile differences of orientation between different authors. This book is intended to offer to those active in research and treatment a broad view of the many factors and levels of discourse in the field, which in turn may lead to wider involvement in research and rehabilitation programming.

What emerges from a reading of this volume is that alcoholism is not simply a disease but an array of disorders of similar topography. The causes of alcoholism are multiple and involve a complex and little understood interaction between genetics and environment. Its manifestations are similarly multifaceted, directly or indirectly affecting most systems of the body. Psychological impairment, social ostracism, crime, family disintegration, and absenteeism are among the most readily observed overt manifestations. The number and variations of treatment strategies reflect the current state of our attempts at rehabilitation.

To present an up-to-date and thorough presentation of every topic is not feasible for a single volume. Our primary objective is to give the reader a perspective of the subject matter so that a critical appreciation of techniques and current directions in research can be achieved. Furthermore, we made a strong effort to recruit scholars from the international arena so as not to bias or constrict the field of view.

We have organized the material so that the reader might be aware of techniques and treatment pertinent to his areas of interest. For example, although such topics as alcoholism in industry, in schools, and the professions have not been considered specifically, the various chapters supply the multidisciplinary framework and techniques of investigation in these areas of concern. Other subjects, although not dealt with separately, are covered where they relate to the topics of a number of chapters. For instance, nutrition is considered under the headings of nervous system disorders, sleep, psychiatric manifestations, pharmacology, and psychological deficits.

Our thanks are due to many persons who gave their time or supported our work. In particular we thank Dr. Henry Murphree for editorial consultation, Lawrence Klein for ready assistance, and Sharon Tarter for her help in preparing the Index. Cynthia Sansom functioned as editorial assistant; her work made ours possible. Wanda Czarcinski had the heavy responsibility of preparing the manuscript here reproduced; her commitment and initiative were invaluable. Special gratitude is offered to Paul Cameron, President of the Carrier Clinic Foundation, and Robert S. Garber, M.D., Secretary of the Foundation, for their support and dedication to research and education in mental health, which enabled us to undertake the preparation of this work. And finally the editors invite readers to comment on how this book has met their specific needs and to make suggestions for future progress. While we have given the authors as much flexibility as possible in presenting a chosen balance between theory, data, and speculation, we have above all endeavored to structure their chapters so that an appreciation of the breadth of the subject can be acquired along with factual content.

Acknowledgment

We gratefully acknowledge permission extended to us by the Association for Research in Nervous and Mental Disease and Dr. M. Victor to reproduce Figure 2 in Chapter 5.

INTRODUCTION

Archer Tongue

The title of this book aptly describes its subject as an enduring problem. Alcoholic beverages have been used continuously from the earliest periods of recorded history. Their value in social life in promoting good fellowship and relaxing men's tensions has been recognized in primitive and developed societies throughout the world. There is every indication at the present time that, in spite of the introduction in recent years of many other substances into the range of drugs available for social use, alcohol consumption has not substantially decreased anywhere. In fact, it seems to be penetrating cultures hitherto maintaining strong sanctions against its use, such as the Moslem and Buddhist worlds, and to encounter no barriers of age, sex, race, or political system.

However, throughout history man has been perplexed by

Ralph E. Tarter and A. Arthur Sugerman (eds.), Alcoholism

ISBN: 0-201-08146-6
ISBN: 0-201-08145-8 (pbk.)

the apparent contradictions involved in the use of alcohol as a beverage. While possessing the positive values aforementioned, the use of alcohol in society has been accompanied by excess in the form of drunken behavior or compulsive drinking manifesting what now is termed alcohol dependence. This bewilderment at the apparently contrasting values of alcohol, on the one hand an enhancer of social life and on the other a danger to health and well-being, has been at the root of man's ambivalent attitude to drunken behavior. This ambivalence, characterized by amusement at one time and disgust at another, mirrors the age-old dilemma posed by alcohol use. Resulting from this situation many societies throughout history have attempted to regulate alcohol consumption in the interests of society's welfare with little conspicuous success. It was due to pioneers at the end of the eighteenth and during the nineteenth century that a change in the approach to this perennial problem emerged. Men like Benjamin Rush in America, Thomas Trotter in Scotland, and Magnus Huss in Sweden laid the foundations of a scientific and medical approach to alcoholism. Although these pioneer efforts led to recognition of alcoholism as a health or medico-social problem in a number of countries in the second half of the nineteenth century with the consequent establishment of some facilities for the treatment of alcoholic persons, the belief that control methods could solve the problems of alcohol in society was still the belief of the majority.

Consequently measures such as prohibition, state control, licensing systems in many variants, continued to be operated with little lasting success. It was not until thirty years ago that the concept of alcoholism as a health question really revived on the international scene. Due in large measure to the impetus given by the World Health Organization's acceptance of alcoholism in its program towards the end of the nineteen-forties, the setting up of alcoholism services in country after country developed and continues at the present day.

Today we may rightly feel a certain cause for satisfaction in that over the last quarter-century more and more persons having drinking problems have been brought into alcoholism treatment programs and that facilities to help the alcoholic person, supplemented by Alcoholics Anonymous and kindred bodies, are to be found all over the world. Moreover, the stigma formerly attached to the person suffering from alcoholism is gradually being removed. Naturally, in this area progress differs according to country and traditions.

What is not so reassuring is the world-wide situation relative to the prevention of alcoholism. In spite of many programs of alcohol education in numerous countries, there is no evidence of a significant diminution of the problem anywhere. Indeed, as indicated earlier, the alcohol consumption would appear to be on the increase almost everywhere. Up to now the educational and informational approaches utilized have been based on varying concepts. These have involved presentation of the facts about alcohol with strong emphasis on the value of abstinence or strict moderation, warning-sign education on the dangers of alcoholism as an illness, the encouragement of healthy drinking habits to mention only some of the concepts prevailing. The lack of success in this important area of prevention could be attributed to the fact that in spite of considerable research carried on over the years in numerous countries, the gaps in our knowledge about alcoholism are still significant and frustrating. The etiology of alcoholism is a case in point. Why some persons who use alcohol become dependent on it and others remain social drinkers all their lives is a question of obvious fundamental importance. A clear concept and definition of alcoholism are badly needed in an educational presentation of the subject, but up to now lack of agreement among specialists in the field is illustrated by the varying concepts and attempts at definition. The opening chapters of this book shed valuable light on these aspects of the problem.

One does not want here to go into the question as to whether alcoholism is a disease or illness. Suffice it to say that the disease formulation has been of unquestioned pragmatic value in transferring alcoholism from the moralistic, judgmental area to that of health.

Also of interest internationally is the allied question of whether there is really a so-called "French" or "Latin" alcoholism as distinct from the Anglo-Saxon type. In other words is the latter, stressing alcoholism as a symptom of personality disorder needing treatment of a psychiatric or psychological type, the real alcoholism? Or is the other concept of alcoholism, an excessive daily intake of alcohol over a number of years without personality disorder resulting in liver cirrhosis and other physical damage to the individual, also valid? These two emphases which have been discernible during the last decades have important bearing on the basis of educational programs.

The contrast can be seen very distinctly when the informational material of the government and private bodies concerned with alcoholism in the United States of America and France are examined. The American emphasis the past twenty-five years has been on alcoholism as a disease and the need to encourage the sufferer to be able to recognize his illness and to seek early advice and treatment. In France the emphasis has been on advising the citizen to be moderate in his consumption and to watch over his drinking habits. This view is based on the belief that individual over-consumption will make the person more vulnerable to alcohol related illness and alcoholism. It is interesting to note that the development of a concern to encourage "responsible" drinking in the U.S.A. in recent years is not so far removed from the French concept. In any case one would feel that educational programs could very appropriately combine the two approaches. Any adequate educational program must be concerned both with those who already have an alcohol problem and with the majority of the population who do not have the problem but need advice on how to evaluate their own drinking habits. Behavioral and motivational patterns are clearly an important subject of research since without understanding of these any educational approach will surely be incomplete.

To return to the area of treatment and rehabilitation of the alcoholic person, a priority is the stimulation of epidemiological research. The determination of the alcoholic population in any country or region is desirable when decisions have to be taken concerning the setting up of treatment programs whether public or private. Unfortunately the definitional basis for statistical estimation of alcoholism frequency varies considerably. Since the epidemiological approach is obviously an imperative in developing adequate treatment facilities, it is necessary to provide the epidemiologist in the alcoholism field with a reasonably clear-cut definition of the population he is required to assess. It is not only, therefore, in the educational field that definition is required. The position may be taken, of course, that the alcoholic person has been helped and must continue to be helped without waiting for a precise definition of his condition. While accepting this, the practical considerations mentioned above as well as others, such as the definition of incapacity due to alcoholism for sickness insurance purposes, demand continuing interdisciplinary research to arrive at a satisfactory operational definition of alcoholism or alcohol dependence and alcohol related problems.

One interesting phenomenon to be observed is the surprising variety of facilities which exist at the present time throughout the world to help the person having alcohol problems. These include units in psychiatric and general hospitals and clinics, specialized hospitals, consultation and information bureaus, sobering-up stations, acute intoxication treatment centers and emergency care units, hangover clinics, day hospitals, therapeutic communities, half-way houses, hostels, impaired driving programs, short-term and long-term residential programs, mobile clinics, Alcoholics Anonymous, Alcoholics Clubs, and similar associations for recovered alcoholics.

The role of the community is crucial to the impact which any society makes on its alcohol problem. Insufficiency of services as well as overlapping of agencies concerned with the problem are both to be avoided in any community. The community may well ask, however, what is the most effective and economically viable modality of treatment and type of service. This poses the need for evaluation of the different types of facility referred to above. Research in this case will not only be of practical value to communities in industrialized countries, but will be invaluable for the developing countries where programs do not exist and where the economic sources of support are extremely limited.

It is fitting that this book should terminate with a chapter on family therapy. The environment of the alcoholic person and his or her interaction with those who compose it must be taken into account in any thorough treatment program. It is often stated that the life of one alcoholic person impinges on and affects a given number of other persons. It is clear that the relation of the patient or client, however we may wish to describe him or her, with the family is such that the involvement of family members in the treatment and rehabilitation process is a logical and desirable procedure.

It is evident that in modern society alcoholism and alcohol related problems can only be satisfactorily approached on an interdisciplinary basis. The historical experience alluded to earlier underlines this approach. There are a wide range of disciplines involved - medicine, sociology, social work, biochemistry and pharmacology, epidemiology, jurisprudence, administration, economics, and history to mention only some. It may seem unnecessary to dwell on this point in a volume where the title indicates this approach. However, in the past too often, lip-service has been paid to the principle of interdisciplinary cooperation without the reality existing. It is to be hoped that this book will reinforce the urgency of active participation of the disciplines in a cooperative endeavor to tackle some of the basic enduring problems connected with man's use of alcoholic beverages.

Over a period of seventy years or more some nations such as the Scandinavian countries and Switzerland have developed a defined national alcohol policy. This has been built up on the theory that problems of alcoholism cannot be compartmentalized. In other words treatment, education, law enforcement, traffic safety, agriculture programs, taxation, production, retail distribution, control systems, etc. involve policies which must be harmonized in the interest of the public health and well-being of the people. In some countries, such as Finland, this has led to the financing of research, treatment, and prevention, from income accruing from the production and sale of alcoholic beverages themselves. What is vital however is that all authorities concerned in some way with problems involving alcohol should be associated in a national body whose task is to formulate an alcohol policy to the best interest of the nation. An interdisciplinary advisory panel is naturally an eminently desirable part of such a body's functioning. In this way the decision makers have access to interdisciplinary knowledge and experience and contact with the different areas of research. Only with such an interdepartmental, interdisciplinary approach can an effective national policy directed to all citizens and encompassing the whole area of alcohol consumption and its resulting problems be structured.

Alcohol would seem to be the preferred social drug or, at any rate, the most used in the majority of countries. We can assume that this situation is not likely to change in the foreseeable future. The task everywhere is to find adequate means to limit or contain the harm to which such usage will give rise. The issues which this book discusses are essential elements in a constructive approach to the problem.

Part 1

Orientation and Perspective

CHAPTER 1

THE HISTORY OF THE CONCEPT OF ALCOHOLISM

Alfonso Paredes

It is of practical importance to examine the historical development of the theoretical constructs that define the problems that affect our society. The redundancy of our conceptual efforts does not seem to inhibit their translation into social action. When empirical data are unavailable or insufficient to anchor our ideas in a valid position, our formulations oscillate between distant points. We abandon one position, at a given moment in history, returning to it later as the moods of the scholars and, occasionally, valid information demand. Paraphrasing Chaslin's aphorism "*chacun fait de l' alcoholisme a sa façon*," we may say that throughout the years, scholars and lay people have defined alcohol-related problems in their own way, depending on the time, fashions, and their personal inclinations (Barbé, 1950).

Those engaged in scientific pursuits seldom picture themselves as social activists. In reality, their cogitations

Ralph E. Tarter and A. Arthur Sugerman (eds.), Alcoholism

ISBN: 0-201-08146-6
ISBN: 0-201-08145-8 (pbk.)

and definitions of problems often lead to political action. Observations or validated empirical data organized along particular conceptual framework are often picked up by the public and translated into political decisions. On the other hand, there is a marked contrast between the level of technical knowledge available to master a problem and the nature of the social action aimed at the same problem. For these reasons it will be useful to review some of the prevailing concepts of alcoholism and the attempts at social control that resulted or coexisted with these formulations. My review will be selective to honor limitations of space. I will refer primarily to the American scene and to events which have occurred within the last two centuries, which are the most accessible to me. The consequences of American experiments usually extend to other nations. In limiting myself to the recent American scene, I do not underestimate the sagacity and importance of early contributions from abroad to our understanding of alcoholism. The ancients made interesting observations about the problem. Seneca (4 B.C. - 65 A.D.) maintained that the word *drunken* refers to two situations: in one case to that of a man who is loaded with wine and has no control of himself; in the other to that of a man who is accustomed to getting drunk and is a slave to the habit (Seneca, 1942). This is perhaps one of the earliest distinctions made between a person who drinks heavily and a person who is addicted to alcohol.

A few basic conceptual models may be identified in the views of physicians and scientists presented through the various historical periods. Some of them have conceptualized the problem which we now call alcoholism as an expression of the free will of individuals or the result of transcendental influences on the person. For others, alcoholism is a psychological response to experiential stresses related to developmental factors, distorted early relationships, or poor interpersonal communication. Alcoholism also has been understood as learned behavior or as an epiphenomenon of disturbances in the social system. One more model views alcoholism as a disorder much like any other medical disease with a biological dysfunction of the brain and other organs (Lazare, 1973). A more detailed discussion of these models may be found in chapter 3.

ALCOHOL AND ALCOHOLISM IN EARLY AMERICA

The use of alcoholic beverages was an important activity during the birth and early development of the United States of America. It would be negligent to omit references to drinking, to the concept of inebriety, and to the social controls utilized to regulate this problem in any discussion of these historical moments. Stanley Baron (1962) has noted that "to speak of the origins of brewing (beer) in America, is to speak of the origins of the nation itself." The early colonists, cheered by beer and singing Dayton's merry ballad, "And ours to hold Virginia, earth's only paradise," boarded the ships Susan, Constant, Godspeed, and Discovery on December 20, 1606. Once in America, low morale compromised the very existence of the first colony. In particular, the colonists sadly complained that "our drinke was water." Drinking water, they lamented, was "contrary to the nature of the English." Providentially, Lord Delaware assured abundant supplies, and a new company of settlers delivered "the First

Supply," which arrived from England in a ship under the command of Captain Christopher Newport. Naturally, beer was among its provisions. The London Company advertised in 1609 for two brewers to be sent to improve the morale of the colony. A few years later, in 1620, an important chapter of the history of America began when the Mayflower, threatened by terrifying shoals and with "our victuals much spent, especially beer..." had to drop anchor in Cape Cod (Provincetown) harbor (Morrison, 1965).

Drinking alcoholic beverages was one of the facts of daily life of early New England. Increase Mather, an early colonist, was reported to say in 1673, "Drink is in itself a creature of God." It was, indeed, a very prominent creature in New England's daily life, trade, and local economy. The New Englanders consumed ale and beer, fermented cider, perry, cider brandy or applejack. Wines like canary, claret, sack, and sack-posset were also appreciated. Aqua vitae liquors such as brandy, whiskey and rum, creams and elixirs, ratafias and spirituous waters were well-liked (Brown, 1966). Merchants of rum and molasses were respected: for example, in the North Church in Boston, where the famous ride of Paul Revere started, all the pews are made of stark wood except one which is upholstered with red velvet. This pew was reserved for the rum and molasses traders.

In early America, drunkenness was frowned upon but not drinking. It has been said that the two basic social institutions of Colonial America were the church and the tavern. Not only were these institutions founded simultaneously; geographically they were close neighbors. Not infrequently, tavern licenses were issued on the understanding that the tavern must be close to the meeting house. In 1651, for example, a Boston ordinary-keeper was given permission to operate a "house of common entertainment" provided "he keepe it neare the new meeting house." Interestingly, the personnel of these institutions were often interchangeable. The ordinary-keeper at Cambridge, Massachusetts, first "home of entertainment," was also a deacon of the church and later steward of Harvard College. The physical structures at times served both purposes. Governor Winthrop's residence at Charlestown, Massachusetts, became a meeting house in 1633 and later a tavern, called The Three Cranes. The location, incidentally, did not improve attendance at religious services. For the pragmatic colonist it was important to have the tavern near the religious meeting place. The tavern served as an excellent retreat from a long sermon or an unheated church.

"Going to the tavern" was found by many, more attractive than attending church. This practice became a problem so serious in Massachusetts that a law was passed stating that tavern keepers within a mile of church were required to ask all persons able to go to church to leave the tavern during the hours of service. In large cities, such as Philadelphia, the tavern met definite needs because of the large numbers of visitors and immigrants. By 1648, in New Amsterdam, also a port of entry for immigrants, one-fourth of the buildings were tap-houses where brandy, beer, and tobacco were sold.

Matters of public concern were expressed in the tavern. The innkeeper was a man of considerable influence. He knew the lawyers well, and he was the first one to learn about actions of the legislature. He was well informed on everything from the governor's health to a sheriff's sale of wood lots. He was attentive to his guests and performed special services such as watching for runaway slaves. The innkeeper often had civic responsibilities. He held public office; was selectman, road commissioner, tax assessor, tax collector, constable, or town moderator. In summary, the early tavern had social, political, and military functions. It was the meeting place for the clergy and the laity, the politician and the merchant. The ensign of the Royal Army, the Puritan, the Quaker, the Huguenot refugee, and the Indian chief from a neighboring place, all assembled there (Baron, 1962).

Liquor brought with it problems; its frequent companion, drunkenness, challenged the social order. Drunkenness was carefully defined by the early colonists. In 1646, the government of Plymouth defined a drunkard as "a person that lisps or faults in his speech by reason of drink, or that staggers in his going, or that vomits or cannot follow his calling." Alcohol abuse was a condition among certain "common drunkards" which "tended to impoverish such offenders." The repetitive nature of the behavior of this person was well recognized, as well as the economic, social, and health consequences. These were the first conceptualizations of alcohol problems; intoxication was a sin, and Puritan jeremiads were used to chastise the wayward drinkers. The clergy publicly emphasized the individual's deliberate choice of sin. Repentence, an individual effort to sin no more, was the only way to avoid calamity. Excessive drinking was also attributed to transcendental causes. Deeply troubled by a rash of drunkenness in Plymouth, William Bradford reasoned that because of the holy mission of New England, the devil was bent to discredit them in the eyes of the world. Satan was a mighty power in the creation of alcohol troubles. Treatment was appropriate to the causes. The church handled those afflicted through admonition, suspension, and finally excommunication. Civil authorities concurred with the aim of the churches to control debauchery; taverns were closely supervised by the government. A story is told of a Robert Coles who was expelled from his congregation for drunkenness and disfranchised by civil authorities. According to an account, "Robert Coles was fyned ten shillings and enjoyned to stand with a white sheet on his back, whereon Drunkard shall be written in great lynes, and to stand therewith soe long as the Court find meet for abusing himself shamefully with drink" (Lender, 1973).

For 17th century New Englanders, habitual drunkenness was a problem of individual responsibility, morality, and religion. Appropriately, the disorder was treated with fines, whippings, imprisonments, social disapproval, and religious sanctions. Alcoholics were thrust into the bilboes, which were long bars or bolts of iron with sliding shackles, or subjected to the sanctions mentioned above.

ALCOHOL PROBLEMS AFTER INDEPENDENCE

When the American Revolution arrived, taverns served as court rooms where court martials took place and as military prisons. Some served as barracks, some as officers' headquarters, others as places for secret meetings of patriots; many were used as hospitals. The Green Dragon Inn, according to Daniel Webster, became the headquarters of the Revolution. In the same building, the first Grand Lodge of the Masons held its meetings. It was at the Sudbury Wayside Inn and Winchester's Black Horse Tavern that soldiers reassembled after the battle of Lexington. Two years previously, those planning the Boston Tea Party had assembled where Samuel Cole's first ordinary had stood in 1634. The very first attempts at dramatic production in New England were performed in taverns and coffeehouses. Hunters would gather there with their hounds. Taverns were the locale for executions, and execution day was a "grand day for the taverns" (Baron, 1962).

The arrival of Independence found Americans preoccupied with alcohol problems. An example of this concern is reflected in the book, *An Inquiry into the Effects of Ardent Spirits upon the Human Body and Mind* published in 1786 by Benjamin Rush. This physician, one of the signers of the Declaration of Independence, lectured at the University of Pennsylvania. His book is the first American scientific treatise on inebriety. Inebriety, according to Rush, is an "odious" disease which appears with the following symptoms: (1) unusual garrulity; (2) unusual silence; (3) captiousness and a disposition to quarrel; (4) uncommon good humor, an insipid simpering or laugh; (5) profane swearing and cursing; (6) a disclosure of their own, or other people's secrets; (7) a rude disposition to tell those persons in company whom they know, their faults; (8) certain immodest actions, the sign of the first stage of drunkenness, sometimes appears in women, who, when sober, are "uniformily remarkable for chaste and decent manners"; (9) a clipping of words; (10) fighting; a black eye, or a swelled nose, often mark this level of drunkenness; (11) certain extravagant acts which indicate a temporary fit of madness. These are singing, "hallooing," "roaring," imitating the noises of brute animals, jumping, tearing of clothes, dancing naked, breaking glasses and china, and dashing other articles of household furniture upon the ground or floor. This description is one of the early disjunctive or "laundry list" definitions of alcoholism.

To the symptoms mentioned, Rush added a description of the many physical signs characteristic of habitual drunkenness. According to him the drinking paroxysms of the disease occur at certain periods and after longer or shorter intervals. These often begin as annual occurrences and gradually increase in their frequency, until they appear in quarterly, monthly, weekly and quotidian or daily periods. Finally, they show hardly any signs of remission even during the night.

Rush conceptualized drunkenness as a progressive disorder that develops slowly. He was well aware of the phenomenon of tolerance. The body, he stated, particularly the sense of taste and the stomach, progressively adapts to the noxious liquor until the person becomes habituated. The main cause of the disorder was attributed to the use of ardent spirits, the consumption of which he castigated vehemently.

Rush provided an inventory of therapeutic measures, most of them rather drastic, including: plunging the body into cold water, terror, the excitement of anger, severe whippings, sweats, bleeding, shaming, etc. He seemed to have pioneered aversive conditioning as we may surmise from his statement, "The association of the idea of ardent spirits, with a painful or disagreeable impression upon some part of the body, has sometimes cured the love of strong drink. I once tempted a Negro man, who was habitually fond of ardent spirits, to drink some run (which I had placed in his way) and in which I had placed a few grains of tartar emetic - the tartar sickened and puked him to such a degree, that he supposed himself to be poisoned. I was much gratified by observing he could not bear the sight nor smell of spirits for two years afterwards." Although inebriety was, in his opinion, a disease, he still appealed to transcendental forces to contain this problem. His cry was eloquent: "Ministers of the Gospel of every denomination in the United States! Aid me with all the might that you possess in society, from the dignity and usefulness of your sacred office, to save our fellow men from being destroyed by the greater destroyer of their lives and souls (inebriety)." (This exhortation, as we will see later, did not go unheeded.) At the same time, Rush requested compassion for the drunkard, "Let us not pass by the prostrate sufferer from strong drink, but administer to him the same relief we would afford to a fellow creature, in a sinister state from an accidental and innocent cause." Benjamin Rush recommended proscription of ardent spirits and advised the use of substitutes such as cider, malt liquors, and wines (Rush,1943). His strong condemnation of strong drinks carried much power. According to one historian, the 19th century worldwide temperance movement can be traced to him (Baron, 1962).

ALCOHOL AND ALCOHOLISM IN EMERGENT AMERICA

America continued to labor and grow. Alcohol beverages remained widely in use. The manufacture of beer, which in its beginnings was a home operation, became a large national industry which modeled our systems of taxation. The profits of this industry contributed to the public coffers, created educational institutions, and supported wars (Baron, 1962).

Throughout these years, physicians demonstrated little interest in drunkenness as a health problem. A few vaguely admitted that the disorder was a "disease produced by a remote cause and giving birth to actions and movements in the living body that discover the functions of health." Thomas Trotter, who had made this statement in 1832, perceptively remarked that "Mankind ever in pursuit of pleasure have reluctantly admitted into the catalogue of their diseases, those evils which were the immediate offsprings of their luxuries" (Trotter, 1941). The visibility of many social problems which appear closely associated with the excessive use of alcohol, and what is more important, the conceptualization of drunkenness as a problem of individual responsibility and morality, assisted by the theorizing or interpretation of alcohol problems by people like Rush, gave impetus to one of the most far reaching experiments of social control undertaken in this country.

On February 13, 1826, the American Temperance Society was born, spearheaded by Justin Edwards, pastor of the Park Street Church in Boston. The movement experienced important changes during a period of thirty years. At first it espoused temperance; later it preached complete abstinence from all intoxicants; eventually it proposed prohibition. This was a genuinely religious movement from which only a few churches remained aloof. The American Temperance Society exhibited successful growth; by the end of 1829, it claimed 100,000 members. At the beginning of 1833, there were reported to be more than 5,000 temperance societies in the United States with a membership of 290,000. Under the pressure of the adverse public opinion created by this movement, many distilleries went out of business, and a great number of merchants were persuaded to stop selling spirituous liquors. The temperance movement led to the formation of an American Congressional Temperance Society with similar societies in state legislatures. Temperance societies were started in colleges and factories, and among blacks, women, and even children. The organizations eventually evolved into the American Temperance Union which included groups in most of the North American Continent.

Attempts were made around 1840 to prohibit by law the sale of liquor. Maine enacted prohibition legislation which was imitated in other states. The territory of Minnesota, Rhode Island, Massachusetts, Vermont, and several states ranging from New York to the Nebraska Territory embraced this law, but eventually all of these legislative actions were declared unconstitutional or were repealed. The temperance movement changed from a spiritual crusade to a political campaign directed toward the goal of universal legal prohibition. The movement lost momentum and entered a period of relative quiescence until the summer of 1865 when the National Temperance Society and Publication-house was born. The movement gained new impetus in 1873 from the founding of a Women's Crusade by Dio Lewis, a minister from Boston. Lewis, whose father had been a drunkard, persuaded women to go in bands to barrooms, saloons, and beer gardens and, armed with prayers and hymns, attempt to free from evil the owners, barkeepers, and patrons of the sinful places. This early form of peaceful protest had a great appeal throughout the country. Their holy crusade developed into the Women's Christian Temperance Union.

The last and most effective of the prohibition movements developed later, based upon religious principles. One of its founders, Rev. Howard Hyde Russell, considered himself to be divinely inspired to lead the movement. The strategy was changed at this point, making saloons the target. The

Anti-Saloon League was founded in Ohio in 1893, becoming a national organization in 1895 in Washington, D.C. The ultimate goal of the league was the suppression of all the liquor traffic. The saloon was identified as the focus of drunkenness, political chicanery, corruption, and seduction of the young. The Anti-Saloon League acquired considerable power. Gradually a campaign was organized to promote national prohibition. Several political victories followed, including overriding President Taft's veto against the Webb-Kenyon bill designed to prohibit interstate shipment of alcoholic beverages into dry states. In December of 1913, 4,000 men and women marched on the Capitol in Washington carrying a resolution asking for the submission of a constitutional amendment to prohibit liquor in the United States. On August 10, 1917, a resolution for a prohibition constitutional amendment was passed in the Senate, and in December, 1917, by the House. The 18th Amendment to the United States Constitution was ratified by the required thirty-six states on January 16, 1919.

Prohibition, characterized by cartoonists of the time as a tall, gaunt, red-nosed, stovepipe-hatted monster, had arrived. The monster begat speakeasies, rum-runners, illicit stills, smugglers, bootleggers, gangsters, and racketeers. Difficult to enforce, the 18th Constitutional Amendment was eventually repealed (Bacon, 1967; Baron, 1962).

Prohibition, an ill-fated social experiment of drinking control, illustrates the consequences of conceptualizing alcohol-related problems as matters of morality and religious concern. The temperance-prohibitionist movement shows how certain conceptual formulations of a problem are accepted by the citizenry and translated into social action. Society has numerous evangelistic social reformers who push concepts to their ultimate consequences. The reluctance of health professionals to accept alcohol problems within their area of serious concern and lack of information about their nature most likely invited the intervention of social reformers and their constituency.

MODERN CONCEPTS OF ALCOHOLISM

In the meantime, Europeans were performing elegant intellectual exercises to explain the complex pattern of behavior which is now called alcoholism. We owe to Marconi (1959) an excellent review of these endeavors. The French, for example, were particularly impressed by the apparently compelling nature of the desire to drink observed in habitual drunkards. Esquirol (1838) called the disease a "monomania of drunkenness, a mental illness whose principal character is an irresistible tendency toward fermented beverages." In this illness, "the wish to drink is instinctive and imperious...and persists during the whole duration of the paroxysm, after which the convalescent becomes sober again and resumes all the habits of temperate life." For Magnan (1893), the patients were incessantly affected by the most overwhelming desire for stimulants. The disease of their concern was called dipsomania (dipso = thirst) or more specifically oinomania (oinos = wine) a morbid insatiable craving for alcohol. The disorder was thought to be the expression of an underlying circular psychosis. Similar conceptions were shared by psychiatrists in Germany. Gaupp (1901), in a scholarly publication, characterized the syndrome by attacks in which, after a period of changed mood, an irresistible craving for alcohol appears, followed by alcoholic excesses, coupled with, or leading to a more or less serious clouding of consciousness, lasting a few hours or days, or in rare cases weeks. The attack usually ends spontaneously. The most important sign of dipsomania was, in his opinion, depression of periodic nature. This periodic disorder was said to have an epileptic origin. Most of Gaupp's contemporaries postulated fundamental disturbances of the central nervous system as causative factors. Presumably, an underlying factor was damage to the "vegetative centers of the hypothalamus." As recently as 1946, Charlin, Gardien and Marty (1946) postulated a disturbance of that region of the brain that commands the "mood and the thirst instincts."

Magnus Huss, Professor at the University of Stockholm, and, incidentally, a temperance advocate, made an important contribution in 1852. In a book titled *Cnronische Alkoholskrankheit, oder Alcoholismus Chronicus,* he coined the expression "chronic alcoholism" (Huss, 1852). The designation encompassed not only the neurologic sequelae to habitual excessive drinking, but certain behavioral manifestations which did not have a direct connection with morphologic changes in the central nervous system. Huss observed that there was not a definite boundary between the symptoms of alcoholism and mental disease in general. The term was a felicitous discovery. Physicians in the past had felt that they committed certain impropriety by being interested in drunkenness and drunkards. Like Trotter, many wondered if inebriety was the proper subject for academic exercises. The word "alcoholism" achieved rapid success, allowing physicians to acknowledge their scholarly and clinical interest in the disorder without having to apologize.

Kurtz and Kraepelin (1901) applied the term "alcohol addiction" to the disorder observed in those persons whose will, allegedly, is not sufficiently strong to abandon the use of alcohol even if drinking results in serious somatic, economic, and social changes. Bleuler (1924) conceptualized alcoholism as a disorder with the characteristic somatic and behavioral changes observed by others. In addition, he was particularly impressed with the ethical deterioration of the alcoholic and with the incongruence of their affective responses. An alcoholic, he indicated, might be deeply moved by a sad story, but shortly afterwards, he would beat his wife and children showing considerable callousness in this real situation. The alcoholic shows emotional incontinence; he is happy one moment and angry the next with little provocation.

The conceptual constructs of the late 19th and beginning of the 20th century emphasized three main aspects in the alcoholism syndrome: (1) the biological and behavioral symptoms resulting from the damage caused by the excessive ingestion of alcohol, (2) the irresistible drive to drink (dipsomania), and (3) functional disturbances of the central nervous system which were the postulated causes of the disorder. Basically, a medical model was utilized to explain the "disease."

CONTEMPORARY CONCEPTS OF ALCOHOLISM

Our contemporary conceptions of alcoholism owe much to the contributions of E.M. Jellinek. In his early publications in collaboration with Karl Bowman, a distinction was made between two types of alcoholism: chronic alcoholism and alcohol addiction. The first entity covers all the physical and psychological changes resulting from the prolonged use of alcohol beverages. The second is a disorder characterized by an urgent craving for alcohol. The patients afflicted by this disorder reportedly have lost control of the situation to such an extent that they are not able to give up drinking even in the presence of "a sincere desire to do so and following a definitely declared resolution" (Bowman & Jellinek, 1941). A few years later, Jellinek (1946) defined more precisely the symptoms and the natural history of the pathological process. His formulations were based on responses to a questionnaire on the symptomatology of alcoholism administered to 98 members of Alcoholics Anonymous in the United States. He later revised his description utilizing observations derived from 2,000 patients. According to Jellinek, alcohol problems adopt two main patterns, alcohol addiction, which is a disorder accessible to medical-psychiatric treatment, and other forms of excessive drinking, which can be best managed through the application of measures of social control including law enforcement. In his opinion, it was unwise to use the term "alcohol addiction" indiscriminately. Unwarranted extensions of the disease conception could be harmful because, eventually, these misuses of the concept would affect unfavorably the social sanctions against drunkenness and their ethical basis. He acknowledged that the nonaddictive alcoholic (habitual symptomatic excessive drinker) is a sick person; his ailment is not excessive drinking per se, but rather the psychological and social difficulties which are partially relieved by the actions of alcohol (Jellinek, 1962). Jellinek's diagnostic formulation of alcoholism includes physical signs and symptoms, psychological and social symptomatology, as well as interpretations deriving from all these areas. In the prodromal phase, the alcoholic experiences relief in drinking and suffers blackouts; he drinks surreptitiously and is preoccupied with alcohol. The alcoholic gulps drinks and experiences guilt about his behavior. As the alcoholic enters into a more critical phase, the frequency of blackouts increases. The characteristic and almost pathognomonic element in the crucial phase of the disorder is loss of control. This symptom means that "any drinking of alcohol starts a chain reaction which is felt by the drinker as a physical demand for alcohol." Prominent accompanying symptoms during this phase are: rationalized drinking behavior, grandiose behavior (extravagant expenditures and grandiloquence), aggressivity, and remorse. Also typical are periods of total abstinence and loss of friends and jobs. The entire behavior of the person becomes alcohol centered. The individual may use alcohol substitutes; he experiences fears and tremors and has religious preoccupations. He may notice a decrease in sexual drive and exhibits displays of jealousy. Commonly observed are marked ethical deterioration and impaired thinking. This complex disease is a progressive disorder (Jellinek, 1962).

Jellinek's characterization of the disorder is what philosophers of science would call disjunctive construct. Several combinations of signs and symptoms are expected to be present in persons affected by the disorder; not every subject labeled alcoholic is expected to display *all* of these features. This taxonomic device contrasts with a conjunctive construct in which certain defined features or conditions (symptoms, positive test results, behaviors, etc.) all have to be present to include the member in a class or category. The signs and symptoms described under the label "alcoholism" belong to various universes of discourse complicating the construct even more. Since Jellinek's alcoholism concept derives from responses to a questionnaire administered to members of Alcoholics Anonymous, we may assume that persons responding, like this group, to a similar questionnaire are alcoholics. An alcoholic then is a person sharing the characteristics of members of Alcoholics Anonymous which is a group of persons who are self-designated alcoholics.

In spite of the methodological limitations of Jellinek's alcoholism model, his conceptions were assimilated and interpreted by the lay public and, in particular, by lay self-help groups such as Alcoholics Anonymous. Alcoholism, according to a prominent lay leader in this field, is a disease which manifests itself chiefly by the uncontrollable drinking of the victim, who is known as an alcoholic. It is a progressive disease which, if left untreated, grows more virulent year by year, driving its victims further and further from the normal world and deeper and deeper into an abyss which has only two outlets, insanity or death. Alcoholism is a treatable disease that can be arrested. This lay person's point of view, like that of Jellinek and Bowman in their early writings, draws sharp distinctions between the heavy drinker and the alcoholic. The heavy drinker drinks by choice; the alcoholic does not choose. He allegedly has lost the power of choice in the matter of drinking. The alcoholic, to his horror and dismay, ends up drunk entirely against his will and intention. Although treatable, the alcoholic cannot be cured of his disease so that he can drink again. This outlook seems to divide humankind into two classes, those who can drink without consequences and those who cannot drink. There is little room for compromises. The heavy drinker is not necessarily an alcoholic; in his case progression is not observed. Reportedly, many people consistently drank more than is considered social drinking over "an indefinite number of years," and did not slide down the incline of alcoholism. These drinkers may have hurt their health and/or their careers, but it has usually been "an invisible hurt, not directly attributable to their drinking, although that may actually be the root of it." In the case of other heavy drinkers (nonalcoholic), the progressive element actually is reversed; they gradually cut their consumption as they grow older, almost inconspicuously and with no apparent effort to do so (Mann, 1959).

The lay conceptions seem to imply that drinking is nothing to fear. Moderate drinking does not disrupt people's lives. Even heavy drinking, although not enjoying a completely clean bill of health, does not have to be seen with apprehension, unless one happens to be an "alcoholic."

RESPONSES IN SOCIAL POLICY TO ALCOHOL PROBLEMS

A series of public reactions appeared concurrent to the increasing appreciation of alcoholism as a disease process rather than as a matter of morality. One of the first responses was the establishment of the Laboratory of Applied Physiology at Yale University in 1923. If alcoholism is a disease, it was appropriate to implement a program for the purpose of collecting scientific information on the physiological and behavioral effects of alcohol and inquiring into the cause of alcoholism. The Yale Laboratory pioneered scientific techniques in the examination of alcohol-related problems, and by 1930, it had organized extensive archives of the world alcohol literature. Training and education were also provided and the Laboratory became a forum for discussion of alcohol-related problems at a time when the scholarly study of these issues was not popular. The Yale effort expanded into the clinical area. In 1944, two clinics, the Yale Plan Clinics, devoted to the treatment of alcoholics, were established in New Haven and Hartford, Connecticut. These clinics have provided models for other rehabilitative centers. In 1962, with the help of the Christopher Smithers Foundation, the National Institute of Health, and additional private support, the Yale Center of Alcohol Studies was moved to Rutgers-The State University of New Jersey. This move, reportedly triggered by the administration of Yale University, at a point in time when the Center was vigorously growing in scientific standing, size, budget, and favorable publicity, is in itself an intriguing event. The University seemed more interested in "academically oriented goals" than in the multidisciplinary study of some of the most serious problems that affect our society (Bacon, 1966). The scholarly activities of the Center have continued and have had a considerable influence in the alcoholism field.

From the Yale Center, a National Committee on Education about Alcoholism emerged, supported by a five year grant. This committee, known as the National Council on Alcoholism, rapidly became one of the outstanding voluntary agencies in the country. At the beginning, leadership in the Council came from persons inspired by the Yale Center and Alcoholics Anonymous. In 1950, the National Council became fully independent of the Yale plan. The Council has evolved into a nation-wide organization comprised of people from all walks of life, including professionals. This outstanding organization now has chapters in most communities of significant size. The organization has been dedicated to the premise that the alcoholic can recover and that alcoholism is a major public health problem and community responsibility (Cross, 1968).

In 1935, a remarkable fellowship was born through the efforts of a New York stockbroker and an Akron physician, both acknowledged alcoholics. This fellowship, named "Alcoholics Anonymous," rapidly became a large organization with groups in most communities in the United States and in many cities abroad. This is a self-help organization based on the principles that an alcoholic has to admit that his life has become unmanageable. Having accepted this, the alcoholic is asked to place reliance in a power greater than himself. This power may be conceived of as God, the inner-self, the miracle of growth, a tree, man's wonderment at the physical universe, the structure of the atom, or a mathematical infinity. To this power, the alcoholic is to pray for strength. This acceptance is followed by other steps, such as taking a moral inventory of oneself. Eventually, those successfully affiliated with the fellowship may engage in "rescuing" other alcoholics. This is done not as an altruistic endeavor, but as a way to help oneself to remain sober.

With no salaried staff, no dues, and no central control, this organization has become the most ubiquitous resource available to alcoholics who wish to stop drinking. Alcoholics Anonymous has played a major role in bringing to public attention the problem of alcoholism and the predicaments of alcoholics (Alexander, 1941).

Simultaneously with the Council and Alcoholics Anonymous' efforts, individual states began to assume responsibility for assessing the seriousness of the problem of alcoholism, taking inventory of the resources available for the handling of this disorder and outlining plans of action. The first state to inaugurate a commission addressed to this problem was Connecticut in 1945. The creation of this Commission was followed by other states who developed similar organizations such as the Michigan State Board on Alcoholism, the Georgia Commission on Alcoholism, the Minnesota Interim Commission on Alcoholism, and many others. These groups were official or semi-official bodies with strong lay representation. By 1955, thirty-one states had alcoholism commissions; some of these were single state agencies, others were incorporated within larger state agencies (Lewis, 1955).

In 1961, a Cooperative Commission on the Study of Alcoholism was created as a preliminary to later Federal efforts. This group was supported by a grant from the National Institute of Mental Health. The Commission had members belonging to several professions and scientific disciplines. From their deliberations, a series of recommendations was drafted. The first suggestion was that a national organization should be established to help bring about changes in American drinking patterns. The second recommendation advised the establishment of an interdepartmental committee within the Federal Government to ensure collaboration among the departments and agencies doing work related to alcohol problems and the establishment of a Center on Alcoholism within the National Institute of Health. The mission of this Center would be to coordinate the activities of the "Institute on Problem Drinking," encourage community mental health centers to establish services for problem drinkers, and provide funds through formula grants for demonstration projects and program support. The Commission also indicated the need for support of research and research training (Plaut, 1967).

The first organized federal action took place in 1966 when President Lyndon Johnson announced the creation of the National Center for Prevention and Control of Alcoholism. The Center initiated its activities with relatively modest fiscal support. Most of the resources of the Center were directed to fund intra- and extramural research, and for the establishment of research centers. A smaller proportion was allocated for training. In 1970, the Federal Government made a more substantial commitment to the control of alcoholism and related problems by the enactment of Public Law 91-616. The law mandated the development and implementation of comprehensive health, education, training, research, and planning programs for the prevention and treatment of alcohol abuse and alcoholism and the rehabilitation of alcohol abusers and alcoholics. This law, titled *Comprehensive Alcohol Abuse and Alcoholism Prevention, Treatment, and Rehabilitation Act of 1970*, created The National Institute on Alcohol Abuse and Alcoholism (NIAAA) with a director appointed by the Secretary of the Department of Health, Education and Welfare (Public Law 91-616). This law was amended in 1974 and its provisions extended through Public Law 93-282.

A significant aspect of the Comprehensive Alcohol Abuse law is the appropriation and assignment of grant funds to states to assist them in planning, establishing, maintaining, coordinating, and evaluating projects for prevention, treatment, and rehabilitation of alcoholics. Each state was asked to designate an authority to administer the funds. The amount of funds is allocated to each state on the basis of population and several social indicators. From the beginning, one of the main goals of the Institute has been the promotion and support of community based alcoholism treatment centers for alcoholics. In addition to the formula grant funded programs, many other programs across the nation receive direct funding from NIAAA. The Institute has created an elaborate rhetoric to describe the expected mission of the federally supported programs. The centers should "make effective, quality treatment available to every alcoholic person who needs it." The programs are encouraged to offer "services required to nurture human motivation to meet the range of needs, as perceived by the individual in trouble with alcohol, and by those family members, friends, associates, and community closest to him." Needs for food, clothing and shelter, health care, legal services, vocational opportunity, health, social interaction and acceptance, need to be assessed to provide "a new and more effective approach to problems associated with alcoholism." The Institute admonishes that to "focus and treat only the alcoholic symptoms" is a limited approach (NIAAA, From Programs to People, 1974).

An important feature of the alcoholism programs supported by the Federal Government has been to encourage local citizens to become actively involved in planning, developing, promoting, and helping to sustain the programs. The citizens' groups participating in these efforts must be representative of the demographic and social characteristics of the community. Their efforts should assure visibility to the programs, stimulate use, secure community support including help with finances, government cooperation, and liaison with community leaders. The governmental support has financed institution affiliated programs, as well as freestanding clinics. Many of these programs are targeted toward particular groups in the population such as the poor, black, American Indian, and public inebriate. NIAAA has promoted programs in the occupational area aimed at the early identification and rehabilitation of alcoholic employees. The drunken driver has been a concern of NIAAA, but the most significant efforts in this area have been sponsored by the U.S. Department of Transportation.

More recently, primary prevention has received considerable attention from NIAAA. The philosophy of this program is that drinking can be defined, prescribed, and taught. Drinking, reportedly, is an individual responsibility, and a person must have freedom of choice in this matter. There is value in disseminating information on the patterns of problem drinking, the effects of alcohol, and alcoholism. Peer groups and social pressures must be created to deal successfully with these problems. Responsible alcohol consumption for those who choose to drink and the right not to drink are important positions adopted in this prevention strategy.

Perhaps one of the most important contributions of the Institute was the development of a centralized computer-based data collection system to evaluate the performance of alcoholism programs supported by NIAAA. One of the objectives of this information system is to gather information about changes in the clients receiving services. Data are collected on the socioeconomic and drinking-related characteristics of clients at intake, follow-up, and middle points during treatment. Other measures regarding manpower utilization and cost accounting are also obtained. During its first year of operation, the system collected data on more than 40,000 clients. This sample size is one of the largest ever collected on problem drinkers and alcoholics (Towle, Bosley, Borgeson, Gray, Mothershead, & Norwood, 1973).

THE GROWING CONSTITUENCY OF ALCOHOLISM SERVICES PROGRAMS

Federal support for alcoholism programs has increased from $17,000,000 in 1971 to over $200,000,000 in 1974. These substantial outlays of funds have led to the emergence of a large constituency of service providers, advocate organizations, and clients receiving services. Organizations such as the North American Association of Alcohol Programs, founded in 1960 by directors of alcoholism programs, have grown considerably. This group recently adopted the new name of Alcohol and Drug Abuse Problems Association of North America to accommodate a larger membership. Of recent formation is the Council of State and Territorial Alcoholism Authorities, Inc. The aims of this organization are to foster the development of alcoholism and drug abuse programs; to assist Federal, State, and Territorial Governments in the design, development, and implementation of cooperative Federal-State alcohol abuse programs; to identify and provide technical assistance to the states regarding licensure, certification, and accreditation of alcoholism rehabilitative personnel; to identify the evaluation needs of the States and Territories in the area of alcoholism treatment services; and to provide technical and financial assistance to selected states in the development of compatible program reporting and management information systems. Several other organizations have been created under the sponsorship or encouragement of the NIAAA. For instance, four Alcohol Education Training Projects have been established in four sections of the U.S.A. A number of private consulting firms have received contracts from the NIAAA to fulfill educational and training objectives, to abstract literature on alcoholism, or to conduct evaluative monitoring or alcoholism treatment programs, occupational alcoholism projects, Indian alcoholism programs, and others. Former U.S. Senator Harold Hughes, an advocate of greater support for alcoholism programs, observing the growth of this large constituency of alcoholism rehabilitators recently commented: "We have in effect, a new civilian army that has now become institutionalized. The alcohol and drug industrial complex is not as powerful as its military-industrial counterpart, but nonetheless, there are some striking similarities. We have a growing body of trained and skilled counselors who are the soldiers in the field. We have the ever-enlarging structure of scientists, 'think tank' personnel, administrators, governmental funding agencies, lobbyists, associations, consultants, evaluators, technical evaluators, technical assistants, and so on. A huge and influential empire produces most of the substances we are engaged in trying to control" (The Alcoholism Report III, 1974).

ALCOHOLISM AS THE TARGET OF THERAPEUTIC AND REHABILITATIVE PROGRAMS

The gallant commitment of the Federal Government to control alcoholism might raise several questions in the critical minds of many (Mendelson, 1972). Considering the status of our scientific knowledge and rehabilitative technology, is it justified to invest substantial financial and manpower resources in the treatment and control of "alcoholism"? Do we have a concept of alcoholism sufficiently precise to aim our efforts and expect measurable outcomes? Is the nature of our preventive and rehabilitative efforts congruent with the scientific knowledge and therapeutic technology currently available?

An examination of our present concepts suggests that alcoholism has an inadequately validated working definition. (Naturally, this is the point of view of the author; the other chapters in this book should provide material for a more balanced opinion on this matter and on some of the issues which I will raise in the following pages). The definitions presented by scientific authorities contain few objective criteria to clearly delimit alcoholism as a disease. Many elements incorporated in conceptions of alcoholism have been found to lack an empirical basis. For example, according to authorities, alcoholism "is characterized by the repeated drinking of alcoholic beverages to an extent that exceeds customary use or compliance with the social customs of the community..." (Keller & Efron, 1955; World Health Organization, 1952). Unfortunately, customs change with communities and within communities. Drinking standards are inadequately codified; it is known that within a community drinking behavior is interpreted differently depending upon whether it is exposed to public agencies of control or shielded from public scrutiny. Socioeconomic status of the drinker, site of drinking, and several other variables affect how drinking is interpreted by others. To complicate matters, individuals are often willing to accept the fact that their drinking behavior is deviant to regain social acceptance or to justify the sick role (Lovald & Neuwirth, 1968). Other definitions are not more precise: Alcoholism "is characterized by repeated drinking that interferes with the drinker's health or social functioning" (Keller & Efron, 1955). Health is not seriously impaired in many alcoholics, and the nature of the relationship between drinking and social impairment is not easy to establish in many cases. "Alcoholism is repeated implicative drinking of alcoholic beverages, so as to cause injury to the drinker's health or to his social or economic functioning" (Keller, 1960). The author of this definition acknowledges that terms like implicative, suspicion, arousing, leaves the epidemiologist or public health worker to his own resources. Even elements seemingly more objective, such as the presence of diagnostic pointers (e.g., blackouts) are not pathognomonic of alcoholism since these phenomena also occur in social drinkers (Goodwin, 1969). Drinking to experience relief is not peculiar to alcoholics as the research to test the tension reduction hypothesis in alcoholism seems to indicate (Cappell & Herman, 1972). Other elements incorporated in concepts of alcoholism like drinking surreptitiously, rationalized drinking behavior, gulping drinks, fears and religious preoccupation, etc., are even more difficult to validate and are hardly exclusive to the alcoholic.

The loss of control considered almost pathognomonic in Jellinek's definition of alcoholism, is a concept that has been severely criticized and challenged by several recent studies. Merry (1966), one of the earliest critics of the concept, demonstrated that the intensity of reported craving was not greater among patients who received alcohol than in those who received a placebo beverage. Paredes and Cornelison (1968) and Paredes, Ludwig, Hassenfeld, and Cornelison (1971) administered 180 ml of 80 proof Vodka to outpatient and inpatient alcoholics without precipitating bender drinking. Cutter, Schwaab, and Nathan (1970) also failed to induce greater alcohol consumption in alcoholics who received a priming dose of alcohol. Engle and Williams (1972) demonstrated that informing alcoholics that there was alcohol in a drink had a greater effect in their stated desire to imbibe than the actual presence of alcohol in the beverage. Gottheil, Corbett, Grasberger, and Cornelison (1972) observed that a significant number of patients who had alcohol available in a closed ward setting were able to initiate and discontinue drinking "at will." Mello and Mendelson (1972) demonstrated that alcoholics placed in a situation with unrestricted access to alcohol do not drink all the alcohol available and challenged most convincingly the loss of control idea. Finally, Paredes, Hood, Seymour, and Gollog, (1973) have shown that alcoholics who were exposed to substantial amounts of alcohol in an open institutional setting were not driven to seek more alcohol in the environment surrounding the hospital. Only one recent study (Ludwig, Wikler, & Stark, 1974) has offered evidence in support of the idea that alcohol induces craving as a function of appropriate interoceptive and extroceptive cues.

A committee from the National Council on Alcoholism has attempted to introduce some preciseness by defining criteria for the concept. The criteria includes three major diagnostic levels: Diagnostic Level 1 include classical, definite, obligatory symptoms clearly associated with alcoholism (e.g., gross tremor, hallucinosis, withdrawal, seizures, delirium tremens); diagnostic Level 2 includes probable, frequent or indicative symptoms that provide basis for a strong suspicion of alcoholism (e.g., major alcohol-associated illnesses: alcoholic hepatitis, Laennec's cirrhosis, etc.); and diagnostic Level 3, includes potential, possible or incidental symptoms, that are common to alcoholism but do not by themselves give a strong indication of its existence (e.g., choice of employment that facilitates drinking, frequent automobile accidents, major family disruptions, separation, divorce, etc.). The committee's criteria strongly rely on physical parameters for the diagnosis. Considerable diagnostic weight is ascribed to withdrawal, tolerance, and blackouts, as well as to major clinical alcohol-associated illnesses. The diagnostic importance of behavioral and attitudinal manifestations is relegated to a more peripheral role. The reliability and validity of the criteria developed by the National Council Committee have not been tested. The criteria assume that alcoholism is a disease, an assumption challenged by some authorities (Robinson, 1972; Steiner, 1969). The criteria also seem to focus on the more chronic or late stages of alcoholism, thus losing their usefulness in the less severe cases where establishment of the diagnosis is perhaps more important. Some critics have complained about the "laundry list approach" to the criteria (the criteria include 93 diagnostic items), arguing that confusion is caused by the assignments of diagnostic levels and the equivalence of "several minor criteria." For example, the Committee has stated that we could arrive at a diagnosis on the basis of one or more major and "several" minor criteria. No guidance is offered as to how many criteria are "several." An example of the uncertainty surrounding the concept are some of the conclusions of the sixty-five noted medical scholars and the fourteen authorities of the Committee. According to them, we do not know: whether anyone who drinks a sufficient quantity over a sufficient period of time will develop alcoholism; whether a specific biochemical or psychological difference leads to alcoholism, or if these are necessary to cause alcoholism; whether there is a continuous or discontinuous progression from drinking alcoholic beverages to dependence on alcohol (Criteria Committee, National Council on Alcoholism, 1972; Jacobson, 1975).

As we move through the maze of definitions and attempts to give specificity to the concept of alcoholism, one thing seems certain, alcoholics *do* consume or have consumed alcoholic beverages. Considering the ideas expressed above, it is difficult to see how large fiscal resources can be successfully applied to deal with an entity which is to a great extent an abstraction, an ill-defined medical concept, sometimes a self-labeling process, frequently an appellative based on a heterogeneous array of medical, legal, and social considerations. To alleviate the effects of such an entity, national policy has been defined, fiscal resources have been mobilized, and a vast inventory of medical, psychological, and social techniques notwithstanding appeals to a transcendental power, have been mustered.

THE IMPACT OF ALCOHOLISM PROGRAMS

The foresight of the leadership of NIAAA has given priority to the development of the information system mentioned earlier which has been permitted to initiate a large scale objective evaluation of the impact of the federal programs. Summaries and interpretation of the data collected by the information system have not been reported in the scientific literature; however, a number of preliminary conclusions have been published in various communications from the NIAAA. The reports illustrate the type of problems reached by the federally supported programs.

From a description of the patients evaluated and treated by the programs, it is possible to derive the concept of alcoholism which is shared by the providers of services. Most clients who receive services in the federally supported programs are middle-aged males (mean age 47 years, 84% male). Seventy percent are white. The median number of years of school attended is 11. Thirty-seven percent of the men are married and 42% divorced. The mean income of these people is above the poverty level ($6,280). Clients report an average of 14 years of heavy drinking. Sixty-one percent are unemployed. From these data we surmise that alcoholism is a disease of the middle-aged, poorly educated, family disaffiliated, low income, or unemployed drinker. Interestingly, surveys conducted in the general population do not identify the groups with these demographic characteristics as those with greater risk of alcohol-related problems (Cahalan, Cisin, & Crossley, 1969). The effects of the treatment programs on the type of client mentioned are worthy of mention. A study of 2,300 clients from representative treatment centers located in various states was done; specially collected data utilizing the information system described earlier were utilized to evaluate therapeutic outcome. Measures were available at intake and 18 months later on follow-up. It was found that 26% of the clients reported having remained abstinent throughout the 18-month period. The vast majority reported drinking at follow-up an amount of alcohol substantially less than that reported at intake, with many clients (70% of those admitted to treatment) drinking less than one ounce of absolute alcohol a day. The changes in alcohol consumption were not related to the type of setting or type of treatment received. However, patients who received more exposure to treatment reported greater changes in the favorable direction. Similar improvement was observed in verbally reported indices of physical and psychological impairment. The last changes, like those involving drinking variables, were not related to site or type of treatment (Ruggels, Armor, Polich, Mothershead, & Stephen, 1975; Towle et al., 1973).

Disappointingly, clients changed little in measures of social adjustment. Marital stability deteriorated, mean number of days of employment did not improve significantly between intake and follow-up, and the rates of unemployment remained high. Average income showed small increases, but these probably were related to general wage increases experienced in the labor market during the study period. The best predictor of improvement in drinking behavior was a high level of psychosocial functioning prior to treatment. Younger clients with fewer years of heavy drinking and better employment records and education showed more improvement. When the clinical and demographic characteristics of the clients were statistically controlled, small differences were observed between various treatment modalities. In other words, changes in outcome were related to the characteristics of the client rather than to the type of treatment received. The statistical validity of these data is open to question; however, the findings are in agreement with those of well controlled studies reported in the literature (Emrick, 1975).

There are intriguing features in several aspects of

national policy in regard to alcoholism programs. The therapeutic effectiveness of the ethnic and social class orientation promoted in the formulation and implementation of programs needs to be assessed. The low priority given to formal education requirements for providers of alcoholism services (nonacademically trained professionals) also needs to be researched. The assumption that the involvement of local citizens will affect favorably the appeal, quality, and effectiveness of therapeutic and rehabilitative services also needs to be proven empirically. Even generally accepted concepts, such as, that the employment setting is an appropriate area for the identification and referral of the problem drinker before his illness has progressed to a stage in which the probability of effective intervention is reduced, have not been sufficiently validated (Schlenger, 1975).

E pur si muove! SOME HOPEFUL SIGNS

Certain facts remain: an overwhelming amount of statistics continue to associate the use of alcohol to a broad range of human problems such as marital disruption, occupational difficulties, crime, accidents, and serious health impairment. The use of alcohol as a beverage brings with it a significant risk that the person will be seriously affected in some department of his life (Hayman, 1967). Alcohol-related problems are quite visible, and, not surprisingly, this visibility has led to the social action just described.

An examination of the behavior of the major statistical indices of alcohol-related problems in our society will very likely indicate that the twelve-fold increase in fiscal support for alcoholism programs in four years has not resulted in a proportional or even in a modest diminution of these problems in this country. In some areas, such as teenage drinking, the problems are worse (U.S. Department of Health, Education and Welfare, Alcohol and Health, 1974).

In conclusion, we cannot help but find a contemporary tone in a document of the Reformation Period published in Germany in 1531 by Sebastian Frank. The document was titled "On the Horrible Vice of Drunkenness." In the book, Frank wryly remarked, speaking of the elimination of drunkenness, "Much has been tried among Germans, but nothing has been achieved. The legislators have failed, although they have made promises" (Frank, 1941).

In spite of the panorama just presented, significant progress has been made. The establishment of the National Center for Prevention and Control of Alcoholism in 1966, signaled a change in the attitude toward alcohol-related problems as the subject of scholarly inquiry. Under the leadership of Jack Mendelson, the interest of scientists in these problems was revitalized. The Center not only contributed to increase the amount of research activity, it also improved the level of scientific standards of work done in this area. Since Mendelson, the quality of alcohol-related work has shown remarkable improvement. Research effort, a form of social activism at its best, has generated a substantial amount of data which no doubt will be eventually incorporated in the thinking of decision makers and will influence national policy encouraging society to take a more objective view of alcohol use and of the associated problems.

Of parallel importance is the development of the centralized computer-based data collection system by the

NIAAA described earlier in this chapter. The importance of such a system created under the administrative leadership of Morris Chafetz cannot be underestimated. At a time when so many priorities in the field of health and human services are competing for support, a strong data base is needed to justify the investment of financial resources and manpower in the treatment of persons with alcohol-related problems. It is quite apparent that no nation can afford to support all the health services made possible by our technology. In order to define priorities and predict costs, we need reliable information on the performance of alcoholism programs including outcome data. Collection of these data requires adequate information systems. In the past, providers of rehabilitative services have assumed that the therapeutic manipulations or rehabilitative procedures incorporated in their programs would benefit their patients. This expectation might not be fulfilled in practise. Without ongoing outcome evaluations, we cannot reliably ascertain if we are helping induce favorable changes, if we are doing harm, or if we are just contributing to support greater numbers of care-givers and sheltering more people from the responsibilities of productive daily living (Paredes, Lange, Gregory, & Stratton, 1974). Reliable information is necessary to make rational decisions and to alter programs if the therapeutic objectives are not reached.

Coming back to Sebastian Frank and his 16th century thinking, our difficulties defining alcoholism notwithstanding, we must agree with him that "Bacchus is killing more men than wars" and that "more men get drowned in the glass than in the sea." Impressive statistical data indicate that a significant segment of the American population, whether labeled alcoholics or not, is negatively affected by the beverage alcohol (Cahalan, et al.,

1969; Hayman, 1967). Drinking alcoholic beverages is an integral part of our culture; society has to accept the fact that the use of alcoholic beverages involves considerable risks for drinkers. From the point of view of public health and of social policy, the original recommendation of the Cooperative Commission on the Study of Alcoholism might have considerable merit. The Commission suggested that a national effort be made to bring about changes in American drinking patterns. The most recent preventive program of the NIAAA seems to go along with this aim. Is this a utopian goal? We have lessons from history. The Arabs were prone to wine drinking and debauchery before Islam. They danced, gambled, and fought as they drank. Caravans lost their way in the desert, and valuable loads on camels were used to carry wine instead of more vital goods. These harmful drinking habits disappeared when the Arabs accepted the strong stand of Mohammed: "O ye who believe! Strong drink and games of chance, idols and disarming arrows are only an infamy of Satan's handiwork. Leave it aside in order that ye may succeed" (Koran, 43-83). With the remarkable power of our present tools of public information, we should be able to influence the cultural patterns that regulate the use of alcohol. In the meantime, we must be sure that the conceptual models which we elaborate do not deceive us from thinking that, for most, the risks of alcohol are small. Sociocultural analyses have shown that drinking behavior is deeply enmeshed within the cultural framework of society. An attempt to change drinking behavior is an attempt to change a culture. This is a challenge that we will have to meet if we wish to cope effectively with the problem (Mandelbaum, 1965; Paredes, 1975).

REFERENCES

The Alcoholism Report, Vol. III. No. 5, December 27, 1974

Bacon, S. The classic temperance movement in the U.S.A.: Impact today on attitudes, action and research. *British Journal on Addictions*, 1967, *62*, 5-18.

Bacon, S. Summer school welcome. Unpublished manuscript, 1966, Rutgers-The State University, New Brunswick, N.J.

Barbé, A. *Précis de psychiatrie*. Paris: G. Doin & Cie, 1950.

Baron, S. *Brewed in America: A history of beer and ale in the United States*. Boston: Little, Brown & Co., 1962.

Bleuler, E. *Tratado de psiquiatría*. (J.M. deVillarerde, Trans.) Madrid: Calpe, 1924.

Bowman, K.M., & Jellinek, E.M. Alcohol addiction and chronic alcoholism. *Quarterly Journal of Studies on Alcohol*, 1941, *2*, 98-176.

Brown, J.H. *Early American beverages*. New York: Bonanza Books, 1966.

Cahalan, D., Cisin, I.H., & Crossley, H.M. American drinking practices: A national survey of drinking behavior and attitudes. New Brunswick, N.J.: Rutgers Center of Alcohol Studies, 1969, (Monograph No. 6).

Cappell, H., & Herman, C.P. Alcohol and tension reduction: A review, *Quarterly Journal of Studies on Alcohol*, 1972, *33*, 33-64.

Charlin, A., Gardien, P., & Marty, P. Dipsomanies-données pathogéniques. *Annales Médico-Psychologiques*, 1946, *104*, 38-47.

Criteria Committee, National Council on Alcoholism. Criteria for the diagnosis of alcoholism. *American Journal of Psychiatry*, 1972, *129*, 127-135.

Cross, J.N. *Guide to the community control of alcoholism*. New York: American Public Health Association, 1968.

Cutter, H.S.G., Schwaab, E.L., Jr., & Nathan, P.E. Effects of alcohol on its utility for alcoholics and nonalcoholics. *Quarterly Journal of Studies on Alcohol*, 1970, *31*, 369-378.

Emrick, C.D. A review of psychologically oriented treatment of alcoholism. II. The relative effectiveness of different treatment approaches and the effectiveness of treatment versus no treatment. *Quarterly Journal of Studies on Alcohol*, 1975, *36*, 88-108.

Engle, K.B., & Williams, T.K. Effect of an ounce of Vodka on Alcoholics' desire for alcohol. *Quarterly Journal of Studies on Alcohol*, 1972, *33*, 1099-1105.

Esquirol, E. *Des maladies mentales*. Paris: Bailliere, 1838.

Frank, S. On the horrible vice of drunkenness. A document of the Reformation Period on inebriety. Classics of the alcohol literature. *Quarterly Journal of Studies on Alcohol*, 1941, *2*, 391-395.

Gaupp, R. *Die Dipsomanie. Eine Klinische Studie*. Jena: Fisher, 1901.

Goodwin, D.W., Crane, J.B., & Guze, S.B. Alcoholic "blackouts": A review and clinical study of 100 alcoholics. *American Journal of Psychiatry*, 1969, *126*, 191-198.

Gottheil, E., Corbett, L.O., Grasberger, J.C., & Cornelison, F.S., Jr. Fixed interval drinking decisions. I. A research and treatment model. *Quarterly Journal of Studies on Alcohol*, 1972, *33*, 311-324.

Hayman, M. The myth of social drinking. *American Journal of Psychiatry*, 1967, *124*, 585-594.

Huss, M. *Chronische Alkoholskrankheit, oder Alcoholismus Chronicus*. (Van dem Busch, Trans.) Stockholm: C.E. Fritze, 1852.

The Jack Alexander article about A.A., New York: Alcoholics Anonymous World Services, Inc. (Reprinted from *The Saturday Evening Post*, March 1, 1941, p. 9)

Jacobson, G.R. *Diagnosis and assessment of alcohol abuse and alcoholism. A report to the National Institute on Alcohol Abuse and Alcoholism*. Rockville, Maryland: National Institute on Alcohol Abuse and Alcoholism, DHEW Publication No. (ADM) 75-228, 1975.

Jellinek, E.M. Phases in the drinking history of alcoholics. Analysis of a survey conducted by the official organ of Alcoholics Anonymous. *Quarterly Journal of Studies on Alcohol*, 1946, *7*, 1-88.

Jellinek, E.M. Phases of alcohol addiction. In: *Society, culture, and drinking patterns*. D. Pittman & C.R. Snyder, (Eds.), New York: John Wiley & Sons, Inc., 1962.

Keller, M. Definition of alcoholism. *Quarterly Journal of Studies on Alcohol*, 1960, *21*, 125-134.

Keller, M., & Efron, V. The prevalence of alcoholism. *Quarterly Journal of Studies on Alcohol*, 1955, *16*, 619-644.

Kurtz, E., & Kraepelin, E. Über die Beeinflussung psychicher Vorgänge durch regelmässigen Alkoholgenuss. *Psychologische Arbeiten*, 1901, *3*, 417-457.

Lazare, A. Hidden conceptual models in clinical psychiatry. *New England Journal of Medicine*, 1973, *288*, 345-351.

Lender, M. Drunkenness as an offense in early New England: A study of "Puritan" attitudes. *Quarterly Journal of Studies on Alcohol*, 1973, *34*, 353-366.

Lewis, J.A. Summary of Federal and State alcoholism programs in the United States. *American Journal of Public Health*, 1955, *45*, 1417-1419.

Lovald, K., & Neuwirth, G. Exposed and shielded drinking--drinking as role behavior and some consequences for social control and self-concept. *Archives of General Psychiatry*, 1968, *19*, 95-103.

Ludwig, A.M, Wikler, A., & Stark, L.H. The first drink. Psychobiological aspects of craving. *Archives of General Psychiatry*, 1974, *30*, 539-547.

Magnan, V. *Leçons cliniques sur les maladies mentales*. Paris: Bataille, 1893.

Mandelbaum, D.C. Alcohol and culture. *Current Anthropology*, 1965, *6*, 281-293.

Mann, M. *New primer on alcoholism*. New York: Rinehart & Co., Inc., 1959.

Marconi, J.T. The concept of alcoholism. *Quarterly Journal of Studies on Alcohol*, 1959, *20*, 216-235.

Mello, N.K., & Mendelson, J.H. Drinking patterns during work-contingent and non-contingent alcohol acquisiton. *Psychosomatic Medicine*, 1972, *34*, 139-164.

Mendelson, J.H. Alcoholism: Some contemporary issues and problems. *Annals of the New York Academy of Sciences*, 1972, *197*, 11-12.

Merry, J. The "Loss of Control" myth. *Lancet*, 1966, *1*, 1257-1258.

Morrison, S.E. *The Oxford history of the American people* New York: Oxford University Press, 1965.

National Institute on Alcohol Abuse and Alcoholism. From programs to people; toward a national policy on alcoholism services, DHEW Publication No. (ADM) 75-155, 1974.

Paredes, A. Social control of drinking among the Aztec Indians of Mesoamerica. *Journal of Studies on Alcohol*, 1975, *36*, 1139-1153.

Paredes, A., & Cornelison, F.S. Development of an audiovisual technique for the rehabilitation of alcoholics. *Quarterly Journal of Studies on Alcohol*, 1968, *29*, 84-92.

Paredes, A., Hood, W.R., Seymour, H., & Gollob, M. Loss of control in alcoholism: An investigation of the hypothesis, with experimental findings. *Quarterly Journal of Studies on Alcohol*, 1973, *34*, 1146-1161.

Paredes, A., Lange, D.K., Gregory, D., & Stratton, R. *The deviation amplifying model and the contract management system*. Paper presented at the North American Congress on Alcohol and Drug Problems, San Francisco, California, 1974.

Paredes, A., Ludwig, K.D., Hassenfeld, I.N., & Cornelison, F.S. Filmed representations of behavior and responses to self-observation in alcoholics. In N.K. Mello & J.H. Mendelson (Eds.), *Recent advances in studies of alcoholism*, Washington, D.C., 1971. U.S. Government Printing Office.

Plaut, T.F.A. *Alcohol problems: A report to the nation by the Cooperative Commission on the Study of Alcoholism*. New York: Oxford University Press, 1967.

Public Law 91-616, 91st Congress, S. 3835, December 31, 1970.

Public Law 93-282, 93rd Congress, S. 1125, May 14, 1974.

Robinson, D. The alcohologist's addiction. Some implications of having lost control over the disease concept of alcoholism. *Quarterly Journal of Studies on Alcohol*, 1972, *33*, 1028-1042.

Ruggels, W.L., Armor, D.J., Polich, J.M., Mothershead, A., & Stephen, M. *A follow-up study of clients at selected alcoholism treatment centers funded by NIAAA*. Menlo Park, California: Stanford Research Institute, 1975.

Rush, B. An inquiry into the effects of ardent spirits upon the human body and mind. The first American medical work on the effects of alcohol. Classics of the alcohol literature. *Quarterly Journal of Studies on Alcohol*, 1943, *4*, 321-341.

Seneca. Epistle LXXXIII: On drunkenness. Classics of the alcohol literature. *Quarterly Journal of Studies on Alcohol*, 1942, *3*, 302-307.

Schlenger, W.E. *Occupational programming: A review of the literature.* Raleigh, North Carolina: The Human Ecology Institute, 1975.

Steiner, C. The alcoholic game. *Quarterly Journal of Studies on Alcohol*, 1969, *30*, 920-938.

Towle, L.H., Bosley, J.J., Borgeson, N.S., Gray, J.H., Mothershead, A.A., & Norwood, C.R. *Alcoholism program monitoring system development - Evaluation of the ATC Program.* Menlo Park, California: Stanford Research Institute, 1973.

Trotter, T. T. Trotter's essay, medical, philosophical, and chemical on drunkenness. Classics of the alcohol literature. *Quarterly Journal of Studies on Alcohol*, 1941, *2*, 584-591.

U.S. Department of Health, Education, and Welfare. Second special report to the U.S. Congress on alcohol and health. DHEW Publication No. (ADM) 74-124, 1974.

World Health Organization, Expert Committee on Mental Health. Report on the first session of the Alcoholism Subcommittee. WHO Org. Tech. Rep., Ser. No. 48, August 1952.

CHAPTER 2

DEFINITIONAL ISSUES IN ALCOHOLISM

David L. Davies

It is unthinkable, if not altogether impossible, to discuss what is meant by the word alcoholism without referring to E.M. Jellinek (1960), whose thinking on this subject was predominant for decades before his death in 1963. It may be worthwhile, therefore, to follow his approach to this problem, looking perhaps a little more critically at his steps with hindsight and in the light of developments since his death.

Jellinek's first difficulty was that there were so many definitions of alcoholism, even in those days. Moreover, there has been not so much a reluctance to employ definitions in this field, as a determination to use labels and catch phrases. As Wexberg (1951) observed, "In no other area of research and social or medical endeavour have slogans so extensively replaced theoretical insights as a basis for

Ralph E. Tarter and A. Arthur Sugerman (eds.), Alcoholism

ISBN: 0-201-08146-6
ISBN: 0-201-08145-8 (pbk.)

therapeutic action, as in alcoholism."

As a start, Jellinek looked at alcoholism as any use of alcoholic beverage that caused any damage to the individual, or society, or both. He never endorsed this definition; it is obviously far too comprehensive. Under it, a boy of 15 who takes alcohol for the first time and becomes tipsy, so that he fails to avoid a passing motor car in time and is killed, might have to be regarded as an alcoholic. It does so much violence to common sense that it is patently absurd.

Yet Jellinek realized that there are so many divergent views about alcoholism that a definition almost as broad as this is needed if one is to accommodate such varying views under one definition. Not only has one to think about the carefully considered statements of those who have made alcoholism a special study by scientific means, but also one has to remember that it is a word in current use. There are popular views about the quantity of alcohol intake as well as the frequency which would seem to mark it off from "normal drinking."

In a hard-drinking society, few, if any, might seem obviously to separate themselves off in this respect. In an abstinent or near-abstinent society, as in certain Muslim countries, almost any drinking is reprehensible, and even criminal. Equally, the behavior of people who have imbibed may be subject to little criticism or constraint in some groups, while subject to severe criticism or constraint in others. Also, the manifestations of such behavior may be different in different groups, which is easily conceived when social behavior is at issue. Academic and professional people generally are less likely to pose problems of violent behavior than, perhaps, unskilled laborers when they become "alcoholics."

In the sphere of physical damage resulting from alcohol usage, national differences are evident. In some countries, gastro-intestinal disorders predominate; in others, nervous, and in still others, psychiatric.

Patterns of drinking differ from country to country, to say nothing of types of beverages consumed, and the idea of alcoholism as something different may seem to lay people, at all events, as an aberration in this area. Thus, one commonly hears it said that solitary drinking has something sinister about it, especially from people who see drinking as essentially a group activity. Therefore, Jellinek had little option but to begin with the crude definition which he quoted.

Some of the patent absurdity of Jellinek's definition, perhaps all, would disappear if one were to qualify the word *use*, by adding some such adjective as *repeated*. Since those who are called alcoholics use alcohol either in bouts or regularly (usually daily), a phrase such as *intermittent or continual use* would be appropriate. It would do justice to the more commonly encountered patterns of use and exclude the unfortunate youth referred to earlier.

Jellinek knew the problem as well as the suggested solution to it since the Alcoholism Subcommittee of the Expert Committee on Mental Health of the World Health Organization (1951) had before it the then accepted definition of drug addiction (and, after all, alcohol is a drug), which ran as follows:

> Drug addiction is a state of periodic or chronic intoxication, detrimental to the individual and to society, produced by the repeated consumption of a drug (natural or synthetic). Its characteristics include:

(1) an overpowering desire or need (compulsion) to continue taking the drug and to obtain it by any means;
(2) a tendency to increase the dose;
(3) a psychic (psychological) and sometimes a physical dependence on the effects of the drug.

Jellinek was prevented by illness from attending, as a member of its secretariat, the first session of that Subcommittee, which came up with the statement that alcoholism is:

> Any form of drinking which in its extent goes beyond the traditional and customary 'dietary' use, or the ordinary compliance with the social drinking customs of the whole community concerned, irrespective of the etiological factors leading to such behaviour and irrespective also of the extent to which such etiological factors are dependent upon heredity, constitution, or acquired physiopathological and metabolic influences.

In essence, this view demarcates alcoholism as drinking which deviates from the socially acceptable norm by its extent (where the drinking is purposeful) or by its direction (i.e., where the aim is other than "traditional" or "customary"). There is no explicit mention of harm, nor of addiction, both of which elements were present in the contemporary definition of drug addiction which this Subcommittee presumably regarded as unsatisfactory to define any part of alcoholism.

The second report of this Subcommittee appeared eleven months later, in August 1952. Jellinek was present at its deliberations, and perhaps because of his presence, the Subcommittee had second thoughts. The members now considered it more appropriate to use their earlier formulation to define not alcoholism but "excessive drinking" and added the following definition of alcoholism.

> Alcoholics are those excessive drinkers whose dependence upon alcohol has attained such a degree that it shows a noticeable mental disturbance or an interference with their bodily and mental health, their interpersonal relations, and their smooth social and economic functioning, or who show the prodromal signs of such developments. They therefore require treatment.

The previous omissions are rectified. In addition to alcoholics being excessive drinkers (whether measured by quantity, frequency, or purpose) there are the two additional elements, dependence and harm. Whether the Subcommittee equated *dependence* with the *addiction* in the definition of drug addiction before them, is a very fine point. In later years, to be precise, in 1964, the World Health Organization recommended that the term *addiction* be replaced by *dependence*, (a matter which will be discussed later) so that perhaps no significance should be attached to the appearance of the less sinister-sounding term in relation to alcohol. The term *harm*, of course, is not used in the second definition of alcoholism quoted above, but is, in fact, spelled out in relation to physical, psychological, social, and economic well-being. This definition will not be evaluated further here, since it is quite misleading. Those who are interested in pursuing that aspect in detail should read the excellent critique by Seeley (1959).

The conclusion reached in that definition - that alcoholics require treatment - implies that they are ill, and so leaves no room for discussion of that contentious issue since the definition asserts it. Yet it was in the context of considering just this - *The Disease Concept of Alcoholism* - that Jellinek revealed in fascinating detail his own views on the nature of alcoholism.

Before leaving that earlier second report of the Alcoholism Subcommittee of the Expert Committee on Mental Health, it should be noted that it proposed a view on how alcoholism develops. Briefly, this view, based to some extent on the progression of the condition in a selected group of drinkers (members of Alcoholics Anonymous) which Jellinek had reported earlier, states that the initial stage is to be called *symptomatic drinking*.

The very term *symptomatic* is a good example of how clear thinking in this area is to be bedevilled endlessly by attributing unusual meanings to medical terms. (Another word is *compulsive*, which in the literature on alcoholism has been similarly debased.) Having been told that this initial phase may be "symptomatic of psychological or physical pathology or of social conditions" any useful meaning the term could have is immediately negated by the statement that "all forms of drinking - even the most moderate forms - are by definition symptomatic at least of social form and convention." Nevertheless, it is proposed that this term *symptomatic* be used to throw some light on excessive drinking.

Introducing a completely unnecessary term like symptomatic in this way would not matter too much if there were no other useful role for this adjective, which of course there is. All medical men, especially psychiatrists, are familiar with illnesses in which disinhibition, dementia, or severe affective disturbances are reflected in heavy alcohol intake, and the consequent features of alcoholism. Mania, schizophrenia, and general paresis, are examples of illnesses identifiable independently of the drinking behavior to which they give rise. The alcoholism which follows is accurately and helpfully to be termed as *symptomatic*. It is increasingly difficult to describe such states today, so successfully has bad verbal currency driven out the good in accordance with Gresham's well-known law.

The Alcoholism Subcommittee then went on to separate off the "irregular symptomatic excessive drinkers" from the "habitual" and "addictive" drinkers, adding that the last two groups "comprise the alcoholics proper."

It is useful to pause here at yet another error into which seekers of the truth in this field are led by the thoughtless use of words. If there are "alcoholics proper," what other sorts are there, and if none, why bring in this phrase? It suggests that there is a nuclear group, recognizable by some but lacking precise definition, and perhaps not even needing such. It follows that serious research findings can be dismissed, especially if they offer a challenge to the folklore of alcoholism, with the glib statement that the cases investigated were not "proper or real alcoholics." It cannot be too strongly emphasized that the great value of a sound definition of alcoholism is that it should preclude this all-too-easy way of avoiding distasteful facts, and, instead, should open the way to a more scientific appreciation of the subject under discussion. In effect, those who fall back on such verbal devices to avoid recognizing facts usually have a stereotype in mind when using the word *alcoholic*. If the person under discussion does not conform, then he is not "a real alcoholic." To say what he is, involves the invention of special categories to recognize his abnormality while preserving the stereotype. For example, the term *problem drinker*, as distinguished from *real alcoholic*, has become customary in many reputable and valuable research studies, e.g. Wilkins (1974). Yet reference to the *Dictionary of Words about Alcohol* by Keller and McCormick (1968) reveals that this term includes the alcoholics. It is seriously suggested that the multiplicity of terms used to describe alcoholism (of which only a few have been given so far) is itself a serious bar to clear thinking on this topic.

One cannot leave the World Health Organization definition of alcoholism without making yet another comment. It clearly envisages three steps, (a) excessive drinking, (b) dependence, (c) harmful drinking, leading to the established state. It says nothing about harmful drinking which is unaccompanied by dependence, which is at least a theoretical possibility, and, even more disconcertingly, it says nothing about dependence without harmful drinking. Suppose that the Subcommittee had eschewed the term *addiction* deliberately, because, as has already been pointed out, at that time addiction implied harm. Are we to understand that the term alcoholic cannot be applied to the individual who takes alcohol regularly, perhaps on a daily basis, because he feels physically or mentally uncomfortable without it; who is unable to reduce his intake though he tries; but who, nevertheless, appears to cause no harm to himself or others? Do such people exist? If so, what are we to call them?

If the drug such people use is opium, or barbiturates, we have no hesitation. These people have been known for decades as addicts, way back into the days when the term addiction implied harm by definition. The contradiction in their styling had to be faced, simply because there were so many of them. The Brain Report (1961) referred to this group as "stabilized addicts." The phenomenon has also been called *controlled addiction*. In this regard it is appropriate to quote Seevers (1968), "Almost any individual can be made to be drug dependent in the most serious sense of the term, even against his will". This leads, he says, to primary psychological dependence, a condition which exists for a majority of the world population. He believes that "certain susceptible individuals" will go beyond this in their abuse of the drug (a matter which will be discussed below), and he goes on to estimate that possibly 70% of the U.S. adult population is using alcohol "in moderation, even to the point of strong psychological dependence, with minimal personal injury and social consequence." In other words, the stabilized or controlled drinkers are the vast majority.

Yet stabilized drinkers are hardly, if ever, referred to in discussions about alcoholism: The *Dictionary of Words about Alcohol* (Keller & McCormick, 1968) makes no reference to them. Realizing that the definition of addiction had been framed when narcotics were the drugs in question and that more liberal legislation and the advent of new drugs made that no longer tenable, WHO first (1964) substituted the word *dependence* for *addiction*, and then (1969) defined dependence solely in terms of the individual's perceived need to go on taking the drug to avoid psychological or physical discomfort. All reference to harm, as well as the other features of narcotic addiction, has been dropped from the definition. What was separately labelled as an innocuous form of addiction, stabilized or controlled addiction, now becomes the norm, dependence. Harm may or may not be associated.

The term alcoholism clearly must embrace those who are merely dependent, even if only psychologically, whose need to continue taking alcohol is to avoid mental and not physical sequalae. There could be no argument on this score were the drug opium, which, like alcohol, far more often results in stabilized addiction than the harmful form. What else but dependency are we trying to treat when the patient recovers from his delirium tremens, or his alcoholic gastritis? Surely he did not cease to be an alcoholic just at that point in time. Though this may seem a pretty obvious point to make, some medical men of the U.S. National Council on Alcoholism (1972) have put forward a definition of alcoholism which is based on *pathological dependence*, evident from *physical* withdrawal symptoms. Therefore, an element which must appear in our definition of alcoholism is dependence, as understood universally with regard to all drugs which have the power to produce such.

Common sense dictates that harmful drinking must clearly be yet another element in the definition. The WHO definition quoted does not actually use this phrase but spells it out. The effects of harm are to mental well-being, physical well-being, and social well-being, including in the latter economic, occupational, and marital aspects.

How essential is dependency as a forerunner of harmful drinking, as has been implied in the WHO definition? Clinical experience suggests that by the time a man is experiencing harm, there is frequently associated dependency. It need not necessarily be so. We have all at some time encountered the man who, at this stage, has accepted advice and given up entirely or moderated his drinking with no special effort. After all, social harm, especially, may come on early and give rise to disproportionate effects in some situations. Frequently, however, there are no means of determining the issue. Let us suppose the man is sleeping badly and has put on a great deal of weight, since he stepped up his drinking a year ago from four to eight pints of beer daily. One might satisfy oneself, as a doctor, that there is no other likely cause to explain this other than alcohol. If the man refuses to accept this view and does not even try to moderate or give up his drinking, one cannot say that he is dependent. If, some years later, he is found at autopsy to have cirrhosed liver, the diagnosis of alcoholism on the score of harmful drinking is confirmed, but one is still unable to say the man was dependent, as the word is proposed. It would be so much simpler to regard dependence and harm as drinking outcomes, either of which constitutes alcoholism, leaving it to be determined in any individual case of harm whether or not dependency co-exists, and even in that case leaving the exact sequence of these two outcomes to be determined by the facts of the case.

How then are these facts to be determined? As already mentioned, the need to take alcohol to avoid unpleasant physical effects is one aspect of dependency. Such withdrawal symptoms, as they are called, may have been experienced by the man when he was not drinking, for some reason. In that case he is able to provide the necessary information on enquiry. If he reports that he has to take a morning drink to settle his tremulous hands, then the issue is not in doubt. However, if there is no information on either of these scores, then he can be requested to leave off drink, and the issue of physical dependence will be settled in that way.

If he reports that without such physical sequalae, withdrawal has caused him mental discomfort so that he has had to resume, or simply that he is aware that he needs his regular drink, then he is psychologically dependent. If he does not know, then again, he can be requested to try abstinence and report back.

Some think this is too simple an approach to dependence, they argue that a great many people "enjoy a drink," adding, "I would be reluctant to give it up myself, though I drink only occasionally and in moderation." This objection lacks force if one takes the view, which seems not unreasonable, that dependence is not an all-or-none phenomenon. True, that was implied in the phrase *overwhelming desire*, which was included in the now discarded addiction definition, framed with the narcotics in mind. That it is not even true of the narcotics has recently been elegantly demonstrated by the report of Robins, Davis and Goodwin (1974) on G.I.'s returning from Vietnam where they were hooked on heroin. Back in their home environment they have either given up or become occasional users with no special fuss. Experience suggests that dependency is of varying strength in different people and at different times for the same drug, so that we can talk of mild, moderate, or severe dependency. Equally, the extent to which the individual is prepared to grapple with it may vary. We talk of this, rightly or wrongly, as motivation.

In treatment, what do we do but encourage the individual to struggle harder against his subjective feeling of need for the drug? True, we do, or think we do, other things as well, according to our orientation (e.g., psychotherapy) which would seem not to be just directed in this way. What about the men, and there are many, who have struggled successfully against their drinking without help from others? The cigarette smoking habit is a form of drug dependence with which a great many ex-smokers are familiar. They will tell in various degrees of the struggle they had to give up, and most of them did so without psychotherapy.

This is not to say that drug-dependent people cannot benefit by assistance from others, nor that they should go it alone. It merely illustrates the obvious point that dependency may vary in its strength from one case to another. The man who says,"I drink moderately because frankly I would miss it and feel uncomfortable without it" probably is dependent, in our sense, but he may be only mildly so. If anyone should say that it is ludicrous to call him an alcoholic, one may reply that obviously the overtones of that word have already become muted with further understanding over recent years; that it may be the stereotype which is at fault and should be dispelled; and that one could refer to the man as (mildly) dependent on alcohol. It is a licit drug after all, and a great many of us really are mildly dependent, as Seevers said, and, not only on alcohol but also on caffeine, not to mention hypnotics of one sort or another.

Of course, it makes no sense to call him alcoholic if, as part of one's thinking, alcoholics must become abstinent, this being regarded as the goal of treatment of these "sick people." It is nonsense to regard 70% of the adult U.S. population as alcoholics, if we are to imply that they are sick and should become abstinent.

It is much more sensible to regard these people as dependent, a harmless state by definition. In that case there is no need for medical men to fuss about them as being in need of medical aid. The sensible thing to do would be to enlighten them, and society, about dependence, pointing out that constantly some of these dependent people move on to a stage of harmful drinking. It would be as well if they monitored their drinking, aiming first at maintaining it rather than giving it up. If necessary, because the quantity of alcohol involved is marginally high, they might be advised to diminish it, surely an easier task now than later, and anyway easier than abstinence for many. This is a preventive approach to alcoholism of the harmful variety, hitherto largely untried except in the extreme, ineffective, and unacceptable form of prohibition. It adds a new dimension to our approach to the problem, and emerges inevitably from semantic considerations.

Such considerations suggest an earlier approach also to prevention. Since alcohol is a drug of dependency, there is no reason to think it should not be subject to restrained use to avoid that state developing. As medical men, nurses, pharmacists and many others know, certain drugs (the so-called Dangerous Drugs in Britain) are prescribed with great care, the aim being to obtain say their analgesic effect but to avoid dependence developing. Thus, we have a fairly good idea of when to stop prescribing such drugs (i.e. in relation to surgical operations) knowing that there is a safe limit to quantity and frequency of prescribing, not to be exceeded. Perhaps a safe limit of alcohol ingestion, specified in terms of quantity and frequency, could be established, below which no significant dependence would develop. Such a limit for the occurrence of harmful drinking has been established by de Lint and Schmidt (1971). Below a daily intake of 15 centiliters of absolute alcohol over an extended period of time (rather less than half a bottle of spirits in the U.K.) no one is likely to be labelled alcoholic in the sense of harmful drinking. Sadly, it is also well known that diagnosed alcoholics have been drinking steadily and heavily for about

15 years, as a rule, before coming under notice in their fifth decade of life. Presumably, a great many of these exceeded the hypothetical dependency limit much earlier, but no one paid much attention because no harm was evident at that point.

One accepted route to alcoholism, perhaps the most common, begins with regular drinking. The amounts taken are higher in some individuals for a variety of reasons, such as occupation, access by price and licensing hours, and the cultural attitudes toward drinking of the group to which the individual belongs, to mention only some. Jellinek (1960) was well aware of this when he stated that "the cultural patterns of a nation or a cultural subgroup play a greater role than individual anomalies" in the genesis of some forms of alcoholism.

Number of drinking years, or stepping up of intake for any reason, will exert their effects on the quantity/frequency factor, the final common path leading to dependence, or harm, or both. It seems more likely that Seeley's 70% of adult U.S. population have been treading this path, than that they are psychopathic, allergic, anxious, or suffering from some mysterious illness yet to be elucidated. So much for the concept of dependence and its implications for action in that sphere and in relation to harmful drinking.

Returning to harmful drinking, there is the difficulty of establishing that the harm and the drinking are related. This is no problem where the drinking is heavy by any standard, and the harm is one of the psychoses traditionally associated with such (e.g. Korsakoff's psychosis) or polyneuropathy of the classical alcoholic type. It is quite another matter when the extent of the drinking is marginal and the harm is in the social sphere, such as breakup of marriage or loss of job, which could result from any number of causes. Usually the harm is evident. It is linking it to the drinking that becomes difficult. Whereas previously, each therapist had his own personal concept of what drinking had to be to be regarded as excessive, we now have an objective criterion, the 15 centiliter absolute alcohol daily level, which is a better general guide, though somewhat unreliable in individual cases. We can now probe the relationship between drinking and the harm by asking the person concerned to cut down or give up his drinking for a period of time (i.e., weeks or months) to see the effect of less alcohol on the harm, be it marital discord, troubles at work, or child behavior disorder. This is likely to throw light on his state of dependency, if any. Of course, if before this, evidence of earlier dependency as described above had been forthcoming, much of the doubt would already have been dispelled.

Harm clearly calls for help. If the damage is in the medical sphere, the doctor will be the chief agent to help. If the harm is in the social or occupational spheres, then other professionals will need to play the major role. Sometimes the harm can be dealt with successfully in a period when drinking is precluded (e.g., gastritis, in hospital), and then the focus of attention shifts to the underlying dependency, if present. Sometimes the harm cannot be dealt with in this way until the dependency is dealt with satisfactorily. Economic difficulties arising from drinking would illustrate this.

It is essential, however, to know what one is aiming to do at any particular time, and once again, a working definition is essential for this purpose. The definition proposed is one that emerges from the foregoing: *Alcoholism is intermittent or continual use of alcohol associated with dependency (psychological or physical) or harm in the sphere of mental, physical, or social activity.*

The illustrations given above are a guide to the application of this relatively simple concept. One looks at the drinking, particularly in relation to chronicity and quantity. It is chronic use which concerns us. Drunkenness is acute intoxication, and relatively unimportant. Many people are drunk from time to time, are no problem to themselves or others, and should not concern us overmuch. Many alcoholics rarely get drunk, and this is certainly true if one thinks of the dependence limit of our definition. One looks for dependency, assessing it from the history and, if necessary, by actively testing by imposing abstinence. One looks at the harm similarly, and especially at the necessary link to the alcohol intake.

Is this all? It seems as though almost anyone could do it. Surely, alcoholism is a disease and so has a cause, symptoms, signs, outcome, and prescribed treatment. Perhaps, like measles, it has a pathognomonic sign: Some say, that "loss of control" is the Koplik's spots of the condition. Do alcoholics not drink in secret (or in groups) so that we shall know them in this way? Have they not a psychopathology we can recognize, and of course a psychogenesis (stress?). Do they not tell lies, or hide away bottles, have red noses, or live on the wrong side of the tracks? Is it not true that they may become abstinent but never resume normal drinking (not the "real alcoholics" anyway), and is it not futile to adopt any other goal of treatment (though, curiously, the alcoholic is expected to give up his "symptom" of drinking before we can start to treat him). Surely, the truth is that we cannot say who is alcoholic, but we all recognize him when we see him.

To try to overcome some of these difficulties, attempts have been made, chiefly by medical men approaching alcoholism conventionally as a disease, to arrange signs and symptoms in long lists of increasing significance. The most extreme example of this is provided by the U.S. National Council on Alcoholism (1972) already mentioned.

Unfortunately, there is no steady progression of the kind one sees in diseases like measles. How could there be, with manifestations of harm in the social, marital, occupational, and economic spheres, at least until the condition is so far advanced that it is obvious to everybody (and some well protected individuals may never come to notice at any time)? To wait for the progression to emerge is to do no better than we do at present.

The pathognomonic sign should help: "Loss of control" is said to be such. Alas, about one-third of alcoholics in the series reported by Stein, Niles, and Ludwig (1968) failed to show such, and of course it is only one aspect of dependence, as Jellinek well knew when he proposed to limit the disease forms of alcoholism to such cases as did show it. He was well aware that even in these forms he could not prove predisposing factors of a physical or psychological kind, and he concluded from the overwhelming evidence available to him that many alcoholics became so, simply by drinking in accordance with the social customs of a hard drinking group to which they belonged. At some point, whatever the genesis of the excessive drinking, "alcohol progressively takes over until it becomes the decisive factor in what the addict may or may not do." Thus the slogan that "alcoholism is not in the bottle but in the man" is a dangerous one.

To misread Jellinek and to come to the conclusion that alcoholism is a disease, which has an ordered progression by which it can be recognized, is to ignore the warning that Jellinek gave precisely against this development when he said:

> The lay public uses the term alcoholism as a designation for any form of excessive drinking, instead of as a label for a *limited and well-defined area of excessive drinking behavior.* Automatically, the disease conception of alcoholism becomes extended to all excessive drinking, irrespective of whether or not there is any physical or psychological pathology involved in the drinking behavior. Such an unwarranted extension of the disease conception can only be harmful because, sooner or later, the misapplication will reflect on the legitimate use, too, and more importantly, will tend to weaken the ethical basis of social sanctions against drunkenness. (1952)

More than anyone, Jellinek was aware that the progression he had done so much to elucidate was possibly true of only one among the very many groupings of alcoholics which exist. He said (1960), "In spite of the respect and admiration to which Alcoholics Anonymous have a claim on account of their great achievements, there is every reason why the student of alcoholism should emancipate himself from accepting the exclusiveness of the picture of alcoholism as propounded by Alcoholics Anonymous." (p.38)

All this suggests that the use of a disease model to define alcoholism is misleading. It is likely to narrow our horizons and prevent early recognition, and it is inefficient because it is too elaborate in the medical and social circumstances in which the problem arises. The truth is that the disease concept of alcoholism is a red herring. How far it is true at all is a separate question, and those interested in pursuing it further might consult, among other writers, Davies (1974).

The concept is usually invoked to elicit sympathy for alcoholics, to alter society's treatment of them, and to query their responsibility in law for some of their acts. It has no bearing at all on the framing of a definition, satisfactory for everyday working purposes and heuristically valuable. Indeed, in the absence of such a definition, no one will ever be able to say whether alcoholism is a disease or not, but that is the very least merit claimed for the definition proposed here.

To recapitulate: Alcoholism is intermittent or continual use of alcohol associated with dependency (psychological or physical) or harm in the sphere of mental, physical, or social activity. This definition, it is submitted, is economical and simple. It provides an essential framework into which to fit the problem, and allows us to go ahead with fact finding to ascertain the truth (as distinct from the legends which surround the subject).

REFERENCES

Brain report. Drug addiction report of the Interdepartmental Committee, London: H.M.S.O., 1961.

Davies, D.L. Is alcoholism really a disease? *Contemporary Drug Problems*, 1974, *3*, 197-212.

deLint, J., & Schmidt, W. Consumption averages and alcoholism prevalence. *British Journal of Addiction*, 1971, *66*, 97-107.

Jellinek, E.M. *The disease concept of alcoholism.* New Haven: Hillhouse Press, 1960.

Jellinek, E.M. Phases of alcohol addiction. *Quarterly Journal of Studies on Alcohol*, 1952, *13*, 673-684.

Keller, M., & McCormick, M. *A dictionary of words about alcoholism.* New Brunswick: Rutgers Center of Alcohol Studies, New Jersey, P. 160.

Robins, L.N., Davis, D.H., & Goodwin, D.W. Drug use by U.S. Army enlisted men in Vietnam - a follow-up on their return home. *American Journal of Epidemiology*, 1974, *99*, 235-249.

Seeley, J.R. The WHO definition of alcoholism. *Quarterly Journal of Studies on Alcohol*, 1959, *20*, 352-365.

Seevers, M.H. Psychopharmacological elements of drug dependence. *The Journal of the American Medical Association*, 1968, *206*, 1263-1266.

Stein, L.I., Niles, D., & Ludwig, A.M. Loss of control phenomenon in alcoholics. *Quarterly Journal of Studies on Alcohol*, 1968, *29*, 598-602.

U.S. National Council on Alcoholism. *American Journal of Psychiatry*, 1972, *129*, 127-135.

Wexberg, L.E. Alcoholism as a sickness. *Quarterly Journal of Studies on Alcohol*, 1951, *12*, 217-230.

Wilkins, R.H. *The hidden alcoholic in general practice.* London: Elek Science, 1974.

World Health Organization, Expert Committee on Mental Health. Technical Report Series No. 42, Geneva: WHO, 1951.

World Health Organization, Expert Committee on Mental Health. Report on the first session of the Alcoholism Subcommittee, Technical Report Series No. 48, Geneva: WHO, August 1952.

World Health Organization, Expert Committee on Mental Health. Technical Report Series No. 273, Geneva: WHO, 1964.

CHAPTER 3

MODELS AND THEORIES OF ALCOHOLISM

Ralph E. Tarter
Dorothea U. Schneider

Throughout recorded history, mankind has made a continuing effort to understand and control natural events. The degree of comprehension and mode of interpretation of phenomena have, however, always been influenced by the social context in which the observer formulated his hypothesis, theory, or explanation. Within the broad field of inquiry pertaining to psychopathology, there has been a progressive evolution of ideas. Beginning with supernatural explanations, man has subsequently advanced moral, medical, and recently, psychosocial theories of maladjustment and deviance.

The study of the chronic inebriate or alcoholic has taken a similar historical course. The indulgent individual has been viewed by society as a morally weak person or degenerate, and consequently banished into exile or other physically remote place, such as "skid row." He has been viewed as a

Ralph E. Tarter and A. Arthur Sugerman (eds.), Alcoholism

ISBN: 0-201-08146-6
ISBN: 0-201-08145-8 (pbk.)

public nuisance in even such restricted places and subsequently placed in prisons, workhouses, or other institutions of detention. More recently, the alcoholic has been considered "sick" and hence afflicted with a disease to be treated by physicians in clinics and hospitals. The chronic inebriate also has been considered a victim of pressures from a demanding society, job insecurity, and breakdown of the family unit, to be treated in community centers by psychologists, social workers, and family counselors. Thus it can be seen that the problem drinker, one whose personal and/or interpersonal efficacy is disrupted by alcohol, has been viewed by society in different ways at different times.

Throughout history, however, there has always been the factor of values in our appraisal of the alcoholic. Thus, even today, the notion of spiritual emptiness is widely accepted as being a significant problem in the alcoholic and hence is integrated into Alcoholics Anonymous ideology. Our values also influence how we relate to the inebriate and plan his rehabilitation as a more productive (and conforming) member of society. Should he be viewed as responsible for his own plight or merely the passive victim of disease? Should he be expected to assert more self-control over his excesses or, alternatively, accept his weaknesses and seek strength from other similarly indulgent persons or from a Power greater than himself? Are the causes for his problems within himself, or is it the stress from his environment that triggers his abusive drinking? These latter questions and how they are dealt with by both the professional and lay communities influence to a large extent whom we label an alcoholic and how we relate to him. The remainder of this chapter will focus on the various models and theories of alcoholism that are currently engaging the interests and efforts of scientists, clinicians, and administrators who are attempting to understand and help the afflicted and often maligned individual.

CHARACTERISTICS OF MODELS AND THEORIES

In order to explain complex and poorly understood events, we often construct a model of the way we think things should work that is based on a simpler scheme of which we have a greater knowledge. Observations are thus described through analogy by placing them within a better understood system of factual events. As conceptual analogues, employed to initiate empirical research, models assume several important functions. They are instrumental in selecting the events relevant for study and those which are irrelevant. Models also shape the manner in which events are described, that is, the language used. Lastly, models assist us in organizing events, to the point where theory building becomes possible. Thus, models stimulate experimentation and theory building and can ultimately influence treatment modality.

Models change over time and reflect the dominant mode of thought at a given time in history. For example, supernatural and moral explanations of behavior were most prominent and accepted when the Catholic Church asserted its authority in regulating virtually all aspects of daily life, that is, prior to the Renaissance. Recently, cybernetics has been applied to psychological inquiry since such concepts proved fruitful in the development of the computer. Man's behavior is thus readily compared to the operations of the computer (which are well known) in the attempt to better understand behavior (which is not well known). As social and technological changes occur, so are new models introduced and old ones abandoned in the continuing effort to better appreciate mysterious events. Changes from one model to another occur when the old model can no longer explain an event. In order to accommodate new data, it may then be necessary to construct an entirely new model. This, according to Kuhn (1962) is the primary reason for the advancement and rejection of models in scientific inquiry.

By way of clarification, it is useful at this junction to illustrate how model utilization has influenced our views and interpretations of abnormal behavior. Consider for a moment Freud's (1966) dilemma when, relatively early in his career, it became evident to him that his training in neurology was inadequate in explaining certain disorders, such as anxiety and hysteria. Similarly, medical knowledge also proved incapable of formulating a comprehensive explanation of psychopathology. Having rejected the concepts and language of medicine, he proceeded to devise the most comprehensive theory of personality to date, based upon a model of the mind derived from nineteenth century classical physics. He conceptualized the human psyche as a closed energy system in which various counteracting forces differentiate from a basic biological source (libido). How the manifestations of this energy become discharged or internalized is what determines a particular psychopathological disturbance. Thus the conceptual model is that of a closed system of energy. However, lacking also an adequate means of description, Freud again set a revolutionary precedent by referring to the deployment of psychic energy (e.g., libido, eros, etc.) as well as to stages of personality development (e.g., Oedipus complex) in the language and myths of ancient Greece.

Although Freud was trained as a physician and was accustomed to thinking and analyzing problems from that standpoint, that perspective was not suitable for explaining certain events. He then made a conscious decision to reject the medical model. This served as impetus in the subsequent development of his complex theories of personality, psychodynamics, and psychopathology by proposing an analogue of mental life and behavior based upon the origins, development, and dispersion of psychic energy. In the *Postscript to a Discussion on Lay Analysis* Freud (1927/1966) cogently summarized this process: "After forty-one years of medical activity, my self-knowledge tells me that I have never really been a doctor in the proper sense. I became a doctor through being compelled to deviate from my original purpose; and the triumph of my life lies in my having, after a long and round-about journey, found my way back to my earliest path."

Scientists who utilize the energy analogue or model of the human psyche have come to be identified with the psychodynamic viewpoint of abnormal behavior. Within this general framework, many different theories have been advanced in addition to the one first articulated by Freud, but essentially, all psychodynamic theories employ an energy model and view psychopathology as a product of the disordered interplay of various psychic forces.

From this example of the relationship between a model and a theory, it is clearly evident that the model is in essence a metaphor. Its value is judged by its usefulness in generating theories which in turn are evaluated by criteria of truthfulness. The model provides us with a perspective, a mode of representation. Theories, on the other hand, enable us to organize our observations and test hypotheses within the specific mode of representation or model. Models are valuable as demonstrated by the range of theories they generate in efforts to clarify a particular phenomenon, but because they lack truth status as such, their limitation is in their very metaphorical quality, which can lead to misinterpretation and error in explicating events. Thus, the advantages and disadvantages of a model are ultimately weighed against the objectives of the observer in elucidating a particular set of natural events. Subsequent sections of this chapter will deal with the different models that have been advanced as they apply to alcoholism. Within each model, the most prominent theories will be presented.

MORAL MODEL

Prior to the development of the hypothetico-deductive method of science, religious concepts and philosophical ideals served as models for differentiating behavior society considered normal from the abnormal. The individual who consumed quantities of alcohol or otherwise behaved in a nonconforming manner was identified as a deviant, basically immoral, and consequently, he had to suffer the legal, physical, and psychological consequences of his actions. Today, those adhering to this model implicitly assume that the alcohol abuser is a "willful sinner" who freely chooses to drink. It is maintained that the individual is responsible for his vice, and that drinking is a sign of moral weakness and not the product of physical, psychological, or social factors.

Because abusive drinking cannot be objectively defined within the context of the moral model, there remains both ambivalence and vagueness as to what constitutes alcoholism.

For example, in cultures where drinking is totally prohibited one is likely to be identified as an alcoholic more readily than in cultures where drinking is tolerated and sanctioned on both religious and secular occasions. Moralists tend to adopt an "all or none" attitude towards alcohol consumption, viewing the beverage itself as evil.

It is also assumed that drinking is under voluntary control and that the abuser is consuming alcohol for his own narcissistic pleasures; consequently the inebriate should expect neither sympathy nor help from society at large. In actual fact, adherents to this model, such as the Salvation Army and Women's Christian Temperance Union, do offer the rudiments of assistance in the form of shelter, food, and spiritual advice. However, it was not uncommon for inebriates during the sixteenth and seventeenth centuries to be socially castigated and loaded on a "ship of fools" with other socially deviant persons to be banished to distant places.

While the moral model had its roots in a prescientific era, it still is accepted today by certain missionary and religious organizations. Even Alcoholics Anonymous accepts in its philosophy a moral deficiency in the problem drinker and so recommends a change in life style by abstaining from alcohol, making restitution to injured others, accepting a higher power or spiritual being, and by transmitting "the word" to other similarly indulgent persons. Although traces of a moral dimension of alcoholism still persist, it is today not a formidable factor in shaping our thinking about alcoholics. Its decline as the dominant mode of thought coincides with the emergence of the medical model of alcoholism. Concepts of evil and wickedness have given rise to concepts of sickness and disease. However, its effects in influencing the course of historical events should not be underestimated. Within this century, the Volstead Act introduced an era of abstinence and prohibition that was ultimately predicated on the immorality of alcohol consumption. Prior to that time enforcers of the moral model (eg., the Church) also exerted social control over the population by defining right from wrong. By refusing to excuse alcohol excesses they may have had some preventative effect on the potential abuser, but considered in total, the moral model has added nothing to a scientific understanding of the etiology and intrinsic processes of alcoholism.

MEDICAL MODEL

With the ascendance of the medical model, alcoholism came to be viewed as a disease entity. Alcohol abuse was regarded as a symptom of an underlying physiological or structural disturbance. This model applies disease terminology, places responsibility for the care of alcoholics in the hands of physicians, and prods the research establishment to find a cure for the disease. Of the many theories that are subsumed under the medical model, they can all be classified as either genetic, endocrinological, brain dysfunctional, or biochemical in nature.

GENETIC THEORIES. Genetic theories attempt to explain alcoholism as an inherited disease. The observations that (a) alcoholism seems to occur more frequently in some families than others; (b) concordance rates for alcoholism are higher in monozygotic twin pairs than in dizygotic pairs (Kaij, 1960);

(c) other pathologies are prevalent in parents of alcoholics (Winokur & Clayton, 1968); (d) animal strains can be bred to prefer alcohol (McClearn & Rogers 1959); (e) racial differences exist in alcohol sensitivity (Wolff 1972); and (f) adopted children with a biological parent who is alcoholic have higher rates of alcoholism than adopted children without a biological alcoholic parent (Goodwin, Hill, Powell, & Viamontes, 1973) are advanced to support the theory of a genetic predisposition to alcoholism.

The type of predisposition and its mechanism are, however disputed among adherents of this perspective. It may be that certain genetic factors play a role in the origin of alcoholism such that: (a) an inherited weak constitution leads to proneness (Jellinek, 1954), (b) an inherited autonomic nervous system responsivity (Wolff 1972) or enzymatic malfunction create the necessary conditions for alcoholism (Williams, 1959), or that (c) the genetic factors may only be relevant as to consumption or nonconsumption of large amounts of alcohol (Jonsson & Nilsson, 1970). The mechanism of inheritance is not known but has been posited to be sex-linked recessive (Winokur & Clayton, 1968), multiple allele (Mardones, 1951), and multiple gene system, or both (Rogers & McClearn, 1962). The genetotrophic theory of Williams (1959) for instance, posits an inherited metabolic defect that interacts with environmental events which may eventually lead the individual to drink and become alcoholic. In this theory, the defect is hypothesized to express itself as a dietary deficiency. Enzymes necessary to metabolize certain nutrients are hypothesized to be lacking due to impaired production and so nutritional deficiencies occur. The dietary deficiency has been speculated to be in the Vitamin B complex (Brady &

Westerfield, 1947), thermolabile elements of the Vitamin B complex (Mardones, 1951), as well as niacin, thiamine, and pyridoxine (Brown, 1969). The presumed deficiency leads to a craving for alcohol as well as cellular and metabolic changes.

ENDOCRINOLOGICAL THEORIES. Another set of theories within the medical model of alcoholism conceptualizes alcoholism as if it were a self-perpetuating glandular disorder (Tintera & Lovell, 1949). There is an initial shock to the endocrine system that is caused by alcohol ingestion and the resulting disequilibrium may be due to either constitutional or environmental factors. Continued drinking however leads to adrenal cortex insufficiency resulting in hypoadrenocorticism. Thus this process toward alcoholism may be initiated by alcohol intoxication which leads at first to a rise in adrenocortical hormones, but a decrease subsequently ensues, resulting in subnormal levels of these hormones. This in effect is a stressful condition which leads to further drinking and so continues the chain of events resulting in adrenal insufficiency. This chronic imbalance results in repetitive alcohol consumption which in itself is labeled as the disease.

BRAIN DYSFUNTION THEORIES. A pathognomic feature in the progression of events in alcoholism is the loss of control phenomenon (Jellinek, 1960). Constitutional theories have been proposed to account for this aspect of the disease (Lemere, 1956). The theory posits heavy controlled drinking as a prerequisite which eventually causes cerebral damage, destroying "willpower" and "judgement" cells. After this point has passed, one drink is sufficient to "paralyze" the healthy cells involved in willpower to the point where the alcoholic is unable to stop drinking.

Recently, evidence has been obtained to suggest that genetic and possibly neurochemical factors may be operating in the alcoholism process. Tarter, McBride, Buonpane, and Schneider (in preparation) found that severe drinkers reported more symptoms of childhood hyperactivity and other indices of minimal brain dysfunction than less severe drinkers. The former group also had a parent or other relative who drank excessively. These findings are congruent with those of Goodwin, Schulsinger, Hermansen, Guze, and Winokur (1975) and Morrison and Steward (1973a, 1973b) who studied adopted children and found that genetic factors play a dominant role in the induction of alcoholism. Alcoholic parents also had children who more frequently exhibited symptoms of minimal brain dysfunction (Cantwell, 1972). Thus the mode of inheritance in alcoholism may be a neurochemical deficiency which in childhood is manifest as minimal brain damage.

BIOCHEMICAL THEORIES. The biochemical approach can also be subsumed under the medical model. The essential tenet of a biochemical theory is that alcoholism reflect some form of dysfunction of appetitive regulation. As such, alcoholism has been viewed as a food addiction (Randolph 1956). Such a theory attempts to explain the alcoholic process as follows: A predisposed individual is one with a sensitivity to certain foods which serve as "pick-ups" and whose elements are also present in alcohol. Drinking affords access to these food elements which, because of their presence in alcohol, are rapidly absorbed, thus accelerating the effect of the "pick-up." However, when these elements are excreted a letdown occurs leading to further drinking to stave off this stressful state. Hence, the addiction is to a food substance, though the alcohol is essential through its quick absorption effect.

The medical model has been applied to describe the behaviors of an alcoholic, speculate about the etiology and pathogenesis of alcoholism, and initiate treatment and prevention programs. Much debate however has centered around the utility of the model and whether it is applicable to alcoholism, and what the actual benefits and deficiencies are that result from its use. By labeling the alcoholic as sick it can be argued that we are robbing him of his freedom, his responsibility for himself and his acts, and deluding him with the hopes of a cure (Szasz, 1972). The model is also questioned on the grounds that by presuming a physiological causation the emphasis is placed erroneously upon the individual, thus ignoring the social milieu which may have been instrumental in establishing a response of excessive drinking in the first place and in maintaining that response. Not only may it be a false premise to call an alcoholic "sick" but it may also hinder more than aid the helping agents who are reluctant to apply pressure on a "sick" person (Finlay, 1974). One answer to the critics would have us believe that the medical model is not purely somatic and that it can incorporate or be complemented by other theoretical constructions. (Van Dijk, 1974). In any event, with the exception of studies pertaining to genetics, there is a significant paucity of experimental evidence that implicates a somatic disturbance in alcoholics in the form of metabolic, biochemical, or endocrinological deficiency (Roebuck & Kessler, 1972).

PSYCHOLOGICAL MODEL

The ascendance of scientific psychology in the twentieth century has had a profound impact upon theory, research, and treatment in the field of alcoholism. The psychological model defines alcoholism as an individual phenomenon but yet does not exclude or minimize social factors and the impact of significant individuals in the development of the addiction.

PSYCHODYNAMIC THEORIES. Within the energy model, alcohol may serve a variety of psychodynamic functions as outlined by Levy (1958). It allows the individual to discharge impulses which are incongruent with his self-image by diminishing the effectiveness of existing repressing forces; it is a means of producing a catharsis which keeps the unconscious ego conflicts from reaching consciousness; it serves symbolic functions related to oral needs and dependency; it allows the person to simulate infantile models of experience, and it can also serve a need for self-punishment. Alcohol intake has been viewed as an expression of hostility and homosexuality. Or alcohol can be a means of identification with a significant other individual.

It has long been hypothesized that oral frustrations originating in childhood lead to a fixation producing a personality type that becomes oral dependent (Bertrand & Masling, 1969). Fenichel (1945) theorized that the alcoholic searches to satisfy his needs for security and self-esteem through an unsatisfied oral drive. It has also been speculated that alcohol enables the drinker to experience a temporary restful equilibrium with his environment and concomitant reduction of psychic pain (Wolowitz & Barker, 1968), by recreating the earlier experience of passive gratification. Alcohol may function as a coping device to relieve stress initially brought on by denial of the mother to provide milk and therefore security (Menninger, 1963). As a symbol of the milk and because of its objective chemical effects, alcohol is then imbibed to relieve stress. Alcoholics have also been hypothesized to experience intense guilt and unacceptable aggressive wishes they attempt to resolve by self-punishment. The aggressive wishes are inappropriately displaced onto one's own body. Thus alcohol intake becomes a manifestation of gradual self-destruction with its concurrent social and psychological deterioration (Menninger, 1963).

Alcoholics have been considered to be latent homosexuals. An overindulgent mother supposedly stimulates intense oral libidinization to the extent that these needs cannot realistically be met and this subsequently results in traumatic weaning. The child then unsuccessfully turns to the father. The rejection and associated deprecation from unsatisifed needs for oral indulgence create feelings of inferiority and envy of masculine potency. Drinking then becomes a strategy in allaying anxiety over masculine inadequacy and also facilitates self-assertion (Machover, Russo, Machover, & Plumeau, 1959).

Another theory views the alcoholic as being deficient in ego functions, and using the alcohol effects to attain a sense of security as a substitute for external object attachments (Chordorkoff, 1964). This theory assumes that the parental environment and constitutional factors cause the individual to be inadequate in forming object relations or attachments. The prealcoholic attempts to adapt by viewing his body as an object. Because of instability in the ego-body relationship, the person must somehow strive to reassure himself of the existence of such a bond. Alcohol, by producing physiological changes of a certain type, provides such an experience of assurance of the ego-body relationship.

LEARNING THEORIES. Psychological learning theories of alcoholism emerged from the larger corpus of reinforcement theory and from attempts to explain alcoholism not as if it were a disease or moral shortcoming, but rather that it is a result of a certain history of learning in which the operant of drinking alcohol has been increased in frequency, duration, and intensity for the psychological benefits it affords. There are many divergent theories. A drive reduction theory defines the stimulus as internal tension which, regardless of its cause, creates a drive state. Drinking becomes a prepotent response (habit) in an effort at drive reduction. The psychological effects of alcohol are thus initially tension reducing and, therefore, reinforcing. The reinforcement in turn strengthens the drinking response which will therefore occur more frequently in response to tension, this cycle eventually leading to habitual drinking (Conger, 1956; Dollard & Miller, 1950).

This homeostatic theory assumes that equilibrium is in itself a desirable or needed bodily state. A disturbance of homeostasis (e.g., physiological arousal or emotional reactions such as fear, anger, depression, etc.) is a drive state that the person strives to reduce. If alcohol is available, the individual will respond with drinking, given that it is socially and culturally tolerated and economically accessible.

The alcohol effects an approximate return to homeostasis and hence is drive reducing thus reinforcing the drinking response. This drinking pattern is further strengthened by transfer to other states of body tension that are different from the original precipitating state of tension. The drinking response may also be strengthened by being elicited in numerous situations through response generalization. The intensity level of the stress gives the alcohol effect either high or low reinforcing qualities. Those individuals who are stress resistant will receive little benefit from alcohol. Highly stressed individuals will receive greater reinforcement effect from the central depressant and anesthetic effects of alcohol and will consequently exhibit faster and more durable learning of the drinking response to stress than others and hence be predisposed to alcoholism (Kingham, 1958).

Learning theory also deals with the seeming incongruence that excessive alcohol drinking brings on social punishment in the forms of job loss, social ostracism, emotional upset, as well as physiological and physical deterioration. This incongruence is explained by the principle of delayed reinforcement. Thus the morning-after hangover or social punishment will not be effective in stopping a drinking response because of the delayed negative reinforcing effects. Secondly, if the drive level is sufficiently high, the immediate drive reducing effects of alcohol will be more heeded than competing social punishment, which may actually create new stress and lead to more drinking.

A comprehensive theory of alcoholism has been advanced by Bandura (1969). He maintains that excessive alcohol consumption is initiated by environmental stress and subsequently is maintained by the central depressant and anesthetic properties of alcohol. The prealcoholic has acquired alcohol consumption as a widely generalized dominant response to aversive stimulation (stress) as a result of its reinforcing qualities through differential reinforcement and modeling. This reinforcement establishes a primary maintaining mechanism of drinking. Excessive drinking as a frequent response to stress eventually leads to metabolic alterations that result in symptoms of physiological aversion when drinking abruptly stops. Thus, drinking is continued so as to allay withdrawal which in turn alleviates physiological aversion. Aversion reduction is itself a reinforcement of drinking and thus becomes a secondary maintaining mechanism for excessive consumption. One advantage of learning theory is that it can be integrated with other theories that posit a drive (physiological or psychological) that can be reduced (or reinforced) by alcohol ingestion. Whatever the source of tension, psychosocial or physiological, learning theory can be invoked to explain excessive alcohol consumption.

PERSONALITY THEORIES. Personality theories of alcoholism view the disturbance as if it were a personality disorder. Alcoholics are described as having a specific type of personality configuration. One theory sees all alcoholics as comprising a specific personality type whose personality traits can be identified as causative factors with the clinical picture being one of high emotionality, immaturity in interpersonal relationships, low frustration tolerance, inability to express anger adequately, anger over dependence with ambivalence to authority, low self-esteem with grandiose behavior, perfectionism, compulsivity, feelings of isolation, and sex role confusion (Catanzaro, 1967). It is interesting to note that this picture very much resembles the psychoanalytic description of dependence. Zwerling and Rosenbaum (1959) posit a matrix composed of five character traits: (a) schizoid, (b) depressed, (c) dependent, (d) hostile, and (e) sexually immature which are necessary but not sufficient conditions for addiction. The temporal ordering of these personality traits was hypothesized by Buhler and Lefever (1947) and commences with an ambitious and rational individual who is intolerant of pressure and has conflicting goals. He then experiences difficulty establishing and attaining his goals. Frustration develops from the thwarted desire for success which leads to anxiety and eventually drinking as an escape response.

The finding that alcoholics as a group are perceptually more field dependent than non-alcoholics (Witkin, Karp, & Goodenough, 1959) has become the basis of a theory which hypothesizes that alcoholic individuals manifest this perceptual inclination toward dependency and passivity as an antecedent trait in their personality development. However the great variability in performance on perceptual dependency measures among alcoholics has led others (Goldstein & Chotlos, 1965) to hypothesize that the dependent cognitive style is a consequence of heavy drinking, probably due to brain damage.

Among personality theorists are those who, instead of attributing one set of characteristics to all alcoholics, find them to form several distinct subgroups (Jellinek, 1960; Parthington & Johnson, 1969). Alcoholics have been divided into essentials or reactives (Knight, 1937). The former group has been shown by Sugerman, Reilly, and Albahary (1965) to be more immature and unstable than the latter group, who have merely turned to alcohol later in life in an attempt to relieve stress during an acute psychiatric disturbance or life stress.

Continuing in the vein that alcoholics do not exhibit one specific cluster of personality traits, Sherfey (1955) concluded that alcoholism is but a symptom of an underlying psychiatric disturbance. Thus alcoholics should not differ qualitatively from the personality profiles of psychiatric patients. Alcoholism is thus not considered as a specific "disease" entity but instead is one manifestation in a molar typology of psychopathology. The typological theory does not view alcoholism as a primary disorder; alcoholics are not considered to be a homogeneous group, and alcoholics are not believed to be diagnostically different from psychiatric patients.

TRANSACTIONAL THEORIES. The transactional approach seeks to find the causes of alcoholism in interpersonal behavior rather than in intrapsychic processes. In this sense it is a social-psychological theory because of its emphasis on the individual's interactions with his social environment. Its basic premise is that alcoholics are individuals who engage in distinct, repetitive, interpersonal behavior sequences (games) which necessitate the excessive use of alcohol insofar as it promotes game playing. It is not the effect from alcohol which initiates and maintains drinking behavior, rather it is the appropriate social reinforcement from significant others that is at the root of alcoholism. Support for this notion comes from Keehn (1969) who found no conclusive evidence of the reinforcing properties of alcohol but rather maintains that it is the reinforcing contingencies set up by the community that maintain excessive drinking. In the sequence of events detailed by Steiner (1969), the individual assumes a life plan or "script" in early childhood which becomes a blueprint for future behavior. The life script is based on his self-concept, perception of self-worth, and the concept of himself as others see him. In promoting his script, the individual engages in repetitive patterns of transactions which lead to rewards. The alcoholic engages in specific games which allow him to express guilt-free anger, to avoid inadequacies, and to satisfy sexual and oral needs. Without the transactions of the game and their attendant payoffs the need for alcohol is hypothesized to drop out.

The transactionalist approach is similar to Bandura's (1969) social learning theory in that both postulate social reinforcement as a crucial factor in abusive drinking. However, Steiner (1969) does not attribute positive reinforcement to the alcohol effects per se whereas Bandura does give consideration to the psychopharmacological effects of ethanol.

SOCIOLOGICAL MODEL

The failure of traditional models to fully explain the causation and development of alcoholism was primarily responsible for sociological involvement in alcoholism research. Indeed it seems necessary to view alcoholism in a social context, whether one has a learning, psychodynamic, or biological bias. The impact of the environment upon the biological and psychological individual must be assessed specifically with reference to the importance of membership in certain social groups. The assumption underlying sociological inquiry is that there exists a relationship between social structure and prevalence of alcoholism.

SUB-STRUCTURAL THEORIES. The social factors which directly influence whether a person will drink and how he views himself after drinking have been studied in the hope of finding explanations for the diversity in alcoholism rates among individuals of differing age, sex, ethnicity, socioeconomic class, religion, and family background. These variables have a profound impact upon the individual to start, continue, or stop drinking by determining: (a) childhood exposure to alcohol and drinking models, (b) quantity of alcohol considered appropriate or excessive, (c) drinking customs, (d) type of alcoholic beverage used, (e) levels of imbibition considered safe, (f) symbolic meaning of alcohol (g) attitude toward public intoxication, (h) the social group associated with drinking, (i) activities associated with drinking, (j) the amount of pressure exerted upon the individual to drink and continue drinking, (k) use of alcohol in social or private context, (l) the individual's mobility in changing drinking reference groups, (m) the permanence of a deviancy label, and (n) the social rewards or punishments for drinking.

The role of social variables has been investigated by Cahalan (1970) in a national survey of drinking habits, and he concluded that the social environment to a large extent determines whether an individual will drink or not. Social-psychological variables also determine the level of drinking maintained. Such variables include: (a) an attitude favorable to drinking, (b) the amount and type of environmental support for heavy drinking, (c) the individual's impulsivity to act and his desire for conformity or nonconformity, (d) his degree of alienation and maladjustment, (e) his expectations for success, and (f) the looseness of social controls. Cahalan proposed two theoretical paradigms to explain the process of becoming a problem drinker and the loss of control phenomenon. To become a problem drinker an individual must permit heavy drinking under at least some circumstances. The social variables of age, sex, ethnicity, and social position will influence the probability of turning to drinking as a dominant response. Labeling occurs next, expecially if the drinker changes to a social reference group which labels him a heavy drinker even though his drinking pattern has not changed, but rather only the reference group. Once labeled as a "heavy drinker" he may continue to drink even under social condemnation given that (a) his impulsivity toward seeking short-term gratification in the form of alcohol effects is sufficiently strong, and (b) his subjective feelings alter drastically between sober and intoxicated conditions such that the physiological effects are more reinforcing than the minimal social reward for not drinking. The problem drinker may under strong social pressure contine to drink by changing his reference group to a more permissive one or, if enough pressure is exerted by significant others, he may terminate or reduce his drinking behavior. The occurrence of loss of control drinking is explained as a psychological dependence which develops after the individual has reached the problem drinking stage described above. Loss of control is hypothesized to occur when the positive reinforcement of the alcoholic effects of euphoria is stronger than the negative effect of the physiological and psychological dysphoria which follows termination of drinking. The drinker learns that hangovers can be forestalled by continued drinking.

When investigating sociological variables that may aid in the prediction of alcoholic behavior, demographic variables such as age and sex are often lumped with factors such as the family structure or religious group. It would seem that a group such as the family would have multiple ways of influencing drinking behavior. A family, especially parents, may contribute to the development of an alcohol problem by providing a dearth of appropriate role models because of parental absence, deprivation, or pathology (Winokur & Clayton, 1968). Parental attitudes toward alcohol, such as ambivalence or strong approval, will be communicated to the child and shape his own attitude toward alcohol (Jackson & Connor, 1953). Conflict in the home or antisocial behavior may create stress conditions that invite the use of alcohol as an escape (McCord, McCord, & Gudeman, 1960). Thus, the parents' roles may not only help create personality adjustment problems in the child which will result in those characteristics found in many alcoholics (dependence, unexpressed anger, tension), but also directly encourage the use of alcohol to deal with the resultant problems.

DEVIANT BEHAVIOR THEORY. Deviant behavior theory has been touched upon in the formulations of Cahalan (1970) as it combines elements of the psychological and social spheres to explain alcoholism. It recognizes the fact that a diagnosis of alcoholism is a judgement made against a social norm and contingent upon social variables. The classification of a person as an alcoholic (therefore, deviant) depends on his social status, visibility, locale, age, and the juncture in time (Goldstein & Goldstein, 1975). Alcoholism is hypothesized to be more than a physical dependency or psychological escape. It is the result of a career of deviancy established through transactions between the individual and other persons, his family, and institutions. These relationships are hypothesized to be deviance-producing and because of the quality of interdependence, the participants may go to extremes to protect their transactions. The needs, motives, and gains of all the participants of an interaction must be taken into account in assessing the development and maintainance of the alcoholic's deviant role.

In the development of an alcoholic career, deviant behavior theory ascribes to social relationships the roles of contributing to the primary deviancy and secondly, of labeling that behavior. Labeling itself may produce deviance or secondary deviance. The label states that specific behaviors assume an importance such that one's identity is defined by these limited behaviors. The label becomes an ever inclusive way of life until the process becomes a commitment to self-justification by rejecting the reference group that can take the form of alienation, retreat, aggression, manipulation of reality, and unity with other deviant subcultures.

CULTURAL THEORIES. There are several general ways in which the social organization at the cultural and suprastructural levels influences rates of alcoholism. It has been postulated that if the primary function of alcohol is to reduce anxiety, then alcoholism will be more prevalent in a culture where anxiety is prevalent (Horton, 1943). This is supported by data which show that tribes with very primitive hunting and gathering economies and therefore greater "subsistence anxiety" tend to have more drunkenness than agricultural tribes (Field, 1962; Horton, 1943). Field (1962) interpreted this phenomenon in terms of social organization rather than anxiety, per se. Drunkenness was found to be related to an informal, loose, individual-oriented type of social organization, rather than a corporate type of organization with strict social controls.

The oft-cited work of R.F. Bales (1946) also provides some general hypotheses for the ways in which culture and social organization influence alcoholism rates. Bales proposed that a society which produces acute inner tensions, such as guilt, suppressed aggression, sexual tension, and whose attitudes condone the use of alcohol in a utilitarian manner to relieve those tensions, is susceptible to high rates of alcoholism. Bales also cited the collective attitudes toward alcohol as influencing drinking practices. These attitudes include: (a) abstinence; (b) ritual use connected with religious rites: (c) convivial drinking in a social setting; and (d) utilitarian, the purpose of drinking being for personal, self-interested reasons. The utilitarian attitude is thought the most likely to lead to problem drinking, especially in a society which induces inner tension. Similar to this formulations is Glad's (1947) "affectivity-instrumentality" hypothesis which states that societies approving the use of alcohol for affective consequences will have higher rates of alcohol than if drinking is used for instrumental, that is, ritualistic or socially practical reasons.

The third variable cited by Bales (1946) is the degree to which the culture offers alternatives to the release of tension and provides substitute means of satisfaction. A society which offers few alternatives to drinking as a tension releaser will have a high rate of inebriation or insobriety. If tension includes the frustration of failure then Merton's (1957) and Cloward's (1959) work should be considered. They focused upon the discrepancy between the socially desirable aspirations instilled in an individual and the choices toward their achievement that a society provides. For example, a society with a strong emphasis on upward social and economic mobility will excessively frustrate the individual if there are no consistent or available methods for achieveing success. The individual who cannot attain a highly socially desirable goal through either legitimate or illegitimate means may abandon both goal and means and retreat into alcoholism. The intervening variables of personality are not considered here, nor is the case of the individual who comes up against incongruence in the social structure but who does not become alcoholic.

The role of societal consensus regarding the use of alcohol is another variable to consider. When there is little unanimity among members as to drinking limits and customs, the norms and controls thus being widely divergent, a higher rate of alcoholism is expected. (Trice, 1962, Ullman, 1958). The importance of conflicting societal attitudes in Ullman's (1953) formulation is that the individual experiences ambivalence and, as a result, emotional arousal with regard to drinking, which is a necessary step in the conditioning process toward heavy drinking. For Trice (1962) however, cultural ambivalence is significant because it results in weak social controls, allowing the drinker to avoid a deviancy label by changing his drinking group easily until he is a problem drinker.

INTERDISCIPLINARY APPROACHES

One significant advance in the study of alcoholism is the realization that it may not be a unitary disorder. Even though there is a similar behavior topography in all alcoholic individuals in that they exhibit excessive drinking to the point where personal and social functioning are impaired, the etiology and motivation for abusive drinking may differ widely. Considered in terms of levels of analysis, the available evidence points to the possibility that alcoholism (heretofore thought of as a single entity) may in fact be manifest via different mechanisms; hence multiple causality in the induction of alcoholism. For some individuals, a genetic predisposition and associated physiological-biochemical dysfunction is a necessary condition for abusive drinking. Such an individual indeed exhibits somatic pathology and can be legitimately labeled as "sick." The medical model best fits the available data in this instance. On the other hand, there are persons with no known predisposition or physiological aberration but with identifiable disturbances in personal development, learning history, and interpersonal orientation. Such individuals can best be understood within a sociopsychological framework; the disease model does not apply. Thus, if alcoholism is viewed as not a single disorder but instead as comprising a set of disorders whose topography is similar but causation varies, it becomes readily apparent that the current debate over which is the best model becomes irrelevant.

From this discussion, an interdisciplinary model appears to be of most heuristic value. If alcoholism is a complex of disorders, then the selection of a model and subsequent derivation of theories would depend primarily upon the particular aspect of alcoholism under inquiry. No one model or theory could suffice. No single mode of treatment would prove universally beneficial. The goals of future investigations should therefore be directed towards graphical differentiation of alcoholics according to etiological factors, process characteristics, and overt manifestations. By shifting from a molar to an atomistic emphasis, we can eventually expect to evolve more specific and circumscribed theories and models of the various alcoholisms.

REFERENCES

Bales, R. Cultural differences in rates of alcoholism. *Quarterly Journal of Studies on Alcohol*, 1946, *6*, 480-499.

Bandura, A. *Principles of behavior modification*. New York: Holt, Rinehart, & Winston, 1969.

Bertrand, S., & Masling, J. Oral imagery and alcoholism. *Journal of Abnormal Psychology*, 1969, *74*, 50-53.

Brady, R., & Westerfield, W. The effects of B complex vitamins on voluntary consumption of alcohol by rats. *Quarterly Journal of Studies on Alcohol*, 1947, *7*, 499-505.

Brown, R. Vitamin deficiency and voluntary alcohol consumption. *Quarterly Journal of Studies on Alcohol*, 1969, *30*, 592-597.

Buhler, C. & Lefever, D. A Rorschach study on the psychological characteristics of alcoholics. *Quarterly Journal of Studies on Alcohol*, 1947, *8*, 197-260.

Cahalan, D. *Problem drinkers*: *A national survey*. San Francisco: Jossey-Bass, 1970.

Cantwell, D. Psychiatric illness in the families of hyperactive children. *Archives of General Psychiatry*, 1972, *27*, 414-417.

Catanzaro, R. Psychiatric aspects of alcoholism, in D.J. Pittman (Ed.), *Alcoholism*, New York: Harper & Row, 1967.

Chordorkoff, B. Alcoholism and ego function. *Quarterly Journal of Studies on Alcohol*, 1964, *25*, 292-299.

Cloward, R. Illegitimate means, anomie, and deviant behavior. *American Sociological Review*, 1959, *24*, 164-176.

Conger, J. Reinforcement theory and the dynamics of alcoholism. *Quarterly Journal of Studies on Alcohol*, 1956, *17*, 296-305.

Dollard, J. & Miller, N. *Personality and psychotherapy*, New York: McGraw Hill, 1950.

Fenichel, O. *The Psychoanalytic theory of neuroses*. New York: Norton, 1945.

Field, P. A new cross-cultural study of drunkenness. In D. J. Pittman & C.R. Snyder, (Eds.), *Society, culture, and drinking patterns*. New York: John Wiley & Sons, 1962.

Finlay, D. *Constructive coercion and the problem-drinking employee: Prospects and problems*. Vancouver: Alcoholism Foundation of B.C., April 1974.

Freud, S. Postscript to a discussion on lay analysis (1927). *On the history of the psychoanalytic movement*(J. Strachey, Trans.) New York: Collier Books, 1966.

Glad, D. Attitudes and experiences of American-Jewish and American-Irish male youths as related to adult rates of inebriety. *Quarterly Journal of Studies on Alcohol*, 1947, *8*, 406-471.

Goldstein, G., & Chotlos, J. Dependency and brain damage in alcoholics. *Perceptual and Motor Skills*, 1965, *21*, 135-150.

Goldstein H., & Goldstein, L. The concept of deviancy revisited. *Canada's Mental Health*, 1975, *23*, 10-14.

Goodwin, D.W., Hill, S., Powell, B., & Viamontes, J. Effect of alcohol on short-term memory in alcoholics. *British Journal of Psychiatry*, 1973, *122*, 93-94.

Goodwin, D., Schulsinger, F., Hermansen, L., Guze, S., & Winokur, G. Alcoholism and the hyperactive child syndrome. *Journal of Nervous and Mental Disease*, 1975, *160*, 349-353.

Horton, D. The functions of alcohol in primitive societies: A cross-cultural study. *Quarterly Journal of Studies on Alcohol*, 1943, *4*, 199-320.

Jackson, J., & Connor, R. Attitudes of parents of alcoholics, moderate drinkers, and nondrinkers toward drinking. *Quarterly Journal of Studies on Alcohol*, 1953, *14*, 596-613.

Jellinek, E.M. Heredity of the alcoholic. In Yale University Center of Alcohol Studies. *Alcohol, science, and society*. Westport, Conn.: Greenwood Press, 1972. (Orig. pub., 1945)

Jellinek, E.M. *The disease concept of alcoholism*. New Haven: Hillhouse Press, 1960.

Jonsson, E., & Nilsson, T. Alcohol consumption in monozygotic and dizygotic pairs of twins. *Quarterly Journal of Studies on Alcohol*, 1970, *31*, 774 (Abstract)

Kaij, L. *Alcoholism in twins: Studies on the etiology and sequels of abuse of alcohol*. Stockholm: Almquist & Wiksell, 1960.

Keehn, J. Voluntary consumption of alcohol by rats. *Quarterly Journal of Studies on Alcohol*, 1969, *30*, 320-329.

Kingham, R. Alcoholism and reinforcement theory of learning. *Quarterly Journal of Studies on Alcohol*, 1958, *19*, 320-330.

Knight, R. The dynamics and treatment of chronic alcohol addiction. *Bull Menninger Clinic*, 1937, *1*, 233-250.

Kuhn, T. *The structure of scientific revolution*. Chicago: University of Chicago Press, 1962.

Lemere, F. What causes alcoholism. *Journal of Clinical Experimental Psychopathology*, 1956, *17*, 202-206.

Levy, R. The psychodynamic functions of alcohol. *Quarterly Journal of Studies on Alcohol*, 1958, *19*, 649-659.

Machover, S., Russo, F., Machover, K., & Plumeau, F. Clinical and objective studies of personality variables in alcoholism. III. An objective study of homosexuality in alcoholism. *Quarterly Journal of Studies on Alcohol*, 1959, *20*, 528-542.

Mardones, J. On the relationship between deficiency of B vitamins and alcohol intake in rats. *Quarterly Journal of Studies on Alcohol*, 1951, *12*, 563-575.

McClearn, G., & Rogers, D. Differences in alcohol preference among inbred strains of mice. *Quarterly Journal of Studies on Alcohol*, 1959, *20*, 691-695.

McCord, W., McCord, J., & Gudeman, J. *Origins of alcoholism*. Stanford University Press, 1960.

Menninger, K. *The vital balance*. New York: Viking Press, 1963.

Morrison, J., & Stewart, M. Evidence for polygenetic inheritance in the hyperactive child syndrome. *American Journal of Psychiatry*, 1973, *130*, 791-792. (a)

Morrison, J., & Stewart, M. The psychiatric status of the legal families of adopted hyperactive children. *Archives of General Psychiatry*, 1973, *28*, 888-891. (b)

Parthington, J., & Johnson, F. Personality types among alcoholics. *Quarterly Journal of Studies on Alcohol*, 1969, *30*, 21-33.

Randolph, T. The descriptive features of food addiction: Addictive eating and drinking. *Quarterly Journal of Studies on Alcohol*, 1956, *17*, 198-224.

Roebuck, J., & Kessler, R. *The etiology of alcoholism*. Springfield, Ill.: C. Thomas, 1972.

Rogers, D., & McClearn, G. Mouse strain differences in preference for various concentrations of alcohol. *Quarterly Journal of Studies on Alcohol*, 1962, *23*, 26-35.

Sherfey, M. Psychopathology and character structure in chronic alcoholism. In W.O. Diethelm, (Ed.), *The etiology of chronic alcoholism*, Springfield: Ill. C. Thomas, 1955.

Steiner, C. The alcoholic game. *Quarterly Journal of Studies on Alcohol*, 1969, *30*, 920-938.

Sugerman, A., Reilly, D., & Albahary, R. Social competence and essential-reactive distinction in alcoholism. *Archives of General Psychiatry*, 1965, *12*, 552-556.

Szasz, T. Bad habits are not diseases. *Lancet*, 1972, *7766*, 83-84.

Tarter, R., McBride, H., Buonpane, N., & Schneider, D. Differentiation of alcoholics according to childhood history of minimal brain dysfunction, family history, and drinking pattern. (In preparation)

Tintera, J., & Lovell, H. Endocrine treatment of alcoholism. *Geriatrics*, 1949, *4*, 274-280.

Trice, H. *Alcoholism in America*. New York: McGraw Hill, 1962.

Ullman, A. The first drinking experiences of addictive and of "normal" drinkers. *Quarterly Journal of Studies on Alcohol*, 1953, *14*, 181-191.

Ullman, A. Sociocultural background of alcoholism. *The Annals of the American Academy of Political and Social Science*, 1958, *351*, 22-30.

Van Dijk, W. Problems concerning the application of the medical model in alcoholism. *Journal of Alcoholism*, 1974, *9*, 9-14.

Williams, R. *Alcoholism: The nutritional approach*. Austin: University of Texas Press, 1959.

Winokur, G., & Clayton, P. Family history studies. IV. Comparison of male and female alcoholics. *Quarterly Journal of Studies on Alcohol*, 1968, *29*, 885-891.

Witkin, H., Karp, S., & Goodenough, D. Dependence in alcoholics. *Quarterly Journal of Studies on Alcohol*, 1959, *20*, 493-504.

Wolff, P. Ethnic differences in alcohol sensitivity. *Science*, 1972, *175*, 449-450.

Wolowitz, H., & Barker, M. Alcoholism and oral passivity. *Quarterly Journal of Studies on Alcohol*, 1968, *29*, 592-597.

Zwerling, I., & Rosenbaum, M. Alcoholic addiction and personality. In S. Arieti (Ed.), *American handbook of psychiatry*. New York: Basin Books, 1959.

Part 11

Processes in Alcoholism

CHAPTER 4

MEDICAL COMPLICATIONS OF ALCOHOLISM: HEPATIC SYSTEM

Mark A. Korsten
Charles S. Lieber

Chronic ethanol exposure results in profound biochemical and morphologic hepatic changes prior to the development of liver disease. Some of these persistent changes are the consequences of the injurious effects of ethanol, whereas others may represent adaptive responses to changes in intermediary metabolism consequent to ethanol oxidation. These adaptive responses may involve pathways of ethanol oxidation other than alcohol dehydrogenase.

PATHWAYS OF ALCOHOL METABOLISM

ALCOHOL DEHYDROGENASE (ADH). Most ingested alcohol is metabolized in the liver by the cytosolic enzyme alcohol dehydrogenase (Figure 1A). This enzyme catalyzes the conversion

Ralph E. Tarter and A. Arthur Sugerman (eds.), Alcoholism

ISBN: 0-201-08146-6
ISBN: 0-201-08145-8 (pbk.)

of ethanol to acetaldehyde and the reduction of cofactor NAD to NADH. Although this enzyme is found in other tissues of the body, the present discussion is limited to hepatic ADH activity. The increased NADH/NAD ratio has important consequences on intermediary metabolism by changing the ratio of those metabolites that are in equilibrium with it (Lieber & Davidson, 1962). In vitro, purified ADH has a K_m (the substrate concentration at which the reaction velocity is half maximal) varying from .5 to 2 mM (Reynier, 1969; Makar, & Mannering, 1970) which is similar to the in vivo values derived from the non-linear, terminal portion of the alcohol clearance curve (Lundquist & Wolthers, 1958). Although the equilibrium constant of ADH actually favors reduction of acetaldehyde to ethanol (Theorell & Bonnichsen, 1951), ethanol oxidation proceeds because of the rapid removal of acetaldehyde. The amount of ADH is probably not the rate limiting step in the metabolism of ethanol. Rather, the availability of cofactor NAD and the rate of mitochondrial reoxidation of NADH has been shown to limit this pathway (Theorell & Bonnichsen, 1951). There are numerous examples of the lack of correlation between rates of ethanol oxidation and hepatic ADH activity. Despite acceleration of ethanol metabolism by chronic ethanol consumption (Kater, Carulli, & Iber, 1969; Lieber & DeCarli, 1970b; Misra, Lefevre, Ishii, Rubin, & Lieber, 1971; Tobon & Mezey, 1971), levels of hepatic ADH activity have been found to be unchanged or even decreased (Carulli, Manenti, Gallo, & Salvioli, 1971; Figueroa & Klotz, 1962, Greenberger, Cohen, & Isselbacher, 1965; Lieber & De Carli, 1970b; Morrison & Brock, 1967; Singlevich & Barboriak, 1971; Videla & Israel, 1970). The nature and significance of non-ADH pathways of alcohol oxidation will be discussed. Although ADH is the main pathway for ethanol oxidation in vivo, several lines of evidence support the notion of alternate, non-ADH pathways. Despite inhibition of ADH by pyrazole, 20-22% of ethanol metabolism remains (Lieber & DeCarli, 1972) and this residual metabolism does not affect the cytosolic redox state (Grunnet & Thieden, 1972).

ALTERNATIVE PATHWAYS OF ETHANOL METABOLISM (MEOS). Other systems that may mediate ethanol oxidation are shown in Figures 1A and 1B. They include the microsomal ethanol oxidizing system (MEOS) and the peroxidation of ethanol by catalase.

FIGURE 1

A.

$$CH_3CH_2OH + NAD^+ \xrightarrow[\text{ADH}]{} CH_3CHO + NADH + H^+$$

B.

$$CH_3CH_2OH + NADPH + H^+ + O_2 \xrightarrow[\text{MEOS}]{} CH_3CHO + NADP^+ + 2H_2O$$

C.

$$NADPH + H^+ + O_2 \xrightarrow[\text{NADPH Oxidase}]{} NADP^+ + H_2O_2$$

$+$

$$H_2O_2 + CH_3CH_2OH \xrightarrow[\text{Catalase}]{} 2H_2O + CH_3CHO$$

FIGURE 1: Pathways of ethanol oxidation: A. Alcohol dehydrogenase (ADH). B. The microsomal ethanol oxidizing system (MEOS). C. The combination of NADPH oxidase and catalase.

Ethanol feeding results in a proliferation of the smooth endoplasmic reticulum (SER) (Iseri, Gottlieb, & Lieber, 1964, 1966) and this resembles the adaptive increase in SER that is seen after the administration of other exogenous compounds (Conney, 1967; Lane & Lieber, 1967). These findings suggested that ethanol might be metabolized in the microsomal fraction as well as in the cytosol. Indeed, microsomal oxidation of ethanol via MEOS resembles other drug metabolizing systems in its requirement for NADPH and oxygen (Lieber & DeCarli, 1970b). An opposing view has been that MEOS activity could be accounted for on the basis of microsomal contamination by enzymes capable of ethanol metabolism, e.g., catalase in association with an H_2O_2 generating system such as NADPH oxidase. However, MEOS activity has now clearly been differentiated from catalase by utilizing inhibitors (Lieber & DeCarli, 1968, 1970b; Lieber, Rubin, & DeCarli, 1970) by DEAE-cellulose column chromatography (Mezey, Potter, & Reed, 1973; Teschke, Hasumura, Joly, Ishii, & Lieber, 1972; Teschke, Hasumura, & Lieber, 1974) and by substrate specificity (Teschke, Hasumura, & Lieber, 1975). The relationship between MEOS and NADPH oxidase activity has also been clarified. Since both systems are enhanced by chronic ethanol feeding (Carter & Isselbacher, 1971; Lieber & DeCarli, 1970d), it has been proposed that microsomal ethanol oxidation is due to the peroxidation of ethanol by H_2O_2 generated in the microsomes (via NADPH oxidase) and contaminating catalase (Khanna, Kalant, & Lin, 1970; Thurman, Ley, & Scholz, 1972). This implies that the activity of NADPH oxidase should be rate limiting for microsomal oxidation of ethanol. However, this was not the case in rats given an acute dose of ethanol after chronic ethanol feeding. Under these conditions, MEOS activity was increased significantly, whereas, NADPH oxidase activity was unchanged (Hasumura, Teschke, & Lieber, 1975). In any case, it is generally accepted that the H_2O_2 - mediated ethanol peroxidation by catalase is limited by the rate of H_2O_2 generated, rather than the amount of catalase itself. The actual capacity of the liver to generate H_2O_2 has been estimated (Boveris, Oshino, & Chance, 1972) and is too low to sustain the residual rate of ethanol metabolism observed after ADH inhibition by pyrazole.

After ADH inhibition by pyrazole in vivo, the apparent K_m of blood ethanol disappearance is 8.8 mM (Lieber & DeCarli, 1972). This coincides with the K_m of MEOS found in vitro (Lieber & De Carli, 1970b). Therefore, compared to ADH, MEOS requires higher ethanol levels for full saturation and maximal velocity. Although ADH remains the main pathway for ethanol metabolism, with increasing concentration of ethanol there is a striking increase in the contribution of this non-ADH fraction (Grunnet, Quistorf, & Thieden, 1973; Matsuzaki & Lieber, 1975; Thieden, 1971). It has been suggested that at very high ethanol concentrations, as much as 80% of ethanol metabolism could proceed via a non-ADH (presumably MEOS) pathway (Thieden, 1971).

Whereas ADH catalyzed ethanol oxidation generates NADH and can be coupled to oxidative phosphorylation, MEOS activity generates heat without apparent conservation of chemical energy. Since MEOS activity is induced by chronic ethanol exposure, this may explain (a) the higher BMRs (and O_2 consumption) of alcoholics compared to non-alcoholic controls (Tremolieres & Carre, 1961), (b) the lesser growth in animals fed ethanol (Lieber, Jones, & DeCarli, 1965; Saville & Lieber, 1965) and, at least in part (c) the weight loss of volunteers upon an isocaloric substitution of food by ethanol and their failure to gain weight when ethanol is given as isocaloric supplementation (Pirola & Lieber, 1972). Thus, in alcoholics in whom ethanol represents a large fraction of the total calories and in whom MEOS is induced, ethanol may not fully count (Lieber, 1973a) in a caloric sense.

METABOLIC CONSEQUENCES OF ALCOHOL OXIDATION

A variety of metabolic effects have been traced to the hepatic metabolism of ethanol. These effects may be mediated by the generation of reducing equivalents as NADH and/or by the production of a toxic metabolite (i.e., acetaldehyde). Moreover, to the extent that ethanol is oxidized by the alternate MEOS pathway, changes in lipoprotein synthesis and drug disposal may be due to microsomal mechanisms.

ACETALDEHYDE. Acetaldehyde is the first major specific oxidation product of ethanol whether derived from the ADH or MEOS pathways. Acetaldehyde itself is oxidized (by acetaldehyde dehydrogenase) to acetate and acetylCoA. Since numerous toxic effects have been attributed to acetaldehyde (Truitt & Walsh, 1971), this compound may contribute to the complications of alcoholism. Recently, a relationship between blood acetaldehyde and ethanol levels was found in humans after intravenous administration of alcohol (Korsten, Matsuzaki, Feinman, & Lieber, 1975). This study revealed that acetaldehyde levels remained relatively constant despite wide variations in blood ethanol concentrations above 150 mg/100 ml. The acetaldehyde plateau abruptly terminated when ethanol concentration reached a mean level of 110 mg/100 ml. Moreover, the plateau level of acetaldehyde was significantly higher in alcoholics than in non-alcoholics. Increased production or decreased disposition may have resulted in the higher levels of acetaldehyde in the alcoholic. The effect of ethanol feeding on acetaldehyde dehydrogenase activity is controversial, with some investigators reporting increases (Dajani, Danielski, & Orten, 1963; Horton, 1971) and others, no changes (Raskin & Sokoloff, 1972; Redmond & Cohen, 1971). Recently, decreased rates of acetaldehyde dehydrogenation were observed using intact mitochondria of chronically alcohol fed rats (Hasumura et al., 1975a). Whether due to increased generation or decreased elimination, the high levels of blood acetaldehyde in the alcoholic may have important metabolic consequences since acetaldehyde reduces the activity of various shuttles involved in the disposition of reducing equivalents and inhibits oxidative phosphorylation (Cederbaum, Lieber, & Rubin, 1974).

CITRIC ACID CYCLE (FIGURE 2). Using a variety of experimental models, ethanol has been found to inhibit the citric acid cycle. This inhibition is due, at least in part, to the increased intra-mitochondrial NADH/NAD ratio that results from ethanol oxidation. On the one hand, increased NADH/NAD slows those reactions of the cycle that require NAD. A major site of inhibition by this mechanism is α-keto-glutarate dehydrogenase (Ontko, 1973). On the other hand, the redox change may reduce the availability of certain intermediaries such as pyruvic acids (Forsander, 1970; Krebs, 1968) or oxaloacetate

(Forsander, 1967; Williamson, Scholz, Browning, Thurman, & Fukami, 1969) both of which serve as substrates for the cycle. Under these circumstances, hydrogen equivalents derived from ethanol oxidation must be utilized for oxidative phosphorylation. Since citric cycle requirements for two carbon fragments are lowered, fatty acid oxidation is secondarily suppressed (Lieber, 1974a).

FIGURE 2

METABOLIC EFFECTS OF ETHANOL IN THE HEPATOCYTE

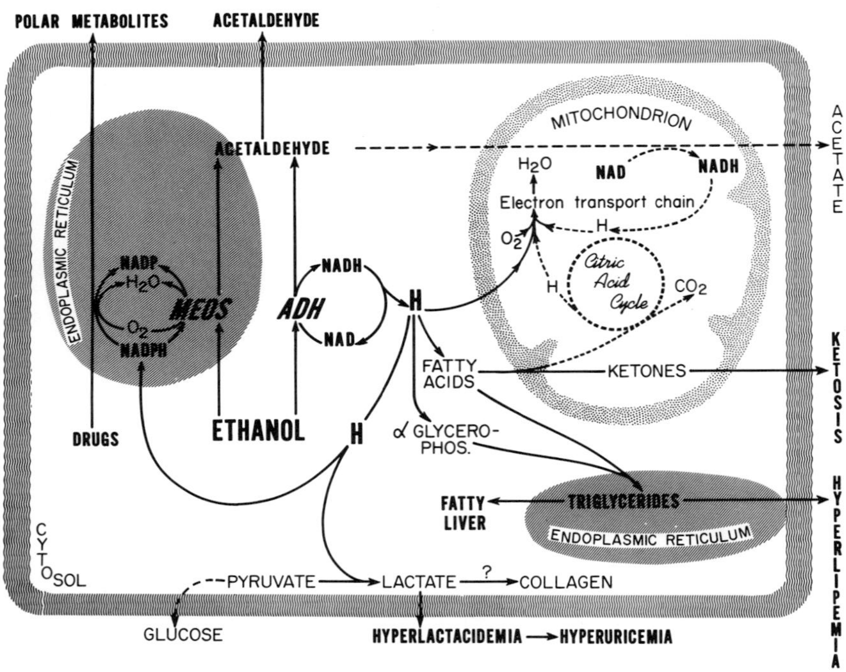

FIGURE 2: Metabolism of ethanol in the hepatocyte and schematic representation of its link to fatty liver, hyperlipemia, hyperuricemia, hyperlactacidemia and ketosis. Pathways decreased by ethanol are represented by dashed lines (see text).

LIPID METABOLISM: HYPERLIPIDEMIA. The suppression by ethanol of fatty acid oxidation has been demonstrated in liver slices (Blomstrand, Kager, & Lantto, 1973; Lieber & Schmid, 1961), perfused liver (Lieber, Lefevre, Spritz, Feinman, & DeCarli, 1967), isolated hepatocytes (Ontko, 1973) and in vivo (Blomstrand & Kager, 1973). This reduction results in the deposition in the liver of dietary fat, when available, or fatty acids derived from endogenous synthesis in the absence of dietary fat (vide infra). Increased synthesis (Baroana & Lieber, 1970) and release of lipoprotein into the blood produces hyperlipemia and tends to counteract lipid accumulation in the liver (Lieber, 1974a). Hyperlipemia may also be due to defective clearance of serum lipids (Chait, February & Mancini, 1972; Losowsky, Jones, Davidson, & Lieber, 1963) and intestinal release or synthesis of lipid (Mistilis & Ockner, 1972). However, the role of these alternate hyperlipemic mechanisms has been questioned (Lieber, 1974b).

In both man (Lieber, Jones, Mendelson, & DeCarli, 1963) and rats (Baraona & Lieber, 1970) the hyperlipemia of chronic ethanol administration usually involves moderate increases in the very low density lipoprotein fraction. It appears that in both alcoholic (Mendelson & Mello, 1973) and non-alcoholic subjects (Ginsberg, Olefsky, Farquhar & Reaven, 1974), the magnitude of the hypertriglyceremic response to ethanol is greater in individuals with preexisting primary type IV hyperlipoproteinemia. Since patients with type IV hyperlipemia are at higher risk for the development of ischemic heart disease (Carlson & Bottiger, 1972), the avoidance of alcohol must be emphasized.

To a great extent, chronic ethanol ingestion also affects lipid metabolism at the microsomal level. These effects include increase in hepatic lipoprotein synthesis (Baraona, Pirola, & Lieber, 1973), and increase in cholesterol synthesis (Lefevre, DeCarli, & Lieber, 1972) and an enhanced activity of hepatic microsomal L-α-glycerophosphate acyl-transferase (Joly, Fienman, Ishii, & Lieber, 1973). It is possible that these alterations in microsomal lipid metabolism are due to the fact that ethanol is oxidized at this metabolic site (Lieber, 1973a).

HYPERURICEMIA. The awareness of an association between alcohol and gout dates back at least to Garrod's description in 1863 (Newcombe, 1972). It is now known that alcoholic hyperuricemia is due, at least in part, to a decrease in uric acid excretion secondary to the increase in blood lactate levels (Lieber, Jones, & Losowsky, 1962). Ethanol metabolism results in an increased lactate-pyruvate ratio since these metabolic intermediaries are linked to the NADH/NAD redox couple. The reduction of pyruvate to lactate regenerates NAD and can be considered another mechanism for disposing of excess hydrogen equivalents. Excess serum lactate contributes to acidosis and leads to secondary hyperuricemia by reducing the capacity of the kidney to excrete uric acid (Lieber et al., 1962). It has been pointed out that ketonemia (MacLachlan & Rodnan, 1967) may have an additive and/or potentiating effect on hyperuricemia. Alcoholic hyperuricemia can be readily distinguished from the primary variety by its reversibility upon abstinence from alcohol (Lieber et al., 1962). It is mandatory to question all patients presenting with hyperuricemia about their alcohol intake.

ALCOHOLIC KETOSIS AND KETOACIDOSIS. The action of ethanol on ketone metabolism is characterized by a delayed change which is not due to the effects of alcohol oxidation on the redox potential (Lieber, 1974b). Although formerly attributed to poor nutrition (Dillon, Dyer, & Smelo, 1940), it is now clear that ketonemia may be induced by the chronic administration of ethanol in association with calorically adequate diets (Lefevre, Adler, & Lieber, 1970). Although the biochemical mechanism is obscure, ketogenesis may reflect a persistent effect of alcohol, in part, perhaps, an alteration in mitochondrial function (Cederbaum, Lieber, Beattie, & Rubin, 1975).

Clinically, alcoholic ketoacidosis is characterized by a history of nausea, vomiting and diminished food consumption. The patient is likely to be female (Cooperman, Davidoff, Spark, & Pallota, 1974) and usually admits to a drinking binge just prior to admission. Physical signs include confusion, dehydration, tachycardia, Kussmaul respiration, and diffuse abdominal tenderness. Initial laboratory values are consistent with metabolic acidosis with depressed bicarbonate and a mean anion gap of 18 (Cooperman et al., 1974). Unlike diabetic ketoacidosis, the ratio of β-hydroxybutyrate to acetoacetate is increased and may not be appreciated if full reliance is placed on the nitroprusside test (Acetest) which is not sensitive to β-hydroxybutyrate. (Levy, Chen, & Zetterman, 1973). During the acute episode, serum free fatty acids are elevated (Cooperman et al., 1974; Levy et al., 1973) and circulating levels of insulin are somewhat low (Cooperman et al., 1974; Levy et al., 1973). Lipolysis and ketogenesis cannot be attributed to insulin deficiency since blood glucose levels are also generally depressed

(Cooperman et al., 1974).

Treatment is generally supportive and consists of intravenous fluid and small amounts of bicarbonate. Insulin therapy is not required.

GLUCOSE METABOLISM. The effects of ethanol on glucose homeostasis differ in the "fed" and "starved" state. Thus, when hepatic stores of glycogen are adequate, glycogenolysis is enhanced and serum glucose is elevated by ethanol administration. Increased glycogenolysis under these circumstances may be mediated by catecholamine secretion (Perman, 1958) or by decreased peripheral utilization of glucose (Lochner, Wulff, & Madison, 1967). After prolonged fasting ethanol consumption may result in symptomatic hypoglycemia (Arky & Freinkel, 1966); this has been attributed to both inhibition of gluconeogenesis and decreased hepatic reserves of glycogen (Arky, 1971). At least in part, ethanol oxidation limits the availability of gluconeogenic precursors by increasing hepatic NADH and altering the ratio of various redox couples (Axelrod, 1974).

Ethanol appears to influence insulin secretion indirectly by its other effects on glucose metabolism. Serum insulin levels appear to reflect rather than mediate changes in circulating glucose (Axelrod, 1974), but this is still controversial. Prompt treatment of alcoholic hypoglycemia with intravenous glucose is of utmost importance. Ethanol-induced hyperglycemia is usually completely reversible but may recur with alcohol abuse (Jenkins, Eckel, & Craig, 1971).

DRUG METABOLISM. As already mentioned, chronic ethanol

administration results in hypertrophy of the smooth endoplasmic reticulum which may be adaptive in nature. This hypertrophy is accompanied by an increased content of microsomal cytochrome P-450 (Rubin, Bacchin, Gang, & Lieber, 1970) and of NADPH-cytochrome P-450 reductase (Joly, Ishii, Teschke, Hasumura, & Lieber, 1973b). These components, which play a key role in the microsomal hydroxylation of various drugs, are also found in purified fractions of MEOS (Teschke et al., 1972; Teschke et al, 1974). These observations offer a likely explanation for the enhanced rate of drug clearance after chronic ethanol consumption (Carulli et al., 1971; Kater, Roggin, Tobin, Zieve, & Iber, 1969; Misra et al., 1971; Vesell, Page, & Passananti, 1971). Conversely, drugs (such as barbiturates) which increase total hepatic MEOS activity (Lieber & DeCarli, 1970a) enhance rates of blood ethanol clearance (Lieber & DeCarli, 1972; Mezy & Robles, 1974). These mechanisms may explain the increased tolerance of the sober alcoholic to a variety of drugs (Lieber, 1973a). The opposite occurs when the individual is intoxicated, namely, drug metabolism may be slowed (Rubin, Gang, Misra, & Lieber, 1970). Possibly due to competition for a common detoxification process (Cohen & Mannering, 1973; Rubin, Gang, Misra & Lieber, 1970), ethanol may augment the toxicity of a variety of frequently used psychoactive drugs (Lieber, 1973b).

ALCOHOLIC LIVER INJURY

INTRODUCTION. The spectrum of alcoholic liver injury involves hepatic steatosis (fatty liver), parenchymal inflammation (alcoholic hepatitis) and cirrhosis. Fatty liver is the earliest, most predictable and least permanent hepatic response to alcohol. Although considerably less is known about the pathogenesis of alcoholic hepatitis and cirrhosis, these lesions are ultimately more significant in terms of morbidity and mortality. Indeed, in an urban area such as New York City, alcoholic cirrhosis now ranks as the third or fourth leading cause of death in males between the ages of 25 and 45 years (Lieber, 1975).

Alcoholic liver injury has been attributed to the malnutrition that accompanies alcoholism rather to than to the toxicity of alcohol per se. Although foodstuff may be supplanted and its digestion and absorption disrupted, recent experimental work has clearly demonstrated the direct, hepatotoxic potential of alcohol. Dietary deficiencies may accentuate the effects of alcohol on the liver, but it is more in the nature of "adding insult to injury".

FATTY LIVER. *Pathology*. Parenchymal accumulation of lipid is indicated by the presence of clear intracytoplasmic vacuoles on hematoxylin and eosin stained sections, or as black globules using various Sudan stains. If sufficient fat is present, the cell nucleus may be eccentrically placed. Subcellular changes that are characteristic of alcohol induced fatty liver include: enlarged and distorted mitochondria containing crystalline inclusions, disarray of the cristae and dilatation of the endoplasmic reticulum (both rough and smooth). Despite adequate nutrition, alcohol can induce these alterations in both alcoholic (Lane & Lieber, 1966; Rubin & Lieber, 1967) and non-alcoholic (Rubin & Lieber, 1968) human volunteers.

Pathogenesis. As noted already, early human and animal studies suggested the primacy of malnutrition in the production of alcoholic fatty liver. Hepatic steatotosis occurring in human Kwashiorkor and rodent choline-deficiency seemed to support this view. Furthermore, clinical studies on recuperating alcoholics with liver disease found that the beneficial effects of bed rest and high protein diet persisted despite continued alcohol intake (Summerskill, Wolfe, & Davidson, 1957; Volwiler, Jones, & Mallory, 1948). These observations contributed to the impression that the injurious effects of alcohol were indirect and due to supplantation of essential dietary nutrients. This concept has not withstood critical epidemiological and experimental evaluation.

Sherlock and Walshe (1948) reported a group of German civilians who had subsisted on meagre protein rations. Despite a diet with less than 35 grams of protein per day, significant weight loss and peripheral edema, none of the individuals had evidence of fatty liver, necrosis or cirrhosis on percutaneous liver biopsy. Similarly, despite widespread malnutrition in Trans-Saharan Africa, adults rarely exhibit fatty liver (Davidson, 1970). Experimentally, it has been shown that the primate has far less requirement for choline than the rat (Hoffbauer & Zaki, 1965) and that dietary supplementation of protein (and choline) fails to prevent alcohol-induced fatty liver in well-nourished human volunteers (Lieber & Rubin, 1968; Lieber & Spritz, 1966; Lieber et al., 1963; Lieber et al., 1965; Rubin & Lieber, 1968). Studies in the rat and human that discounted the direct toxicity of alcohol administered the drug in doses far below those usually consumed by the chronic alcoholic. Given the rats' natural aversion towards alcohol, it must be incorporated into totally liquid diets to assure adequate ingestion. When alcohol is isocalorically substituted for carbohydrate in this manner, alcohol can supply up to 36% of the rats' daily caloric intake in a diet that is otherwise of normal composition. With this experimental design, rats develop an average 8-fold rise of hepatic triglycerides after 24 days (Lieber et al., 1965). Studies in the human that fail to detect a deleterious effect of alcohol in patients recovering from fatty liver suffered from the same methodologic oversight. Although dietary deficiencies have been shown to increase the severity of alcohol-related fatty liver (Klatskin, Krehl, & Conn, 1954; Lieber, Spritz, & DeCarli, 1969), present evidence clearly indicates that alcohol has direct hepatotoxicity regardless of nutritional status.

As already discussed the steatogenicity of ethanol relates to its effect on intermediary and microsomal metabolism. Alcohol decreases fatty acid oxidation (Lieber, et al., 1967; Lieber & Schmid, 1961), stimulates lipogenesis (Lieber & Schmid, 1961; Mendenhall, Bradford, & Furman, 1969) and promotes formation of triglycerides (Nikkila & Ojala, 1963). These effects are mediated by the increased ratio NADH/NAD and the reactions that depend on this redox couple. Under controlled conditions, the degree of steatosis is a function of the amount and type of dietary lipid. Both in the rat (Lieber & DeCarli, 1970c) and man (Lieber & Spritz, 1966), the degree of steatosis increases with the amount of fat present in the diet. When medium chain triglycerides (MCT) are substituted for long chain triglycerides (LCT), less steatosis is observed (Lieber et al., 1967). Preferential oxidation of MCT relative to LCT is the probable explanation for this finding. Fatty acids in the steatotic liver reflect those in the diet under normal conditions of fat intake. When dietary lipid is reduced, the fat that accumulates during alcohol ingestion represents endogenous synthesis (Lieber & Spritz, 1966; Lieber, Spritz, & DeCarli, 1966; Lieber et al., 1969). Fatty acid composition of the liver reflects adipose stores only after large, single doses of alcohol (Horning, Williams, Maling, & Brodie, 1960).

Clinical Aspects. Alcoholic fatty liver is a benign, reversible condition if alcohol consumption is discontinued. Non-tender hepatomegaly is a common mode of presentation. Actually, in a quantitative sense, accumulation of protein may be as important as increased lipid in causing hepatomegaly (Baroana, Leo, Borowsky, & Lieber, 1975). When abdominal pain occurs, it is typically in the upper right quadrant and may also be perceived in the upper gastric or periumbilical areas. Severe forms of fatty liver may present a clinical picture mimicking extrahepatic obstructive jaundice especially if pain, jaundice, dark urine and acholic stools are prominent symptoms (Ballard, Bernstein, & Farrar, 1961; Phillips & Davidson, 1957). In such suspicious cases, percutaneous biopsy of the liver or endoscopic retrograde cholangiopancreatogram (ERCP) may clarify the intrahepatic nature of the cholestasis.

Liver function tests such as SGOT, SGPT, alkaline phosphatase and bilirubin correlate poorly with the degree of hepatic steatosis (Bradus, Korn, Chomet, & West, 1963). The alkaline phosphatase is elevated in about one-half of cases and is rarely more than three times the normal value. The serum levels of bilirubin, SGOT and SGPT are minimally elevated in 35%, 40%, and 10% of patients respectively; a certain proportion (approximately 25%) of patients with fatty liver will have no increases in any of these parameters (Devenyi, Rutherdale, Sereny, & Olin, 1970). Rarely, alcoholic fatty liver may be complicated by hyperlipemia and transient hemolytic anemia, so-called Zieve's syndrome (Zieve, 1958).

Treatment. The goal of therapy is to restore nutritional status to normal and to encourage abstinence from alcohol. Choline and methionine supplementation have no proven efficacy in the prevention or treatment of fatty liver. Since dietary fat influences the degree of steatosis, reduction in dietary fat may be beneficial; however, this question has not been rigorously studied (Feinman & Lieber, 1974). The role of anabolic steroids in this entity is controversial (Fenster, 1966; Jabbari & Levy, 1967; Mendenhall, 1968). It is apparent that these steroids may be effective when parenchymal function is intact but are not useful when hepatic integrity is marginal. In any case, the side-effects of this therapeutic modality (mainly androgenic and cholestatic) make its long-term use both impractical and potentially harmful. Other approaches to the treatment and prevention of alcoholic fatty liver have been reviewed (Lieber, et al., 1971).

ALCOHOLIC HEPATITIS. Acute hepatic failure in the chronic alcoholic has been designated in many ways. Since the clinicopathological picture is quite variable, no single expression is inclusive enough to achieve unanimous approval. Some stress one or more components of the pathological lesion, e.g., "Steatonecrosis-Mallory Body Type" (Harinasuta, Chomet, Ishak, & Zimmerman, 1967) or "Sclerosing Hyaline Necrosis" (Edmondson, Peters, Reynolds, & Kuzma, 1963), whereas others emphasize functional or prognostic features, e.g. "Progressive

Alcoholic Cirrhosis" (Hall & Ophuls, 1925) or "Acute Hepatic Insufficiency" (Phillips & Davidson, 1954). Sufficiently vague and noncommittal, the term "alcoholic hepatitis" (Beckett, Livingstone, & Hill, 1961) is now popular with most clinicians and pathologists.

The significance of alcoholic hepatitis as a precursor of cirrhosis is still unsettled since the lesion of alcoholic hepatitis does not invariably precede the cirrhotic stage. Furthermore, alcoholic hepatitis may persist unchanged without progression to cirrhosis despite long periods of follow-ups in humans (Galambos, 1972b).

Pathology. Pathologic hallmarks of alcoholic hepatitis include parenchymal and portal infiltration with polymorphonuclear leukocytes, intracytoplasmic clumping of hyaline-like material (Mallory bodies) and varying degrees of necrosis, sclerosis, steatosis, and cholestasis (Edmondson et al., 1963; Hall & Ophuls, 1925; Phillips & Davidson, 1954; Popper, Szanto, & Parthasarathy, 1955). Sclerosis in the centrolobular zone may obliterate the central veins and sinusoids (Edmondson et al., 1963). Ultrastructural changes in alcoholic hepatitis include variation in mitochondrial size and shape, and disorientation and elongation of cristae. The smooth endoplasmic reticulum is vesiculated and frequently increased in quantity (Svoboda & Manning, 1963). Collagenous material may be found in the space of Disse and may be associated with loss of the microvilli that normally project from the hepatocyte (Edmondson, Peters, Frankel, & Borowsky, 1967; Klion & Schaffner, 1968). Ultrastructurally, Mallory material is fibrillar (Biava, 1964; Flax & Tisdale, 1964; Iseri & Gottlieb, 1971; Smuckler, 1968), not bound by a limiting membrane

(Yokoo, Minick, Batti, & Kent, 1972) and bears no resemblance to giant mitochondria (Yokoo et al., 1972) or any other subcellular organelle. Three fibrillar arrangements have been delineated. Fibrils may be arranged parallel to one another (Type I) or have a random orientation (Type II). In Type III hyaline, fibrillar debris is found in an amorphous background. Types II and III hyaline may represent degenerative forms of Type I (Yokoo et al., 1972). There is no consensus regarding the origin of the fibrillar material in alcohol hepatitis. Investigators have both found (Biava, 1964; French & Davies, 1975; Horvath, Kovacs, & Ross, 1973; May 1972) and not found (Gerber, Orr, Denk, Schaffner, & Popper, 1973; Smuckler, 1968; Yokoo et al., 1972) a relationship between hyaline material and contiguous cell organelles. Recent data suggests that the fibrillar material may be part of a subcellular contractive system (Yokoo et al., 1972) but this is also controversial (French & Davies, 1975).

Alcoholic hyaline is considered diagnostic (especially when centrolobular) of alcoholic hepatitis. By electron microscopy, however, it is also observed in primary biliary cirrhosis (Gerber et al., 1973; Monroe, French, & Samboni, 1973), hepatocellular carcinoma (Keeley, Iseri, & Gottlieb, 1972) and Indian childhood cirrhosis (Roy, Ramalingaswami, & Nayak, 1971). Moreover, hyaline is not necessary for diagnosis of alcoholic hepatitis, (Harinasuta & Zimmerman, 1971; Lischner, Alexander, & Galambos, 1971). If alcoholic hepatitis is defined on clinical grounds, e.g., jaundice, fever, anorexia, and pain (vide infra) or on histologic criteria that only require parenchymal inflammation with polymorphonuclear leukocytes, hyaline is found in approximately 30% of patients (Lischner et al., 1971). However, it is not known to what extent fixation techniques affect detection of alcoholic hyaline.

Early retrospective studies indicate that the prognosis of patients with Mallory bodies is poor. The inclusion of autopsy material contributed heavily to the mortality statistics and led to this overly grim conclusion (Harinasuta et al., 1967; Phillips & Davidson, 1954). In alcoholics well enough to be biopsied antemortem, mortality as low as 4% has been reported (Green, Mistilis, & Schiff, 1963) and there is no significant difference in mortality rates between those with and without Mallory bodies in the liver studied either retrospectively (Harinasuta & Zimmerman, 1971) or prospectively (Birschbach, Harinasuta, & Zimmerman, 1974). However, Mallory bodies are generally accompanied by more severe degrees of necrosis, steatosis, and cholestasis (Birschbach et al., 1974; Harinasuta & Zimmerman, 1971).

Pathogenesis. As shown in the baboon, alcohol per se can cause the development of alcoholic hepatitis in the absence of poor diet. The link between alcohol consumption and hepatic injury is obscure. It is likely, however, that the subcellular changes seen in alcoholic fatty liver and alcoholic hepatitis reflect the striking biochemical modifications that accompany ethanol metabolism. If sufficiently severe or prolonged, these alterations may cause cell death (necrosis) and inflammation (hepatitis). The association of leukocytes with cells containing hyaline has suggested that hyaline itself may be leukotactic (Popper & Orr, 1970). Alterations in cellular immunity may also play a role in the pathogenesis of alcoholic liver injury (Leevy et al., 1975). Changes in cellular immunity that have been documented include a decrease in the percentage of T lymphocytes and a decreased response (blast transformation) to phytohemagglutinin. Despite this relative state of cellular anergy, migration inhibition of lymphocytes from patients with alcoholic hepatitis has been demonstrated using either normal human liver (Mihas, Bull, & Davidson, 1975) or alcoholic hyaline (Zetterman, Chen, & Leevy, 1974) as antigen. Finally it has recently been shown that lymphocytes from baboons with alcoholic hepatitis are cytotoxic against autologous liver cells in tissue culture (Paronetto & Lieber, unpublished observations). Although the in vivo significance of these reactions is by no means established, they might contribute to the perpetuation of injury in the absence of alcohol.

Clinical aspects. The clinical presentation of patients with alcoholic hepatitis varies greatly. The fulminant and fatal nature of the lesion was necessarily stressed by studies based on autopsy material. It is now clear, however, that patients well enough to have a percutaneous liver biopsy may have a benign clinical course and indeed may be relatively asymptomatic. More serious cases present with fever, jaundice, and abdominal pain. These symptoms may be superimposed on signs of cirrhosis. Laboratory tests reveal hyperbilirubinemia (sometimes predominantly direct-reacting) and moderate elevations of serum alkaline phosphatase (3 times normal or less) and transaminases (500 units or less) (Galambos, 1974). Characteristically, the SGOT is more elevated than the SGPT but neither enzyme approaches the high levels that occur in acute viral hepatitis (Harinasuta et al., 1967). The correlation between serum enzyme levels and the degree of inflammation is generally poor (Edmondson et al., 1963). Prolongation of the prothrombin time, hypoalbuminemia and mild to severe leukocytosis (at times exceeding 40,000 WBC/mm^3) are associated findings. The symptoms and signs of alcoholic hepatitis may occasionally mimic those of extrahepatic biliary obstruction (Mikkelsen, Turrill, & Kern, 1968). Surgical exploration carries considerable risk in this setting and can only be avoided by a high index of suspicion.

The acute mortality in more seriously ill patients is 33% (Hardison & Lee, 1966). Patients in this category commonly succumb to hepatic encephalopathy, hepatorenal syndrome, or variceal hemorrhage. Where the clinical condition permits diagnostic biopsy, acute mortality falls dramatically (Green et al., 1963). Although the frequency of abdominal pain, anorexia, fever, jaundice, and hepatomegaly is almost the same in this group, the intensity of these symptoms is less pronounced (Feinman & Lieber, 1974). As discussed above, the optimistic outlook in this relatively compensated group of patients does not depend on the presence or absence of Mallory bodies (Birschbach, et al., 1974; Harinsuta & Zimmerman, 1971). Mean five year survival in these individuals is approximately 56%. The following variables, however, reduce expected longevity: continued alcohol consumption, ascites, severe inflammation or fibrosis on initial biopsy (Alexander, Lischner, & Galambos, 1971). Encephalopathy (Alexander et al., 1971), alcoholic hyaline (Alexander et al., 1971; Winkel, Juhl, & Tygstrup, 1970) and the severity of steatosis (Alexander et al., 1971; Winkel et al., 1970) have no long-term prognostic value. In a small number of patients with alcoholic hepatitis who abstained from alcohol, serial liver biopsies have shown persistence of parenchymal inflammation without progression to cirrhosis (Galambos, 1972b). Galambos

(1972a) has termed this the "chronic persistent" form of alcoholic hepatitis.

Treatment. Treatment principles in uncomplicated alcoholic hepatitis are the same as with alcoholic fatty liver: abstinence from alcohol and improved nutrition. If anorexia or vomiting prevent adequate oral intake, intravenous therapy may be necessary. Hepatic encephalopathy and ascites, both of which may complicate alcoholic hepatitis, will be discussed below.

Controlled, therapeutic trials using glucocorticoids have generally been disappointing (Porter, Simon, Pope, Volwiler, & Fenster, 1971; Reynolds & Edmondson, 1971). However, Helman, Temko, Nye, and Fallon (1971) found that steroids increased the survival rate but did not prevent progression to cirrhosis in a selected group of very ill patients with hepatic encephalopathy. The efficacy of prednisolone (40 mg/day) was attributed to increased appetite and caloric intake. In a follow-up study (Lesesne, Bozynski, & Fallon, 1974), prednisolone was compared with caloric supplementation in the treatment of alcoholic hepatitis complicated by encephalopathy. Caloric supplementation (1600 calories/day via various routes) by itself was associated with 0% (0 /6) survival whereas 71% (5/7) patients treated with prednisolone recovered from the acute episode. Thus, the efficacy of steroids cannot be attributed to its effect on nutrition alone.

ALCOHOLIC CIRRHOSIS. Cirrhosis is the most harmful hepatic complication of alcoholism and may be accompanied by many serious and intractable complications. The incidence of cirrhosis is related to the amount and duration of alcohol consumption; neither the type of beverage nor the protein content of the diet are important in this respect (Lelbach, 1975). According to Lelbach's data, a 70 kg man who drinks approximately 210 grams/day of alcohol for 20 years has a 50% risk of developing cirrhosis.

Pathology. The gross appearance of the liver depends on the duration of the cirrhosis. A fine, uniform nodularity of the liver is characteristic of early cirrhosis (micronodular or Laennec's cirrhosis). Later, nodules of many different sizes are present giving the liver surface an irregular appearance. At this stage, the pathologic picture may closely resemble that of post-necrotic cirrhosis. The size of the cirrhotic liver depends on the degree of co-existent steatosis (Feinman & Lieber, 1974). Microscopically, the parenchymal architecture is distorted by bands of connective tissue joining central and portal zones (Rubin, Krus, & Popper, 1962). The nodules partitioned off may be regular (micronodular cirrhosis) or irregular (macronodular cirrhosis). In addition, various admixtures of fat, inflammation, Mallory bodies, cholestasis, and siderosis may be found. An etiologic diagnosis may not be possible at this stage in the absence of these clues (Garceau & Boston Inter-Hospital Group, 1964). The transition from micronodular to macronodular cirrhosis has been traced (Rubin et al., 1962) and appears to result from the differential growth of regenerative nodules (Rubin & Lieber, 1975). These nodules, by compression of the hepatic veins, may impede the flow of blood out of the liver (post-sinusoidal portal hypertension).

Cirrhosis results in a decrease in both total and effective hepatic blood flow (Bradley, Ingelfinger, & Bradley,

1952; Conn, Lindenmuth, May, & Ramsby, 1972; Rubin & Popper, 1967). Whereas total blood flow is reduced by extrahepatic porto-systemic shunts, effective circulation is limited by neovascularization of connective tissue septae. These new vessels act as intrahepatic shunts, reducing blood flow to the parenchymal cells. Collagenization of the space of Disse may further isolate the hepatocyte from its blood supply (Edmondson et al., 1967; Klion & Schaffner, 1968). As a result of these changes in the hepatic vasculature, marked deterioration in residual hepatic function may result from minor decrements in cardiac output and/or circulating blood volume.

Pathogenesis. In the baboon, alcoholic hepatitis, commonly but not invariably precedes the appearance of cirrhosis (Lieber et al., 1975). It is still not clear whether hepatitis causes or merely accompanies this fibrotic process (Feinman & Lieber, 1974). It is noteworthy that the activity of peptidyloproline hydroxylase, an enzyme active in the initial steps of fibrogenesis, is increased in alcohol-induced fatty liver prior to histologic signs of inflammation (Feinman & Lieber, 1974). On the other hand, there is a correlation between the severity of alcoholic hepatitis and the degree of subsequent fibrosis (Galambos, 1972b); this could imply that inflammation per se is a fibrogenic stimulus (Popper & Orr, 1970). The respective role of alcohol and malnutrition in the production of alcoholic cirrhosis has been studied in the baboon. Baboons fed a nutritionally adequate diet containing alcohol (50% of total calories) demonstrate the entire spectrum of alcohol-related liver injury, including cirrhosis. Under these experimental conditions, baboons maintained their weight and had adequate intake of protein, minerals, and vitamins. Thus, the alcoholic cannot fully prevent the development of liver injury by adequate or even supplemented nutrition (Lieber et al., 1975).

Clinical Aspects. The signs and symptoms of cirrhosis are often more suggestive of superimposed fatty liver and/or alcoholic hepatitis (Feinman & Lieber, 1974). Features of cirrhosis per se include abdominal distension, variceal hemorrhage, and hepatic coma.

Physical signs of cirrhosis include spider angiomata, palmar erythema, Dupuytrens contractures, and parotid enlargement. In the male, there may be signs of feminization: gynecomastia, redistribution of hair and testicular atrophy. When portal hypertension complicates cirrhosis, ascites, splenomegaly, and venous collateral circulation may be prominent. An arterial bruit heard over the liver may suggest the presence of hepatocellular carcinoma. The small, firm and nodular liver of classical cirrhosis is uncommon until late in the clinical course.

Serum levels of bilirubin, transaminases, and alkaline phosphatase may be only minimally elevated. Hyperglobulinemia is common and reflects, at least in part, elevations in the γ and β-globulin fractions. This may result in so-called "β-γ bridging" (Ritzmann, 1975).

COMPLICATIONS OF ALCOHOLIC LIVER INJURY

ASCITES. The appearance of ascites is a serious prognostic sign in the alcoholic with cirrhosis. The lower survival rates of those with ascites may, at least in part, reflect an association between it and the hepatorenal syndrome. Functional renal failure rarely occurs in the absence of ascites (Summerskill, 1966).

Pathogenesis. The transudation of fluid across capillary membranes is a function of at least four variables: (a) hydrostatic pressure, (b) colloid oncotic pressure, (c) pericapillary tissue pressure, and (d) capillary permeability. In the cirrhotic with ascites, portal hypertension and hypoalbuminemia increase the net filtration of fluid into the peritoneal cavity by upsetting the equilibrium between hydrostatic and osmotic forces (Atkinson & Losowsky, 1962). Other factors that may determine the degree and type of ascitic fluid include (a) secondary hyperaldosteronism and (b) the anatomic locus of the increased portal pressure (pre or post sinusoidal). The stimulus initiating hyperaldosteronism is not clearly understood since blood volume is normal or increased in cirrhosis (Lieberman & Reynolds, 1967). Instead, it was proposed that decreased "effective" blood volume led to secondary hyperaldosteronism and distal tubular reabsorption of sodium. The concept of effective blood volume and its role in ascites has been challenged (Lieberman, Ito, & Reynolds, 1969).

The likelihood of ascitic accumulation is dependent, at least in part, on the anatomic locus of pressure development in the hepatoportal vasculature. In addition, the protein concentration of the ascitic fluid is a function of this anatomical consideration. Obliteration of portal venules (as in schistosomiasis) leads to pre-sinusoidal hypertension; obstruction of hepatic venules and sinusoids (as in macronodular cirrhosis or sclerosing hyaline necrosis) eventuates in intrahepatic sinusoidal hypertension (Sherlock, 1974). Ascites formation is more common in the latter type of obstruction and the protein content of the fluid is considerably higher owing to the presence of hepatic lymph (Witte, Dumont, Cole, Witte, & Kinter, 1969). Although very low protein (<1.0 gr.%) levels suggest presinusoidal inflow obstruction alone, higher levels may arise from combined pre and post sinusoidal obstruction as occurs in advanced alcoholic cirrhosis (Conn, 1972). Esophageal varices and splenomegaly are common in both types of portal hypertension.

Clinical aspects. Large amounts of ascitic fluid may cause anorexia, abdominal discomfort, dyspnea and increases in the incidence of umbilical, hiatal, and inguinal hernias. On physical examination fluid waves and shifting dullness are well known signs of ascites. Minimal amounts of ascites may be detected by percussion in the knee chest position - the-so-called "puddle" sign (Lawson & Weissbein, 1959). Recently, as little as 100 ml of free ultra abdominal fluid has been reliably detected using A-mode ultrasonography (Goldberg, Clearfield, Goodman, & Morales, 1973). Liver and spleen size is difficult to evaluate in the presence of ascites as is the recognition of concomitant abdominal pathology. Common laboratory abnormalities include hyponatremia, hypochloremia, hypokalemia, and hypoalbuminemia. Depending on its course, hypokalemia may be associated with either metabolic alkalosis (e.g., vomiting or diuresis) or metabolic acidosis (e.g., in the course of renal tubular acidosis).

Treatment. The dietary restriction of sodium is the cornerstone of the medical management of ascites. Restriction of sodium to as little as 250 mg/day may be necessary. Limitation of water intake may be necessary in cases complicated by hyponatremia. Severe degrees of hyponatremia (serum sodium $<$ 120 mEq/L) may require the intravenous administration of hypertonic sodium chloride. A weight loss of about two pounds per day is considered optimal. This corresponds to the maximum resorption rate of ascites from the peritoneal cavity (approximately 950 cc/day).

Diuretics should only be necessary in the resistant cases. Spironolactones, which inhibit the renal tubular effects of aldosterone, are added to the therapeutic regimen initially. The potassium retention induced by these agents is advantageous since many cirrhotics with ascites have total body deficiencies of potassium (Casey, Summerskill, Bickford, & Rosevear, 1965). The maximum dose of 400 mg/day of spironolactone produces a response in 75% of cases (Conn, 1972), but hyperkalemia may be a complication. The dose of the medication is adjusted according to daily weight loss and urinary sodium concentration. Sodium excretion may be further augmented by the addition of thiazides or "loop" diuretics (ethacrynic acid and furosemide). However, these agents may accentuate hypokalemia and induce azotemia. Azotemia is especially likely when weight loss exceeds two pounds per day in a decompensated cirrhotic without dependent peripheral edema since weight loss occurs at the expense of intravascular volume. As will be discussed azotemia may result in increased ammonia production and concurrent hypokalemia may augment ammonia toxicity by induction of metabolic alkalosis (Stabenau, Warren, & Rall, 1959). Other therapeutic modalities include albumin infusion (Wilkinson & Sherlock, 1962), ascites re-infusion alone (Clermont, Vlahcevic, Chalmers, Adham, Curtis, & Morrison, 1967) and in combination with diuretics (Eknoyan,

Martinez-Maldonado, Yium, & Suki, 1970). Increased plasma oncotic pressure may facilitate diuresis but may also increase the risk of variceal bleeding by increasing plasma volume (Faloon, Ecknardt, Murphy, Cooper, & Davidson, 1949).

Surgical approaches to intractable ascites include portacaval anastomosis and peritoneo-venous shunting. If retrograde flow is demonstrated in the portal system, a side to side portacaval anastomosis is indicated (Warren, Foman, Viamonte, Martinez, & Kalser, 1968). Peritoneovenous shunting may be effective but is limited by shunt clotting and valve failure (Hyde & Eiseman, 1967; Leveen, Christoudias, Moon, Luft, Falk, & Grosberg, 1974; Mortenson, & Lawton, 1968).

VARICEAL HEMORRHAGE. Esophageal and gastric varices are almost always an expression of portal hypertension in a patient with pre or post-sinusoidal obstruction. Although often asymptomatic, acute rupture of these vessels is a significant cause of mortality in the cirrhotic population. Given the limited nature of hepatic reserves in cirrhosis, bleeding is poorly tolerated; hepatic encephalopathy and the hepatorenal syndrome frequently follow in its wake. When portal hypertension is due to presinusoidal reasons (e.g., schistosomiasis or portal vein thrombosis), hemorrhage is better tolerated.

Diagnosis. Radiographically, esophageal varices produce distortion of the barium column. In the stomach, varices appear as thickened mucosal folds which may simulate infiltrating processes. The radiographic visualization of esophageal varices may be enhanced by various maneuvers (Valsalva and/or Mueller) which increase intra abdominal pressure or by administration of antispasmodics (Pro-Banthine or Buscopan)

(Liu, 1974).

Endoscopically, varices are gray or bluish, tortuous and nodular. The caliber of the varix may be underestimated when the esophageal lumen is over distended with air (Dagradi, Lee, Rodiles, & Lockareff, 1973). Gastric varices are sometimes confused with neoplasms, so-called "tumorous varices". (Okuda, Yasumoto, Goto, & Kunisaki, 1973). In such cases, angiography may clarify the diagnosis and avoid the danger of variceal laceration during biopsy.

Endoscopy is considered more reliable than radiography in the detection of small or moderate size varices (Demling, Ottenjann, & Elster, 1972; Reynolds, 1969). In one study, the esophagram correctly identified only 50% of endoscopically proven varices (Katon & Smith, 1973). Endoscopic examination is considered essential during upper G.I. bleeds in patients known to have varices. Endoscopy provides direct visualization of variceal hemorrhage and excludes other significant sources of blood loss in the upper G.I. tract (e.g., acute erosive gastritis or peptic ulceration).

Management. The management of varices is controversial. It was hoped that prophylactic surgical decompression of the portal system would decrease the incidence of variceal hemorrhage and thereby prolong survival in cirrhotics. Unfortunately, despite a reduction in variceal blood loss, portacaval anastomosis has not improved long-term outcome compared with that of non-operated controls (Conn et al., 1972; Resnick, Chalmers, Ishihara, Garceau, Callow, Schimmel, & O'Hara, 1969). Portacaval anastomosis performed electively after an initial variceal bleed (therapeutic shunt) also fails to increase life expectancy significantly in randomized controlled studies (Resnick, Iber, Ishihara, Chalmers, & Zimmerman, 1974). In both prophylactic and therapeutic portacaval anastomosis, diversion of portal flow from the liver increases the risk of hepatocellular failure and hepatic encephalopathy. Together, these complications of portosystemic shunting offset the beneficial effects of surgery on variceal hemorrhage (Conn et al., 1972; Resnick et al., 1974). Encephalopathy also develops in about 35% of non-operated patients but tends to be acute and follows gastrointestinal hemorrhage. Post-shunt encephalopathy is more severe and recurrent; coma is often spontaneous or is related to the intake of dietary protein (Mutchnick, Lerner, & Conn, 1974). The prognostic value of hemodynamic staging is unsettled (Smith, 1974). Although it has been suggested that the risk of hepatocellular failure and encephalopathy should be higher in those with better pre-operative indices of portal circulation (Warren, Restrepo, Respess, & Muller, 1963) a prospective surgical study has not confirmed this prediction (Smith, 1974). Procedures that selectively decompress esophageal varices such as the distal end-side splenorenal (Warren, Zeppa, & Fomon, 1967) and central side to side splenorenal (Britton, Voorhees, & Price, 1970) shunts are designed to maintain hepatic blood flow. These operations are technically more difficult than portacaval anastomosis and especially in patients with ascites, are associated with high operative mortality (Conn, 1974). Emergency transthoracic ligation of esophageal varices has also been advocated (Ottinger & Moncure, 1974). In good risk patients, portosystemic shunt can then be carried out with lower mortality. Arterialization of the intrahepatic portal system is a novel approach to maintain sinusoidal perfusion after portacaval shunt. In this procedure, the right gastroepiploic artery is anastomosed to the reopened umbilical vein (Adamsons, Kinkhabwala, & Moscowitz, 1972). Long-term controlled studies to evaluate these operations have not yet appeared.

The failure of shunt surgery to improve long-term survival has resulted in a renewed emphasis on medical management. Protocols that have been evaluated include use of the Sengstaken-Blakemore tube, systemic and selective infusion of Pitressin. The efficacy of the Sengstaken-Blakemore tube has been improved by various modifications and by the recognition (Conn, & Simpson, 1967) and prevention of its potential hazards (Pitcher, 1971).

Vasopressin is thought to lower portal venous pressure by producing splanchnic vasoconstriction. Given systemically as an intravenous infusion, vasopressin has short-term effectiveness (Shaldon & Sherlock, 1960) but is limited by tachyphylaxis and cardiotoxicity (Beller, Trevino, & Ruban, 1971). An enhanced effect on splanchnic vasoconstriction and a reduction in cardiac effects and tolerance was anticipated by constant infusion of vasopressin directly into the superior mesenteric artery. (Baum & Nusbaum, 1971). In a controlled, prospective study, intra-arterial infusion of vasopressin was successful in checking variceal hemorrhage, but survival was not improved over that obtained by conventional medical therapy (Conn, Ramsby, Storer, Mutchnick, Joshi, Phillips, Cohen, Fields, & Petroski, 1975). This conclusion however has been challenged on several methodologic grounds (Resnick, 1975). Moreover, recent studies have detected systemic effects during selective vasopressin therapy (Barr, Lakin, & Rosch, 1975; Millette, Huet, & Lavoie, 1975) and the assumption that the therapeutic effects of vasopressin are mediated by a decline in portal pressure has also been questioned (Millette et al., 1975).

HEPATORENAL SYNDROME. *Clinical aspects.* The insidious onset of oliguria and azotemia in a cirrhotic with medically intractable ascites has been termed the hepatorenal syndrome. Although commonly found in association with alcoholic liver injury, fulminant viral hepatitis and chronic active hepatitis may be complicated by a similar process. It is important to distinguish the hepatorenal syndrome from other forms of renal failure that may occur in the setting of cirrhosis. For example, review of the hospital course may reveal that the patient is receiving or had been administered nephrotoxic antibiotics. The acute onset of oliguria (or anuria) may be due to acute tubular necrosis, a complication for which the cirrhotic is particularly susceptible. Determination of urinary sodium and osmolality and examination of the urinary sediment will usually permit these distinctions to be made. Reflecting the state of intense sodium retention, urinary sodium concentrations are vanishingly low in the hepatorenal syndrome. As a result of impaired diluting capacity, the urine osmolality is usually greater than that of plasma. The urinary sediment is unremarkable. The lack of structural change in kidneys of patients with this syndrome, the normal appearance (both macro and microscopically) of the kidneys in fatal cases and the normal performance of these organs in transplant recipients underscores the functional nature of this type of renal failure.

Paracentesis, vigorous diuresis, and gastrointestinal hemorrhage often precede the appearance of the hepatorenal syndrome. However, the role of diuretics in this syndrome has been questioned (Lieberman & Reynolds, 1966). Although renal failure typically occurs in the context of severe hepatic decompensation and intractable ascites, hyperbilirubinemia per se is not correlated with indices of renal function. (Baldus, Feichter, & Summerskill, 1964). Hepatic encephalopathy may precede (Shear, Kleinerman, & Gabuzda, 1965), accompany or follow the appearance of renal failure (Baldus, 1972).

Pathogenesis. Changes in renal circulatory dynamics and renal tubular function have been implicated in the hepatorenal syndrome. By a variety of techniques, it has been shown that both glomerular filtration rate and renal plasma are reduced in a predictable fashion. They are normal or minimally reduced in cirrhotics who have never had ascites or whose ascites is medically responsive, and they are markedly reduced in the presence of both ascites and azotemia (Baldus, Feichter, Summerskill, Hunt, & Wakim, 1964). Since cardiac output is normal or increased in cirrhotics and arterial blood pressure is unchanged, (Baldus, Summerskill, Hunt, & Maher, 1964; Lancestremere, Davidson, & Earley, 1962), the decline in renal blood flow reflects increased renal vascular resistance (Baldus, Summerskill, Hunt, & Maher, 1964; Tristini & Cohn, 1967). In addition to an overall decline in renal blood flow, there is a redistribution of renal blood flow away from cortical nephrons. This was deduced on the basis of decreased PAH extraction (Schroeder, Shear, Sancetta, & Gabuzda, 1967), and later confirmed by xenon washout in both azotemic (Epstein, Berk, Hollenberg, Adams, Chalmers, Abrams, & Merrill, 1970) and nonazotemic (Kew, Brunt, Varma, Hourigan, Williams, & Sherlock, 1971) subjects with cirrhosis. The cause for the increase in renal vasular resistance and redistribution of blood flow is not known but may involve the following variables: (a) neurohumoral or sympathetic stimulation of cortical nephrons, (Hori, Austin, & McDermott, 1965), (b) decreased "effective" blood volume (Vlahcevic, Adham, Jick, Moore, & Chalmers, 1965), (c) increased renal vein pressure (Mullane & Gliedman, 1966). In favor of the first is the observation that phenoxybenzamine (an α-adrenergic blocking agent) increases renal blood flow in cirrhosis (Baldus, 1970). The second factor is unlikely since blood volume is generally normal or increased in cirrhosis (McCloy, Baldus, Tauxe, & Summerskill, 1967); plasma expansion increases renal flow only when cardiac output is depressed (Tristani & Cohn, 1967). With respect to the third variable, renal vein catheterization has not detected a relationship between renal vein pressure and renal hemodynamics (Baldus, Summerskill, Hunt, & Maher, 1964). In any case, pressures considerably higher than those observed in the hepatorenal syndrome are required before renal flow patterns are altered.

Increased reabsorption of sodium is observed in cirrhosis prior to changes in renal circulatory parameters (Baldus, Feichter, Summerskill, Hunt, & Wakim, 1964). It is therefore unlikely that diminished glomerular filtration initiates sodium retention although it may secondarily aggravate it. Alternate mechanisms involve the action of aldosterone and renin on the distal tubule (Barnado, Summerskill, Strong, & Baldus, 1970; Schroeder, Eich, Smulyan, Gould, & Gabuzda, 1970) and "third factor" on the proximal tubule (Baldus, 1972). Intra-renal shunting of blood to medullary nephrons may also contribute to increased sodium reabsorption. Compared to cortical nephrons, medullary nephrons have longer loops of

Henle and tend to conserve more sodium (Barger & Herd, 1971).

Treatment. Prognosis is poor in patients with the syndrome although there are several reports of recovery after portacaval shunt (Schroeder, Numann, & Chamberlain, 1970) and prednisone therapy (Conn, 1973). General principles of therapy include protein restriction, low doses of Neomycin (to minimize toxicity), and electrolyte management. Judicious plasma volume expansion may be attempted but improvement is generally transient. In the presence of ascites, paracentesis alone and paracentesis in combination with plasma volume expansion (Conn, 1973) may be efficacious. Pharmacologic agents that increase renal blood flow and glomerular filtration rate (GFR) such as dibenzyline, dopamine and octapressin are promising but require further study (Conn, 1973).

HEPATIC ENCEPHALOPATHY. Hepatic encephalopathy in the alcoholic with cirrhosis and portosystemic shunting is usually a chronic, recurrent and reversible neuropsychiatric syndrome. In contrast, the encephalopathy of acute hepatic failure is more fulminant and less readily overcome. A third, more unusual type of encephalopathy, termed "acquired hepatocerebral degeneration" is irreversible and resembles Wilson's disease. Dementia is prominent and symptoms such as ataxia and choreathetosis suggest extrapyramidal involvement.

Clinical aspects. Changes in personal habits or sleep patterns may be the earliest symptoms of encephalopathy. More severe manifestations include confusion, drowsiness and, finally, various degrees of unresponsiveness. Signs of encephalopathy include constructional apraxia, hypothermia, hyperventilation and fetor hepaticus. Asterixis (flapping tremor) is characteristic of hepatic encephalopathy but is not specific. Among others, it can be elicited in uremia, heart failure, hypoglycemia and respiratory insufficiency (Conn, 1960). Asterixis is usually elicited at the metacarpophalangeal joints. Fetor hepaticus is a characteristic sweet or musty odor, the intensity of which reflects the degree of encephalopathy (Schenker, Breen, & Hoyumpa, 1974). The odor has been attributed to the exhalation of mercaptans (Chen, Zieve, & Mahadevan, 1970), a bacterial degradation product of methionine. Elevated arterial ammonia levels and characteristic EEG changes support the diagnosis of hepatic encephalopathy but, again, neither is specific (Schenker, et al., 1974). Moreover, arterial ammonia may not correlate well with the state of consciousness (Schenker, et al., 1974). Cerebrospinal fluid may reveal xanthochromia (in the presence of hyperbilirubinemia) and elevated pressure (due to cerebral edema). Cerebrospinal fluid ammonia (Caesar, 1962) glutamine (Hourani, Hamlin, & Reynolds, 1971) and α-keto glutaramate (Vergara, Plum, & Duffy, 1974) levels are increased.

Pathogenesis. Although other cerebral toxins have been implicated in hepatic encephalopathy, the role of ammonia is still favored. Both the G.I. tract and kidney are important sites of ammonia production. In the colon, bacterial urease generates ammonia from urea. Colonic absorption of urea is pH-dependent; a low pH favors trapping of ammonia (as ammonium ion) in the colonic lumen with subsequent excretion in the stool. Dietary protein, gastrointestinal bleeding, and azotemia by increasing the colonic load of urea results in greater ammonia production. Constipation, by prolonging transit time, may also facilitate the accumulation of ammonia. In the presence of hepatic injury and/or portosystemic shunting, the clearance of blood ammonia is reduced and encephalopathy may be precipitated. In the kidney, hypokalemia increases renal vein ammonia levels by either augmentation of glutaminase activity (Gabuzda & Hall, 1966) or a pH-dependent mechanism similar to that in the colon (Shear, Bonkowsky, & Gabuzda, 1969).

The toxicity of ammonia is related, at least in part, to its regional effects on cerebral energy metabolism (Schenker, et al., 1974). After an intoxicating dose of ammonia, the level of high energy phosphates (ATP and phosphocreatine) is lower in the brain stem than in the cortex. The significance of these findings is apparent in as much as arousal has been related to brain stem integrity.

The rate of ammonia detoxification rather than ammonia concentration per se may disrupt cerebral energy metabolism (Bessman & Bessman, 1955). Detoxification of ammonia involves the consumption of ATP and α-ketoglutarate (a normal citric acid cycle intermediary) and formation of glutamine (via glutamic acid). Since α-ketoglutarate depletion may slow the citric acid cycle and secondarily impair electron transport, ATP stores will be further depressed. It has been suggested that the disruption of ATP-dependent metabolism and neuronal repolarization engenders the signs and symptoms of cerebral dysfunction (Schenker, et al., 1974). This is consistent with the finding that rodents administered methionine sulfoximine (which prevent ammonia detoxification by inhibiting glutamine synthetase) are protected from ammonia toxicity (Warren & Schenker, 1964). However, a direct neuronal effect of ammonia has also been postulated (Hawkins, Miller, Nielsen, & Veich, 1973).

Other substances that have been implicated in the development of hepatic encephalopathy include certain short chain fatty acids such as butyric, valeric, and octanoic acids (Chen, Mahadevan, & Zieve, 1970), methionine and its derivatives (Chen, Zieve, & Mahadevan, 1970) and biogenic amines (ß-hydroxylated phenylethylamines) which are structural analogues of norepinephrine (Fischer & Baldessarini, 1971). Increased quantities of all these potential toxins have been found in body fluids of patients with hepatic coma. The effects of short chain fatty acids are probably not mediated at the energy level. Rather, they appear to directly effect neuronal membranes and synaptosomes directly (Rissoli & Golzigna, 1970). Finally, acting as false neurochemical transmitters, biogenic amines may interfere with synaptic function. The experimental treatment of hepatic encephalopathy using L-dopa is based on this premise. The role of methionine or its derivatives in producing coma is unclear but does not appear related to increase in blood ammonia (Phear, Rubner, Sherlock, & Summerskill, 1956).

Treatment and prevention. Hepatic encephalopathy is commonly precipitated by azotemia, gastrointestinal bleeding, dietary protein excess, overly vigorous diuresis, infection, and constipation (Schenker, et al., 1974). Correction and/or prevention requires that these factors be properly identified. The goal of active therapy is to reduce the gastrointestinal and renal contributions to ammonia production. To this end, protein restriction, antibiotics (Neomycin), and bowel cleansing are routinely instituted. Lactulose, a synthetic disaccharide that is metabolized to lactic and acetic acid, has also been shown to be effective in controlled clinical trials (Elkington, Floch, & Conn, 1969; Simmons, Goldstein, & Boyle, 1970). It has been assumed that lactulose lowers colonic pH and traps ammonia within the lumen (Bircher, Haemmerli, Scollo-Lavizzari, & Hoffmann, 1971). However, this may not be the case since stool ammonia was not increased after lactulose administration in one study (Agostini, Down, Murison, & Wrong, 1972). The use of corticosteroids has been advocated (Katz, Velasco, Klinger, & Alessandri, 1962) but controlled trials have been disappointing (Schenker et al., 1974). Therapy with L-Dopa is also controversial, but striking, albeit temporary, improvement has been reported (Fischer et al., 1971; Parkes, Sharpstone, & Williams, 1970).

REFERENCES

Adamson, R.J., Kinkhabwala, M., & Moskowitz, H. Portacaval shunt with arterialization of the hepatic portion of the portal vein. *Surgery, Gynecology, Obstetrics*, 1972, *135*, 529-535.

Agostini, L., Down, P.F., Murison, J., & Wrong, O.M. Faecal ammonia and pH during lactulose administration in man: A comparison with other cathartics. *Gut*, 1972, *13*, 859-866.

Alexander, J.F., Lischner, M.W., & Galambos, J.T. Natural history of alcoholic hepatitis. II. The long term prognosis. *American Journal of Gastroenterology*, 1971, *56*, 515-525.

Arky, R.A. The effect of alcohol on carbohydrate metabolism: Carborhydrate metabolism in alcoholics. In H. Kissen & H. Begleiter (Eds.), *The biology of alcoholism* (Vol. 1). New York: Plenum Press, 1971.

Arky, R.A., & Freinkel, N. Alcohol hypoglycemia. V. Alcohol infusion to test gluconeogenesis in starvation, with special reference to obesity. *New England Journal of Medicine*, 1966, *274*, 426-433.

Atkinson, M., Losowsky, M.S. Plasma colloid osmotic pressure in relation to the formation of ascites and edema in liver disease. *Clinical Science*, 1962, *22*, 383-389.

Axelrod, D.R. Metabolic and endocrine aberrations in alcoholism. In B. Kissen & H. Begleiter (Eds.), *The biology of alcoholism* (Vol.3). New York: Plenum Press, 1974.

Baldus, W.P. Etiology and management of renal failure in cirrhosis and portal hypertension. *Annals of The New York Academy of Sciences*, 1970, *170*, 267-279.

Baldus, W.P. Renal failure in advanced liver disease. In H.K. Popper & F. Schaffner, (Eds.), *Progress in liver disease* (Vol. 4). New York & London: Grune & Stratton, 1972.

Baldus, W.P., Feichter, R.N., & Summerskill, W.H.J. The kidney in cirrhosis. I. Clinical and biochemical features of azotemia in hepatic failure. *Annals of Internal Medicine*, 1964, *60*, 353-365.

Baldus, W.P., Feichter, R.N., Summerskill, W.H.J., Hunt, J.C., & Wakim, K.G. The kidney in cirrhosis. II. Disorders of renal function. *Annals of Internal Medicine*, 1964, *60*, 366-377.

Baldus, W.P., Summerskill, W.H.J., Hunt, J.C., & Maher, F.T. Renal circulation in cirrhosis: Observations based on catheterization of the renal vein. *Journal of Clinical Investigation*, 1964, *43*, 1090-1097.

Ballard, H., Bernstein, M., & Farrar, J.T. Fatty liver presenting as obstructive jaundice. *American Journal of Medicine*, 1961, *30*, 196-201.

Baraona, E., Leo, M., Borowsky, S.A., & Lieber, C.S. Alcoholic hepatomegaly: Accumulation of protein in the liver. *Science*, 1975, *190*, 794-795.

Baraona, E., & Lieber, C.S. Effects of chronic ethanol feeding on serum lipoprotein metabolism in the rat. *Journal of Clinical Investigation*, 1970, *49*, 769-778.

Baraona, E., Pirola, R.C., & Lieber, C.S. The pathogenesis of postprandial hyperlipemia in rats fed ethanol containing diets. *Journal of Clinical Investigation*, 1973, *52*, 296-303.

Barger, A.C., & Herd, J.A. The renal circulation. *New England Journal of Medicine*, 1971, *284*, 482-490.

Barnardo, D.E., Summerskill, W.H.J., Strong, C.G., & Baldus, W.P. Renal function, renin activity and endogenous vasoactive substances in cirrhosis. *American Journal of Digestive Diseases*, 1970, *15*, 419-425.

Barr, J.W., Lakin, R.C., & Rosch, J. Similarity of arterial and intravenous vasopressin portal and systemic hemodynamics. *Gastroenterology*, 1975, *69*, 13-19.

Baum, S., & Nusbaum, M. The control of gastrointestinal hemorrhage by selective mesenteric arterial infusion of vasopressin. *Radiology*, 1971, *98*, 497-505.

Beckett, A.G., Livingstone, A.V., & Hill, K.R. Acute alcoholic hepatitis. *British Medical Journal*, 1966, *2*, 1113-1119.

Beller, B.M., Trevino, A., & Urban, E. Pitressin-induced myocardial injury and depression in a young woman. *American Journal of Medicine*, 1971, *51*, 675-679.

Bessman, S.P., & Bessman, A.N. The cerebral and peripheral uptake of ammonia in liver disease with an hypothesis for the mechanism of hepatic coma. *Journal of Clinical Investigation*, 1955, *34*, 622-628.

Biava, C. Mallory alcoholic hyalin. A heretofore unique lesion of hepatocellular ergastoplasm. *Laboratory Investigation*, 1964, *13*, 301-320.

Bircher, J., Haemmerli, U.P., Scollo-Lavizzari, G., & Hoffman, K. Treatment of chronic portal-systemic enchephalopathy with lactulose. *American Journal of Medicine*, 1971, *51*, 148-159.

Birschbach, H.R., Harinasuta, U., & Zimmerman, H.J. Alcoholic steatonecrosis. II. Prospective study of prevalence of Mallory bodies in biopsy specimens and comparison of severity of hepatic disease in patients with and without this histological feature. *Gastroenterology*, 1974, *66*, 1195-1202.

Blomstrand, R., & Kager, L. The combustion of triolein-1-^{14}C and its inhibition by alcohol in man. *Life Sciences*, 1973, *13*, 113-123.

Blomstrand, R., Kager, L., & Lantto, O. Studies on the ethanol-induced decrease of fatty acid oxidation in rat and human liver slices. *Life Sciences*, 1973, *13*, 1131-1141.

Boveris, A., Oshino, N., & Chance, B. The cellular production of hydrogen peroxide. *Biochemical Journal*, 1972, *128*, 617-630.

Bradley, S.E., Ingelfinger, F.J., & Bradley, G.P. Hepatic circulation in cirrhosis of the liver. *Circulation*, 1952, *5*, 419-429.

Bradus, S., Korn, R.J., Chomet, B., & West, M. Hepatic function and serum enzyme levels in association with fatty metamorphosis of the liver. *American Journal of the Medical Sciences*, 1963, *246*, 35-41.

Britton, R.C., Voorhees, A.B., & Price, J.B. Selective portal decompression. *Surgery*, 1970, *67*, 104-113.

Caesar, J. Levels of glutamine and ammonia and the pH of cerebrospinal fluid and plasma in patients with liver disease. *Clinical Science*, 1962, *22*, 33-41.

Carlson, L.A., & Bottiger, L.E. Ischemic heart disease in relation to fasting values of plasma triglycerides and cholesterol. *Lancet*, 1972, *1*, 865-866.

Carter, E.A., & Isselbacher, K.J. The role of microsomes in the hepatic metabolism of ethanol. *Annals of the New York Academy of Sciences*, 1971, *179*, 282-294.

Carulli, N., Manenti, F., Gallo, M., & Salvioli, G.F. Alcohol-drugs interaction in man: Alcohol and tolbutamide. *European Journal of Clinical Investigation*, 1971, *1*, 421-424.

Casey, T.H., Summerskill, W.H.J., Bickford, R.G., & Rosevear, J.W. Body and serum potassium in liver disease. II. Relationship to arterial ammonia, blood pH and hepatic coma. *Gastroenterology*, 1965, *48*, 208-215.

Cederbaum, A.I., Lieber, C.S., Beattie, D.S., & Rubin, E. Effect of chronic ethanol ingestion on fatty acid oxidation by hepatic mitochondria. *Journal of Biological Chemistry*, 1975, *250*, 5122-5129.

Cederbaum, A.I., Lieber, C.S., & Rubin, E. The effect of acetaldehyde on mitochondrial function. *Archives of Biochemistry and Biophysics*, 1974, *161*, 26-39.

Chait, A., February, A.W., Mancini, M., & Lewis, B. Clinical and metabolic study of alcoholic hyperlipidaemia. *Lancet*, 1972, *2*, 62-64.

Chen, S., Mahadevan, V., & Zieve, L. Volatile fatty acids in the breath of patients with cirrhosis of the liver. *Journal of Laboratory and Clinical Medicine*, 1970, *75*, 622-627.

Chen, S., Zieve, L., & Mahadevan, V. Mercaptans and dimethyl sulfide in the breath of patients with cirrhosis of the liver. *Journal of Laboratory and Clinical Medicine*, 1970, *75*, 628-635.

Clermont, R.J., Vlahcevic, Z.R., Chalmers, T.C., Adham, N.F., Curtis, G.W., & Morrison, R.S. Intravenous therapy of massive ascites in patients with cirrhosis. II. Long term effects on survival and frequency of renal failure. *Gastroenterology*, 1967, *53*, 220-228.

Cohen, G.M., & Mannering, G.J. Involvement of a hydrophobic site in the inhibition of the microsomal p-hydroxylation of aniline by alcohols. *Molecular Pharmacology*, 1973, *9*, 383-397.

Conn, H.O. Asterixis in non-hepatic disorders. *American Journal of Medicine*, 1960, *29*, 647-661.

Conn, H.O. The rational management of ascites. In H. Popper & F. Schaffner (Eds.), *Progress in liver diseases* (Vol. 4). New York and London: Grune & Stratton, 1972.

Conn, H.O. A rational approach to the hepatorenal syndrome. *Gastroenterology*, 1973, *65*, 321-340.

Conn, H.O. The rational evaluation and management of portal hypertension. In F. Schaffner, S. Sherlock, & C.M. Leevy (Eds.), *The liver and its diseases*. New York: Intercontinental Book Corp., 1974.

Conn, H.O., Lindenmuth, W.W., May, C., & Ramsby, G.R. Prophylactic portacaval anastomosis: A tale of two studies. *Medicine*, 1972, *51*, 27-40.

Conn, H.O., Ramsby, G.R., Storer, E.H., Mutchnick, M.G., Joshi, P.H., Phillips, M.M., Cohen, G.A., Fields, G.N., & Petroski, D. Intrarterial vasopressin in the treatment of upper gastrointestinal hemorrhage: A prospective, controlled clinical trial. *Gastroenterology*, 1975, *68*, 211-221.

Conn, H.O., & Simpson, J.A. Excessive mortality associated with balloon tamponade of bleeding varices: A critical reappraisal. *Journal of the American Medical Association*, 1967, *202*, 587-591.

Conney, A.H. Pharmacological implications of microsomal enzyme induction. *Pharmacological Reviews*, 1967, *19*, 317-366.

Cooperman, M.T., Davidoff, E., Spark, R., & Pallotta, J. Clinical studies of alcoholic ketoacidosis. *Diabetes*, 1974, *23*, 433-439.

Dagradi, A.F., Lee, E.R., Rodiles, D., & Lockareff, S. "Open-tube" vs fiberoptic esophagoscopy for evaluation of esophageal varices. *American Journal of Gastroenterology*, 1973, *60*, 240-249.

Dajani, R.M., Danielski, J., & Orten, J.M. The utilization of ethanol. II. The alcohol dehydrogenase systems in the livers of alcohol treated rats. *Journal of Nutrition*, 1963, *80*, 196-204.

Davidson, C.S. Nutrition, geography, and liver diseases. *American Journal of Clinical Nutrition*, 1970, *23*, 427-436.

Demling, L., Ottenjann, R., & Elster, K. *Endoscopy and biopsy of the esophagus and stomach.* Philadelphia: W.B. Saunders Company, 1972.

Devenyi, P., Rutherdale, J., Sereny, G., & Olin, J.S. Clinical diagnosis of alcoholic fatty liver. *American Journal of Gastroenterology*, 1970, *54*, 597-602.

Dillon, E.S., Dyer, W.W., & Smelo, L.S. Ketone acidosis in nondiabetic adults. *Medical Clinics of North America*, 1940, *24*, 1813-1822.

Edmondson, H.A., Peters, R.L., Frankel, H.H., & Borowsky, S. The early stage of liver injury in the alcoholic. *Medicine*, 1967, *46*, 119-129.

Edmondson, H.A., Peters, R.L., Reynolds, T.B., & Kuzma, O.T. Sclerosing hyaline necrosis of the liver. A recognizable clinical syndrome. *Annals of Internal Medicine*, 1963, *59*, 646-673.

Eknoyan, G., Martinez-Maldonado, M., Yium, J.J., & Suki, W.N. Combined ascitic-fluid and furosemide infusion in management of ascites. *New England Journal of Medicine*, 1970, *282*, 713-717.

Elkington, S.G., Floch, M.H., & Conn, H.O. Lactulose in the treatment of chronic portal-systemic encephalopathy. A double-blind clinical trial. *New England Journal of Medicine*, 1969, *281*, 408-413.

Epstein, M., Berk, D.P., Hollenberg, M.K., Adams, D.F., Chalmers, T.C., Abrams, H.L., & Merrill, J.P. Renal failure in the patient with cirrhosis. The role of active vasoconstriction. *American Journal of Medicine*, 1970, *49*, 175-185.

Faloon, W.W., Eckhardt, R.D., Murphy, T.L., Cooper, A.M., & Davidson, C.S. An evaluation of human serum albumin in the treatment of cirrhosis of the liver. *Journal of Clinical Investigation*, 1949, *28*, 583-594.

Feinman, L., & Lieber, C.S. Liver disease in alcoholism. In B. Kissen & H. Begleiter (Eds.), *The biology of alcoholism* (Vol. 3). New York: Plenum Press, 1974.

Fenster, L.F. The nonefficacy of short-term anabolic steroid therapy in alcoholic liver disease. *Annals of Internal Medicine*, 1966, *65*, 738-744.

Figueroa, R.B., & Klotz, A.P. Alterations of alcohol dehydrogenase and other hepatic enzymes in alcoholic cirrhosis. *Metabolism*, 1962, *11*, 1169-1180.

Fischer, F.E., & Baldessarini, R.J. False neurotransmitters and hepatic failure. *Lancet*, 1971, *2*, 75-81.

Flax, M.H. & Tisdale, W.A. An electron microscopic study of alcoholic hyalin. *American Journal of Pathology*, 1964, *44*, 441-453.

Forsander, O.A. Influence of some aliphatic alcohols on metabolism of rat liver slices. *Biochemical Journal*, 1967, *105*, 93-97.

Forsander, O.A. Influence of ethanol on the redox state of the liver. *Quarterly Journal of Studies on Alcohol*, 1970, *31*, 550-570.

French, S.W., & Davies, P.L. The Mallory body in the pathogenesis of alcoholic liver disease. In J.M. Khanna, Y. Israel, & H. Kalant (Eds.), *Alcoholic liver pathology*. Toronto: Addiction Research Foundation, 1975.

Gabuzda, G.J., & Hall, P.W. Relation of potassium depletion to renal ammonium metabolism and hepatic coma. *Medicine*, 1966, *45*, 481-491.

Galambos, J.T. Alcoholic hepatitis: Its therapy and prognosis. In H. Popper & F. Schaffner (Eds.), *Progress in liver diseases*(Vol. 4). New York & London: Grune and Stratton, 1972.

Galambos, J.T. Natural history of alcoholic hepatitis. III. Histological changes. *Gastroenterology*, 1972, *63*, 1026-1035.

Galambos, J.T. Alcoholic hepatitis. In F. Schaffner, S. Sherlock, & C.M. Leevy (Eds.), *The liver and its diseases*. New York: Intercontinental Medical Book Corp., 1974.

Garceau, A.J. & Boston Inter-Hospital Group. The natural history of cirrhosis. II. The influence of alcohol and prior hepatitis on pathology and prognosis. *New England Journal of Medicine*, 1964, *271*, 1173-1179.

Gerber, M.A., Orr, W., Denk, H., Schaffner, F., & Popper, H. Hepatocellular hyalin in cholestasis and cirrhosis: Its diagnostic significance. *Gastroenterology*, 1973, *64*, 89-98.

Ginsberg, H., Olefsky, J., Farquhar, J.W., & Reaven, G.M. Moderate ethanol ingestion and plasma triglyceride levels: A study in normal and hypertriglyceridemic persons. *Annals of Internal Medicine*, 1974, *12*, 134-149.

Goldberg, B.B., Clearfield, H.R., Goodman, G.A., & Morales, J.O. Ultrasonic determination of ascites. *Archives of Internal Medicine*, 1973, *131*, 217-220.

Green, J., Mistilis, S., & Schiff, L. Acute alcoholic hepatitis. *Archives of Internal Medicine*, 1963, *112*, 67-78.

Greenberger, N.J., Cohen, R.B., & Isselbacher, K.J. The effect of chronic alcohol administration on liver alcohol dehydrogenase activity in the rat. *Laboratory Investigation*, 1965, *14*, 264-271.

Grunnet, N., Quistorf, B., & Thieden, H.I.D. Rate - limiting factors in ethanol oxidation in isolated rat-liver parenchymal cells. *European Journal of Biochemistry*, 1973, *40*, 275-282.

Grunnet, N., Thieden, H.I.D. The effect of ethanol concentration upon in vivo metabolite levels of rat liver. *Life Sciences*, 1972, *11*, (Part 2), 983-993.

Hall, E.M., & Ophuls, W. Progressive alcoholic cirrhosis: Report of four cases. *American Journal of Pathology*, 1925, *1*, 477-493.

Hardison, W.G., & Lee, F.I. Prognosis in acute liver disease of the alcoholic patient. *New England Journal of Medicine*, 1966, *275*, 61-66.

Harinasuta, U., Chomet, B., Ishak, K., & Zimmerman, H.J. Steatonecrosis - Mallory body type. *Medicine*, 1967, *46*, 141-162.

Harinasuta, U., & Zimmerman, H.J. Alcoholic steatonecrosis. I. Relationship between severity of hepatic disease and presence of Mallory bodies in the liver. *Gastroenterology*, 1971, *60*, 1036-1046.

Hasumura, Y., Teschke, R., & Lieber, C.S. Acetaldehyde oxidation by hepatic mitochondria: Its decrease after chronic ethanol consumption. *Science*, 1975, *189*, 727-729. (a)

Hasumura, Y., Teschke, R., & Lieber, C.S. Hepatic microsomal ethanol oxidizing system (MEOS): Dissociation from reduced nicotinamide adenine dinucleotide phosphate oxidase and possible role of form I of cytochrome P-450. *Journal of Pharmacology and Experimental Therapeutics*, 1975, *194*, 469-474. (b)

Hawkins, R.A., Miller, A.L., Nielsen, R.C., & Veigh, R.L. The acute action of ammonia on rat brain metabolism in vivo. *Biochemical Journal*, 1973, *134*, 1001-1008.

Helman, R.A., Temko, M.H., Nye, S.W., & Fallon, H.J. Alcoholic hepatitis: Natural history and evaluation of prednisolone therapy. *Annals of Internal Medicine*, 1971, *74*, 311-321.

Hoffbauer, F.W., & Zaki, G. Choline deficiency in baboons and rat compared. *Archives of Pathology*, 1965, *79*, 364-369.

Hori, M., Austin, W.G., & McDermott, W.V., Jr. Role of hepatic arterial blood flow and hepatic nerves on renal circulation and function. I. Acute studies in the dog. *Annals of Surgery*, 1965, *162*, 849-962.

Horning, M.G., Williams, E.A., Maling, H.M., & Brodie, B.B. Depot fat as source of increased liver triglycerides after ethanol. *Biochemical and Biophysical Research Communications*, 1960, *3*, 635-640.

Horton, A.A. Induction of aldehyde dehydrogenase in a mitochondrial fraction. *Biochimica et Biophysica Acta*, 1971, *253*, 514-517.

Horvath, F., Kovacs, K., & Ross, R.C. Subcellular features of alcoholic liver lesion: Alcoholic hyalin. *Journal of Pathology*, 1973, *110*, 245-250.

Hourani, B.T., Hamlin, E.M., & Reynolds, T.B. Cerebrospinal fluid glutamine as a measure of hepatic encephalopathy. *Archives of Internal Medicine*, 1971, *127*, 1033-1036.

Hyde, G.L., & Eiseman, B. Peritoneal-atrial shunt for intractable ascites. *Archives of Surgery*, 1967, *95*, 369-373.

Iseri, O.A., & Gottlieb, L.S. Alcoholic hyaline and megamitochondria as separate and distinct entities in liver disease associated with alcoholism. *Gastroenterology*, 1971, *60*, 1027-1035.

Iseri, O.A., Gottlieb, L.S., & Lieber, C.S. The ultrastructure of ethanol-induced fatty liver. *Federation Proceedings*, 1964, *23*, 579.

Iseri, O.A., Lieber, C.S., & Gottlieb, L.S. The ultrastructure of fatty liver induced by prolonged ethanol ingestion. *American Journal of Pathology*, 1966, *48*, 535-555.

Jabbari, M., & Leevy, C.M. Protein anabolism and fatty liver of the alcoholic. *Medicine*, 1967, *46*, 131-139.

Jenkins, J.S., Eckel, R.E., & Craig, J.W. Alcoholic keto-acidosis. *Journal of the American Medical Association*, 1971, *217*, 177-183.

Joly, J.G., Feinman, L., Ishii, H., & Lieber, C.S. Effect of chronic ethanol feeding on hepatic microsomal glycerophosphate acyltransferase activity. *Journal of Lipid Research*, 1973, *14*, 337-343.

Joly, J.G., Ishii, H., Teschke, R., Hasumura, Y., & Lieber, C.S. Effect of chronic ethanol feeding on the activities and submicrosomal distribution of reduced nicotinamide adenine dinucleotide phosphate (NADPH)-cytochrome P-450 reductase and the demethylases for aminopyrine and ethyl morphine. *Biochemical Pharmacology*, 1973, *22*, 1532-1535.

Kater, R.M.H., Carulli, N., & Iber, F.L. Difference in the rate of ethanol metabolism in recently drinking alcoholic and nondrinking subjects. *American Journal of Clinical Nutrition*, 1969, *22*, 1608-1617.

Kater, R.M.H., Roggin,G., Tobon, F., Zieve, P., & Iber, F.L. Increased rate of clearance of drugs from the circulation of alcoholics. *American Journal of the Medical Sciences*, 1969, *258*, 35-39.

Katon, R.M., & Smith, F.W. Panendoscopy in the early diagnosis of acute upper gastrointestinal bleeding. *Gastroenterology*, 1973, *65*, 728-734.

Katz, R., Velasco, M., Klinger, J., & Alessandri, H. Corticosteroids in the treatment of acute hepatitis in coma. *Gastroenterology*, 1962, *42*, 258-266.

Keeley, A.F., Iseri, O.A., & Gottlieb, L.S. Ultrastructurel of hyaline cytoplasmic inclusions in a human hepatoma: Relationship to Mallory's alcoholic hyalin. *Gastroenterology*, 1972, *62*, 280-293.

Kew, M.C., Brunt, P.W., Varma, R.R., Hourigan, K.J., Williams, H.S., & Sherlock, S. Renal and intrarenal blood-flow in cirrhosis of the liver. *Lancet*, 1971, *2*, 504-509.

Khanna, J.M., Kalant, H., & Lin, G. Metabolism, of ethanol by rat liver microsomal enzymes. *Biochemical Pharmacology*, 1970, *19*, 2493-2499.

Klatskin, G., Krehl, W.A., & Conn, H.O. The effect of alcohol on the choline requirement. I. Changes in the rat's liver following prolonged ingestion of alcohol. *Journal of Experimental Medicine*, 1954, *100*, 605-614.

Klion, F.M., & Schaffner, F. Ultrastructural studies in alcoholic liver disease. *Digestion*, 1968, *1*, 2-14.

Korsten, M.A., Matsuzaki, S., Feinman, L., & Lieber, C.S. High blood acetaldehyde levels following ethanol administration: Differences between alcoholic and non-alcoholic subjects. *New England Journal of Medicine*, 1975, *292*, 386-389.

Krebs, H.A. The effects of ethanol on the metabolic activities of the liver. *Advances in Enzyme Regulation*, 1968, *6*, 467-480.

Lancestremere, R.G., Davidson, P.L., & Earley, L.F. Renal failure in Laennec's cirrhosis. II. Simultaneous determination of cardiac output and renal hemodynamics. *Journal of Clinical Investigation*, 1962, *41*, 1922-1927.

Lane, B.P., & Lieber, C.S. Ultrastructural alterations in human hepatocytes following ingestion of ethanol with adequate diets. *American Journal of Pathology*, 1966, *49*, 593-603.

Lane, B.P., & Lieber, C.S. Effects of butylated hydroxytoluene on the ultrastructure of rat hepatocytes. *Laboratory Investigation*, 1967, *16*, 342-348.

Lawson, J.D., & Weissbein, A.S. The puddle sign - an aid in the diagnosis of minimal ascites. *New England Journal of Medicine*, 1959, *260*, 652-654.

Leevy, C.M., Chen, T., & Zetterman, R. Alcoholic hepatitis, cirrhosis and immunologic reactivity. *Annals of New York Academy of Sciences*, 1975, *252*, 106-115.

Lefevre, A.F., Adler, H.M., & Lieber, C.S. Effect of ethanol on ketone metabolism. *Journal of Clinical Investigation*, 1970, *49*, 1775-1782.

Lefevre, A.F., DeCarli, L.M., & Lieber, C.S. Effect of ethanol on cholesterol and bile acid metabolism. *Journal of Lipid Research*, 1972, *13*, 48-55.

Lelbach, W.K. Cirrhosis in the alcoholic and its relation to the volume of alcohol abuse. *Annals of the New York Academy of Sciences*, 1975, *252*, 85-105.

Lesesne, H.R., Bozynski, E., & Fallon, H.J. Treatment of alcoholic hepatitis with encephalopathy: Comparison of prednisolone with caloric supplements. *Gastroenterology*, 1974, *67*, 808. (Abstract)

Leveen, H.H., Christoudias, G.K., Moon, I.P., Luft, R., Falk, G., & Grosberg, S. Peritoneo-venous shunting for ascites. *Annals of Surgery*, 1974, *180*, 580-591.

Levy, L.J., Duga, J., Girgis, M., & Gordon, E.E. Ketoacidosis associated with alcoholism in nondiabetic subjects. *Annals of Internal Medicine*, 1973, *78*, 213-219.

Lieber, C.S. Hepatic and metabolic effects of alcohol (1966-1973). *Gastroenterology*, 1973, *65*, 821-846. (a)

Lieber, C.S. Liver adaptation and injury in alcoholism. *New England Journal of Medicine*, 1973, *288*, 356-362. (b)

Lieber, C.S. Contrast between the acute and chronic effects of ethanol on lipid, ketone, and drug metabolism. In F. Lundquist & N. Tygstrup (Eds.), *Proceedings of the Alfred Benzon Symposium VI: Regulation of hepatic metabolism May 22-24, 1973*. Copenhagen: Munksgaard International Publishers, Ltd., 1974. (a)

Lieber, C.S. Effects of ethanol upon lipid metabolism. *Lipids*, 1974, *9*, 103-116. (b)

Lieber, C.S. Liver disease and alcohol: Fatty liver, alcoholic hepatitis, cirrhosis, and their interrelationships. *Annals of the New York Academy of Sciences*, 1975, *252*, 63-84.

Lieber, C.S., & Davidson, C.S. Some metabolic effects of ethyl alcohol. *American Journal of Medicine*, 1962, *33*, 319-327.

Lieber, C.S., & DeCarli, L.M. Ethanol oxidation by hepatic microsomes: Adaptive increase after ethanol feeding. *Science*, 1968, *162*, 917-918.

Lieber, C.S., & DeCarli, L.M. Effect of drug administration on the activity of the hepatic microsomal ethanol oxidizing system. *Life Sciences*, 1970, *9*, (Part 2), 267-276. (a)

Lieber, C.S., & DeCarli, L.M. Hepatic microsomal ethanol-oxidizing system: In vitro characteristics and adaptive properties in vivo. *Journal of Biological Chemistry*, 1970, *245*, 2505-2512. (b)

Lieber, C.S., & DeCarli, L.M. Quantitative relationship between the amount of dietary fat and the severity of the alcoholic fatty liver. *American Journal of Clinical Nutrition*, 1970, *23*, 474-478. (c)

Lieber, C.S., & DeCarli, L.M. Reduced nicotinamide-adenine dinucleotide phosphate oxidase: Activity enhanced by ethanol consumption. *Science*, 1970, *170*, 78-79. (d)

Lieber, C.S., & DeCarli, L.M. The role of the hepatic microsomal ethanol oxidizing system (MEOS) for ethanol metabolism in vivo. *Journal of Pharmacology and Experimental Therapeutics*, 1972, *181*, 279-287.

Lieber, C.S., DeCarli, L.M., & Rubin, E. Sequential production of fatty liver, hepatitis, and cirrhosis in sub-human primates fed ethanol with adequate diets. *Proceedings of the National Academy of Sciences of the U.S.A.*, 1975, *72*, 437-441.

Lieber, C.S., Jones, D.P., & DeCarli, L.M. Effects of prolonged ethanol intake: Production of fatty liver despite adequate diets. *Journal of Clinical Investigation*, 1965, *44*, 1009-1021.

Lieber, C.S., Jones, D.P., & Losowsky, M.S. Interrelation of uric acid and ethanol metabolism in man. *Journal of Clinical Investigation*, 1962, *41*, 1863-1870.

Lieber, C.S., Jones, D.P., Mendelson, J., & DeCarli, L.M. Fatty liver, hyperlipemia, and hyperuricemia produced by prolonged alcohol consumption, despite adequate dietary intake. *Transactions of the Association of American Physicians*, 1963, *76*, 289-300.

Lieber, C.S., Lefevre, A., Spritz, L., Feinman, L., & DeCarli, L.M. Difference in hepatic metabolism of long-and medium-chained fatty acids: The role of fatty acid chain length in the production of the alcoholic fatty liver. *Journal of Clinical Investigation*, 1967, *46*, 1451-1460.

Lieber, C.S., & Rubin, E. Alcoholic fatty liver in man on high protein-low fat diet. *American Journal of Medicine*, 1968, *44*, 200-206.

Lieber, C.S., Rubin, E., & DeCarli, L.M. Hepatic microsomal ethanol oxidizing system (MEOS): Differentiation from alcohol dehydrogenase and NADPH oxidase. *Biochemical and Biophysical Research Communications*, 1970, *40*, 858-865.

Lieber, C.S., Rubin, E., & DeCarli, L.M. Effects of ethanol on lipid, uric acid, intermediary and drug metabolism, including the pathogenesis of alcoholic fatty liver. In B. Kissen & H. Begleiter (Eds.), *The biology of alcoholism*. New York: Plenum Press, 1971.

Lieber, C.S., & Schmid, R. The effect of ethanol on fatty acid metabolism: Stimulation of hepatic fatty acid synthesis in vitro. *Journal of Clinical Investigation*, 1961, *40*, 394-399.

Lieber, C.S., & Spritz, N. Effects of prolonged ethanol intake in man: Role of dietary, adipose, and endogenously synthesized fatty acids in the pathogenesis of alcoholic fatty liver. *Journal of Clinical Investigation*, 1966, *45*, 1400-1411.

Lieber, C.S., Spritz, N., & De Carli, L.M. Role of dietary, adipose and endogenously synthesized fatty acids in the pathogenesis of the alcoholic fatty liver. *Journal of Clinical Investigation*, 1966, *45*, 51-62.

Lieber, C.S., Spritz, N., & DeCarli, L.M. Fatty liver produced by dietary deficiencies: Its pathogenesis and potentiation by ethanol. *Journal of Lipid Research*, 1969, *10*, 283-287.

Lieberman, F.L., & Reynolds, T.B. Renal failure with cirrhosis: Observations on the role of diuretics. *Annals of Internal Medicine*, 1966, *64*, 1221-1228.

Lieberman, F.L., & Reynolds, T.B. Plasma volume in cirrhosis of the liver: Its relation to portal hypertension, ascites, and renal failure. *Journal of Clinical Investigation*, 1967, *46*, 1297-1308.

Lieberman, F.L., Ito, S., & Reynolds, T.B. Effective plasma volume in cirrhosis with ascites. Evidence that a decreased value does not account for renal sodium retention, a spontaneous reduction in glomerular filtration rate (GFR), and a fall in GFR during drug-induced diuresis. *Journal of Clinical Investigation*, 1969, *48*, 975-981.

Lischner, M.W., Alexander, J.F., & Galambos, J.T. Natural history of alcoholic hepatitis. I. The acute disease. *American Journal of Digestive Diseases*, 1971, *16*, 481-494.

Liu, C.I. Enhanced visualization of esophageal varices by buscopan. *American Journal of Roentgenology, Radium Therapy, and Nuclear Medicine*, 1974, *121*, 232-235.

Lochner, A., Wulff, J., & Madison, L.L. Ethanol-induced hypoglycemia. I. The acute effects of ethanol on hepatic glucose output and peripheral glucose utilization in fasted dogs. *Metabolism*, 1967, *16*, 1-18.

Losowsky, M.S., Jones, D.P., Davidson, C.S., & Lieber, C.S. Studies of alcoholic hyperlipemia and its mechanism. *American Journal of Medicine*, 1963, *35*, 794-803.

Lundquist, F., & Wolthers, H. The kinetics of alcohol elimination in man. *Acta Pharmacologica et Toxicologica*, 1958, *14*, 265-289.

Ma, M.H. Ultrastructural pathologic findings of the human hepatocyte. I. Alcoholic liver disease. *Archives of Pathology*, 1972, *94*, 554-571.

MacLachlan, M.J., & Rodnan, G.P. Effect of food, fast, and alcohol on serum uric acid and acute attacks of gout. *American Journal of Medicine*, 1967, *42*, 38-57.

Makar, A.B., & Mannering, G.J. Kinetics of ethanol metabolism in the intact rat and monkey. *Biochemical Pharmacology*, 1970, *19*, 2017-2022.

Matsuzaki, S. & Lieber, C.S. ADH-independent ethanol oxidation in the liver and its increase by chronic ethanol consumption. *Gastroenterology*, 1975, *69*, 845. (Abstract)

McCloy, R.M., Baldus, W.P., Tauxe, W.N., & Summerskill, W.H.J. Plasma volume and renal circulatory function in cirrhosis. *Annals of Internal Medicine*, 1967, *66*, 307-311.

Mendelson, J.H., & Mello, N.K. Alcohol-induced hyperlipemia and beta lipoproteins. *Science*, 1973, *180*, 1372-1374.

Mendenhall, C.L. Anabolic steroid therapy as an adjunct to diet in alcoholic hepatic steatosis. *American Journal of Digestive Diseases*, 1968, *13*, 783-791.

Mendenhall, C.L., Bradford, R.H., & Furman, R.H. Effect of ethanol on glycerolipid metabolism in rat liver. *Biochimica et Biophysica Acta*, 1969, *187*, 501-509.

Mezey, E., & Robles, E.A. Effects of phenobarbital administration on rates of ethanol clearance and on ethanol-oxidizing enzymes in man. *Gastroenterology*, 1974, *66*, 248-253.

Mezey, E., Potter, J.J., & Reed, W.D. Ethanol oxidation by a component of liver microsomes rich in cytochrome P-450. *Journal of Biological Chemistry*, 1973, *248*, 1183-1187.

Mihas, A.A., Bull, D.M., & Davidson, C.S. Cell-mediated immunity to liver in patients with alcoholic hepatitis. *Lancet*, 1975, *1*, 951-956.

Mikkelsen, W.P., Turrill, F.L., & Kern, W.H. Acute hyaline necrosis of the liver: A surgical trap. *American Journal of Surgery*, 1968, *116*, 266-272.

Millette, B., Huet, P.M., & Lavoie, P. Portal and systemic effects of selective infusion of vasopression into the superior mesenteric artery in cirrhotic patients. *Gastroenterology*, 1975, *69*, 6-12.

Misra, P.S., Lefevre, A., Ishii, H., Rubin, E., & Lieber, C.S. Increase of ethanol, meprobamate and pentobarbital metabolism after chronic ethanol administration in man and in rats. *American Journal of Medicine*, 1971, *51*, 346-351.

Mistilis, S.P., & Ockner, R.K. Effects of ethanol on endogenous lipid and lipo-protein metabolism in small intestine. *Journal of Laboratory and Clinical Medicine*, 1972, *80*, 34-46.

Monroe, S., French, S.W., & Zamboni, L. Mallory bodies in a case of primary biliary cirrhosis. An ultrastructural and morphogenetic study. *American Journal of Clinical Pathology*, 1973, *59*, 254-262.

Morrison, G.R., & Brock, F.E. Quantitative measurement of alcohol dehydrogenase activity within the liver lobule of rats after prolonged ethanol ingestion. *Journal of Nutrition*, 1967, *92*, 286-292.

Mortenson, R.A., & Lawton, R.L. Surgical treatment for intractable ascites. *American Journal of Surgery*, 1968, *116*, 929-932.

Mullane, J.R., & Gliedman, M.L. Elevation of the pressure in the abdominal inferior vena cava as a cause of a hepatorenal syndrome in cirrhosis. *Surgery*, 1966, *59*, 1135-1146.

Mutchnick, M.G., Lerner, E., & Conn, H.O. Portal-systemic encephalopathy and portacaval anastomosis: A prospective, controlled investigation. *Gastroenterology*, 1974, *66*, 1005-1019.

Newcombe, D.S. Ethanol metabolism and uric acid. *Metabolism*, 1972, *21*, 1193-1203.

Nikkila, E.A., & Ojala, K. Role of hepatic L-aglycerophosphate and triglyceride synthesis in production of fatty liver by ethanol. *Proceedings of the Society for Experimental Biology and Medicine*, 1963,*113*, 814-817.

Okuda, K., Yasumoto, M., Goto, A., & Kunisaki, T. Endoscopic observations of gastric varices. *American Journal of Gastroenterology*, 1973, *60*, 356-357.

Ontko, J.A. Effects of ethanol on the metabolism of free fatty acids in isolated liver cells. *Journal of Lipid Research*, 1973, *14*, 78-86.

Ottinger, L.W., & Moncure, A.C. Transthoracic ligation of bleeding esophageal varices in patients with intrahepatic portal obstruction. *Annals of Surgery*, 1974, *179*, 35-38.

Parkes, J.D., Sharpstone, P., & Williams, R. Levodopa in hepatic coma. *Lancet*, 1970, *2*, 1341-1343.

Perman, E.S. The effect of ethyl alcohol on the secretion from the adrenal medulla in man. *Acta Physiologica Scandinavica*, 1958, *44*, 241-247.

Phear, E.A., Rubner, B., Sherlock, S., & Summerskill, W.H.J. Methionine toxicity in liver disease and its prevention by chlortetracycline. *Clinical Science*, 1956, *15*, 93-117.

Phillips, G.B., & Davidson, C.S. Acute hepatic insufficiency of the chronic alcoholic. *Archives of Internal Medicine*, 1954, *94*, 585-603.

Phillips, G.B., & Davidson, C.S. Liver disease of the chronic alcoholic simulating extrahepatic biliary obstruction. *Gastroenterology*, 1957, *33*, 236-244.

Pirola, R.C., & Lieber, C.S. The energy cost of the metabolism of drugs, including ethanol. *Pharmacology*, 1972, *7*, 185-196.

Pitcher, J.L. Safety and effectiveness of the modified Sengstaken-Blakemore tube: A prospective study. *Gastroenterology*, 1971, *61*, 291-298.

Popper, H., & Orr, W. Current concepts in cirrhosis (4th World Congress of Gastroenterology). *Scandinavian Journal of Gastroenterology*, 1970, *5*, (Suppl. 6), 203-222.

Popper, H., Szanto, P.B., & Parthasarathy, M. Florid cirrhosis. A review of 35 cases. *American Journal of Clinical Pathology*, 1955, *25*, 889-901.

Porter, H.P., Simon, F.R., Pope, C.E, Volwiler, W., & Fenster, F. Corticosteroid therapy in severe alcoholic hepatitis: A double-blind drug trial. *New England Journal of Medicine*, 1971, *284*, 1350-1355.

Raskin, N.H., & Sokoloff, L. Ethanol-induced adaptation of alcohol dehydrogenase activity in rat brain. *Nature*, 1972, *236*, 138-140.

Redmond, G., & Cohen, G. Induction of liver acetaldehyde dehydrogenase: Possible role in ethanol tolerance after exposure to barbiturates. *Science*, 1976, *171*, 387-389.

Resnick, R.H. Intrarterial vasopressin: A continuing challenge. *Gastroenterology*, 1975, *68*, 411-412.

Resnick, R.H., Chalmers, T.C., Ishihara, A.M., Garceau, A.J., Callow, A.D., Schimmel, E.M., & O'Hara, E.T. A controlled study of the prophylactic portacaval shunt: A final report. *Annals of Internal Medicine*, 1969, *70*, 675-688.

Resnick, R.H., Iber, E., Ishihara, A.M., Chalmers, T.C., & Zimmerman, H. A controlled study of the therapeutic portacaval shunt. *Gastroenterology*, 1974, *67*, 843-857.

Reynier, M. Pyrazole inhibition and kinetic studies of ethanol and retinol oxidation catalyzed by rat liver alcohol dehydrogenase. *Acta Chemica Scandinavica*, 1969, *23*, 1119-1129.

Reynolds, T.B., Portal hypertension. In L. Schiff (Ed.), *Diseases of the liver* (3rd ed.). Philadelphia: J.B. Lippincott Company, 1969.

Reynolds, T.B., & Edmondson, H.A. Alcoholic hepatitis. *Annals of Internal Medicine*, 1971, *74*, 440-442.

Ritzmann, S.E. Immunoglobulin abnormalities. In S.E. Ritzmann & J.C. Daniels (Eds.), *Serum protein abnormalities. Diagnostic and clinical aspects*. Boston: Little, Brown, & Co., 1975.

Rizzoli, A.A., & Golzigna, L. Molecular mechanism of unconscious state induced by butyrate. *Biochemical Pharmacology*, 1970, *19*, 2727-2736.

Roy, S., Ramalingaswami, V., & Nayak, N.C. An ultrastructural study of the liver in Indian childhood cirrhosis with particular reference to the structure of cytoplasmic hyaline. *Gut*, 1971, *12*, 693-701.

Rubin, E., Bacchin, P., Gang, H., & Lieber, C.S. Induction and inhibition of hepatic microsomal and mitochondrial enzymes by ethanol. *Laboratory Investigation*, 1970, *22*, 569-580.

Rubin, E., Gang, H., Misra, P.S., & Lieber, C.S. Inhibition of drug metabolism by acute ethanol intoxication. A hepatic microsomal mechanism. *American Journal of Medicine*, 1970, *49*, 801-806.

Rubin, E., Krus, S., & Popper, H. Pathogenesis of post-necrotic cirrhosis in alcoholics. *Archives of Pathology*, 1962, *73*, 288-299.

Rubin, E., & Lieber,C.S. Early fine structural changes in the human liver induced by alcohol. *Gastroenterology*, 1967, *52*, 1-13.

Rubin, E., & Lieber, C.S. Alcohol-induced hepatic injury in non-alcoholic volunteers. *New England Journal of Medicine*, 1968, *278*, 869-876.

Rubin, E., & Lieber, C.S. Relation of alcoholic liver injury to cirrhosis. *Clinics in Gastroenterology*, 1975, *4*, 247-272.

Rubin, E., & Popper, H. The evolution of human cirrhosis deduced from observations in experimental animals. *Medicine*, 1967, *46*, 163-183.

Saville, P.D., & Lieber, C.S. Effect of alcohol on growth, bone density, and muscle magnesium in the rat. *Journal of Nutrition*, 1965, *87*, 477-488.

Schenker, S., Breen, K.J., & Hoyumpa, A.M. Hepatic encephalopathy: Current status. *Gastroenterology*, 1974, *66*, 121-151.

Schroeder, E.T., Shear, L., Sancetta, S.M., & Gabuzda, G.J. Renal failure in patients with cirrhosis of the liver. III. Evaluation of intrarenal blood flow by para-aminohippurate extraction and response angiotensin. *American Journal of Medicine*, 1967, *43*, 887-896.

Schroeder, E.T., Eich, R.H., Smulyan, H., Gould, A.B., & Gabuzda, G.J. Plasma renin level in hepatic cirrhosis; Relation to functional renal failure. *American Journal of Medicine*, 1970, *49*, 186-191.

Schroeder, E.T., Numann, P.J., & Chamberlain, B.E. Functional renal failure in cirrhosis. *Annals of Internal Medicine*, 1970, *72*, 923-928.

Shaldon, S., & Sherlock, S. The use of vasopressin ("Pitressin") in the control of bleeding from oesophageal varices. *Lancet*, 1960, *2*, 222-225.

Shear, L., Kleinerman, J., & Gabuzda, G.J. Renal failure in patients with cirrhosis of the liver. I. Clinical and pathologic characteristics. *American Journal of Medicine*, 1965, *39*, 184-198.

Shear, L., Bonkowsky, H.L., & Gabuzda, G.J. Renal tubular acidosis in cirrhosis. A determinant of susceptibility to recurrent hepatic precoma. *New England Journal of Medicine*, 1969, *280*, 1-7.

Sherlock, S. Classification and functional aspects of portal hypertension. *American Journal of Surgery*, 1974, *127*, 121-128.

Sherlock, S., & Walshe, V. Effect of undernutrition in man on hepatic structure and function. *Nature*, 1948, *161*, 604.

Simmons, E., Goldstein, H., & Boyle, J.D. A controlled clinical trial of lactulose in hepatic encephalopathy. *Gastroenterology*, 1970, *59*, 827-832.

Singlevich, T., & Barboriak, J.J. Ethanol and induction of microsomal drug-metabolizing enzymes in the rat. *Toxicology and Applied Pharmacology*, 1971, *20*, 284-290.

Smith, G.W. Use of hemodynamic selection criteria in the management of cirrhotic patients with portal hypertension. *Annals of Surgery*, 1974, *179*, 782-790.

Smuckler, E.A. The ultrastructure of human alcoholic hyalin. *American Journal of Clinical Pathology*, 1968, *49*, 790-797.

Stabenau, F.R., Warren, K.S., & Rall, D.P. The role of pH gradient in the distribution of ammonia between blood and cerebrospinal fluid, brain, and muscle. *Journal of Clinical Investigation*, 1959, *38*, 373-383.

Summerskill, W.H.J. Hepatic failure and the kidney. *Gastroenterology*, 1966, *51*, 94-107.

Summerskill, W.H.J., Wolfe, S.J., & Davidson, C.S. Response to alcohol in chronic alcoholic liver disease. Clinical, pathological and metabolic changes. *Lancet*, 1957, *1*, 335-343.

Svoboda, D.J., & Manning, R.T. Chronic alcoholism with fatty metamorphasis of the liver. *American Journal of Pathology*, 1963, *44*, 645-662.

Teschke, R., Hasumura, Y., Joly, J.G., Ishii, T.T., & Lieber, C.S. Microsomal ethanol-oxidizing system (MEOS): Purification and properties of a rat liver system free of catalase and alcohol dehydrogenase. *Biochemical and Biophysical Research Communications*, 1972, *49*, 1187-1193.

Teschke, R., Hasumura, Y., & Lieber, C.S. Hepatic microsomal ethanol-oxidizing system: Solubilization, isolation, and characterization. *Archives of Biochemistry and Biophysics*, 1974, *163*, 404-415.

Teschke, R., Hasumura, Y., & Lieber, C.A. Hepatic microsomal alcohol-oxidizing system. *Journal of Biological Chemistry*, 1975, *250*, 7397-7404.

Theorell, H., & Bonnichsen, R. Studies on liver alcohol dehydrogenase. I. Equilibria and initial reaction velocities. *Acta Chemica Scandinavica*, 1951, *5*, 1105-1126.

Thieden, H.I.D. The effect of ethanol concentration on ethanol oxidation in rat liver slices. *Acta Chemica Scandinavica*, 1971, *25*, 3421-3427.

Thurman, R.G., Ley, H.G., & Scholz, R. Hepatic microsomal ethanol oxidation: Hydrogen peroxide formation and the role of catalase. *European Journal of Biochemistry*, 1972, *25*, 420-430.

Tobon, E., & Mezey, E. Effect of ethanol administration on hepatic ethanol and drug - metabolizing enzymes and on rates of ethanol degradation. *Journal of Laboratory and Clinical Medicine*, 1971, *77*, 110-121.

Tremolieres, J., & Carre, L. Etudes sur les modalites d'oxydation de l'alcool chez l'homme normal et alcoolique. *Revue de l'alcoolisme (Paris)*, 1961, *7*, 202-227.

Tristani, F.E., & Cohn, J.N. Systemic and renal hemodynamics in oliguric hepatic failure: Effect of volume expansion. *Journal of Clinical Investigation*, 1967, *46*, 1894-1906.

Truitt, E.B. Jr., & Walsh, M.J. The role of acetaldehyde in the actions of ethanol. In B. Kissin & H. Begleiter (Eds.) *The biology of alcoholism*. New York: Plenum Press, 1971.

Vergara, F., Plum, F., & Duffy, T.E. α-ketoglutaramate: Increased concentrations in the cerebrospinal fluid of patients in hepatic coma. *Science*, 1974, *183*, 81-83.

Vesell, E.S., Page, J.G., & Passananti, G.T. Genetic and environmental factors affecting ethanol metabolism in man. *Clinical Pharmacology and Therapeutics*, 1971, *12*, 192-201.

Videla, L., & Israel, Y. Factors that modify the metabolism of ethanol in rat liver and adpative changes produced by its chronic administration. *Biochemical Journal*, 1970, *118*, 275-281.

Vlahcevic, Z.R., Adham, N.F., Jick, H., Moore, E.W., & Chalmers, T.C. Renal effects of acute expansion of plasma volume in cirrhosis. *New England Journal of Medicine*, 1965, *272*, 387-391.

Volwiler, W., Jones, C.M., & Mallory, T.B. Criteria for the measurement of results of treatment in fatty cirrhosis. *Gastroenterology*, 1948, *11*, 164-182.

Warren, K.S., & Schenker, S. Effect of an inhibitor of glutamine synthesis (methionine sulfoximine) on ammonia toxicity and metabolism. *Journal of Laboratory and Clinical Medicine*, 1964, *64*, 442-449.

Warren, W.D., Fomon, J.J., Viamonte, M., Martinez, L.O., & Kalser, M. Spontaneous reversal of portal venous blood flow in cirrhosis. *Surgery, Gynecology, Obstetrics*, 1968, *126*, 315-323.

Warren, W.D., Restrepo, J.E., Respess, J.C., & Muller, W.H. The importance of hemodynamic studies in management of portal hypertension. *Annals of Surgery*, 1963, *158*, 387-409.

Warren, W.D., Zeppa, R., & Fomon, J.J. Selective transsplenic decompression of gastro-esophageal varices by distal splenorenal shunt. *Annals of Surgery*, 1967, *166*, 437-455.

Wilkinson, P., & Sherlock, S. The effect of repeated albumin infusions in patients with cirrhosis. *Lancet*, 1962, *2*, 1125-1128.

Williamson, J.R., Scholz, R., Browning, E.T., Thurman, R.G., & Fukami, M.H. Metabolic effects of ethanol in perfused rat liver. *Journal of Biological Chemistry*, 1969, *244*, 5044-5054.

Winkel, P., Juhl, E., & Tygstrup, N. Copenhagen study group for liver diseases: The prognostic value of clinical and laboratory data in patients with cirrhosis. *Scandinavian Journal of Gastroenterology*, 1970, *5*, (Suppl. 7) 181-187.

Witte, M.H., Dumont, A.E., Cole, W.R., Witte, C.L., & Kintner, K. Lymph circulation in hepatic cirrhosis: Effect of portacaval shunt. *Annals of Internal Medicine*, 1969, *70*, 303-310.

Yokoo, H., Minick, O.T., Batti, F., & Kent, G. Morphologic variants of alcoholic hyalin. *American Journal of Pathology*, 1972, *69*, 25-40.

Zetterman, R.K., Chen, T., & Leevy, C.M. Role of altered lymphocyte function in alcoholic liver disease. *Gastroenterology*, 1974, *67*, 837. (Abstract)

Zieve, L. Jaundice, hyperlipemia, and hemolytic anemia: A heretofore unrecognized syndrome associated with alcoholic fatty liver and cirrhosis. *Annals of Internal Medicine*, 1958, *48*, 471-496.

CHAPTER 5

DISEASES OF THE NERVOUS SYSTEM ASSOCIATED WITH ALCOHOLISM

Gerhard Freund

Our civilization is based on the control of electrons and molecules. The control of conception, pneumonia, and mood is only a pill away, and so are the "diseases of progress." Alcohol consumption occupies but a small, although numerically important, part of the spectrum of our chemistry-based civilization.

The clinical and social consequences of chronic, heavy alcohol consumption interact in many complex ways. These consequences may, under some conditions, reinforce heavy consumption and help perpetuate a self-sustaining cycle. Chronic alcohol consumption may be associated with diseases involving almost every organ of the body (Kissin & Begleiter, 1971-1974), including the central and peripheral nervous systems. In each particular case several questions arise: (a) Is the chronic alcohol consumption the cause of the disease; is it a coincidental, causally unrelated finding or is the alcohol consumption a result of the

Ralph E. Tarter and A. Arthur Sugerman (eds.), Alcoholism

ISBN: 0-201-08146-6
ISBN: 0-201-08145-8 (pbk.)

disease (Figure 1)? Clearly, association does not prove a cause-effect relationship. (b) If chronic alcohol consumption were proved to be the cause of a clinical disease, is it the ethanol per se, or a metabolite, or is it malnutrition that may accompany chronic alcohol consumption; or is it some chemical, other than alcohol, contained in a particular alcoholic beverage ("congener")? (c) Not all chronic alcohol consumers develop all diseases associated with chronic alcohol abuse, and many develop none. What are the factors that in a particular patient enhance the development of a particular disease--are they genetic or environmental, or is there a specific interaction between both? (d) Does alcohol consumption cause a disease, or does it only permit (or facilitate) the development of a disease that in other patients occurs without alcohol? (For example, does alcohol accelerate aging processes or atherosclerosis of the CNS, or does it activate a latent virus infection of the brain, pancreas, or liver?) (e) If a pathogenetic factor for a disease is identified, where does it fit into the predetermined chain of biological events that leads from the interactions of molecules, including enzymes and receptors, to the patients' symptoms? Such knowledge would obviously enable one to interrupt prophylactically the chain of events leading to the overt disease.

It is clearly a desirable objective for the alcoholic patient, as well as society, to prevent brain damage and institutionalization in a mental hospital. Some persons, however, would or could not abstain from alcohol even if they knew that it is harmful, as is evident from continued cigarette consumption despite its inherent risks. The idea of preventing alcohol-induced brain damage by preventing alcohol consumption appears as simplistic as suggesting that the solution to marital problems is the abolition of marriage.

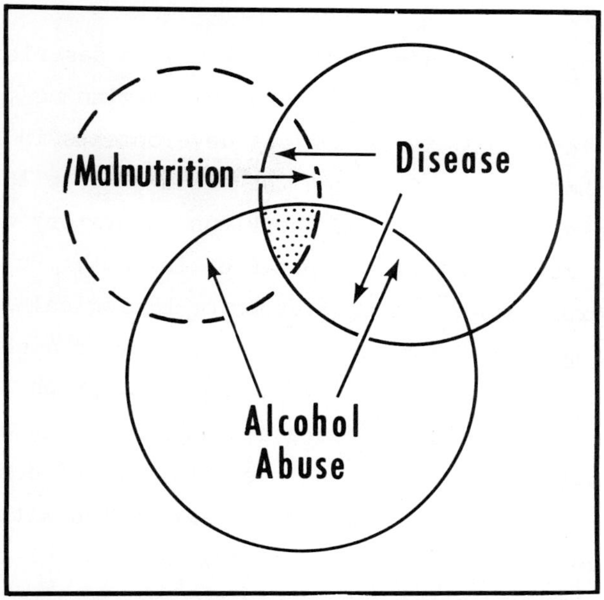

POSSIBLE PATHOGENETIC RELATIONSHIPS IN A PATIENT OR PATIENT POPULATION

NO OVERLAP: INDEPENDENT COEXISTENCE

OVERLAP: CAUSE ⟶ EFFECT

FIGURE 1. Venn diagram of inter-relationships between three potentially separate and independent conditions that may merely coexist or may interact in a particular patient or in a patient population. Arrows indicate which condition potentially causes the other--e.g., alcohol abuse may cause malnutrition that, in turn, may cause a disease. This order may be reversed in other patients: many chronic diseases may result in poor dietary intake and in malnutrition (that may not be severe enough to cause a disease). The cross-hatched areas in the center indicates the presence of all three conditions in the same patient or population, without defining the causal relationships, if any, between them. "Malnutrition" may be caloric, protein, vitamin, or mineral deficiencies, either singly or in various combinations.

The present "state of the art" may be described by saying that the above questions are only beginning to be explored. In analogy to historical developments in poliomyelitis, there was a time when the value of iron lungs was widely recognized but that of the virus laboratory was not. Serendipity may cast a little piece of insight. But only intensive explorations at all levels of biological organization, ranging from the molecular to the body as a whole, will give us the basis for planning rational prophylaxis and treatment of the alcohol-related diseases. In the state of present knowledge, the physical presentations of central and peripheral nervous system impairment associated with chronic alcohol abuse are little more than taxonomic descriptions.

Impairment of the nervous system may manifest itself at the various levels of biological organization: morphological (histology, ventriculography, arteriography, blood-flow studies), electrophysiological (electroencephalography, peripheral nerve conduction velocity), neurological (physical signs, subjective symptoms), psychological, and social. Some of these will be discussed in other chapters. A tentative clinical-pathogenetic classification of diseases of the nervous system is outlined in Table 1. The clinical features of each disease will be briefly described, followed by a consideration of pathogenesis and relevant animal experimentation.

ACUTE INTOXICATION

The acute effects of alcohol intoxication on the central nervous system have been described in several

TABLE 1

Pathogenic Classification of Alcohol-Related Nervous System Disease

I. Acute Intoxication

  A. Stupor
  B. Coma
  C. Death: respiratory paralysis, hypothermia, ketoacidosis.

II. Acute Withdrawal

  A. Tremulousness ("shakes")
  B. Hallucinosis
  C. Delirium tremens
  D. Death: withdrawal seizures, activation of epileptic focus.

III. Chronic Malnutrition

  A. Thiamine deficiency: Wernicke's syndrome.

IV. Degenerative Syndromes

  A. Cerebellum
  B. Corpus callosum
  C. Central pontine myelinolysis

V. Chronic Organic Brain Syndrome

  A. Korsakoff's syndrome
  B. Dementia
    1. Hepatic encephalopathy
    2. Subdural hematoma

VI. Effects on Developing Brain

VII. Peripheral Neuropathy

comprehensive books (Kissin & Begleiter, 1971, 1972, 1974; Thompson, 1956; Wallgren & Barry, 1970). Death in man from respiratory center paralysis may occur at blood-ethanol concentrations of approximately 500 mg/100 ml following a single dose of about 4 g/kg by mouth. However, death may occur at much lower blood-alcohol concentrations when men or animals are exposed to low environmental temperatures, because ethanol impairs the function of the temperature-regulating center (Freund, 1973c; Weyman, Greenbaum, & Grace, 1974). Similarly, alcoholic patients may die in coma from hypoglycemia associated with modest elevation of blood-alcohol concentrations (Madison 1968). It is important to be aware of the effects of alcohol in decreasing blood sugar (primarily by depressing gluconeogenesis in the liver): death is easily preventable by intravenous administration of glucose. The potential danger of alcohol consumption inducing ketoacidosis has been recognized only recently because the standard laboratory tests used in the diagnosis of diabetic ketoacidotic coma result in artificially low "ketone" values (Cooperman, Davidoff, Spark, & Pallotta, 1974). It is self-evident that an alcoholic patient may be in coma, with or without ethanol in the blood, as a result of the many causes of coma (including other drugs) found in the general population.

ACUTE ALCOHOL WITHDRAWAL

The abrupt discontinuation of alcohol following prolonged consumption results in a gradual disappearance of the signs of intoxication over a period of hours, partially overlapped and followed by a variable set of clinical signs and symptoms of withdrawal persisting for days. Historically this group of illnesses was attributed to a variety of causes including malnutrition, direct toxicity of alcohol, and toxins (Kaim, 1971; Victor, 1973). Isbell, Fraser, Wikler, Belleville, and Eisenman (1955) proved in their classical studies that typical withdrawal signs could be induced after prolonged alcohol consumption in well-nourished nonalcoholic subjects taking vitamin supplements. Mendelson and colleagues (1964) confirmed and extended these observations. Withdrawal illnesses are unique in that they occur promptly after the *discontinuation* of the toxic agent.

Clinically, the signs and symptoms specific for withdrawal can be classified and grouped according to type, severity, and temporal order of emergence after the cessation of alcohol consumption. Victor and Adams (1953) first related the various signs to the beginning of abstinence (Figure 2). In its mildest forms, ethanol withdrawal occurs after only a few days of steady drinking and after only a few hours (overnight) of withdrawal in the form of tremulousness and irritability ("morning shakes") (Victor, 1973). According to Victor and Adams (1953), the severity of withdrawal may progress to three subsequent stages of increasing severity (Figure 2): (a) Tremors and hallucinations (initially auditory, later visual and tactile) reach peak intensity 24 hours after cessation of drinking. In "hallucinosis," hallucinations dominate the clinical picture usually in the form of visual misperception and often involving animals or insects. Auditory hallucinosis is characterized by hearing voices, often threatening. While these patients do not appear to be disoriented or confused, they have lost insight and often act inappropriately. (b) Generalized (single or multiple) convulsive seizures, usually of the grand-mal type, occur between 7 and 48 hours. (c) Delirium (clouding of sensorium, disorientation) with persistent tremors, agitation, nausea, vomiting, diarrhea, and excessive perspiration begin 72 to 96 hours following cessation of drinking. Victor and Adams (1953) reserve the term "delirium tremens" for this stage. A similar staging has been proposed by Johnson (1961). Salum (1972) in a retrospective study of 1,026 male alcoholics treated on 1,907 occasions distinguishes progression through three stages: tremulousness without psychosis, acute hallucinosis, and disorientation combined with the two preceding stages (called delirium tremens). The incidence of seizures is 6% in the first two stages and ranges from 21% to 41% in the delirium tremens stage, depending upon its severity. However, Gross, Rosenblatt, Malenowski, Broman, and Lewis (1972) found the stages less clearly defined and more variable, visual and auditory hallucinations occurring simultaneously, and clouding of sensorium difficult to quantify. Fever, present in about 25% of patients, seems usually attributable to medical causes, including pneumonia or dehydration (Rose, Gobert, Sanz, & Leitschuh, 1970). The mortality may be as high as 20%, but this depends upon the type of patient (lower socioeconomic groups tend to reach the hospital in more advanced stages) and the type and severity of associated medical disease that may have forced cessation of drinking. During the last decades mortality has progressively declined, but death may ensue during delirium tremens even in the absence of medical complications (Tavel, Davidson, & Batterton, 1961). Other clinical aspects of withdrawal, including sleep disturbances and treatment, are discussed elsewhere in this volume. The activation of a coexisting seizure disorder, such as epilepsy, by alcohol withdrawal has been discussed by Victor (1970).

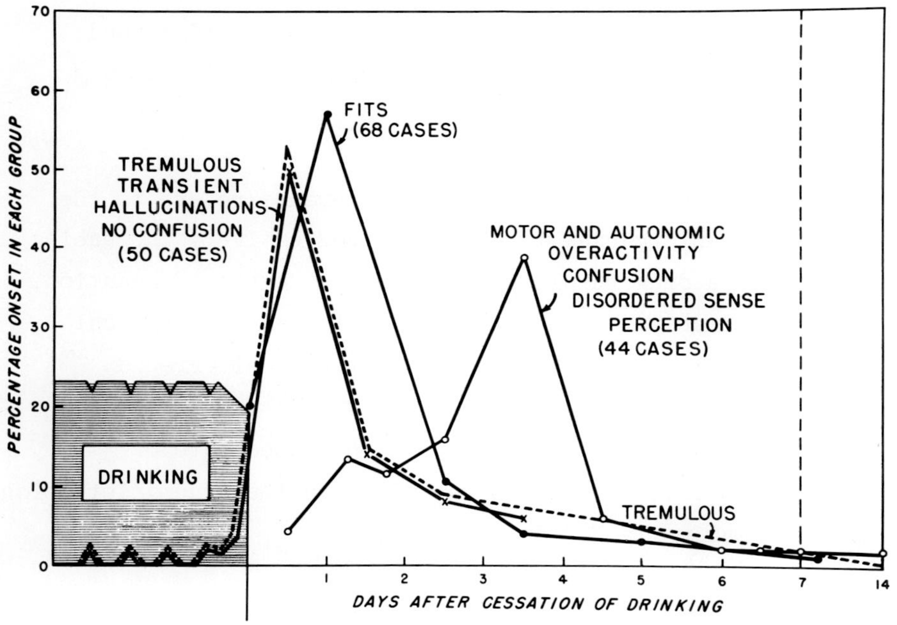

FIGURE 2. Onset of clinical manifestations after alcohol withdrawal (Victor & Adams, 1953).

Various animal models of physical dependence on alcohol have recently been developed (for reviews see Freund, 1973b, 1975a, 1975c, in press). These experiments have confirmed the conclusion of Isbell et al. (1955) that the pathogenesis is based on the sudden release of the CNS from depression by alcohol and not on malnutrition. In addition, they promise to be useful for the development of new treatment modalities, other than the presently practiced substitution of cross-addicting sedatives for alcohol (Freund, 1973d, 1975a).

Several alternate first steps in the pathogenetic chain of events leading to withdrawal syndromes have been suggested but not conclusively proved: Ethanol or acetaldehyde (the first and only specific metabolite of ethanol) mediated effects (a) on any one of several brain neurotransmitters, (b) on brain intermediary metabolism, and (c) on the physical state of brain membranes without any primary chemical reaction (as in CNS depression with chemically inert anesthetics).

Functional or "behavioral" tolerance refers to the ability of an organism to tolerate progressively increasing amounts of a drug resulting in the same degree of sedation. The relationship, if any, to the development of physical dependence on alcohol is not clear at present (Freund, 1975a; Kalant, LeBlanc, & Gibbins, 1971). The term "metabolic tolerance" refers to an increased rate of alcohol metabolism in the liver with continued administration (perhaps maximally 35% in man).

EFFECTS OF CHRONIC MALNUTRITION ON CNS

Disorders of malnutrition (deficiencies of protein, calories, vitamins, or minerals) are encountered in alcoholic patients. While these disorders are most important in the skid-row type of alcoholics, comprising about 5% of all problem drinkers (Congressional Report, 1970), the great majority of alcoholic patients of higher socioeconomic groups are not significantly malnourished (Figueroa, Sargent, Imperiale, Morey, Paynter, Vorhaus, & Kark, 1953; Neville, Eagles, Sampson, & Olson, 1968).

Many alcohol studies in the literature are based on skid-row alcoholics because these unfortunate individuals are most willing and able to remain hospitalized for prolonged studies in the charity type of institution where many investigators are located. The problems encountered in this group are not necessarily representative of other types of alcoholics.

That acute hemorrhagic superior polioencephalitis (clinically designated as Wernicke's Syndrome) is clearly secondary to thiamine deficiency is based on two observations: (a) This acute syndrome may occur without any alcohol consumption in patients on vitamin-deficient diets (Drenick, Joven, & Swendseid, 1960; Mancall & McEntee, 1965) or after depletion by hemodialysis (Lopez & Collins, 1968). (b) This syndrome is reversible within hours by thiamine administration, unless the syndrome is not recognized and therapy is delayed until irreversible brain changes have occurred (Phillips, Victor, Adams, & Davidson, 1952; Victor, Adams, & Collins, 1971) or when liver disease slows the conversion of thiamine to its active metabolite (Cole, Turner, Frank, Baker, & Leevy, 1969). Therefore, it should be routine to administer immediately 100 mg of thiamine parenterally to every ill alcoholic patient at the time of admission to the hospital to prevent this serious complication. This should be followed by multivitamin therapy because vitamin deficiency almost invariably involves a combination of several vitamins that occur together in natural foods. (c) The syndrome has been induced in animals by thiamine deficiency (McCandless & Schenker, 1968; Robertson, Wasan, & Skinner, 1968).

The clinical picture has been described and extensively correlated with histopathological data by Victor et al. (1971). The presenting complaints develop over a period of several days or weeks (or rarely within a day) and consist of confusion (90% of patients), loss of memory, staggering gait, and inability to focus eyes. Objective signs include: (a) ataxia, (b) ophthalmoplegia resulting in bilateral ptosis of eyelids and in impaired lateral and upward gaze, (c) horizontal and vertical nystagmus. Hypothermia with temperatures ranging from 95° to 85° F is uncommon (Philip & Smith, 1973). These findings may be associated with those of withdrawal syndromes, chronic brain syndromes, other types of malnutrition, liver disease, and other medical diseases often encountered in an alcoholic patient population. The incidence of fever in a predominantly skid-row type of population was approximately 12% (Victor et al., 1971). Because of the frequent association of the acute Wernicke's syndrome, malnutrition, and the chronic Korsakoff amnestic syndrome in their patient population, Victor et al. (1971) consider both syndromes to have the same nutritional etiology, and they designate the combination as Wernicke-Korsakoff syndrome.

DEGENERATIVE SYNDROMES

Cerebellar degeneration is clinically manifested by the gradual development of ataxic gait; incoordination, spasticity, and tremors of arms and legs; nystagmus; and dysarthria in which the speech is thick and gait is broad-based and halting (Victor, Adams, & Mancall, 1959). In the absence of alcohol consumption, cerebellar degeneration may occur, either isolated or in association with degeneration of a variety of other related structures in the CNS, in the form of various characteristic syndromes described in the neurological literature. When cerebellar degeneration is associated with chronic alcoholism, it may also be associated with Wernicke's encephalopathy (six of seven cases) or pontine myelinolysis (one of seven cases (Allsop & Turner, 1966). It has been speculated that malnutrition, rather than ethanol per se, is the cause of this syndrome (Victor et al., 1959). However, no history or evidence of malnutrition was found in 11 of 50 patients in one series (Victor et al., 1959) and in 0 of 3 patients in another report (Martin, 1965). Perhaps these discrepancies simply reflect the variable prevalence of malnutrition in a particular population of alcoholics.

Degeneration of the corpus callosum (Marchiafava-Bignami disease) is clinically suggested by an insidious onset of psychosis (manic, depressive, or paranoid) and by dementia and focal neurological signs, such as grand mal seizures, paresis, aphasia, and apraxia. Death usually ensues within 3 to 6 years after onset. Marchiafava-Bignami disease is very rare (Ironside, Bosanquet, & McMenemey, 1961). It was originally described in Italy and blamed on drinking wine. The rarity of this syndrome suggests that alcohol, perhaps uniquely, activates an underlying disease or that alcohol has nothing to do with the diseases and that most Italians at the time of this discovery merely drank wine.

Central pontine myelinolysis was first described by Adams et al. (1959). Clinically there is an acute onset of quadriplegia and pseudobulbar palsy, manifested by nystagmus, slurring of speech, impaired ocular convergence, dysphagia, nasal regurgitation, and diminished cough and gag reflexes. Since this diagnosis is based on the histological changes at autopsy, the in vivo diagnosis can only be suspected on clinical grounds. For example, a patient who was well nourished and received vitamin supplements until the day he drank one-half pint of Zippo lighter fluid (petroleum distillates, alcohols, and naptha) developed the complete clinical syndrome and eventually recovered (Khurana, Post, & Araman, 1974).

CHRONIC ORGANIC BRAIN SYNDROMES

KORSAKOFF'S SYNDROME. Korsakoff's amnestic syndrome is characterized by disorientation, mental confusion, loss of recent memory, and tendency to confabulation in alert, responsive patients with no clouding of sensorium (Victor et al., 1971). Korsakoff's syndrome may follow an episode of an acute organic brain syndrome in association with temporary clouding of consciousness (as in Wernicke's syndrome), or it may arise insidiously without such evidence. Korsakoff's syndrome may be associated clinically with disorders of malnutrition or with other disease often encountered in alcoholic patient populations, including peripheral polyneuropathy and acute abstinence syndromes. When an acute episode leads to hospitalization, the course of the illness during the subsequent two months of observation may result in complete, significant, slight, or no recovery (in up to 10-year follow-up) in approximately one-quarter of patients in each category (Victor et al., 1971). Histological lesions may be those of associated illnesses (Wernicke's): they may be concentrated in the central periventricular gray structures, and they may occur in the cerebral cortex.

The controversy regarding the etiology of Korsakoff's syndrome has been discussed elsewhere in more detail (Freund,

1973a). This is not only of academic interest, because if vitamin deficiency is the only cause of brain impairment in chronic alcoholic patients, then brain damage should be easily preventable by adequate vitamin intake--e.g., by fortifying alcoholic beverages with vitamins. Evidence for a nutritional etiology of Korsakoff's syndrome is seen by the proponents of this hypothesis as follows:

(a) Association with malnutrition and with other disorders of clearly nutritional origin--e.g., Wernicke's syndrome.

(b) Some improvement of Korsakoff's syndrome may occur with time and may be the result of vitamin therapy. Treatment failures are attributed to irreversible anatomical changes in far-advanced lesions.

(c) Lesions produced by other illnesses in the anatomical areas usually involved in Wernicke's syndrome may cause impairment of memory (mammillary bodies, fornices, and around the third and fourth ventricle and their connecting aqueduct).

None of the above observations are intrinsically unequivocal proof for the nutritional hypothesis, although they may appear to be plausible and they may be correct. Alternate interpretations of the observations are possible. Besides the fact that association does not prove a cause-and-effect relationship (Figure 1), the following observations may be difficult to reconcile with the nutritional hypothesis:

(a) Persisting Korsakoff's syndrome is extremely rare in cases of even the most severe degrees of vitamin deficiencies on a nutritional basis alone without alcohol consumption (Cruickshank, 1950; Denny-Brown, 1947; DeWardener & Lennox, 1947; Smith, 1946; Spillane & Riddoch, 1947).

(b) In the absence of controlled therapeutic trials,

improvement of Korsakoff's syndrome with time and with vitamin treatment may be a result of time itself, rather than any specific treatment. Lack of response to vitamin treatment could be interpreted as evidence against a pathogenetic role of vitamins, rather than anatomical irreversibility of the lesions.

(c) Not all patients with extensive anatomical involvement, typical for Wernicke's Syndrome, have the Korsakoff's syndrome (Victor et al., 1971).

(d) Clinically, the Korsakoff's syndrome is not confined to lesions in the central diencephalic areas considered to be characteristically involved in Wernicke's syndrome. Korsakoff's syndrome has been described with cortical involvement alone (Carmichael & Stern, 1931). The induction of clinical Korsakoff's syndrome by specific localized lesions does not preclude the induction of the same clinical syndrome by lesions, perhaps more extensive, elsewhere in the brain (Lindqvist & Norlen, 1966) or by toxic agents (Minogue, 1956). The histological, radiological, and electroencephalographic evidence for diffuse brain involvement in alcoholic patients has been reviewed elsewhere (Freund, 1973a).

CHRONIC BRAIN SYNDROMES OTHER THAN KORSAKOFF'S, INCLUDING DEMENTIA. It is indisputable that vitamin deficiencies, when present in alcoholic patients, may cause neuropsychiatric disorders. In addition, does alcohol itself contribute to the pathogenesis of neuropsychiatric disorders in alcoholic patients? There is no reason to assume that the two possibilities are mutually exclusive. A direct alcohol toxicity is strongly suggested by the fact that malnutrition has become rare in alcoholics (Neville et al., 1968), even in skid-row populations (Figueroa et al., 1953). In contrast, the rate of admission to state mental hospitals for alcoholic patients suffering from the irreversible "chronic brain syndrome associated with alcohol intoxication" was rapidly increasing at a time when admission rates for other mental disorders were declining (Locke & Duvall, 1963). If malnutrition were the only cause of the chronic brain syndrome in alcoholic patients, one would have predicted a declining rather than an increasing incidence. It is difficult to determine the true prevalence of a disease from hospital admission diagnoses alone because of shifts of admissions from one type of psychiatric facility to another (Redick, 1973), changes in diagnostic criteria, and changes in criteria required for institutionalization of a patient in different institutions. It is also well established that the frequency of the diagnosis of alcoholism increases appreciably when this information is actively searched for at the time of admission to the hospital (Nolan, 1965).

The rate of decline of mental functions with aging is variable, ranging from slightly increased forgetfulness at one end of the spectrum to severe senility and dementia at the other (Busse & Pfeiffer, 1973). This decline in function with advancing age has been attributed to loss of a critical number of neurons in the brain because of the inability of neurons to replenish losses by cell division. Courville (1955) has demonstrated in autopsy material that brain atrophy is common in severe alcoholic patients. He suggested that alcohol abuse may accelerate the brain atrophy that occurs with aging (Bowen, Smith, & Davison, 1973; Himwich, 1962). However, a functional decline of surviving cells has not been excluded. A great number of diverse diseases can all lead to the same end result--dementia (Watson & Heilman, 1974). Dementia is a decline of intellectual function, including problem solving, that requires acquisition, storage, and retrieval of information, as well as adequate attention (arousal). Some of these diseases are partially reversible, lending support to the concept of functional impairment of living neurons under some conditions. Just as inflammation is the uniform response to a great many diverse noxious stimuli, it is conceivable that the decline of brain function is the end result of many diverse etiological factors, including genetic predisposition. Alcohol could be one of those factors. Unfortunately, quantitative data on alcohol consumption in patients admitted to mental hospitals for dementia ("non-alcohol-related") are not available, although heavy consumption of alcohol has been found in histories of mental hospital patients with primary diagnoses other than alcoholism (Redick, 1973).

It is possible that chronic alcohol abuse may result in mental impairment less dramatic than dementia that leads to admission to mental hospitals. Clinical evidence reviewed by Tarter, Chapter 11 in this volume, suggests that this may be the case. Conclusive evidence regarding the etiology could be obtained by a prospective clinical study of perhaps 100 subjects--matched by age, sex, race, body build, intelligence, and schooling--randomly assigned to either control or alcohol group. After appropriate baseline studies, one group would consume large amounts of alcohol for perhaps 20 years. At annual intervals the alcohol group would be temporarily withdrawn from alcohol, and following recovery from withdrawal illnesses, various test results could be compared with the nutritionally matched control group. Such a study would, of course, be unethical. An indirect, but practically feasible, approach is to find clues for biological, alcohol-specific effects in animals and to search for such markers in alcoholic patients. Every drug, food additive, or industrial chemical to which humans are exposed is or should be tested for safety in animals. Vast experience indicates that toxicity in animals usually predicts toxicity in man.

Animal models. Even a casual reader of the animal experimental literature should be aware that a number of problems arise when standard pharmacological procedures are applied to a toxicological evaluation of alcohol in animals (Freund, 1973a):

(a) Alcohol is aversive to animals, and only small amounts are consumed voluntarily (despite anecdotal reports to the contrary).

(b) Alcohol is a source of "empty" calories (5.5 Cal/ml, 6.9 Cal/gm). When rodents are fed aqueous solutions of alcohol as the only source of water, only relatively small amounts of alcohol are consumed (20% of total caloric intake); very low blood-ethanol concentrations result (Freund, 1969; Lieber, Jones, & DeCarli, 1965); and no evidence of physical addiction is apparent. If the alcohol- and water-drinking groups consume the same number of total calories, the alcohol group will also have consumed 20% less laboratory chow--with its protein, vitamins, and minerals--than will the water group. Four types of malnutrition may be potentially induced--calorie (weight loss), protein, vitamin, and mineral. Without the pair-fed controls it is impossible to determine whether observed differences between the two groups are a result of alcohol or decreased chow consumption or both.

(c) Alcohol is very irritating to tissues when administered parenterally.

(d) Some forms of alcohol administration cause nonspecific stress (adrenocortical, adrenomedullary stimulation), the biological effects of which may be erroneously attributed to ethanol per se.

(e) Problems with growing, immature animals are discussed in section VI.

Evidence suggests that chronic ethanol consumption per se in the absence of malnutrition and other complications leads to impairment of learning in rodents and has been reviewed elsewhere (Freund, 1973a). Since then it has been demonstrated that timing behavior, a task that requires no external cues or painful stimuli, is impaired by chronic ethanol comsumption (Walker & Freund, 1973). Chronic sedation with phenobarbital does not impair learning performance under the same conditions that alcohol consumption does (Freund, 1974). Retention of a task, once acquired, is also impaired, whether prolonged alcohol consumption precedes or follows the learning event (Freund, 1975b). The biochemical basis for these alcohol effects may be altered brain protein metabolism induced by chronic ethanol consumption (Noble & Tewari, 1973).

DISEASES INDIRECTLY RELATED TO ALCOHOLISM. *Hepatic encephalopathy*. Severe liver disease, acute or chronic and irrespective of etiology, may cause a syndrome characterized by a disturbance of consciousness that may range from mild lethargy to profound coma. Personality changes are nonspecific and range from depression to euphoria and may be associated with anxiety and paranoid features. Intellectual function may be impaired, as evidenced by an inability to concentrate, remember, and think abstractly. Neurological impairment may consist of dysphasia; slow, slurred speech; apraxia; a characteristic (but not pathognomonic) flapping tremor of the outstretched hands ("asterixis"); ataxia; and hyperreflexia. Characteristically, the severity of all the above manifestations may fluctuate rapidly within minutes or hours, apparently as a result of concurrent metabolic fluctuations, such as rate of ammonia absorption from the bowel and its disposition; pH of the blood as determined by respiration; and others.

The clinical course varies with the acuity of the underlying liver disease. Fulminant hepatitis may cause death in deep coma preceded by convulsions and decerebrate rigidity. Chronic cirrhosis of the liver may have a variable course with either improvement of encephalopathy or progression to paraplegia or to dementia over a period of years.

The cause of the neurological and psychiatric manifestations appears to be toxic substances (including ammonia) from the gastrointestinal tract and from the intermediary metabolism that are normally detoxified in the liver (Plum, 1974).

Subdural hematoma. As a result of slow venous bleeding, subdural hematoma following (often minor) head trauma is a not uncommon cause of death in alcoholics. Death is preventable if surgical drainage is done promptly. Symptoms of the chronic subdural hematoma may begin several weeks after the often trivial head injury that by then may have been forgotten. Headaches (in 90% of cases), confusion, and irritability are insidiously followed by drowsiness, urinary incontinence, and stupor, all of which may be erroneously attributed to deterioration as a result of alcoholism or to senescence. The course may fluctuate for weeks or months but may terminate in sudden coma and death. The presence of a subdural hematoma can now be diagnosed with such noninvasive techniques as echoencephalography combined with electroencephalography. This disorder is mentioned here because a high index of suspicion is a necessary prerequisite for early referral and successful surgical treatment.

EFFECTS OF ALCOHOL CONSUMPTION ON THE MATURING BRAIN

It has been reported that offspring of alcoholic mothers "fail to thrive" (Ulleland, 1972) and that perinatal mortality is high. A syndrome of congenital malformation, including cardiovasular, craniofacial, and limb defects has been described (Jones, Smith, & Streissguth, 1974). Again, it is difficult to assess the potentially contributory effects of protein-calorie malnutrition and vitamin deficiencies in these cases. If vitamin deficiencies accompany alcoholism during pregnancy, they may also be present in the offspring (Burgess, 1958).

The great susceptibility of the growing brain (prenatal or early postnatal, "vulnerable period") to the damaging effects of malnutrition (Bass, 1971; Rappoport, Fritz, & Yamagami, 1971) and drugs (Sparber, 1972) is well established. In contrast to the immature brain, the mature brain is remarkably resistant to calorie-protein malnutrition. This "brain-sparing" effect in calorie-protein malnutrition applies to brain protein (Dallman & Spirito, 1972) and brain lipids (Dobbing, 1968). Behavioral performance also does not appear to be significantly affected by adult protein-calorie malnutrition, unless gross motor impairment is induced (Brozek & Vaes, 1961). However, specific and very severe degrees of vitamin deficiencies (niacin, pyridoxin, B-12), in addition to thiamine deficiency, may cause psychoses in the adult human. Because mouse and rat brains do not mature until the ages of approximately 5 to 7 weeks postpartum (Bass, 1971; Folch, 1955) and mouse brain cortex protein is not at maximum level until 80 to 90 days of age (Benjamins & McKhan, 1972), results from animal experiments using such immature rodents may not be relevant to alcohol abuse in adult humans even if appropriate nutritional controls have been applied. The alcohol concentration in mother's milk equals the concentration in mother's blood. The alcohol consumption by milk is therefore minute (Kesaniemi, 1974).

PERIPHERAL POLYNEUROPATHY

Manifestations of disorders of the peripheral nervous system may be classified according to its functional divisions--motor, sensory, and autonomic. In severity they may range from impairment--detectable only by nerve condition velocity studies in clinically asymptomatic patients--to clinically overt neuropathy of varying degrees of severity and disability. Most chronic alcoholic patients have no detectable impairment of the peripheral nervous system at all.

The development of clinical manifestations is usually slow, extending over a period of weeks or months and, rarely, days. Typically the involvement is symmetrical; it begins and is most severe in the lower rather than upper extremities and in the distal rather than proximal extremities. Sensory manifestations--paresthesias, pain, numbness, hyperesthesia upon pressure--are usually followed, but sometimes preceded, by motor involvement--weakness, muscle atrophy, foot drop, ataxic gait. Vibratory and position sense and reflexes become impaired. In extreme cases, cranial nerves may become involved, resulting in scotomas; pupil abnormalities; visual impairment; and paresis of ocular, facial, and pharyngeal muscles. Autonomic nervous system involvement (Novak & Victor, 1974) may manifest itself by paralysis of urethral and rectal sphincters, by vocal cord palsy (hoarseness, weak voice), and by persistent hypotension. As usual, peripheral neuropathy may be associated with other nutritional, neurological, and nonneurological diseases common in alcoholic patients. And. again, a reminder that a neuropathy in an alcoholic patient is not necessarily "alcoholic neuropathy": it may be caused by a spinal cord tumor or degenerated intervertebral disc.

The incidence of clinically significant peripheral neuropathy as usual depends upon the population from which the sample is drawn. In a recent study it was approximately 5% of patients requiring admission for chronic alcoholism to a neuropsychiatric hospital (Niedermeyer & Prokop, 1959). In another study it was 80 of 25,000 (0.3%) patients referred to a university neurology outpatient clinic in Hamburg over a 12-year period (Janzen & Balzereit, 1968). A third survey of 451 skid-row alcoholics consecutively admitted to a correctional institution found only 7 cases of "possible nutritional polyneuropathy," even though 23% of the subjects were judged to be underweight (Figueroa et al., 1953). The unexpectedly low incidence was attributed to enrichment of bread with vitamins, started in 1940.

Neurophysiological studies demonstrated impairment in asymptomatic alcoholic patients of motor (Wanamaker & Skillman, 1966) and sensory (Casey & LeQuesne, 1972) nerve conduction velocities, generally associated with degeneration of the myelin sheets of peripheral nerves. But the nerve axons themselves (and by implication the associated nerve cells) may also be damaged, as evidenced by reduced amplitudes of nerve action potentials and nerve biopsy (Bischoff, 1971; Casey & LeQuesne, 1972; Walsh & McLeod, 1970).

The usual controversy exists regarding the pathogenetic roles of vitamin deficiencies and of direct toxic effects of alcohol. Those who favor the nutritional etiology cite three facts: (a) vitamin deficiencies alone may cause peripheral neuropathies in man and animals (Denny-Brown, 1947; Spillane & Riddoch, 1947); (b) vitamin deficiencies are commonly associated with neuropathy in chronic alcoholic patients; (c) peripheral nutritional neuropathy may improve if vitamin therapy is instituted before irreversible damage has occurred (Denny-Brown, 1947; Spillane & Riddoch, 1947). Authors who favor a direct toxic effect of alcohol per se, base their opinions on the following: (a) the clinical picture of the vitamin deficiency polyneuropathies is somewhat different from that encountered in alcoholic patients (for discussion see Novak & Victor, 1974); (b) not all patients with alcoholic polyneuropathy show evidence or have a history of malnutrition (Bischoff, 1971; Walsh & McLeod, 1970); and (c) experimental vitamin deficiency causes a demyelination of nerve fibers with axonal involvement in only the final stages (Robertson et al., 1968; Zimmerman, 1956). In contrast, patients with alcoholic polyneuropathy frequently have a primary axonal degeneration (Bischoff, 1971). The lack of uniformity of the clinical and histopathologic picture suggested to Bischoff a variety of different pathogenetic factors in alcoholic polyneuropathy. As is self-evident, inferences about pathogenetic mechanisms cannot be made with certainty from associations alone. The relative contributions of malnutrition and direct toxic alcohol effects must be elucidated by further experiments.

REFERENCES

Adams, R.D., Victor, M., & Mancall, E.L. Central pontine myelinolysis. *American Medical Association Archives of Neurology and Psychiatry*, 1959, *81*, 154-172.

Allsop, J., & Turner, B. Cerebellar degeneration associated with chronic alcoholism. *Journal of Neurological Sciences*, 1966, *3*, 238-258.

Bass, N.H. Influence of neonatal undernutrition on the development of rat cerebral cortex: A microchemical study. In R. Paoletti & A.N. Davison (Eds.), *Chemistry and brain development advances in experimental medicine and biology* (Vol. 13). New York: Plenum Press, 1971.

Benjamins, J.A., & McKhann, G.M. Neurochemistry of development. In R.W. Albers, G.J. Siegel, R. Katzman, & B.W. Agranoff (Eds.), *Basic neurochemistry*. Boston: Little, Brown, 1972.

Bishoff, A. Die alkoholische Polyneuropathie (Alcoholic polyneuropathy). *Deutsch Medizinische Wochenschrift*, 1971, *96*, 317-322.

Bowen, D.M., Smith, C.B., & Davidson, A.N. Molecular changes in senile dementia. *Brain*, 1973, *96*, 849-856.

Brozek, J., & Vaes, G. Experimental investigations on the effects of dietary deficiencies on animal and human behavior. *Vitamins and Hormones*, 1961, *19*, 43-94.

Burgess, R.C. Infantile beriberi. *Federation Proceedings*, (Part 2, Suppl. 2), 1958, *17*, 39-43.

Busse, E.W., & Pfeiffer, E. (Eds.), *Mental illness in later life*. Washington, D.C.: American Psychiatric Association, 1973.

Carmichael, E.A., & Stern, R.O. Korsakoff's syndrome: Its histopathology. *Brain*, 1931, *54*, 189-213.

Casey, E.B. & LeQuesne, P.M. Electrophysiological evidence for a distal lesion in alcoholic neuropathy. *Journal of Neurology, Neurosurgery, and Psychiatry*, 1972, *35*, 624-630.

Cole, M., Turner, A., Frank, O., Baker, H., & Leevy, C.M. Extraocular palsy and thiamine therapy in Wernicke's encephalopathy. *American Journal of Clinical Nutrition*, 1969, *22*, 44-51.

Congressional Report. *Substantial cost savings from establishment of alcoholism program for federal civilian employees*. Washington, D.C.: U.S. Government Printing Office, 1970.

Cooperman, M.T., Davidoff, F., Spark, R., & Pallotta, J. Clinical studies of alcoholic ketoacidosis. *Diabetes*, 1974, *23*, 433-439.

Courville, C.B. *Effects of alcohol on the nervous system of man*. Los Angeles: San Lucas Press, 1955.

Cruickshank, E.K. Wernicke's encephalopathy. *Quarterly Journal of Medicine*, 1950, *19*, 327-338.

Dallman, P.R., & Spirito, R.A. Brain response to protein undernutrition. Mechanism of preferential protein retention. *Journal of Clinical Investigation*, 1972, *51*, 2175-2180.

Denny-Brown, D. Neurological conditions resulting from prolonged and severe dietary restriction. *Medicine*, 1947, *26*, 41-113.

DeWardener, H.E., & Lennox, B. Cerebral beriberi (Wernicke's encephalopathy). *Lancet*, 1947, *1*, 11-17.

Dobbing, J. Vulnerable periods in developing brain. In A.N. Davison & J. Dobbing (Eds.), *Applied neurochemistry*, Philadelphia: F.A. Davis, 1968.

Drenick, J.E., Joven, C.B., & Swendseid, M.E. Occurrence of acute Wernicke's encephalopathy during prolonged starvation for the treatment of obesity. *New England Journal of Medicine*, 1960, *247*, 937-939.

Figueroa, W.G., Sargent, F., Imperiale, L., Morey, G.R., Paynter, C.R., Vorhaus, L.J., & Kark, R.M. Lack of avitaminosis among alcoholics: Its relation to fortification of cereal products and general nutrition status of the population. *Journal of Clinical Nutrition*, 1953, *1*, 179-199.

Folch, P.J. Composition of the brain in relation to maturation. In H. Waelsch (Ed.), *Biochemistry of the developing nervous system*, New York: Academic Press, 1955.

Freund, G. Alcohol withdrawal syndrome in mice. *Archives of Neurology*, 1969, *21*, 315-320.

Freund, G. Alcohol consumption and its circadian distribution in mice. *Journal of Nutrition*, 1970, *100*, 30-36.

Freund, G. Alcohol, barbiturate and bromide withdrawal syndromes in mice. *Annals of the New York Academy of Sciences*, 1973, *215*, 224-234. (a)

Freund, G. Chronic central nervous system toxicity of alcohol. *Annual Review of Pharmacology*, 1973, *13*, 217-227. (b)

Freund, G. Hypothermia after acute ethanol and benzyl alcohol administration. *Life Sciences*, 1973, *13*, 345-349. (c)

Freund, G.: The prevention of ethanol withdrawal seizures in mice by lidocaine. *Neurology*, 1973, *23*, 91-94. (d)

Freund, G. Normal shuttle box avoidance learning after phenobarbital intoxication in mice. *Psychopharmacologia*, 1974, *40*, 199-203.

Freund, G. Animal models of ethanol withdrawal syndromes and their relevance to pharmacology. In H.D. Cappell & A.E. LeBlanc (Eds.), *Biological and behavioural approaches to drug dependence.* Toronto: Alcoholism and Addiction Research Foundation of Ontario, 1975. (a)

Freund, G. Impairment of memory after prolonged alcohol consumption in mice. In M.M. Gross (Ed.), *Alcohol intoxication and withdrawal*. New York: Plenum Press, 1975.(b)

Freund, G. Induction of physical dependence on alcohol in rodents. In E. Majchrowicz (Ed.), *Biochemical pharmacology of alcohol*. New York: Plenum Press, 1975. (c)

Freund, G. Alcohol withdrawal syndromes and chronic central nervous system toxicity in rodents. In S. Gabey & F. Ellinwood, Jr. (Eds.), *Animal models in neuropsychopathology*. New York: Raven Press, in press.

Gross, M.M., Rosenblatt, S.M., Malenowski, B., Broman, M., & Lewis, E. Classification of alcohol withdrawal syndromes. *Quarterly Journal of Studies on Alcohol*, 1972, *33*, 400-407.

Himwich, W.A. Neurochemistry of aging. *Postgraduate Medicine*, 1962, *31*, 195-200.

Ironside, R., Bosanquet, F.D., & McMenemey, W.H. Central demyelination of the corpus callosum (Marchiafava-Bignami disease). With report of a second case in Great Britain. *Brain*, 1961, *84*, 212-217.

Isbell, H., Fraser, H.F., Wikler, A., Belleville, R.E., & Eisenman, A.J. An experimental study of the etiology of "rum fits" and delirium tremens. *Quarterly Journal of Studies on Alcohol*, 1955, *16*, 1-33.

Janzen, R., & Balzereit, F. Polyneuropathie bei Alkoholabusus (Polyneuropathy in alcohol abuse.) *Internist (Berlin)*, 1968, *9*, 260-263.

Johnson, R.B. The alcohol withdrawal syndromes. *Quarterly Journal of Studies on Alcohol*. (Suppl. No. 1), 1961, 66-76.

Jones, K.L., Smith, D.W., Streissguth, A.P., & Myrianthopoulos, N.C. Outcome in offspring of chronic alcoholic women. *Lancet*, 1974, *1*, 1076-1078.

Kaim, S.C. Drug treatment of the alcohol withdrawal syndrome. In N.K. Mello & J.H. Mendelson (Eds.), *Recent advances in studies of alcoholism*. Washington, D.C.: U.S. Government Printing Office, 1971.

Kalant, H., LeBlanc, A.E., & Gibbins, R.J. Tolerance to and dependence on some non-opiate psychotropic drugs. *Pharmacological Reviews* , 1971, *23*, 135-191.

Kesaniemi, Y.A. Ethanol and acetaldehyde in the milk and peripheral blood of lactating women after ethanol administration. *Journal of Obstetrics and Gynaecology of the British Commonwealth*, 1974, *81*, 84-86.

Khurana, R., Post, J.C., & Araman, K.K. Bulbar paralysis in chronic alcoholism with recovery. *Diseases of the Nervous System*, 1974, *35*, 135-137.

Kissin, B., & Begleiter, H. (Eds.). *The biology of alcoholism* (Vol. 1-3). New York: Plenum Press, 1971, 1972, 1974.

Lieber, C.S., Jones, D.P., & DeCarli, L.M. Effects of prolonged ethanol intake: Production of fatty liver despite adequate diets. *Journal of Clinical Investigation*, 1965, *44*, 1009-1021.

Lindqvist, G., & Norlen, G. Korsakoff's syndrome after operation on ruptured aneurysm of the anterior communicating artery. *Acta Psychiatrica Scandinavica*, 1966, *42*, 24-34.

Locke, B.Z., & Duvall, H.J. Alcoholism among first admissions to Ohio public mental hospitals. *Quarterly Journal of Studies on Alcohol*, 1964, *25*, 521-534.

Lopez, R.I., & Collins, G.H. Wernicke's encephalopathy. A complication of chronic hemodialysis. *Archives of Neurology*, 1968, *18*, 248-259.

Madison, L.L. Ethanol-induced hypoglycemia. In R. Levine & R. Luft (Eds.), *Advances in metabolic disorders*(Vol. 3). New York: Academic Press, 1968.

Mancall, E.L., & McEntee, W.J. Alterations of the cerebellar cortex in nutritional encephalopathy. *Neurology*, 1965, *15*, 303-313.

Martin, E.A. Alcoholic cerebellar degeneration: A report of 3 cases. *Journal of the Irish Medical Association*, 1965, *56*, 172-175.

McCandless, D.W., & Schenker, S. Encephalopathy of thiamine deficiency: Studies of intracerebral mechanisms. *Journal of Clinical Investigation*, 1968, *47*, 2268-2280.

Mendelson, J.H. (Ed.) Experimentally induced chronic intoxication and withdrawal in alcoholics. *Quarterly Journal of Studies on Alcohol* (Suppl. No. 2), 1964, 1-129.

Minogue, S.J. Korsakoff's disease due to lead and arsenic poisoning. *Medical Journal of Australia*, 1956, *43*, 16-17.

Neville, J.N., Eagles, J.A., Sampson, G., & Olson, R.E. Nutritional status of alcoholics. *American Journal of Clinical Nutrition*, 1968, *21*, 1329-1340.

Niedermeyer, E., & Prokop, H. Ueber die Alkoholpolyneuritis und deren Stellung im Rahmen chronischer Alkoholschaden des gesamten Nervensystems. (On alcohol polyneuritis and its place among chronic alcohol injuries of the entire nervous system.) *Wiener Klinische Wochenschrift*, 1959, *71*, 267-268.

Noble, E.D., & Tewari, S. Protein and ribonucleic acid metabolism in brains of mice following chronic alcohol consumption. *Annals of the New York Academy of Sciences*, 1973, *215*, 333-345.

Nolan, J.P. Alcohol as a factor in the illness of university service patients. *American Journal of the Medical Sciences*, 1965, *249*, 135-142.

Novak, D.J., & Victor, M. The vagus and sympathetic nerves in alcoholic polyneuropathy. *Archives of Neurology*, 1974, *30*, 273-284.

Philip, G., & Smith, J.F. Hypothermia and Wernicke's encephalopathy. *Lancet*, 1973, *2*, 122-124.

Phillips, G.B., Victor, M., Adams, R.D., & Davidson, C.S. A study of the nutritional defect in Wernicke's syndrome. The effect of a purified diet, thiamine, and other vitamins on the clinical manifestations. *Journal of Clinical Investigation*, 1952, *31*, 859-871.

Plum, F. (Ed.). *Brain dysfunction in metabolic disorders.* Proceedings Association for Research in Nervous and Mental Disease (Vol. 53). New York: Raven Press, 1974.

Rappoport, D.A., Fritz, R.R., & Yamagami, S. Development. In A. Lajtha (Ed.), *Handbook of neurochemistry* (Vol. 5). New York: Plenum Press, 1971.

Redick, R.W. *Utilization of psychiatric facilities by persons diagnosed with alcohol disorders; analytical and special study reports* (DHEW publication No. HSM 73-9114). Washington, D.C.: U.S. Government Printing Office, 1973.

Robertson, D.M., Wasan, S.M., & Skinner, D.B. Ultrastructural features of early brain stem lesions of thiamine-deficient rats. *American Journal of Pathology*, 1968, *52*, 1081-1097.

Rose, H.D., Gobert, T.M., Sanz, C.J., & Leitschuh, T.H. Fever during acute alcohol withdrawal. *American Journal of the Medical Sciences*, 1970, *260*, 112-121.

Salum, I. Delirium tremens and certain other acute sequels of alcohol abuse. *Acta Psychiatrica Scandinavica* (Suppl. 235), 1972, 1-145.

Smith, D.A. Nutritional neuropathies in the civilian internment camp, Hong Kong, January 1942-August 1945. *Brain*, 1946, *69*, 209-222.

Sparber, S.B. Effects of drugs on the biochemical and behavioral responses of developing organisms. *Federation Proceedings*, 1972, *31*, 74-80.

Spillane, J.D., & Riddoch, G. *Nutritional disorders of the nervous system.* Baltimore: Williams & Wilkins, 1947.

Tavel, M.E., Davidson, W., & Batterton, T.D. A critical analysis of mortality associated with delirium tremens. Review of 39 fatalities in a 9-year period. *American Journal of the Medical Sciences*, 1961, *242*, 18-29.

Thompson, G.N. (Ed.). *Alcoholism.* Springfield, Ill.: C.C. Thomas, 1956.

Ulleland, C.N. The offspring of alcoholic mothers. *Annals of the New York Academy of Sciences*, 1972, *197*, 167-169.

Victor, M. The role of alcohol in the production of seizures in epilepsy. *Modern problems in pharmacopsychiatry* (Vol. 4). Basel: S. Karger, 1970.

Victor, M. In F.A. Seixas & S. Eggleston (Eds.), Alcoholism and the central nervous system (Introductory remarks). *Annals of the New York Academy of Sciences*, 1973, *215*, 210-213.

Victor, M., & Adams, R.D. The effect of alcohol on the nervous system. *Research Publication of the Association for Research in Nervous and Mental Diseases*, 1953, *32*, 526-573.

Victor, M., Adams, R.D., & Collins, G.H. The Wernicke-Korsakoff syndrome. In F. Plum & F.H. McDowell (Eds.), *Contemporary Neurology Series* (Vol. 7). Philadelphia: F.A. Davis, 1971.

Victor, M., Adams, R.D., & Mancall, E.L. A restricted form of cerebellar cortical degeneration occurring in alcoholic patients. *Archives of Neurology*, 1959, *1*, 579-688.

Walker, D.W., & Freund, G. Impairment of timing behavior after prolonged alcohol consumption in rats. *Science*, 1973, *182*, 597-599.

Wallgren, H., & Barry, H., III. *Actions of Alcohol* (Vol. 1 & 2). New York: Elsevier, 1970.

Walsh, J.C., & McLeod, J.G. Alcoholic neuropathy. An electrophysiological and histological study. *Journal of the Neurological Sciences*, 1970, *27*, 457-469.

Wanamaker, W.M., & Skillman, T.G. Motor nerve conduction in alcoholics. *Quarterly Journal of Studies on Alcohol*, 1966, *27*, 16-22.

Watson, R.T., & Heilman, K.M. The differential diagnosis of dementia. *Geriatrics*, 1974, *29*, 145-154.

Weyman, A.E., Greenbaum, D.M., & Grace, W.J. Accidental hypothermia in an alcoholic population. *American Journal of Medicine*, 1974, *56*, 13-21.

Zimmerman, H.M. Neuropathies due to vitamin deficiency. *Journal of Neuropathology and Experimental Neurology*, 1956, *15*, 335-339.

CHAPTER 6

PSYCHIATRIC DESCRIPTION AND EVALUATION OF THE ALCOHOLIC

Donald W. Goodwin

The definition of alcoholism has been discussed at length elsewhere in this book. Nevertheless, in order to properly introduce the subject matter of this chapter, a word needs to be said about the definition of alcoholism from a clinical perspective.

Most definitions of alcoholism today focus on problems. Theoretically, a person can drink enormous amounts of alcohol, but if he has no problems from drinking, he is not an alcoholic. Of course, truly heavy drinkers almost always have problems, so in a sense the distinction is academic. Traditionally, the problems are divided into categories, such as psychological problems, domestic and social problems, medical problems, and so forth. Although necessary for establishing research criteria for the study of alcoholism, in "real life" these problems interact in complicated ways to produce the condition

Ralph E. Tarter and A. Arthur Sugerman (eds.), Alcoholism

ISBN: 0-201-08146-6
ISBN: 0-201-08145-8 (pbk.)

called alcoholism.

Disagreement about diagnosis usually comes from two sources: (a) the diagnostic criteria are not purely descriptive and phenomenological but have etiological connotations, and (b) mild, early, and atypical cases lead to disagreement, just as they do in virtually every disease category in medicine. An example of the first arises whenever the definition begins with a phrase like "alcoholism is a biological condition. . ." when in fact the term biological is meaningless unless it refers to some strictly physical process, and there is as yet no evidence that alcoholism is the result of any physical abnormality. A third, presumably less common, source of disagreement about diagnosis arises when physicians attempt to apply research criteria to a clinical condition. If, for example, they adopt the research criteria used in our Department of Psychiatry at Washington University, they could only make the diagnosis of alcoholism if there were symptoms in three of four groups. These groupings are purely arbitrary, and whereas they are necessary for research purposes, their ritualistic application to clinical cases is a mistake.

For this reason, this chapter opens with a case history similar to what one might hear at a meeting of Alcoholics Anonymous. The patient is "four-plus," meaning severe indeed. When we picture a typical patient with practically any illness, we are usually thinking of the four-plus case, and what follows is such a case, with one proviso: "David" represents a severe form of American bender alcoholic, and, as will be discussed later, the term alcoholism can also be applied to other patterns of excessive drinking.

CLINICAL PICTURE

"I am David," the AA member begins. "I am an alcoholic. I will always be an alcoholic. I cannot touch alcohol. It will destroy me. It is like an allergy - not a real allergy - but like an allergy.

I had my first drink at 16. I got drunk. For several years I drank every week or so with the boys. I didn't always get drunk, but I know now that alcohol affected me differently than other people. I looked forward to the times I knew I could drink. I drank for the glow, the feeling of confidence it gave me. But maybe that's why my friends drank, too. They didn't become alcoholics. Alcohol seemed to satisfy some specific need I had, which I can't describe. True, it made me feel good, helped me forget my troubles, but that wasn't it. What was it? I don't know, but I know I liked it, and after a time, I more than liked it, I needed it. Of course, I didn't realize it. It was maybe 10 or 15 years before I realized it, let myself realize it.

My need was easy to hide from myself and others (maybe I'm kidding myself about the others). I only associated with people who drank. I married a woman who drank. There were always reasons to drink. I was low, tense, tired, mad, happy. I probably drank as often because I was happy as for any other reason. Occasions for drinking - when drinking was appropriate, expected - were endless. Football games, fishing trips, parties, holidays, birthdays, Christmas, or merely Saturday night. Drinking became interwoven with everything pleasurable - food, sex, social life. When I stopped drinking, these things, for a time, lost all interest for me, they were so tied to drinking. I don't think I will ever enjoy them as much as I did when drinking. But if I had kept drinking, I wouldn't be here to enjoy them. I would be dead.

So, drinking came to dominate my life.

By the time I was 25 I was drinking every day, usually before dinner, but sometimes after dinner (if there was a reason), and more on weekends, starting in the afternoon. By 30, I drank all weekend, starting with a beer or Bloody Mary in the morning, and drinking off and on, throughout the day, beer or wine or vodka, indiscriminately. The goal, as always, was to maintain a glow, not enough, I hoped, that people would notice, but a glow. When 5 o'clock came, I thought, well, now it's cocktail hour and I would have my two or three scotches or martinis before dinner as I did on nonweekend nights. After dinner I might nap, but just as often I felt a kind of wakeful calm and power and happiness that I've never experienced any other time. These were the dangerous moments. I called friends, boring them with drunken talk; arranged parties; decided impulsively to drive to a bar. In one year, at the age of 33, I had three accidents, all on Saturday night, and was charged with drunken driving once (I kept my license, but barely). My friends became fewer, reduced to other heavy drinkers and barflies. I fought with my wife, blaming her for her drinking, and once or twice, I hit her (or so she said. Like many things I did while drinking, there was no memory afterward.)

And by now I was drinking at noontime, with the lunch hour stretching longer and longer. I began taking off whole afternoons, going home potted. I missed mornings at work because of drinking the night before, particularly Monday mornings. And I began drinking weekday mornings to get going. Vodka and orange juice. I thought vodka wouldn't smell (it did). It usually lasted until an early martini luncheon, and I then suffered through until cocktail hour, which came earlier and earlier.

By now I was hooked and knew it, but desperately did not want others to know it. I had been sneaking drinks for years - slipping out to the kitchen during parties and such - but now I began hiding alcohol, in my desk, bedroom, car glove compartment, so it would never be far away, ever. I grew panicky even thinking I might not have alcohol when I needed it, which was just about always.

For years, I drank and had very little hangover, but now the hangovers were gruesome. I felt physically bad - headachy, nauseated, weak - but the mental part was the hardest. I loathed myself. I was waking early and thinking what a mess I was, how I had hurt so many others and myself. The words *guilty* and *depression* sound superficial in trying to describe how I felt. The loathing was almost physical - a dead weight that could be lifted in only one way, and that was by having a drink, so I drank, morning after morning. After two or three, my hands were steady, I could hold some breakfast down, and the guilt was gone, or almost.

Despite everything, others knew. There was the odor, the rheumy eyes, and flushed face. There was missing work and not working well when there. Fights with wife, increasingly physical. She kept threatening to leave and finally did. My boss gave me a leave of absence after an embarrassed remark about my 'personal problems'. At some point I was without wife, home, or job. I had nothing to do but drink. The drinking was now steady, days on end. I lost appetite and missed meals (besides, money was short). I awoke at night, sweating and shaking, and had a drink. I awoke in the morning, vomiting, and had a drink. It couldn't last. My ex-wife found me in my apartment shaking and seeing things, and got me in the hospital. I dried out, left, and went back to drinking. I was hospitalized again, and this time stayed dry for six months. I was nervous and couldn't sleep, but got some of my confidence back and found a part-time job. Then my ex-boss offered my job back and I celebrated by having a drink. The next night I had two drinks. In a month I was drinking as much as ever and again unemployed. That was three years ago. I've had two big drunks since then but don't drink other times. I think about alcohol and miss it. Life is gray and monotonous. The joy and gaiety is gone.

But drinking will kill me. I know this and have stopped - for now."[1]

Alcoholism in this chapter refers to the David-type alcoholism, granting that patterns of human behavior are bewilderingly variable, even patterns of illness. Not all Davids, for example, reach bottom (in A.A. terms). Some stop drinking long before. Others drink, but with enough control to prevent the big problems from happening. The essence of the David-type alcoholism is a vulnerability to alcohol that sets him apart from other drinkers. By taking extreme measures, such as total abstinence, he may prevent alcohol problems; but if he drinks at all, the chance of developing problems is high, and this vulnerability appears to be lifelong.

To recapitulate and amplify some of the points made above in the David story: Alcoholism is a behavioral disorder. The specific behavior that causes problems is the consumption of large quantities of alcohol on repeated occasions. The motivation underlying this behavior is often obscure. When asked why they drink excessively, alcoholics occasionally attribute their drinking to a particular mood, such as depression or anxiety, or to situational problems. They sometimes describe an overpowering "need" to drink, variously described as a craving or compulsion. Just as often, however, the alcoholic is unable to give a plausible explanation of his excessive drinking (Ludwig, 1972).

Like other drug dependencies, alcoholism is accompanied

---

1 Like the other clinical vignettes in this chapter, David is a composite portrait drawn from multiple observations. This as well as some of the material that follows has appeared in revised form in several other works, principally Woodruff, Goodwin, and Guze (1973) and Goodwin (1976).

by a preoccupation with obtaining the drug in quantities sufficient to produce intoxication over long periods. It is especially true early in the course of alcoholism that the patient may deny this preoccupation or attempt to rationalize his need by assertions that he drinks no more than his friends. As part of this denial or rationalization, alcoholics tend to spend their time with other heavy drinkers.

As alcoholism progresses and problems from drinking become more serious, the alcoholic may drink alone, sneak drinks, hide the bottle, and take other measures to conceal the seriousness of his condition. This is almost always accompanied by feelings of guilt and remorse which in turn may produce more drinking, temporarily relieving the feelings. Remorse may be particularly intense in the morning, when the patient has not had a drink for a number of hours, and this may provoke morning drinking (Jellinek, 1952).

Prolonged drinking, even if initiated to relieve guilt and anxiety, commonly produces anxiety and depression (Davis, 1971). The full range of symptoms associated with depression and anxiety neurosis, including terminal insomnia, low mood, irritability, and anxiety attacks with chest pain, palpitations, and dyspnea, often appears. Alcohol temporarily relieves these symptoms, resulting in a vicious cycle of drinking-depression-drinking which may ultimately result in a classical withdrawal syndrome. Often the patient makes a valiant effort to stop drinking and may succeed for a period of several days or weeks, only to "fall off the wagon" again.

Repeated experiences like this easily lead to feelings of despair and hopelessness. By the time the patient consults a physician, he has often reached rock bottom. His situation seems hopeless and, after years of heavy drinking, his problems have become so numerous that he feels nothing can be done about them. At this point he may be ready to acknowledge his alcoholism, but feels powerless to stop drinking.

Alcohol is one of the few psychoactive drugs that produce, on occasion, classical amnesia. Nonalcoholics, when drinking, also experience this amnesia (blackouts), but much less often, as a rule, than do alcoholics (Goodwin, Crane, & Guze, 1969). These episodes of amnesia are particularly distressful to the alcoholic, since he may fear that he has unknowingly harmed someone or behaved imprudently while intoxicated. Studies of blackouts (Goodwin, 1971; Tamerin, Weiner, Poppen, Steinglass, & Mendelson, 1971) indicate that the amnesia is anterograde. During a blackout, the person has relatively intact remote and immediate memory but experiences a specific short term memory deficit in which he is unable to recall events that happened five or ten minutes before. Since his other intellectual faculties are well preserved, he can perform complicated acts and appears normal to the casual observer. Present evidence suggests that alcoholic blackouts represent impaired consolidation of new information rather than repression motivated by a desire to forget events that happened while drinking (Goodwin, 1971).

Blackouts are a curious phenomenon. They represent one of the most dramatic features of alcoholism, as the following stories illustrate:

> A 39-year-old salesman awoke in a strange hotel room. He had a mild hangover but otherwise felt normal. His clothes were hanging in the closet; he was clean-shaven. He dressed and went down to the lobby. He learned from the clerk that he was in Las Vegas and that he had checked in two days previously. It had been obvious that he had been drinking, the clerk said, but he hadn't seemed very drunk. The date

> was Saturday the 14th. His last recollection was of sitting in a St. Louis bar on Monday the 9th. He had been drinking all day and was drunk, but could remember everything perfectly until about 3 p.m., when "like a curtain dropping," his memory went blank. It remained blank for approximately five days. Three years later, it was still blank. He was so frightened by the experience that he abstained from alcohol for two years.

Some people forget and do not realize when sober that they have forgotten anything. Someone tells them and then they remember a little.

> A 53-year-old member of Alcoholics Anonymous said that he had experienced many blackouts during his 25 years of heavy drinking. He could not remember his first blackout, but guessed it had happened about 15 years before. The memory loss had not bothered him, he said; he assumed everyone who drank had trouble with memory. Sometimes, however, it was embarrassing to be told he had said something or gone somewhere and not recalled it. Upon being told, he would sometimes remember the event and sometimes not. Occasionally, months later, something would remind him of the event and his memory would snap back. Typically, he could remember some parts of a drinking episode and not others; a half hour might be blanked out and the next hour remembered. The forgotten parts appeared to have no more emotional significance than the remembered ones. "It's like turning a switch on and off."

Sometimes a curious thing happens when a person is drinking: The drinker recalls things that happened during a previous drinking period which, sober, he had forgotten. For example, alcoholics often report hiding money or alcohol when drinking, forgetting it when sober, and having their memory return when drinking again. This is reminiscent of "state dependent learning."

> A 47-year-old housewife often wrote letters when she was drinking. Sometimes she would jot down notes for a letter and start writing it, but not finish it. The next day, sober, she would be unable to decipher the notes. Then she would start drinking again, and after a few drinks the meaning of the notes would become clear and she would resume writing the letter. "It was like picking up the pencil where I had left off."

By the time the alcoholic consults a physician, he has often developed medical and social complications from drinking. These will be discussed under the section *Complications*.

NATURAL HISTORY

The natural history of alcoholism seems to be somewhat different in men and women (Pemberton, 1967). In men the onset is usually in the late teens or twenties, the course is insidious, and the alcoholic may not be fully aware of his dependency on alcohol until his thirties. The first hospitalization usually occurs in the late thirties or forties (Drew, 1968).

The above observations are based on studies conducted a number of years ago. In the past few years there appears to be a shift toward more youthful heavy drinking, with what appears to be frank alcoholism developing in the mid or late teens. Although frequency of drinking among teenagers has definitely increased, it is still too early to estimate how often teenage alcoholism occurs, at least alcoholism as defined in the introduction to this chapter.

Symptoms of alcoholism rarely occur for the first time

after age 45 (Amark, 1951). If they do occur, the physician should be alerted to the possibility of primary affective disorder or brain disease.

Alcoholism has a higher spontaneous remission rate than is often recognized. Even among alcoholics sick enough to be hospitalized, many remit without further treatment (Gerard & Saenger, 1966).

The incidence of first admissions to psychiatric hospitals for alcoholism drops markedly in the sixth and seventh decades as do first arrests for alcohol-related offenses. Although the mortality rate among alcoholics is perhaps two to three times that of nonalcoholics, this is probably insufficient to account for the apparent decrease in problem drinking in middle and late middle life (Drew, 1968).

Female alcoholics have been studied less extensively than male alcoholics, but the evidence suggests that the course of the disorder is more variable in women. The onset often occurs later, and spontaneous remission apparently is less frequent (Pemberton, 1967). Female alcoholics are also more likely to have a history of primary affective disorder (Schuckit, Pitts, Reich, King, & Winokur, 1969).

On the basis of questionnaire data obtained from alcoholics, Jellinek promulgated the view that manifestations of alcoholism follow a natural chronological order, with blackouts being one of the early "prodromal" symptoms of the illness (Jellinek, 1952). Later studies (Goodwin et al., 1969) have challenged this view, and it is now believed that problems from drinking may occur in various sequences and that blackouts have no special significance as a sign of incipient alcoholism. Frequently, after years of heavy problem-free drinking, a person may experience a large number of problems in a brief period.

Patterns of drinking also are variable, and it is a mistake to associate one particular pattern exclusively with alcoholism. Jellinek (1960) divided alcoholics into various species depending on their pattern of drinking. One species, the so-called gamma alcoholic, is common in America and conforms to the stereotype of the Alcoholics Anonymous alcoholic. Gamma alcoholics have problems with control: once they begin drinking, they are unable to stop until poor health or depleted financial resources prevent them from continuing. Once the bender is terminated, however, the person is able to abstain from alcohol for varying lengths of time. Jellinek contrasted the gamma alcoholic with a species of alcoholic common in France. He has control but is unable to abstain; he must drink a given quantity of alcohol every day, although he has no compulsion to exceed this amount. He may not recognize that he has an alcohol problem until, for reasons beyond his control, he has to stop drinking, whereupon he experiences withdrawal symptoms.

There are more men alcoholics than women alcoholics, but women may be catching up. At any rate, people who treat alcoholics say they are seeing more women patients.

Black alcoholics start drinking younger - often in their early and mid-teens. By twenty they may be floridly alcoholic and need hospitalization. They have withdrawal hallucinations more often than do white alcoholics, and, for unknown reasons, are less suicidal in middle age.

The French alcoholic might describe himself as follows:

> "My name is Pierre. I am not an alcoholic. I do not know alcoholics. There are no alcoholics in France, except tourists.
>
> I have drunk wine since I was a child.

> Wine is good for you. I drink it with meals and when I am thirsty. Since I was a young man, I have drunk three or four liters of wine every day. I also enjoy an occasional aperitif, especially on Sunday mornings and after work. I never drink more than this. I have no problems from alcohol.
>
> Once, when I was in the Army, no wine was permitted. I started shaking all over and thought bugs were crawling on me. I think it was the Army food. My doctor says my liver is too large. My father and grandfather had large livers. It probably means nothing."

Although these pure types of alcoholism do exist, many individuals who do not conform to the stereotypes still have serious drinking problems. Among American alcoholics, one drink does not invariably lead to a binge; a person may drink moderately for a long time before his drinking begins to interfere with his health or social functioning.

This diversity in drinking patterns explains the current emphasis on problems rather than a single set of symptoms, as the basis for diagnosing alcoholism.

COMPLICATIONS

Since alcoholism is defined by the problems it creates, symptoms and complications inevitably overlap. For present purposes, we will consider social and medical complications separately.

Alcoholics have a high rate of marital separation and divorce (Woodruff, Guze, & Clayton, 1972). They often have job troubles, including frequent absenteeism and job loss.

They also have a high frequency of accidents - in the home, on the job, and while driving automobiles. Of the more than 55,000 highway fatalities each year in the United States, about half involve a driver who has been drinking, usually an alcoholic (Selzer, Payne, Westervelt, & Quinn, 1967). Nearly half of convicted felons are alcoholic (Goodwin, Crane, & Guze, 1971), and about half of police activities in large cities are associated with alcohol-related offenses.

Medical complications fall into three categories: (a) acute effects of heavy drinking; (b) chronic effects of heavy drinking; and (c) withdrawal effects.

Consumption of very large amounts of alcohol can lead directly to death by depressing the respiratory center in the medulla. Acute hemorrhagic pancreatitis occasionally occurs from a single heavy drinking episode.

Nearly every organ system can be affected, directly or indirectly, by chronic, heavy use of alcohol. Gastritis and diarrhea are common reversible effects. Gastric ulcer may also occur, although the evidence that alcohol directly produces ulceration is equivocal (Wallgren & Barry, 1970).

The most serious effect of alcohol on the gastrointestinal tract is liver damage. After many years of study, however, it is still not clear whether alcohol alone has a direct toxic effect on the liver. At present, it appears that cirrhosis results from the combined effect of alcohol and diet, plus other factors, possibly including heredity. Human and animal studies indicate that a single large dose of alcohol, combined with a diet rich in fat, produces a fatty liver (Lieber, 1968; Wallgren & Barry, 1970). Conversely, alcohol together with fasting can result in a fatty liver. The connection between fatty liver and cirrhosis, however, is unclear. The fatty changes in the liver after acute alcohol intoxication are reversible. Most patients with Laennec's cirrhosis, in Western countries, are excessive drinkers. Most severe alcoholics, however, do not develop cirrhosis (probably less than 10%).

Alcoholism is associated with pathology of the nervous system, principally due to vitamin deficiencies and not to a direct toxic effect of alcohol. Peripheral neuropathy, the most common neurological complication, apparently results from multiple vitamin B deficiencies (Victor & Adams, 1953). It is usually reversible with adequate nutrition. Retrobulbar neuropathy may lead to amblyopia (sometimes called tobacco-alcohol amblyopia), which is also usually reversible with vitamin therapy.

Other neurological complications include anterior lobe cerebellar degenerative disease (Romano, Michael, & Merritt, 1940) and the Wernicke-Korsakoff syndrome (Victor, Adams, & Collins, 1971). The latter almost certainly results from thiamine deficiency. The acute Wernicke state consists of ocular disturbances (nystagmus or sixth nerve palsy), ataxia, and confusion. It usually clears in a few days but may progress to a chronic brain syndrome (Korsakoff psychosis). Short-term memory loss (anterograde amnesia) is the most characteristic feature of Korsakoff's psychosis. Confabulation (narration of fanciful tales) may also occur but is not the pathognomic feature that it is often said to be. The Wernicke-Korsakoff syndrome is associated with necrotic lesions of the mammillary bodies, thalamus, and other brain stem areas. Thiamine corrects early Wernicke signs rapidly and may prevent development of an irreversible Korsakoff dementia.

Other medical complications of alcoholism include cardiomyopathy, thrombocytopenia and anemia, and myopathy.

The term alcohol withdrawal syndrome is preferable to delirium tremens (DT's). The latter refers to a specific manifestation of the syndrome. The most common withdrawal symptom is tremulousness, which usually occurs only a few hours after cessation of drinking and may even begin while the person is still drinking (relative abstinence). Transitory hallucinations also may occur. If so, they usually begin 12 to 24 hours after drinking stops (Victor & Adams, 1953). Grand mal convulsions ("rum fits") occur occasionally, sometimes as long as two or three days after drinking stops. As a rule, alcoholics experiencing convulsions do not have epilepsy, they have more or less normal electroencephalograms when not drinking and experience convulsions only during withdrawal (Marinacci, 1956).

Delirium tremens is infrequent, and when it does occur is often associated with an intervening medical illness. For a diagnosis of delirium tremens, gross memory disturbance should be present in addition to other withdrawal symptoms, such as agitation and vivid hallucinations. Classically, delirium tremens begins two or three days after drinking stops and subsides within one to five days (Victor & Adams, 1953). One must always suspect intercurrent medical illness when delirium occurs during withdrawal. The physician should be particularly alert to hepatic decompensation, pneumonia, subdural hematoma, pancreatitis, and fractures.

Psychiatric patients are rarely dangerous, but delirious patients are an exception. They may be dangerous indeed, as was the case of Huckleberry Finn's alcoholic father, whose DT's were described by Mark Twain as follows:

> "I don't know how long I was asleep, but all of a sudden there was an awful scream and I was up. There was Pap looking wild, and skipping around and yelling about snakes. I couldn't see no snakes, but he said they was crawling up his legs; and then he would give a jump and scream, and say one had bit him on the cheek. I never see a man look so wild. Pretty soon he was all fagged out, and fell down panting; then he rolled over and over, screaming and saying there was devils a-hold of him. He wore out by and by, and laid still awhile, moaning. Then he laid stiller, and didn't make a sound. I could hear the owls and the wolves away off in the woods, and it seemed terrible still. He was laying over by the corner. By and by he raised up partway and listened, with his head to one side. He wails, very low:
>
> 'Tramp-tramp-tramp; that's the dead; tramp-tramp-tramp; they're coming after me; but I won't go. Oh, they're here! Don't touch me - don't. Hands off - they're cold; let go. Oh, let a poor devil alone!'
>
> He rolled himself up in his blanket and went to crying. But by and by he rolled out and jumped up to his feet looking wild, and he see me and went for me. He chased me round and round the place with a clasp knife, calling me the Angel of Death, and saying he would kill me.. I begged, and told him I was only Huck; but he laughed such a screech laugh, and roared and cussed, and kept on chasing me. Once when I turned short and dodged under his arm he got me by the jacket between my shoulders, and I thought I was gone; but I slid out of the jacket and saved myself. Pretty soon he was all tired out, and dropped down with his back against the door, and said he would rest a minute and then kill me. He put his knife under him, and pretty soon he dozed off."

So-called chronic alcoholic hallucinosis refers to the persistence of hallucinations, usually auditory, for long periods after other abstinence symptoms subside and after the patient has stopped heavy drinking (Victor & Hope, 1958). This occurs rarely and, after 75 years of debate concerning the etiology, it has not been resolved whether drinking actually produces the condition.

Suicide is an important complication of alcoholism. About one-quarter of suicides are alcoholic, predominantly men over age 35. Apparently alcoholics (unlike patients with primary affective disorder) are especially likely to commit suicide after loss of a wife, close relative, or other serious interpersonal disruption (Goodwin, 1973).

DIFFERENTIAL DIAGNOSIS

Chronic excessive use of alcohol produces a wide range of psychiatric symptoms which, in various combinations, can mimic other psychiatric disorders. Therefore, while a person is drinking heavily and during the withdrawal period, it is difficult to determine whether he suffers from a psychiatric condition other than alcoholism.

The diagnosis of alcoholism itself is relatively easy. However, many alcoholics also use other drugs, and it may be difficult to determine which symptoms are produced by alcohol and which by barbiturates, amphetamines, and so on. If a patient has been drinking heavily and not eating, he may become hypoglycemic (Freinkel & Arky, 1966), and this condition may produce symptoms resembling those seen in withdrawal.

The two psychiatric conditions most commonly associated with alcoholism are primary affective disorder and sociopathy. Female alcoholics apparently suffer more often from primary affective disorder than do male alcoholics (Schuckit et al., 1969). The diagnosis of primary affective disorder usually can be made by past history or by observing the patient during long periods of abstinence. According to one study, about one-third of patients with manic depressive illness drink more while depressed and another third drink less (Cassidy, Flanagan, Spellman, & Cohen, 1957). Studies indicate that small amounts of alcohol administered to a depressed patient relieve depressive symptoms, but large amounts worsen depression (Mayfield, 1968).

Many sociopaths drink to excess, although how many would be considered alcoholic is uncertain. A follow-up study of convicted felons, about half of whom had alcohol problems, indicates that sociopathic drinkers have a higher "spontaneous" remission rate than do nonsociopathic alcoholics (Goodwin et al., 1971). When sociopaths reduce their drinking, their criminal activities are correspondingly reduced.

Various personality disorders have been associated with alcoholism particularly those in which dependency is a feature. The consensus at present is that alcoholism is not connected with a particular constellation of personality traits. Longitudinal studies (of those available) help little in predicting what types of individuals are particularly susceptible to alcoholism (Jones, 1968; McCord & McCord, 1962).

This work was supported, in part, by U.S.P.H.S. grant DA4RG008 and a Research Scientist Development Award AA47325 from the National Institute of Alcohol Abuse and Alcoholism.

REFERENCES

Amark, C. A study in alcoholism: Clinical, social-psychiatric, and genetic investigations. *Acta Psychiatrica Scandinavica*, 1951, Suppl. 70, 7-283.

Cassidy, W.L., Flanagan, N.B., Spellman, M., & Cohen, M.E. Clinical observations in manic-depressive disease. *Journal of the American Medical Association*, 1957, *164*, 1535-1546.

Davis, D. Mood changes in alcoholic subjects with programmed and free-choice experimental drinking. *Recent Advances in Studies of Alcoholism*. Washington, D.C.: U.S. Government Printing Office, 1971.

Drew, L.R.H. Alcoholism as a self-limiting disease. *Quarterly Journal of Studies on Alcohol*, 1968, *29*, 956-967.

Freinkel, M., & Arky, R.A. Effects of alcohol on carbohydrate metabolism in man. *Psychological Medicine*, 1966, *28*, 551-563.

Gerard, D.L., & Saenger, G. *Out-patient treatment of alcoholism*. Toronto: University of Toronto Press, 1966.

Goodwin, D.W. Blackouts and alcohol-induced memory dysfunction. *Recent Advances in Studies of Alcoholism*. Washington, D.C.: U.S. Department of Health, Education and Welfare, 1971.

Goodwin, D.W. Alcohol in suicides and homicides. *Quarterly Journal of Studies on Alcohol*, 1973, *34*, 144-156.

Goodwin, D.W. *Is alcoholism hereditary*? New York: Oxford University Press, 1976.

Goodwin, D.W., Crane, J.B., & Guze, S.B. Alcoholic "blackouts": A review and clinical study of 100 alcoholics. *American Journal of Psychiatry*, 1969, *126*, 191-198.

Goodwin, D.W., Crane, J.B., & Guze, S.G. Felons who drink. *Quarterly Journal of Studies on Alcohol*, 1971, *32*, 136-147.

Jellinek, E.M. Phases of alcohol addiction. *Quarterly Journal of Studies on Alcohol*, 1952, *13*, 673-684.

Jellinek, E.M. *The disease concept of alcoholism*. New Haven: Hillhouse Press, 1960.

Jones, M.C. Personality correlates and antecedents of drinking patterns in adult males. *Journal of Consulting and Clinical Psychology*, 1968, *32*, 2-12.

Lieber, C.S. Metabolic effects produced by alcohol in the liver and other tissues. *Advances in Internal Medicine*, 1968, *14*, 151-199.

Ludwig, A.M. On and off the wagon. *Quarterly Journal of Studies on Alcohol*, 1972, *33*, 91-96.

Marinacci, A.A. Electroencephalography in alcoholism. *Alcoholism*. Springfield, Ill.: CC. Thomas, 1956.

Mayfield, D.G. Psychopharmacology of alcohol. I. Affective change with intoxication, drinking behavior, and affective state. *Journal of Nervous and Mental Diseases*, 1968, *146*, 314-321.

McCord, W., & McCord, J. A longitudinal study of the personality of alcoholics. *Society, culture, and drinking patterns*. New York: Wiley, 1962.

Pemberton, D.A. A comparison of the outcome of treatment in female and male alcoholics. *British Journal of Psychiatry*, 1967, *113*, 367-373.

Romano, J., Michael, M., Jr., & Merritt, H.H. Alcoholic cerebellar degeneration. *Archives of Neurology and Psychiatry*, 1940, *44*, 1230-1236.

Schuckit, M., Pitts, F.N., Jr., Reich, T., King, L.J., & Winokur, G. Alcoholism. *Archives of Environmental Health*, 1969, *18*, 301-306.

Selzer, M.L., Payne, C.E., Westervelt, F.H., & Quinn, J. Automobile accidents as an expression of psychopathology in an alcoholic population. *Quarterly Journal of Studies on Alcohol*, 1967, *28*, 505-516.

Tamerin, J.S., Weiner, S., Poppen, R., Steinglass, P., & Mendelson, J.H. Alcohol and memory: Amnesia and short-term memory function during experimentally induced intoxication. *American Journal of Psychiatry*, 1971, *127*, 1659-1664.

Victor, M., & Adams, R.D. The effect of alcohol on the nervous system. *Research Publication of The Association for Research in Nervous and Mental Disease*, 1953, *32*, 526-573.

Victor, M., & Hope, J.M. The phenomenon of auditory hallucinations in chronic alcoholism. *Journal of Nervous and Mental Diseases*, 1958, *126*, 451.

Victor, M., Adams, R.D., & Collins, G.H. The Wernicke-Korsakoff syndrome. In F. Plum & F.H. McDowell (Eds.), *Contemporary neurology series* (Vol. 7). Philadelphia: F.A. Davis, 1971.

Wallgren, H., & Barry, H. III. *Actions of alcohol* (Vol. 1). Amsterdam: Elsevier, 1970.

Woodruff, R.A.,Jr., Goodwin, D.W., & Guze, S.B. *Psychiatric diagnosis*. New York: Oxford University Press, 1973.

Woodruff, R.A., Jr., Guze, S.B., & Clayton, P.J. Divorce among psychiatric out-patients. *British Journal of Psychiatry*, 1972, *121*, 289-292.

CHAPTER 7

GENETIC DETERMINANTS OF ALCOHOLISM

Remi J. Cadoret

Evidence for genetic factors in alcoholism comes from a wide variety of approaches. By and large in human inheritance studies we must be content with the experiments which nature and society provide us. Selection of breeding stock, types of crosses, rigid control of environmental factors, and the like are not part of the experimental armamentarium. However, by capitalizing on accidents of nature (such as twins) and social rearrangements (such as adoption), it is possible to give some tentative answers to the question of a genetic etiology in alcoholism.

The following sections will consider the evidence available from many sources.

Ralph E. Tarter and A. Arthur Sugerman (eds.), Alcoholism

ISBN: 0-201-08146-6
ISBN: 0-201-08145-8 (pbk.)

FAMILIAL FACTORS IN ALCOHOLISM - THE CONTRIBUTION OF FAMILY STUDIES TOWARD STUDY OF TRANSMISSION OF ALCOHOLISM

Studies of alcoholics and their relatives have shown an increased incidence of alcoholism in relatives when compared to population or some other control value. The comparison group or population value is obviously critical to prove that alcoholism runs in families, i.e., that there is increased prevalence in certain families, which would be consistent with a familial factor (genetic, or family environmental, or both). Ideally the comparison group should reflect or be a measure of population values, and comparisons should take into account such important factors as sex and socio-economic status by careful sampling. The factor of age difference in a sample can be controlled to a considerable degree by expressing the probability of individuals having alcoholism in terms of the "morbid risk", a value corrected for the age distribution of the sample, and this is what we have endeavored to do in the following data. Table 1 presents the findings of a number of family studies from Europe and North America, representing several different cultures and socio-economic levels. These studies were selected because they included suitable control groups. Each study presents morbid risks for alcoholism among first degree relatives (parents and siblings) of both alcoholic probands and a comparison group: in some cases population values; in others, a different psychiatric condition. The risks for alcoholism follow a definite pattern: (a) male risks, whether for parents or sibs are higher than female; and (b) for both male and

Table 1

Family Studies of Alcoholism

Risks for Alcoholism in Relatives of Alcoholic and Comparison Probands

Study and Source	Parents		Siblings	
	Father	Mother	Brothers	Sisters
Brugger, 1934				
Alcoholic probands N=70	24.3	5.5	11.3	
Population values				
4 groups N-1303 families	6.9-12.4	-	0.8-1.6	
M. Bleuler, 1955				
Alcoholic probands N=50	22.0	6.0	11.8	8.0
Surgical probands N=200	13.0	3.0	4.6	0.0
Schizophrenic probands N=100	3.0	1.0	1.3	0.7
Pohlisch, 1933				
Alcoholic probands N=86	46.5	2.3	30.7	4.8
Morphine probands N=66	6.0	0.0	7.8	0.0
Amark, 1951				
Alcoholic probands	26.3	2.0	21.1	0.86
Population (after Fremming cited in Amark)	3.5	0.75	3.5	0.75
Pitts and Winokur, 1966				
Alcoholic probands N=62	16.1	1.6	7.0[a]	
Control probands N=62	1.6	0.0	0.5	

[a]12.4% of brothers; 1.0% of sisters

female relatives, alcoholic risks are usually higher than corresponding population or control values. The population or control values given in the table vary considerably from series to series and undoubtedly reflect differences in sampling, population values, and methodologic factors such as varying definitions of alcoholism. However, the risks, for the most part, fall within the range usually cited for population values in other studies (Brugger, 1933; Fremming, 1947; Lunenburger, 1928; Slater, 1935).

Thus, the family study permits the conclusion that risks for alcoholism are higher in families who are selected by having at least one alcoholic member. Although the family study does not prove a genetic or cultural transmission, the family study method can elucidate familial factors important in alcoholism. Most studies cited in Table 1 started with many probands who were described as having serious personality problems (Amark, 1951; Bleuler, 1955; Brugger, 1934). More recent studies also attest to the ubiquity of serious personality disturbances in alcoholic individuals (Schuckit, Rimmer, Reich, & Winokur, 1970). If personality disorders were a familial factor in alcoholism, then we might expect that the incidence of personality disorders in families of alcoholics should be higher than population or control values. Table 2 shows that personality disorders are also higher in alcoholic families when compared to population values (Bleuler and Amark studies). Comparison with other conditions, such as schizophrenia (Bleuler) or morphine addiction (Pohlisch), does not show increased incidence of personality disorder in families of alcoholics; however, the family study data of Bleuler and Amark suggest that personality disorders are a familial factor in alcoholism.

The definition of personality disorder by these European

Table 2

Risks for Personality Disorder in Relatives of Alcoholics

Study and Source	Parents		Siblings	
	Father	Mother	Brothers	Sisters
Bleuler, 1955				
Alcoholic probands	22.0		12.0	
Surgical probands	1.8		1.5	
Schizophrenic probands	11.9		20.5	
Pohlisch, 1933				
Alcoholic probands	7.0	7.0	7.8	6.8
Morphine probands	16.7	18.2	23.5	15.0
Amark, 1951				
Alcoholic probands	17.7	13.5	14.9	15.1
Population values (after Fremming, 1947)	3.1	2.8	3.1	2.8

and Scandinavian psychiatrists is much different and broader than current North American usage. They tend to follow the classification of Schneider (1940) and designate as psychopaths those individuals with lifelong personality traits which are so deviant that they cause distress to the individual or to society. This definition certainly includes those who in both America and the United Kingdom would be termed antisocial (sociopaths), or obsessive compulsive (anankastic), and probably includes other less well defined conditions such as passive aggressive, passive dependent personality, and hysterical personality.

One other condition has appeared to be a familial factor in alcoholism: affective disorder. Table 3 shows the

Table 3

Risks for Affective Disorder in Relatives of Alcoholics

Study and Source	Parents: Father	Parents: Mother	Siblings: Brothers	Siblings: Sisters
Bleuler, 1955				
Alcoholic Probands	4.7[a]		1.3[a]	
Surgical probands	0.6		0.2	
Schizophrenic probands	2.2		0.0	
Amark, 1951				
Alcoholic probands	3.7[b]		6.4[a,b]	
Population values (after Fremming, 1947)	2.6		2.6	
Pitts and Winokur, 1966				
Alcoholic probands	4.8	4.8	8.0[a]	
Control probands	3.2	1.6	0.5	

[a]indicates significant difference with control value
[b]includes risk for manic-depressive disease plus psychogenic psychoses because latter category contained mostly depressive illnesses with remitting courses similar to other affective disorders

evidence from family studies. Some of the earlier studies, such as Brugger (1933, 1936) or Pohlisch (1933), do not report increased affective disorder in the families of their alcoholic probands. It is not apparent why these investigators report negative results, but the positive findings in at least three well-designed series (Table 3) constitute good evidence for the importance of affective disorder as a factor in alcoholism. Other supporting evidence is available to connect alcoholism with affective disorder. Starting with affective disorder probands, Winokur and Pitts (1965) found that alcoholism was significantly increased in fathers and sibs compared to the same relatives in a matched control group of patients with medical illness only.

Thus, from family studies we can determine that not only does alcoholism occur more frequently in families of alcoholics but several other important psychiatric conditions as well: affective and personality disorders. In a study of severe alcoholics admitted to a large public hospital, Winokur, Reich, Rimmer, and Pitts (1970) were able to sort out three types of alcoholism based upon these familial factors of personality and affective disorder. Definitions of these three classes are: (a) primary alcoholics - individuals who meet criteria for alcoholism and do not have any other pre-existing psychiatric condition, (b) depressive alcoholics - individuals who meet criteria for alcoholism and have an affective disorder (in this study the affective condition was unipolar depression) which was present prior to the onset of alcoholism or independent in time from alcoholism, (c) sociopathic alcoholics - individuals who meet criteria for alcoholism and whose antisocial behavior occured prior to the onset of alcoholism. Table 4 shows some important familial differences found in this study: increased depression in first degree relatives of sociopathic alcoholics (Table 4, line 2); and increased sociopathy in first degree relatives of sociopathic alcoholics (Table 4, line 3) thus confirming the importance of sociopathy and affective disorder in alcoholics. Clinically, the three groups of alcoholics demonstrated very important and significant differences, some of which are shown in Table 4, the last four lines.

This tripartite division of alcoholics assumes

Table 4

Familial and Clinical Differences between Three Types of Alcoholism

Risks in 1° Relatives	Primary Alcoholics	Depressive Alcoholics	Sociopathic Alcoholics
Alcohol	184/807(22.8)	18/130(13.8)	18/106(7.0)
Depression	78/535(14.6)	24/89(27.0)	14/72(19.4)
Sociopathy	19/516[a](3.7)	3/70[a](4.3)	15/68[a](22.1)
Clinical Characteristics in Proband			
Sex of proband	male:female 2:1	almost all female	male:female 4:1
Median age onset alcoholism	male = 24 female = 30	male = 40 female = 37	male = 18 female = 24
Suicide attempts	26%	62%	31%
Driving problem due to drinking	29%	19%	59%

Note: data from Winokur, Rimmer, and Reich (1971)

[a]incidence of sociopathy computed for male relatives only

importance when we consider that the familial factors of depression and sociopathy have a genetic element. Three recent adoptee studies have demonstrated that antisocial personality has a definite genetic factor (Crowe, 1974; Hutchings & Mednick, 1974; Schulsinger, 1972). In the case of affective disorders, a genetic factor has been proven for the bipolar type of illness (manic-depressive disease) but not for other types, though on the basis of twin and family studies a genetic factor is extremely likely (Cadoret & Winokur, 1975). Thus, considerations of inheritance of alcoholism must take into account the association of alcoholism with these other conditions. One way in which the frequency of conditions like depression and sociopathy can be increased in alcoholic families is through the operation of assortative mating: non-random selection by alcoholics of spouses with higher prevalence of affective and personality disorder. Rimmer and Winokur (1972) studied the spouses of 57 alcoholics and compared them to blood relatives of the alcoholics and to a control sample. Alcoholism and depression were found to be increased in the spouses compared to the control group. Sociopathy did not appear to be increased. However, other studies of alcoholics' spouses have noted increased prevalence of personality disorders in the spouse Amark, 1951; Brugger, 1936).

Obviously, family studies of the type described so far do not permit conclusions concerning the relative importance of genetic factors, environmental factors, or their interaction. However, one type of family study does permit some unraveling of these factors: that is by investigating half-siblings. Using this approach, the outcome regarding alcoholism can be studied in children with a biologic alcoholic parent but raised in a foster home with no alcoholic parent figure. Conversely, the alcoholic outcome can be determined in children without alcoholic biologic antecedent but who were raised in a home with an alcoholic foster parent. We are fortunate in having a study of such half-sibs starting from probands who had primary alcoholism as defined above (Schuckit, Goodwin, & Winokur, 1972). Figures 1 and 2 show the results of that study. In Figure 1, alcoholism

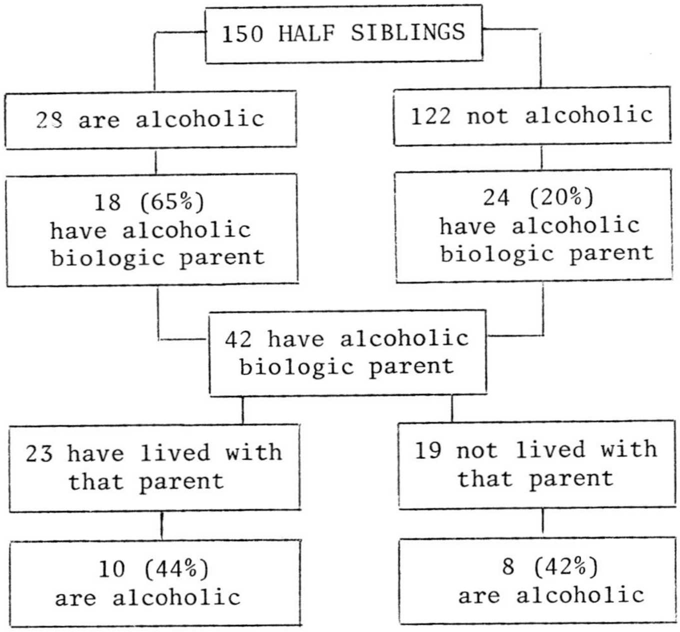

Figure 1. Nature and nurture I. Adopted from: Schuckit, M., Goodwin, D., & Winokur, G. Genetic investigation in alcoholism. In Forsander, O., & Eriksson, K. (Eds.), *International symposijm on biological aspects of alcohol consumption, 27-29 September 1971, Helsinki* (Vol. 20). Helsinki: Finnish Foundation for Alcohol Studies, 1972.

in half-sibs is significantly associated with an alcoholic biologic parent (line 3), but there is no evidence that the alcoholism in the half-sibs was related to living with the alcoholic parent (Figure 1, last line). Figure 2 shows that similar proportions of alcoholic and non-alcoholic half-sibs had lived with an alcoholic parent (Figure 2, line 3) and that sharing the same childhood environment as the alcoholic proband did not result in increased alcoholism (Figure 2, last line). Thus, the half-sib study is consistent more with a genetic influence in primary alcoholism than an environmental effect.

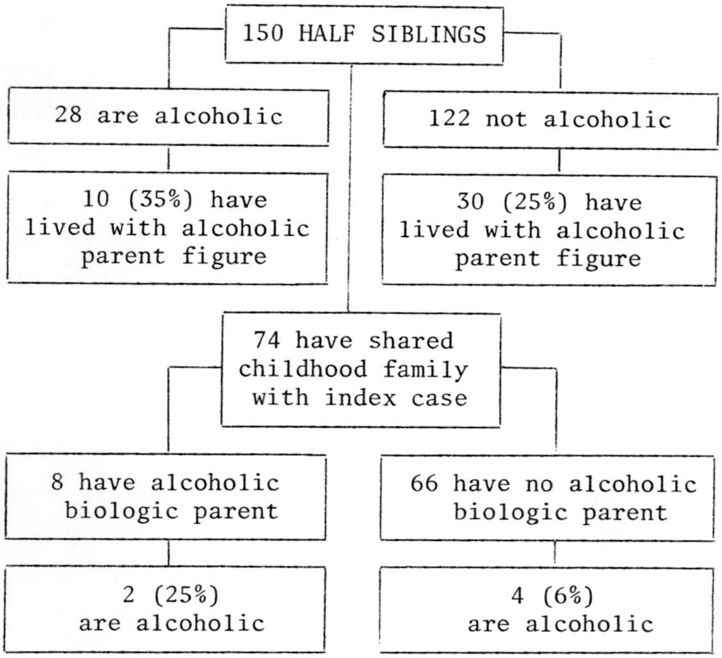

Figure 2. Nature and nurture II. Adopted from: Schuckit, M., Goodwin, D., & Winokur, G. Genetic investigation in alcoholism. In Forsander, O., & Eriksson, K. (Eds.), *International symposium on biological aspects of alcohol consumption, 27-29 September 1971, Helsinki* (Vol. 20). Helsinki: Finnish Foundation for Alcohol Studies, 1972.

EVIDENCE OF GENETIC ETIOLOGY IN STUDIES OF TWINS

The comparison of concordance in monozygotic (MZ) versus dizygotic (DZ) twin pairs has long been used as a way to assess the importance of genetic factor by varying the genetic factor while keeping the environmental relatively constant. Over the years, methodology of ascertaining zygosity and of obtaining a representative sample of the twin population have improved; and the two twin studies we report here in detail have utilized adequate techniques, in both ascertaining zygosity and in obtaining their samples. However, in interpreting results of such well-designed studies there is still controversy about how similar the environment may be for MZ and DZ partners. The commonest objection is that because of the greater physical (and constitutional) resemblance between MZ partners, they are more likely to be treated more similarly by their social environment than would DZ pairs. There is no absolute answer at present to this and similar objections, and the current evidence must be interpreted accordingly. Studies of twins who have been separated from childhood would help answer the environmental question, and some cases have been reported whose results suggest that the genetic factor is more important. However, this conclusion must be tempered by the possibility of sampling bias: MZ twins separated from birth who are concordant for alcoholism might be more likely to be reported than a discordant pair.

The twin study of Kaij (1960) analyzed drinking habits of same-sexed twins (males only) selected as an unbiased sample of twin pairs registered with County Temperance Boards in Sweden. Concepts such as primary alcoholism, etc., were not in use in this study which obviously included all types of alcoholics. The sample is probably not representative of alcohol abusers in general, but results such as MZ versus DZ rates for alcoholism would give a valid idea of the importance of a genetic factor. Table 5 shows the concordance found by Kaij. The two contingency tables, one for MZ and the other for DZ pairs, correlate the drinking score of one twin with that of the remaining partner. The distribution of degrees of concordance appears in the botton of the table: 53.5% of the MZ twins show complete concordance versus 28.3% of the dizygotic; discordance is more frequent in the DZ twins. The difference is highly significant and is consistent with a genetic factor. From data given in Chapters 8-10 in Kaij's monograph (Kaij, 1960) it is possible to partly assess the importance of factors such as personality disorders and affective illness. Thirty-seven MZ pairs were closely examined for personality traits and other psychiatric conditions and could be divided into two groups. In the first, 18 of the examined pairs had marked personality or affective (depressive) diagnoses in both members of the twin pair thus testifying to the inclusion of personality disorder and depression in alcoholism; 19 pairs in the second group were normal regarding personality traits or had other conditions such as organic brain syndromes. Table 6 shows the comparative distribution of concordances for the two groups. There is no demonstrable difference between the two concordant distributions. Unfortunately we cannot subdivide the DZ group similarly, but in as much as we can determine from the above comparison, personality disorder and affective illness do not appear to be important factors in explaining the high MZ concordance rate. Further, affective disorder

Table 5

Drinking Habits of Probands and Twin Sib (Kaij, 1960)

Drinking Score Twin	DZ Probands, Drinking Score Proband: 0	1	2	3	4	MZ Probands, Drinking Score Proband: 0	1	2	3	4
4		1	2	1	10			1	1	10
3	1	3	7	6	3		1	4	7	1
2		6	4	6	6		3	10	3	2
1	1	19	22	10	7		4	5	2	1
0		7	5	6	5		1	2		

Concordance Rate from Above Tables

	DZ n	DZ %	MZ n	MZ %
Concordant (main diagonal)	39	28.3	31	53.5
Discordant 1 (1 off main diagonal)	53	38.4	18	31.0
Discordant 2 (2 off main diagonal)	26	18.8	8	13.8
Discordant 3 + 4 (3 or 4 off main diagonal)	20	14.5	1	1.7

$X^2=13.81$ df=3 $p<.001$

Code for Severity of Drinking

0 = abstainers and below average use

1 = average user, rarely or never drinks but may drink regularly

2 = heavy weekend drinkers and above average consumers

3 = heavy abusers

4 = chronic alcoholics: 1 or more cardinal symptoms (loss of control, regular blackouts, physical dependence) or liver cirrhosis or DT's

alcoholism would be a minimal factor in this study because only male probands were selected. Thus this study provides some support for a genetic factor in primary alcoholism.

Table 6

Concordance Rates in MZ Twin Pairs Divided into Those with Personality or Affective Diagnoses Versus Other Conditions or "Normal" Pairs

Degree of Concordance of Drinking Score	Affective or Personality Diagnoses	No or Other Diagnoses
C1	10 (55.6%)	8 (42.1%)
D1	5 (27.8%)	7 (36.8%)
D2 to 4	3 (16.7%)	4 (21.1%)

$X^2 = .68$ df = 2 p = N.S.

Note: data from Kaij (1960)

The other twin study relevant to alcoholism was done by Partanen (1966) and sampled drinking behavior in male twin pairs born between 1920 and 1929 who still resided in Finland in 1958. The sample of 902 twin pairs included individuals with all degrees of drinking--from alcoholics to teetotalers. Answers to 13 questions about drinking were factor analyzed and three factors extracted to describe drinking behavior: (a) Density - the frequency and regularity of drinking; (b) Amount - amount, duration of drinking occasion, and degree of intoxication reached; and (c) Lack of Control - ability to stop drinking and to control amount.

Using individual scores for each of these three factors, hereditability measures were computed by comparing the within pair variances for MZ twins with corresponding variances for DZ pairs. Significant hereditability in the Partanen study was found for two of the three drinking behavior factors: Density and Amount. Lack of control was not significant in the overall analysis but was for younger twin pairs. Thus the study was consistent with a genetic factor in several important drinking behaviors. Interestingly, no evidence of hereditability was found for social complications of drinking such as arrests for drunkenness.

EVIDENCE FROM ADOPTEE STUDIES OF A GENETIC FACTOR IN ALCOHOLISM

Adoptees have figured in a number of designs for isolating genetic factors from environmental ones in psychiatry (Crowe, 1974). In the most commonly reported design, adoptees from varied biologic backgrounds who have lived with adoptive parents are examined for behavior which is then correlated with that shown by biologic parents. If such adoptees are separated at birth and raised entirely by non-relatives, then obviously the biologic parent social environment is minimized, although the unborn child has still been exposed to an intrauterine environment which could conceivably be a factor. In order to determine the importance of the biologic background, a control or comparison group is usually employed from a different biologic source, generally of normal parentage, and matched for factors of known importance such as age and sex of the child and early childhood experiences.

There are two adoptee studies of alcoholics similar to the above description. The first study by Roe (1945) involved a sample of male and female adoptees whose biologic fathers were "heavy drinkers with syndrome" (syndrome = "a picture of over aggressive, disorganized, or escape behavior such as repeated loss of jobs or disorderly conduct"). The contrast group of 22 adoptees had a biologic background without known alcoholism in either parent. At the time of follow-up at an average age of 32 there was no significant difference in drinking habits between the control adoptees and those from the alcoholic biologic backgrounds. The conclusion from this study was that there was no evidence of hereditary or genetic factor. The fact that many of these adoptees were female in the alcoholic parentage group (15 out of 36) makes it less likely that alcoholism would be found because of the preponderance of the condition in males (see family studies above), and this could partly account for the essentially negative results. Furthermore, from the standpoint of design, these were less than optimal features which makes interpretation even more difficult. For example, some children spent considerable time with biologic parents, and children from alcoholic backgrounds were more likely to be placed in rural environments and at later ages.

The second adoptee study made the detection of alcoholism more likely by using an all male adoptee sample. In this study done in Denmark by Goodwin, Schulsinger, Hermansen, Guze, and Winokur (1973), children were obtained by screening 5,483 adoptions for biologic parents who had been hospitalized for alcoholism. Children separated from biologic parents before the first six weeks of life were selected. Adoptees for comparison came from the same pool of subjects. Two control groups were selected. In one, none of the biologic parents had a record of psychiatric hospitalization; in the second, one parent had a psychiatric hospitalization for a condition other than alcoholism. Adoptees were age and sex matched. Psychiatrists interviewed adoptees without knowing to which group each belonged.

Elimination of biologic parents with other psychiatric conditions makes it more likely that primary alcoholism was present in the parents selected for the study. The types of other psychiatric illness found in the adoptees would tend to confirm this. As shown in Table 7 there is no evidence

Table 7

Psychopathology in Adoptees

	Probands N=55	Controls N=78
Depression	2%	3%
Sociopathy	5%	3%
Other personality disturbances	51%	53%
Drinking behavior		
Moderate drinker	51%	45%
Heavy drinker (ever)	22%	36%
Problem drinker (ever)	9%	14%
Alcoholic (ever)	18%	5%[a]

Note: data from Goodwin, Schulsinger, Hermansen, Guze, and Winokur (1973)
[a]difference significant at 2% level

of increased incidence of depression or sociopathy in the proband adoptees, as might be expected if sociopathic or depressive alcoholics had been included in large numbers among the alcoholic biologic parents. The only psychopathology to be significantly increased in the proband group is drinking which met rigid criteria for alcoholism (Table 7, last line). Of note, is that lesser degrees of drinking were no different between the two groups. Additional objective evidence of increased alcohol-related problems in the proband group was a fact that six of eight probands with psychiatric hospitalizations suffered from alcoholism, whereas only two controls had a psychiatric hospitalization and none of these was alcoholic. Probands also had more divorce than controls, again most likely related to alcohol-correlated problems.

The findings of this study, relating to drinking, are compatible with a genetic factor in primary alcoholism. However, there is little evidence for such a factor in other drinking patterns which share some of the features of alcoholism: the heavy drinker and the problem drinker (Table 7, lines 5 & 6).

EVIDENCE OF INTERACTION OF GENETIC WITH ENVIRONMENTAL FACTORS

By studying the fate of children who remain with alcoholic biologic parents and comparing their outcome with sibs who were adopted into "normal" families it is possible to arrive at some estimate of an environmental contributor to drinking behavior. Such a study has been reported by Goodwin, Schulsinger, Moller, Hermansen, Winokur and Guze (1974) comparing full siblings who had no contact with each other but did have in common an alcoholic parent. Table 8 contains the important results of this comparison. As expected,

Table 8

Home Experience and Psychopathology in Adopted and Non-Adopted Sons of Alcoholics

	Adopted Sons N=20	Non-Adopted Sons N=30
Home experience		
Parental psycho-pathology (any)	60%	88%
Parental economic status		
Above average	50%	4%
Psychopathology in sons		
Personality disturbances	60%	20%
Drinking Behavior		
Moderate drinker	60%	77%
Heavy drinker (ever)	15%	3%
Problem drinker (ever)	0%	3%
Alcoholic (ever)	25%	17%

Note: data from Goodwin, Schulsinger, Hermansen, Guze, and Winokur, (1975)

there was more reported parental psychopathology in the homes of the non-adopted sons, with most of the difference due to fathers' conditions.

The adopted sons enjoyed an above average socio-economic class (Table 8, line 2) which was reflected in the higher class of the adoptees as well. Other than this the sons were well matched on other demographic variables. Except for personality disturbances (In Denmark, characterologic diagnoses are commonly made; e.g., compulsive personality, sensitive-insecure personality, etc.) being more common in adopted sons (Table 8, line 3), there were no other differences in psychopathology, including drinking behavior (Table 8, last 4 lines). The increased psychopathology in the adopted sons was confounded with different interviewers, making interpretation difficult. Increased duration of exposure to the alcoholic parent did not appear to be associated with alcoholism in the non-adopted sons. To some extent, severity of the parent's drinking problem did correlate with the son's alcoholism, with more severe drinking in parents associated with increased incidence of alcoholism in sons.

Thus the findings do not support an independent environmental factor in this alcoholic sample. This conclusion must be tempered both by the small sample size as well as confounded factors such as the reasons for giving one son up for adoption. However, this is compatible with the half-sib study cited earlier which found little evidence of an environmental factor (having an alcoholic foster father).

LINKAGE AND ASSOCIATION STUDIES IN ALCOHOLISM

Association studies generally demonstrate that a genetic trait, such as a particular blood group or serum protein, is more likely to be correlated with a particular illness: for example, if individuals having type A blood are more likely to develop peptic ulcer than individuals with other blood types. A positive association such as this does not, however, necessarily imply that genetic linkage is responsible for the correlation. Linkage describes a situation where a known genetic trait lies close enough on the chromosome to a second gene (which is a factor in a different condition) that both genes from the same chromosome are passed on together to progeny. Linkage is detected by measuring the correlation of both traits or conditions within sibships or by more sophisticated analyses of transmission from one generation to another (Li, 1961). Association, as defined above, and linkage are thus not equivalent; for example, in association there is obviously no need for the genes to be located physically on the same chromosome; in linkage the known genetic trait usually serves as a marker only--its presence is not considered a factor in the manifestation of the condition related to the linked gene.

In alcoholism both association and linkage studies have been done. Cruz-Coke and co-workers have explored extensively the possibility of an association between alcoholism and color vision in individuals with liver cirrhosis due mainly to alcoholism (Cruz-Coke & Varela, 1966). Later these investigators found increased incidence of this color vision deficit in non-alcoholic relatives of alcoholic probands compared to control groups (Varela, Rivera, Mardones, & Cruze-Coke, 1969), so that the abnormality did not appear to be a consequence of alcohol abuse or cirrhosis. Inconsistent results by others in efforts to duplicate these findings have been attributed by Cruz-Coke to insensitive color vision tests (Cruz-Coke & Mardones, 1972). More recent studies by Cruz-Coke detail increased incidence of blue-yellow disturbances in males with habitual heavy drinking patterns compared to males with lesser degrees of drinking or those who abstained (Cruz-Coke, Rivera, Varela, & Mardones, 1972). Unfortunately Cruz-Coke has published no analyses of family pedigrees or of sib pairs for linkage using the color vision abnormality as a marker gene.

Association studies between blood groups and alcoholism have been reported but with conflicting results (see review in Hill, Goodwin, Cadoret, Osterland, & Doner, 1975). A recent study has found an association between the presence of S blood antigen (part of the MNSs system) and alcoholism; the same study did not find evidence for genetic linkage of the S*x* system with alcoholism (Hill et al., 1975). This type of isolated association finding requires extensive replication because it usually represents one significant difference out of many tests for possible differences.

One study has been published which sought for evidence of linkage between 11 serological markers known to be genetically determined, and alcoholism in members of 35 families (Hill et al., 1975). No positive evidence of genetic linkage was reported in this study. Only one marker on the X-chromosome was studied (the Xg system) and unfortunately too few cases were available for linkage analysis so that the hypothesis of an X-linked factor suggested by the Cruz-Coke findings could not be tested.

THE NATURE OF THE GENETIC TRANSMISSION OF ALCOHOLISM

The type of genetic transmission in some kinds of alcoholism should logically be associated with the transmission of the primary psychiatric condition: affective disorder or antisocial personality. We have no known studies looking at transmission in relatively homogeneous groups of alcoholics, e.g., primary alcoholics, etc.

Studies of alcoholics in general have produced conflicting results. Any model of alcoholic transmission should explain the marked sex difference which is a hallmark of alcoholism. One way to explain such differences in sex incidence of alcoholism is by a transmission involving a recessive gene on the X-chromosome, as for example occurs with red-green color blindness or hemophilia. The work of Cruz-Coke supports this hypothesis (see previous section).

Several of the consequences of an X-linked gene (recessive) have been pursued; some of the data support the hypothesis, and other data go against it. One consequence of an X-linked recessive gene is that the population frequency of affected females will be the square of that of affected males. Actual data fit this model well (Cruz-Coke, & Mardones, 1972). However, other testable consequences do not. Winokur (1967) reported that the number of affected sisters and brothers in alcoholic families was not consistent with that expected by an X-linked recessive hypothesis. One obvious problem in interpreting these inconsistent results is the probable heterogeneity of the alcoholic samples.

Again using data which included depressive and sociopathic alcoholics, Reich, Winokur, and Mullaney (1975) fitted mathematical models of inheritance in order to test hypotheses about the pattern of inheritance. The model fit was patterned after the multi-factoral model of Falconer. The authors concluded that the male-female difference in incidence was explainable on the basis of similar genotypes which were affected by individual, non-familial environmental sources of variation. This conclusion is obviously at variance with the X-linked recessive factor hypothesis. The authors did, however, find that within-family correlations (which include genetic transmission) accounted for a large portion of the variation in the data, with correlation for first-degree relatives in the range found for other hereditable conditions such as peptic ulcer and essential hypertension. Thus, the type of transmission in alcoholism is not clear at the present time.

WHAT IS TRANSMITTED IN ALCOHOLISM

There have been hypotheses to account for transmission in alcoholism. Specific genetic factors have been proposed for years; for example, the metabolic hypotheses of Williams, Berry, and Beerstecher (1949) and the subsequent animal work demonstrating genetically controlled taste preferences for alcohol (Whitney, 1972). To date such factors have not been demonstrated in man. However, the data reviewed in the present paper suggest the heterogeneity of alcoholism and the importance of inherited conditions such as affective disorder, antisocial personality, and possibly other personality features as important factors in alcoholism.

In depressed individuals, the depressive symptoms might lead to use of alcohol as self-medication. But there is still another possibility with depressives: Winokur and co-workers (Winokur, 1974; Winokur, Cadoret, Baker, & Doryab, 1975) have described an early onset (prior to age 40) unipolar depressive familial illness in which female family members suffer from depression but males have alcoholism or antisocial personality. This condition has been named "depressive spectrum illness" and could account for the increased affective disorder and alcoholism in certain families.

Several possibilities might account for the associattion of personality disorders with alcoholism. In the case of individuals with sociopathy, the very personality traits which predispose to antisocial behavior could also predispose to excessive drinking. As mentioned before, many earlier European investigations of alcoholics (e.g., Amark and Bleuler) have remarked upon the frequency of personality diagnoses in alcoholism. Only some of these personality disorders would come under our rubric of sociopathy or antisocial personality. Thus, we are left with a significant portion of primary alcoholics who have deviant personality traits or features. Many of these traits could have a genetic factor; there is some evidence from twin studies to suggest this for some personality features (Shields, 1973). Accordingly, we might be able to continue our present approach of carving out from the primary alcoholics additional personality disorder types associated with alcoholism (analogous to our separation of sociopathic or antisocial alcoholics). This possibility is supported from two sources. Amark (1951) compared the personality deviations of his alcoholics with a group of patients from a surgical clinic and reported the differences shown in Table 9. There is a very significant increase in psychopathy or serious personality deviations in the alcoholic probands. More detailed breakdown of the psychopathy into types revealed in the alcoholics a preponderance of traits in which anxiety and uneasiness appeared as important symptoms. Also, those types with a disposition for depressive states were more common among the alcoholics than the control group.

The second source is the study of Danish adoptees reported by Goodwin, Schulsinger, Hermanse, Guze, and Winokur, (1975). Their 14 adopted alcoholics reported higher incidences of such behaviors as childhood hyperactivity, shyness, etc.,

Table 9

Incidence of Psychopathy in Alcoholics and Controls

Personality Diagnosis	Alcoholics N=610	Surgical Patients N=85
Psychopathy	295(48.4)	7(8.2)
Deviating personality	263(43.1)	39(45.9)
Without considerable personality deviation	43(7.0)	37(43.5)
Subnormal intelligence	9(1.5)	2(2.47)

Note: data from Amark (1951)

as shown in Table 10. The important fact about these behaviors is that for many of them there is evidence of a genetic factor. Childhood hyperactivity has been reported to have a genetic etiology on the basis of an adoption study (Cunningham, Cadoret, Loftus, & Edwards, 1975) which is further supported by several family studies (Morrison & Stewart, 1971, 1973) that in turn have connected hyperactivity with alcoholism. Shyness and social insecurity have a strong genetic component as evidenced by a number of twin investigations (Shields, 1973). Other childhood temperament variables, including antisocial types of behavior, have been shown to have a genetic factor in an adoption study (Cadoret, Cunningham, Loftus, & Edwards, 1975). However, McCord, McCord, and Gudeman (1959) failed to find an association with childhood hyperactivity and later problem drinking.

Thus, it appears quite reasonable to predict that

Table 10

Significant Childhood Behavioral Differences Between Alcoholic and Non-Alcoholic Adoptees[a]

Childhood Behavior	Alcoholic N=14	Non-Alcoholic N=119
Hyperactive	50%[a]	15%
Often truant or antisocial	21%	2%
Combination of above	57%	15%
Shy, sensitive, insecure	64%	20%
Aggressive, impulsive, hot tempered	50%	18%
Often disobedient	29%	4%

Note: data from Goodwin, Schulsinger, Hermansen, Guze, and Winokur, 1975.

[a]All differences shown in table between alcoholic and non-alcoholic groups are statistically significant at the 5% level.

further study may show that alcoholism is associated with many genetically determined temperament and behavioral traits other than the antisocial. If true, this would mean clinically that some prediction of future alcohol problems could be made in childhood, and intervention attempted, since these traits might be manifested and detectable in childhood.

REFERENCES

Amark, C. A study in alcoholism: Clinical, social, psychiatric and genetic investigations. *Acta Psychiatrica Neurologica Scandinavica*, 1951, *Suppl. 70*, 1-283.

Bleuler, M. Familial and personal background of chronic alcoholics. In O. Drethelm (Ed.), *Etiology of chronic alcoholism*. Springfield, Ill.: Charles C Thomas, 1955.

Brugger, C. Psychiatrisch-genealogische untersuchungen an einer Allgauer Landbevolkerung im Gebiet eines psychiatrischen Zensus. *Zeitschrift fur die gesamte Neurologie und Psychiatrie*, 1933, *150*, 516-540.

Brugger, C. Familien untersuchungen bei chronischen Alkoholikern. *Zeitschrift fur die gesamte Neurologie und Psychiatrie*, 1934, *151*, 103-129.

Brugger, C. Untersuchungen an Kindern, Neffen, Nichten und Enkeln von chronischen Trinkern. *Zeitschrift fur die gesamte Neurologie und Psychiatrie*, 1936, *154*, 223-241.

Cadoret, R., Cummingham, L., Loftus, R., & Edwards, J. Studies of adoptees from psychiatrically disturbed biologic parents, II. Temperament, hyperactive, antisocial, and developmental variables. *Journal of Pediatrics*, 1975, *87*, 301-306.

Cadoret, R., & Winokur, G. Genetic studies of affective disorders. In F. Flach & S. Draghi (Eds.). *The nature and treatment of depression.* New York: Wiley & Sons, 1975.

Crowe, R. An adoption study of antisocial personality. *Archives of General Psychiatry*, *31*, 785-791.

Cruz-Coke, R., & Mardones, J. Evidence for genetic factors in alcoholism. In O. Forsander & K. Eriksson (Eds.), *International symposium on biological aspects of alcohol consumption, 27-29 September 1971 Helsinki* (Vol. 20). Helsinki: Finnish Foundation for Alcohol Studies, 1972.

Cruz-Coke, R., Rivera, L., Varela, A., & Mardones, J. Correlation between color vision disturbance and appetite for alcohol. *Clinical Genetics*, 1972, *3*, 404-410.

Cruz-Coke, R., & Varela, A. Inheritance of alcoholism, its association with color-blindness. *Lancet*, 1966, *2*, 1282-1284.

Cunningham, L., Cadoret, R., Loftus, R., & Edwards, J. Studies of adoptees from psychiatrically disturbed biologic parents. I. Psychiatric conditions in childhood and adolescence. *British Journal of Psychiatry*, 1975, *126*, 534-549.

Fremming, K.H. *Sygdomsrisikoen for Sindslidelser og andre sjaelelege Abnormtilstande i den danske Sennemsnitsbefolksung.* Copenhagen: Munksgaard, 1947.

Goodwin, D., Schulsinger, F., Hermansen, L., Guze, S., & Winokur, G. Alcohol problems in adoptees raised apart from alcoholic biological parents. *Archives of General Psychiatry*, 1973, *28*, 238-243.

Goodwin, D., Schulsinger, F., Hermansen, L., Guze, S., & Winokur, G. Alcoholism and the hyperactive child syndrome. *Journal of Nervous and Mental Disorders*, 1975, *160*, 349-353.

Goodwin, D., Schulsinger, F., Moller, N., Hermansen, L., Winokur, G., & Guze, S. Drinking problems in adopted and non-adopted sons of alcoholics. *Archives of General Psychiatry*, 1974, *31*, 164-169.

Hill, S., Goodwin, D., Cadoret, R., Osterland, C., & Doner, S. Association and linkage between alcoholism and eleven serological markers. *Journal of Studies on Alcohol*, 1975, *36*, 981-992.

Hutchings, B., & Mednick, S. Registered criminality in the adoptive and biological parents of registered male adoptees. In S. Mednick, F. Schulsinger, J. Higgins, & B. Bell (Eds.), *Genetics environment and psychopathology*. Amsterdam: North-Holland Publishing Co., 1974.

Kaij, L. *Alcoholism in twins: Studies on the etiology and sequels of abuse of alcohol*. Stockholm: Almquist & Wiksell, 1960.

Li, C. *Human genetics - principles and methods*. New York: McGraw Hill, 1961.

Luxenburger, H. Demographische und psychiatrische Untersuchungen in der engeren biologischen Familie von Paralytikerehegatten. *Zeitschrift fur die gesamte Neurologie und Psychiatrie*, 1928, *112*, 331-491.

McCord, W., McCord, J., & Gudeman, J. Some current theories of alcoholism: A longitudinal evaluation. *Quarterly Journal of Studies on Alcohol*, 1959, *20*, 717-749.

Morrison, J., & Stewart, M. A family study of the hyperactive child syndrome. *Biological Psychiatry*, 1971, *3*, 189-195.

Morrison, J., & Stewart, M. The psychiatric status of the legal families of adopted hyperactive children. *Archives of General Psychiatry*, 1973, *28*, 888-891.

Partanen, J., Bruun, K., & Markkanen, T. *Inheritance of drinking behavior. A study on intelligence, personality, and use of alcohol in adult twins* (Vol. 14). Helsinki: The Finnish Foundation for Alcohol Studies, 1966.

Pitts, F.N., Jr., & Winokur, G. Affective disorder - VII: Alcoholism and affective disorder. *Journal of Psychiatric Research*, 1966, *4*, 37-50.

Pohlisch, K. *Social und Persönliche Bedingungen des chronischen Alkoholismus.* Leipzig: Georg Thieme Verlag, 1933.

Reich. T., Winokur, G., & Mullaney, J. The transmission of alcoholism. In R. Fieve, D. Rosenthal, & H. Brill (Eds.), *Genetic research in psychiatry*. Baltimore: Johns Hopkins University Press, 1975.

Rimmer, J., & Winokur, G. The spouses of alcoholics: An example of assortative mating. *Diseases of the Nervous System*, 1972, *32*, 509-511.

Roe, A. The adult adjustment of children of alcoholic parents raised in foster homes. *Quarterly Journal of Studies on Alcohol*, 1945, *5*, 378-393.

Schneider, K. Die psychopathischen personlichkeiten. In G. Aschaffenburg (Ed.). *Handbook der psychiatrie*(Vol. 7:1, 5th ed.). Vienna: F. Deuticke, 1940.

Schuckit, M., Goodwin, D., & Winokur, G. A study of alcoholism in half siblings. *American Journal of Psychiatry,* 1972, *128*, 122-216.

Schuckit, M., Rimmer, J., Reich, T., & Winokur, G. Alcoholism: Antisocial traits in male alcoholics. *British Journal of Psychiatry*, 1970, *117*, 575-576.

Schulsinger, F. Psychopathy: Heredity and environment. *International Journal of Mental Health*, 1972, *1*, 190-206.

Shields, J. Heredity and psychological abnormality. In H. Eysenck (Ed.), *Handbook of abnormal psychology*(2nd ed.). London: Pitman, 1973.

Slater, E. The incidence of mental disorder. *Annals of Eugenics*, 1935, *6*, 172.

Varela, A., Rivera, L., Mardones, J., & Cruz-Coke, R. Color vision defects in non-alcoholic relatives of alcoholic patients. *British Journal of Addictions*, 1969, *64*, 67-73.

Whitney, G. Relationships between alcohol preference and other behaviors in laboratory mice. In O. Forsander & K. Eriksson (Eds.), *International symposium on biological aspects of alcohol consumption, 27-29 September 1971, Helsinki* (Vol. 20). Helsinki: Finnish Foundation for Alcohol Studies, 1972.

Williams, R., Berry, L., & Beerstecher, E.,Jr. *Proceedings of the National Academy of Science*, 1949, *35*, 265-271.

Winokur, G. X-borne recessive genes in alcoholism. In *Lancet*(Letters to Editor), 26 August 1967.

Winokur, G. The division of depressive illness into depression spectrum disease and pure depressive disease. *International Pharmaco-psychiatry*, 1974, *9*, 5-13.

Winokur, G., Cadoret, R., Baker, M., & Doryab, J. Depression spectrum disease versus pure depressive disease: Some further data. *British Journal of Psychiatry*, 1975, *127*, 75-77.

Winokur, G., & Pitts, F.N.,Jr. Affective disorder: VI. A family history study of prevalences, sex differences, and possible genetic factors. *Journal of Psychiatric Research*, 1965, *3*, 113-123.

Winokur, G., Reich, T., Rimmer, J., & Pitts, R.N.,Jr. Alcoholism: III. Diagnosis and familial psychiatric illness in 259 alcoholic probands. *Archives of General Psychiatry*, 1970, *23*, 104-111.

Winokur, G., Rimmer, J., & Reich, T. Alcoholism IV: Is there more than one type of alcoholism? *British Journal of Psychiatry*, 1971, *118*, 525-531.

CHAPTER 8

SLEEP DISTURBANCES IN ALCOHOLISM

Milton M. Gross
John M. Hastey

OVERVIEW. Sleep disturbances are probably among the most frequently occurring symptoms associated with alcoholism. Insomnia is the most common of these complaints. Severe insomnia, for example, was reported as a current symptom in approximately one third of a sample of almost 300 alcoholic males applying to an outpatient clinic in New York City (Baekeland, Lundwall, Shanahan, & Kissin, 1974). A similar incidence of insomnia was reported in samples of alcoholics in Germany (Feuerlein, 1974).

This suggests that among alcoholics across nations and cultures there may be a particular subgroup prone to suffering from insomnia, or, alternatively, that at any one time some percentage of these patients tends to be experiencing

Ralph E. Tarter and A. Arthur Sugerman (eds.), Alcoholism

ISBN: 0-201-08146-6
ISBN: 0-201-08145-8 (pbk.)

insomnia. Direct observations, during experimental prolonged heavy drinking and withdrawal, would tend to support the latter possibility; the clinical findings were consistent with the experimental findings. Thus, insomnia is likely to occur in most alcoholics during the course of their illness, with variations over time in the frequency and severity of this symptom. Non-alcohol related etiologies of insomnia may also contribute to the incidence and severity. We may conclude that insomnia is widespread among alcoholics and that its management is an important aspect of the treatment of these patients.

Wider possible implications are suggested by the paradoxical statement in the preceding paragraph, that the use of alcohol appears to contribute to insomnia. Alcohol is a central nervous system depressant and as such, should tend to increase the amount of sleep. Is the paradoxical decrease of sleep an effect of alcohol, or is it limited only to the effect of alcohol on alcoholics? It seems most likely that the insomnia is not specific for the alcoholics but probably occurs most frequently among them. Even if the incidence and characteristics of alcohol-related insomnia in the general populations of the countries with high per capita alcohol intake were found primarily among alcoholics, it would still probably be one of the most common causes of sleep disturbances among the adult men of the high alcohol consumption nations. This indicates the value of considering the possibility of an alcohol-related etiology in the general differential diagnosis of insomnia.

Insomnia is not the only clinical sleep disturbance associated with alcoholism. Others have been described, though less frequently. These include disruptions of the sleep-wake cycle, hypersomnia (prolonged sleep), sleep talking, and organized motor phenomena related to sleep walking which may be designated as "somnokineses." Finally, there is that clinical phenomenon which is particularly fascinating, the occasion where the dream during sleep appears to continue uninterrupted into a waking hallucinatory and illusionary delirium.

Advances in the general area of sleep psychophysiology have been applied to studies of sleep disturbances among alcoholics. They have contributed substantially to a deeper understanding of these clinical disturbances. They have also revealed disturbances which are not clinically observable but which may be identified on the basis of the deviation from normal of the rhythmicity, or of the composition, or both, of the sleep electroencephalogram (EEG).

COMPOSITION AND RHYTHMS OF SLEEP IN THE ADULT. It was more than 20 years ago that a new era in the scientific study of sleep was ushered in by the findings of Aserinsky and Kleitman (1953). They identified a recurring activity during sleep in which concomitantly there were low voltage, predominantly fast EEG activity, conjugate rapid eye movements, and dreaming. This was followed by another landmark report by Dement and Kleitman (1957) which delineated the stages and rhythms of sleep. Since than an extensive international research effort has sought to determine the nature of sleep in normal and pathological states. Before examining the alcohol-related sleep disturbances, a brief discussion of the psychophysiology of sleep is necessary. A number of comprehensive reviews are available (Jouvet, 1972; Moruzzi, 1972;

Weitzman, 1974; Williams, Karacan, & Hursch, 1974).

Sleep composition. The staging of sleep is delineated on the basis of EEG criteria, which for the differentiation of stages 1 and REM also involves electroculographic (EOG) and electromyographic (EMG) criteria (Rechtschaffen & Kales, 1968). Stage 1 is characterized by low voltage, predominantly high frequency EEG activity without conjugate rapid eye movements, sleep spindles, or K-complexes; stage 2 is characterized by bursts of sleep spindles (13-16 Hz) and K complexes in the EEG which tends otherwise to be similar to stage 1; stages 3 and 4 are characterized by the presence of large quantities of slow, high voltage, delta waves (0-2 Hz and greater than 75 microvolts) in which 20%-49% slow wave sleep is stage 3, and 50% or more is stage 4: REM is characterized by essentially the same EEG as stage 1, combined with intermittent bursts of rapid conjugate eye movements and a marked reduction of muscle tonus.[1]

---

[1]The designation for stage REM has changed over the years and may be a source of confusion when reading the literature. An early designation was "stage 1 REM." In conjunction with that usage, "REM" was at times used to refer only to the conjugate rapid eye movements per se regardless of whether or not it was during sleep when they occur as part of "stage 1 REM," or during wakefulness, when they are the eye movements which characterize normal visual scanning behavior (viz. Gross, Goodenough, Tobin, Halpert, Lepore, Perstein, Sirota, Dibianco, Fuller, & Kishner, 1966). Readers are also likely to be confused by the use of multiple designations in current usage as may be noted in an excellent recent multiple-authored review volume (Weitzman, 1974) where the terms "REM sleep," "Stage REM sleep," "Stage REM," "Paradoxical sleep," "active sleep," "D (REM) Sleep," "D sleep," "desynchronized sleep (D)" appear along with the simultaneous use of "REM" to also refer to the rapid conjugate eye movements only. In this chapter, "REM" will be used for the sleep stage and "rapid conjugate eye movements" will be used for the eye movements.

The various rhythmic EEG sleep stages tend to be associated with concomitant rhythmic patterns of physiological, neurophysiological, neurochemical, neuroendocrine, and psychological activity. It was on this basis that it was inferred that the EEG sleep stages may reflect complex states of central nervous system function. This concept of the stages of sleep as complex multidimensional states of central nervous system and organismic function has been applied most often to REM where the terms REM state and D state are used. The degree and consistency of the concomitance appears to be less fixed than was assumed earlier (see Kripke, 1974 for review).

In examining the effects of alcohol on the composition of sleep, particular emphasis will be given to REM, and stages 3 and 4 (both of which are collectively referred to as a slow wave sleep (SWS)). Unlike stages 1 and 2, after REM or SWS are selectively prevented or suppressed, or generally prevented by total sleep deprivation, there is a tendency for REM as well as SWS to demonstrate a subsequent compensatory "rebound," i.e., to be present in quantities exceeding the pre-deprivation levels (in the normal adult usually 20%-25% of total sleep time for each).

Sleep rhythmicity. Many of the psychobiological activities associated with sleep have a periodicity regulated by biological clocks. Those activities which have 24-hour cycles are referred to as having circadian rhythms; those periodic activities with shorter cycles are ultradian rhythms. The cyclic alternation of sleep and wakefulness in the normal adult is a circadian rhythm. During sleep there tends to be a recurring succession of stages 1 and 2, SWS and REM with ultradian cycles of approximately 90 minutes; data suggest that the ultradian rhythms of the specific sleep stages may be time-locked to specific neuroendocrine activities such as SWS and growth hormone secretion (Parker, Sassin, Mace, Gotlin, & Rossman, 1969; Quabbe, Helge, & Kubicki, 1971; Quabbe, Schilling, & Helge, 1966), REM and luteinizing hormone secretion (Boyar, Perlow, Hellman, Kapen, & Weitzman, 1972; Rubin, Kales, & Adler, 1972), and REM and suppression of ADH secretion (Mandell, Mandell, Rubin, Brill, Rodnick, Sheff, & Chaffey, 1966). (For further discussion see Kripke, 1974).

An interaction exists between the ultradian and circadian rhythms. Napping during the latter part of the day and the sleep of the first half of the night demonstrate an increased tendency for SWS, while the sleep of the second half of the night and napping during the early part of the day demonstrate an increased tendency for REM. Thus, during the first half of the night, periods of SWS are long and periods of REM are short, while in the second half of the night this is reversed; napping during the early part of the day tends to consist predominately of REM, while in the latter part of the day naps tend to be predominately SWS. This would suggest a circadian rhythm of SWS predisposition alternating with REM predisposition, each of which relates to adjacent segments of both the sleep and wake cycle. This indication of a continuity between sleep and wakefulness suggests that alterations of sleep EEG composition may at times reflect general changes of central nervous system functioning rather than changes limited only to the time of sleep. This is demonstrable normally for SWS where the delta waves (which when of sufficient amplitude characterize SWS) are detectable around the clock, but vary in prevalence and amplitude in relation to the circadian and ultradian rhythms of SWS.

Operational Considerations. The consideration of sleep in terms of its composition and rhythms is to a certain extent artificial since changes in one are likely to be related to changes in the other. It is, nevertheless, often heuristically useful to treat the composition and rhythmicity separately. The usefulness is further enhanced by the fact that the precise interrelationships between the two remain to be established.

However, several interrelationships have been demonstrated which are relevant to the examination of alcohol-related sleep disturbances. One such interrelationship has been observed in studies of REM. When REM has been suppressed, one may subsequently observe either no evidence of compensatory activity or several compensatory REM phenomena either singly or in combination with the others. These compensatory phenomena include: rebound increases of % REM; decreases in REM onset latency (in which REM may first occur at sleep onset or shortly thereafter instead of approximately 90 minutes after sleep onset); and an increase in the number of eye movements during REM. The change in REM latency clearly involves an alteration of the ultradian rhythm of sleep which, nevertheless, implies an underlying "moreness" of REM even if it is not necessarily associated with an increase in % REM.

SLEEP DISTURBANCES

Sleep disturbances have been consistently recognized and reported as prominent features of the alcohol withdrawal syndrome (which includes impending delirium tremens, acute alcoholic hallucinosis, and delirium tremens). For example, the earliest description of delirium tremens, by Lettsom (1787), stated, "if these horrors seize him in bed, when waking from slumber he springs up like an elastic body." Pearson (1813) noted that the onset of delirium tremens "is preceded by tremors of the hands, restlessness, irregularity of thought, anxiety to be in company, dreadful nocturnal dreams." Restoration of sleep has often been and continues to be an important criterion for assessing the treatment of and recovery from the withdrawal syndrome.

It is noteworthy that far less has been reported about the sleep disturbances among alcoholics outside of the periods immediately adjacent to, and during the florid withdrawal syndrome. There is considerable recent evidence which indicates that this neglect has been unjustified. How then might we account for this neglect? Perhaps the complaints of sleep disturbances, particularly insomnia, in the absence of blatant withdrawal, were considered a non-alcohol related psychological symptom of anxiety or depression or of an addictive personality clamoring for pills for sleep. The widespread occurrence of the withdrawal syndrome among alcoholics was probably markedly underestimated as a result of the failure to sufficiently recognize that the withdrawal syndrome existed on a continuum extending from very mild to very severe, and consequently a tendency to overlook the milder degrees of withdrawal. Furthermore the importance of partial withdrawal was not sufficiently appreciated. The propensity for an early onset and a progressive increase of the partial withdrawal syndrome on consecutive drinking days (with falling blood alcohol concentrations) was not recognized.

These more subtle clinical characteristics of the partial withdrawal syndrome have emerged with gradually increasing clarity in a series of studies over a period of more than 20 years (Begleiter, Gross, & Porjesz, 1973; Gross, Goodenough, Hastey, Rosenblatt, & Lewis, 1971; Gross & Lewis, 1973; Gross, Lewis, Best, Young, & Feuer, 1975; Gross, Lewis & Hastey, 1974; Isbell, Fraser, Wikler, Belleville, & Eisenman, 1955; Mello, 1972; Mello & Mendelson, 1970; Mendelson & coworkers, 1964; Victor & Adams, 1953). It is now clear that signs and symptoms of withdrawal, including sleep disturbances, may occur during non-drinking intervals (such as sleep) of drinking days. There is, thus, a continuity of the withdrawal disturbances extending from the drinking period into the subsequent period of abstinence. Finally, the duration of the alcohol withdrawal syndrome has probably been underestimated since recent sleep EEG studies suggest that a subacute, mild withdrawal syndrome may persist after the onset of abstinence for periods varying from days to months. Embedded in this more broadly identified withdrawal syndrome is a series of clinically and instrumentally detectable sleep disturbances.

SOME GENERAL COMMENTS ON ALCOHOL-RELATED EFFECTS ON SLEEP. Several considerations tend to apply broadly to the effects of alcohol and alcohol withdrawal on sleep. In relation to sleep, we are dealing with effects of alcohol upon the central nervous system. In these effects, a key factor, perhaps even the primary one, is the blood alcohol concentration. The effects of the alcohol will vary with the concentrations attained and the degree to which the concentrations are sustained (i.e., for how many consecutive days). These blood alcohol concentration (BAC) effects will vary between individuals as a result of a number of factors, some of which have been identified, such as differences in the level of functional tolerance and other residual effects of previous drinking. Furthermore, evidence suggests that the central nervous system actions of alcohol are not all continuous, so that lower BACs may have effects which are opposite to those of higher BACs. For example, lower BACs may tend to "normalize" some disturbances while the higher BACs may tend to intensify such disturbances. In addition, at the higher BACs there may be yet other discontinuities of alcohol effects in which increasing levels and durations of BACs may produce not only an increasing severity of certain disturbances but may also result in producing a hierarchical sequence of different disturbances.

At relatively low BACs, alcohol is a CNS stimulant. Beyond that alcohol is a CNS depressant related to the barbiturates, opiates, and anesthetics. In many of its actions as a CNS depressant, alcohol tends to be biphasic, i.e., when the BAC falls and after it reaches zero, the functions which had been effected by alcohol tend to shift in the opposite direction beyond the return to the pre-alcohol level of function. The likelihood and magnitude of the "overshoot" increases or decreases depending in part upon whether the rate of fall of the BAC is abrupt or gradual, respectively.

DISTURBANCES OF CIRCADIAN RHYTHMICITY. The most readily apparent alcohol-related sleep disturbances are the clinically observable disruptions of the circadian sleep-wake cycle. These consist of hypersomnia, insomnia, and circadian instability (periods asleep and periods awake occur during both day and night). All of the circadian disturbances of sleep occur in degrees of severity.

Hypersomnias. Three types of hypersomnia have been observed in alcoholics, two associated with the epoch of alcohol intake, while the third is associated with the abstinence-withdrawal phase. The first and most common type is the expression of the pharmacologic action of alcohol as a CNS depressant. Thus, one would anticipate that the effect of alcohol would tend to be increased durations of sleep and that withdrawal would tend to be associated with decreased amounts of sleep, i.e., intoxication hypersomnia followed by withdrawal insomnia.

Three series of experimental studies involving prolonged heavy alcohol intake in human volunteers shed light on the intake hypersomnia. Isbell et al., (1955) studied the effects of scheduled, regulated, and increasing doses of alcohol under conditions of self-regulated times of sleep, and observed hypersomnia during the alcohol intake phase. Mello and Mendelson (1970) studied the effects of self-regulated times and quantities (with a fixed maximum) of alcohol intake and self-regulated times of sleep, and observed hypersomnia during the intake phase. Gross, Goodenough, Hastey, and Lewis (1973), Gross, Goodenough, Nagarajan, and Hastey (1973), and Gross and Lewis (1973) studied the effects of scheduled fixed dosage of alcohol intake and scheduled times of sleep, and observed a paradoxical group trend of moderate progressive reduction of sleep during the intake phase. Had the alcoholics, studied in our laboratory, demonstrated insomnia during baseline conditions, it might have been possible to examine the matter of alcohol-induced hypersomnia in our studies which, unlike the other two, involved scheduled times of sleep only. This was not the case, and our data do not permit any conclusions to be drawn regarding alcohol intake hypersomnia. Therefore our data in no way contradict the very clear experimental findings of Isbell et al. (1955) and Mello and Mendelson (1970) as well as a great body of pharmacological and clinical data demonstrating that heavy alcohol intake induces hypersomnia. Lester, Rundell, Cowden, and Williams (1973), in a study of the effects of regulated moderate amounts of alcohol for two consecutive days in alcoholics under conditions of scheduled sleep with EEG monitoring, observed a moderate increase of sleep time. It is noteworthy that the two sets of findings with scheduled sleep and EEG monitoring, those of Lester et al. (1973), and our own, reported trends in opposite directions regarding effects of alcohol on sleep time. One of the factors involved was probably the difference in blood alcohol concentrations resulting from moderate vs. heavy alcohol intake in the two alcoholic samples. Where moderate concentrations tended to "normalize" the sleep characteristics, the high concentrations did not demonstrate this. Another source of the difference was probably in the sampling of the participants. The group studied by Lester et al. (1973) were different in a number of ways, of which their being older may well have been the most critical. Finally, the difference in the number of days of exposure to the alcohol was probably also important.

The second type of hypersomnia during the epoch of

alcohol intake was observed in alcoholics by Mello and Mendelson (1970) during those 1-2 day intervals during the course of drinking, which were preceded and followed by days of drinking, when patients were permitted to ingest alcohol but did not. They noted that such interruptions during extended periods of self-regulated alcohol intake tended to be a self-imposed interval of abstinence or reduced intake between recurring cycles of 6-8 days of alcohol intake. It was on such days of abstinence between cycles of drinking that patients occasionally slept for most of the 24 hours and then resumed drinking. This intake cyclicity has also been observed in self-regulatory alcohol intake studies in primates (Woods & Winger, 1971) and rats (Goldstein, private communication). The nature of this intermittent brief-abstinence hypersomnia of the drinking period is undetermined.

The third type of hypersomnia has been observed during the epoch of withdrawal. This is the terminal sleep which occurs in some of the patients some of the time. It has been described as a period of prolonged, restful, deep sleep, following which the patient awakens markedly improved. On one occasion when it was observed with sleep EEG monitoring, the striking features were prolonged sleep (approximately 14 hours) and an abundance of slow wave sleep (48%) in contrast to alcohol coma where slow wave sleep is essentially absent (Gross & Goodenough, 1968). During sleep, the patient seldom moved and appeared extremely relaxed, in contrast to the flaccidity of alcohol coma. The patient also had a zero BAC prior to sleep, which was the most obvious contrast to alcohol coma. Whether what was observed in this instance characterizes terminal sleep, and what relationship if any exists between this phenomenon and the intermittent brief-abstinence hypersomnia of the drinking phase, remain to be established.

Insomnias. The alcohol-related insomnias are probably most often withdrawal insomnias. These withdrawal insomnias may occur on days of alcohol intake at times of receding BACs such as are most likely to occur during sleep. Thus, during an episode of prolonged alcohol intake, both the hypersomnias and insomnias may occur. The pattern of hypersomnia vs. insomnia during such an alcohol intake phase is likely to be related to the levels and patterns of the BACs.

The same design constraints which made our data non-applicable to examining the hypersomnia effects of alcohol intake, also made the same data optimal for examining the insomnia of partial withdrawal during the alcohol intake phase. Alcohol administration was limited to 1400 to 2400 hours and sleep was limited to 2400 to 0600 hours. The early part of the night usually coincided with the highest BACs. There was thus a relative concordance and reinforcement of the BACs and the circadian regulatory mechanism of sleep onset. As the days of drinking continued, there was a gradual tendency for increased awakenings and progressive sleep reduction under these conditions (Gross, Goodenough, Hastey, & Lewis, 1973; Gross, Goodenough, Nagarajan, & Hastey, 1973; Gross & Lewis, 1973. The design constraints of Isbell et al. (1955) do not allow for conclusions to be drawn about the relationship between insomnia and partial withdrawal since they used progressively increasing doses of alcohol. The findings of Mello and Mendelson (1970) are difficult to interpret in this connection. The method which they employed for behaviorally determining the amount of sleep, a nurse's observation of the patient in his private room once/hour, would be very likely to miss the multiple brief awakenings from sleep which characterize the insomnia of partial withdrawal. It is nevertheless of interest to note that in their data, during the alcohol intake phase there was a shift in the range of daily hours of sleep which not only included an increase at the upper end (which one would expect with the hypersomnia of intake) but also a decrease at the lower end which would suggest intermittent hyposomnia. However, the data presented do not permit any conclusions to be drawn regarding the possible relationship of the sleep reductions to partial withdrawal.

To complicate matters further, there are also two insomnias associated with alcohol intoxication during phases of alcohol intake. The first and probably more common form appears to be a high BAC phenomenon associated with considerable agitation. In contrast to the insomnia of partial withdrawal, it appears to be more likely to occur during the early part of the night and the first few days of heavy drinking. The nature of this insomnia is unclear.

A second, less frequently observed and etiologically different form of sleep reduction associated with epochs of alcohol intake, is related to acute somatic distress of various sorts associated with the toxic effects of the alcohol. It also tends to be a sleep onset insomnia.

The most frequent occurrence and greatest severity of insomnia tend to occur as manifestations of the abstinence withdrawal syndrome. As previously noted, this has been repeatedly observed since the eighteenth century. This was reaffirmed clinically by Victor and Adams (1953). It was also apparent in the experimental studies of Isbell et al. (1955) and Mendelson and coworkers (1964), where behavioral but not EEG sleep measurements were used. A striking relationship was noted between the severity of insomnia and the severity of withdrawal in the data of Isbell et al. (1955). A similar relationship was observed in the EEG monitored sleep of patients entering hospital in alcohol withdrawal (Gross et al., 1966; Gross & Goodenough, 1968; Laverty, 1973). Mello and Mendelson (1970) frequently used medication during the withdrawal period in their patients, and these data therefore do not permit any conclusions to be drawn regarding insomnia during alcohol abstinence and withdrawal. With EEG monitoring of sleep, both under the experimental conditions of brief moderate regulated alcohol intake and scheduled sleep (Lester et al., 1973) and prolonged heavy regulated scheduled alcohol intake and scheduled sleep (Gross, Goodenough, Hastey, & Lewis, 1973; Gross, Goodenough, Nagarajan, & Hastey, 1973), a reduction of sleep time was observed during the period of abstinence withdrawal.

The progressive sleep reduction during partial and abstinence withdrawal, which we frequently observed, was an additive result of difficulty staying asleep, difficulty returning to sleep following an awakening, and then difficulty falling asleep at sleep onset. In the experimental situation, during the abstinence withdrawal, participants anticipating or experiencing the greater degrees of withdrawal occasionally expressed a fear of going to sleep because they feared the possibility of severe nightmares or delirium when emerging from sleep.

In the clinical situation patients have reported similar responses when they had no access to alcohol during the night or found that the alcohol no longer counteracted the tendency toward nightmares and delirium. (Since partial withdrawal tends to increase progressively on the succession of drinking days it can attain major magnitudes of severity even without abstinence). However, a much more frequent complaint during withdrawal is the fear of not sleeping which at times is of such magnitude as to merit being designated insomnophobia. Such patients react as though their lives were jeopardized by the insomnia, and they clamor for medication. At home they describe attempting to deal with the insomnia either through particularly heavy intake of alcohol at bedtime, the use of medication, or the dangerous combination of alcohol and medication. This insomnophobia may frequently be observed in patients during the first few nights of hospitalization for treatment of withdrawal.

Total sleeplessness, confirmed by EEG monitoring, is not uncommon as a manifestation of severe withdrawal (Gross et al., 1966; Gross & Goodenough, 1968; Laverty, 1973).

Mello and Mendelson (1970) have suggested that the sleep reduction of the withdrawal may be secondary to anxiety which is increased as a manifestation of withdrawal. While withdrawal anxiety may very well contribute to the insomnia, there are also likely to be primary direct sources of the insomnia in the profound alcohol-related disturbances of the sleep mechanisms which may occur. Such sleep disturbances are likely to increase anxiety so that the relationship between anxiety and sleep disturbances during withdrawal probably involves a flow in both directions.

In a large clinical sample of almost 300 patients at the time of their application to an alcohol clinic, approximately one third complained of severe insomnia. The evidence pointed to a central role of withdrawal in these insomnias since the severe sleep disturbances were positively correlated with previous histories of hospitalization for treatment of severe withdrawal, current or recent drinking, quantity of current drinking, anxiety, and depression (Baekeland et al., 1974).

Circadian instability. The final alcohol-related circadian disturbance is circadian instability which Mello and Mendelson (1970) aptly described as "fragmentation." During heavy alcohol intake they noted that there tended to be shorter though more numerous episodes of sleep which were also less likely to be confined to the usual hours of sleep. Thus there was a decreasing tendency for intervals of sleep to occur by night and an increasing tendency for intervals of sleep to occur by day. Presumably, the fluctuating levels of BAC interacted with and disrupted the normal intrinsic circadian sleep regulatory mechanisms. They also observed similar circadian sleep instability during the abstinence withdrawal.

There are indications that there may be prolonged circadian instability. Lester et al. (1973) observed a much greater number of brief awakenings in alcoholics who were dry and medication-free for three weeks than in a matched normal group. Also, clinical observations suggest that there may be a propensity for daytime naps among alcoholics for several weeks after withdrawal. However, napping among dry alcoholics has not been systematically studied. In any case, the increased number of awakenings suggest a prolonged alcohol withdrawal effect upon the stability of the circadian sleep-wake cycle.

DISTURBANCES OF ULTRADIAN RHYTHMICITY AND SLEEP COMPOSITION. Unlike the direct clinical observability of the disturbances of the circadian sleep rhythms, the alcohol-related disturbances of the ultradian rhythms and of the composition of sleep are observed in the laboratory. These laboratory studies of sleep afford an opportunity to track the multisynaptic CNS changes reflected in the sleep EEG during alcohol intake and withdrawal and to examine the relationships between the sleep disturbances and the clinical disturbances. In this way we may come to discern some of the mechanisms underlying the clinical disturbances, sleepwise and otherwise, of the alcoholic. In examining these findings it becomes evident that the sleep disturbances not only show a considerable range of magnitude but also a considerable range of duration. We are thus faced with how much disturbance is present, and how long the disturbance will persist. As will be seen below, some of the sleep EEG disturbances may last for months, indicating that prolonged post-ingestional neurophysiologic disturbances may at times be a consequence of prolonged intake, evidence of subacute alcohol withdrawal syndrome.

With few exceptions changes in ultradian rhythmicity are so closely linked to changes in sleep composition that the two parameters are difficult to separate. It is only the broadest view of ultradian rhythms, total number of stage changes, that can be examined outside the context of specific stages of sleep.

General disturbances of ultradian rhythmicity. In a comparison with a matched normal group, a sample of alcoholics after three weeks of abstinence showed an increased number of sleep stage changes (Lester et al., 1973). These alcoholics tended to have the greatest increase in stage changes during the withdrawal which followed two days of alcohol administration, suggesting that the baseline increase observed after three weeks of abstinence may have been residual withdrawal effects. The possible relation between withdrawal and increased stage changes was further supported by the finding that the two days of moderate alcohol intake resulted in "normalizing" the number of stage changes, i.e., decreased them to where they were more similar to the control group. Prolonged heavy alcohol intake also tended to produce a reduction of stage changes during the drinking phase and a greater increase during the withdrawal phase (Gross, Goodenough, Hastey, & Lewis, 1973; Gross, Goodenough, Nagarajan, & Hastey, 1973). The increased number of stage changes during withdrawal are a result of ultradian instability or fragmentation analogous to the circadian instability previously described.

Rapid eye movement (REM). The quantity and cyclicity of REM are affected by alcohol. The effects of alcohol are biphasic and vary in direct relation to the BACs. The effects of alcohol on REM have been studied in normals (Gresham, Webb, & Williams, 1963; Knowles, Laverty, & Kuechler, 1968; Lester et al., 1973; Rundell, Lester, Griffith, & Williams, 1972; Williams & Salamy, 1972; Yules, Freedman, & Chandler, 1966; Yules, Lippman, & Freedman, 1967) and in alcoholics (Allen & Wagman, 1975; Allen, Wagman, Faillace, & McIntosh, 1971; Greenberg & Pearlman, 1967; Gross, 1973; Gross et al., 1966; Gross et al., 1971; Gross et al., 1974; Gross & Goodenough, 1968; Gross, Goodenough, Hastey, & Lewis, 1973; Gross, Goodenough, Nagarajan, & Hastey, 1973; Gross & Hastey, 1975a; Gross, Hastey, Lewis, & Young, 1975; Johnson, 1971; Johnson, Burdick, & Smith, 1970; Laverty, 1973; Lester et al., 1973; Lester, Rundell, Cowden, & Williams, 1975; Zarcone, Barchas,

Hoddes, Montplaisir, Sack, & Wilson, 1975; Zarcone & Hoddes, 1975).

During epochs of alcohol intake, increasing BACs tended to produce increasing reductions of % REM and increased delays in the appearance of the first REM of the night. At relatively low bedtime BACs (approximately 80-100 mg/100 ml) this effect tended to be limited to the first half of the night; at intermediate bedtime BACs (approximately 150 mg/100 ml) REM was decreased and delayed throughout the night; at high bedtime BACs (approximately 200-350 mg/100 ml) REM was likely to be almost or totally absent all night.

When the BACs fell, a series of opposite effects tended to occur. After the relatively low bedtime BACs, the second half of the night (partial withdrawal) was likely to demonstrate a rebound increase in % REM. With lesser rebound, the increased % REM was likely to be due to lengthening of the individual REM periods without altering the number of these periods or the interval between them; with greater rebound the inter-REM intervals were also modified at times. When alcohol intake was maintained over several successive days, the effects on the first half of the night tended to diminish while the effects on the second half of the night tended to increase. Thus, over a period of successive nights the trend was toward a net increase in % REM during the period of drinking. In this REM pattern one can discern in the course of successive days of drinking that both functional tolerance (diminished first half of the night effect) and physical dependence and withdrawal (enhanced second half of the night effect) increased progressively.

After the intermediate bedtime BACs, when REM was diminished throughout the night, the rebound effect was often not observed until the night of the first non-drinking day. It was noted, however, that on such first nights of abstinence sometimes the % REM simply returned to normal but did not exceed it. When REM rebound did occur, it was primarily during the first half of the night with increased % REM and earlier REM onset.

After the high bedtime BACs, when alcohol was administered for a number of successive days, decreased % REM and delayed REM onset were still usually present on the first withdrawal night. As with the intermediate BACs, at times % REM rebound was not observed throughout the first week of withdrawal. Feinberg, Hibi, Cavness, and March (1974) have drawn attention to the problem of the inconstancy of REM rebound following the withdrawal of barbiturates and other CNS depressants. They emphasized the need to determine predictors of REM rebound so that we may better understand the effects of the CNS depressants, and the "extraordinarily intense REM activity (during delirium tremens) which is perhaps the most striking abnormality of brain physiology apparent in human delirium." (p.535) We have observed (Gross & Hastey, 1975a) that the group of alcoholic volunteers with total absence of REM during the entire heavy drinking period had a significant REM rebound during withdrawal while that group which had markedly reduced, but not total absence of REM during the heavy drinking phase, did not demonstrate rebound during withdrawal. All of those in the former group had REM rebound while only a minority of those in the latter group did. The BACs were significantly higher for the group with total absence of REM during drinking and REM rebound during withdrawal. Thus, the magnitude of the BACs appears to be a significant determinant of whether or not REM rebound is likely to occur.

Whether or not there was a rebound increase in % REM during withdrawal, there was likely to be a reduction of the interval between sleep onset and REM onset, and between subsequent REM periods. REM at sleep onset rather than the normal interval of approximately 90 minutes was not uncommon during the first 2-3 nights of withdrawal.

How did the REM findings in normals compare with those of the alcoholics? During baseline, Lester et al. (1973) compared a group of alcoholics (free of alcohol and psychoactive medication for three weeks) with a matched group of non-alcoholics. The alcoholics demonstrated a higher % REM (26.5% vs. 20% in the controls) and a phenomenon first described in alcoholics by Johnson et al. (1970), REM fragmentation or instability -- frequent brief interruptions of REM. Although our own data were not matched with a control group, they were consistent with those reported by Lester et al. (1973). The average % REM baseline levels observed in our alcoholic sample tended to be slightly higher than the alcoholics in the group of Lester et al. (1973) (Gross et al., 1973; Gross et al., 1974). A possible link of withdrawal and these baseline REM increases in the alcoholics was suggested by their being diminished by moderate BACs and by their tending to be most severe during acute alcohol withdrawal. In fact, very high levels of % REM (75% and 100%) have been observed during severe alcohol withdrawal in some patients entering the hospital after presumed prolonged heavy drinking (Gross et al., 1966; Johnson et al., 1970).

It should be noted that along with the previously cited increased number of awakenings and of stage changes, the increased % REM and REM fragmentation that Lester et al.

(1973) reported during the baseline of the alcoholics provide further evidence suggestive of prolonged residual alcohol withdrawal effects.

There has been considerable interest in the increased % REM during alcohol withdrawal and its relation to the hallucinations of withdrawal. Sleep studies of clinical patients who had consumed alcohol up to the time of admission indicated a tendency for hallucinations to be related to high levels of REM, with the obvious exception of those who were totally sleepless (Greenberg & Pearlman, 1967; Gross et al., 1966; Gross & Goodenough, 1968; Johnson et al., 1970). Greenberg and Pearlman suggested that during withdrawal the dream intruded into the waking state because of alcohol-induced REM rebound and created the hallucinations of the delirium. Gross and coworkers (1966) suggested that the elevated REM may contribute to hallucinogenesis but that other conditions, particularly low slow wave sleep and altered states of consciousness, were probably also necessary. Gross (1973) later suggested that increased % REM and the hallucinations may at times be parallel processes both of which were partially related to cortical sensory superexcitability and hyperactivity during withdrawal. Such a mechanism most likely might be involved in the more fragmentary and fleeting hallucinations. If increased % REM is more directly involved in hallucinogenesis during withdrawal, perhaps it might be in connection with those hallucinatory episodes which are more global in nature, especially when the hallucinations appear to emerge directly from the dream (Gross et al., 1966).

Our experimental data suggested a direct relationship between higher bedtime BACs, a greater REM reduction during the drinking period, a greater incidence of nightmares during the latter days of drinking and even more so during the early part of withdrawal, a greater likelihood of REM rebound during the first three days of withdrawal and a greater likelihood of hallucinations during withdrawal (Gross et al., 1971; Gross et al, 1974; Gross, Goodenough, Hastey, & Lewis, 1973; Gross & Hastey, 1975a; Gross & Lewis, 1973).

The experimental data of Wolin and Mello (1973) and our own data agreed insofar as they suggested a link between the development of hallucinations and prolonged exposure to high BACs (greater than 200 mg/100 ml). However, the data of Wolin and Mello appeared to show no relationship between BACs, the period of drinking or withdrawal, REM reduction during drinking, REM rebound, nightmares, or hallucinations. There does not appear to be a clear basis for explaining the difference between their findings and the clinical and experimental data previously cited. We may speculate that some basis for the differences between the findings of Wolin and Mello and of others may emanate from differences in experimental design. One factor of possible importance was their unscheduled and unregulated alcohol intake in contrast to our own design which synchronized alcohol intake to sleep. The less regulated alcoholization would tend to result in less clarity and control of the shifts between intoxication and partial withdrawal, and less clear "visibility" of these processes in the sleep EEG. This raises an important issue.

It seems plausible that on occasion the CNS changes underlying the partial or abstinence alcohol withdrawal effects may continue to take place during the day or non-sleeping periods of the night. As the sleep EEG reflects function of the brain during sleep, so too is the brain activity not observable by means of the sleep EEG "window" when it occurs outside of sleep. The CNS effects of alcohol or alcohol withdrawal do not wait for sleep. If, during experimental alcoholization, the alcohol intake and sleep are synchronized, we may be more likely to view the effects as they are reflected by sleep. With diminished synchronization of alcohol intake and sleep, the sleep EEG is less likely to provide an informative "window." Furthermore, there is no equally precise way to regulate the rate at which the withdrawal develops so as to assure its coincidence with the time of sleep. The failure to observe a withdrawal effect, such as REM rebound, does not establish that changes did not take place in those mechanisms which regulate sleep since, as was noted earlier in the comments on napping, certain of those mechanisms appear to have some continuity from the sleeping to the non-sleeping state. This currently unresolvable issue is an exceedingly important one since it also relates to the question of how close to the nature intoxication and withdrawal are the reflections observed in the sleep EEG changes. Are the sleep changes a bit of sea spray from a wave washing over a shore after a distant splash of sufficient magnitude and under certain conditions of wind and tide? Or, are the sleep changes more like the height of the waves or tides or the velocity of the winds from which we can examine the nature of a storm, albeit measurable only at limited times of the day?

Two final aspects of the REM disturbances of alcohol withdrawal are of interest. Both are phenomena which have been observed rarely, and then only in conjunction with very high levels of REM (Gross et al., 1966). The first was designated as a "REM storm" and consisted of extremely frequent rapid eye movements over an extended period of time, which was associated with marked salivation and diaphoresis.

The second involved organized motor activities which were purposively related to dream content during a REM period. This was fully established by the sleep talking which also occurred during this episode. The activities involved cupping both hands around the penis and raising the cupped hands to the mouth as though they contained a vessel with liquid in it, which the patient then appeared to drink. The activities appeared related to sleep walking and were designated "somnokineses." They were preceded for several minutes by a progression of movements in both upper extremities which were initially distal and small and gradually became more expansive and involved increasingly proximal muscular components as well. In non-alcoholics sleep talking and sleep walking have been found to occur most often in non-REM (see Williams et al., 1974 for review). We know nothing of the relation between these phenomena and the sleep stages in the non-delirious alcoholic.

Each of these phenomena have been reported only on one occasion. Their mechanism is unknown as is the frequency of their occurrence in "nature."

Slow wave sleep (SWS). The quantity and cyclicity of SWS are affected by alcohol. The effects of alcohol are biphasic and vary in direct relation to the BACs. These effects have been studied in normals (Knowles et al., 1968; Lester et al., 1973; Rundell et al., 1972; Williams & Salamy, 1972; Yules et al., 1966; Yules et al., 1967) and in alcoholics (Adamson & Burdick, 1973; Allen et al., 1971; Gross et al., 1966; Gross et al., 1971; Gross et al., 1974; Gross & Goodenough, 1968; Gross, Goodenough, Hastey, & Lewis, 1973; Gross, Goodenough, Nagarajan, & Hastey, 1973; Gross & Hastey, 1975b;

Gross, Hastey, Lewis, & Young, 1975; Johnson, 1971; Johnson et al., 1970; Lester et al., 1973; Lester et al., 1975; Wagman & Allen, 1975; Zarcone, Barchas, Hoddes, Montplaisir, Sack, & Wilson, 1975).

During epochs of alcohol intake, increasing BACs tended to produce increasing elevations of the % SWS, earlier onset of SWS, more prolonged SWS periods, and increasing SWS activity during the second half of the night. The SWS appeared to be less affected than REM by low BACs since at low bedtime concentrations significant reduction of % REM could be demonstrated without changes of % SWS. The effects of alcohol resulting in increased SWS tended to be observed at the intermediate and high bedtime BACs. At high bedtime BACs the % SWS even occasionally approached 100% of total sleep time, particularly during the first few nights of alcoholization. When the intermediate and high bedtime BACs were prolonged for several consecutive days, the % SWS gradually tended to decrease.

The reduction of % SWS during the drinking epoch appeared related to the progressive increase of both functional tolerance and partial withdrawal. The relation between the rising and falling of the % SWS during the alcohol intake epoch and intoxication and partial withdrawal respectively, was consistent with concomitant clinical observations (Gross et al., 1971, Gross & Best, 1975; Gross, Hastey, Lewis, & Young, 1975).

During the epoch of abstinence withdrawal, the % SWS tended to be reduced. Compared to baseline and drinking, the quantities of SWS tended to be lowest during the first few days of abstinence. This was particularly true following those drinking epochs characterized by high bedtime BACs.

The % SWS tended to recover more slowly than the REM. Furthermore, SWS "rebound" appeared to be less frequent than REM "rebound." Evidence compatible with SWS "rebound" has thus far been observed only in alcoholics after inferred prolonged heavy drinking. The possibility that SWS rebound may occur during abstinence was suggested by the elevated levels of % SWS observed during terminal sleep (Gross & Goodenough, 1968) and after several weeks of abstinence (Gross, Hastey, Lewis, & Young, 1975).

How does SWS in the "dry" alcoholic compare to the normal. Under conditions of abstinence, i.e., baseline and beyond the first week of post-drinking abstinence, the alcoholics have most frequently been observed to have reduced quantities of SWS. The evidence suggests that this is a withdrawal effect. The shorter the period of abstinence, the lower the amount of baseline % SWS which tended to be observed in the alcoholic (Allen et al., 1971; Gross et al., 1971; Gross et al., 1974; Gross, Goodenough, Hastey, & Lewis, 1973; Lester et al., 1973). Recovery of SWS may occur in as quickly as several days but more usually takes weeks to months and even years of abstinence (Adamson & Burdick, 1973; Allen et al., 1971; Gross et al., 1971; Gross, et al., 1974; Gross & Goodenough, 1968; Gross, Goodenough, Hastey, & Lewis, 1973; Gross, Goodenough, Nagarajan, & Hastey, 1973; Gross & Hastey, 1975b, Gross, Hastey, Lewis, & Young, 1975; Johnson, 1971; Johnson et al., 1970; Lester et al., 1973; Lester et al., 1975; Wagman & Allen, 1975).

Thus, in addition to the evidence previously cited of increased numbers of awakenings, increased numbers of sleep stage changes, increased % REM, and REM fragmentation or instability, prolonged reductions of % SWS are also indications of prolonged withdrawal effects. Lester et al. (1975) recently reported that the reduction of % SWS appears to represent a decrease in the amplitude of the 0-3 Hz activity to below the 100 uV SWS criterion level, rather than a reduction of the occurrence of slow waves.

Until recently the literature had been confusing on the effects of alcohol on the SWS of alcoholics. It is now clear that the amount of increased % SWS which follows alcohol intake tends to be positively related to the baseline level of SWS and the magnitude of bedtime BACs during drinking (Gross & Hastey, 1975b; Wagman & Allen, 1975; Zarcone, Barchas, Hoddes, Montplaisir, Sack, & Wilson, 1975). Thus, at very low levels of SWS, moderate bedtime BACs were not likely to produce increases in % SWS, thereby explaining the findings of Johnson et al. (1970) and Allen et al. (1971). With lesser reductions of SWS at baseline, moderate bedtime BACs tended to bring the % SWS toward the level of matched normal controls, i.e., had a "normalizing" effect, as was described by Lester et al. (1973). At baseline levels in alcoholics which were within or above the normal levels of % SWS, high bedtime BACs tended to produce greater increases in % SWS in direct relation to the baseline level. In addition to baseline levels of % SWS, bedtime BAC levels also tended to be positively related to increases in % SWS (Gross & Hastey, 1975b; Wagman & Allen, 1975). On successive days of high bedtime BACs, after the initial tendency for increases of % SWS, the % SWS tended to gradually decrease.

Clinically, the dose-related (BAC) increases of % SWS appeared positively related to the dose-related (BAC) evidence of intoxication. The alcoholics with lower baseline % SWS and the lesser duration of % SWS increment during alcohol intake also tended to show less intoxication (Gross, Hastey, Lewis, & Young, 1975). Thus, there was an indication of both SWS and behavioral tolerance as concomitant processes.

Evidence of a continuity of the effects of alcohol on sleep and waking function is perhaps more suggestive for SWS than any other aspect of sleep. Rosadini, Rodriguez, and Siani (1974) administered substantial quantities of alcohol to young healthy subjects. BACs ranged from 84-233 mg/100 ml with an average of 145 mg/100 ml. (It seems reasonable to assume that the values reported in the publication were in error at the stated levels of 9.84, 2.33 and 1.45 mg/100 ml). They observed, particularly at the anterior scalp, that a spectral EEG analysis demonstrated a marked increase in delta activity between 1 and 2 hours after alcohol intake. Evidence of intoxication was present in all subjects and they noted that, "Drowsiness and/or full sleep also featured in all subjects" (p. 275). However, no comment was made about a possible relationship to SWS. Similarly, Kalant (1975) discussed the direct effects of alcohol on the CNS and cited findings in the cat by Sauerland and Harper (1970) similar to those reported by Rosadini et al., (1974). Once again, no comment was made in relation to SWS. Yet it is the anterior scalp leads which also are the primary sites for recording SWS. It is tempting to speculate that the continuity of the increased SWS during the waking, drowsy, and sleep states may reflect alcohol effects on closely related or identical CNS mechanisms.

K-complexes and sleep spindles. Data on the landmarks of stage 2 sleep, the K-complexes and sleep spindles, are sketchy. Gross and Goodenough (1968) reported one instance in which, following a day of inferred extremely high BACs prior to hospitalization, all sleep landmarks including sleep spindles were absent during the first half of the night. The sleep spindles returned during the second half of the night but no count of spindle bursts was made. Johnson et al. (1970) reported a reduced number of sleep spindles throughout the ten days of monitored withdrawal in their alcoholic sample.

Johnson et al. (1970) reported a low incidence of K-complexes throughout the period of monitoring although the number of K-complexes did tend to increase in the course of ten days of withdrawal. Allen et al. (1971) observed an absence of K-complexes in their sample of alcoholics over a period of abstinence lasting from 15-30 days.

Further studies of spindles and K-complexes are needed in order to determine more precisely the nature of their occurrence in alcoholics during baseline, drinking, and withdrawal.

SUBACUTE ALCOHOL WITHDRAWAL SYNDROME. It has been noted in the preceding discussion of the sleep disturbances of the alcoholic, that most of the alcoholics demonstrated prolonged residual disturbances of numerous aspects of the sleep EEG following episodes of prolonged alcohol intake. These prolonged disturbances included circadian instability (increased number of awakenings), ultradian instability (increased number of stage changes, increased numbers of brief REM interruptions) increased % REM, and decreased % SWS. These disturbances tended to diminish with moderate BACs; tended to be most severe during acute withdrawal; and also tended to diminish as the duration of abstinence increased. It remains to be established whether or not these prolonged disturbances of the sleep EEG have clinical correlates or clinical consequences or both. Preliminary data suggest that the degree of prolonged SWS reduction may be related to and predict some of the characteristics of a subsequent drinking episode (Gross & Best, 1975; Gross, Hastey, Lewis, & Young, 1975). The rates and sequence of recovery of these prolonged disturbances need to be determined. Although our knowledge of the prolonged sleep disturbances of the alcoholics is limited, there are sufficient data available to indicate that the disturbances are prolonged alcohol withdrawal effects.

Taken together, these sleep disturbances strongly suggest the existence of a subacute alcohol withdrawal syndrome which may persist for variable lengths of time, from weeks to months, and even perhaps years.

A subacute withdrawal syndrome may contribute to an increased risk of returning to alcohol use. This is suggested by two studies of craving in samples of alcoholics. There are data which indicate that the intensity and frequency of experiences of craving for alcohol in alcoholics are positively related to the severity of the withdrawal experienced during the most recent drinking episode and are negatively related to the duration of abstinence (Hore, 1974; Ludwig & Stark, 1974).

SLEEP IN THE ALCOHOLIC VS. SLEEP IN THE NON-ALCOHOLIC. Frequent evidence has been cited thus far of a multiplicity of sleep disturbances in the alcoholic. The most prominent of these were noted during periods of prolonged high blood alcohol concentrations and the acute withdrawal period that followed. Many of the sleep disturbances persisted for extended periods of abstinence. We have presented data consistent with the interpretation that the baseline disturbances observed in the alcoholics were the selfsame persistent withdrawal effects. May we conclude from this that the alcoholic differs from the non-alcoholic in having the functional tolerance which permits him to drink sufficiently to induce the high blood alcohol concentrations? In other words, would a non-alcoholic fall asleep or pass out before reaching the high concentrations and therefore be spared effects which will only occur at high concentrations? This may be the case, but we do not know at this time if the high blood alcohol concentration sleep effects seen in the alcoholic occur at lower concentrations in the less tolerant non-alcoholic, or are indeed specific to high BACs. The more specific the relationships of the profound sleep disturbances are to high BACs, the more readily will we be able to conclude that the differences are substantially attributable to the differences of degree of functional tolerance. In connection with this last possibility it is important to keep in mind that alcohol behaves almost as though it were multiple substances. For example, BACs exceeding 200 mg/100 ml have quite different pharmacologic actions (such as effects on cellular and intracellular membranes in the CNS) than low BACs (Gross, 1975a, 175b; Lundquist, 1975). It seems most likely that both types of consequences of functional tolerance, i.e., a "moreness" of alcohol effects as well as a "newness" of alcohol effects, occur at high BACs compared to lower BACs. This in turn also creates the possibility for a third group of effects, namely the interaction of those increased continuous effects with the new effects.

BIOPATHOLOGY AND MANAGEMENT

The findings reviewed in the preceding section lead to the conclusion that among alcoholics every element of sleep composition and rhythmicity may be disturbed. These disturbances are not random but are related to the clinical state and the effects of alcohol intake and withdrawal. Our understanding of the "what" of alcohol-related sleep disturbances is substantial compared to the "how" of it.

BIOPATHOLOGY. A number of descriptive and explanatory models have been proposed for the basis of the relationships between alcohol, alcoholism, and sleep. Most of these models are mutually compatible since they approach the problem, not with different formulations in the same frame of reference, but from different frames of reference. Furthermore, the frames of reference differ in levels of abstraction. Thus, the alcohol-sleep interactions have been formulated in descriptive clinical process terms such as: shifts in sleep EEG rhythms and composition in relation to clinical stages of intoxication and withdrawal (the primary approach we have taken); acute and chronic disturbances of homeostasis (Johnson et al., 1970), possibly related to aging (Johnson et al., 1970; Lester et al., 1973; Lester et al., 1975). The alcohol-sleep interactions have also been conceptualized in explanatory theoretical system process terms. From a neurophysiological frame of reference (Evarts, 1962; Hobson, 1974; McGinty, Harper, & Fairbanks, 1974; Moruzzi, 1972) this has focused upon effects of alcohol and other CNS depressants and their withdrawal on inhibitory vs. excitatory sleep CNS systems

(Feinberg & Evarts, 1969; Feinberg, Wender, Koresko, Gottlieb, & Piehuta, 1969; Gross et al., 1971). From a neurochemical frame of reference (Jouvet, 1972; Morgane & Sterne, 1974), the focus has been upon the interactions of alcohol and the serotoninergic vs. catecholaminergic systems (Johnson et al., 1970; Kissen et al., 1973; Lester et al., 1973; Williams & Salamy, 1973; Zarcone, Barchas, Hoddes, Montplaisir, Sack, & Wilson, 1975; Zarcone & Hoddes, 1975).

Furthermore, in the many-sided effects of alcohol and its metabolites, about which knowledge is limited, practically nothing is known regarding which of the effects are sequential (and what the sequence is), which are parallel, which are primary for sleep effects, and which are concomitant. Finally, the basic neurophysiology and neurochemistry of sleep per se are not yet fully understood. An adequate review of the evidence and the theoretical formulations would require a chapter, if not a monograph in itself. A brief discussion would do too much violence to the issues and will only become possible when the nature of the underlying biopathological mechanisms are more firmly established.

MANAGEMENT. Effective management of the sleep disturbances requires recognition of the alcohol-related etiology, diagnosis regarding the relation to alcohol intoxication or withdrawal, careful assessment of the severity of the sleep disturbances, and rational treatment.

Recognition. Awareness of the frequent, varied sleep disturbances which may be alcohol-related should prompt the examining physician to consider such a possible etiology when confronted by patients complaining of sleep problems. Men between 25 and 55 are probably a high risk group for such difficulties, but these difficulties are probably not rare in women of the same age group or in both sexes above age 55. Ironically, patients are often aware that alcohol at bedtime appears to relieve the sleep difficulties but may not be aware that the daily drinking may be causing the sleep difficulties in the first place. The recognition of the physician should also extend to the possibility that alcohol-related sleep disturbances may signal the presence of other alcohol-related pathologies and of alcoholism.

Diagnosis. Once the alcohol-related etiology of the sleep disturbance is established, the task remains to specifically diagnose the disturbance as intoxication-related or withdrawal-related. Furthermore, even when it can be established that a particular sleep disturbance is intoxication-related, it must be kept in mind that it may be followed by a withdrawal-related sleep disturbance. Finally, it should be remembered that the sleep disturbances of withdrawal may be long-lasting and may continue to be the primary diagnosis even though by current history it may appear to be intoxication-related.

Although a complete diagnostic evaluation should ideally include a blood alcohol determination and sleep EEG studies, much can be done with a careful history and physical examination. Relevant history would include past, recent, and present quantities and patterns of alcohol intake; current nutritional intake; use of hypno-sedatives; and past, recent, and present symptomatology of alcohol withdrawal.

Poor nutrition is likely to increase the likelihood of higher BACs and thereby, increase the likelihood of alcohol-related sleep disturbances in general. If the alcohol intake is limited to a brief span of time in the course of a day, particularly in the evening, the former will be conducive to higher BACs, the latter, to a greater likelihood of affecting sleep. If the current heavy intake has been present for more than two consecutive days the likelihood is great that the current sleep disturbance is withdrawal-related. Did the use of hypno-sedatives (including a single generous "night-cap" which may be for some the nocturnal equivalent of the "hair of the dog" used to start the day) begin after an episode of withdrawal during the past year or even two? Past history of withdrawal increases the likelihood of recurrence of withdrawal. It is also important to determine if there has been a recent episode of withdrawal, since this would increase the likelihood of residual withdrawal and of withdrawal-related sleep disturbances. As for the present history of withdrawal symptomatology, it is helpful to keep in mind that the severity of such symptoms is subject to considerable fluctuation, and the entire preceding 24 hours should be assessed.

The history of the sleep disturbances must be evaluated in the context of collateral history of intake and withdrawal. A current history of excessive sleep would be most likely to occur in relation to alcohol intoxication, although it may occur as a "terminal sleep" after withdrawal. The milder insomnias may be manifestations of intoxication, partial withdrawal, or abstinence withdrawal. The milder insomnias of intake are most likely to be sleep onset insomnias, while those of partial and abstinence withdrawal are more likely to involve awakenings in the latter part of the night with difficulty returning to sleep. The mild withdrawal insomnias may take the form of earlier rising than usual. The more severe insomnias are likely to be withdrawal (partial or withdrawal)-related. Instability, or fragmentation of circadian sleep-wake rhythms, may be intake or withdrawal related and is manifest in its milder forms by multiple awakenings during the night. the circadian disturbances may also result in an increased tendency to nap during the day.

Prominent complaints of vivid dreams or nightmares are most liekly to be related to partial or abstinence withdrawal. The instability of ultradian rhythms, which tends to be associated with diminished slow wave sleep and instability of circadian sleep rhythms, frequently is clinically experienced as a complaint of "poor sleep" without feeling refreshed or restored upon awakening. It is likely to be a manifestation of partial or abstinence withdrawal and appears to be a particularly prominent feature of the prolonged subacute withdrawal syndrome.

The interpretation of the sleep EEG requires that as much care be given to the clinical staging as to the sleep staging. Careful history and examination provide the essential context within which the sleep EEG can be interpreted. To give one very simple example, the history and even more, the BAC are essential in distinguishing the high levels of SWS of intoxication from those of "terminal sleep." Nevertheless, high levels of SWS are most likely to be indications of intoxication. (The absence of increased SWS does not rule intoxication out since those starting to drink with low SWS levels may not demonstrate such an increase). Likewise, diminished REM is most likely to be a concomitant of intoxication. The absence or reduction of K-complexes and sleep spindles may occur during severe intoxication. The reduction of SWS and REM are likely to be manifestations of abstinence withdrawal. Sleep onset REM, reduced time of REM onset, increased eye movement density, and the instability or fragmentation of the individual REM periods appear to be especially likely to occur within the first week of withdrawal. SWS reduction is likely to occur during this period as well. The findings suggest that while the most dramatic EEG concomitants of acute withdrawal are the REM disturbances, the reduction of SWS is perhaps the most consistent feature.

A variety of EEG disturbances are observed during the subacute withdrawal syndrome; reduced sleep time, increased awakenings, increased stage changes, increased REM, REM instability, and decreased SWS. Of all of these we know that decreased SWS can be especially long lasting but less information is available for the other manifestations. Thus, at the present time the most sensitive measure of prolonged withdrawal appears to be the monitored SWS.

Assessment of severity and rational treatment. Because of the risk of contributing to the development of multiple substance addiction and the potential lethality of alcohol combined with hypno-sedatives, the management of the sleep disturbances should be characterized by therapeutic restraint.

The greatest single error is likely to be the failure to diagnose the sleep disturbance as alcohol-related. Once the correct etiological diagnosis is made, the task of management becomes clearer if not necessarily simpler. In the narrowest context, i.e., the sleep disturbances per se, it is the management of intoxication and of withdrawal, both of which are self-limiting processes for each episode. It is because of this self-limiting nature that the issue of severity is critical. If the symptomatology is not severe, or the patient's distress regarding the symptoms, when they are mild or moderate in severity, is not great, medication may not be necessary. When medication is used to prevent withdrawal in the patient with intoxication-related sleep disturbances who is advised to sharply reduce or stop alcohol intake, or to treat the withdrawal-related sleep disturbances, supplementary hypno-sedatives should not be necessary. While it is true that improved sleep may not occur in the first 24 hours of treatment, the patient will be better served by being informed that the sleep disturbance will diminish as his condition improves than by hastily supplementing the medication. What is true of the acute episode of alcohol-related sleep disturbances is true also of its frequently prolonged moderate and milder stages. Informing the patient of the link of the sleep disturbances to alcohol use, and that continued lesser alcohol intake or the use of hypno-sedatives may provide transient relief but is likely to perpetuate the distress, will provide the patient with credible reasons for enduring the discomfort. This gradually becomes self-reinforcing when the patient experiences the relief promised. Such sharing of understanding and encouragement by the physician will generally be effective, even in those instances alluded to previously as insomnophobias.

Essentially then, the treatment of alcohol-related sleep disturbances is the treatment of alcohol intoxication and withdrawal. If the decision is made that medication is needed, it is medication for the treatment of profound alcohol intoxication or for prevention or treatment of withdrawal, without supplementary hypno-sedatives. Every effort should be made to discontinue all medication as soon as it is clinically feasible, and the patient should be encouraged to maintain abstinence and thus allow the residual withdrawal to gradually clear.

In some instances, however, the severity of the

prolonged withdrawal and associated sleep disturbances or the patient's difficulty in tolerating them, may require prolonged use of medication after first re-evaluating for other possible causes of sleep disturbance. Here too, the less medication the better. Chlordiazepoxide, 10 mg at bedtime may be helpful, particularly when the patient is advised to take it no more than 5 evenings per week so as to diminish the likelihood of developing tolernace.

In its broadest context, the management of the alcohol-related sleep disturbances is the diagnosis and treatment of alcoholism, which is a topic addressed elsewhere in this volume. If the patient who is suffering from alcohol-related sleep disturbances is not found to be an alcoholic, he should be informed that this may be a prodromal warning and encouraged to decrease or stop alcohol intake.

CONCLUSION

Alcohol-related sleep disturbances are extremely common among alcoholics and, to a lesser extent, probably among non-alcoholics as well. These sleep disturbances may be brief or prolonged, range from mild to severe, and are manifestations of alcohol intoxication or withdrawal effects on the CNS. The likelihood and nature of the disturbances has been demonstrated to vary in relation to blood alcohol concentrations and duration of exposure, but there are undoubtedly other factors involved as well. The symptoms include hypersomnia, insomnia, "poor sleep," increased napping by day, increased awakenings at night, and nightmares. Sleep EEG recordings are desirable for precise evaluation and, even more, for monitoring the recovery.

All aspects of sleep may be disrupted. This is particularly evident in sleep EEG studies where the following alcohol-related effects have been described: instability or fragmentation of the circadian and ultradian sleep rhythms, mild to marked upward and downward deviations of the quantitative composition of REM and SWS, and reduction or even absence of characteristic landmarks of sleep, such as K-complexes and sleep spindles. Prolonged sleep EEG manifestations of alcohol withdrawal across a broad range of sleep dimensions, of which the SWS reduction has been most extensively studied, appear to support the reality of a subacute alcohol withdrawal syndrome. This may last for as long as several years although more commonly clears in several months and may have important implications for the prognosis and treatment of alcoholism.

The alcohol-related sleep disturbances tend to be self-limiting. Medication should be used with restraint and should be medication for the treatment of the intoxication or withdrawal. Hypno-sedative use should be discouraged. When the sleep disturbances are consequences of alcoholism the primary treatment should be the treatment of the alcoholism.

ACKNOWLEDGMENT

Preparation of this manuscript was partially supported by NIMH Grant #AA01236.

REFERENCES

Adamson, J., & Burdick, J.A. Sleep of dry alcoholics. *Archives of General Psychiatry*, 1973, *28*, 146-149.

Allen, R.P., & Wagman, A.M.I. Do sleep patterns relate to the desire for alcohol? In M.M. Gross (Ed.), *Alcohol intoxication and withdrawal: Experimental studies II, Advances in experimental medicine and biology* (Vol. 59). New York: Plenum Press, 1975.

Allen, R.P., Wagman, A., Faillace, L.A., & McIntosh, M. Electroencephalographic (EEG) sleep recovery following prolonged alcohol intoxication in alcoholics. *Journal of Nervous and Mental Disease*, 1971, *153*, 424-433.

Aserinsky, E., & Kleitman, N. Regularly occurring periods of eye-motility, and concomitant phenomena, during sleep. *Science*, 1953, *118*, 273.

Baekeland, F., Lundwall, L., Shanahan, T.J., & Kissin, B. Clinical correlates of reported sleep disturbance in alcoholics. *Quarterly Journal of Studies on Alcohol*, 1974, *35*, 1230-1241.

Begleiter, H., Gross, M.M., & Porjesz, B. Recovery function and clinical symptomatology in acute alcoholization and withdrawal. In M.M. Gross (Ed.), *Alcohol intoxication and withdrawal: Experimental studies I, Advances in experimental medicine and biology* (Vol. 35). New York: Plenum Press, 1973.

Boyar, R., Perlow, M., Hellman, L., Kapen, S., & Weitzman, E. Twenty-four hour pattern of luteinizing hormone secretion in normal men with sleep stage recording. *Journal of Clinical Endocrinology and Metabolism*, 1972, *35*, 73-81.

Dement, W.C., & Kleitman, N. Cyclic variations in EEG during sleep and their relation to eye movements, body motility, and dreaming. *Electroencephalography and Clinical Neurophysiology*, 1957, *9*, 673-690.

Evarts, E.V. A neurophysiologic theory of hallucinations. In L.J. West (Ed.), *Hallucinations*. New York: Grune & Stratton, 1962.

Feinberg, I., & Evarts, E.V. Some implications of sleep research for psychiatry. In J. Zubin & C. Shagass (Eds.), *Neurobiological aspects of psychopathology*. New York: Grune & Stratton, 1969.

Feinberg, I., Hibi, S., Cavness, C., & March, J. Absence of REM rebound after barbiturate withdrawal. *Science*, 1974, *185*, 534-535.

Feinberg, I., Wender, P.H., Koresko, R.L., Gottlieb, F., & Piehuta, J.A. Differential effects of chlorpromazine and phenobarbital on EEG sleep patterns. *Journal of Psychiatric Research*, 1969, *7*, 101-109.

Feuerlein, W. The acute alcohol withdrawal syndrome: Findings and problems. *British Journal of Addictions*, 1974, *69*, 141-148.

Goldstein, D. Personal communication.

Greenberg, R., & Pearlman, C. Delirium tremens and dreaming. *American Journal of Psychiatry*, 1967, *124*, 133-142.

Gresham, S.C., Webb, W.B., & Williams, R.C. Alcohol and caffeine: Effect on inferred visual dreaming. *Science*, 1963, *140*, 1226-1227.

Gross, M.M. Sensory superactivity; A preliminary report on an hypothetical model for an hallucinogenic mechanism in alcohol withdrawal. In M.M. Gross (Ed.), *Alcohol intoxication and withdrawal*: *Experimental studies* I, *Advances in experimental medicine and biology* (Vol. 35). New York: Plenum Press, 1973.

Gross, M.M. Physical dependence and alcohol withdrawal syndrome in man. In M. Airaksinen (Ed.), *Proceedings of the Sixth International Congress of Pharmacology* (Vol. 3), *CNS and Behavioural Pharmacology*. Finland: International Union of Pharmacology, 1975. (a)

Gross, M.M. Psychobiological contributions to the alcohol dependence syndrome, with particular emphasis on toxicity, tolerance, dependence and withdrawal. OMH/C/75.17, World Health Organization, 1975. (b)

Gross, M.M., & Best, S. Behavioral concomitants of the relationship between baseline slow wave sleep and carry-over of tolernace and dependence in alcoholics. In M.M. Gross, (Ed.), *Alcohol intoxication and withdrawal*: *Experimental studies*, II, *Advances in experimental medicine and biology* (Vol. 59). New York: Plenum Press, 1975.

Gross, M.M., & Goodenough, D.R. Sleep disturbances in the acute alcoholic psychoses. *Psychiatric Research Report No. 24* of the American Psychiatric Association, 1968, 132-147.

Gross, M.M., Goodenough, D.R., Hastey, J.M., & Lewis, E. Experimental study of sleep in chronic alcoholics before, during and after 4 days of heavy drinking with a non-drinking comparison. In F. Seixas (Ed.), *Alcoholism and the central nervous system* (Vol. 215). New York: New York Academy of Science, 1973.

Gross, M.M., Goodenough, D.R., Hastey, J.M., Rosenblatt, S.M., & Lewis, E. Sleep disturbances in alcohol intoxication and withdrawal. In N.K. Mello & J.H. Mendelson (Eds.), *Recent advances in studies of alcoholism* . Washington, D.C.: U.S. Government Printing Office, 1971.

Gross, M.M., Goodenough, D.R., Nagarajan, M., & Hastey, J.M. Sleep changes induced by 4 and 6 days of experimental alcoholization and withdrawal in humans. In M.M. Gross (Ed.), *Alcohol intoxication and withdrawal: Experimental studies* II, *Advances in experimental medicine and biology* (Vol. 35). New York: Plenum Press, 1973.

Gross, M.M., Goodenough, D.R., Tobin, M., Halpert, E., Lepore, D., Perstein, A., Sirota, M., Dibianco, J., Fuller, R., & Kishner, I. Sleep disturbances and halluncinations in the acute alcoholic psychoses. *Journal of Nervous and Mental Disease*, 1966, *142*, 493-514.

Gross, M.M., & Hastey, J.M. A note on REM rebound during experimental alcohol withdrawal in alcoholics. In M.M. Gross, (Ed.), *Alcohol intoxication and withdrawal: Experimental studies* II, *Advances in experimental medicine and biology* (Vol. 59). New York: Plenum Press, 1975. (a)

Gross, M.M., & Hastey, J.M. The relation between baseline slow wave sleep and the slow wave sleep response to alcohol in alcoholics. In M.M. Gross (Ed.), *Alcohol intoxication and withdrawal: Experimental studies* II, *Advances in experimental medicine and biology* (Vol. 59). New York: Plenum Press, 1975. (b)

Gross, M.M., Hastey, J.M., Lewis, E., & Young, N. Slow wave sleep and carry-over of functional tolerance and physical dependence in alcoholics. In M.M. Gross (Ed.), *Alcohol intoxication and withdrawal: Experimental studies* II, *Advances in experimental medicine and biology* (Vol. 59). New York: Plenum Press, 1975.

Gross, M.M., & Lewis, E. Observations on the prevalence of the signs and symptoms associated with withdrawal during continuous observation of experimental intoxication and withdrawal in humans. In M.M. Gross (Ed.), *Alcohol intoxication and withdrawal: Experimental studies* I, *Advances in experimental medicine and biology* (Vol. 35). New York: Plenum Press, 1973.

Gross, M.M., Lewis, E., Best, S., Young, N., & Feuer, L. Quantitative changes of signs and symptoms associated with acute alcohol withdrawal: Incidence, severity, and circadian effects in experimental studies in alcoholics. In M.M. Gross (Ed.), *Alcohol intoxication and withdrawal: Experimental studies* II, *Advances in experimental medicine and biology* (Vol. 59). New York: Plenum Press, 1975.

Gross, M.M., Lewis, E., & Hastey, J.M. Acute alcohol withdrawal syndrome. In B. Kissin & H. Begleiter (Eds.), *The biology of alcoholism* (Vol. 3). New York: Plenum Press, 1974.

Hobson, J.A. The cellular basis of sleep cycle control. In E.D. Weitzman (Ed.), *Advances in sleep research*, (Vol. 1). New York: Spectrum Publications, 1974.

Hore, B.D. Craving for alcohol. *British Journal of Addictions*, 1974, *69*, 137-140.

Isbell, H., Fraser, H., Wikler, A., Belleville, R., & Eisenman, A. An experimental study of the etiology of "rum-fits" and delirium tremens. *Quarterly Journal of Studies on Alcohol*, 1955, *16*, 1-33.

Johnson, L.C. Sleep patterns in chronic alcoholics. In N.K. Mello & J.H. Mendelson (Eds.), *Recent advances in studies of alcoholism*. Washington, D.C.: U.S. Government Printing Office, 1971.

Johnson, L.C., Burdick, J.A., & Smith, J. Sleep during alcohol intake and withdrawal in the chronic alcoholic. *Archives of General Psychiatry*, 1970, *22*, 406-418.

Jouvet, M. The role of monoamines and acetylcholine-containing neurons in the regulation of the sleep-waking cycle. *Neurophysiology and neurochemistry of sleep and wakefulness, Reviews of physiology* (Vol. 64). Berlin: Springer-Verlag, 1972.

Kalant, H. Direct effects of ethanol on the nervous system. *Federation Proceedings*, 1975, *34*, 1930-1041.

Kissin, B., Gross, M.M., & Schutz, I. Correlation of urinary biogenic amines with sleep stages in chronic alcoholization and withdrawal. In M.M. Gross (Ed.), *Alcohol intoxication and withdrawal: Experimental studies* I, *Advances in experimental medicine and biology* (Vol. 35). New York: Plenum Press, 1973.

Knowles, J.B., Laverty, S.G., & Keuchler, H.A. Effects of alcohol on REM sleep. *Quarterly Journal of Studies on Alcohol*, 1968, *29*, 342.

Kripke, D.F. Ultradian rhythms in sleep and wakefulness. In E.E. Weitzman (Ed.), *Advances in sleep research* (Vol. 1). New York: Spectrum Publications, 1974.

Laverty, S.G. Sleep disorders and delirium associated with the use of ethanol. In P.D. MacLean (Ed.), *A triune concept of the brain and behaviour: Clarence M. Hincks Memorial Lectures*, 1969. University of Toronto Press, 1973.

Lester, B.K., Rundell, O.H., Cowden, L.C., & Williams, H.L. Chronic alcoholism, alcohol and sleep. In M.M. Gross (Ed.), *Alcohol intoxication and withdrawal: Experimental studies* I, *Advances in experimental medicine and biology* (Vol. 35). New York: Plenum Press, 1973.

Lester, B.K., Rundell, O.H., Cowden, L.C., & Williams, H.L. Alcohol and sleep in the chronic alcoholic. In Niel & H.L. Altshuler, (Eds.) *Behavior and brain electrical activity*. New York: Plenum Press, 1975.

Lettsom, J.C. Some remarks on the effects of lignum guassie amarae. *Memoirs Medical Society*, London, 1787, *1*, 151-165.

Ludwig, A.M., & Stark, L.H. Alcohol craving. *Quarterly Journal of Studies on Alcohol*, 1974, *35*, 899-905.

Lundquist, F. Interference of ethanol in cellular metabolism. In F. Seixas, K. Williams, & S. Eggleston (Eds.), *Medical consequences of alcoholism* (Vol. 252). New York: New York Academy of Sciences, 1975.

Mandell, M.P., Mandell, A.J., Rubin, R.T., Brill, P., Rodnick, J., Sheff, R., & Chaffey, B. Activation of the pituitary-adrenal axis during rapid eye movement sleep in man. *Life Science*, 1966, *5*, 583-587.

McGinty, D.J., Harper, R.M., & Fairbanks, M.K. Neuronal unit activity and the control of sleep states. In E.D. Weitzman (Ed.), *Advances in sleep research* (Vol. 1). New York: Spectrum Publications, 1974.

Mello, N.K. Behavioral studies of alcoholism. In B. Kissin & H. Begleiter (Eds.), *Biology of alcoholism*, (Vol. 2). New York: Plenum Press, 1972.

Mellow, N.K., & Mendelson, J.H. Experimentally induced intoxication in alcoholics: A comparison between programmed and spontaneous drinking. *Journal of Pharmacological and Experimental Therapies*, 1970, *173*, 271-298.

Mendelson, H.H. Experimentally induced chronic intoxication and withdrawal in alcoholics. *Quarterly Journal of Studies on Alcohol*, 1964, *Suppl. No. 2*, 1-126.

Morgane, P.J., & Sterne, W.C. Chemical anatomy of brain circuits in relation to sleep and wakefulness. In E.D. Weitzman (Ed.), *Advances in sleep research*(Vol. 1). New York: Spectrum Publications, 1974.

Moruzzi, G. The sleep-waking cycle. *Neurophysiology and neurochemistry of sleep and wakefulness, Reviews of physiology* (Vol. 64). Berlin: Springer-Verlag, 1972.

Parker, D.C., Sassin, J.F., Mace, J.W., Gotlin, R.W., & Rossman, L.G. Human growth hormone release during sleep: Electroencephalographic correlation. *Journal of Clinical Endocrinology and Metabolism*, 1969, *29*, 871-874.

Pearson, S.B. Observations on brain fever: Delirium tremens. *Edinburgh Medical & Surgical Journal*, 1813, *9*, 326-332.

Quabbe, H.J., Helge, H., & Kubicki, S. Nocturnal growth hormone secretion: Correlation with sleeping EEG in adults and pattern in children and adolescents with non-pituitary dwarfism, overgrowth, and with obesity. *Acta Endocrinology*, 1971, *67*, 767-783.

Quabbe, H.J., Schilling, E., & Helge, H. Pattern of growth hormone secretion during a 24-hour fast in normal adults. *Journal of Clinical Endocrinology and Metabolism*, 1966, *26*, 1173-1177.

Rechtschaffen, A., & Kales, A. Manual of standardized terminology. Techniques, and scoring system for sleep stages of human subjects. *National Institute of Health Publication No. 204*, Book 1-62. Washington, D.C. U.S. Government Printing Office, 1968.

Rosadini, G., Rodriguez, G., & Siani, C. Acute alcohol poisoning in man: An experimental electrophysiological study. *Psychopharmacologia*, 1974, *35*, 273-285.

Rubin, R.T., Kales, A., Adler, R. Gonadotropin secretion during sleep in normal adult men. *Science*, 1972, *175*, 116-198.

Rundell, O.H., Lester, M.K., Griffith, W.J., & Williams, H.L. Alcohol and sleep in young adults. *Psychopharmacologia*, 1972, *26*, 201-218.

Sauerland, E.K., & Harper, R.M. Effects of ethanol on EEG spectra of the intact brain and isolated forebrain. *Experimental Neurology*, 1970, *27*, 490.

Victor, M., & Adams, R.D. Effects of alcohol on the nervous system. In H.H. Merritt & C.C. Hare (Eds.), *Metabolic and toxic diseases of the nervous system*. Baltimore: Williams & Wilkins, 1953.

Wagman, A.M.I., & Allen, R.P. Effects of alcohol ingestion and abstinence. In M.M. Gross (Ed.), *Alcohol intoxication and withdrawal*: *Experimental studies* II, *Advances in experimental medicine and biology* (Vol. 59), New York: Plenum Press, 1975.

Weitzman, E.D. (Ed.) *Advances in sleep research* New York: Spectrum Publications, 1974.

Williams, R.L., Karacan, I., Hursch, C.J. *Electroencephalography(EEG) of human sleep--clinical applications*. New York: John Wiley & Sons, 1974.

Williams, , & Salamy, A. Alcohol and sleep. In B. Kissin & H. Begleiter (Eds.), *Biology of alcoholism* (Vol. 2). New York: Plenum Press, 1972.

Wolin, S.J., & Mello, N.K. The effects of alcohol on dreams and hallucinations in alcohol addicts. In F. Seixas (Ed.), *Alcoholism and the central nervous system*, (Vol. 215). New York: New York Academy of Sciences, 1973.

Woods, J.H., & Winger, G.D. A critique of methods for inducing ethanol self-intoxication in animals. In N.K. Mello & J.H. Mendelson (Eds.), *Recent advances in studies of alcoholism* Washington, D.C.: U.S. Government Printing Office, 1971.

Yules, R.B., Freedman, D.X., & Chandler, K.A. The effect of ethyl alcohol on man's electroencephalographic sleep cycle. *Electroencephalography Clinical Neurophysiology*, 1966, *20*, 109-111.

Yules, R.B., Lippman, M.E., & Freedman, D.X. Alcohol administration prior to sleep: The effect on EEG sleep stages. *Archives of General Psychiatry*, 1967, *16*, 94.

Zarcone, V.P., Jr., Barchas, J., Hoddes, E., Montplaisir, J., Sack, R., & Wilson, R. Experimental ethanol ingestion: Sleep variables and metabolites of dopamine and serotonin in the cerebrospinal fluid. In M.M. Gross (Ed.), *Alcohol intoxication and withdrawal: Experimental studies* II (Vol. 59). New York: Plenum Press, 1975.

Zarcone, V.P., Jr., & Hoddes, E. The effects of 5-OH tryptophane on fragmentation of REM sleep in alcoholics. *American Journal of Psychiatry*, 1975, *132*, 74-76.

CHAPTER 9

PERSONALITY MEASUREMENT FOR THE EVALUATION AND PREDICTION OF ALCOHOLISM

Helmut Hoffmann

Chapters on alcoholism in modern psychiatric textbooks sometimes provide the reader with baffling statements. For example: "No single personality configuration is found in alcoholism" (Freedman, Kaplan, & Sadock, 1972). "If there is such a thing as an 'alcoholic personality' or a 'pre-alcoholic personality', its specifications are poorly defined and often contradictory" (Masserman, 1963). "There is no agreement on the identity of those traits of an alcoholic personality nor on whether they may be the cause or the result of excessive drinking" (NIAAA, 1972).

In two reviews of the literature on the personality of alcoholics, Sutherland, Schroeder, and Tordella (1950), and Syme (1957), all sociologists, concluded that research had not demonstrated significant differences in personality characteristics between alcoholics and non-alcoholics.

Ralph E. Tarter and A. Arthur Sugerman (eds.), Alcoholism

ISBN: 0-201-08146-6
ISBN: 0-201-08145-8 (pbk.)

Further, they suggested that the differences which had been found might be results rather than causes of alcoholism. Admitting that the studies they reviewed left something to be desired methodologically, they nevertheless concluded that "there is no alcoholic personality prior to alcoholism" (Sutherland et al., 1950). To arrive at such a conclusion via such a route is certainly not warranted. One might even call it deplorable when one considers that these reviews are often cited as arguments against the concept of an alcoholic personality.

Two questions occur immediately. Why is it expected that alcoholic personality traits should be spelled out in terms of what is cause and what result of excessive drinking? No such demands are made of other psychiatric entities, i.e., are schizophrenic personality traits the cause or the result of the psychotic state? And certainly rather large groups of neuroses show a variety of facets. The second question: why should investigators be satisfied with nothing less than a "single personality" for alcoholics? Just as there is no such thing as a personality unique to any particular group of persons, so is there none for alcoholics. While the answers to these questions are unclear, the message from those who would try to separate cause and result and find the unique alcoholic personality seems to be: the personality of the alcoholic is a will o' the wisp. Such being the case, would it not be better to concentrate on other areas more fruitful to the study of alcoholism?

On the other hand, alcoholics are frequently described by clinicians, as well as by journalists and other non-professionals in the field as being maladjusted, emotionally immature, socially isolated, and poorly integrated; as lacking impulse control, having difficulties coping with frustration or tension, and suffering from feelings of unworthiness, guilt, and depression--all personality characteristics.

There is considerable literature dealing with the alcoholic personality by psychologists, both clinicians and researchers. Most assume that alcoholism is a symptom of an underlying personality disorder, fueled by an intricate interplay of emotional, social, and physiological factors (Chafetz, Blane, & Hill, 1970). And there is increasing interest in the subject of alcoholic personality research as indicated by Dahlstrom, Welsh, and Dahlstrom (1975) in their handbook on the clinically most frequently used instrument, the Minnesota Multiphasic Personality Inventory (MMPI). The handbook chapter concerning diagnosis and classification notes the following number of references for methods of differential diagnosis for alcoholism: between 1943 and 1963: 37 references; between 1964 and 1968: 58 references; and between 1970 and 1973: 60 references. The total number of studies quoted on alcoholism exceeds by nearly twice those given for any other diagnostic categories, e.g., depressive states or schizophrenic reactions.

The purpose of this chapter is to review the main findings in the field of alcoholic personality measurement, their theoretical and methodological problems, and their applications for evaluation and prediction, with the hope of bringing some clarity and perspective to the issue. Emphasis will be given here to findings based on the MMPI, although other psychological personality measurements will be considered to supplement the big bulk of MMPI research. Other types of psychological measurements which may belong within the framework of personality, e.g., cognitive tests and intelligence tests, are not reviewed here.

THEORIES ABOUT THE CAUSES OF ALCOHOLISM

This chapter deals mainly with personality measurement and also with personality theory. Personality measurement is primarily concerned with what a person is like at a given time (Edwards, 1970). However, before problems of personality measurement are dealt with in detail, common theories about the causes of alcoholism should be mentioned briefly.

The Genotropic theory (Williams, 1954, 1959) suggests that alcoholism is related to a genetically determined, biochemical deficit; that the desire to drink is an inner urge, mediated by nervous structures, perhaps in the hypothalamus of the brain. The physiological functioning of the nervous system is then deranged by alcohol and malnutrition, and in individuals who are prone to be alcoholic, these structures are particularly susceptible to alcohol.

Genetic theories rely on the fact that the children of alcoholic parents have a greater chance of becoming alcoholic than the children of non-alcoholic parents (Bleuler, 1955; Hoffmann & Noem, 1975a, 1975b; Jellinek, 1946). This fact was also confirmed by McCord and McCord (1960) in a longitudinal study. In addition to the likelihood of alcoholics' children becoming alcoholics themselves, it was also found that alcoholism was more strongly related to paternal criminality than it was to paternal alcoholism. All these genetic studies, however, face a methodological problem which consists of difficulty in determining whether the pathological behavior patterns being observed are caused by heredity, or whether the behavioral pathology is learned from parents who manifested similar behavioral abnormalities. Future studies dealing with adopted children, however, might give the answer to such complex questions by investigating, with longitudinal methods, the characteristics of natural parents, adoptive parents, and the behaviors of the children themselves.

Psychoanalytical theories as presented by Fenichel (1945) suggest that an oral fixation is the cause of alcoholism. Oral frustrations during childhood produce a passive, dependent, self-centered individual. Such individuals experience unconscious desires for warmth and nurturance which cannot be satisfied in ordinary interpersonal relationships. These individuals, when experiencing frustrations, are more likely to turn to alcohol than to other people. Ansbacher and Ansbacher (1946) adapted Adler's theory of personality and suggest that the alcoholic, when he faces coping problems, uses alcohol to produce feelings of self-esteem and power, thereby attempting to overcome his feelings of inferiority. In addition, the psychoanalytic point of view asserts that alcohol is used for the expression of repressed desires and that there exists a correlation between oral dependence and latent homosexuality and the usage of alcohol.

Cultural learning theories stress that societal norms involve conditions which produce anxiety in the members of any given society. The use of alcohol is accepted within the societal norms, norms which are then applied by the alcoholic to the use of alcohol for the reduction of anxieties and tensions produced by that society. Cultural theories rely heavily on the fact that the usage of alcohol differs among societies and also among diverse cultural subgroups within a given society. According to Merton's (1957) theory of social structure, deviant behavior is more likely to occur when the expectation of maximizing one's attainment of goals or preferred outcomes through deviant behavior is higher than the expectation of attaining one's goals through more conforming behavior. The sociological hypothesis of Jessor, Graves, Hanson, and Jessor (1968) is this: "The magnitude of the deviance rates at a given location in society will vary directly with the degree of value-excess disjunction, anomie, and access to illegitimate means characterizing that location" (p. 78). In connection with the social learning theory approach to behavior deviancy, Bandura (1969) perceives alcoholism as being a social learning process rather than a deviant type of behavior:

> Although drinking behavior is most often acquired under non-stress conditions, a habitual social drinker will experience stress reduction on many occasions. Once alcohol consumption is thus intermittently reinforced, it will be readily elicited under frustration or adverse conditions. Therefore, alcoholism typically results from habituation after prolonged heavy social drinking acquired within the context of familial alcoholism. (p. 535)

In this framework, the point of view given by MacAndrew and Edgerton (1969) might be mentioned.

> Rather than viewing drunken comportment as a function of toxically disinhibited brains operating in impulse driven bodies, we have recommended that what is fundamentally at issue are the learned relations among men living living together in a society....The way people comport themselves when they are drunk is determined not by alcohol's toxic assault upon the seat of moral judgment, conscious or the like, but what society makes of and imparts to them concerning the state of drunkenness. (p. 164)

Analyzing historical source material concerning contact between fur traders and Indian tribes, MacAndrew and Edgerton noted that Indians were reported to handle alcohol rather well when first introduced to it. Drinking and drunkenness did not seem to lead to any breakdown in interpersonal relations, nor did they seem to interfere with the performance of social roles by individuals, but after being accustomed to the usage of alcohol, behavior patterns appeared to be changing, and the drunkenness became associated with criminality and obscure acting-out behaviors.

BLANE'S DEPENDENCY CONCEPT

Dependency conflicts, in Blane's (1968) view, play the key role in the personality of the alcoholic. He suggests that three common methods of resolving these conflicts result in three distinctive kinds of behavior: open-dependent, counter-dependent, and dependent-independent.

The open-dependent alcoholic has strong dependent needs for which he seeks direct gratifications, relying openly on others and seeking their care and solicitude. The counter-dependent alcoholic shows quite opposite behavior, studiously avoiding relationships which involve open expression of dependency needs. The dependent-independent type falls midway between these extremes, his behavior tending to fluctuate, according to circumstances, between displaying and denying dependent needs.

Blane goes on to give detailed attention to six areas in which one or more types of dependent behavior apparently play a part. (a) The conflict between dependency feelings and concepts, both personal and social, of masculinity; (b) The etiology of anger and its frequent corollary, depression; (c) Denial and the part dependency feelings play in its tone and amplification; (d) The relationship between impulsivity, a low frustration threshold, and dependency needs; (e) The ambiguous landscape which exists between over-evaluation and under-evaluation of the self; (f) Marred social and personal relationships, and the role dependency plays in them.

Most of his presentation centers on men, but he devotes one chapter to the woman alcoholic. Here he notes that she usually displays open-dependent behavior, that her excessive use of alcohol often results from her uncertain position in today's society, and that unlike men, she tends to use alcohol primarily as a medicine.

Blane also devotes chapters to treatment, prevention, and social attitudes about alcoholism. His presentation, avowedly "a work about the personality of the alcoholic for the general reader," contains no empirical studies, but his theory that the crucial problems for the alcoholic lie in the area of dependency conflicts is rich in both implications and ramifications for such studies.

McCLELLAND'S MOTIVATION THEORY

McClelland and his co-workers (McClelland, Davis, Kalin, & Wanner, 1972), using an adaptation of the Thematic Apperception Test (TAT), conducted a variety of studies over a ten-year period, the data from which provide a theory which attempts to explain alcohol and human motivation. The TAT is a method which requires a subject to tell stories about a series of pictures presented to him. The stories are then scored to provide a measure of his fantasies.

The authors conclude that men drink primarily out of a need for personalized power. They note that such a theory may not apply to women or to specialized types of drinking patterns, since the data considered focused on drinking among American males. Except for 20 men recruited for a pilot study to try out the theory, none of the subjects of the other studies had been diagnosed as alcoholic, their drinking habits ranging from "moderate" or "social" to "heavy" or "problem." Thus, one might question whether it is possible to construct a personality theory applicable to alcoholics which is based on data obtained from drinkers who may or may not be alcoholic.

Conclusions reached by McClelland on the basis of these studies dispute some common answers to the question of why men drink, some excessively. Reduction of anxiety is not an adequate answer. Neither do men drink primarily as an excuse for irresponsible or childish behavior, or for oral gratification, or for indulgence of dependency feelings. Indeed, McClelland argues, "The fact that heavy drinkers are commonly counter-dependent and aggressive need not be interpreted as meaning that they have a repressed need for dependence....It may be taken at its face value as evidence for a personalized power drive" (p. 333).

The question of why some men drink to excess while others do not can be illuminated, according to this theory, by examining the strength of an individual's personalized power drive. Why some men choose drinking rather than other available power outlets, e.g., acting-out aggressive impulses, gambling, or accumulating material goods associated with prestige, is not explained by the findings of these studies; but an attempt is made to explain some of the factors contributing to an accentuated need for personalized power. They include aging, a culture which stresses machismo, and "the war between the sexes"--to name a few. "In short, whatever makes power important or salient--in the family, in the culture, in the society, or in the current life situation--may lead to an accentuated power concern in some men which leads them to drink to increase their sense of personalized power" (p. 335).

The simplest way to cure excessive drinking, according to McClelland, is to socialize these power drives. Some examples: an individual might be encouraged to choose an outlet less damaging than alcohol to gratify his power drive; he might be encouraged to join an organization in which the emphasis is on doing things for others; or he might be helped to gain insight into why he drinks, then assisted in choosing his own methods of socializing his power drive. However, judging from results of a four-month and eight-month follow-up on 6 of the 20 subjects in the pilot study mentioned earlier, the particular didactic approach used did not seem to be notably successful either as a therapeutic tool or as a didactic exercise. McClelland summarized his theory in these words:

> The alcoholic experience has a common core for men everywhere and they drink to get it. While individuals in different cultures embroider and interpret the experience in different ways, and while it is more marked for distilled liquors than for wine or beer, the experience centers everywhere in men on increased thoughts of power which, as drinking progresses, become more personal and less socialized and responsible. And societies and individuals with accentuated needs for

> personalized power are most likely to drink more heavily in order to get the feeling of strength they need so much more than others. (p. 336)

DRAW A PERSON TEST

Irgens-Jensen's (1971) study of 593 men called up for service in the Royal Norwegian Navy in 1957 and 1958 showed that there is a clear relationship between excessive drinking and the typical ways in which male and female figures are drawn, the relationship indicating a connection between problem drinking and certain psychological characteristics.

Table 1 shows correlations between problem drinking and graphic items on the Draw a Person (DAP) test.

All subjects in this study served on ships engaged in overseas trade and were 20 or 21 years old. They were culled from a larger group of 3500 called up for service on the basis of availability of detailed background information. In addition, it should be noted that all 3500 were interviewed by a psychologist, one of the objects of the interview (part of a regular induction procedure) being to elicit information about drinking habits--information considered important by the Navy in assessing an individual's suitability for service. It should also be noted that Jensen defined a "problem drinker" as a man "who showed clear signs of regularly drinking to the point of heavy intoxication, often accompanied by overt outbursts of aggressiveness leading in some cases to arrest" (p. 21). He points out that while all alcoholics are "problem drinkers", not all "problem drinkers" can be called alcoholics. Since his sample consists of fairly young

TABLE 1

Correlations between Problem Drinking and Graphic Items in the DAP Test Score

	r	*p*
Male figure incomplete	.36	.01
Female figure incomplete	.47	.001
Male hands abnormal	.43	.001
Female hands abnormal	.34	.01
Poor sophistication score	.35	.01
High body-disturbance score	.32	.01
Male age indeterminable	.34	.01
Female age indeterminable	.56	.001
Female larger than male	.31	.01
Female nude	.39	.001
Female figure obscene	.58	.001
Female conventional	-.48	.001
Female figure "john-wall" style	.61	.001
Female aggressively dominant	.44	.01
Male caricatured eyes	.47	.01

Note: Adapted from Irgens-Jensen (1971).

men, he suggests that alcoholism may not yet have had time to develop. He also emphasizes that his sample is not only young but also exclusively male and because of the selection factor may not be a representative sample even of young Norwegian men.

With these limitations in mind, he goes on to state that his data suggest that excessive use of alcohol may have three main functions: (a) It relieves anxiety and tension. (b) It enables satisfaction of dependency needs without damaging an image of manliness, thus allowing an adult male to behave with impunity like an irresponsible child. (c) It facilitates an indulgence in fantasies about personal worth and achievements.

He concludes that three principal personality factors seem to be closely related to problem drinking: (a) conflicts arising from a need to be both dependent and independent, (b) conflicts arising from a hostile attitude towards women, and (c) a lack of self-confidence coupled with an undeveloped self-concept. He also mentions a fourth factor--inability to control emotional impulses, adding that these symptoms and conflicts do not exist independently of one another and may reflect different aspects of the same personality pattern.

Irgens-Jensen (1971) summarizes as follows:

> Although the conclusions that have been drawn have had to be formulated as hypotheses that need to be further investigated, there is reason to believe that these hypotheses are quite widely applicable--at least within the framework of Norwegian traditions and the Norwegian cultural pattern. This pattern has, however, many features in common with other Western cultural patterns, especially the Anglo-American one. (p. 147)

Kirchner and Marzolf (1974) report about four studies of measures of the alcoholic personality by the Sixteen Personality Factor questionnaire (16 PF) and the House-Tree-Person test. This study is of particular interest because the correlations between 16 PF traits and House-Tree-Person color choice characteristics among alcoholic and college men show differences between both samples. These results demonstrate the need for caution in applying data obtained from non-alcoholic samples and generalizing these data to alcoholic samples. Comparison of the data from alcoholics and college students led to the conclusion that, in general, relationships between drawing characteristics and personality traits may well depend upon the type of sample used.

MEASUREMENTS OF SELF-ESTEEM

Using the Multi-Dimensional Successive Intervals Scaling Model, Parthington (1970) required alcoholic and student subjects to judge all possible pairs of a set of stimulus persons. The target stimuli in this set were sober-self and high-self. The resulting matrix of relative inter-point distances treated by multi-dimensional scaling resembles a matrix of factor analysis. The students judged their sober-self and their high-self to be quite similar, but their high-self was closer to the warm stimulus person than was their sober-self. Finally, there was a great polarity between sober-self and alcoholic stimulus, which suggested that students perceive a great deal of psychological distance between themselves and alcoholics. The alcoholics, on the other hand, judged greater dissimilarities between their sober and high self-images than did the students. Also, alcoholics identified their sober-self within a network of relationships which included the physically healthy, warm, and purposeful stimulus people. In contrast, their high-self was located within an entirely different semantic space, in the neighborhood of dominant and alcoholic stimulus people. This means that alcoholics judge their high-self to be stronger yet less desirable than their sober-self. The alcoholics' stimulus person was also judged very similar to other undesirable stimulus persons such as psychopathic, passive-aggressive, and neurotic individuals.

Parthington (1970) concludes from this experiment of rating personal concepts that alcoholics tend to think of themselves in dualistic terms (sober-high). This means an alcoholic person possesses two kinds of self-orientation preferences. The alcoholic might perceive himself as "being an alcoholic" and describe himself with high-self adjectives, which usually include being careless, impulsive, immature, etc. On the other hand, he also has a tendency to identify himself with all the characteristics describing a sober self-orientation which is relatively similar to the concepts of physically healthy, warm, purposeful, etc.

Parthington concludes that it is possible for alcoholics to answer personality statements describing themselves at any point along a line of the polarity sober-high, depending on which kind of self-orientation they choose to identify with. Parthington suggests that research designs for investigating the personalities of alcoholics should provide careful controls for subject self-orientation, and that one aspect of psychotherapy should be directed toward helping alcoholics to recognize and understand the meaning of dualism in their interpersonal perceptions. As long as alcoholics can hypothesize their high-self along the line, "I drink because I am an alcoholic," they will be handicapped in understanding their own behavior.

MMPI PROFILES AND MMPI CODES

The MMPI was constructed for the purpose of providing an effective and practical instrument which would aid routine psychiatric casework by providing objective measurements for determining the severity of a patient's condition and for measuring possible changes in his condition, as well as the magnitude of therapeutic effect. The MMPI is routinely scored for three validity scales: Lie (*L*), Infrequency (*F*), Correction (*K*), and ten clinical scales: Hypochondriasis (*Hs*, 1), Depression (*D*, 2), Conversion Hysteria (*Hy*, 3), Psychopathic Deviate (*Pd*, 4), Masculinity-Femininity (*Mf*, 5), Paranoia (*Pa*, 6), Psychasthenia (*Pt*, 7), Schizophrenia (*Sc*, 8), Hypomania (*Ma*, 9), and Social Introversion (*Si*, 0).

Behind the abbreviation of the clinical scales the traditional code number was provided. Within the last 30 years there were literally hundreds of new experimental scales developed based on the large item pool which the MMPI provided. Alcoholics being in treatment demonstrated in dozens of studies a quite consistent group profile which is characterized by high T-score elevations on the scales *Pd* and *D* and to a lesser extent, *Pt*, *Sc*, and *Ma* (Brown, 1950; Hill, Haertzen, & Davis, 1962; Rosen, 1960; Williams, 1968). Such findings were interpreted by diverse authors in terms of neurotic depression, sociopathy, and neurotic anxiety.

The clinical interpretations of single MMPI scale elevations, however, results often in difficulties because individual MMPI clinical scales are factorially complex (Comrey, 1958). Astin (1959) investigated the factorial structure of individual items of the Psychopathic Deviate scale and identified five factors called (a) self-esteem, (b) hypersensitivity, (c) social maladaption, (d) impulse control, and (e) emotional deprivation. This means a given elevated *Pd* scale leads to difficulties in interpretation because such a score may result from any one of these several facets of behavior as determined by factor analysis of items. To determine and to identify both dimensions of psychopathology in alcoholic patients, Hoffmann, Jackson, and Skinner (1975) factor analyzed the MMPI in conjunction with the Differential Personality Inventory (DPI) consisting of twenty-eight scales. The DPI is a construct-oriented test in the tradition of the Personality Research Form (Jackson, 1967). The analysis resulted in seven distinct factors which were interpreted as reflecting the dimensions of (a) hypochondriacal complaining, (b) denial, (c) depressed withdrawal, (d) interpersonal conflict and social alienation, (e) persecutory ideas, (f) cognitive dysfunction, and (g) response bias. The identification of a variety of dimensions in a sample of alcoholic patients demonstrated that considerable heterogeneity of psychopathology existed within the sample tested.

The MMPI was found to be useful in differentiating between patient populations of diverse alcoholism treatment programs. English and Curtin (1975) compared alcoholics from a V.A. Hospital, a halfway house, and a state hospital and found differences for the various scales and suggested that different types of programs attract different types of clients. Wilkinson, Prado, Williams, and Schnadt (1971) used the MMPI and the Edwards Personal Preference Schedule EPPS) to predict dropouts from programs. Both tests were of limited value. However, the MMPI was found to be most useful for measuring significant improvement in the personal adjustment of alcoholics who completed treatment. Changes in pre and posttreatment MMPI scores, with the most marked difference in the Depression scale, were verified by Ends and Page (1959). This appears to be a common finding.

Libb and Taulbee (1971) demonstrated that MMPI profiles

of alcoholics are more malignant when the patients are tested before detoxification. To assess changes in psychopathology during detoxification and in a treatment program after detoxification, Hoffmann, Nelson, and Jackson (1974) used the Differential Personality Inventory with two groups of consecutively admitted male alcoholics. They were found to decrease after detoxification in those personality scales which reflect gross pathology. The change in personality measures during and after detoxification is due mainly to DPI scales which measure psychotic and neurotic dimensions rather than those which measure dimensions of personality disorder or sociopathic reactions, both of which tend to be unaffected by treatment. Measures of psychopathology showed further decrease with treatment after detoxification had been accomplished. Relatively high test retest correlations revealed that although systematic mean changes in both groups occurred, individuals showed marked tendencies to retain their relative position within a group after detoxification and treatment.

Recently, Huber and Danahy (1975) found significant differences on the *Pd* scale between alcoholics who completed a treatment program and those who did not, the former showing a significant reduction of pathology on most MMPI scales.

Even though a relationship between treatment outcome and the MMPI *Pd* scale was found by Kurland (1968), the relationship found by Pokorny, Miller, and Cleveland (1968) consisted only of a trend. However, the authors concluded on the basis of the MMPI that the abstinent are more neurotic while the drinkers are more psychopathic. Hoffmann and Jansen (1973) found that hospitalized alcoholics, categorized on the basis of selected discharge variables, differ significantly with regard to MMPI scale scores. Among the MMPI scales, the *Pd* scale was found to be the best predictor.

In summary then, it might be concluded that the MMPI appears to be a very sensitive instrument for measuring improvement of alcoholics during treatment and that personality measurements in terms of its clinical scales are useful in predicting treatment outcome.

Many investigators realize that measurements obtained from individual personality scales neglect the true personality profile of individuals. Thus, many clinicians and researchers give a higher degree of interpretive value to the relative elevation on scales than to absolute elevation. Such a distribution of percentages of two-point code-types of two alcoholic populations are presented in Table 2. The comparison of the 1959 and the 1971 populations reveals a relatively high stability of MMPI two-point codes in alcoholics over a period of 12 years. The inspection of Table 2 also reveals that a variety of psychopathological symptoms are present in alcoholics. Furthermore, it can be seen that certain code combinations are more prevalent, such as 4-2, 4-9, 9-4, and 4-7. A similar result was obtained by Goss and Morosko (1969). Table 3 presents the frequency of MMPI *T* score areas and combinations which demonstrates that the scales 4-2, 2-4, and 7 are most frequently elevated in groups of alcoholics. In addition, a variety of other MMPI scale score combinations are listed as being elevated which demonstrates again the large variety of psychopathology possible within alcoholic populations.

TABLE 2

Percentage of MMPI Codes from Two Groups of Male Minnesota State Hospital Alcoholics from Consecutive Admissions in 1959 and 1971

Second Point	High Point										
	1	2	3	4	5	6	7	8	9	0	Total
			Group I: 1959 (*N* = 393)								
1 *Hs*	-	2.5	0.8	3.8	0.3	-	-	0.8	1.0	0.3	9.4
2 *D*	1.5	-	0.5	10.7	1.0	0.3	0.8	0.8	0.8	1.5	17.8
3 *Hy*	1.5	0.5	-	4.0	-	-	-	0.3	0.3	-	7.4
4 *Pd*	1.8	5.1	0.3	-	0.8	2.0	0.8	1.8	5.3	1.5	19.3
5 *Mf*	-	0.5	0.3	2.3	-	0.5	0.3	0.3	1.8	-	5.9
6 *Pa*	-	3.1	0.3	2.0	-	-	-	1.5	2.3	0.8	9.9
7 *Pt*	0.3	2.0	-	4.1	0.3	0.5	-	1.0	1.3	0.5	9.9
8 *Sc*	-	1.8	-	1.5	-	0.8	-	-	0.5	-	4.6
9 *Ma*	-	0.3	-	8.4	0.5	0.8	0.5	-	-	-	10.4
0 *Si*	-	2.8	-	1.0	-	0.8	-	0.3	0.5	-	5.3
Total	5.1	18.6	2.0	38.7	2.8	5.6	2.3	6.6	13.7	4.6	100.0
			Group II: 1971 (*N* = 279)								
1 *Hs*	-	3.2	0.7	2.9	-	-	-	0.4	0.7	-	7.9
2 *D*	1.1	-	0.7	11.5	0.4	1.1	2.2	1.4	0.4	0.4	19.0
3 *Hy*	0.7	3.2	-	6.1	-	-	0.4	-	-	-	10.4
4 *Pd*	2.2	5.0	0.4	-	0.7	2.2	0.7	1.1	2.9	0.4	15.4
5 *Mf*	0.4	0.4	0.4	3.2	-	-	-	0.4	1.4	0.4	6.5
6 *Pa*	-	2.9	0.7	3.6	1.1	-	0.4	1.4	1.1	0.7	11.8
7 *Pt*	0.4	3.2	-	3.9	0.4	-	-	1.8	-	-	9.7
8 *Sc*	0.7	0.7	0.4	1.1	-	0.4	0.7	-	0.4	-	4.3
9 *Ma*	0.7	0.7	-	7.2	0.4	-	0.4	0.7	-	0.7	10.8
0 *Si*	-	2.2	-	1.1	0.4	0.4	-	-	0.4	-	4.3
Total	6.1	21.5	3.2	40.5	3.2	4.0	4.7	7.2	7.2	2.5	100.0

Note: Adapted from Hoffmann (1973)

TABLE 3

Frequency of MMPI T-Score Areas and Combinations above 70 (N = 200)

T-scores and T-score combinations above 70	Total N	T-scores and T-score combinations above 70 (cont.)	Total N
4	127	123	44
2	114	6	38
24	87	4271	36
7	72	4273	34
1	64	42781	32
3	64	5	31
27	64	42783	28
47	58	0	27
8	57	19	27
9	57	427813	25
427	56	39	24
49	47	427819	17
4278	46	427839	14
13	45	4278139	13

Note: Adapted from Goss and Morosko (1969).

MMPI ALCOHOLISM SCALES

In order to identify alcoholism among various psychiatric populations, several investigators have developed alcoholism scales based on MMPI items. The scales developed by Hampton (1953), Hoyt and Sedlacek (1958), and Holmes (1953) were found in replication studies not to discriminate between alcoholics and other psychiatric patient populations, the prime reason for the failure being that these scales were developed using normal populations for control groups. Thus, it is not too surprising to find that they measure mainly general maladjustment. However, MacAndrew's scale (1965) was found to distinguish between alcoholics and psychiatric outpatients. There is some evidence that this scale might also measure the general addictive process (Kranitz, 1952). Rosenberg (1972) developed a composite scale consisting of common items from the three most promising alcoholism scales: Holmes (1953), Hoyt and Sedlacek (1958), and MacAndrew (1965).

In a longitudinal study (Hoffmann, Loper, Kammeier, 1974), alcoholism scales were used on college students who later became alcoholics and on controls. None of the scales, with the exception of MacAndrew and the Rosenberg composite, seemed to differentiate between prealcoholics and controls. It was also found in this study that results based on the MacAndrew scale did not change significantly between time of college and time of treatment. It was concluded, therefore, that the MacAndrew scale and the Rosenberg composite would be valuable in detecting alcoholism prior to the onset of overt symptoms. Several other investigators (Huber & Danahy, 1975; Rohan, Tatro, & Rotman, 1969; Vega, 1971) demonstrated that the MacAndrew scale remains elevated for alcoholic subjects after treatment. These special characteristics of the MacAndrew scale--ability to differentiate between alcoholics and non-alcoholics, between prealcoholics and controls, and its stability from time prior to alcoholism to treatment--suggest that it may indeed uniquely measure personality traits of alcoholics.

Apfeldorf (1974) suggested that the construction of scales to measure alcoholic sub-types, such as neurotic and psychopathic alcoholics, be extended. Alcoholics and their sub-types ought then to be considered as relevant nosologies which are most appropriately assessed by empirically derived alcoholism scales.

PERSONALITY OF ALCOHOLICS AND ADDICTS

While there have been many MMPI research studies using both alcohol and drug abuser samples, relatively few investigations of such samples have compared the personality characteristics of alcoholics and narcotic addicts. Black and Heald (1975) performed such a comparison of MMPI profiles of alcohol and drug abusers drawn from similar vocational populations and identical treatment programs. The profile configuration in the two samples was found to be similar, with a relatively higher elevation on the *D* scale in the alcoholic sample and relatively higher elevations on the *Mf*, *Pa*, *Pt*, *Sc* and *Ma* scales in the drug samples. A large percentage of alcoholics appeared to be normal or only psychopathic on the MMPI, and an equal percentage produced MMPI profiles which suggest depression, psychoneurosis, and marked emotional maladjustment. The drug user sample had a greater percentage of psychopathic MMPI profiles, and it also showed a greater incidence of general personality maladjustment and significant emotional dysfunction. This means that drug abusers appeared to be somewhat more psychiatrically disturbed than alcoholics. On the other hand, the two samples could not be differentiated to any significant degree with regard to current personality dysfunctioning.

Overall (1973) averaged MMPI profiles of groups of narcotic addicts and alcoholics as compiled by Lanyon (1968) and applied a discriminant function analysis of differences in MMPI profiles of addicts and alcoholics. Both groups had elevated *Pd* components. The alcoholics' profile had substantially more *D*, *Hy*, *Pt*, *Pa*, and *Sc* MMPI scale elevations, whereas the addicts' profile had higher *K* and *Ma* components.

The narcotic addict MMPI profile is then characterized in terms of the MMPI coding system as manifesting a 4-9 "type". Marks and Seeman (1963) describe this type as a "sociopathic-emotionally unstable personality" with a long history of socially deviant behavior and a poor treatment outcome. The alcoholics' prototype profile then consists of a typical MMPI 2-4-7 code type. This code type is characterized by Marks and Seeman (1963) as being "depressive" with "passive-aggressive personality" features. This includes childhood health problems, a depressed and labile emotional tone, with feelings of inferiority, guilt, and anxiety. Overall (1973) concludes that alcoholics and narcotic addicts have very different personality characteristics. The alcoholics are more neurotic, depressed, anxious, passive, and dependent, whereas the narcotic addicts are more antisocial, amoral, impulsive, irritable, hostile, and psychopathic. The main difference between the groups on the basis of MMPI profiles consists of the stronger neurotic depressive profile pattern in the alcoholic group. Overall (1973) adds a word of caution, however: the majority of today's drug addicts and alcohol addicts are very different personalities.

Finally, a study by Toler (1975) investigating the personal values of addicts and alcoholics should be mentioned. The Rokeach Value Survey showed for only one value, "Independent", a statistically significant difference between the addict and the alcoholic group. The values of alcoholics and drug addicts are quite similar, but the two groups are quite different from the general population with respect to their value systems.

THE SIXTEEN PERSONALITY FACTOR QUESTIONNAIRE

The Sixteen Personality Factor Questionnaire (16 PF) was used by Fuller (1966) on a large group of state hospital alcoholics. Alcoholics were found to score in the direction of the scales, Less Intelligent, Emotionally Unstable, Humble, Sober, Shy, Imaginative, Apprehensive, and Tense. This profile indicates that the alcoholic person is aware of and concerned about the effects of inadequate adjustment. He is guilt prone and unable consistently to express this guilt in adjustive constructive behavior. In addition to frustration, alcoholics are high on anxiety. They have an inability to release tension or to control it. The amount of ego weakness found might result from adolescent attitudes or failures to assume mature social roles. Fuller (1966) found the alcoholic profile was correlated .62 with the profile of neurotics, .20 with narcotic addicts and -.11 with sociopaths. Therefore, he concludes that the alcoholic is neither a psychotic nor a psychopath although his "social nuisance value" may have misled some psychiatrists into so classifying him. Furthermore, it was concluded that neurotic drinking is a relief seeking or comfort seeking effort to eliminate the symptomatology of the neurotic personality. High waves of anxiety and depression, so concluded Fuller (1966), are experienced by the majority of alcoholics, and the threshold of tolerance for these anxiety waves has tended to make this type of neurotic individual seek an escape for the discomfort of his experience.

Golightly and Reinehr (1969) replicated Fuller's (1966) study but could not find such a high correlation of an alcoholic profile with a neurotic profile. Nevertheless, the authors agreed that 64% of the total sample were classified as "neurotic", 20% as "psychotic," and 15% as "character disorder".

Gross and Carpenter (1971) used also the 16 PF and concluded that chronic alcoholics are a distinct personality type. Lind (1972) compared 16 PF profiles obtained from a prison alcoholic sample with a profile elaborated by Fuller (1966) and found a positive similarity between the profiles.

The 16 PF was finally used by Hoy (1969) for treatment evaluation purposes. Alcoholics who left from a treatment program were found to be more surgent and extraverted than those who remained. The treatment effect as demonstrated by a test retest evaluation showed a significant decrease in the factor, Ergic Tension, and only a low or medium test retest correlation for individual 16 PF scales. It was concluded that the 16 PF questionnaire appears to be relatively insensitive to changes due to hospitalization and treatment.

Lawlis and Rubin (1971) used the 16 PF for the purpose of cluster analysis of the profiles in order to help investigate whether or not a unitary group of personality characteristics among alcoholics could be identified. Factor analysis of the 16 PF profiles identified three groups described as having inhibited-neurotic, aggressive-neurotic, and sociopathic symptoms. These types could be cross validated within two samples; in a third sample, a schizoid type could also be identified. However, it became apparent that all types of alcoholics have maladaptive ways of dealing with anxiety.

In a similar vein, to identify distinctive subgroups among male alcoholics based on 16 PF profiles, Nerviano and Gross (1973) used a multivariate typing technique developed by Lorr and found two highly discriminative types which could be replicated within two samples. The first type was described in terms of high anxiety and introversion, and the second type was characterized by dependency and conformity.

Further studies, which attempted to identify a number of personality types among alcoholic populations on the basis of the MMPI and other psychometric personality tests, will be referred to later on.

ALCOHOLIC PERSONALITY TYPES

Most studies consider alcoholics as a unitary group and assume, thereby, within-group homogeneity. In other words, the personality measurements of a group of persons being studied are usually averaged, resulting in a group personality profile. Such group profiles, however, could wash out meaningful individual variations. Although many individual test profiles might be similar to the group profile, a considerable number of tests might be not at all similar to the group average. Theoretically, there is no reason to believe that all alcoholics are more or less alike with respect to their personality pattern. Rather the possibility might be assumed that within a larger group of persons there may exist several kinds of smaller groups, each one characterized by a high similarity with the other, and in addition that these subgroups may have little in common when compared with each other. Recently, several investigators devoted themselves to the search for distinct personality patterns within alcoholic samples.

Hill, Haertzen, and Davis (1962) used the MMPI profiles of 199 Willmar State Hospital alcoholics, Lexington Public Health Service Hospital narcotic addicts, and 200 Stillwater Minnesota State Prison criminals. The factor analysis of the scale *T*-scores identified three major factors: (a) "undifferentiated psychopaths," characterized by social deviance and an elevation on the *Pd* scale, (b) "primary psychopaths," characterized by an elevation in the *Pd* and *Ma* scales, (c) "neurotic psychopaths, depressed," characterized by considerable elevation on the neurotic triad scales, especially on depression, including the *Pd* scale. It was concluded that differentiation can be made between the groups investigated and other nosological groups on factor one, but on no other factor. It was also concluded that except for behavior which is peculiarly determined by the particulr activity, no other personality characteristic is associated specifically with alcoholism, narcotic addiction, or criminality. Social deviance appears to be the common characteristic.

Applying the correlational trust procedure of MMPI profiles on alcoholics, Goldstein and Linden (1969) found four different personality types: (a) psychopathic personality and emotional instability, characterized by a *Pd* elevation; (b) psychoneurosis in terms of anxiety reaction or reactive depression, with the highest elevation in the MMPI scales, *D*, *Pt*, *Sc*, and *Pd*; (c) psychopathic personality, mixed type, with a long history of chronic alcoholism and multiple hospital admissions, characterized by a little deviance in the MMPI, but low elevations for the scales *Pd*, *Ma*, and *D*; and finally (d) alcoholism with secondary characteristics of drug addiction and paranoid features, characterized by MMPI elevation of the scales *Pd* and *Ma*. The four cluster types were cross validated by splitting the sample and computing the cluster analyses separately for both alcoholic groups.

Cluster analysis methods on the MMPI profiles from male alcoholics were used by Whitelock, Overall, and Patrick (1971). Of the four types identified, the first three were identical with Goldstein and Linden's (1969) types. In addition, it was found that patients with different MMPI profile patterns differed in the levels of self-reported alcohol abuse. The most severe self-report, as measured by a 38-item alcoholic questionnaire, was associated with anxiety and depression; lower abuse scores were associated with psychopathy and poor impulse control. A further attempt to elaborate alcoholic types was undertaken by Parthington and Johnson (1969) using responses to the

Differential Personality Inventory (DPI). This earlier developed experimental form of the DPI consisted of 18 pathological and personality constructs and was composed of 371 true-false items.

Parthington and Johnson (1969) were able to identify and replicate five types: (a) young, unstable, antisocial alcoholics (b) well motivated alcoholics who tend to lose emotional and cognitive control; (c) older, hypochrondiacal alcoholics with poor motivation for abstinence; (d) highly defensive alcoholics; and (e) extremely heavy drinkers with relatively little evidence of maladjustment. Parthington and Johnson (1969) interpreted these findings in terms of McQuitty's (1966) hierarchical model of types, which assumes that every person is a combination of "imperfect types" as distinct from a "pure type." Whereas pure types are hypothetical constructs, imperfect types consist of a given number of persons with internally consistent categories.

Skinner, Jackson, and Hoffman (1974) used a more recently developed form of the DPI consisting of 26 clinical scales and two validity scales. The personality profiles of three equal samples of alcoholics were intercorrelated and a Q technique factor analysis was conducted to identify preliminary model types. A sequential factor analytic strategy then identified eight bipolar dimensions. The five most important dimensions were: (a) acute anxiety versus denial and blunted affect, represented by the personality scales Defensiveness, Repression, and Shallow Affect versus Irritability, Panic Reaction, and Mood Fluctuation; (b) antisocial attitudes versus hypochondriacal preoccupation, represented by the personality scales Health Concern, Hypochondriasis, Somatic Complaints versus Rebelliousness,

Socially Deviant Attitudes, Impulsivity, and Desocialization; (c) hostile-hallucinatory syndrome versus neurotic depression, represented by the personality scales Self-depreciation, Cynicism, Depression, and Health Concern versus Perceptual Distortion, Headache Proneness, Hostility, and Irritability; (d) neurotic disorganization versus hostile paranoid, represented by the personality scales Health Concern, Sadism, Broodiness, Ideas of Persecution, Hostility, Familial Discord, and Cynicism versus Insomnia, Self-depreciation, Neurotic Disorganization, and Defensiveness; (e) emotional instability versus interpersonal conflict and depression, represented by the personality scales Depression, Rebelliousness, and Familial Discord versus Insomnia, Sadism, Health Concern, and Neurotic Disorganization. These personality types were finally correlated with MMPI marker profiles elaborated by Goldstein and Linden (1969), Whitelock et al. (1971) and the MMPI codes elaborated by Gilberstadt and Duker (1965) and Marks and Seeman (1963), and Lanyon (1968) group profiles which had been averaged by Overall (1973). The common types elaborated on the basis of the DPI showed marked correspondence with MMPI profiles from prior research by the authors mentioned above with a variety of psychiatric groups.

The typological studies demonstrate that it is possible to distinguish among many alcoholic types with differing personality characteristics and psychopathology. In a recent study, Skinner, Reed, and Jackson (1974) cross validated the above described alcoholic types with female alcoholics, male prisoners, psychiatric patients, and groups of college students and found that the typology elaborated on alcoholics can be replicated in other psychiatric samples. The classification for the male prison inmates was virtually identical to the alcoholic sample. These findings lend some credence to the assertion that common types exist in various diversely labeled psychiatric samples. Skinner et al. (1974), however, found small typological differences between the alcoholic and the prison sample; they hypothesize that these two types might be unique to alcoholics. These unique alcoholic features consist of the two dimensions of neurotic depression versus hostile-hallucinatory syndrome, and the hostile and sadistic temperament versus the impulsive, unstable personality. Contrary to these possible specific alcoholic personality types, the main general dimensions which were visible across all samples consisted of (a) repression versus the rebellious, antisocial syndrome, and (b) general symptom severity.

In connection with these typological findings, it should be noted that only 25% of the college population fit the typologies described above, whereas 53% of the prison population and 56% of the alcoholic population do fit into such typological classifications. This means that a very large percentage of a population, particularly among the college population, do not fit any kind of experimental personality classification. Prisoners and alcoholics who receive treatment, however, do fit to a much larger percentage into this typological system. Furthermore, this indicates that there exist in each population, to a greater or lesser extent, persons who do not fit any kind of typological system. The personality profiles of those subjects are evidently unique in that they have little resemblance to others.

LONGITUDINAL STUDIES

McCord and McCord (1960) undertook a comparative study of 29 male pre-alcoholics and 158 controls who had been part of the original group of 255 lower-class boys of the Cambridge-Somerville Youth Study, a project designed to prevent delinquency and to collect data on child training practices in this population segment of these two Massachusetts cities. The subjects were first studied in 1935 and followed up in 1956 when their average age was 30. The study included a variety of records on each subject and interviews by trained social workers during a five-year period. The investigators found that alcoholism symptoms were definable at this age level and that as pre-alcoholics the group was more self-contained and tended to be more over-confident than the control group. They concluded that this kind of behavior was probably a masculine facade which collapsed during the addiction stage.

Robins, Bates, and O'Neal (1962) and Robins (1966) in a follow-up study of 503 men and women who had, 30 years earlier, been patients in the St. Louis Municipal Psychiatric Clinic, classified 84 as alcoholics and 74 as heavy drinkers. They found that the childhoods of the alcoholics had been characterized by many symptoms of antisocial behavior, but none were specifically predictive of alcoholism. The behavior of alcoholics as adults appeared somewhat similar to the behavior of sociopaths. The alcoholics, however, did not usually indulge in the kinds of antisocial behavior that brought on serious legal consequences. Robins also concluded that the subjects showed very few symptoms that might have been a direct result of an excessive intake of alcohol. A similar history in sociopaths and alcoholics may have appeared not because both may have had a common disease, but rather because both had treatment in a child guidance clinic. Robins (1966) theorized that other alcoholics may have had origins of behavior more consistent with neurotic patterns which, during their childhoods, did not lead them to treatment clinics.

Jones (1968), working with data from the Oakland Growth Study (OGS), explored the alcohol-related behavior of 66 men in their mid-forties for whom childhood records from the OGS were available. From this group, six problem drinkers were identified. They showed numerous signs of maladjustive behavior in their childhood ratings. Jones indicated that potential problem drinkers had difficulty with dependency relationships and consequently tended to overplay an assertive masculine role.

Jones (1971) also explored alcohol-related behavior of more than 100 women, again working with data from the OGS. These women, preponderantly urban, middle class, and middle aged, had been part of the OGS for more than 30 years. Both their childhood and their adult personality characteristics were assessed by the California Q sort and by behavior ratings. It was found that the problem drinkers and the abstainers had certain traits in common, suggesting inadequate coping devices. Heavy drinkers seemed to share a history of social and manipulative competence, while moderate drinkers had similar likable and self-sufficient qualities. The data suggested to her that adult alcohol-related behavior may be an expression of personality tendencies already present before drinking patterns have been established.

Such findings have been interpreted by Sanford (1968) and Lisansky-Gomberg (1968) in terms of sex-role confusion and dependence associated with the increasing addictive process. McCord (1972) suggested, however, that an "interactionist approach" to an understanding of alcoholism is inadequate, that alcoholics might share a weak sense of self-esteem which, when challenged, results in an alcoholic "breakdown". This conclusion was reached when it was found that families of alcoholics from broken homes differed from those who came from intact homes in evidencing greater frequency of maternal promiscuity, other sexual deviances, and mutual parental role dissatisfaction. The sex-role confusion was evident among alcoholics from broken homes but not among alcoholics from intact homes.

In spite of differences in methodology, data gathering, and socioeconomic status of the samples, all these studies showed some degree of agreement concerning the preadolescent and adolescent characteristics of problem drinkers. However, all lacked comparative data from standardized personality measures administered to the subjects before and after the overt onset of alcoholism.

In an attempt to provide such data, three longitudinal studies, using Minnesota Multiphasic Personality Inventory (MMPI) profiles of 38 male alcoholics, were undertaken (Hoffmann, Loper, & Kammeier, 1974; Kammeier, Hoffmann, & Loper, 1973; Loper, Kammeier, & Hoffmann, 1973). From the late 1940's until 1962, the MMPI was administered routinely to all entering freshmen in many colleges at the University of Minnesota. Subjects selected for these studies had MMPI records at the University and also at one of two Minnesota treatment centers, where they had been admitted as alcoholics. Time span between the two recorded profiles averaged 13 years.

TABLE 4

Means, Standard Deviations, *T*-Scores, *t* Tests, and Test-Retest Correlations of MMPI Scales of Alcoholics at College Orientation and at Treatment

	Orientation			Treatment				
Scales	*M*	*SD*	*T*	*M*	*SD*	*T*	*t*	*r*
L	2.89	2.21	45	2.11	1.54	43	1.81	.62
F	5.11	3.61	55	7.92	4.11	62	-3.18**	.29
K	14.89	4.55	55	15.75	5.33	57	-0.69	.46
Hs	12.03	4.68	52	14.58	4.68	58	-2.38*	.22
D	18.74	5.44	55	24.26	6.76	68	-3.93**	.33
Hy	20.05	4.46	56	23.84	5.23	63	-3.40**	.35
Pd	23.37	6.94	60	29.18	4.27	74	-4.41**	.43
Mf	26.39	5.74	61	28.08	5.14	65	-1.35	.49
Pa	9.24	3.02	54	12.38	3.87	62	-3.93**	.36
Pt	25.98	8.16	56	30.58	6.55	65	-2.40*	.32
Sc	26.11	7.97	57	29.79	7.62	64	-1.76	.25
Ma	20.84	6.37	59	22.92	4.16	66	-1.89	.52
Si	22.77	9.41	47	31.17	9.49	57	-3.64**	.29

Note: Adapted from Kammeier, Hoffmann, and Loper (1973).

*$p < .05$.

**$p < .01$.

The first study (Kammeier et al., 1973) compared the college entrance profile with the treatment center profile for each subject. Table 4 gives the raw score means, standard deviations, T-scores, *t* values, and test-retest correlations on the MMPI validity and clinical scales of alcoholics at college orientation and at treatment. The mean scores on scales *F*, *Hs*, *D*, *Hy*, *Pd*, *Pa*, *Pt* and *Si* were significantly higher for the treatment profiles. These changes might suggest that "a progression to overt alcoholic symptomatology was accompanied by an increase in irritability, depression, hostility, anxiety, impulsivity, and resentment; by a strong need to manipulate and use others; and by difficulties with interpersonal relationships" (Kammeier et al., 1973). The combination of scale elevations describes the "neurotic patterns of a self-centered, immature, dependent, resentful, irresponsible kind of person who has been unable to face reality."

Preaddiction profiles were characterized by a lack of obvious deviance. Moderate test-retest correlations showed a relative stability in spite of the progressive nature of the addictive process, and this stability was supported by the clinical evaluation of the profiles by three psychologists. Four key scales--*Pd*, *D*, *Pt*, and *Sc*--showed the greatest changes in frequency of elevation, three of the scales--*Pd*, *D*, and *Sc*, and the *Ma* scale, being elevated frequently enough to suggest that they may be indicators of dependency problems.

The second study (Loper et al., 1973) compared college entrance scores of the alcoholic subjects with scores of 148 male classmates for MMPI clinical scales, Wiggins content scale, and item differences. Preaddiction profiles of the alcoholic subjects were significantly higher on scales *F*, *Pd*, and *Ma* and the content scales Authority, Conflict, and

TABLE 5

MMPI Items with Percentage "True" Difference > 20 between Prealcoholic Freshman Males and Classmates

Booklet No.	Item	Pre-alcoholics	Classmates
124	Most people will use somewhat unfair means to gain profit or an advantage rather than to lose it.	72	36
322	I worry over money and business.	50	28
12	I enjoy detective or mystery stories.	87	56
118	In school I was sometimes sent to the principal for cutting up.	56	29
502	I like to let people know where I stand on things.	97	70
25	I would like to be a singer.	59	32
329	I almost never dream.	25	54
116	I enjoy a race or game better when I bet on it.	56	30
435	Usually I would prefer to work with women.	34	9
294	I have never been in trouble with the law.	50	74
224	My parents have often objected to the kind of people I went around with.	34	10
117	Most people are honest chiefly through fear of being caught.	43	20

135	If I could get into a movie without paying and be sure I was not seen, I would probably do it.	65	41
95	I go to church almost every week.	34	57
481	I can remember "playing sick" to get out of something.	72	49
438	There are certain people whom I dislike so much that I am inwardly pleased when they are catching it for something they have done.	68	45
126	I like dramatics.	71	49
64	I sometimes keep on at a thing until others lose their patience with me.	62	39
521	In a group of people I would not be embarassed to be called upon to start a discussion or give an opinion about something I know well.	93	73
424	I feel hungry almost all the time.	41	19
131	I do not worry about catching diseases.	47	67
348	I tend to be on my guard with people who are somewhat more friendly than I had expected.	38	18

Note: Adapted from Loper, Kammeier, and Hoffmann (1973).

Poor Health, suggesting that the college prealcoholic is more likely to be impulsive, nonconforming, and gregarious than his peers. However, otherwise he does not appear to be grossly maladjusted. An item analysis showed 35 items differentiating prealcoholics from classmates (Table 5). The prealcoholic group was found to be less conventional, showed more health concern, and reflected attitudes of social cynicism and romanticism.

The third study (Hoffmann et al., 1974) examines MMPI content scales, MMPI alcoholism scales, and item changes in the same subjects from the time of college orientation to the time of treatment. In addition, it examines the performance of MMPI alcoholism scales, comparing the prealcoholic sample at the time of college with a classmate control group to determine to what degree these scales might be able to identify future alcoholics.

At the time of treatment, alcoholics scored significantly higher on the MMPI content scales Social Maladjustment, Depression, Feminine Interests, Poor Morale, and Family Problems, but significantly lower on Religious Fundamentalism. Also 13 MMPI items were found to indicate changes from the time of college testing to the time of treatment (Table 6). The item content suggests an increase of the depressive symptomatology over time. A decrease of endorsement for the item "I feel hungry almost all the time" might be of interest for a psychoanalytical interpretation suggesting alcohol consumption as a substitute for oral needs.

The authors conclude, on the basis of the findings in all three studies, that prior to an addictive stage there are already certain characterological elements associated with persons who develop alcoholism. In the prealcoholic

TABLE 6
MMPI Item Endorsement Frequencies (Percentage Responding "True") of Alcoholics at College and at Treatment

Booklet No.	Item	College	Treatment	$P <$
215	I have used alcohol excessively.	36	96	.0001
460	I have used alcohol moderately (or not at all).	84	24	.0001
46	My judgment is better than it ever was.	80	36	.001
549	I shrink from facing a crisis or difficulty.	4	48	.002
397	I have sometimes felt that difficulties were piling up so high that I could not overcome them.	36	80	.002
61	I have not lived the right kind of life.	28	72	.002
86	I am certainly lacking in self-confidence.	8	48	.002
264	I am entirely self-confident.	32	0	.002
424	I feel hungry almost all the time.	40	4	.005
67	I wish I could be as happy as others seem to be.	24	68	.005
102	My hardest battles are with myself.	56	92	.005
506	I am a high-strung person.	16	56	.005
442	I have had periods in which I lost sleep over worry.	52	88	.005

Note: Adapted from Hoffmann, Loper, and Kammeier (1974).

stage, however, we find a certain lack of neurotic symptomatology, depression, and environmental conflict. It appears that between the prealcoholic stage and the time of hospitalization for alcoholism, further drinking leads to cumulative stresses of life which are reflected in an increase of symptomatology connected with general distress.

The authors suggest further experimentation is needed with the MacAndrew and similar alcoholism scales as applied to college and non-college samples within the same age categories.

> Such experimentation should be done in light of the probability multiple-causation theory of the alcoholism process. The personality component is only one factor in the development of the eventual condition of alcoholism, but it is our conclusion that the role of personality factors is no longer speculative. (Hoffman et al., 1974, p. 497)

A recent study (Goldstein & Sappington, 1975) investigated whether the prealcoholic MMPI profiles described by Loper et al. (1973) could be replicated on a sample of college students who later became drug users and whether there might be the possibility of an antecedent personality constellation in preusers. All of the 33 students entered the university between 1962 and 1965 and had become regular users of marijuana and hallucinogens during their college years. Preusers were found to score significantly higher on the MMPI scales *Hy*, *Pd*, *Pa*, and *Ma* than the control group. This result would describe the drug preusers as being verbally skillful and socially outgoing individuals who are also reluctant to reveal themselves because of ideas of persecution. Preusers also showed a greater expression of impulse and conflict with societal norms and aggressiveness.

It has to be noted, however, that the differences found between the two groups were rather small and were characterized by an absence of obvious psychopathology.

There exists a remarkable similarity of group profiles between both the prealcoholics and the preusers as well as between both kinds of control subjects. The current findings, together with those of Loper et al. (1973), provide some credence to the existence of a personality constellation prior to addiction. Unlike the prealcoholic personality, the preaddictive personality might be characterized by an additional paranoid component which does not exist in prealcoholics.

CONCLUSIONS

It might appear that simple generalizations about personality in alcoholism are unwarranted. However, certain pathological personality traits, investigated with a variety of personality measurements, occur repeatedly in alcoholic populations. There is relative agreement that the broad symptom complex describes people with depressive, neurotic-depressive, sociopathic, and anxiety features. Yet there are many different personality types prevalent in alcoholic populations which can also be found in other psychiatric populations. MMPI alcoholism scales, in particular the MacAndrew scale, were found to be quite effective in identifying alcoholics prior to addiction, either before or after a period of treatment and might, therefore, measure a substantive personality characteristic unique to addiction.

Longitudinal studies demonstrate the pre-existence

of personality within the etiology of alcoholism. However, at present, it is not quite clear whether these kinds of personality traits prior to alcoholism are a result of heredity, family background, or both. Absence of impulse control, combined with aggressiveness, antisocial symptoms, authority conflict, and gregariousness are personality features which the prealcoholic shares with the normal adolescent. Prolonged drinking and the development of an alcoholic career result in an increase of psychiatric symptoms, most notably those connected with depression, insecurity, and defensive behaviors. In short, alcoholism might be viewed as a life-style chosen by a person in order to cope with his own needs and the pressures of his environment.

For future research, it might be well to elaborate further on the development of typologies among alcoholic populations and to investigate suitable and effective treatment techniques, taking into account the individual differences between personality types.

REFERENCES

Ansbacher, H., & Ansbacher, R. *The individual psychology of Alfred Adler*. New York: Basic Books, 1946.

Apfeldorf, M. Contrasting assumptions and directions in MMPI research on alcoholism. *Quarterly Journal of Studies on Alcohol*, 1974, *35*, 1375-1379.

Astin, A.W. A factor study of the MMPI Psychopathic Deviate Scale. *Journal of Consulting Psychology*, 1959, *23*, 550-554.

Bandura, A. *Principles of behavior modification*. New York: Holt, Rinehart, & Winston, 1969.

Black, F.W., & Heald, A. MMPI characteristics of alcohol and illicit drug-abusers enrolled in a rehabilitation program. *Journal of Clinical Psychology*, 1975, *31*, 572-575.

Blane, H.T. *The personality of the alcoholic: Guises of dependency*. New York: Harper & Row, 1968.

Bleuler, M. Familial and personal background of chronic alcoholics. In O. Diethelm (Ed.), *Etiology of chronic alcoholism*. Springfield, Ill.: Charles C Thomas, 1955.

Brown, M.A. Alcoholic profiles on the Minnesota Multiphasic. *Journal of Clinical Psychology*, 1950, *6*, 266-269.

Chafetz, M.E., Blane, H.T., & Hill, M.J. *Frontiers of alcoholism*. New York: Science House, 1970.

Comrey, A.L. A factor analysis of items on the MMPI Psychopathic Deviate Scale. *Educational and Psychological Measurement*, 1958, *18*, 91-98.

Dahlstrom, W.G., Welsh, G.S., & Dahlstrom, L.E. *An MMPI handbook, Volume 2, research applications*. Minneapolis: University of Minnesota Press, 1975.

Edwards, A.L. *The measurement of personality traits by scales and inventories*. New York: Holt, Rinehart, & Winston, 1970.

Ends, E.J., & Page, S.W. Group psychotherapy and concomitant psychological change. *Psychological Monograph*, 1959, *73*, (10, Whole No. 480).

English, G.E., & Curtain, M.E. Personality differences in patients at three alcoholism treatment agencies. *Quarterly Journal of Studies on Alcohol*, 1975, *36*, 52-61.

Fenichel, O. *The psychoanalytic theory of neurosis*. New York: Norton, 1945.

Freedman, A.M., Kaplan, H.I., & Sadock, B.J. *Modern synopsis of comprehensive textbook of psychiatry*. Baltimore: The Williams & Wilkins Co., 1972.

Fuller, G.B. Research in alcoholism with the 16 PF Test. *IPAT information bulletin* No. 12, Champaign, Ill.: Institute for Personality and Ability Testing, 1966.

Gilberstadt, H., & Duker, J. *A handbook for clinical and actuarial MMPI interpretation*. Philadelphia: Saunders, 1965.

Goldstein, J.W., & Sappington, J. *Personality characteristics of students who became heavy drug users*. Unpublished manuscript, Carnegie-Mellon University, 1975.

Goldstein, S.G., & Linden, J.D. Multivariate classification of alcoholics by means of the MMPI. *Journal of Abnormal Psychology*, 1969, *74*, 661-669.

Golightly, C., & Reinehr, R.C. 16 PF profiles of hospitalized alcoholic patients: Replication and extension. *Psychological Reports*, 1969, *24*, 543-545.

Goss, A., & Morosko, T.E. Alcoholism and clinical symptoms. *Journal of Abnormal Psychology*, 1969, *74*, 682-684.

Gross, W.F., & Carpenter, L.L. Alcoholic personality: Reality or fiction? *Psychological Reports*, 1971, *28*, 375-378.

Hampton, P.J. The development of a personality questionnaire for drinkers. *Genetic Psychological Monographs*, 1953, *48*, 55-115.

Hill, E.H., Haertzen, C.A., & Davis, H. An MMPI factor analytic study of alcoholics, narcotic addicts, and criminals. *Quarterly Journal of Studies on Alcohol*, 1962, *23*, 411-431.

Hoffmann, H. MMPI changes for a male alcoholic state hospital population -- 1959 to 1971. *Psychological Reports*, 1973, *33*, 139-142.

Hoffmann, H., Jackson, D.N., & Skinner, H.A. Dimensions of psychopathology among alcoholic patients. *Journal of Studies on Alcohol*, 1975, *36*, 825-837.

Hoffmann, H., & Jansen, D.G. Relationships among discharge variables and MMPI scale scores of hospitalized alcoholics. *Journal of Clinical Psychology*, 1973, *29*, 475-477.

Hoffmann, H., Loper, R., & Kammeier, M.L. Identifying future alcoholics with MMPI alcoholism scales. *Quarterly Journal of Studies on Alcohol*, 1974, *35*, 490-498.

Hoffmann, H., Nelson, P.C., & Jackson, D.N. The effects of detoxification on psychopathology for alcoholics as measured by the Differential Personality Inventory (DPI). *Journal of Clinical Psychology* , 1974, *30*, 89-93.

Hoffmann, H., & Noem, A.A. Alcoholism among parents of male and female alcoholics. *Psychological Reports*, 1975, *36*, 322. (a)

Hoffmann, H., & Noem, A.A. Alcoholism and abstinence among relatives of American Indian alcoholics. *Journal of Studies on Alcohol*, 1975, *36*, 165. (b)

Holmes, W.O. *The development of an empirical MMPI scale for alcoholism.* M.A. thesis, San Jose State College, 1953.

Hoy, R.M. The personality of inpatient alcoholics in relation to group psychotherapy as measured by the 16 PF. *Quarterly Journal of Studies on Alcohol*, 1969, *30*, 401-407.

Hoyt, D.P., & Sedlacek, G.M. Differentiating alcoholics from normals and abnormals with the MMPI. *Journal of Clinical Psychology*, 1958, *14*, 69-74.

Huber, N.A., & Danahy, S. Use of the MMPI in predicting completion and evaluating changes in a long-term alcoholism treatment program. *Journal of Studies on Alcohol*, 1975, *36*, 1230-1237.

Irgens-Jensen, O. *Problem drinking and personality. A study based on the Draw-a-Person Test.* New Brunswick, N.J.: Rutgers Center of Alcohol Studies, 1971.

Jackson, D.N. *Personality research form manual.* Goshen, N.Y.: Research Psychologists Press, 1967.

Jellinek, E.M. Phases in the drinking history of alcoholics. *Quarterly Journal of Studies on Alcohol*, 1946, *7*, 1-88.

Jessor, R., Graves, T.D., Hanson, R.C., & Jessor, S.L. *Society, personality, and deviant behavior: A study of a tri-ethnic community.* New York: Holt, Rinehart & Winston, 1968.

Jones, M.C. Personality correlates and antecedents of drinking patterns in adult males. *Journal of Consulting and Clinical Psychology*, 1968, *32*, 2-12.

Jones, M.C. Personality antecedents and correlates of drinking patterns in women. *Journal of Consulting and Clinical Psychology*, 1971, *36*, 61-69.

Kammeier, M.L., Hoffmann, H., & Loper, R.G. Personality characteristics of alcoholics as college freshmen and at time of treatment. *Quarterly Journal of Studies on Alcohol*, 1973, *34*, 390-399.

Kirchner, J.H., & Marzolf, S.S. Personality of alcoholics as measured by Sixteen Personality Factor questionnaire and House-Tree-Person color-choice characteristics. *Psychological Reports*, 1974, *35*, 627-642.

Kranitz, L. Alcoholics, heroin addicts, and nonaddicts: Comparisons on the MacAndrew alcoholism scale of the MMPI. *Quarterly Journal of Studies on Alcohol*, 1972, *33*, 807-809.

Kurland, A.A. Maryland alcoholics: Follow-up study 1. *Psychiatric Research Report* 24. Washington, D.C.: American Psychological Association, March 1968.

Lanyon, R.I. *A handbook of MMPI group profiles*. Minneapolis: University of Minnesota Press, 1968.

Lawlis, G.F., & Rubin, S.E. 16 PF study of personality patterns in alcoholics. *Quarterly Journal of Studies on Alcohol*, 1971, *32*, 318-327.

Libb, J.W., & Taulbee, E.S. Psychotic-appearing MMPI profiles among alcoholics. *Journal of Clinical Psychology*, 1971, *27*, 101-102.

Lind, C.W., Jr. 16 PF screening instrument for alcoholics. *Journal of Clinical Psychology*, 1972, *28*, 548-549.

Lisansky-Gomberg, E.S. Etiology of alcoholism. *Journal of Consulting and Clinical Psychology*, 1968, *32*, 18-20.

Loper, R.G., Kammeier, M.L., & Hoffmann, H. MMPI characteristics of college freshman males who later became alcoholics. *Journal of Abnormal Psychology*, 1973, *82*, 159-162.

MacAndrew, C. The differentiation of male alcoholic outpatients from nonalcoholic psychiatric outpatients by means of the MMPI. *Quarterly Journal of Studies on Alcohol*, 1965, *26*, 238-246.

MacAndrew, C., & Edgerton, R.B. *Drunken comportment: A social explanation*. Chicago: Aldine, 1969.

Marks, P.A., & Seeman, W. *Actuarial description of abnormal personality*. Baltimore: Williams & Wilkins, 1963.

Masserman, J.H. Alcohol and neurotic behavior. In S.P. Lucia (Ed.), *Alcohol and civilization*. New York: McGraw Hill, 1963.

McClelland, D., Davis, W., Kalin, R., & Wanner, E. *The drinking man*. New York: The Free Press, 1972.

McCord, J. Etiological factors in alcoholism; Family and personal characteristics. *Quarterly Journal of Studies on Alcohol*, 1972, *33*, 1020-1027.

McCord, W., & McCord, J. *Origins of alcoholism*. California: Stanford University Press, 1960.

McQuitty, L.L. Single and multiple hierarchical classification by reciprocal pairs and rank order types. *Educational and Psychological Measurement*, 1966, *26*, 253-266.

Merton, R.K. *Social theory and social structure*. Glencoe, Ill.: Free Press, 1957.

National Institute on Alcohol Abuse and Alcoholism. *Alcohol & Alcoholism: Problems, programs, & progress*. Washington, D.C.: U.S. Government Printing Office, 1972.

Nerviano, V.J., & Gross, W.F. A multivariate delineation of two alcoholic profile types on the 16 PF. *Journal of Clinical Psychology*, 1973, *29*, 371-374.

Overall, J.E. MMPI personality patterns of alcoholics and narcotic addicts. *Quarterly Journal of Studies on Alcohol*, 1973, *34*, 104-111.

Parthington, J.T. Dr. Jekyll and Mr. High: Multidimensional scaling of alcoholics' self-evaluations. *Journal of Abnormal Psychology*, 1970, *75*, 131-138.

Parthington, J.T., & Johnson, F.G. Personality types among alcoholics. *Quarterly Journal of Studies on Alcohol*, 1969, *30*, 21-33.

Pokorny, A.D., Miller, B.A., & Cleveland, S.E. Response to treatment of alcoholism. A follow-up study. *Quarterly Journal of Studies on Alcohol*, 1968, *29*, 364-381.

Robins, L.N. *Deviant children grown up*. Baltimore: Williams & Wilkins, 1966.

Robins, L.N., Bates, W., & O'Neal, P. Adult drinking patterns of former problem children. In D. Pittman, & C. Snyder, (Eds.), *Society, culture and drinking patterns*. New York: John Wiley & Sons, Inc., 1962.

Rohan, W.P., Tatro, R.L., & Rotman, S.R. MMPI changes in alcoholics during hospitalization. *Quarterly Journal of Studies on Alcohol*, 1969, *30*, 389-400.

Rosen, A.C. A comparative study of alcoholic and psychiatric patients with the MMPI. *Quarterly Journal of Studies on Alcohol*, 1960, *21*, 253-266.

Rosenberg, N. MMPI alcoholism scales. *Journal of Clinical Psychology*, 1972, *28*, 515-522.

Sanford, N. Personality and patterns of alcohol consumption. *Journal of Consulting and Clinical Psychology*, 1968, *32*, 13-17.

Skinner, H.A., Jackson, D.N., & Hoffmann, H. Alcoholic personality types: Identification and correlates. *Journal of Abnormal Psychology*, 1974, *83*, 658-666.

Skinner, H.A., Reed, P.L., & Jackson, D.N. *Generalizability of personality types derived from alcoholic patients.* (Research Bulletin 303), London, Canada: University of Western Ontario, Department of Psychology, August 1974.

Sutherland, E.H., Schroeder, H.C., & Tordella, C.L. Personality traits and the alcoholic. *Quarterly Journal of Studies on Alcohol*, 1950, *11*, 547-561.

Syme, L. Personality characteristics and the alcoholic: A critique of current studies. *Quarterly Journal of Studies on Alcohol*, 1957, *18*, 288-302.

Toler, C. The personal values of alcoholics and addicts. *Journal of Clinical Psychology*, 1975, *31*, 554-557.

Vega, A. Cross-validation of four MMPI scales for alcoholism. *Quarterly Journal of Studies on Alcohol*, 1971, *32*, 791-797.

Whitelock, P.R., Overall, J.E., & Patrick, J.H. Personality patterns and alcohol abuse in a state hospital population. *Journal of Abnormal Psychology*, 1971, *78*, 9-16.

Wilkinson, A.E., Prado, W.M., Williams, W.D., & Schnadt, F.W. Psychological test characteristics and length of stay in alcoholism treatment. *Quarterly Journal of Studies on Alcohol*, 1971, *32*, 60-65.

Williams, J.H. Characterization and follow-up of alcoholic patients. In R.J. Catanzaro (Ed.), *Alcoholism; The total treatment approach*. Springfield, Ill.: Charles C Thomas, 1968.

Williams, R.J. The genotropic concept: Nutritional deficiencies and alcoholism. *Annals of the New York Academy of Science*, 1954, *54*, 794-811.

Williams, R.J. Biochemical individuality and cellular nutrition: Prime factors in alcoholism. *Quarterly Journal of Studies on Alcohol*, 1959, *20*, 452-463.

CHAPTER 10

EMPIRICAL INVESTIGATIONS OF PSYCHOLOGICAL DEFICIT

Ralph E. Tarter

Throughout history, alcoholic beverages have been consumed by members of almost all cultural groups for religious, social, or recreational reasons. The extent to which alcohol has been integrated into Western society is readily illustrated by its universal availability at private clubs, public drinking houses, athletic events, and business functions. Social gatherings are often organized specifically for drinking; for example, the cocktail hour and the wine tasting party. Perhaps more than any other single substance, alcohol has been woven into our social fabric and significantly influences our life style.

While alcohol consumption is a common and accepted practice, surprisingly little is known of its consequences from chronic and unrestrained intake. For most addicted individuals, there are deleterious social, economic, marital,

Ralph E. Tarter and A. Arthur Sugerman (eds.), Alcoholism

ISBN: 0-201-08146-6
ISBN: 0-201-08145-8 (pbk.)

and vocational effects resulting from chronic inebriation, but a vital question that remains to be answered concerns the consequences to the individual in terms of behavioral efficiency and psychological functioning. This chapter will focus on the nature and extent of psychological deficit in chronic alcoholics as it pertains to neurological integrity. As such, the neuropsychological sequelae of alcoholism will be discussed with the primary objective of systematically elucidating the intrinsic processes of alcoholism as they affect brain-behavior relationships.

PSYCHOLOGICAL DEFICIT

INTELLIGENCE MEASURES OF COMPETENCY. The concept of psychological deficit as first advanced by Hunt and Cofer (1944) refers to a performance decrement on intellectual and laboratory tasks. Alcoholics are deficient on a variety of psychological and behavioral tasks, but intellectual capacity is strikingly intact. On standardized psychometric tests of intelligence, such as the Wechsler Adult Intelligence Scale and Wechsler-Bellevue Intelligence Scale, alcoholics typically perform in the average (Bauer & Johnson, 1957; Fitzhugh, Fitzhugh, & Reitan, 1960, 1965; Goldstein & Shelley, 1971; Murphy, 1953; Peters, 1956; Wechsler, 1941, 1958) to superior ranges (Halpern, 1946; Kaldegg, 1956; Malerstein & Belden, 1968; Plumeau, Machover, & Puzzo, 1960). In one study (Kaldegg, 1956), it was observed that over half of the alcoholic subjects obtained an IQ score greater than 120.

Alcoholics do not appear to suffer from an intellectual deterioration in any generalized or global fashion. On the

Shipley Institute of Living Scale, Tarter and Jones (1971a) and Kish (1970) found no differences between alcoholics, normals, and psychiatric patients on the conceptual quotient, an index of deterioration. Tarter and Jones (1971a) also found no relationship between the conceptual quotient and number of years the person admitted to being alcoholic or total number of years of alcohol consumption.

Other tests of mental ability, however, have revealed certain impairments in alcoholics. Jones and Parsons (1971b) found that alcoholics performed less well than normals on the 1963 version of the Raven's Progressive Matrices, a test with factor loadings on general intelligence and perceptual organization (Burke & Bingham, 1969). In another investigation (Jones, 1971b), it was observed that the severity of performance deficit on this test was associated with duration of alcoholism history. The General Aptitude Test Battery has also been administered to alcoholics (Kish, 1970; Kish & Cheney 1969). In addition to General Intelligence, alcoholics also performed competently on the Verbal, Spatial, Perceptual, and Clerical subtests. Decrements were, however, manifested on the Numerical, Motor Coordination, Finger Dexterity, and Manual Dexterity subtests.

From the above cited investigations, it is apparent that alcoholics do not suffer from a pervasive intellectual deterioration. Standard tests of intelligence yielding global measures of intellectual capacity have not been particularly useful in elucidating the nature and extent of impairment in alcoholics because of their relative lack of specificity. The IQ scores of alcoholics are typically within the normal ranges of functioning. In order to determine if performance decrements exist on specific aspects of intelligence, Tarter,

Buonpane, and Wynant (1975) administered a battery of 23 factorially pure tests derived from the Kit of Reference Tests for Cognitive Factors (French, Ekstrom, & Price, 1963) and found no differences between alcoholics and psychiatric patients. Performance on other tests, such as the Block Design Subtest of the WAIS and Wechsler-Bellevue, has, however, been shown to be somewhat deficient (Fitzhugh et al., 1960, 1965; Goldstein, Neuringer, & Klappersack, 1970). On other measures that tap specific aspects of intellectual capacity, deficits have also been observed (Jones, 1971b; Jones & Parsons, 1971b).

LABORATORY TESTS OF COMPETENCY. Many experimental investigations have been conducted with the primary objective of determining the competency of alcoholics in perceptual, motor, and cognitive functions. Several reviews of the literature have been published (Kleinknecht & Goldstein, 1972; Tarter 1975a, 1975b).

On tasks of perceptual speed, alcoholics exhibited intact performance on the Stroop Test (Goldstein & Chotlos, 1965) and Street Gestalt and Figure Identification Tests (Claeson & Carlsson, 1970). Perceptual synthesis on the other hand has been shown to be impaired. On tasks where the subject must assemble the visual elements of a field into a specific pattern, alcoholics have been observed to be impaired. Thus on the Block Design Subtest of the WAIS (Goldstein et al., 1970) and Wechsler-Bellevue (Fitzhugh et al., 1960, 1965), deficient performance has been observed. Similarly, alcoholics performed poorly on the Kohs Block Design Test (Claeson & Carlsson, 1970) and Grassi Block Substitution Test (Grassi, 1953; Jonsson, Cronholm, &

Izikowitz, 1962).

Perceptual orientation, that is the ability to appreciate verticality and tilt of a visual stimulus, has frequently been found to be impaired in alcoholics. Thus on the Rod and Frame test, alcoholics perform more poorly than normals (Witkin, Karp, & Goodenough, 1959). Whether this deficiency is the result of a personality trait of the dependent individual (Karp & Konstadt, 1965; Karp, Witkin, & Goodenough, 1965a, 1965b; Witkin et al., 1959) or a product of neurological dysfunction (Bailey, Hustmyer, & Kristofferson, 1961, Goldstein & Chotlos, 1965) is not clear. Improvement in performance has been reported after alcoholics had an opportunity to focus attention on kinesthetic cues during a period of perceptual deprivation (Jacobson, 1968). Cognitive factors have also been shown to play a significant role in perceptual field orientation studies. Tarter, Sheldon, and Sugerman (1975) reported that general reasoning ability alone could account for 25% of RFT performance variance. By adding other factors such as sensitivity to problems, mechanical knowledge, speed of closure, and length estimation, one could account for over 52% of RFT variance. For a more detailed discussion of this subject, the reader is referred to Tarter (1975b) and Sugerman and Schneider (Chapter 11 of this volume).

An impairment has also been observed on tasks that require spatial scanning and planning. Thus deficits were noted on the Trail Making Test of the Halstead-Reitan Battery (Fitzhugh et al., 1960, 1965; Goldstein & Chotlos, 1965) and Maze Tracing Speed Test (Tarter, 1971). Intact performance on the other hand was observed on tests that measure perceptual flexibility, such as the Embedded Figures Test (Jones & Parsons,

1971b; Rhodes, Carr, & Jurji, 1968; Rudin & Stagner, 1958), Gottschaldt Test (Claeson & Carlson, 1970) and Copying Test (Tarter, 1971).

The studies in which perceptual-motor coordination was tested are less conclusive. For example, a perceptual-motor deficit has not been found on the Bender-Gestalt Test in which the subject must copy simple geometric figures (Hirschenfang, Silber, & Benton, 1967, 1968; Kates & Schmolke, 1953; Silber, Hirschenfang, & Benton, 1968), but has been found on a star tracing task (Vivian, Goldstein, & Shelly, 1973) and Purdue Pegboard where the subject must place pegs into holes (Tarter & Jones, 1971b).

Tests of motor capacity have also been useful in discriminating alcoholics from normals. On a test of finger tapping, Tarter and Jones (1971b) and Vivian et al. (1973) noted that alcoholics were deficient. Finger and manual dexterity (Kish & Cheney, 1969) has also been shown to be impaired. Muscle strength as measured by the dynanometer has also been found to be reduced (Tarter & Jones, 1971b).

Learning and memory capacity has received the attention of various investigators. On the Graham-Kendall Memory for Designs Test, May, Urquhart, and Watts (1970) found no evidence for impairment; however, on the Benton Visual Retention Test, Claeson and Carlsson (1970) noted that 65% of their alcoholic subjects were impaired. Chandler, Vega, and Parsons (1973) found intact memory on a dichotic memory task, but alcoholics who were previously suspected of being brain damaged were deficient on this task. On paired associate tasks, Jonsson et al., (1962) and Claeson and Carlsson (1970) were also unable to detect signs of a memory disturbance. Similar results have been reported by Weingartner, Faillace, & Markley (1971) for serial and free recall tasks.

One aspect of memory functioning that has engaged the curiosity of researchers and clinicians is the alcoholic blackout. This phenomenon has been assumed to be a basic characteristic of the addictive process (Jellinek, 1960) and refers to an inability to recall in a sober state events that occurred while inebriated. In a series of provocative studies, (Goodwin, Crane, & Guze, 1969; Goodwin, Hill, Powell, & Viamontes, 1973; Goodwin, Othmer, Halikas, & Freemon, 1970), it was found that the blackout reflected a form of antegrade amnesia after a threshold quantity of ethanol was ingested. Tarter and Schneider (in preparation) found that the number of alcoholic blackouts reported by the individual was unrelated to memory capacity while in the sober condition. The blackout was on the other hand associated with drinking history and current drinking pattern. For example, those persons who reported the greatest number of blackouts were more inclined to drink until they were inebriated or until they fell asleep. They also admitted more frequently to a craving for alcohol and reported both a loss of control over their drinking and an increased tolerance to alcohol during their years of abuse. Similar results have been obtained by Goodwin et al. (1969), who also noted that loss of control, increased tolerance, and extreme intoxication (benders) were related to blackouts. In addition they observed that gulping drinks was associated with blackouts; a finding also replicated by Tarter and Schneider (in preparation), although the results did not quite attain statistical significance. Thus the blackout does not appear to be related to cognitive or memorial factors while in the sober condition. Rather, this curious but frequently observed manifestation of amnesia appears to be more a function of drinking history and present drinking behavior.

A cognitive deficit has also been noted in chronic alcoholics. For example, alcoholics typically perform in the impaired ranges on the Category Test of the Halstead-Reitan Battery (Fitzhugh et al., 1960, 1965; Jones & Parsons, 1971a). They have also been observed to be impaired on the Query Brain Damage Scale, a variant of the Goldstein Object Sorting Test (Lovibond & Holloway, 1968). In one study, alcoholics also manifested a deficit in a test of proverb appreciation (Jonsson et al., 1962). Intact performance has been reported on other cognitive tasks such as Thurstone's Figure Classification Test (Claeson & Carlsson, 1970; Jonsson et al., 1962), synonym identification (Claeson & Carlsson, 1970; Jonsson et al., 1962; Tarter & Jones, 1971a), and in a rule learning concept identification test (Pishkin, Fishkin, & Stahl, 1972). In another investigation, Tarter et al., (1975) observed intact capacity on tests that measure comprehension, memory, inductive reasoning, and syllogistic reasoning.

In an attempt to further clarify the status of cognitive competency of alcoholics, Tarter and Parsons (1971) and Tarter (1973) administered the Wisconsin Card Sorting Test, a task that requires the identification of simple concepts and also measures the ability of the person to shift concepts. It was found that alcoholics were not impaired in concept acquisition, but were unable to switch cognitive sets as readily as normals. In addition, the alcoholics were unable to maintain or persist with a concept despite the fact that they were positively reinforced for a correct mode of responding. It was also observed that the alcoholic subjects were less capable than normals in using the information contained in an erroneous response to achieve a correct mode of responding later. And finally, it was found that the alcoholics were inclined to perseverate, according to the physical position or place of the stimulus cards, rather than to sort them according to their intrinsic characteristics of color, shape, or number.

Thus it can be seen that deficits are manifested by alcoholics on a variety of psychological and behavioral measures. Is the pattern of deficits systematic and suggestive of CNS pathology? Theories and evidence pertaining to this question are presented in the next section.

NEUROPSYCHOLOGICAL INTERPRETATION

Two essential questions concerning the performance deficits of alcoholics merit consideration. First, on the basis of psychological and behavioral measures, do alcoholics manifest a performance pattern indicative of a central neurological disturbance? If so, can the available evidence be conceptualized so as to implicate a specific anatomical site or neurophysiological system?

With the respect to the first question, there is now abundant information. Testing alcoholics on the Halstead-Reitan Battery reveals a neuropsychological impairment, although not as severe as that seen in patients who have suffered traumatic brain injury (Fitzhugh et al., 1960, 1965; Goldstein & Shelly, 1971). The Halstead-Reitan Battery is a frequently utilized clinical instrument for the assessment of brain damage. Originally developed by Halstead (1947), who first advanced the concept of "biological intelligence" as a means of quantitatively describing neurological efficiency, his test battery has since been modified by Reitan (1955) and validated numerous times. Presently the battery occupies a central position in the clinical neuropsychology laboratory. The individual tests comprising the battery assist in the diagnosis of focal brain lesions and enable quantitative summarization of neuropsychological competence in the form of an impairment index. For example, the Tactual Performance Test can identify neurological pathology in the parietal regions of the brain; the Rhythm Test and Speech Perception Test can assess possible temporal lobe dysfunction; and the Aphasia Screening Test can diagnose linguistic disturbance associated with either frontal or temporal lobe disturbance. Other tests can localize specific regions of brain dysfunction. Thus, the fact that alcoholics perform in the impaired ranges is strongly supportive of a neuropsychological deficit that may be brought about through excessive ethanol intake.

A second source of behavioral evidence pointing to a neurological disturbance is derived from the observation, on some measures at least, of a progressive decline in competency with increasing duration of alcohol abuse. On the Wisconsin Card Sorting Test (Tarter, 1973; Tarter & Parsons, 1971), it was found that the alcoholics exhibited an increasing loss of ability to maintain and shift acquired concepts as the duration of alcoholism increased. Similar results have been obtained in the investigation of motor skills, particularly speed and strength, where the alcoholism history extends beyond ten years duration (Tarter & Jones, 1971b).

In two important studies (Jones & Parsons, 1971a, 1971b), it was found that alcoholics do not exhibit a global neuropsychological impairment, but rather they demonstrate deficits on tasks which require visual-spatial information processing. An item analysis of the Category Test of the Halstead-Reitan Battery revealed deficits only on subtest IV, where a positional concept must be identified. Similarly, deficits were observed on the Raven's Progressive Matrices, a test of visual-spatial capacity, but also demanding a relatively high level of intellectual efficiency. In a related study, Jones (1971b) found that the cognitive disturbances were primarily manifested by older alcoholics, leading to the speculation that alcohol abuse over extended periods leads to accelerated aging of the nervous system. The notion that the aging brain might be more susceptible to the effects of alcohol (Jones & Parsons, 1971b) has also been advanced by other investigators who evaluated alcoholics on motor capacity (Goldstein & Shelly, 1971), aptitude (Kish & Cheney, 1969), neuropsychological competence (Fitzhugh, et al., 1965), EEG (Smith, Johnson, & Burdick, 1971), and neuropathological disturbance (courville, 1955).

Considering the information presented up to this point, it can be concluded with some degree of confidence that alcoholics: (a) manifest impairments on neuropsychological tests (b) exhibit a progressive decline on some measures with increasing duration of alcoholism; and (c) reveal a premature form of senescent process upon psychological test performance, EEG tracings, and neuropathological study. These observations lead to the second general question; namely, whether or not the evidence allows for conceptualization of the available literature so as to implicate a specific anatomical site and/or neurophysiological system. To date three distinct hypotheses have been advanced.

1. Chronic alcohol abuse exerts a global effect on the

brain, resulting in diffuse cerebral atrophy (Brosin, 1967).

2. The right hemisphere of the brain is particularly vulnerable to disruption from chronic alcohol consumption (Jones & Parsons, 1971a; Parsons, Tarter, & Edelberg, 1972).

3. The frontal-limbic-diencephalic system of the brain is differentially disrupted from extended alcohol abuse (Tarter, 1971, 1973, 1975a, 1975b; Tarter & Parsons, 1971).

Before embarking upon a critical evaluation of each of these hypotheses, it is important to elaborate upon their fundamental differences. Hypotheses 1 and 2 are essentially structural insofar as they specify anatomically what is impaired; the former implying a nonspecific deficit throughout the brain, while the second confines the pathology to the right hemisphere. The third hypothesis attempts to identify a functional neurophysiological system and its anatomical substrate which are adversely affected by alcohol.

Turning our attention to each of the hypotheses, it becomes apparent that any conclusion about the neuropsychological processes involved must at this time still be considered tentative. As a superficial inspection of the bibliography of this chapter will indicate, it is only since the 1960's that psychological studies of alcoholics began appearing in the scientific literature with any degree of frequency. Nonetheless, the notion that alcohol has a disruptive neuropsychological effect has been generally accepted despite a conspicuous paucity of studies designed to examine this experimentally. Historically, first among the hypotheses advanced was the thesis that alcoholics suffered from a diffuse cerebral atrophy. As late as 1967 this position was widely accepted (Brosin, 1967), even though evidence accrued from neuropathological (Courville, 1955), neurophysiological

(Lereboullet, Pluvinage, & Anstutz, 1956), and neuropsychological (Fitzhugh et al., 1960, 1965) investigations was not entirely supportive of this position. As detailed by Brosin (1967), the symptoms accompanying generalized cerebral atrophy are memory impairment, clouding of consciousness, disorientation, poor judgment, and reduced intellectual competence. While alcoholics do manifest many of these symptoms while in a state of intoxication, no such permanent and pervasive disturbance is observed once sobriety has been achieved.

A second hypothesis, evolved out of clinical neuropsychological research maintains that alcoholics suffer from a differentially greater impairment of the right than left hemisphere of the brain. Two lines of supportive evidence have been advanced. First, the majority of deficits in alcoholics have been circumscribed to nonverbal types of tasks. On the WAIS and Wechsler-Bellevue tests, alcoholics have consistently been found to exhibit a decrement in performance IQ relative to verbal IQ which is larger than would be expected on a chance basis alone or simply as the result of aging (Wechsler, 1941). That an inferiority of performance scale scores is indicative of a right hemisphere disorder has already been clearly demonstrated (Vega & Parsons, 1969). Spatial deficits are most pronounced in patients with right hemisphere lesions and have often been observed in alcoholics (Tarter, 1975b). Where both verbal and nonverbal forms of the same test have been administered, deficits are more readily observed on the nonverbal or spatial form (Jones, 1971a). The second source of evidence, implicating a right hemisphere involvement, derives from the observation that on manual tasks alcoholics tend to exhibit a differentially greater degree of impairment with the left hand than with the right. In fact, it has been found that right hand performance is equivalent to that of nonalcholics on a test of motor regulation (Parsons et al., 1972). Other authors (Tarter & Jones, 1971b) have observed a trend in this direction as well. Goodglass and Peck (1972) observed in a dichotic memory task that only the items presented to the left ear were recalled less well by alcoholics than normals. Although the evidence is still far from conclusive, the available information is suggestive of a greater vulnerability of the right hemisphere. However, it is not at all clear why the right hemisphere should have a greater predilection to neurological damage from alcohol than the left hemisphere. Furthermore, it should also be noted that the behavioral deficits that have been demonstrated are not entirely supportive of a lateralized deficit. On several visuo-spatial tasks, such as the Bender-Gestalt and Embedded Figures Test, no substantial impairment has been observed.

The third hypothesis to be advanced asserts that alcoholics suffer from a neurological impairment of the frontal-limbic-diencephalic system of the brain. That these structures are in fact morphologically and functionally integrated has been known for quite some time (Brutkowski, 1965; Fulton, 1952; Marsala & Grofova, 1962; Nauta, 1964; Pribram, 1958). In addition, it has been observed that lesions in various locations of this system result in similar behavioral deficits (Brutkowski, 1965), suggesting that the anterior-basal region of the brain is responsible for mediating common behaviors.

The evidence in support of a frontal-limbic-diencephalic deficit in alcoholics is gleaned from several sources. First, patients exhibiting the Wernicke-Korsakoff Syndrome are known to have neurological damage in the limbic and diencephalic regions (Meissner, 1967; Talland, 1965). It is therefore not improbable that alcoholics manifest a less severe though still detectable impairment in this area of the brain as well. A second source of information is based on clinical neurological investigation. Segal, Kushnarev, Urakov, and Misionzhnik (1970) report that alcohol withdrawal symptoms are similar to those seen in patients with structural lesions of the diencephalon. Haug (1968), and Brewer and Perrett (1971), observed from pneumoencephalographic measurements that the area surrounding the third ventricle is atrophic, resulting in an enlargement or dilatation of that ventricle.

There is also supportive evidence for a frontal focus of impairment as well. Brewer and Perrett (1971) and Lereboullet et al. (1956) found from EEG tracings that there were definite indications of frontal lobe atrophy. Direct neuropathological assessments have confirmed these findings. Alexander (1941) and Courville (1955) observed that on autopsy alcoholics were most atrophic in the anterior frontal lobes. Creutzfeldt (1928) reported that the frontal-diencephalic tracts were disrupted in alcoholics. Thus there is substantial evidence from the neurological literature to support the hypothesis of a frontal-limbic-diencephalic disorder.

The behavioral evidence complements the above cited neurological findings. Tarter (1975a, 1975b) compared the psychological characteristics and deficits that are manifest by alcoholics, brain injured persons, and experimentally lesioned animals and concluded that there were many similarities between these disparate groups. Of the various impairments, it has been found that there is a marked inability of alcoholics to temporally organize behavior and persist with a cognitive set. The capacity to temporally organize behavior has been hypothesized by Pribram (1969) to depend on the functional integrity of the anterior frontal lobes. Confirmation of this notion is derived from the observations of Stamm (1964) and Tubbs (1969) who found that frontally lesioned animals were impaired in a discrimination learning task. When the stimuli were "chunked" or parsed into discrete units, no deficit was noted. An impairment in temporal integration has also been reported in Korsakoff patients (Lidz, 1942; Talland, 1965; Williams & Zangwill, 1950). Luria (1966) reports a similar deficit in humans with anterior frontal brain damage. Thus there is concensus that a deficit in behavioral persistence is manifested by chronic alcoholics and Korsakoff patients as well as humans and animals with frontal lesions.

Alcoholics are also deficient in utilizing the information contained in an erroneous response to achieve a subsequent correct response (Tarter, 1973). Konow and Pribram (1970) have observed a similar impairment in frontally brain damaged humans, while Miles (1964) reported that monkeys were also impaired in this regard in a discrimination learning task.

One of the behavioral characteristics of a frontal lesion is spatial perseveration (Mishkin, 1964). That is, the subject continues to respond to a particular place or location (e.g., left or right) regardless of the properties of the particular stimuli or discriminanda. Such a response propensity has been reported in alcoholics (Tarter, 1973) as well as in animals (Mishkin, 1964; Tubbs, 1969). There is also a great tendency in alcoholics to perseverate with a concept after it has been switched or shifted (Tarter, 1973).

Notably, a similar impairment has been reported in persons with anterior frontal lesions (Milner, 1963, 1964).

Spatial scanning, as measured by maze tests, has been reported to be disrupted in alcoholics (Fitzhugh et al., 1960, 1965; Goldstein & Chotlos, 1965; Tarter, 1971) and frontally lesioned humans (Milner, 1963; Porteus, 1959). It is worthwhile to point out that maze tests also measure a planning factor or capacity for foresight, a function which has been reported to be deficient in alcoholics as well as frontally damaged humans (Milner, 1963; Porteus, 1959) and animals (Pribram, 1960, 1969).

Motor regulation is impaired in alcoholics (Parsons et al., 1972). Comparable decrements have been observed by Zangwill (1966) and Luria (1966) in brain damaged humans. In a similar vein, it has been reported that initiative is reduced in alcoholics (Malerstein, 1969) and in frontally lesioned subjects (Luria, 1966).

Field orientation, as measured by the Rod and Frame Test, is also sensitive to detecting brain damage. Teuber (1964) stated that the only region of the brain which results in behavioral deficit, that is field dependency, occurs after pathology to the anterior lobes or specifically to the frontal eye fields. Alcoholics have consistently been shown to behave in a field-dependent manner (Bailey et al., 1961; Goldstein & Chotlos, 1965; Karp & Konstadt, 1965; Karp, Poster, & Goodman, 1963; Karp et al., 1965a, 1965b). While several authors have interpreted the impairment as being due to personality factors (Karp & Konstadt, 1965; Karp et al., 1965a, 1965b), it should be pointed out that Goldstein, Neuringer, Reiff, and Shelly (1968) were unable to observe any correlation between performance on the Rod and Frame Test and several personality measures of dependency needs and motivation. Although a conclusive statement about the cause of the field dependency is not yet warranted, it is at least congruent with other data to consider this mode of perceptual functioning as a consequence of chronic alcohol abuse.

Another source of evidence which implicates a frontal-basal involvement concerns the performance of alcoholics on tests which specifically and differentially tap frontal, limbic, and diencephalic functions. Halstead (1964) noted that 75% of patients with frontal damage perform in the impaired range on the Categories and Tactual Performance Tests. It is noteworthy that Fitzhugh et al., (1960, 1965) observed an impairment in alcoholics on these two measures. Porteus (1959) has maintained that the Porteus Maze Test is sensitive to differentially detecting anterior cerebral deficits. While only a transient impairment has been observed in alcoholics on this test by one group of investigators (Jonsson et al., 1962), other maze-type tests have been able to reveal a deficit (Fitzhugh et al., 1960, 1965; Goldstein & Chotlos, 1965; Tarter, 1971). Thus, while there is a paucity of neuropsychological measures of frontal lobe functioning, the tests that are available and have been applied to alcoholics are indeed supportive of a disturbance to that system.

And finally, an admittedly weak test of the anterior-basal hypothesis is based upon personality assessment. There is strong evidence in the literature which demonstrates that damage to the frontal lobes results in a personality change toward extraversion (Meyer, 1961; Petrie, 1949; Tow, 1965). Smart (1965) assigned a group of alcoholics to one of two groups after a pre-selection based on their WAIS performance.

Subjects whose verbal IQ exceeded the performance IQ by at least 18 points were placed in one group, and those for whom the verbal-performance difference was less than 5 points were assigned to a second group. It was hypothesized that the former group, manifesting greater intellectual and presumably neurological deterioration, would be more extraverted as measured by the Maudsley Personality Inventory. The hypothesis was in fact confirmed, thus indirectly providing a link between the hypothesized focus of the brain dysfunction, personality, and intellectual competence.

While there is substantial support for an anterior-basal focus of impairment, some information has been accrued which may not be consistent with such a neurological interpretation. Tarter (1971), for example, observed that alcoholics were not impaired in "learning to learn" or interproblem improvement across cognitive sets. This finding appears, initially at least, to be at variance with results obtained in animals with anterior frontal lesions (Warren & Akert, 1964). Where familiarity with the stimuli is minimal, no decrement in "learning to learn" is evident in frontally ablated animals (Miles, 1964; Oxbury & Weiskrantz, 1962). Thus the intact capacity of alcoholics to improve across cognitive sets may not reflect the absence of anterior basal disorder but may, instead, be related to the nature of the task employed.

A second finding which is perhaps more critical to the anterior-basal hypothesis concerns the observation by Tarter (1971) that no decrement in goal-directed behavior was noted in alcoholics. Luria (1966) asserts that one of the cardinal features of an anterior frontal focus of impairment is the inability to sustain a train of thought towards a goal.

Administering the Goal Directed Serial Alternation Test (Melges, Tinklenberg, Hollister, & Gillespie, 1970) in which the subject must perform a sequence of serial arithmetic calculations until a specific number is reached, Tarter (1971) was unable to demonstrate a performance decrement in alcoholics. This procedure is quite similar to that of Luria's (1966) in which he requires the subject to perform serial subtractions of a given number. The fact that Luria (1966) reports a significant impairment in his subjects with frontal damage, while no such deficit is observed in chronic alcoholics, is at this point unclear. Although a slight difference in procedure was employed, it is not likely that this discrepancy was crucial to the obtained results. Further research is needed to clarify this issue.

In conclusion, it appears that the psychological deficits in alcoholics are amenable to a neuropsychological interpretation. Of the three hypotheses advanced to date, there is little specific confirmatory evidence for a diffuse and generalized cerebral impairment. Some information has been obtained which is suggestive of a greater vulnerability to disruption of the right over the left hemisphere, but the results at this stage should be considered tentative. The notion that alcoholics suffer from an anterior-basal focus of impairment is supported by neuroanatomical, neurological, and behavioral evidence. The findings, although not entirely confirmatory, do account for most of the observed psychological deficits and can thus be conceptualized into a systematic and coherent framework.

One issue of both theoretical and empirical importance concerns the source or underlying mechanisms for the observed psychological impairments. A basic presumption maintained throughout the preceding discussion has been that ethanol transported to the brain via the vascular or cerebrospinal system exerts a permanent adverse effect on neural functioning and associated behavioral capacity. However, one factor which has been observed to contribute to the reduced psychological competence of Korsakoff patients is that of nutritional status (Meissner, 1967; Talland, 1965). Avitaminosis in the form of thiamine deficiency may exist in chronic alcoholics, thereby reducing neural efficiency and causing the manifest psychological impairments.

Methodologically, it may not be feasible to accurately tease apart the effects of the ethanol and vitamin deficiency on psychological competence in humans. There is, however, strong experimental evidence from animal studies which demonstrates the deleterious consequences of alcohol on behavioral processes, such as learning and timing behavior, when nutritional status is controlled (Freund, 1970; Walker & Freund, 1973). In conducting research on a clinical population where nutrition is considered to be a relevant factor, it is imperative that the experimental and control groups be drawn from the same general population, since it has been shown in at least one study that alcoholics are nutritionally similar to normals who are similar in health, social, history, and economic class (Neville, Eagles, Samson, & Olson, 1968).

In conclusion, there is substantiative experimental evidence of a psychological nature to implicate a neurological impairment in chronic alcoholics. For a further discussion of the neurological literature the reader is referrred to Chapter 5. While the current status of research does not permit a final statement, it is apparent that a longstanding history of alcoholism is detrimental to neurological integrity, either by alcohol effects or nutritional deficiency or both.

MINIMAL BRAIN DAMAGE AS AN ETIOLOGICAL FACTOR

The preceding discussion has focused on the consequences of alcohol abuse on neuropsychological capacity. Within the past few years there has been developed a body of knowledge which suggests that some alcoholics may suffer from hyperactivity and other "soft" neurological signs indicative of brain damage prior to their drinking onset. As such, antecedent neuropsychological factors may play a role in the etiology and maintenance of abusive drinking. Hyperactivity symptoms in childhood have been proposed by Guze (1975) to lead to hysterical disorders in women and sociopathic conditions in men. It is, therefore, not too surprising that alcoholism as a subtype of sociopathy according to DSM-II criteria would be associated with symptoms of minimal brain damage.

In one study, Mendelson, Johnson, and Stewart (1971) found that 15% of hyperactive children between the ages of 12 and 16 were exhibiting excessive alcohol consumption. In another investigation, Tarter, McBride, Buonpane, and Schneider (in preparation) found that severe alcoholics reported four times as many symptoms of MBD in childhood as less severe drinkers. Severe drinkers in that study were characterized by early onset of alcohol abuse, positive psychic effect from alcohol, withdrawal symptoms, daily drinking, increased tolerance, and loss of control. The severe drinkers also reported a significantly higher incidence of alcoholism in a parent, suggesting a genetic link between MBD and alcoholism. Other researchers have noted a similar association. For example, in two studies where environmental factors were minimized (Goodwin, Schulsinger, Hermansen, Guze & Winokur, 1975; Morrison & Stewart, 1973), it was found that adopted children with a hyperactivity disorder more frequently had a biological parent who was alcoholic. Similar results demonstrating a relationship between alcoholism and hyperactivity have been reported by Cantwell (1972).

In the study by Tarter et al. (in preparation), it was also found that the severe drinker was not as disturbed in terms of psychiatric symptoms as the less severe alcoholic. In fact, the former group presented a general picture of assertiveness and well-being as compared with the latter group. Thus, while they endorsed more symptoms of MBD (dyslexia, aggressiveness, distractibility, antisocial behavior, etc.), these characteristics were unrelated to psychiatric status, at least as measured by the MMPI.

From these studies there is tentative evidence to suggest an association between alcoholism and childhood minimal brain damage. The fact that MBD may also be a precursor to other clinical disorders implicates a possible common neurobehavioral mechanism in hysteria, depression, sociopathy, and alcoholism and hence points to the important role played by these etiological factors in various psychopathological conditions. The possibility that such disparate disorders may have a common etiological basis that is expressed phenotypically as MBD in early life indicates that social learning processes may also be involved in the ultimate expression of the adult disorder. Sex role learning in the form of hysteria in women and sociopathy in men are two examples. In conclusion, it appears that there exists an association between childhood MBD and adult alcoholism. Further research, however, is needed to clarify this relationship. In addition, it is important to develop techniques to identify high risk individuals. Once the neurochemical defect is discovered, it is hoped that corrective procedures in the form of pharmacological manipulations could be introduced as a preventative measure.

REVERSIBILITY OF IMPAIRMENT

Although alcoholics have been shown to be impaired on a variety of psychological and behavioral tasks, the possibility that the observed deficits may be reversible has not received much attention until recently. Does an extended period of abstinence from alcohol lead to recovery?

In one comprehensive study, Long and McLachlan (1974) administered the Halstead-Reitan Battery and WAIS to a sample of alcoholics. They noted a significant improvement on the Category Test and Finger Tapping Test after a one year period of sobriety. The overall impairment index also indicated substantial improvement from test to retest. In another investigation, McLachlan and Levinson (1974) observed improved performance on the WAIS Block Design Test after one year of sobriety. Page and Linden (1974) tested alcoholics on the WAIS, Bender-Gestalt, Trail Making Test, Shipley Institute of Living Scale, and Halstead-Reitan Battery. They reported improvements in test performance after two weeks of abstinence but no subsequent changes after another two months of sobriety. The authors concluded that "abstract reasoning, short-term memory and coding, sequencing ability, and general mental flexibility are depressed in alcoholics to a severely disruptive extent for about a week, after which partial recovery occurs rapidly and remains essentially asymptotic for at least two months" (p. 105). Clarke and Houghton (1975) examined a group of alcoholics on the Wechsler Memory Scale and several subtests of the WAIS. They found that performance decrements on these tests were still apparent after ten weeks of sobriety.

Other investigators have similarly reported marked improvements after sobriety. Smith et al. (1971) found improvements on the Shipley Institute of Living Scale, Hidden Figures Test, and Embedded Figures Test from test to retest. Allen, Faillace, and Reynolds (1971) reported that there were no signs of a memory deficit in a free recall procedure after their alcoholics had been detoxified for two weeks. Weingartner, et al. (1971) noted that any retentive deficits that were present at the time of hospital admission disappeared after three weeks.

On tests of motor performance, Tarter and Jones (1971b) found improvements in motor speed, muscle strength, and perceptual-motor coordination after the subjects were sober for ten weeks. The improvement was most pronounced in those persons whose alcoholism history did not exceed ten years. Goldstein, Chotlos, McCarthy, and Neuringer (1968) reported that gait instability diminished with sobriety and that practice accelerated the recovery process. In one electrophysiological study, Bennett (1960) found that approximately 50% of alcoholics manifest abnormal EEG tracings. Changes toward normality on these measures were also found to take place after a period of abstinence from alcohol.

Other investigators have failed to observe any appreciable improvement with sobriety. Carlsson, Claeson, and Pettersson (1973) could not detect significant improvement within the first two weeks of hospitalization on a battery of cognitive and perceptual tests. In two animal studies no improvement with sobriety was observed. In the first investigation (Freund & Walker, 1971) it was found that mice were still impaired at an avoidance task after over four months of abstinence. In the second study (Walker & Freund, 1973) it was found that timing behavior in rats was still deficient after 30 days of sobriety.

From these studies it appears that significant recovery does take place in alcoholics after detoxification and that improvement may continue for up to one year. In the two animal studies reported, the effects of the alcohol appear to be more debilitating than in humans to the extent that reversibility of impairment is not readily seen. The reasons for this discrepancy cannot be ascertained at this time. It is possible that ethanol is more toxic to animals than humans. Also the human brain, being more developed and allowing for greater flexibility than other animals, may make it possible for the individual to compensate for lost capacity by developing new learning strategies and thereby circumvent the manifestation of an impairment. Whatever the reason, it should be reassuring to both the clinician and afflicted individual that improvement can and does take place although the mechanism for this may not be understood at this time.

REFERENCES

Alexander, L. Neuropathological findings in the brain and spinal cord of chronic alcoholics. *Quarterly Journal of Studies on Alcohol*, 1941, *1*, 798.

Allen, R., Faillace, L., & Reynolds, D. Recovery of memory functioning in alcoholics following prolonged alcohol intoxication. *Journal of Nervous and Mental Disease*, 1971, *153*, 417-423.

Bailey, W., Hustmyer, F., & Kristofferson, A. Alcoholism, brain damage, and perceptual dependence. *Quarterly Journal of Studies on Alcohol*, 1961, *22*, 387-393.

Bauer, R., & Johnson, D. The question of deterioration in alcoholism. *Journal of Consulting Psychology*, 1957, *21*, 296.

Bennett, A. Diagnosis of intermediate stage of alcohol brain disease. *Journal of American Medical Association*, 1960, *172*, 1143-1146.

Brewer, C., & Perrett, L. Brain damage due to alcohol consumption: An airencephalographic, psychometric, and electroencephalographic study. *British Journal of Addictions*, 1971, *66*, 170-182.

Brosin, H. Acute and chronic brain syndromes. In A. Freedman & H. Kaplan (Eds.), *Comprehensive textbook of psychiatry*. Baltimore: Williams & Wilkins, 1967.

Brutkowski, S. Functions of prefrontal cortex in animals. *Physiological Reviews*, 1965, *45*, 721-746.

Burke, H., & Bingham, W. Raven's progressive matrices: More on construct validity. *Journal of Psychology*, 1969, *72*, 247-251.

Cantwell, D. Psychiatric illness in the families of hyperactive children. *Archives of General Psychiatry*, 1972, *27*, 414-417.

Carlsson, C., Claeson, L., & Pettersson, L. Psychometric signs of cerebral dysfunction in alcoholics. *British Journal of Addictions*, 1973, *68*, 83-86.

Chandler, B., Vega, A., & Parsons, O. Dichotic listening in chronic alcoholics with and without a history of possible brain injury. *Quarterly Journal of Studies on Alcohol*, 1973, *34*, 1099-1109.

Claeson, L., & Carlsson, C. Cerebral dysfunction in alcoholics: A psychometric investigation. *Quarterly Journal of Studies on Alcohol*, 1970, *31*, 317-323.

Clarke, J., & Houghton, H. A study of intellectual impairment and recovery rates in heavy drinkers in Ireland. *British Journal of Psychiatry*, 1975, *126*, 178-184.

Courville, C. *Effects of alcohol on the central nervous system*. Los Angeles: San Lucas Press, 1955.

Creutzfeldt, R. Hirnveränderungen bei Gewohnheitstrinkern. *Zeitschrift für die die gesamte Neurologie und Psychiatrie*, 1928, *50*, 321-324.

Fitzhugh, L., Fitzhugh, K., & Reitan, R. Adaptive abilities and intellectual functioning in hospitalized alcoholics. *Quarterly Journal of Studies on Alcohol*, 1960, *21*, 414-423.

Fitzhugh, L., Fitzhugh, K., & Reitan, R. Adaptive abilities and intellectual functioning of hospitalized alcoholics: Further considerations. *Quarterly Journal of Studies on Alcohol*, 1965, *26*, 402-411.

French, J., Ekstrom, R., & Price, L. *Manual for kit of reference tests for cognitive factors*. Princeton: Educational Testing Service, 1963.

Freund, G. Impairment of shock avoidance learning after long-term alcohol ingestion in mice. *Science*, 1970, *168*, 1599-1601.

Freund, G., & Walker, D. Impairment of avoidance learning by prolonged ethanol consumption in mice. *Journal of Pharmacology and Experimental Therapeutics*, 1971, *179*, 284-292.

Fulton, J. *The frontal lobes and human behavior. The Sherrington Lectures*. Liverpool: Liverpool University Press, 1952.

Goldstein, G., & Chotlos, J. Dependency and brain damage in alcoholics. *Perceptual and Motor Skills*, 1965, *21*, 135-150.

Goldstein, G., Chotlos, J., McCarthy, R., & Neuringer, C. Recovery from gait instability in alcoholics. *Quarterly Journal of Studies on Alcohol*, 1968, *29*, 38-43.

Goldstein, G., Neuringer, C., & Klappersack, B. Cognitive, perceptual, and motor aspects of field dependency in alcoholics. *Journal of Genetic Psychology*, 1970, *117*, 253-266.

Goldstein,, G., Neuringer, C., Reiff, C., & Shelly, C. Generalizability of field dependency in alcoholics. *Journal of Consulting and Clinical Psychology*, 1968, *32*, 560-564.

Goldstein, G., & Shelly, C. Field dependence and cognitive, perceptual and motor skills in alcoholics: A factor-analytic study. *Quarterly Journal of Studies on Alcohol*, 1971, *32*, 29-40.

Goodglass, H., & Peck, E. Dichotic ear order effects in Korsakoff and normal subjects. *Neuropsychologia*, 1972, *10*, 211-217.

Goodwin, D., Crane, J., & Guze, S. Phenomenological aspects of the alcoholic "blackout". *British Journal of Psychiatry*, 1969, *115*, 1033-1038.

Goodwin, D., Hill, S., Powell, B., & Viamontes, J. Effect of alcohol on short term memory in alcoholics. *British Journal of Psychiatry*, 1973, *122*, 93-94.

Goodwin, D., Othmer, E., Halikas, J., & Freemon, F. Loss of short term memory as a predictor of the alcoholic "blackout." *Nature*, 1970, *227*, 201-202.

Goodwin, D., Schulsinger, F., Hermansen, L., Guze, S., & Winokur, G. Alcoholism and the hyperactive child syndrome. *Journal of Nervous and Mental Disease*, 1975, *160*, 349-353.

Grassi, J. *The Grassi Block Substitution Test for Measuring Organic Brain Pathology*. Springfield, Ill.: Charles C Thomas, 1953.

Guze, S. The validity and significance of the clinical diagnosis of hysteria (Briquet's syndrome). *American Journal of Psychiatry*, 1975, *32*, 138-141.

Halpern, F. Studies of compulsive drinkers: Psychological test results. *Quarterly Journal of Studies on Alcohol*, 1946, *6*, 468-479.

Halstead, W. *Brain and intelligence*, Chicago: University of Chicago Press, 1947.

Halstead, W. Unpublished communication to S. Ackerly, 1964. Cited by S. Ackerly in J. Warren & K. Akert (Eds.), *The frontal granular cortex and behavior*. New York: McGraw Hill, 1964.

Haug, J. Pneumoencephalographic evidence of brain damage in chronic alcoholics. *Acta Psychiatrica Scandinavica*, 1968, *203*, 135-143.

Hirschenfang, S., Silber, M., & Benton, J. Comparison of Bender-Gestalt reproductions in patients with peripheral neuropathy. *Perceptual and Motor Skills*, 1967, *24*, 1317-1318.

Hirschenfang, S., Silber, M., & Benton, J. Personality patterns in peripheral neuropathy. *Diseases of the Nervous System*, 1968, *29*, 46-50.

Hunt, J., & Cofer, C. Psychological deficit in schizophrenia. In J. McV. Hunt (Ed.), *Personality and the behavior disorders* (Vol.2). New York: Ronald Press, 1944.

Jacobson, G. Reduction of field dependence in chronic alcoholic patients. *Journal of Abnormal Psychology*, 1968, *73*, 547-549.

Jellinek, E.M. *The disease concept of alcoholism*. New Haven: Hillhouse Press, 1960.

Jones, B. *Performance of chronic alcoholics on the JVAT: A test of the "temporal sequencing deficit" hypothesis using a verbal abstraction task.* Paper presented at the meeting of the western Psychological Association. San Antonio, Texas, 1971. (a)

Jones, B. Verbal and spatial intelligence in short and long-term alcoholics. *Journal of Nervous and Mental Diseases*, 1971, *153*, 292-297. (b)

Jones, B., & Parsons, O. Impaired abstracting ability in chronic alcoholics. *Archives of General Psychiatry*, 1971, *24*, 71-75. (a)

Jones, B., & Parsons, O. Specific vs. generalized deficits of abstracting ability in chronic alcoholics. *Archives of General Psychiatry*, 1971, *24*, 71-75. (b)

Jonsson, C., Cronholm, B., & Izikowitz, S. Intellectual changes in alcoholics Psychometric studies on mental sequals of prolonged intensive abuse of alcohol. *Quarterly Journal of Studies on Alcohol*, 1962, *23*, 221-242.

Kaldegg, A. Psychological observations in a group of alcoholic patients. *Quarterly Journal of Studies on Alcohol*, 1956, *17*, 608-628.

Karp, S., & Konstadt, N. Alcoholism and psychological differentiation: Long-range effect of heavy drinking on field dependence. *Journal of Nervous and Mental Diseases*, 1965, *140*, 412-416.

Karp, S., Poster, D., & Goodman, A. Differentiation in alcoholic women. *Journal of Personality*, 1963, *31*, 386-393.

Karp, S., Witkin, H., & Goodenough, D. Alcoholism and psychological differentiation: Effect of achievement of sobriety on field dependence. *Quarterly Journal of Studies on Alcohol*, 1965, *26*, 580-585. (a)

Karp, S., Witkin, H., & Goodenough, D. Alcoholism and psychological differentiation: Effect of alcohol on field dependence. *Journal of Abnormal Psychology*, 1965, *70*, 262-265. (b)

Kates, S., & Schmolke, M. Self-related and parent related verbalizations and Bender-Gestalt performances of alcoholics. *Quarterly Journal of Studies on Alcohol*, 1953, *14*, 38-48.

Kish, G. Alcoholics GATB and Shipley profiles and their interrelationships. *Journal of Clinical Psychology*, 1970, *26*, 482-484.

Kish, G., & Cheney, T. Impaired abilities in alcoholism measured by the General Aptitude Test Battery. *Quarterly Journal of Studies on Alcohol*, 1969, *30*, 384-388.

Kleinknecht, R., & Goldstein, S. Neuropsychological deficits associated with alcoholism. *Quarterly Journal of Studies on Alcohol*, 1972, *33*, 999-1020.

Konow, A. & Pribram, K. Error recognition and utilization produced by injury to the frontal cortex in man. *Neuropsychologia*, 1970, *8*, 489-491.

Lereboullet, J., Pluvinage, R., & Anstutz, D. Aspects cliniques et electroencephalographiques des atrophies cerebrales alcoliques. *Revue Neurologique*, 1956, *94*, 674-782.

Lidz, T. The amnestic syndrome. *Archives of Neurology and Psychiatry*, 1942, *47*, 588-605.

Long, J., & McLachlan, J. Abstract reasoning and perceptual motor efficiency in alcoholics. Impairment and reversibility. *Quarterly Journal of Studies on Alcohol*, 1974, *35*, 1220-1229.

Lovibond, S., & Holloway, I. Differential sorting behavior of schizophrenics and organics. *Journal of Clinical Psychology*, 1968, *24*, 307-311.

Luria, A. *Human brain and psychological processes*. New York, Harper & Row, 1966.

Malerstein, A. Korsakoff's syndrome and resumption of an interrupted task as an index of initiative. *Journal of Nervous and Mental Diseases*, 1969, *148*, 506-514.

Malerstein, A., & Belden, E. WAIS, SILS, and PPVT in Korsakoff's syndrome. *Archives of General Psychiatry*, 1968, *19*, 743-750.

Marsala, J., & Grofova, I. Connections of the frontal cortex with the basal ganglia, thalamus, hypothalamus, and nesencephalon. In *Theses of the Czechoslovakian Medical Congress*. Prague: State Health Publications House, 1962.

May, A., Urquhart, A., & Watts, R. Memory for Designs Test - a follow up study. *Perceptual and Motor Skills*, 1970, *30*, 753-754.

McLachlan, J., & Levinson, T. Improvement in WAIS Block Design Performance as a function of recovery from alcoholism. *Journal of Clinical Psychology*, 1974, *30*, 65-66.

Meissner, W. Memory functions in the Korsakoff's syndrome. *Journal of Nervous and Mental Diseases*, 1967, *145*, 106-122.

Melges, F., Tinklenberg, J., Hollister, L., & Gillespie, H. Marijuana and temporal disintegration. *Science*, 1970, *168*, 1118-1120.

Mendelson, W., Johnson, N., & Stewart, M. Hyperactive children as teenagers: A follow-up study. *Journal of Nervous and Mental Diseases*. 1971, *153*, 273-279.

Meyer, V. Psychological effects of brain damage. In H.J. Eysenck (Ed.), *Handbook of abnormal psychology*. New York: Basic Books, 1961.

Miles, R. Learning by squirrel monkeys with frontal lesions. In J. Warren & K. Akert (Eds.), *The frontal granular cortex and behavior*. New York: McGraw Hill, 1964.

Milner, B. Effects of different brain lesions on card sorting. *Archives of Neurology*, 1963, *9*, 90-100.

Milner, B. Some effects of frontal lobectomy in man. In J. Warren & K. Akert (Eds.), *The frontal granular cortex and behavior*. New York: McGraw Hill, 1964.

Mishkin, M. Perseveration of central sets after frontal lesions in monkeys. In J. Warren & K. Akert (Eds.), *The frontal granular cortex and behavior*. New York: McGraw Hill, 1964.

Morrison, J., & Stewart, M. The psychiatric status of the legal families of adopted hyperactive children. *Archives of General Psychiatry*, 1973, *28*, 888-891.

Murphy, M. Social class differences in intellectual characteristics of alcoholics. *Quarterly Journal of Studies on Alcohol*, 1953, *14*, 192-196.

Nauta, W. Some efferent connections of the prefrontal cortex in the monkey. In J. Warren & K. Akert (Eds.), *The frontal granular cortex and behavior*. New York: McGraw Hill, 1964.

Neville, J., Eagles, J., Samson, G., & Olson, E. Nutritional status of alcoholics. *American Journal of Clinical Nutrition*, 1968, *21*, 1320-1340.

Oxbury, J., & Weiskrantz, L. Effects of frontal cortex lesions on discrimination learning by monkeys. *Nature*, 1962, *195*, 310-311.

Page, R., & Linden, J. "Reversible" organic brain syndrome in alcoholics: A psychometric evaluation. *Quarterly Journal of Studies on Alcohol*, 1974, *35*, 98-107.

Parsons, O., Tarter, R., & Edelberg, R. Altered motor control in chronic alcoholics. *Journal of Abnormal Psychology*, 1972, *72*, 308-314.

Peters, G. Emotional and intellectual concomitants of advanced chronic alcoholism. *Journal of Consulting Psychology*, 1956, *20*, 390.

Petrie, A. Personality changes after pre-frontal leucotomy. *British Journal of Medical Psychology*, 1949, *22*, 200-207.

Pishkin, V., Fishkin, S., & Stahl, M. Concept learning in chronic alcoholics: Psychophysiological and set functions. *Journal of Clinical Psychology*, 1972, *28*, 328-334.

Plumeau, F., Machover, S., & Puzzo, F. Wechsler-Bellevue performances of remitted and unremitted alcoholics and their normal controls. *Journal of Consulting Psychology*, 1960, *24*, 240-242.

Porteus, S. *The Maze Test and clinical psychology*. Palo Alto, California: Pacific Books, 1959.

Pribram, K. Comparative neurology and the evolution of behavior. In A. Roe & G. Simpson (Eds.), *Behavior and evolution*. New Haven: Yale University Press, 1958.

Pribram, K. A review of theory in physiological psychology. *Annual Review of Psychology*, 1960, *11*, 1-40.

Pribram, K. The primate frontal cortex. *Neuropsychologia*, 1969, *7*, 259-266.

Reitan, R. Investigation of the validity of Halstead's measures of biological intelligence. *Archives of Neurology and Psychiatry*, 1955, *73*, 28-35.

Rhodes, R., Carr, J., & Jurji, E. Interpersonal differentiation and perceptual field differentiation. *Perceptual and Motor Skills*, 1968, *27*, 172-174.

Rudin, S., & Stagner, R. Figure-ground phenomena in the perception of physical and social stimuli. *Journal of Psychology*, 1958, *45*, 213-225.

Segal, B., Kushnarev, V., Urakov, I., & Misionzhnik, E. Alcoholism and disruption of the activity of deep cerebral structures: Clinical-laboratory research. *Quarterly Journal of Studies on Alcohol*, 1970, *31*, 587-601.

Silber, M., Hirschenfang, S., & Benton, J. Psychological factors and prognosis in peripheral neuropathy. *Diseases of the Nervous System*, 1968, *29*, 688-692.

Smart, R. The relationships between intellectual deterioration, extraversion, and neuroticism among chronic alcoholics. *Journal of Clinical Psychology*, 1965, *21*, 27-29.

Smith, J., Johnson, L., & Burdick, J. Sleep, psychological, and clinical changes during alcohol withdrawal in NAD-treated alcoholics. *Quarterly Journal of Studies on Alcohol*, 1971, *32*, 982-944.

Stamm, J. Retardation and facilitation in learning by stimulation of frontal cortex in monkeys. In J. Warren & K. Akert (Eds.), *The frontal granular cortex and behavior*. New York: McGraw Hill, 1964.

Talland, G. *Deranged memory: A psychonomic study of the amnestic syndrome*. New York: Academic Press, 1965.

Tarter, R. *A neuropsychological examination of cognition and perceptual capacities in chronic alcoholics*. Unpublished doctoral dissertation, University of Oklahoma, 1971.

Tarter, R. An analysis of cognitive deficits in chronic alcoholics. *Journal of Nervous and Mental Disease*, 1973, *147*, 138-147.

Tarter, R. Brain damage associated with chronic alcoholism. *Diseases of the Nervous System*, 1975, *36*, 185-187. (a)

Tarter, R. Psychological deficit in chronic alcoholics: A review. *International Journal of the Addictions*, 1975, *10*(2), 327-368. (b)

Tarter, R., Buonpane, N., & Wynant, C. Intellectual competence of alcoholics. *Quarterly Journal of Studies on Alcohol*, 1975, *36*, 381-386.

Tarter, R., & Jones, B. Absence of intellectual deterioration in chronic alcoholics. *Journal of Clinical Psychology*, 1971, *27*, 453-454. (a)

Tarter, R. & Jones, B. Motor impairment in chronic alcoholics. *Diseases of the Nervous System*, 1971, *32*, 632-636. (b)

Tarter, R., McBride, H., Buonpane, N., & Schneider, D. Differentiation of alcoholics according to childhood history of minimal brain dysfunction, family history and drinking patterns. In preparation.

Tarter, R., & Parsons, O. Conceptual shifting in chronic alcoholics. *Journal of Abnormal Psychology*. 1971, *77*, 71-75.

Tarter, R., & Schneider, D. Blackouts: Relationship with memory and alcoholism history. In preparation.

Tarter, R., Sheldon, J., & Sugerman, A. Correlates of perceptual orientation in chronic alcoholics. *Journal of Clinical Psychology*, 1975, *31*(2), 364-366.

Teuber, H. The riddle of frontal lobe function in man. In J. Warren & K. Akert (Eds.), *The frontal granular cortex and behavior*. New York: McGraw Hill, 1964.

Tow, R. *Personality changes following frontal leucotomy*. Oxford: Oxford Medical Publications, 1965.

Tubbs, W. Primate frontal lesions and the temporal structure of behavior. *Behavioral Science*, 1969, *14*, 347-356.

Vega, A., & Parsons, O. Relationships between sensory-motor deficits and WAIS verbal and performance scores in unilateral brain damage. *Cortex*, 1969, *5*, 229-241.

Vivian, T., Goldstein, G., & Shelly, C. Reaction time and motor speed in chronic alcoholics. *Perceptual and Motor Skills*, 1973, *36*, 136-138.

Walker, D., & Freund, G. Impairment of timing behavior after prolonged alcohol consumption in rats. *Science*, 1973, *182*, 597-598.

Warren, J., & Akert, K. (Eds.) *The frontal granular cortex and behavior*. New York: McGraw Hill, 1964.

Wechsler, D. The effect of alcohol on mental activity. *Quarterly Journal of Studies on Alcohol*, 1941, *2*, 479-485.

Wechsler, D. *The measurement and appraisal of adult intelligence*. Baltimore: Williams & Wilkins, 1958.

Weingartner, H., Faillace, L., & Markley, H. Verbal information retention in alcoholics. *Quarterly Journal of Studies on Alcohol*, 1971, *32*, 293-303.

Williams, N., & Zangwill, O. Disorders of temporal judgment associated with amnestic states. *Journal of Mental Science*, 1950, *96*, 484-493.

Witkin, H., Karp, S., & Goodenough, D. Dependence in alcoholics. *Quarterly Journal of Studies on Alcohol*, 1959, *20*, 493-504.

Zangwill, O. Psychological deficits associated with frontal lobe lesions. *International Journal of Neurology*, 1966, *5*, 395-402.

CHAPTER 11

COGNITIVE STYLES IN ALCOHOLISM

A. Arthur Sugerman
Dorothea U. Schneider

COGNITIVE STYLES AND CONTROLS

The terms "cognitive styles" and "cognitive controls" are labels that have been applied to self-consistent modes of functioning which characterize an individual pervasively throughout his perceptual and intellectual activities. The concepts of cognitive style and control exhibit important differences which, when ignored, cause the terms to be used interchangeably, and thus incorrectly (Santostefano, 1969).

In a review of the work of Witkin and his colleagues (Witkin & Oltman, 1967), evidence was summarized which shows that individuals evince consistent and stable styles of cognitive organization which cut across both perceptual and physiological characteristics. The emphasis is upon the approach an individual brings to his experiences, that is,

Ralph E. Tarter and A. Arthur Sugerman (eds.), Alcoholism

ISBN: 0-201-08146-6
ISBN: 0-201-08145-8 (pbk.)

his style. A battery of tests was devised to measure the field dependent-independent dimension of cognitive style. This refers to an individual's ability to separate an item from an organized field or prevailing background, be it a rod in a frame (Rod and Frame Test, RFT) or a simple figure in a more complex one (Embedded Figures Test, EFT). The perceptual style which characterizes an individual who is heavily influenced by the background and so cannot adjust the rod to the true vertical in the RFT, or who has difficulty in disembedding a simple figure from its surroundings in the EFT, is termed field dependent. Conversely, the field independent style of perception describes an individual who perceives an item as discrete from the organized field of which it is a part, and who therefore has relatively little difficulty in correctly performing the tasks.

As Witkin and his colleagues extended the range of variables which were found to correlate with measures of the field dependence-independence styles, they proposed a global versus articulated style which defines a continuum (Witkin, 1965). The individual at one extreme experiences events globally and diffusely, the organization of the surrounding field dictating the way its elements are perceived. The other end of the dimension is represented by a tendency to experience in an analytic, delineated, and structured manner. This concept of psychological differentiation encompasses not only field dependence-independence and the perceptual tasks used to measure it, but also includes social and personality correlates of the RFT and EFT. A similar concept of cognitive style proposed by Kagan, Moss, and Sigel (1963) describes an analytic-nonanalytic dimension. This style finds its extremes in individuals who exhibit articulate and active cognitive behaviors versus those who experience globally and passively.

Cognitive controls also deal with consistent individual differences in performance on perceptual-cognitive tests, but the concept has a different theoretical basis. Klein and Schlesinger (1949) found that in a group of war refugees, some subjects, when asked to estimate the size of discs on which were placed various symbols including a swastika, consistently gave inaccurate estimates, presumably because of the emotional impact of the symbols. In explaining the individual differences, Klein employed a psychoanalytic framework based upon Hartmann's (1958) formulations of the conflict-free sphere of the ego. He postulated that ego functions such as perception, thinking, recall, and comprehension are used by the individual to deal with his environment and that these functions develop outside of conflict. As the individual develops, dissonances occur between the level of the ego functions and the environmental stimulation. Ego control mechanisms emerge which select, rearrange, and block stimulation so as to relieve the dissonance and create a "fit" between the individual's cognitive apparatus and his environment. These mechanisms represent specific cognitive controls. They regulate and manage information by governing and controlling the amount and organization of the information which becomes available. Just as with cognitive styles, they develop as a function of maturation, are enduring in the individual, and mediate the individual's personality in his cognitive encounters.

Specific cognitive controls (Gardner, Holzman, Klein, Linton, & Spence, 1959) include (a) focal attention (scanning), (b) field articulation, (c) leveling-sharpening, and (d) equivalence range. Several cognitive controls can form a configuration representing the cognitive style of an individual. For Klein, then, cognitive style is a configuration of a number of cognitive controls. For Witkin, however, cognitive style represents a single principle, such as field dependence-independence.

FIELD DEPENDENCE-INDEPENDENCE

Before dealing with the concept of cognitive styles and their relevance to alcoholism, the tests of field dependence and the findings in normal and other groups will be outlined. Field dependence is the cognitive style most studied in alcoholics.

The RFT (Witkin, Lewis, Hertzman, Machover, Meissner, & Wapner, 1954) requires the individual seated in a darkened room to adjust a luminous tilted rod to the true upright position. Interference with this task is created by setting a luminous square frame, which surrounds the rod, at various angles of tilt. Great individual differences in performing this task occur. The two extremes of performance are represented by people who adjust the rod with regard to the frame, whatever its tilt, and those who correctly adjust the rod to the true vertical. A score of degrees of deviation from verticality is obtained.

Analogous to the RFT is the Body Adjustment Test (BAT) (Witkin et al., 1954) where the subject is strapped into a chair which can be tilted. This chair is projected into a small room which can also be tilted independently of the chair. The subject's task is to adjust his body to a position where he perceives it to be truly upright. It is apparent that the BAT and RFT are structurally similar tasks, the body acting as rod, and the room as frame. Again, performances are on a continuum between the extremes of field dependence and field independence. When subjects are allowed to close their eyes in the BAT, everyone is able to adjust the body to the upright with very little error.

A third task, the Embedded Figures Test (EFT), is similar to the RFT in that both require disembedding of a figure from an organized field. In the EFT, the subject is required to look at a simple geometric figure and then find it in a more complex figure. The issue again is the extent to which the perceptual field (complex figure) dominates the perception of an item within it. The score is the time taken to find the simple figure. As a paper and pencil measure of field dependence, the EFT would be expected to correlate with the original RFT. Positive correlations between the EFT and RFT (Goldstein, Neuringer, & Klappersack, 1970; Rudin & Stagner, 1958; Witkin, Dyk, Faterson, Goodenough, & Karp, 1962; Witkin et al., 1954; Young, 1959) and factor analytic results (Gardner, Jackson, & Messick, 1960) give considerable support to the assumption that both tests measure a factor of field dependence. However, while each test may be an appropriate measure of this dimension, each has other sources of variance also. Arbuthnot (1972) cites many reported correlations between EFT and RFT; the average of these was .44. Differences in test procedures or uncontrolled variables may affect test results in different ways, as will be seen in reviewing studies with alcoholic patients.

Ramifications of the field dependence dimension have been pursued in development, personality, physiology, and psychopathology. There is a general developmental trend toward field independence from age 5 to 15, leveling off until the early 40's and then decreasing toward more field dependence with increased age.

Small but persistent sex differences have generally been found on RFT performance in Western society, with females scoring more field dependent than males from adolescence. This difference may very well be due to socialization rather than to innate differences (Witkin & Berry, 1975).

Individuals who are extremely field dependent or independent exhibit consistent differences in other areas. For example, field dependent subjects are reported to have a less sophisticated body concept (Witkin et al., 1962) than field independent perceivers, who have a relatively articulated body concept as measured by a Draw-A-Person test. That is, field independent persons conceive of the body as segregated from the field, with discrete yet interrelated body parts formed into a definite structure. In contrast, field dependent subjects have a global, inarticulated concept of the body.

In the social sphere, the person who uses the frame to determine the position of the rod in the RFT will also tend to be more prone to influence by his social context in determining his attitude, feelings, and needs. He is sensitive to social cues, interested in the actions and behaviors of those around him, and more drawn to people. Field dependent persons have been shown to prefer to be physically closer to others than field independent persons (Holley, 1972) and are perceived as warm, tactful, considerate, and socially outgoing by others (Weissenberg & Gruenfeld, 1966).

Cognitive styles have also been related to the nature of defenses. Field independent persons tend to use more specialized defenses such as isolation and intellectualization, while field dependent persons tend to use global defenses such as massive repression and primitive denial (Witkin, 1965).

In the area of physiology, differences in autonomic discharge between field dependent and field independent individuals have been found. Under conditions of sensory isolation both field dependent and field independent subjects exhibited a high level of physiological arousal, as measured by various physiological indicators of autonomic activity including galvanic skin resistance and electroencephalography, at the beginning of the session. The field independent subjects adapted to their surroundings, resulting in lower arousal levels at the end of the session, whereas field dependent subjects did not show such a reduction (Cohen, Silverman, & Shmavonian, 1963). In a situation where a higher arousal level is adaptive, however, field independent subjects may actually show higher levels of physiological arousal (Hein, Cohen, & Shmavonian, 1964). These and many other results in the vast literature on field dependence are consistent with the view that field independent subjects tend to impose their own structure on ambiguous situations. Field dependent subjects are less likely to do this, and for them more situations remain ambiguous.

With regard to psychopathology, a tendency to be more field dependent or field independent is not related to the presence or absence of pathology. Pathology is found at both extremes of the field dependence continuum (Witkin, 1965). Persons who perform at the extremes seem to show different types of psychopathology. Associated with extreme field independence are delusions, outward aggression, expansive and euphoric ideas of grandeur, over-ideation, obsessive-compulsive personality, paranoia, and some types of schizophrenia and neurosis. Associated with field dependent functioning are dependency, unresisted identity problems, hallucinations, passivity and helplessness, character disorders, and hysterical personality.

FIELD DEPENDENCE AND ALCOHOLISM

The finding that alcoholics as a group are more field dependent than controls, with hospitalization, socioeconomic variables, and psychopathology controlled, was first reported by Witkin, Karp, and Goodenough (1959) and has been supported by numerous studies (Bailey, Hustmyer, & Kristofferson, 1959; Chess, Neuringer & Goldstein, 1971: Goldstein & Chotlos, 1965; Goldstein, Neuringer, Reiff, & Shelly, 1968; Goldstein & Shelly, 1971; Karp & Konstadt, 1965; Karp, Poster, & Goodman, 1963; Neale, 1963; Rhodes & Yorioka, 1968; Surrey, 1968).

Two hypotheses have been advanced to explain the relationship between field dependence and alcoholism (Karp, Witkin, & Goodenough, 1965b). The "predisposing hypothesis" suggests that field dependence precedes and may in some way contribute to the development of alcoholism. The second, or "consequence hypothesis," states that prolonged drinking or its physiological and psychological consequences contribute to field dependence.

THE PREDISPOSING HYPOTHESIS: STABILITY OF FIELD DEPENDENCE IN ALCOHOLICS

Witkin, Karp, and Goodenough (1959), in their report of the first study demonstrating field dependence in alcoholics, raise the question of whether a field dependent mode of perceiving reflects an underlying predisposition towards alcoholism or is in some way a consequence of alcoholism. While recognizing that only a longitudinal study of a large group of subjects, beginning early in life before the age when alcoholism appears, could provide definitive answers to this question, Witkin and his colleagues carried out several studies of specific problems aimed at acquiring essential information for assessing the reasonableness of carrying out such a long-term study. The predisposition hypothesis would be supported by findings in a longitudinal study that subjects who later became alcoholic show field dependent perception and the associated characteristic of limited differentiation prior to the onset of alcoholism. A necessary prerequisite before undertaking a longitudinal study is to determine the stability of field dependence and its related characteristics during phases of the alcoholismic cycle. Although, as Karp, Witkin, and Goodenough (1965a) point out, evidence of stability would not directly prove the predisposition hypothesis, it would make this hypothesis more plausible than would the finding of instability. Lack of stability, on the other hand, would make a prediction study unreasonable. One study (Karp, Witkin, & Goodenough, 1965b) checked on stability of field dependence in alcoholics tested on two occasions, once while sober and once after ingestion of controlled doses of alcohol. They did not find differences in field dependence attributable to the acute effects of intoxication. A second study (Karp & Konstadt, 1965) found no significant differences in field dependence among alcoholics differing in duration of drinking history. A third study (Karp, Witkin, & Goodenough, 1965a) examined the effect of cessation of drinking upon field dependence. Two groups of alcoholics who had achieved remission from their alcoholism for at least fifteen months were compared with two groups who were still actively drinking; the measures used were RFT, BAT, and a short form of the EFT, and no significant difference in extent of field dependence was found between drinking and abstaining alcoholics. The investigators concluded from the results of the three studies that considerable stability of field dependence among alcoholics had been demonstrated, suggesting that the hypothesis that field dependence is a prior condition and contributory factor to the development of alcoholism should be further investigated. Other studies carried out since have in part supported and in part questioned this conclusion. The findings of Karp et al. (1965b) were questioned by Kristofferson (1968), who found increased field dependence on the RFT in nonalcoholic college students following alcohol intake of 1.00 ml per kg. Harley, Cohen, and Silverman (1974) challenged Kristofferson's findings by reporting that none of three groups of 10 normal subjects selected for inclusion into field independent, field dependent, and field middle groups by performance on the RFT showed significant changes in RFT performance after alcohol ingestion. However, a high dose (1.00 ml per kg) did result in less accurate RFT performance when computed across all three groups. Intergroup comparisons showed a tendency towards greater accuracy in field dependent subjects than field independent subjects after a low dose of alcohol (0.33 ml per kg). The authors speculated that enhanced perceptual functioning may offer one possible unconscious motive for low or moderate alcohol consumption in field dependent subjects. They point to procedural differences between their study and Kristofferson's; in the latter, the

RFT was given one hour after alcohol ingestion, while in the former it was administered 2 hours and 25 minutes afterwards. Smith and Carpenter (1969) cite Smith (1968) as having found that field middle subjects (mean deviation between 2° and 4°) showed more field dependence after an 0.67 ml per kg dose at one measurement period; how long after alcohol ingestion is not stated. The finding by Jones (1974) that a personality dimension such as intro-extraversion can interact with alcohol ingestion to alter performance on a cognitive task (Raven's Progressive Matrices) may account for some of the variability in reported results.

The major difference between Karp et al. (1965b) and the later studies cited is that the former tested alcoholic subjects; in the latter studies alcohol was administered to nonalcoholic subjects. The reports do not allow direct comparisons of baseline levels of field dependence between the studies; it is conceivable that the alcoholic subjects were considerably more field dependent at baseline than the nonalcoholic subjects, and thus less likely to show a change towards increased field dependence after alcohol administration. It is also possible that alcohol has different effects on field dependence in alcoholics than in nonalcoholics. Resolution of the conflicting evidence in the studies cited would require a study of the effects of different doses of alcohol on alcoholic and nonalcoholic subjects matched for initial level of field dependence.

In the second study from Witkin's group, Karp and Konstadt (1965) investigated the effect of prolonged drinking on field dependence, as measured by the EFT, BAT, and RFT, in a group of male alcoholics divided into long and short duration of excessive drinking. These subjects were compared with two groups of normals whose mean ages corresponded to those of the two alcoholic groups. As expected, the older groups were more field dependent than the younger subjects, and alcoholics were more field dependent than controls. The absence of an interaction between alcoholism and age showed that prolonged drinking has no effect on field dependence. This was interpreted to support the view that field dependence is a stable characteristic of alcoholics and does not change as a result of prolonged drinking.

In contrast, Groden (1970) found that male subjects with a duration of nine years or less of alcoholism performed comparably to matched, nonalcoholic controls on the Gottschaldt Hidden Figures Test. Drinkers with a sixteen year or more history of alcoholism were more field dependent than matched controls.

Although Groden's results appear to challenge those of Karp and Konstadt, it should be noted that the Gottschaldt Hidden Figures Test is not by itself the best means of assessing field dependence; like the EFT, it shares some common variance with other tests of field dependence but the relationship is not strong enough to ensure comparable findings.

The third study from Witkin's group (Karp et al., 1965a), as noted above, found no difference in field dependence between alcoholics who were actively drinking and alcoholics who were abstinent for at least fifteen months. Later studies of test-retest comparisons in the same alcoholic subjects have not entirely supported the notion of stability in the subacute phase of recovery from alcoholic excess.

Utilizing the RFT (upright condition), Chess (1969) reported a significant decline in field dependence in alcoholic inpatients in a seven-week veterans program. Subjects were still field dependent, but significantly less so. Veteran hospital employees, matched for age and general intelligence, served as controls and showed no such improvement over time. Autonomic arousal level, as monitored by skin resistance and heart rate, declined over the seven testing sessions for both alcoholics and controls. Thus, the reduction in field dependence in the alcoholic group was attributed to abstinence and the lessening of anxiety rather than to arousal level.

Goldstein and Chotlos (1966) also found that a significantly greater number of subjects from a sample of 62 alcoholic males became less field independent after 8 to 10 weeks in a treatment facility than could be expected by chance. The authors attributed the improvement to abstinence.

Smith and Layden (1972) administered the RFT to 63 middle class alcoholic inpatients in a 10-day conditioned aversion therapy program. The subjects were tested after withdrawal, one week later, and six weeks after that. Field dependence decreased significantly by the sixth week ($p<.05$). This improvement was accompanied by improvement on reaction time, Shipley-Hartford, color-vision, moods, neurotic symptoms, heart rate, and blood chemistries. McWilliams, Brown, and Minard (1975) studied a group of 54 alcoholic volunteers (47 men, 7 women) in a state hospital alcoholism unit. Of these, 28 had completed a course of treatment with a psychedelic drug (dipropyltryptamine) and individual therapy; 18 had individual therapy with no drug; and 8 had only group and milieu therapy, given to the other two groups also. These patients were the survivors after 6 weeks of an original sample of 143 patients randomly assigned to all three groups. Rod and frame testing (body upright) before and after the 6-week period of treatment showed no significant difference between the 54 survivors and the 89 dropouts at initial testing and a significant decrease in RFT score (less field dependence) in the two groups who had individual therapy with or without drug; the small control group did not show a significant difference, although the magnitude of the decrease in score was of the same order as in the other two groups.

Contrary to these findings, Jacobson, Pisani, and Berenbaum (1970) found no significant differences between performances on RFT ten days after hospitalization and again 33 days later. It must be noted that the RFT procedure was irregular in that it required subjects to stand upright 8 feet away from the RFT apparatus during testing. They concluded that sobriety and abstinence are not significant variables in reducing field dependence in alcoholics, thus supporting Karp's et al. (1965a) findings to this effect. Karp et al., as noted above, did not perform testing and retesting on the same patients; they compared 40 alcoholics who had achieved remission for at least 15 months with 40 who were still actively drinking, and found no significant differences in EFT, RFT, and BAT performance.

In attempting to interpret the meaning of these studies on stability of field dependence in alcoholics, several observations should be made.

David Wechsler, many years ago (1958) stated:

> "In discussing the effects of alcohol on mental activity, it is important to distinguish between the transient changes in psychological functions following the ingestion of restricted amounts of alcohol and those ascribed to its continued use."

Transient and reversible effects of large doses of alcohol on field dependence have been shown in nonalcoholic subjects, although not in alcoholics. These changes cannot be inferred to have any relevance to the question of long-term stability of field dependence in alcoholics subject to continuous repeated intoxication. The immediate acute phase of intoxication caused by recent alcohol ingestion is succeeded by the subacute phase; during a period of weeks or months of abstinence many brain functions show slow recovery; Goodwin and Hill (1975) and Tarter (in press) cite numerous studies to this effect. Improvements have been shown in learning, memory, vocabulary, abstract reasoning, gait instability, electroencephalograms, perceptual-motor, and other functions, so that it is likely that the changes in field dependence reflect a similar reconstitution or recompensation of brain functions temporarily impaired by alcohol excess massive enough to require hospital treatment. The question of whether chronic alcohol excess over many years, with repeated episodes of severe intoxication, can cause increasing field dependence remains open. It has not been tested by repeated administration of RFT and other tests to the same subjects; like the longitudinal study from prealcoholic life onwards, this remains to be done. However, even such a study would not distinguish the effects of alcohol from the effects of alcoholism. Several investigators have pointed out that the alcoholic is usually malnourished, usually a heavy smoker, at risk of repeated trauma to the head, and usually drinks alcoholic beverages rich in congeners which may be particularly toxic. Alcoholics also have particular life styles and habits which distinguish them from other groups. There is little agreement among investigators that the permanent brain damage in alcoholics is due to alcohol per se, although the avitaminosis associated with malnutrition in alcoholics can undoubtedly cause permanent brain damage.

THE PREDISPOSING HYPOTHESIS: THE QUESTION OF HOMOGENEITY

An issue which has been raised by investigators attempting to refute the predisposing hypothesis is the wide range of performance scores on RFT and other tests of field dependence among alcoholics. The fact that some alcoholics score comparably to field independent normals seems to require particular explanation; the assumption appears to be that if field dependence predisposes to alcoholism, all alcoholics must be field dependent. This is, of course, not necessarily so. Field dependence may be one factor among many others which leads through so far undetermined mechanisms, and by interacting with other factors in environment and experience, to alcoholism. The evidence clearly shows that although some alcoholics are field independent, the distribution of scores in alcoholics is skewed in the field dependent direction.

Studies which claim that field independent alcoholics are easily found have not been adequately controlled. Klappersack (1968) for instance, states that he found groups of 20 field independent and 20 field dependent alcoholics in a group of 60 Veterans Administration patients, but he does not state the size of the group from which he selected his groups of 20 field independent and 20 field dependent controls. He also used a mean deviation of 9° or less as his criterion for field independence, while 12° or more identified field dependent alcoholics. For comparison,

Smith and Carpenter (1969) and Harley, Cohen, and Silverman (1974), studying normal subjects, used a cut-off point of less than 2° to identify field independence. Thus, some of Klappersack's field independent alcoholics would have been rated as field dependent by the other investigators. Jacobson (1974) presents a complete distribution for 145 hospitalized male alcoholics tested by his unusual procedure, standing upright 8 feet from the apparatus. Approximately 53% of his group had error deviations of 9° or less, while 34% had deviations of 12° or more. The median was 8.24°. While 13% had deviations of 2° or less, 16.5% had deviations between 2° and 4°. Comparable data are lacking for other alcoholic groups.

In the same paper, Jacobson cites data from other investigators showing comparable distributions for male psychiatric and male normal subjects. Neville, Workman, and Johnson (1969) studied 238 male and female psychiatric in-patients. Pressey (1968) studied 266 normal subjects. Vaught (1968) studied 684 normal subjects. There are certain methodological differences between the studies of Pressey and Vaught on the one hand and Neville et al. on the other, as Vaught (1970) has pointed out. Neville et al. used a head clamp while administering the RFT while Pressey and Vaught did not; the former used a noncommercial RFT while the latter used a commercial apparatus, perhaps differing in calibration. Neville et al. manipulated the rod following subjects' instructions, while the Pressey and Vaught data were collected by subjects using a remote-control switch to move the rod. Jacobson used a commercial apparatus and had the subject adjusting the rod, but the subjects were standing rather than sitting. Thus there are a variety of procedural differences between Jacobson, Neville et al. and Pressey and Vaught. Only if we neglect such differences can we consider comparisons between the distributions presented. If we accept the validity of the distributions for our purposes in spite of these differences, we can conclude that choice of cutting points either at 2° or 9° demonstrates clearly less prevalence of field independent performance among alcoholics (and unspecified psychiatric patients) compared to normals. At the same time it is apparent that a sizable number of alcoholics perform in a field independent manner.

Bellows (1971) compared an Alcoholics Anonymous group with unspecified controls and found no statistically significant difference in RFT performance, although alcoholics exhibited twice as high a ceiling in degrees of deviation from the upright towards field dependence. Burdick (1969) found alcoholics from a higher socioeconomic class to be field independent on Jackson's (1956) EFT short form when compared to normative data from other studies. The lack of a concurrent control group and other methodological problems mitigate against acceptance of Burdick's results.

Goldstein et al. (1970) compared alcoholics with nonalcoholic ambulatory medical patients and community volunteers. When divided into field dependent and field independent groups, they showed different levels of ability on cognitive-analytic (EFT, Block Design, Picture Completion, Object Assembly) and visual-postural tasks (Rod Verticality) regardless of alcoholism. This is not surprising considering the well-known correlates of field dependence with the WAIS "analytic triad," and does not in itself imply brain damage in field dependent groups, alcoholic or nonalcoholic.

A field independent subsample of alcoholics comparable

to normal field independent subjects was again found by Fehr (1971), and a great range in scores among alcoholics on the RFT has been reported (Bellows, 1971; Goldstein & Chotlos, 1965) to support the "heterogeneity effect" in perceptual error among alcoholics. Again it must be emphasized that a variety of scores will be found in a group of alcoholics on any measure. The heterogeneity effect does not in itself refute the predisposing hypothesis, although different explanatory mechanisms may be required for the development of alcoholism in field independent alcoholics.

THE CONSEQUENTIAL HYPOTHESIS: CENTRAL NERVOUS SYTEM DAMAGE OR PREMATURE AGING

Central nervous system damage has been implicated as a factor in field dependence in alcoholics. Goldstein and Chotlos (1965) compared 50 male alcoholic veterans during the second week of hospitalization with 50 VA hospital employees on various tests, attempting to match for age and intelligence. Alcoholics performed significantly more slowly on tests of psychomotor function (Trail Making Test) and speed of speech (Stroop Test), and more field dependently on the RFT than controls. However, no differences were found on the Halstead Category, Seashore Rhythm, Delayed Auditory Feedback, and Autokinetic Phenomenon tests. The authors interpreted these results in conjunction with high D scale scores on the MMPI by alcoholics as a sign of organicity with reactive depression rather than being due to general dependence.

The pattern of a normal pure motor speed with

performance below average on timed manual dexterity found in alcoholics (Goldstein & Shelly, 1971) is often found in old persons, who are also more field dependent than young adults. Thus, field dependence in alcoholics may represent premature aging and/or be attributable to an interaction of aging and excessive drinking (Pisani, Jacobson, & Berenbaum, 1973).

When actually comparing alcoholics, controls, and brain damaged subjects, Klappersack (1968) concluded that if the overall performance of all groups is placed on a continuum of intactness to deterioration, the following order is found: field independent controls, field independent alcoholics, field dependent controls, field dependent alcoholics, and brain damaged subjects. As noted earlier, subjects scoring less than 9° and more than 12° mean deviation were categorized as field independent and field dependent, respectively. Significant differences between performance on Picture Completion and Block Design tests were found between controls and alcoholics. Brain damaged subjects scored comparably to the field dependent alcoholics on Picture Completion and Block Design, but scored inferior to field dependent controls on these tests. Since the Block Design test is considered to be an indicator of organic dysfunction, and since field dependent alcoholics did not differ from brain damaged subjects on this test, the author warned against dismissing the notion of brain damage in alcoholism. However, it would of course be a fallacy to accept this as evidence supporting brain damage as a cause of field dependence in alcoholism.

The differences in performance on the RFT between groups in Klappersack's study were attributed to perceptual and visual-organizational components rather than visual ones. Also, the fact that postural tests (Tilt Chair, Heath Rails) did not differentiate the groups was interpreted as failing to support the equilibratory functioning aspect of the consequential theory. Bellows (1971), however, found that alcoholics and brain damaged (cerebellar neoplasms) subjects performed more poorly on Heath Rails than controls. He noted that Klappersack's failure to reach a significant correlation between RFT and rail walking could well have been due to methodological modifications not in accordance with original instructions for the Heath Rails. Shortcomings cited were (a) scoring length walked instead of number of steps; (b) failure to state whether subjects walked erect, and (c) use of three rail widths instead of six.

Bergman and Agren (1974) provided some evidence of the relationship of field dependence to brain damage in some alcoholics. Ninety male alcoholics, 30 in each of three age groups, 18-30, 31-44, and 45-60, were tested after withdrawal from alcohol on a battery of cognitive tests including Synonyms, Reasoning (figure classifications) and Koh's Block Design, the Grassi Block Substitution Test, the Trail Making Test, the Memory for Designs Test, as well as tests of short-term memory for word pairs and personal data. Field dependence was assessed with the RFT (all three series); the authors also administered two additional control series, one with body erect, no frame (rod-alone series) and one with body tilted, no frame (body-tilt series) to measure the effects of frame exposure and body tilt. The EFT was administered using Jackson's short version (Jackson, 1956). The most advanced symptoms of alcoholism, occurrence of delirium tremens or alcoholic hallucinosis, were found in 24 patients. These did not differ significantly from the other 63 patients for whom data are given in age or results of cognitive testing except in measures of field dependence. They were more field dependent on all three series of the RFT and in the rod-alone and body-tilt series. The authors note that many had great difficulty in perceiving the upright even without the frame; and in fact the difference in performance was most evident on the rod-alone and body-tilt series. The EFT, which they point out, does not demand reference to postural sensations, showed least discriminability. They suggest that the difficulties in these patients were mediated by inability to use the felt position of the body as a reference point in space, possibly because of undiagnosed vestibular, kinesthetic, and tactile malfunctioning. Although a normal control group was not used, the authors stated that their alcoholic patients as a whole were definitely field dependent compared to available (published) control data. Their study provides evidence that one particular group of alcoholics, those with histories of hallucinations or delirium tremens, were clearly more field dependent; the rod-alone and body-tilt conditions without the frame appear to show that the greater field dependence in this group was mediated through neurological impairment consequent on alcohol use. However, the rod-alone and body-tilt measures are mediated through different mechanisms; well-known effects came into play, for instance, in the body-tilt condition but not in the rod-and-frame situation. Some caution, therefore, is required in accepting these results as supporting the consequential hypothesis. It is conceivable, for instance, that more field dependent subjects are more likely to develop delirium tremens or hallucinosis than less field dependent subjects; as noted earlier, hallucinations have been long associated with the psychopathology of extreme field dependence, and the inability of such individuals to structure ambiguous situations may well lead to delirium in withdrawing from alcohol intoxication.

AN ALTERNATIVE HYPOTHESIS

Based on the effect of sensory deprivation, Jacobson (1971) has rejected both predisposing and consequence hypotheses in accounting for the RFT performance of alcoholics. In his study, 96 hospitalized, male chronic alcoholics were assigned to one of five groups subjected to various amounts of stimulus deprivation. Subjects in Group SD were placed under perceptual and sensory deprivation by wearing opaque goggles, arm cuffs, and hearing white noise through earphones while lying in bed. Group SI was subjected to 1 hour of social isolation only, and Group SC received 1 hour of dark adaptation in a normal environment. Control Group UC_1 was administered the RFT once after admission and again 5 weeks later, while subjects in Group UC_2 were tested repeatedly. All groups except UC_1 were tested on the RFT 8 times in the standing position. The results showed that field dependence was significantly reduced for the SD group immediately after sensory deprivation and remained significantly reduced up to four months later, at which time the study was terminated. Jacobson reports a significant correlation between brain damage indices and perceptual field dependence before the experimental condition was imposed, but a reduction in field dependence was not accompanied by a change in the brain damage indices. Field dependence was also reduced in SC (dark adaptation) and UC_2 (repeated testing) groups, thus further questioning the stability hypothesis. It must be noted that the UC_2 group scored significantly more field dependent on the RFT on the initial baseline test, but the author did not comment on this.

Jacobson offers the hypothesis that alcohol serves as a chemical means of suppressing interoceptive, body-generated stimuli that conflict with exteroceptive, environmentally produced stimuli. Thus alcohol acts as a psychophysiological reinforcement for field dependent behavior. In an environment which reduces exteroceptive stimuli, thus creating sensory deprivation, the subject must shift his attention to the interoceptive stimuli, which are always present but usually suppressed, as valid information. Thus, when he is tested immediately after deprivation, his performance is improved due to use of the interoceptive stimuli. Continued improved performance becomes rewarding, extinguishing the reliance on external cues, thus further reducing field dependent performance.

FIELD DEPENDENCE AND PERSONALITY MEASURES

It will be recalled that a cognitive style as measured by perceptual-cognitive tests is considered a pervasive characteristic of an individual's functioning. Field dependent and field independent individuals have been claimed to show differences in abstraction level, social interaction, and physiological functioning. It is plausible that measures of field dependence are tapping a basic characterological tendency which is also expressed as social and psychological dependence. Thus, alcoholics who appear perceptually field dependent are also described as passive, markedly dependent individuals with poor self-differentiation (Witkin, Karp, & Goodenough, 1959).

Initial support for this viewpoint came from comparative clinical studies which report marked field dependence in both obese people (Lolli, 1955) and ulcer patients (Gordon, 1953); both groups reported displaying dependence as part of their personality constellations. However, studies in alcoholics, and in general in other groups, have shown no relationship between field dependence and emotional dependence. Rhodes and Yorioka (1968) presented 19 alcoholic and 19 nonalcoholic tuberculous patients, matched by age, education, and length of hospitalization, with the EFT (12-item) and Navran Dy Scale, a social dependency measure. Alcoholics scored significantly higher on EFT ($p < .05$) than nonalcoholics and scored higher but not significantly so on the Dy Scale. In addition, the correlation between EFT and Dy scores was low ($r = +.30$). The authors felt their data refuted a unitary concept of dependency.

Fisk (1970) used the Navran Scale to determine whether 60 male alcoholics were overtly dependent, counterdependent, or flexible. The counterdependent individual denies dependency by acting independently, and was expected to score extremely low on the dependency scale. The flexible person is genuinely independent and would fall in the middle range of scores. Indeed, subjects at both extremes on the Navran Scale were significantly more field dependent on the EFT (short form) than subjects scoring in the moderate range. Subjects rated overtly dependent were more field dependent than counterdependent subjects, who in turn were more field dependent than flexible subjects.

Attempting also to relate field dependence as measured by the RFT to other forms of dependency, Goldstein et al. (1968) reported 30 male hospitalized alcoholics to be field dependent on the (RFT $\overline{X}$ = 11.7, *SD* = 9.1; no control group included). When tested on a battery of tests of dependency, only dominance and ascendance scales correlated significantly with RFT performance, and this was in a direction opposite to that expected, that is, the greater the field dependence, the lower the dominance and ascendance scores. Factor analysis produced only a negligible relationship between RFT and other measures of dependence. In addition, psychological dependency scales of the MMPI (*Mf*, *Hy*) did not significantly correlate with RFT performance in the expected direction (Goldstein & Chotlos, 1966; Neale, 1963).

Neale (1963) found that essential alcoholics, who are by definition highly socially dependent, scored significantly lower on the RFT than less dependent, reactive alcoholics. The essential alcoholic sample can, by normative standards, still be considered field dependent since their average degrees of deviation from the vertical was 14.7°.

Similarly, other studies have found that field dependence has no stable relationship with neuroticism, extraversion, and anxiety.

The relationship of cognitive style to defense mechanisms was studied in 110 psychiatric outpatients, aged between 20 and 55, who were not medicated, psychotic, or brain damaged and had at least a tenth-grade education (Ihilevich & Gleser, 1971). The Defense Mechanism Inventory (DMI), EFT, and Figure Drawing tests were administered. High scores on a particular defense scale of the DMI indicate a relatively stable response pattern to a range of frustrating events. Sex differences have been reported in normal subjects (Bogo, Winget, & Gleser, 1970) and in alcoholics (Sugerman, Sheldon, & Roth, 1975). It was found that subjects who rely excessively on global defenses (turning against self, reversal) are more field dependent than subjects who employ differentiated defenses (turning against objects, projection).

Donovan, Hague, and O'Leary (1975) extended these findings to alcoholics. Seventy-five male alcoholic in-patients with a mean age of 47.7 (*SD* = 8.7) and educational level of 11.9 years (*SD* = 2.9) were tested on the DMI and Group EFT (GEFT). It was found that although alcoholics exhibited a wide range of scores on the GEFT, field independent alcoholics significantly more often employed the differentiated defenses of turning against object and projection than did field dependent alcoholics, who relied more heavily on turning against self and reversal. The field independent group was significantly younger and better educated.

INTELLIGENCE, COGNITIVE COMPLEXITY AND SELF-ACTUALIZATION

At this juncture we may inquire into the relationship between cognitive style and general intelligence. It has been reported that RFT performance in alcoholics correlates with the WAIS intelligence quotient, greater field independence being associated with higher intelligence (Goldstein et al., 1968). However, when subjects are matched on intellectual ability, alcoholics also exhibit field dependent performance, which thus cannot be attributed to intellectual deficiency. Indeed, intelligence as measured by verbal ability has not been found to correlate with either the EFT (Fehr, 1971) or RFT (Gough & Olton, 1972). Many other investigators have reported similar results.

This does not rule out a qualitative difference in terms of abstraction, problem solving, and cognition in general. Intellectual factors have been shown to be important in perceptual orientation (Tarter, Sheldon, & Sugerman, 1975). Of 23 tests selected from the Kit of Reference Tests for Cognitive Factors, the correlation with RFT performance was significant ($p = < .05$) for General Reasoning (Mathematic Aptitude Test) and Mechanical Knowledge (Tool Knowledge) factors. Over 50% the variance of the RFT could be accounted for by these two factors and Sensitivity to Problems, Length Estimation, and Speed of Closure.

Reilly and Sugerman (1967) found that of 96 hospitalized male alcoholics, those functioning at a low level of cognitive complexity, characterized by dependence or concreteness, were significantly more field dependent on the EFT and also less differentiated on the Sophistication of Body Concept Scale than more cognitively complex individuals. Of the four levels of complexity ranging from concrete to abstract, most of the subjects belonged to Systems I and II, and only two subjects reached System III. Brook (1962) had previously used this conceptual systems approach of Harvey, Hunt, and Schroder (1961) to study the cognitive complexity of alcoholics who were successful and unsuccessful in affiliating with Alcoholics Anonymous. System I subjects, who function at a concrete level and accept external sources of authority, are more successful in A.A. than System II subjects, who question control and test limits. However, Karp et al. (1965a) found

A.A. members, both drinking and in remission, significantly less field dependent than patients attending an alcoholism clinic. The significant differences appeared on EFT, BAT, and a combined index of EFT, BAT, and RFT, but not on RFT alone. Kissin, Rosenblatt, and Machover (1968) studied four groups of alcoholics treated primarily with drug therapy, psychotherapy, as inpatients in a rehabilitation ward (skid-row alcoholics), and as a control group. Their results showed some evidence for greater field independence in subjects who were successful in psychotherapy. Field dependent alcoholics tend to drop out of psychotherapy, while field independent alcoholics remain in therapy (Karp, Kissin, & Hustmyer, 1970; Kissin, Platz, & Su, 1970). However, field dependence is not related to dropping out of drug therapy.

Another personality dimension which has been related to field dependence is that of self-actualization. Doyle (1975) tested the hypothesis proposed by Maslow (1964) that self-actualizers would be less likely to be field dependent. He studied 150 normal volunteers, 75 men, and 75 women between the ages of 21 and 35, using the RFT (Series 3, body upright) and Shostrom's (1966) Personal Orientation Inventory. He found nine statistically significant but small negative correlations between RFT and scores and measures of self-actualization. The I Scale (inner-directedness) showed a correlation of -.35 with field independence, supporting Maslow's hypothesis. He concluded cautiously that self-actualization accounts for a small percentage of the variance in the perceptual style labeled field independent.

McWilliams, Brown, and Minard (1975), in a study mentioned earlier, tested 54 state hospital alcoholic patients on RFT Series 3 and Shostrom's Personal Orientation

Inventory. Groups who received individual therapy with or without a psychedelic drug showed significant increase ($p < .01$) in I Scale score after 6 weeks; a small control group (8 patients) did not show a statistically significant change. The changes in self-actualization paralleled changes towards field independence on the RFT. As the control group also showed changes towards greater inner-directedness, they concluded that the effectiveness of individual insight therapy for alcoholics was not substantiated by their findings. As was noted earlier, the subacute phase of withdrawal from alcohol is characterized by recovery in many cerebral functions; Mc Williams' et al. results do not imply any correlation between field independence and self-actualization.

OVERVIEW

Field dependence has been studied more in alcoholism than in any other area of psychopathology, and it has been studied in alcoholism to the virtual exclusion of other cognitive styles. But the extensive literature shows that field independence has been measured differently by different investigators, and also that alcoholism has not been sufficiently considered as a heterogeneous array of disorders with a variety of etiological mechanisms. Even superficial study of the many papers cited in this chapter will show inconsistencies in the use of the various tests of field dependence, although the authors may claim to be measuring the same dimension. The EFT may be used in its original form, in Witkin's short form, or Jackson's short form; results are presented without concurrent scores for a control group, although differences in administration procedures between different investigators can have significant effects. The RFT procedures, when these are given in detail, are even more variable. The subjects may be tested sitting or standing at different distances from the apparatus, with or without the head held in a clamp; the rod adjustments may be made by subject or investigator; the apparatus itself may be the original apparatus used in a dark room or a portable apparatus used in a lighted room. Correlations among these varying methods of testing field dependence are not always high enough to ensure that the same phenomenon is being measured. It is therefore quite striking to observe the amount of agreement between reports of field dependence in alcoholics. The sheer weight of the evidence is compelling; alcoholics, as a heterogeneous group, show at least as high a degree of field dependence as any other psychopathological group except brain damaged subjects. However, the group of alcoholics is heterogeneous enough to show a sizable number of field independent individuals. Neither the predisposition nor the consequence hypothesis has received enough support to be acceptable alone when applied to all alcoholics, and although a longitudinal study from early childhood on, with assessment of field dependence in large numbers of children and followup to identify those who later became alcoholic, might be invaluable in adding to knowledge of the etiology and nosology of alcoholism, it may be more useful for the present to consider that the two hypotheses are not exclusive and that other hypotheses might have more heuristic value. If the heterogeneity of alcoholism is accepted, it is certainly possible that in some alcoholics field dependence or its personality correlates may predispose to dependence on alcohol.

It is certainly also possible that in some alcoholics (who may overlap with the first group) field dependence may be a consequence of cerebral impairment produced by long continued ingestion of alcohol or its usual concomitant nutritional deficiencies. Studies in alcoholism and field dependence elucidating these issues should pay more attention than heretofore to differences among alcoholic subjects and differences between alcoholic and normal subjects. The effects of alcohol on alcoholics are not the same as those of alcohol on normals. Essential alcoholics are not reactive alcoholics; alcoholics who have shown hallucinosis and delirium tremens should not be grouped with those who have not. The increasing amount of data on genetic factors in alcoholism shows the importance of studying alcoholics with family histories of alcoholism as a separate group. The influence of childhood upbringing in the development of field dependence is strong enough to require a history of alcoholism in parents as an essential item of information in the study of field dependence in alcoholics. Recent interest in minimal brain dysfunction in childhood as a precursor of adult alcoholism suggests another factor which may have a bearing on field dependence in alcoholics; the dysfunction may possibly predispose to both alcoholism and field dependence, and in this group neither the predisposition or consequence hypothesis in their original form would be necessary.

The tremendous size of the problem of alcoholism warrants massive research efforts; the concepts and tools provided by Witkin and his co-workers have been of great benefit to alcoholism research and will undoubtedly lead to much more important work in the future. If investigators are to use these concepts and tools to best advantage, attention must be paid to careful specification of both alcoholic and control samples, standard and reproducible methodology in the measurement of variables, and good research design. Only by such means can answers be found for the many perplexing questions posed by the cognitive style of alcoholics.

ACKNOWLEDGEMENTS

Preparation of this review was supported in part by Research Grant No. AA 00456 (National Institute on Alcohol Abuse and Alcoholism).

We thank Dr. H.A. Witkin for providing ready access to his library on field dependence and for many helpful comments.

REFERENCES

Arbuthnot, J.B. Cautionary note on measurement of field independence. *Perceptual and Motor Skills*, 1972, *35*, 479-488.

Bailey, W., Hustmyer, F., & Kristofferson, A. *Judgement of verticality by alcoholics*. Paper presented at the meeting of the American Psychological Association, Cincinnati, 1959.

Bellows, C.A. *The relationship of alcoholism and cerebellar damage to posture and field dependency*. Unpublished master's thesis, University of Manitoba, 1971.

Bergman, H., & Agren, G. Cognitive style and intellectual performance in relation to the progress of alcoholism. *Quarterly Journal of Studies on Alcohol*, 1974, *35*, 1242-1255.

Bogo, N., Winget, C., & Gleser, G.C. Ego defenses and perceptual styles. *Perceptual and Motor Skills*, 1970, *30*, 599-605.

Brook, R.R. Personality correlates associated with differential success of affiliation with Alcoholics Anonymous. (Doctoral dissertation, University of Colorado, 1962). (University Microfilms No. 62-6262)

Burdick, J.A. A field-independent alcoholic population. *Journal of Psychology*, 1969, *73*, 163-166.

Chess, S.B. The relationship between arousal level and Rod and Frame test performance. (Doctoral dissertation, University of Kansas, 1969). (University Microfilms, No. 70-11,007).

Chess, S.B., Neuringer, C., & Goldstein, G. Arousal and field dependency in alcoholics. *Journal of General Psychology*, 1971, *85*, 93-102.

Cohen, S.I., Silverman, A.J., & Shmavonian, B.M. Psychophysiological studies in altered sensory environments. *Journal of Psychosomatic Research*, 1963, *6*, 259-281.

Donovan, D.M., Hague, W.H., & O'Leary, M.R. Perceptual differentiation and defense mechanisms in alcoholics. *Journal of Clinical Psychology*, 1975, *31*, 356-359.

Doyle, J.A. Field-independence and self-actualization. *Psychological Reports*, 1975, *36*, 363-366.

Fehr, D.H. Perceptual field-dependence and inconsistency of interpersonal perceptions in alcoholics. (Doctoral dissertation, University of Oklahoma, 1971). (University Microfilms, No. 72-3389)

Fisk, C.B. Psychological dependence, perceptual dependence and the establishment of a treatment relationship among male alcoholics. (Doctoral dissertation, Boston University, 1970). (University Microfilms, 1970. No. 70-22,385)

Gardner, R., Holzman, P.S., Klein, G.S., Linton, H., & Spence, D.P. Cognitive control: A study of individual consistencies in cognitive behavior. *Psychological Issues*, 1959, *1* (4), 1-186.

Gardner, R., Jackson, D., & Messick, S. Personality organization in cognitive controls, and intellectual abilities. *Psychological Issues*, 1960, *2*(4), 1-149.

Goldstein, G., & Chotlos, J.W. Dependency and brain damage in alcoholics. *Perceptual and Motor Skills*, 1965, *21*, 135-150.

Goldstein, G., & Chotlos, J.W. Stability of field dependence in chronic alcoholic patients. *Journal of Abnormal Psychology*, 1966, *71*, 420.

Goldstein, G., Neuringer, C., & Klappersack, B. Cognitive, perceptual, and motor aspects of field dependency in alcoholics. *Journal of Genetic Psychology*, 1970, *117*, 253-266.

Goldstein, G., Neuringer, C., Reiff, C., & Shelly, C.H. Generalizability of field dependency in alcoholics. *Journal of Consulting and Clinical Psychology*, 1968, *32*, 560-564.

Goldstein, G., & Shelly, C.H. Field dependence and cognitive, perceptual, and motor skills in alcoholics: A factor-analytic study. *Quarterly Journal of Studies on Alcohol*, 1971, *32*, 29-40.

Goodwin, D.W., & Hill, S.Y. Chronic effects of alcohol and other psychoactive drugs on intellect, learning, and memory. In J.G. Rankin (Ed.), *Alcohol, drugs, and brain damage*. Toronto: Alcoholism and Drug Addiction Research Foundation of Ontario, 1975.

Gordon, B. *An experimental study of dependence-independence in a social and a laboratory setting*. Unpublished doctoral dissertation, University of Southern California, 1953.

Gough, H.G., & Olton, R.M. Field independence as related to nonverbal measures of perceptual performance and cognitive ability. *Journal of Consulting and Clinical Psychology*, 1972, *38*, 338-342.

Groden, G. The performance of alcoholics on the Hidden Figures and the Trail Making tests. (Doctoral dissertation, Purdue University, 1970). (University Microfilms, No. 70-10,645)

Harley, J.P., Cohen, R., & Silverman, A.J. Field dependence and response to alcohol. *Quarterly Journal of Studies on Alcohol*, 1974, *35*, 973-986.

Hartmann, H. *Ego psychology and the problem of adaptation*. New York: International Universities Press, 1958.

Harvey, O.J., Hunt, D.E., & Schroder, H.M. *Conceptual systems and personality organization*. New York: John Wiley & Sons, 1961.

Hein, P., Cohen, S.I., & Shmavonian, B.M. Perceptual mode and Pavlovian typology. In J. Wortis (Ed.), *Recent advances in biological psychiatry, VII*. New York: Plenum Press, 1964.

Holley, M. Field-dependence-independence, sophistication-of-body-concept, and social distance selection. (Doctoral dissertation, New York University, 1972). (University Microfilms, No. 72-20,635)

Ihilevich, D., & Gleser, G. Relationship of defense mechanisms to field dependence-independence. *Journal of Abnormal Psychology*, 1971, *77*, 296-302.

Jackson, D.N. A short form of Witkin's Embedded Figures Test. *Journal of Abnormal and Social Psychology*, 1956, *53*, 254-255.

Jacobson, G.R. Sensory deprivation and field dependence in alcoholics. (Doctoral dissertation, Illinois Institute of Technology, 1971). (University Microfilms, No. 72-22,839)

Jacobson, G.R. Field dependence among male alcoholics: Establishing norms for the Rod-and-Frame Test. *Perceptual and Motor Skills*, 1974, *39*, 1015-1018.

Jacobson, G.R., Pisani, V.D., & Berenbaum, H. Temporal stability of field dependence among hospitalized alcoholics. *Journal of Abnormal Psychology*, 1970, *76*, 10-12.

Jones, B. Cognitive performance of introverts and extraverts following acute alcohol ingestion. *British Journal of Psychology*, 1974, *65*, 35-42.

Kagan, J., Moss, H.A., & Sigel, I.E. Psychological significances of styles of conceptualization. *Monographs of the Society for Research in Child Development*, 1963, *28*, 73-112.

Karp, S.A., Kissin, G., & Hustmyer, F.E. Field dependence as a predictor of alcoholic therapy dropouts. *Journal of Nervous and Mental Disease*, 1970, *150*, 77-83.

Karp, S.A., & Konstadt, N.L. Alcoholism and psychological differentiation: Long-range effect of heavy drinking on field dependence. *Journal of Nervous and Mental Disease*, 1965, *140*, 412-416.

Karp, S.A., Poster, D.C., & Goodman, A. Differentiation in alcoholic women. *Journal of Personality*, 1963, *31*, 386-393.

Karp, S.A., Witkin, H.A., & Goodenough, D.R. Alcoholism and psychological differentiation: Effect of achievement of sobriety on field dependence. *Quarterly Journal of Studies on Alcohol*, 1965, *26*, 580-585. (a)

Karp, S.A., Witkin, H.A., & Goodenough, D.R. Alcoholism and psychological differentiation: Effect of alcohol on field dependence. *Journal of Abnormal Psychology*, 1965, *70*, 262-265. (b)

Kissin, B., Platz, A., & Su, W.H. Social and psychological factors in the treatment of chronic alcoholism. *Journal of Psychiatric Research*, 1970, *8*, 13-27.

Kissin, B., Rosenblatt, S.M., & Machover, S. Prognostic factors in alcoholism. Chapter III. *Psychiatric Research Report 24*, American Psychiatric Association, March 1968.

Klappersack, B. Sources of field dependence in alcoholics. (Doctoral dissertation, University of Kansas, 1968). (University Microfilms, No. 68-17,409)

Klein, G., & Schlesinger, H.S. Where is the perceiver in perceptual theory? *Journal of Personality*, 1949, *18*, 32-47.

Kristofferson, M.V. Effect of alcohol on field dependence. *Journal of Abnormal Psychology*, 1968, *73*, 387-391.

Lolli, G. Centers for research on nutritional habits and for the prevention and correction of their deviations. *Quarterly Journal of Studies on Alcohol*, 1955, *16*, 393-396.

Maslow, A.H. Further notes on the psychology of being. *Journal of Humanistic Psychology*, 1964, *4*, 45-58.

McWilliams, J., Brown, C.C., & Minard, J.G. Field dependence and self-actualization in alcoholics. *Quarterly Journal of Studies on Alcohol*, 1975, *36*, 387-394.

Neale, C.R., Jr. An investigation of perception of visual space among alcoholics. (Doctoral dissertation, University of Utah, 1963). (University Microfilms, 1963. No. 63-7112)

Neville, C.W., Workman, S.N., & Johnson, D.T. Expected scores in the Rod and Frame test: Field dependence is where you find it. *Psychonomic Science*, 1969, *15*, 321-322.

Pisani, V.D., Jacobson, G.R., & Berenbaum, H.L. Field dependence and organic brain deficit in chronic alcoholics. *International Journal of the Addictions*, 1973, *8*, 559-564.

Pressey, A.W. A reply to comments on figural aftereffects, illusions, and the dimension of field dependence. *Psychonomic Science*, 1968, *11*, 364.

Reilly, D.H., & Sugerman, A.A. Conceptual complexity and psychological differentiation in alcoholics. *Journal of Nervous and Mental Disease*, 1967, *144*, 14-17.

Rhodes, R.J., & Yorioka, G.N. Dependency among alcoholics and non-alcoholic institituionalized patients. *Psychological Reports*, 1968, *22*, 1343-1344.

Rudin, S., & Stagner, R. Figure-ground phenomena in the perception of physical and social stimuli. *Journal of Psychology*, 1958, *45*, 213-225.

Santostefano, S. Cognitive controls versus cognitive styles: An approach to diagnosing and treating cognitive disabilities in children. *Seminars in Psychiatry*, 1969, *1*, 291-317.

Shostrom, G.L. *The Personal Orientation Inventory manual*. San Diego: Educational & Industrial Testing Service, 1966.

Smith, G.M. *The effect of alcohol on perception, mood, and heart rate.* Unpublished master's thesis, Department of Psychology, Rutgers University, 1968.

Smith, G.M., & Carpenter, J.A. Alcohol absorption and field dependence. *Quarterly Journal of Studies on Alcohol*, 1969, *30*, 15-20.

Smith, J.W., & Layden, T.A. Changes in psychological performance and blood chemistry in alcoholics during and after hospital treatment. *Quarterly Journal of Studies on Alcohol*, 1972, *33*, 379-394.

Sugerman, A.A., Sheldon, J.B., & Roth, C. Defense mechanisms in male and female alcoholics. *Quarterly Journal of Studies on Alcohol*, 1975, *36*, 422-424.

Surrey, E.S. *An investigation of the relationship of narcotic drug dependence, perceptual style, and stress*. Paper presented at the Eastern Psychological Association meeting, Washington, D.C., April 1968.

Tarter, R.E. Neuropsychological investigations of alcoholism. In preparation.

Tarter, R.E., Sheldon, J., & Sugerman, A.A. Correlates of perceptual field orientation in alcoholics. *Journal of Clinical Psychology*, 1975, *31*, 364-366.

Vaught, G.M. Expected scores in the Rod and Frame test: Fuel for the Immergluck-Pressey fire. *Psychonomic Science*, 1968, *13*, 248.

Vaught, G.M. Expected scores in the Rod and Frame test revisited. *Psychonomic Science*, 1970, *18*, 111.

Wechsler, D. *The measurement and appraisal of adult intelligence*(4th ed.). Baltimore: Williams & Wilkins, 1958. Cited by Goodwin & Hill (1975).

Weissenberg, P., & Gruenfeld, L.W. Relationships among leadership dimensions and cognitive style. *Journal of Applied Psychology*, 1966, *50*, 392-395.

Witkin, H.A. Psychological differentiation and forms of pathology. *Journal of Abnormal Psychology*, 1965, *70*, 317-336.

Witkin, H.A., & Berry, J.W. Psychological differentiation in cross-cultural perspective. *Journal of Cross-Cultural Psychology*, 1975, *6*, 4-87.

Witkin, H.A., Dyk, R.B., Faterson, H.F., Goodenough, D.R., & Karp, S.A. *Psychological differentiation*. New York: John Wiley & Sons, 1962.

Witkin, H.A., Karp, S.A., & Goodenough, D.R. Dependence in alcoholics. *Quarterly Journal of Studies on Alcohol*, 1959, *20*, 493-504.

Witkin, H.A., Lewis, H.B., Hertzman, M., Machover, K., Meissner, P.B., & Wapner, S. *Personality through perception*. New York: Harper, 1954.

Witkin, H.A., & Oltman, P.K. Cognitive style. *International Journal of Neurology*, 1967, *6*, 119-137.

Young, H.H. A test of Witkin's field-dependence hypothesis. *Journal of Abnormal and Social Psychology*, 1959, *59*, 188-192.

CHAPTER 12

PSYCHOPHYSIOLOGICAL CORRELATES OF ALCOHOLISM

Ben Morgan Jones
Oscar A. Parsons
Orvis H. Rundell

This chapter will be divided into four sections related to the psychophysiological correlates of alcoholism. The first section will point out certain methodological considerations in evaluating acute effects of alcohol, review relevant studies reporting the effects of alcohol on psychophysiological systems of social drinkers, and examine several hypotheses related to acute alcohol ingestion. The second section will review the psychophysiological responses of "dried-out" alcoholics during both rest and activity and attempt to relate these findings to a neuropsychological model of brain damage in chronic alcoholics. The third section will examine the acute effects of alcohol on chronic alcoholics primarily during sleep, and relate these findings to the hypothesis that alcohol partly functions to exert a normalizing effect on what may be an abnormally functioning

Ralph E. Tarter and A. Arthur Sugerman (eds.), Alcoholism

ISBN: 0-201-08146-6
ISBN: 0-201-08145-8 (pbk.)

nervous system. The last section will attempt to integrate these three areas and arrive at some conclusion about the usefulness and meaningfulness of the psychophysiological approach in understanding alcoholism.

ACUTE EFFECTS OF ALCOHOL

METHODOLOGICAL CONSIDERATIONS. Psychophysiological effects produced by consuming alcohol depend on a variety of factors such as dose and concentration of the drink. However, another variable which has been emphasized lately is the *direction* of change in the blood alcohol level. Behaviorally, the increasing blood alcohol level (absorptive phase or ascending limb) is usually associated with stimulant-type behavior such as talkativeness, excitement, laughter, and a general euphoric state, while the decreasing blood alcohol level (elimination phase or descending limb) is usually associated with tiredness, sleepiness, and general depression (Ekman, Frankenhaeuser, Goldberg, Hagdahl, & Myrsten, 1964). A good deal of evidence that will be reported later indicates that many psychophysiological systems respond differentially to ascending and descending blood alcohol levels. Thus, apparently conflicting data related to the effect of alcohol on psychophysiological measures may merely be reflecting ascending-descending limb differences. For this reason, methodological factors discussed below generally will be oriented around how experimental procedures influence the ascending and descending phases of acute alcohol intoxication.

Three main considerations related to the actual alcohol preparation are the type of alcoholic drink, the concentration of the drink, and the dose of alcohol. Alcohol administration should include having the subject fast before drinking, controlling drinking time, and determining if the subject is on the ascending or descending limb.

Beverage. The first question to consider is the type of alcoholic drink the subject will consume. It is now considered that the "purest" experimental drink is probably made of 190 proof ethanol (95% USP ethyl alcohol) instead of beer, wine, or whisky. These common sources of alcohol contain other products due to brewing or distillation called congeners. These congeners (Greenberg, 1970) have been reported to be related to some of the effects of alcohol, including hangover (Takala, Pihkanen, & Markkanen, 1957; Takala, Siro, & Toivainen, 1958). Control of impurities may be especially important in psychophysiological research since these other ingredients might influence various measures such as heart rate, muscle tension, or EEG (Lolli, Nencini, & Misiti, 1964). However, a recent study indicates little difference in effects of beer, rye whiskey, or wine on psychophysiological measures (Kalant, LeBlanc, Wilson, & Homatidis, 1975).

Concentration. The next factor to consider is the concentration of the drink. Lolli and Rubin (1943 a,b) reported a curvilinear relation between concentration of alcohol in the ingested beverage and the rate of absorption. A 30% concentration was absorbed more rapidly than the same quantity of alcohol given in 15% or 45% concentrations. The rate of absorption is often associated with degree of intoxication, and a fast absorption rate also may precipitate more dramatic psychophysiological changes than a slow absorption rate. Hence, concentration of the alcohol beverage is very important.

Dose. Alcohol dose is extremely important since alcohol effects are often dose-related: that is, the larger the dose, the greater the effect. This is primarily because different doses produce different blood alcohol levels. Dose is usually calculated on total body weight. A small dose may produce no effects or even a slight improvement in cognitive performance, while a large dose may produce a very large performance impairment (Carpenter, Moore, Snyder, & Lisansky, 1961). Again, the exact effect of a given dose is related to the concentration of the drink, drinking time, and absorption rate. In addition, the tolerance of the subject to alcohol and other drugs may affect psychophysiological responses. A large dose to a moderate social drinker may be effectively a small dose to an alcoholic and thus produce different effects in the two groups.

Fasting. Effects of alcohol also can be modified by eating. Food in the stomach produces a slower absorption rate, thereby reducing the magnitude of alcohol effect. Most experimental studies require the subjects to fast for at least four hours prior to consuming alcohol. This procedure results in a rather rapid absorption rate and reduces variability among subjects. However there is evidence that, if the testing session lasts several hours, alcohol may induce functional hypoglycemia (lowered blood sugar) especially in chronic alcoholics (Kallas & Sellers, 1975). The hypoglycemia seems to be the result of a combination of fasting plus alcohol intake. Functional hypoglycemia can be partly overcome by feeding the subject on the descending limb since food in the stomach should not influence elimination rate once all the alcohol has been absorbed. The other alternative is to feed all subjects the same amount of food based on body weight before drinking alcohol. Since some subjects may digest certain foods at different rates than others, then this procedure might introduce a good deal of variance.

Drinking time. The amount of time the subject takes to consume the beverage is vitally important. If the subject gulps the drink--as opposed to sipping it over a long period of time--then he will absorb it at a higher rate (Mellanby, 1919). We have found that fast drinking results in greater performance decrement and slower elimination rate (Jones & Vega, 1973).

Ascending-descending limb. Goldberg (1943), as well as experimenters in more recent reports, have noted that the direction of change of the blood alcohol level is very important. If subjects are tested 15-20 minutes after drinking (while the blood alcohol level is increasing), then they laugh, act excited, and feel happy much as though they had had a stimulant. However, performance is also more impaired during the ascending limb even though most subjects report they are performing very well. Once the peak has been reached and blood alcohol level begins descending, subjects become quiet, behaviorally depressed, sleepy, and often report a lack of interest in the tasks and ability to perform as well. However, objective data indicate performance is better on the descending limb and is often almost as good as before alcohol (Jones, 1973; Jones & Vega, 1972). Several studies have shown that such performance differences are not due to practice effects. The direction of blood alcohol change may be the critical factor, since giving a second alcohol dose when the subject is on the descending limb appears to reinstate ascending limb effects (Mirsky, Piker, Rosenbaum, & Lederer, 1941). Another interpretation of such data is that there is an acute behavioral tolerance to alcohol during one particular testing session (Kalant, LeBlanc, & Gibbins, 1971).

ALCOHOL EFFECTS ON HEART RATE AND SKIN CONDUCTANCE.

Heart rate. There are probably more studies evaluating the effect of alcohol on heart rate than any other psychophysiological measure. Methodological considerations of several representative studies will be reviewed in this section.

Several studies have reported that over a period of time, the heart rate of placebo groups decreases while heart rate of the alcohol groups remains rather constant. Some reports indicate that alcohol affects heart rate of alcoholics more than social drinkers; however, doses given to alcoholics are usually larger than doses given to nonalcoholics.

Docter and Perkins (1961) administered .5 ml of absolute alcohol per kg of body weight mixed in a 20% solution in orange juice. Drinking time was apparently not controlled. Blood alcohol levels after 30-45 minutes for 10 subjects ranged from .011% to .067%. Heart rate responses were recorded for two stressors: cold-pressor and venipuncture and withdrawal of a blood sample from the right arm. The results indicated that resting heart rate between the alcohol and control groups was not significantly different after drinking. Although both groups displayed an increase in heart rate from time of drinking to the end of the session, the alcohol group demonstrated a greater heart rate change than the control group when compared to the pre-drinking baseline. Since the first post-drinking heart rate measure was taken 23 minutes after consumption of the drink, this measure may indicate heart rate at about the peak blood alcohol level. Heart rate measurements taken later, at 39 and 54 minutes, may represent heart rate on the descending limb of the blood alcohol curve.

Docter and Bernal (1964) studied two male alcoholics for 14 successive days. The subjects reported heavy drinking for about 19 years. Subjects were administered 1.8 ml of absolute alcohol per kg of body weight of 80 proof vodka mixed in a 1:1 solution with Kool-Aid. Breathalyzer samples indicated that morning blood alcohol levels ranged from .01% to .04% before drinking. The mean blood alcohol estimates taken approximately 40 minutes after the daytime vodka drink were .15% and .19% for the two subjects. The results indicated that both subjects had markedly elevated heart rates during the alcohol drink days as compared to the initial control days. These heart rate changes did not appear to covary with estimates of blood alcohol absorption curve. A prolonged effect was observed in that increased heart rate was still apparent up to seven days after the last drinking day.

Docter, Naitoh, and Smith (1966) administered 1.5 ml alcohol per kg of body weight in the form of 80 proof vodka mixed 1:1 with fruit juice to 25 alcoholics. Results indicated a linear relationship between resting heart rate and blood alcohol level which may be attributable to progressive vasodilation. The increase was from 80 beats per minute (bpm) before alcohol to 90 bpm at end of drinking. However, these data were taken at 13-minute intervals as the subject was drinking. At the conclusion of the fifth drink, the mean blood alcohol level was .104%. Therefore, these heart rate data are based entirely on the relationship to blood alcohol level on the ascending limb.

Skin conductance. The majority of studies examining the effects of alcohol on skin conductance level (SCL) and skin conductance response (SCR) have examined the effect of alcohol on "emotional behavior." The findings indicate that, in general, both SCL and SCR increase during absorption of alcohol and then decrease after peak on the descending limb. These results are consistent with behavior during those phases when increased activity is usually observed during the rise of the blood alcohol level and a decrease in activity, often drowsiness and sleepiness, is observed on the descending limb.

Carpenter (1957) administered either 50 ml or 350 ml of wine and ethyl alcohol solution to 8 male moderate social drinkers aged 22-30 years. A control condition consisted of 132 ml of water. Drinking time for the 50 ml was 3 minutes and for the 350 ml was 21 minutes. Although no information was given regarding blood alcohol levels during the actual study, a preliminary blood analysis indicated that the 350 ml of wine would produce a peak blood alcohol level of .054% at about 45 minutes. Subjects were engaged in a card filing task throughout the experiment. An increase in SCL was observed shortly after drinking, followed later by a decrease in SCL. A smaller SCR was found with the larger than smaller dose to a startle stimulus about 60 minutes after drinking.

Coopersmith (1964) administered either .86 ml of 86 proof whisky per kg of body weight or soda water to 24 male moderate social drinkers aged 21-38 years. Subjects were given 25 minutes to drink the beverage. Testing began 30 minutes after beginning of drinking (5 minutes after end of drinking) and continued for 25 minutes. Therefore, testing ended about 55 minutes from beginning of drink. Physiological measures were recorded during the ascending limb to peak. The level of SCR was found to be greater for the alcohol than for the control subjects. However, baseline measures were not recorded so it may have been that subjects in the alcohol group initially had higher SCR scores.

McGonnell and Beach (1968) gave a placebo or a dose of .34 ml of 95% ethanol per pound of body weight to 32 males aged 21-48 years. The placebo consisting of 3 ml ethanol was given to half the subjects. Subjects fasted 3 hours before drinking and consumed the drink in 10-15 minutes. Although alcohol did not suppress responses to a noxious shock stimulus, a significant effect of alcohol on the ascending limb indicated that alcohol reduced the magnitude of the conditioned SCR during training. The authors interpreted these data to mean that alcohol inhibits the acquisition and maintenance of a conditioned galvanic skin response (GSR).

From our review of the acute effects of alcohol on psychophysiological systems, it would appear that reports regarding the direct effects of alcohol are conflicting. This state of affairs may be related to the failure of many investigators to consider a host of methodological variables that influence the results, in particular, the ascending-descending limbs of the blood alcohol curve. When such variables are considered, the data are more consistent.

EVALUATION OF THREE HYPOTHESES. *Tension reduction hypothesis.* Clearly, alcohol must produce some type of pleasant effect or individuals would not drink. The positively reinforcing quality of alcohol is probably associated with the ascending limb, while the more negative subjective aspects of drinking are related to the descending limb. Recent attempts to discredit the tension-reduction hypothesis may be premature, especially since the majority of studies quoted by Cappell and Herman (1972) to test this notion involved animals, and animals normally do not prefer alcohol in the first place. There have been only a very few human studies designed to test the tension-reduction hypothesis, and these studies failed to consider important variables such as the ascending-descending limb phenomenon. In addition, future studies will need to define "tension" in such a way that it can be measured either by self-report (anxiety?) or by psychophysiological responses. If individuals do not demonstrate tension before alcohol, how can tension-reduction be demonstrated? Once experimental manipulations are devised so that given tension levels can be produced, then the tension-reducing effects of alcohol ay be evaluated. As Cappell and Herman (1972) point out, even if alcohol were shown to be a tension-reducer, this does not necessarily imply that the reason individuals drink alcohol is to reduce tension all the time, everytime they drink. Alcohol, being a drug with diverse effects, is probably consumed for a variety of reasons; tension-reduction may be only one of many reasons for drinking which will vary even within a given individual. The principal question may be: why do individuals become alcoholics and how are they different from nonalcoholics? One important factor may be individual differences in psychophysiological reactions to alcohol, perhaps related to some genetic characteristic. This notion prompted research on what has become known as the ethnic sensitivity hypothesis.

Ethnic sensitivity hypothesis. It has been suggested that certain racial groups may have lower incidence of alcoholism since they may be more sensitive to physiological effects and therefore will drink less alcohol. Oriental subjects have been reported to have a greater flushing response to alcohol than Caucasians in both adults and infants, and this difference was suggested to be related to variations in autonomic nervous system responsivity (Wolff, 1972). Similar responses also have been reported in North American Indians and Americans of Mongolian extraction who were born and reared in the United States and raised entirely on Western diets (Wolff, 1973). Eskimos and Indians in Canada also have been reported to metabolize ethanol significantly slower than Caucasians (Fenna, Mix, Schaefer, & Gilbert, 1971). Recent evidence has corroborated these earlier studies by demonstrating that Oriental subjects demonstrated significantly more skin flushing, higher heart rate, a greater drop in blood pressure, and more general discomfort with alcohol than Occidental subjects (Ewing, Rouse, & Pellizzari, 1974). These investigators also reported that while there was no significant difference in alcohol absorption or metabolism, there was a trend for acetaldehyde levels to be higher in Orientals than Occidentals; however, this difference was not statistically significant due to high variance.

These data have been interpreted to support the notion that Orientals may have low alcoholism rates due to their greater psychophysiological reactivity to alcohol. On the other hand, the American Indian also has a greater reactivity to alcohol, but has a high alcoholism rate. This difference indicates that both cultural and physiological factors should be considered when evaluating the magnitude of alcohol abuse within a group (Zeiner, Paredes, & Cowden, 1976).

State-dependent effects. As typically applied, this interesting concept indicates that events learned and experienced during one state (e.g., intoxication) can be better remembered during a subsequent identical state than during a different state (e.g., sober) (Goodwin, Powell, Bremer, Hoine, & Stern, 1969; Overton, 1971). Recent evidence indicates that psychophysiological responses such as heart rate may demonstrate state-dependent effects by being highly correlated between different states (Crow & Ball, 1975; Powell, Goodwin, Janes, & Hoine, 1971). State dependent effects have been reported for heart rate, finger pulse volume, and skin response (Crow & Ball, 1975).

The tension-reduction hypothesis, the ethnic sensitivity hypothesis, and the state-dependent hypothesis are three examples of how psychophysiological responses are currently being employed to understand the acute effects of alcohol and how investigators are attempting to relate these findings to the chronic abuse of alcohol. For predictive purposes, none of the hypotheses have reached a stage of satisfactory confirmation or, indeed, disconfirmation.

PSYCHOPHYSIOLOGICAL CHANGES IN "DRIED-OUT" ALCOHOLICS

The first section described the acute effects of alcohol on various psychophysiological measures in social drinkers. This section is directed at answering the next logical question: Does ingestion of large amounts of alcohol over long periods of time lead to permanent changes in psychophysiological functioning and responsivity? This question is of importance for several reasons. First, assuming that adaptive behavior is a product of the total organism, changes in psychophysiological responsivity could be associated with lowered effectiveness in performance on a variety of life tasks, thus posing problems for the alcoholic's rehabilitation. Second, psychophysiological changes could point to possible central nervous system (CNS) damage which again would have implications for remission and rehabilitation of alcoholics. Third, such change might point to specific organs or systems other than the nervous system whose functioning is impaired by alcoholism, e.g., the heart and/or vasculature. Finally changes in psychophysiological responses could play a role in the alcoholic's recidivism, i.e., drinking might be resumed to "normalize" the pattern of responding. (This last point will be examined in the next section.)

Before considering the empirical evidence, it is necessary to point out that if psychophysiological changes are found in dried-out alcoholics, the question of whether these changes existed premorbidly or whether they are the consequences of the alcoholism, cannot be answered satisfactorily without doing prospective studies. However, whether such prospective studies should be attempted is a question to which the empirical findings will be of decided pertinence. If no psychophysiological alterations exist, then there would be scant justification for prospective studies involving psychophysiological measurements.

BRAIN-DAMAGED HYPOTHESIS. One approach to the empirical evidence is to examine it relevant to a given model or hypothesis. We have chosen the "brain damage" hypothesis as the most promising avenue for examining the data. In brief, this hypothesis asserts that chronic abuse of alcohol with its associated malnutrition, liver dysfunction and the like, leads to damage to the brain, especially to frontal-limbic areas and connections.

Frontal-limbic circuits. There is abundant evidence for neuropathological brain changes subsequent to prolonged alcohol abuse (Freund, 1973; Seixas & Eggelston, 1973; Wallgren & Barry, 1970). Pneumoencephalographic and echo-encephalographic studies of alcoholics have identified both cortical and subcortical atrophy, especially in the frontal and paraventricular areas (Brewer & Perrett, 1971; Ferrer, 1970; Feuerlein & Heyse, 1970; Haug, 1968). These neuropathological changes appear in areas traversed by frontal-limbic circuits. It is known (Naitoh, 1972) that stimulation of certain frontal-limbic areas result in modifications of autonomic functioning. Naitoh (1972), in an excellent review of the effect of alcohol on autonomic nervous system functioning, has cited numerous conclusions which stress the cortical-hypothalamic connections in the regulation of visceral, emotional, and motor behavior. Nauta (1972) has detailed the close connections between the frontal and hypothalamic centers and emphasized the integrating function of the frontal lobe. All of the above evidence, indicating both cortical and subcortical changes in alcoholics, strongly suggests the possibility of psychophysiological changes in alcoholics. Further, this evidence suggests that psychophysiological changes would more likely be found in alcoholics in the integration of somato-visceral activities than in the individual measures of autonomic functioning.

Diencephalic syndrome. There is another type of evidence

which strongly suggests the importance of this line of investigation. Segal, Kushnarev, Urakov, and Misionzhnik (1970) have compared in Russian patients the alcohol withdrawal syndrome with the diencephalic syndrome (post-infectional) as follows: "Both groups are characterized by sleep disorders, vasovegetative paroxysms, disorders of cardiovascular and temperature regulation, changes in the water carbohydrate and ionic balance, damage to the endocrine functions trophic and allergic symptoms, similar EEG changes, vital asthenia, anxiety, and characteristic emotional disturbance..." (p. 597). Segal et al. (1970) consider the prodromal stage of alcoholic encephalopathy to be a reversible diencephalopathy, the symptoms for which were described above. In some patients, however, (the "third" stage alcoholics) prolonged abstinence does not lead to complete restitution of symptoms, but to a mild organic brain syndrome with some similarities to post-infectional encephalopathies.

Withdrawal syndrome and related brain disturbances. Gross and his colleagues have conducted detailed studies of the withdrawal syndrome in alcoholics. Using factor analytic techniques (Rosenblatt, Gross, Malenowski, Broman, & Lewis, 1972), they have isolated three clusters of symptoms (accounting for 66% of the variance) which they identify with CNS dysfunction. Factor I includes tinnitus, tactile hallucinations, visual disturbances, pruritis, hallucinations, agitation, and sleep disturbances. Rosenblatt et al. (1972) suggest that this cluster is related to functions located in the sensory receptors and the cortex. Factor II loads on tremor, perspiration, depression, and anxiety. This factor, they suggest, is related to limbic system and midbrain functions.

Factor III is related to disturbances of consciousness, impaired contact, clouding of sensorium, and disturbances of gait. These disturbances, they conclude, are related to functions located in the brain stem.

There seems to be little doubt that once the alcoholic reaches the stage where withdrawal symptoms are prominent, the central nervous system and the autonomic nervous system are grossly dysfunctional during the withdrawal period. Milder forms of the withdrawal syndrome are present, it should be noted, with less protracted or intense alcoholism (Segal et al., 1970). The question again becomes: after the acute withdrawal syndrome subsides, is there evidence for psychophysiological change of a relatively persistent or permanent nature?

METHODOLOGICAL CONSIDERATIONS. As usual in studies of psychopathological populations, there are a number of methodological issues which must be considered. The typical design for the study of dried-out alcoholics is the comparison of such patients with other groups of patients and/or nonalcoholic control subjects. The first problem is the definition of "alcoholic." Most studies of alcoholics are conducted on patients who have declared themselves to be alcoholic and who indicate that alcohol constitutes a problem for them. The difficulties this creates for the experimenter seeking to establish valid generalizations are commonly recognized in the literature on alcoholism. Fortunately for the experimenter, most patients who present themselves as alcoholics in fact can be distinguished from self-proclaimed nonalcoholics on variables such as frequency of drinking, volume of alcohol ingestion, duration of excessive alcohol intake, and physical signs and symptoms of prolonged intake. Of these variables, duration of excessive drinking is perhaps one of the more critical, but is often ignored. Segal's et al. (1970) report of the withdrawal syndrome appearing after 8 to 9 years of heavy drinking clearly suggests a critical dividing point with respect to duration. Behavioral studies in our laboratories (Jones & Parsons, 1971; Parsons, 1975; Tarter & Parsons, 1971) suggest the same dividing point for differentiating alcoholics who show deficits on abstracting tasks from alcoholics who do not.

A second critical variable in the study of chronic alcoholics is that of possible brain injury from causes other than the direct effects of alcohol. The presence of poor nutrition, liver disease, cardiovascular disorders, and head injury may lead to changes in the central components of the autonomic nervous system which are secondary to alcoholism. Certainly, these variables should be clearly identified or controlled if inferences about the primary or direct effects of alcohol on the nervous system are to be unambiguous.

The third major variable is that of time of examination of the alcoholic with respect to duration of sobriety. While the acute symptoms of withdrawal are usually over within a week or so following cessation of drinking (Cutshall, 1965), the time course for recovery of many behaviors has been shown to last several months (Long & McLachlan, 1974; Page & Linden, 1974) with some functions improving more slowly than others. Indeed, in the case of EEG slow-wave (stage 4) sleep, recovery to age-expected percent may require more than a year (Wagman & Allen, 1975). The implication of these findings is clear: the duration of sobriety before experimental procedures are administered should be determined and reported in every experiment.

Finally, the experimental study of alcoholism is almost solely devoted to men, so much so that in a study of 2,688 alcoholics "sex" of the patient is not even mentioned (Schnall & Wiener, 1958)! In view of the many sex differences in psychophysiological measures (Liberson & Liberson, 1975) and the increasing number of women alcoholics (Beckman, 1975), designation of the sex of the subjects if obviously necessary.

EMPIRICAL FINDINGS: MULTIPLE MEASURES STUDIES. Naitoh (1972) has presented in detail one of the earliest studies of psychophysiological functioning in alcoholics. Wenger (1948) examined 7 alcoholics on his autonomic balance score, $\bar{A}$. This score was designed to reflect the relative dominance of the sympathetic nervous system (SNS) or parasympathetic nervous system (PNS) under resting conditions. The $\bar{A}$ score was calculated from salivary output, sublingual temperature, palmar conductance, volar conductance, log conductance change, diastolic blood pressure, and heart rate. The score for these alcoholics was very close to that of several hundred young normal males. Other analyses indicated that the alcoholics had four scores out of 14 measures which were one standard deviation or more below the mean in the SNS dominance direction: salivary output (low), finger temperature (low), respiration period (short), and pupillary diameter (large). None of the variables were more than one-half a standard deviation above the mean (in the direction of PNS dominance), although five reached that level. Unfortunately, details such as duration of alcoholism, period of sobriety, possible brain injury, etc., were not given.

A similar approach was taken by Kissin, Schenker and Schenker (1959) when they studied three groups of male subjects (*S*s): alcoholics recently sobered, alcoholics sober for 2 years, and control *S*s matched on age. In response to the question of SNS and PNS dominance in alcoholics, psychophysiological and other measures were made under resting conditions. The authors concluded that alcoholics, even those of 2 years abstinence, had impaired SNS activity and increased PNS activity. Variables on which both groups of alcoholics differed significantly from the control *S*s were: the diastolic cold-pressor response (significantly lower in alcoholics); the intravenous glucose tolerance curve (significantly greater percentage drops in alcoholics); and the sodium concentration in saliva (significantly higher in alcoholics than in the controls). Tests of adrenal cortex function in the same groups of *S*s suggested that the alcoholics had diminished urinary excretion of 17-hydroxycorticoids and 17-ketosteroids and increased mineral-acorticoid function. Considering the provocative findings in this experiment, it seems remarkable that there has been no systematic follow-up of what the investigators termed preliminary findings.

Chotlos and Goldstein (1967) compared alcoholics, schizophrenics, hypertensives, and controls (groups of 11 *S*s each) on skin resistance, heart rate, and finger temperature responses to meaningful sound stimuli and silences. The alcoholics were not described as to duration of sobriety, duration of heavy drinking, neurological or other medical diseases status. Neither maximum or minimum heart rates differentiated the groups, although the heart rate for the three psychopathological groups was decidedly higher than the controls. No differences were found for finger temperature, but skin resistance levels were significantly different for groups. Alcoholics had the highest levels of skin resistance (lowest conductance), while schizophrenics had the lowest skin resistance (highest conductance). Paradoxically, then, the alcoholics had the lowest skin conductance (low SNS activity), but the highest heart rate (high SNS activity or low PNS functioning). Assuming that skin conductance levels represent basal arousal and that heart rate represents transient reactions to stress, the authors conclude that alcoholics are not in a state of chronic activation but "dislike" examining or testing situations.

At our Center, Lester, Rundell, Cowden, and Williams (1975) studied the sleep physiological profiles of 20 sober middle-class male alcoholics in good clinical health who were matched on age ($\overline{X}$ = 39 years) to 20 normal controls. The alcoholics had been hospitalized and drug free for a minimum of three weeks. They had a median duration of heavy drinking of 10.5 years. Compared to controls, the sober alcoholic patients had less slow-wave sleep (stages 3 and 4), more stage 1 and stage REM (rapid eye movement) sleep. Sleep quality in the alcoholics was poor as evidenced by frequency of brief arousal, changes of stages and REM disruptions. Significantly higher rates of respiration and non-specific electrodermal responses were found in the alcoholics in both sleeping and waking periods during bed time. The pattern of results led the authors to suggest that chronic abuse of alcohol leads, among other results, to increased autonomic activation and arousal during the sleeping period.

Also at our Center, Chandler, Parsons, and Vega (1975)

studied skin conductance level, skin conductance response, and heart rate in 27 detoxified (at least 2 weeks) male middle-aged alcoholics and 27 closely-matched, paid, non-alcoholic volunteers from community social agencies. Criteria for entering the study included the absence of any neurological, liver, or heart disease. None of the *S*s were receiving medication. All *S*s were given a questionnaire which surveyed possible brain injury in detail. Items covered partial drownings, concussions, periods of unconsciousness, high temperatures (fevers), exposure to low oxygen levels in high altitude flying, etc. Eleven of the alcoholics reported exposure to possible brain insults and were placed in a "Possible Brain Injured" (PBI) group; the remaining 16 were placed in the "Non-Brain Injured History" (NBIH) group. Psychophysiological variables were measured at baseline, during the difficult trials of a dichotic listening task and at rest after the task.

Tonic (basal levels) and phasic (responses to stimuli) measures of skin conductance, skin conductance response, and heart rate were calculated. Tonic and phasic heart rate did not differ among the groups (overall mean = 76 bpm). However, the groups did differ on variability of heart rate as measured by the coefficient of variation (V) calculated on the peak-trough differences (based on within *S* variability) during the dichotic listening task. The NBIH group had almost twice the variability (52.46 ± 27.46) as the PBI (24.07 ± 8.11) or or the Controls (27.10 ± 17.15). Comparison of both tonic and phasic skin conductance levels indicated no significant differences among the groups. However, when skin conductance was corrected for baseline (phasic minus tonic), NBIH had significantly greater skin conductance levels during the dichotic task; PBI and control groups did not differ (Table 1). Finally, Spearman rank-order correlations between perfomance (commission errors) on the dichotic task and the coefficient of variation measures during the task were calculated. The results are presented in Table 2. A significant negative

Table 1

Skin Conductance (micromhos) Tonic, Phasic, and Phasic Minus Tonic Levels for Groups

Group	Phasic	Tonic	Phasic Minus Tonic
PBI	1.737	1.214	.521
NBIH	3.367	2.034	1.333[a]
Controls	2.094	1.854	.240

[a]NBIH differs significantly from both PBI ($U = 47$, $p < .05$) and Controls ($U = 88$, $p < .004$)

Table 2

Rho Correlations of Commission Errors vs. Coefficients of Variation in Dichotic Task

		Heart Rate Peak- (V)	Skin Conductance Response (V)
Controls	(N = 25)	.07	.38
All Alcoholics	(N = 25)	-.55*	-.30
PBI	(N = 10)	-.62*	-.50
NBIH	(N = 15)	-.41	-.08

*$p < .05$

correlation was obtained in the alcoholic group on the heart rate *V* measure ($p = -.55$, $p < .05$), whereas the correlation in the normal group was negligible. On the skin conductance *V* measure, the correlations in the alcoholics were again negative while the correlation in the controls was positive ($p = + .38$) and approached significance.

Overall, the findings indicate no differences in tonic levels of heart rate and skin conductance between controls and alcoholics. However, when subjected to a demanding task, group differences in autonomic responsivity and in the relationship between the responsivity and performance emerged. Further, grouping alcoholics into those with and without possible brain injury gave rise to differences which suggest that this variable be considered in experiments with alcoholics.

EMPIRICAL EVIDENCE: SINGLE SYSTEM STUDIES. One of the largest studies of a psychophysiological response system in alcoholics is that of Schnall and Weiner (1958). Blood pressure was recorded in 2,688 alcoholics at admission and discharge (interval not stated). Comparisons of alcoholics by age groups with norms indicated that the alcoholics over 40 were less hypertensive than the general population of that age, even at time of admission. Hypotension was also much less frequent in the alcoholics. The alcoholics in this study were not described as to health status, duration of heavy drinking, and duration of sobriety before testing. At the least, however, it would appear that if any trend is interpretable, it would be in the direction of alcoholics having a more normotensive blood pressure than the general population!

Another approach was taken by Rosenberg & Buttsworth

(1969) who examined forearm blood flow on 35 middle-aged alcoholics 5 days after cessation of drinking. The alcoholics were considered to have recovered from alcohol withdrawal and were off medication. No screening for other diseases was mentioned and duration of heavy drinking not stated. Control *S*s were hospital personnel including physicians! Resting levels of forearm blood flow (measured by a water filled venous plethysmograph) were not different in the two groups, but under the stress of mental arithmetic, the alcoholics had significantly less rise in blood flow than the control group. The authors point out that the alcoholics rise was similar to other diagnostic groups they had studied. This suggests that their control group was really the "deviant" group, i.e., hospital personnel responding to the challenge by colleagues.

Smith and Layden (1972) examined 60 male, middle-aged patients on a variety of behavioral and biological tests after the acute withdrawal symptoms had subsided but before treatment was instituted. They reexamined the patients one week later and about two-thirds of the sample 6 weeks later. The mean heart rates for the three times were as follows: pretreatment, 84.5 bpm; after one week, 78.4 bpm and finally, 6 weeks later, 73.1 bpm. Thus, there was a significant lowering of heart rate over the three measurements. This finding again emphasizes the importance of specification of duration of sobriety. If alcoholics were sampled at the "before treatment" and "after one week" times, they probably would have significantly higher heart rates than controls. The value of 73 beats per minute (obtained after 6 weeks) is quite within the normal range.

Finally, Lovallo, Parsons, and Holloway (1973) gave

the cold-pressor test to middle-aged male alcoholics, brain-damaged, and control patients. Alcoholics were screened for other medical diseases and neurological signs and had been sober at least three weeks before testing. In general, the plethysmograph rebound responses to the cold-pressor test were markedly different in the brain-damaged compared to the control patients. The alcoholics fell intermediate to the other groups. One additional interesting finding was the effect of introducing a reaction time task during the cold-pressor: the alcoholic and brain-damaged group responded similarly in comparison to the controls.

In summary, studies of psychophysiological responses in alcoholics have been inconclusive and, therefore, our working hypothesis concerning brain-damage could not be confirmed. There is no response system which has been shown to be consistently aberrant in dried-out alcoholics. To take a specific example, compared to controls, Wenger (1948) found no difference on palmar skin conductance levels in his alcoholics, nor did Coopersmith and Woodrow (1967). Chotlos and Goldstein (1967) found skin conductance to be significantly lower in their alcoholics; Lester et al., (1975) found significantly higher "non-specific" skin conductance responses for sleeping alcoholics; Chandler et al. (1975) found significantly higher phasic levels (skin conductance response) to a demanding task, but no differences in skin conductance tonic levels.

This lack of consistency in findings is undoubtedly due in part to the methodological problems noted earlier. It is vitally important that the *S*s be clearly and comprehensively described. What is the age, socioeconomic level, sex, and race of the *S*s? How long have they been drinking heavily? What is the duration of sobriety before testing? Are the *S*s cleared for other medical and neurological diseases (including nutritional status) which could affect the nervous system? Have they been exposed to trauma, fevers, partial drownings, etc., all of which could lead to possible brain injury? Finally, is more than one response system measured? Any one response measure could be grossly misleading. All these variables plus those of differing methods, equipment, and procedures suggest that the definitive studies in answer to the question posed at the beginning of this chapter remain to be conducted.

If these methodological points are observed, there are some questions which deserve further exploration. First, while differences in resting levels of psychophysiological variables appear to be minimal, examining these variables in response to the introduction of stimuli or tasks seems more profitable. Second, if the task introduced has a measurable quality of performance, it is possible to compare performance--psychophysiological response relationships in alcoholics and nonalcoholics. At least two studies have found some suggestive differences. Third, it would appear to the authors that the field needs a comprehensive multiple systems study similar to that performed almost 20 years ago by Kissin et al. (1959). Such a study, with methodological improvements suggested above, could provide us with the data to ascertain the promise of psychophysiological investigations in alcoholics.

PSYCHOPHYSIOLOGICAL EFFECTS OF ALCOHOL IN CHRONIC ALCOHOLICS

Alcohol ingestion results in increases of most psychophysiological measures on the ascending limb and then decreases on the descending limb in social drinkers. In dried-out alcoholics, no consistent differences in psychophysiological responses have been reported. The present section will examine studies reporting the acute effect of alcohol on alcoholics.

A number of investigators have suggested that a profitable line of research would be one targeted on the questions of what alcohol does for the alcoholic (see, Naitoh, 1972). Perhaps, for example, the alcoholic drinks to relieve anxiety. From a psychophysiological perspective, one might first determine the physiological correlates of anxiety and then make the appropriate measurements on sober alcoholics. If the alcoholics showed psychophysiological indicants of anxiety, either at rest or under stress, then the next step would be to give alcohol and repeat the measurements. Assuming that the physiological measures showed signs of decreased anxiety with alcohol, one might then be allowed to speculate that one factor in alcoholic drinking is an attempt on the part of the alcoholic to treat his anxiety. Of course, prospective studies would be necessary to demonstrate that the anxiety preceded the alcoholism, and any causal relationship between anxiety and alcoholism would remain to be demonstrated.

A similar approach, mentioned previously, would be to look for normalizing effects of alcohol on the alcoholics' physiology. Unfortunately, as we have seen, there is little consistent evidence for an alcoholic abnormality in any of the traditional psychophysiological measures. It is difficult, therefore, to imagine how alcohol can exert a normalizing effect when the system is seemingly normal before drinking. However, this effect may be present, not during waking, but during sleep as will be illustrated.

NORMALIZING EFFECTS. One of the most encouraging studies investigating the psychophysiological effects of drinking in alcoholics was published in 1959 by Kissin et al. Their findings, as mentioned previously, led to the conclusion that chronic alcoholics suffer from impaired SNS activity, overactive PNS and muscular systems, along with deviant endocrine activity. When given 1 ml alcohol per kg body weight, their alcoholics showed changes in their pattern of physiologic activity in the direction of normalization. The alcoholics showed less extreme variance in their responses to the Funkenstein mecholyl test, while their PNS activity and muscle tension declined (see also Mizoi, Kimura, Ohga, & Ishido, 1963), and their endocrine functions generally approached control levels. Comparison of the alcoholics' physiologic response patterns to alcohol, chlorpromazine (25 mg), and barbiturates led the authors to suggest that alcohol behaves more like a major tranquilizer than like an hypnotic sedative. Thus, the Kissin et al. (1959) study was encouraging in that a deviant pattern of response was identified in the alcoholic group and the response pattern was normalized by alcohol. Unfortunately, a major variable, direction of change of blood alcohol level, was not controlled in the study. For nonalcoholics (as pointed out in the first section), direction of change of blood alcohol level is of substantial importance in terms of mood and cognitive functioning (Jones & Vega, 1972). This has been demonstrated for some psychophysiological effects in nonalcoholics and probably holds true for alcoholics as well. Thus, for alcoholics as for nonalcoholics, the physiological effects of drinking may be quite different on the ascending and descending limbs of the blood alcohol curve.

A series of investigations by Docter and his associates (Bernal & Docter, 1962; Docter & Bernal, 1964; Docter & Perkins 1961; Docter et al., 1966), have studied a number of psychophysiological variables in sober and intoxicated alcoholics. Briefly, they found increased heart rate, finger pulse volume, rapid eye movements, and EEG alpha frequency activity as a function of alcohol intoxication. Spectral analysis of the EEG indicated that alcohol increased the amplitude of low frequency alpha (8 and 9 H_z), decreased 10 and 11 H_z activity, and had no effect on other EEG frequencies. Forearm flexor EMG and vigilance task performance were maintained in the intoxicated condition relative to controls. Perhaps the alcoholic is seeking some state defined by contrasting excitement and relaxation: high amplitude slow alpha EEG, warm hands, accelerated heart rate, and increased visual scanning (Naitoh, 1972). Such an hypothesis is of a different nature than that proposed by the Kissin (1959) group. Kissin and colleagues proposed that the alcoholic was psychophysiologically deviant and drank to normalize his physiology. Naitoh and associates, on the other hand, are not arguing for normalization. In the main, the hypothesis proposed by Naitoh (1972) is that the alcoholic is seeking a psychophysiological state that is abnormal[1]. There is, for example, no evidence to suggest that alcoholics have low heart rates or chronic peripheral vasoconstriction and that drinking normalizes their cardiovascular system. On the other hand, the data regarding

[1]This state may reflect the "altered state of unconsciousness" that has been described in chronic alcoholics (Parsons, 1975).

EEG alpha activity does seem to support a deficit in chronic alcoholics (Funkhauser, Nagler, & Walke, 1953; Little & McAvoy, 1952; Varga & Nagy, 1960) and increased alpha with intoxication (Docter et al., 1966; Naitoh, 1972; Varga & Nagy, 1960; but see Wikler, Prescor, Fraser, & Isbell, 1956).

Whatever the case, the studies by Kissin, Docter, and their colleagues clearly point out the complex nature of the effects of alcohol on chronic alcoholics. There is little doubt that alcohol can be shown to have widely differing effects on the CNS, PNS, and SNS. Moreover, the effects of alcohol may be opposite or at least contrary on subsystems within, for example, the CNS. Alcohol effects may also be found to vary according to the stress imposed by non-drug factcrs. Thus, it has been suggested (although not demonstrated) by Garfield and McBrearty (1970) that drinking alcohol increases the alcoholic's level of arousal, but decreases his responsiveness to stimuli (cf., Coopersmith & Woodrow, 1967).

The most consistent findings with regard to the psychophysiological effects of alcohol on chronic alcoholics have been those dealing with heart rate and the sleep studies. Increases in heart rate in alcoholics following ingestion of alcohol have been reported in waking by Isbell, Fraser, Wikler, Belleville and Eisenman, (1955); Docter & co-workers (1961, 1964, 1966), and Mendelson and LaDou (1964), and in sleep by Gross, Hastey, Lewis, and Young (1975) and Lester et al., (1975). As mentioned above, alcohol-related increases have been well documented in normals. In 1955, Holmberg and Martens reported increased heart rate for both alcoholics and nonalcoholics when given alcohol. In their study, the alcoholics showed smaller increases than the nonalcoholics, perhaps due to tolerance. Alcohol-related increases may persist for alcoholics over a period of at least several days after cessation of heavy drinking (Docter & Bernal, 1964; Lester et al., 1975; Smith & Layden, 1972).

SLEEP DISTURBANCES. Extreme disturbance of sleep is probably the best documented psychophysiological correlate of chronic alcoholism. The first systematic studies of sleep in alcoholic patients undergoing acute withdrawal were apparently conducted by Gross and his colleagues (Gross & Goodenough, 1968; Gross, Goodenough, Tobin, Halpert, Lepore, Perlstein, Sirota, Dibianco, Fuller, & Kishner, 1966; Gross, see Chapter 8, this volume). Their findings, supported by Greenberg and Pearlman (1967) and Johnson, Burdick, and Smith (1970), indicate a fragmentation of sleep manifested by frequent awakenings, frequent changes of EEG stage, and frequent body movements. The sleep studies have also generally shown an almost total absence of stage 4 sleep (Gross et al., 1966; Greenberg & Pearlman, 1967; Johnson et al., 1970; Lester et al., 1975; Lester, Rundell, Cowden, & Williams, 1973). Gross et al. (1975) have recently suggested that the marked reduction in slow-wave sleep may reflect withdrawal and may be related to "another persistent 'silent' addictive mechanism which Kalant (1973) designated 'carry-over'."

For normal subjects, alcohol generally produces sedative effects on sleep, suppressing stage REM, and reducing the density of such phasic events as non-specific electrodermal responses, sigma spindles, and K-complexes (Gresham, Webb, & Williams, 1963; Rundell, Lester, & Griffiths, & Williams, 1972; Yules, Freedman, & Chandler, 1966). However, sedative effects have not invariably been found when alcoholics were given alcohol. For example, increases in sleep onset latency have been reported by Allen, Wagman, Faillace, and McIntosh (1971); Gross, Goodenough, Hastey, Rosenblatt, and Lewis (1972); and Johnson et al. (1970) for intoxicated alcoholics.

A recent study at our Center (Lester et al., 1975) investigated the effects of two nights of drinking on the sleep of 20 middle-class, healthy male alcoholics who had been dry for a minimum of 3 weeks. Baseline (sober) sleep was compared with that of 20 age-matched controls. One week after the baseline nights, the alcoholics came to the laboratory for four consecutive sessions. On the first two sessions, the alcoholics drank alcohol on a controlled drinking schedule from 1300 hours to 2100 hours. Mean bedtime blood alcohol levels were approximately .15%. Physiological sleep measures were recorded on baseline and alcohol nights and the succeeding two (recovery) nights. A final baseline session occurred one week following the second recovery night.

As compared with controls, the alcoholics had less percent stage 3 sleep and elevated percent stages 1 and REM. Percent stage 4 sleep interacted with age such that the younger alcoholics (ages 24-29) had substantially reduced stage 4 as compared to younger controls. Very little stage 4 was evidenced by either alcoholics or controls in the older group (ages 40-56). The alcoholics also showed more arousals and stage changes, longer sleep onset latency, more non-specific electrodermal responses, and higher respiration rates than controls. REM periodicity was substantially accelerated in the alcoholics.

Alcohol generally had sedative effects on our alcoholics' sleep. Thus, on the alcohol nights, percent stages 1 and REM were reduced and percent stages 3 and 4 were increased in the alcoholic group. With regard to stage 4 sleep, the effects of alcohol interacted with age, producing increased stage 4 only for the younger alcoholics. In addition, alcohol reduced percent time awake, number of arousals, sleep onset latency, non-specific electrodermal responses, and REM disruptions. REM latency was increased, but REM periodicity was unchanged.

For the final baseline session, obtained one week after the alcohol session and five to six weeks after hospitalization, there were some indications of normalization of sleep. Stage 3 sleep had increased significantly and stage 1 had decreased. However, the poor quality of sleep as manifested by frequent brief arousals and frequent stage changes was not much improved on the final baseline. Recent cross-sectional data (Wagman & Allen, 1975) indicate a varying time course for recovery of various aspects of sleep with some abnormalities evidenced after as long as two years of sobriety.

SELF-SUSTAINING DISREGULATION. The alcoholic's sleep is markedly disturbed and fragmented. Under some circumstances, drinking appears to normalize the alcoholic's sleep. Thus, the alcoholic may be faced with a paradoxical situation in which the cure is the disease. Certainly prolonged bouts of drinking lead to further sleep disturbances (Gross, Goodenough, Hastey, & Lewis, 1973). The development of this vicious circle, drinking to sleep which in turn disrupts sleep which leads to further drinking, might be termed the "self-sustaining disregulation" hypothesis (see Yules et al., 1966). This concept probably applies to many aspects of the alcoholic's behavior, but the effect of alcohol on the psychophysiological parameters of sleep best illustrates it.

INTEGRATION, INTERPRETATION, AND CONCLUSION

Our conclusion is that there is very little evidence of consistent psychophysiological correlates of alcoholism. This statement does not imply that there are no differences in psychophysiological systems between alcoholics and non-alcoholics. A variety of methodological problems exist in this area of research and may contribute to the inconsistent and often contradictory findings.

The review of the acute effects of alcohol on nonalcoholics in the first section illustrates some of the methodological effects. These same considerations should be, but most often are not, employed when giving alcohol to alcoholics. Superimposed on the factors that influence the acute effects of alcohol are the factors which relate to the chronic alcoholic as presented in the second section. The proper study of the acute effects of alcohol on the psychophysiological systems of alcoholics requires a knowledge of the psychopharmacological action of alcohol in addition to a proper neuropsychclogical evaluation of the background of the alcoholic.

The acute effects of alcohol on nonalcoholics are consistent, but not very dramatic at the blood alcohol levels usually reported, (viz., 0.02% to 0.10%). The stimulant-like effects that have been reported for most systems are usually observed while the blood alcohol level is rising and is gradually replaced by depressant effects while the blood alcohol level is declining. It is not clear whether alcoholics demonstrate ascending-descending limb differences since there apparently are no reports directly examining these differences in alcoholics. Interestingly, the most consistent effects of alcohol on the alcoholic have been found during sleep, a time following drinking while the alcoholic is on the descending limb. It would be interesting to investigate the effects of alcohol on sleep during the ascending limb by giving alcohol continuously (i.v.) during the night.

However, most interest is in how one can define, differentiate, and treat an alcoholic based on his or her psychophysiological response pattern when dried-out. Our review found no consistent reports of differences between a dried-out alcoholic and a control subject during a resting state. During a time of stress, the alcoholic may respond differently, but this difference is not consistent. With our present knowledge, there certainly is no warrant for attempting to differentiate different kinds or types of alcoholics on the basis of their psychophysiology.

In light of this rather pessimistic review, can we conclude anything of potential value for the worker in this field? We know that small doses of alcohol do, indeed, result in some changes in the psychophysiological systems of non-alcoholics. It does not appear that continued stimulation of these systems with alcohol results in marked, long-term, chronic changes in the psychophysiological system as measured in dried-out alcoholics during resting and waking state, but there may be changes in the way psychophysiological responses and performance are related. Chronic alcoholics do appear to have psychophysiological sleep disturbances that might be the result of long term drinking. The effect of alcohol on alcoholics appears to normalize sleep patterns, but also leads to further disruptions. Future studies should give due consideration to the methodological issues mentioned in this chapter if an adequate assessment of psychophysiological correlates of alcoholism is to be made.

REFERENCES

Allen, R., Wagman, A., Faillace, L., & McIntosh, M. Electroencephalographic (EEG) sleep recovery following prolonged alcohol intoxication in alcoholics. *Journal of Nervous and Mental Disease*, 1971, *153*, 424-433.

Beckman, L.J. Women alcoholics: A review of social and psychological studies. *Journal of Studies on Alcohol*, 1975, *36*, 797-824.

Bernal, M.E., & Docter, R.F. Autonomic studies of sustained alcohol intake. *Psychophysiology Newsletter*, 1962, *8*, 32.

Brewer, C., & Perrett, L. Brain damage due to alcohol consumption: An airencephalographic, psychometric, and electroencephalographic study. *British Journal of Addiction*, 1971, *66*, 170-182.

Cappell, H., & Herman, C.P. Alcohol and tension reduction: A review. *Quarterly Journal of Studies on Alcohol*, 1972, *33*, 33-64.

Carpenter, J. The effects of alcoholic beverages on skin conductance. An exploratory study. *Quarterly Journal of Studies on Alcohol*, 1957, *18*, 1-18.

Carpenter, J., Moore, O., Snyder, C., & Lisansky, E. Alcohol and higher-order problem solving. *Quarterly Journal of Studies on Alcohol*, 1961, *22*, 183-222.

Chandler, B., Parsons, O., Vega, A. Autonomic functioning in alcoholics: A study of heart rate and skin conductance. *Quarterly Journal of Studies on Alcohol*, 1975, *36*, 566-577.

Chotlos, J.W., & Goldstein, G. Psychophysiological responses to meaningful sounds. *Journal of Nervous and Mental Disease*, 1967, *145*, 314-325.

Coopersmith, S. The effects of alcohol on reactions to affective stimuli. *Quarterly Journal of Studies on Alcohol*, 1964, *25*, 459-475.

Coopersmith, S., & Woodrow, K. Basal conductance levels of normals and alcoholics. *Quarterly Journal of Studies on Alcohol*, 1967, *28*, 27-32.

Crow, L.T., & Ball, C. Alcohol state-dependency and autonomic reactivity. *Psychophysiology*, 1975, *12*, 702-706.

Cutshall, B.J. The Saunders-Sutton Syndrome: An analysis of delirium tremens. *Quarterly Journal of Studies on Alcohol*, 1965, *26*, 423-448.

Docter, R.F., & Bernal, M.E. Immediate and prolonged psychophysiological effects of sustained alcohol intake in alcoholics. *Quarterly Journal of Studies on Alcohol*, 1964, *25*, 438-450.

Docter, F.R. Naitoh, P., & Smith, J.C. Electroencephalographic changes and vigilance behavior during experimentally induced intoxication with alcoholic subjects. *Psychosomatic Medicine*, 1966, *28*, 605-615.

Docter, R.F., & Perkins. R.B. The effects of ethyl alcohol on autonomic and muscular responses in humans. *Quarterly Journal of Studies on Alcohol*, 1961, *22*, 374-386.

Ekman, G., Frankenhaeuser, M., Goldberg, L., Hagdahl, R., & Myrsten, A. Subjective and objective effects of alcohol as functions of dosage and time. *Psychopharmacologia*, 1964, *6*, 399-409.

Ewing, J.A., Rouse, B.A., & Pellizzari, E.D. Alcohol sensitivity and ethnic background. *American Journal of Psychiatry*, 1974, *131*, 206-210.

Fenna, D., Mix, L., Schaefer, O., & Gilbert, J.A.L. Ethanol metabolism in various racial groups. *Canadian Medical Association Journal*, 1971, *105*, 472-475.

Ferrer, S. *Complications neurologicas cronicas del alcoholismo*. Santiago, Chile: Editorial Universitaria, S.A., 1970.

Feuerlein, W., & Heyse, H. Die Weite der 3. Hirnkammer bei Alkoholikern. *Archiv fuer Psychiatrie u. Nervenkheiten*, 1970, *213*, 78-85.

Freund, G. Chronic central nervous system toxicity of alcohol. *Annual Review of Pharmacology* , 1973, *12*, 217-227.

Funkhauser, J.B., Nagler, B., & Walke, N.D. The electroencephalogram of chronic alcoholism. *Southern Medical Journal*, 1953, *46*, 423-428.

Garfield, Z.H., & McBrearty, J.F. Arousal level and stimulus response in alcoholics after drinking. *Quarterly Journal of Studies on Alcohol*, 1970, *31*, 832-838.

Goldberg, L. Quantitative studies on alcohol tolerance in man: The influence of ethyl alcohol on sensory, motor, and psychological functions referred to blood alcohol in normal and habituated individuals. *Acta Physiologica Scandinavica*, 1943, *Suppl. No. 16*, 1-128.

Goodwin, D.W., Powell, B., Bremer, D., Hoine, H., & Stern, J. Alcohol and recall: State-dependent effects in man. *Science*, 1969, *163*, 1358-1360.

Greenberg, L.A. Studies of congeners in alcoholic beverages. *Quarterly Journal of Studies on Alcohol*, 1970, *Suppl. No. 5*.

Greenberg, R., & Pearlman, C. Delirium tremens and dreaming. *American Journal of Psychiatry*, 1967, *124*, 133-142.

Gresham, S.C., Webb, W.B., & Williams, R.L. Alcohol and caffeine: Effect on inferred visual dreaming. *Science*, 1963, *140*, 1226-1227.

Gross, M.M., & Goodenough, D.R. Sleep disturbances in the acute alcoholic psychoses. *Psychiatric Research Reports of the American Psychiatric Association*, 1968, *24*, 137-147.

Gross, M.M., Goodenough, D.R., Hastey, J., & Lewis, E. Experimental study of sleep in chronic alcoholics before, during, and after four days of heavy drinking, with a non-drinking comparison. *Annals of the New York Academy of Sciences*, 1973, *215*, 254-265.

Gross, M.M., Goodenough, D.R., Hastey, J.M., Rosenblatt, S.M., & Lewis, E. Sleep disturbances in alcoholic intoxication and withdrawal. In N.K. Mello & J.H. Mendelson (Eds.), *Recent advances in studies of alcoholism*. Washington, D.C.: U.S. Government Printing Office, 1972.

Gross, M.M., Goodenough, D.R., Tobin, M., Halpert, E., Lepore, D., Perstein, A., Sirota, M., Dibianco, J., Fuller, R., & Kishner, I. Sleep disturbances and hallucinations in the acute alcoholic psychoses. *Journal of Nervous and Mental Disease*, 1966, *142*, 493-514.

Gross, M.M., Hastey, J.M., Lewis, E., & Young, N. Slow-wave sleep and carry-over of functional tolerance and physical dependence in alcoholics. In M.M. Gross (Ed.), *Alcohol intoxication and withdrawal: Experimental studies II, Advances in experimental medicine and biology (Vol. 59)*. New York: Plenum Press, 1975.

Haug, J.O. Pneumoencephalographic evidence of brain damage in chronic alcoholics. *Acta Psychologica Scandinavica*, 1968, *203*, 135-143.

Holmberg, G., & Martens, S. Electroencephalographic changes in man correlated with blood alcohol concentration and some other conditions following standardized ingestion of alcohol. *Quarterly Journal of Studies on Alcohol*, 1955, *16*, 411-424.

Isbell, H., Fraser, H., Wikler, A., Belleville, R., & Eisenman, A. An experimental study of etiology of "rum fits" and delirium tremens. *Quarterly Journal of Studies on Alcohol*, 1955, *16*, 1-33.

Johnson, L.C., Burdick, J.A., & Smith, J. Sleep during alcohol intake and withdrawal in the chronic alcoholic. *Archives of General Psychiatry*, 1970, *22*, 406-418.

Jones, B.M. Memory impairment on the ascending and descending limbs of the blood alcohol curve. *Journal of Abnormal Psychology*, 1973, *82*, 24-32.

Jones, B., & Parsons, O.A. Impaired abstracting ability in chronic alcoholics. *Archives of General Psychiatry*, 1971, *24*, 71-75.

Jones, B.M., & Vega, A. Cognitive performance measured on the ascending and descending limb of the blood alcohol curve. *Psychopharmacologia*, 1972, *23*, 99-114.

Jones, B.M., & Vega, A. Fast and slow drinkers: Blood alcohol variables and cognitive performance. *Quarterly Journal of Studies on Alcohol*, 1973, *34*, 797-806.

Kalant, H. Biological models of alcohol tolerance and physical addiction. In M.M. Gross (Ed.), *Alcohol intoxication and withdrawal: Experimental studies, Advances in experimental medicine and biology, Vol. 35*. New York: Plenum Press, 1973.

Kalant, H., LeBlanc, A.E., & Gibbins, R.J. Tolerance to, and dependence on, some non-opiate psychotropic drugs. *Pharmacological Reviews*, 1971, *23*, 135-191.

Kalant, H., LeBlanc, A.E., Wilson, A., & Homatidis, S. Sensorimotor and physiological effects of various alcoholic beverages. *CMA Journal*, 1975, *112*, 953-958.

Kallas, P., & Sellers, E.M. Blood glucose in intoxicated chronic alcoholics. *CMA Journal*, 1975, *112*, 590-592.

Kissin, B., Schenker, V., & Schenker, A. The acute effects of ethyl alcohol and chlorpromazine on certain physiological functions in alcoholics. *Quarterly Journal of Studies on Alcohol*, 1959, *20*, 480-492.

Lester, B.K., Rundell, O.H., Cowden. L.C., & Williams, H.L. Chronic alcoholism, alcohol, and sleep. In M.M. Gross (Ed.), *Alcohol intoxication and withdrawal: Experimental studies, Advances in experimental medicine and biology, Vol. 35.* New York: Plenum Press, 1973.

Lester, B., Rundell, O.H., Cowden, L., & Williams, H.L. Alcohol and sleep in the chronic alcoholic. In N. Burch (Ed.), *Behavior and brain electricl activity.* New York: Plenum Press, 1975. (In press)

Liberson, C.W., & Liberson, W.T. Sex differences in autonomic responses to electric shock. *Psychophysiology*, 1975, *12*, 182-186.

Little, S.C., & McAvoy, M. Electroencephalographic studies in alcoholism. *Quarterly Journal of Studies on Alcohol*, 1952, *13*, 9-15.

Lolli, G., Nencini, R., & Misiti, R. Effects of two alcoholic beverages on the electroencephalographic and electromyographic tracings of healthy men. *Quarterly Journal of Studies on Alcohol*, 1964, *25*, 451-458.

Lolli, G., & Rubin, M. Alcohol and the emptying time of the stomach. *Quarterly Journal of Studies on Alcohol*, 1943, *4*, 64-67. (a)

Lolli, G., & Rubin, M. The effect of concentration of alcohol on the rate of absorption and the shape of the blood alcohol curve. *Quarterly Journal of Studies on Alcohol*, 1943, *4*, 57-63. (b)

Long, J.A., & McLachlan, J.F.C. Abstract reasoning and perceptual-motor efficiency in alcoholics. *Quarterly Journal of Studies on Alcohol*, 1974, *35*, 1220-1229.

Lovallo, W., Parsons, O.A., & Holloway, F. Autonomic arousal in normal, alcoholic, and brain damaged patients as measured by plethysmograph response to cold pressor stimulation. *Psychophysiology*, 1973, *10*, 166-170.

McGonnell, P.C., & Beach, H.D. The effects of ethanol on the acquisition of conditioned GSR. *Quarterly Journal of Studies on Alcohol*, 1968, *29*, 845-855.

Mellanby, E. Alcohol; its absorption into and disappearance from the blood under different conditions. Medical Research Committee, Special Report Series No. 31. London: H.M.S.O., 1919.

Mendelson, J.H., & LaDou, J. Experimentally induced chronic intoxication and withdrawal in alcoholics. I. Background and experimental design. *Quarterly Journal of Studies on Alcohol*, 1964, *Suppl. No. 2*, 1-13.

Mirsky, A., Piker, P., Rosenbaum, M., & Lederer, H. "Adaptation" of the central nervous system to varying concentrations of alcohol in the blood. *Quarterly Journal of Studies on Alcohol*, 1941, *2*, 35-45.

Mizoi, Y., Kimura, A., Ohga, N., & Ishido, T. Electromyographical studies for diagnosis of mild drunkness. *Japanese Journal of Legal Medicine*, 1963, *17*, 1-8.

Naitoh, P. The effects of alcohol on the autonomic nervous system of humans: Psychophysiological approach. In B. Kissin & H. Begleiter (Eds.), *The biology of alcoholism*. New York: Plenum Press, 1972.

Nauta, W.J.H. Neural associations of the frontal cortex. *Acta Neurobiologica Experimentalis*, 1972, *32*, 125-140.

Overton, D.A. State-dependent learning produced by alcohol and its relevance to alcoholism. In B. Kissin & H. Begleiter (Eds.), *The biology of alcoholism, Vol.2, Physiology and behavior*. New York: Plenum Press, 1971.

Page, R.D., & Linden, J.D. Reversible organic brain syndrome in alcoholics. *Quarterly Journal of Studies on Alcohol*, 1974, *35*, 98-107.

Parsons, O.A. Brain damage in alcoholics: Altered states of unconsciousness. In M.M. Gross (Ed.), *Second Biannual International Symposium on Experimental Studies of Alcohol Intoxication and Withdrawal*. New York: Plenum Pres, 1975.

Powell, B.J., Goodwin, D.W., Janes, C.L., & Hoine, H. State-dependent effects of alcohol on autonomic orienting responses. *Psychonomic Science*, 1971, *25*, 305-306.

Rosenberg, C.M., & Buttsworth, F.J. Anxiety in alcoholics. *Quarterly Journal of Studies on Alcohol*, 1969, *30*, 729.

Rosenblatt, S.M., Gross, M.M., Malenowski, B., Broman, M., & Lewis, E. Factor analysis of the daily clinical course rating scale of the acute alcoholic psychoses. *Quarterly Journal of Studies on Alcohol*, 1972, *33*, 1060-1064.

Rundell, O.H., Lester, B.K., Griffiths, W.J., & Williams, H.L. Alcohol and sleep in young adults. *Psychopharmacologia*, 1972, *26*, 201-218.

Schnall, C., & Wiener, J.S. Clinical evaluation of blood pressure in alcoholics. *Quarterly Journal of Social Psychiatry*, 1958, *19*, 432-446.

Segal, B.M., Kushnarev, V.M., Urakov, I.G., & Misionzhnik, E.U. Alcoholism and disruptions of activity of deep cerebral structures. *Quarterly Journal of Studies on Alcohol*, 1970, *31*, 587-601.

Seixas, F.A., & Eggelston, S. Alcoholism and the central nervous system. *Annals of the New York Academy of Sciences*, 1973, *215*, 5-389.

Smith, J.W., & Layden, T.A. Changes in psychological performance and blood chemistry in alcoholics during and after hospital treatment. *Quarterly Journal of Studies on Alcohol*, 1972, *33*, 379-394.

Takala, M., Pihkanen, T.A., & Markkanen, T. The effects of distilled and brewed beverages. A Physiological, neurological, and psychological study. Publication No. 4. Helsinki: The Finnish Foundation for Alcohol Studies, 1957.

Takala, M., Siro, E., & Toivainen, Y. Intellectual functions and dexterity during hangover. Experiments after intoxication with brandy and with beer. *Quarterly Journal of Studies on Alcohol*, 1958, *19*, 1-29.

Tarter, R.E., & Parsons, O.A. Conceptual shifting in chronic alcoholics. *Journal of Abnormal Psychology*, 1971, *77*, 71-75.

Varga, B., & Nagy, T. Analysis of alpha-rhythm in the EEG of alcoholics. *Electroencephalography and Clinical Neurophysiology*, 1960, *12*, 933. (Abstract)

Wagman, A.M.I., & Allen, R.P. Effects of alcohol ingestion and abstinence on slow wave sleep of alcoholics. In M.M. Gross (Ed.), *Alcohol intoxication and withdrawal*. New York: Plenum Press, 1975.

Wallgren, H., & Barry, H., III. *Actions of Alcohol, Vol. 1: Biochemical, physiological, and psychological aspects; Vol. 2: Chronic and clinical aspects*. Amsterdam: Elsevier, 1970.

Wenger, M.A. Studies of autonomic balance in Army Air Forces personnel. *Comparative Psychology Monograph*, 1948, *19*, (Serial No. 101).

Wikler, A., Prescor, F.T., Fraser, H.F., & Isbell, H. Electroencephalographic changes associated with chronic intoxication and the alcohol abstinence syndrome. *American Journal of Psychiatry*, 1956,

Wolff, P.H. Ethnic differences in alcohol sensitivity. *Science*, 1972, *175*, 449-450.

Wolff, P.H. Vasomotor sensitivity to alcohol in diverse mongoloid populations. *American Journal of Human Genetics*, 1973, *25*, 193-199,

Yules, R.B., Freedman, D.X., & Chandler, K.A. The effect of ethyl alcohol on man's electroencephalographic sleep cycle. *Electroencephalography and Clinical Neurophysiology*, 1966, *20*, 109-111.

Zeiner, A.R., Paredes, A., & Cowden, L. Physiological responses to ethanol among the Tarahumara Indians. *Annals of the New York Academy of Sciences*, 1976. (In press)

CHAPTER 13

BEHAVIORAL AND MOTIVATIONAL PATTERNS OF CHRONIC ALCOHOLICS

Peter E. Nathan
Stephen A. Lisman

This chapter reviews the body of behavioral research with human beings, primarily alcoholics, enquiring into the structure and function of alcohol use and abuse by humans. By its nature, most of the work required that it be undertaken within controlled laboratory settings. By structure, we refer specifically to the topography of drinking by chronic alcoholics, including micro and macro patterns of alcohol consumption; by function, both to behavioral concomitants of drinking, including socialization patterns, mood and affect, aggression, and "craving" and "loss of control," and to behavioral determinants of alcohol consumption, which include again social interaction factors and interpersonal anxiety and social stress, as well as "set" and social influence.

Though some of the same issues are also considered by the authors of other chapters in this book, we believe that

Ralph E. Tarter and A. Arthur Sugerman (eds.), Alcoholism

ISBN: 0-201-08146-6
ISBN: 0-201-08145-8 (pbk.)

they belong as well in this chapter because of the unique perspective data from the experimental behavioral laboratory provide the alcohol researcher. By the same token, it is clear that data gathered by other means, in other settings which permit less stringent environmental control, belong as legitimately in this comprehensive book; the two sets of data complement each other to provide more and more precise approximations to the truth. In this case, the truth has to do with the effects of alcohol on certain very human aspects of human behavior.

THE TOPOGRAPHY OF ALCOHOL CONSUMPTION

Although the topography of alcohol consumption by alcoholics has been widely studied by participant observation and field research methods, the reliability of data generated under these uncontrolled circumstances remains a source of concern. For this reason, it was an important step forward when alcohol was first given to experimental subjects on an acute basis under controlled laboratory conditions. Though valuable, acute studies nonetheless focused only on the immediate effects of limited quantities of alcohol on physiological, metabolic, and behavioral functioning, in part simply to demonstrate these effects, in part to contrast alcoholics and nonalcoholics along these dimensions. The first such studies were those of Docter and Bernal (1964), Talland, Mendelson, and Ryack (1964), and Talland and Kasschav (1965). Mello (1972) reviews the results of these and other more recent acute studies in detail.

The pioneering work of Mendelson and Mello, the first research team to give alcohol to alcoholic subjects on a chronic basis, was also the first to permit an unencumbered view of the topography of daily and weekly (macro) alcoholic drinking. The first study of prolonged drinking by these investigators (1964) enabled behavioral observations of 10 chronic skid-row alcoholics at a correctional institution near Boston during programmed administration of 86-proof beverage alcohol. Alcohol was administered over a 24-day period in undiluted form every four hours. Six ounces were consumed the first day of the drinking period, 12 ounces the second day, 18 ounces the third day, 24 ounces the fourth day, and 30 the fifth through 18th days. On the 19th day of drinking, subjects were raised to 40 ounces of beverage, then maintained at that level to the conclusion of the 24-day study period. Though only prior anecdotal data had led Mendelson and Mello to believe that chronic alcoholics could consume such large quantities of alcohol over such a lengthy period of drinking, most of their subjects did in fact consume most or all of the beverage alcohol offered them, confirming clinical lore as to the prodigious capacity of such alcoholics.

Having established that chronic alcoholics can drink very substantial quantities of alcohol for sustained periods of time in a study which also yielded initial data on psychophysiologic, psychiatric, psychomotor, cognitive, EEG, and metabolic correlates of prolonged heavy drinking, Mello and Mendelson went on to conduct a series of additional laboratory studies of sustained drinking within the free-operant experimental paradigm. These studies began with two exploratory projects, each requiring two chronic alcoholic subjects to earn beverage alcohol during, respectively, 14- and 16-day drinking periods. Conclusions from these studies included the following:

> (1) All subjects have shown a striking behavioral tolerance for alcohol, and all have been able to continue to perform operant tasks of varying complexity, despite blood alcohol levels ranging between 200 and 300 mg/100 ml.
>
> (2) A tendency to work for alcohol increasingly at night as the drinking period progresses has been consistently observed.
>
> (3) All subjects have shown severe withdrawal signs and symptoms upon cessation of drinking.
>
> (4) There was no evidence of a compulsive, uncontrollable drinking pattern following initial achievement of high blood alcohol levels.
>
> (5) Subjects worked for and drank relatively small amounts of alcohol (1-2 ounces).
>
> (6) The potential importance of social interactional factors in determining the episodic periodicity of drinking was illustrated by the subject who terminated an unlimited period of drinking after 16 days because his companion had stopped. (Mello, 1972, p. 232)

Following these two pilot projects, Mello and Mendelson initiated a comprehensive program of research designed to identify a range of social, environmental, and physiological factors affecting the drinking patterns of chronic alcoholics. While review and discussion of most of the results of this research properly belongs farther along in this review, the normative patterns of drinking it revealed will be discussed here.

The first study in this series confirmed that systematic variation in the operant work requirement for alcohol affected drinking behavior in a linear fashion (Mello, McNamee, & Mendelson, 1968). This finding suggested that human subjects performing operant work for alcohol were obeying the known laws of operant conditioning. The same study also confirmed that alcoholics earn and drink relatively small amounts of alcohol at a time in an experimental setting in which the amount of operant work directly determinates the amount of alcohol available for consumption.

As before, the ready availability of virtually unlimited quantities of alcohol did not impel any of the chronic alcoholic subjects of this study to try to consume all available alcohol; none drank to oblivion.

The next two studies in this sequence (Mello & Mendelson, 1970, 1972) asked whether groups of chronic alcoholics, given free access to unlimited quantities of alcohol over very lengthy experimental drinking periods (30 to 60 days), would show consistent consumption patterns through these prolonged periods of drinking. In fact, almost all subjects quickly adopted similar patterns of operant work and consumption which they maintained through the study. To this end, they rarely worked at the operant task while they were drinking; all subjects initiated discrete patterns of working and drinking very shortly after drinking began. These patterns were so regular as to be cyclic, with subjects typically spending virtually all tokens earned during the baseline (nondrinking) phase of the study during the early days of the drinking period, doing no operant work at this time, then working and drinking in small units when the initial reservoir of tokens was exhausted. Subjects frequently exhibited partial withdrawal signs during experimental drinking, with decreases in blood alcohol level of 100 mg/100 ml during a 24-hour period sufficient to bring on these withdrawal phenomena.

Nathan and his colleagues (Nathan, O'Brien, & Lowenstein, 1971; Nathan, Titler, Lowenstein, Solomon, & Rossi, 1970; Nathan, Zare, Ferneau, & Lowenstein, 1970; in a contemporaneous but independent series of operant studies of drinking by chronic alcoholics, also observed a comparable cyclic pattern of drinking and working for operant points by their alcoholic subjects, a finding that clearly heightened the credibility and generalizability of this important behavioral phenomenon. Unlike Mello and Mendelson's subjects, however, Nathan's alcoholics failed consistently to experience signs and symptoms of partial withdrawal, perhaps because they tended to work for alcohol every day once the spree period of heavy drinking had ended, rarely going more than a few hours without a drink. The studies by Nathan are reviewed more thoroughly below, where the data they provide on the reciprocal influences of social interaction and drinking are examined in detail.

Nathan and a colleague also observed the drinking patterns of nonalcoholic drinkers drawn from the same population pool as the alcoholics they had previously studied. In a paper reporting this work, Nathan and O'Brien (1971) noted that these nonalcoholic drinkers showed only a monophasic, maintenance drinking pattern instead of the biphasic, spree maintenance pattern demonstrated by the alcoholics. The monophasic pattern, characterized by moderate blood alcohol levels across almost every day of an extended period of drinking, was presumed to reflect a drinking behavior outside the laboratory which permitted these men to support themselves by working even while they continued to drink. By contrast, few of the alcoholic men studied by Nathan and his coworkers worked steadily, largely because their spree maintenance pattern of drinking prohibited it.

In a subsequent additional study, Tracey and Nathan (in press) reported that four chronic alcohoholic women who lived and drank in a laboratory setting similar to that employed in the 1970 and 1971 studies demonstrated a monophasic pattern of maintenance drinking very much like the earlier nonalcoholic drinkers. Tracey and Nathan concluded from these observations that all four women, alcoholics for many years, nonetheless had learned to drink in ways that permitted them to function as members of more-or-less intact families. That is, despite blood alcohol levels that sometimes approached 200 mg/100 ml, these women never lost control of their drinking in the laboratory to the extent of behavioral loss-of-control or unconsciousness. This pattern of drinking, which the women said also characterized their drinking outside the laboratory, was clearly more functional than the biphasic pattern shown by the male alcoholics studied earlier.

In additional studies designed to elucidate environmental factors associated with changes in drinking by chronic alcoholics, Mendelson and Mello examined the impact on drinking patterns of contingent versus noncontingent alcohol (Mello & Mendelson, 1972), eating and drinking (Mello, 1972), and immediate versus delayed reinforcement (Mello et al., 1968; Mello & Mendelson, 1971). They conluded, in the first instance that the biphasic pattern of drinking remains intact whether alcohol is available contingently or noncontingently (though variability of blood alcohol levels decreases substantially in the latter case); in the second, that the biphasic pattern also remains in the face of enforced food consumption, though blood alcohol levels fluctuate with changes in food intake; and, in the third, that immediate reinforcement results in spaced and moderate (controlled) drinking while delayed reinforcement results in more variable, less moderate (uncontrolled) drinking.

The Fixed-Interval Drinking Decision (FIDD) research and treatment model developed by Gottheil and his colleagues at the Coatesville (Pa.) Veterans Administration Hospital has also been employed to reflect normative daily and weekly (macro) patterns of drinking by chronic alcoholics (Gottheil, Corbett, Grasberger, & Cornelison, 1972; Gottheil, Murphy, Skoloda, & Corbett, 1972). The usual FIDD research/treatment cycle lasts six weeks. During their first week of residence on the 12-bed FIDD ward, patients are introduced to ward routine and the treatment regimen (which involves milieu, group, and individual therapy); no alcohol is available to them at this time. A four-week "drinking-decisions" phase then follows. During this time, patients can choose to drink either 0, 1, or 2 ounces of 80-proof ethanol in water each hour on the hour from nine a.m. to nine p.m. Mondays through Fridays. This means that patients can drink from 0 to 26 ounces of beverage alcohol on five of the seven days of each of the four weeks of this phase of the FIDD cycle. Of the 98 patients who participated in the first 14 FIDD treatment/research cycles during the first two years of the project, 55 drank at some time during the program (Skoloda, Alterman, Cornelison, & Gottheil, 1975). Given that every one of these patients had been diagnosed chronic alcoholic prior to admission and that the amount of alcohol that could be consumed each day was substantial, that fewer than six of ten patients drank at all during this extended period of in-patient treatment was quite surprising. And that 32 of these 55 drinkers were categorized as moderate drinkers because they consumed 250 or fewer ounces of beverage alcohol during the four weeks (with a median daily alcohol consumption of just 3.5 ounces) reinforces the impression that these alcoholics chose to moderate their drinking in a setting which did not demand moderation. In fact, only 23 of the 98 patients failed to make a serious effort to moderate their drinking; median daily alcohol consumption by this group of patients was 20.8 ounces, probably not much different from their usual alcohol consumption on the street.

Other behavioral researchers have investigated the moment-to-moment (micro) topography of drinking by alcoholics. In one of the first of these studies, Schaefer, Sobell, and Mills (1971) observed 16 male alcoholics and 15 male social drinkers drinking ad lib at an experimental bar over several sessions. Simultaneously recording several different components of the drinking sequence, these investigators concluded that the alcoholic drinkers they studied differed from the nonalcoholic drinkers in at least three ways: (a) alcoholics chose more often to drink straight than mixed drinks; (b) alcoholics usually consumed their drinks by gulping them; by contrast, nonalcoholics more often sipped their drinks; (c) alcoholics drank beyond the stage of moderate intoxication much more frequently than did the nonalcoholics. Subsequent research by the same researchers has confirmed these initial observations (Sobell, Schaefer, & Mills, 1972).

In the study of women alcoholics briefly described above, Tracey and Nathan (in press) observed that the micro drinking behavior of their female alcoholics was more like that of Schaefer's and Sobell's male social drinkers than their male alcoholics. This observation accords with the conclusion Tracey and Nathan also drew to the effect that these female alcoholics were more like the nonalcoholic men studied by Nathan and O'Brien (1971) in overall consumption patterns and amount (macro drinking).

The newest thrust in behavioral efforts to capture macro and micro features of drinking by alcoholics and non-alcoholics also represents, ironically, a partial return to the old participant observation approach to the problem. Incorporating more precise behavioral observation methods in their research plan, however, Kessler and Gomberg (1974) and Reid (1975) have sent observers into actual drinking establishments to record data on number of drinks ordered by a target subject, time the drink is served, type of drink, number of sips per drink, and total time taken to consume each drink. In the recent study by Kessler and Gomberg, it was reported that the number of drinks ordered by the 53 males they observed was 2.41, with subjects taking from four to nine sips per drink. Most subjects chose to drink beer. Interestingly, these data differ from those reported by Sobell, Schaefer, & Mills (1972) on the social drinkers drinking in their experimental bar setting, suggesting that such factors as setting, geography, socioeconomic status, and age must be taken into account before any effort to draw general conclusions about any category of drinker in such studies can be fully accepted.

BEHAVIORAL CONCOMITANTS OF DRINKING

Although alcohol, expecially excessive amounts of alcohol, affects virtually the full range of behaviors of which men and women are capable, this review will restrict itself to those variables studied by behavioral researchers which appear most consistently to covary with alcohol ingestion by alcoholics. Among these variables are socialization patterns, mood and affect, aggression, psychopathology, and craving and loss of control.

SOCIALIZATION PATTERNS. Patterns of socialization as concomitants as well as determinants of alcohol consumption have been a major focus of research by Nathan and his colleagues, first at Boston City Hospital, more recently at Rutgers University. Initial impetus for his attention to this variable derived from Nathan's observation that the subjects of Mendelson and Mello's early research showed variations in social behavior that stemmed from at least three different variables, the amount of alcohol they consumed, the physical surroundings within which they lived and drank, and their own social learning histories vis-a-vis alcohol. The interaction of these variables, important to a full understanding of the behavioral effects of alcohol on alcoholics, clearly required intensive experimental analysis. For this reason, Nathan and his coworkers designed a research schema that permitted continuous examination of alcoholic and nonalcoholic subjects' operant choice of behavior between alcohol and socialization during varying periods of drinking and under varying environmental circumstances. To this end, Nathan and his colleagues (Nathan, et al., 1970, 1971) reported that their skid-row alcoholic subjects almost invariably chose to translate reinforcement points earned for operant work into beverage alcohol rather than relief from imposed social isolation during the lengthy drinking periods they programmed. Further, the same subjects chose to drink by themselves even during periods of socialization, when they did not have to give up reinforcement points for the opportunity to spend time with each other in the ward dayroom.

This preference for interpersonal isolation increased as drinking continued so that by the end of the three-week drinking period, subjects were drinking by themselves, alone in their bedrooms, during most of every day, regardless of whether the study was in a socialization or isolation phase. Building on these data, Nathan and O'Brien (1971) then contrasted the social isolation demonstrated by their skid-row alcoholic subjects before, during, and after periods of experimental drinking with the much more socially responsive behavior of matched skid-row nonalcoholics. The latter, living in the same experimental laboratory setting as their alcoholic confreres, chose to spend substantial numbers of reinforcement points for socialization before and during the drinking period; in fact, socialization by some of these subjects actually increased as the drinking period progressed.

In view of their macro and micro drinking behavior, it was not surprising that the four alcoholic women in Tracey and Nathan's recent study adopted socialization patterns during experimental drinking that were even more prosocial than those shown by Nathan and O'Brien's male nonalcoholics. In fact, every one of the four invested more reinforcement points in social interaction than in alcohol, an allocation in favor of socialization that increased as drinking continued.

These findings, taken together, suggest that the demographic identity and drinking history of a population of alcoholic subjects, not simply the fact of their alcoholism or the physical stimuli confronting them in an experimental laboratory setting, largely determine their socialization patterns in laboratory settings. Partial confirmation for this statement comes from studies by Bigelow, Griffiths, and their colleagues at the Baltimore City Hospitals. On contrasting a variety of behavioral correlates of alcohol consumption during alternating days of drinking and abstinence, Bigelow (1973) and Griffiths, Bigelow, and Liebson (1974b) reported that most of their male chronic alcoholic subjects (who otherwise resembled Nathan and O'Brien's alcoholic subjects) were significantly more sociable on drinking days than on days they were not permitted to drink. Further support for the view that all chronic alcoholics are not social isolates derives from results of a study by Thornton, Alterman, Skoloda, and Gottheil (1975), which revealed that heavy drinkers in Gottheil's FIDD treatment/research model dramatically increased their social interaction once they began drinking on the FIDD ward.

We conclude that among the variables influencing an alcoholic's socialization pattern during a given drinking episode are the physical and emotional setting within which the drinking occurs (e.g., whether or not the setting is conducive to conviviality); the alcoholic's prior social learning history vis-a-vis alcohol and socialization (the male alcoholics Nathan and his colleagues, Mendelson and Mello, studied had been socially isolated for years; the women alcoholics Nathan and Tracey studied and the male alcoholics Thorton, Bigelow, and Griffiths treated were not interpersonally isolated in the real world); and the amount of alcohol consumed in a given period of time (every study by Nathan, Mendelson, and Mello which reported an increase in interpersonal isolation during periods of experimental intoxication also reported that subjects had been drinking very heavily for substantial periods of time; by contrast, in the studies by Bigelow, Griffiths, and their colleagues, by Thornton and his colleagues, and by Tracey and Nathan, subjects drank substantially less alcohol, either by choice or experimental design).

MOOD AND AFFECT. Just as the "folkways" of alcoholism would have had us believe that many or most chronic alcoholics are social isolates, so has it also been assumed that alcohol makes most people, including most alcoholics, less depressed and less anxious. But during several of their early studies, Mello and Mendelson observed that many of their alcoholic subjects did not experience this predicted decrease in anxiety and depression; instead, several of their subjects, apparently intact before drinking began, became clinically anxious and depressed when they did drink.

In an effort both to confirm and quantify these clinical observations, Nathan and his colleagues (Nathan & O'Brien, 1971; Nathan, O'Brien, & Lowenstein, 1971; Nathan, Titler, Lowenstein, Solomon & Rossi, 1970, 1970) employed a variety of mood-rating scales and behavioral checklists in the context of their experimental drinking studies to determine the precise nature of these concomitants of drinking by alcoholics. These measures revealed that most male alcoholics studied did in fact report marked rises from predrinking levels of anxiety, depression, and anger, but usually only after the first 12 to 24 hours of drinking, during which levels of these moods often decreased. Subsequent studies by this group have confirmed these early findings (Allman, Taylor, & Nathan, 1972; Goldman, Taylor, Carruth, & Nathan, 1973; Martorano, 1974; Nathan, Goldman, Lisman, & Taylor, 1972). Mello and Mendelson also confirmed their early clinical observations in later experimental drinking studies (Mello, 1972). However, Tracey and Nathan (in press) failed to observe either an initial decrease or a subsequent increase in anxiety and depression in the women alcoholics they studied, a finding that accords with other observations of these subjects that clearly differentiated their behavior in important ways from that of male alcoholics studied in similar settings.

Other behavioral investigators have studied affective behavior changes in drinking alcoholics. Vannicelli (1972), for example, administered a variety of objective mood-rating scales to 30 male chronic alcoholic out-patients before and after they had consumed enough beverage alcohol to reach one of four blood alcohol levels; final BALs ranged from 19 to 158 mg/100 ml. Her results--about half her subjects reported an increase in levels of anxiety while the other half experienced a decrease -- led Vannicelli to posit the existence of two distinct types of alcoholics, "anxiety alcoholics" and "anxiety-reduction alcoholics." Though her findings have not been replicated, the hypothesis Vannicelli set forth to explain them does accord with the increasingly widespread belief that diagnostic labels like schizophrenia, manic-depressive psychosis, and alcoholism each encompass a variety of syndromes sharing symptoms but determined by different sets of etiologic factors, some biophysiological, some sociocultural and environmental, some psychological. Another recent study lends equivocal support to prior laboratory data on changes in subjective anxiety and depression in drinking alcoholics. Steffen, Nathan, and Taylor (1974) reported that four male alcoholics given extensive biofeedback on frontalis-muscle activity during periods of experimental intoxication reported significant increase in subjective anxiety at the same time that they were experiencing significantly reduced frontalis muscle activation levels. This paradoxical finding suggests that prior studies employing only subjective or only physiological measures of anxiety may well have revealed but partial truths about relationships between alcohol ingestion and affective change. It also implies that alcoholics and nonalcoholics may differ in the degree to which psychological and physiological cues to the same affect coincide. If this is so, and if this difference between the two groups predates development of alcoholism in one, it would have etiologic significance worth further serious exploration.

AGGRESSION. Another widespread assumption about alcohol's effects on behavior is its supposed ability to enhance assertiveness and induce aggression. To 1972, however, the date of a review of the research area by Carpenter and Armenti, only four empirical studies of alcohol and aggression had been reported. And only one of these studies (Bennett, Buss, & Carpenter, 1969) provided for direct testing of the effects of alcohol on physical aggression by human beings. Bennett's study measured aggression within an experimental paradigm first developed by Buss (1961), in which aggression is defined as the level of electric shock a subject will administer to an experimental confederate in a learning task. Bennett reported that alcohol at three different dosage levels did not facilitate physical aggression in his human subjects. In their review of that study and additional ones, however, Carpenter and Armenti (1972) failed to reach the same conclusion, concluding instead that "aggression, whether direct or indirect, increases with alcohol in social interaction" (Carpenter & Armenti, 1972, p.531). In our view, though, the studies on which Carpenter and Armenti based this conclusion (Hartocollis, 1962; Kalin et al., 1965; Takala, 1957) were so deficient methodologically that it is possible to explain their findings supporting the aggression-facilitation effects of alcohol as functions of these manifold methodologic and conceptual shortcomings rather than as the result of replicable empirical findings.

Spurred by the gap between Bennett's results and Carpenter and Armenti's conclusions, Taylor and his colleagues (Shuntich & Taylor, 1972; Taylor & Gammon, 1975) modified the Buss paradigm Bennett had employed in the attempt to make it more true-to-life. This modification required a confederate (previously, an impotent victim) and the subject (formerly, an all-powerful teacher) to compete with each other in a reaction-time task, with the winner then asked to select any intensity shock to administer to the loser. Trial wins as well as the confederate's choice of shock level were programmed so that the subject lost fifty percent of the trials, for which he received increasingly painful shock. Within this somewhat more true-to-life experimental paradigm, Shuntich and Taylor found that subjects given 0.9 ml/kg body weight alcohol used significantly higher shock levels than placebo-dose or no alcohol controls in response to provocatively escalating shock levels administered by the confederates.

The significance of these findings was diminished by the fact that only one dosage (low) level was employed and that the placebo group was not convinced it had consumed as much alcohol as the experimental group. For these reasons, Taylor and Gammon (1975) returned to the modified aggression paradigm to examine the effects of type and dose of alcohol on physical aggression. Results were that subjects who consumed an amount of bourbon or vodka comparable to Bennett's high dosage condition administered shock at greater intensities than low dosage counterparts. A no-alcohol control group, run subsequently, administered shock at levels of intermediate intensity, suggesting that the low dose of alcohol used in this study had had an inhibiting effect on aggression. Despite the drawbacks of post hoc experimental designs like this one, as well as the study's other methodologic shortcomings, Taylor's design is consistent with Carpenter and Armenti's plea for extrinsic manipulation of aggression via provocation (in this case, competition). As important, his results were the first to suggest a direct link between alcohol and physical aggression on the basis of behavioral evidence, though the bases for this link - expectancy, disinhibition, pharmacology - were not illuminated.

In an unstructured study with the same ends, Smith, Parker, and Noble (1975) arranged for 18 nonalcoholic male-female dyads to consume large or small amounts of alcohol over a 50 minute period. Afterwards, the couples were to engage in extended discussion, which was videotaped for later coding. Coded along several dimensions, including some of the Gottschalk-Gleser (1969) content-analytic system, the dyads' interaction showed no alcohol effects on aggression at high or low dosages. That a no-alcohol control group was not employed in the study, that aggression was not elicited by design, and that a passive coding system for complex behaviors was permitted all detracted from the worth of this study.

Boyatzis (1974) also videotaped, then coded and scored for aggression, interpersonal behavior at different alcohol dosages. In an effort to maximize the generality of his findings, however, Boyatzis filmed his videotapes within pre-arranged cocktail party settings. In an effort to control for some of the methodologic flaws which had marred earlier studies, he ran a large number of subjects of diverse SES's, gave them one of two kinds of beverage alcohol or soft drinks during the test situations, and devoted considerable energy to achieving high inter-rater reliability in coding. During the drinking (test) sessions, subjects participated in competitive games. Mean blood alcohol levels between 75 and 84 mg % were reached following ingestion of distilled spirits; beer led to BALs approximately 10% less. Results were that beer and distilled spirits were associated with higher aggression ratings than soft-drinks throughout the full sessions; during their latter phases, however, distilled spirits alone were related to higher levels of aggression. Further, BALs above 100 mg % were associated with significantly more aggressive behavior than those below that level. Finally, aggressive behavior during the study was significantly related to aggressive acts outside the experimental setting, including self-reports of "trouble due to drinking" and "physical fights." Because of the relative methodologic sophistication of this study, as well as its successful efforts to validate within-study measures of aggression with aggression outside the experimental situation, its results must be viewed carefully.

The final study reviewed in this section (Lang, Goeckner, Adesso, & Marlatt, in press) was like Boyatzis' in its choice of subjects but unlike that study in that it undertook to determine directly the effects of alcohol upon anger and aggressive behavior that were specifically provoked. The design of the study was 2 x 2 x 2 factorial, with half the male social drinker subjects told they were drinking an alcoholic beverage and the other half, that their beverage was simply tonic water; half of each of these groups was actually given beverage alcohol while the other half received tonic water. Finally, half of each of these four groups was provoked to aggression by an insulting confederate, with the other half exposed to a neutral interaction with the confederate. Results were that subjects who believed they had been given alcohol were more aggressive than subjects who thought they had been given tonic water; subjects who had actually consumed alcohol, however, were no more aggressive than subjects who had not. These data, then, emphasize the impact of expectancy on the relationship between alcohol and aggression rather than the pharmacological effect of the drug on this behavior. That blood alcohol levels reached in the study were only in the 100 mg/100 ml range, however, tends further to restrict the generalizability of these data to social drinkers who become moderately intoxicated. In other words, one can conclude little or nothing about aggression in intoxicated alcoholics from these reults.

Unfortunately, it is difficult to conclude much more about aggression in any subject population from the behavioral research just reviewed. While the diverse methodologic shortcomings of these studies are partly responsible for our inability to generalize from them, at the root of the problem may be the difficulty behavioral researchers have had defining, then operationalizing, human behavior as complex, multifaceted, and overdetermined as anger and aggression. It is one thing simply to record frequency of social interaction in a group by recording frequency of prosocial acts by members of that group; it is quite another to comment reliably on the nature of those acts. That behavioral researchers have accelerated their commitment to this and other more complex areas of research attests, however, to their faith that the hastening technology of reliable behavioral measurement will permit them to complete their work.

CRAVING AND LOSS OF CONTROL. Until very recently, the only treatment goal for the chronic alcoholic entering any treatment program was total abstinence. The belief that there could be but one goal for alcoholism treatment derived from a variety of influences. One was the conviction of influential early figures in the field (e.g., Jellinek, 1960; Williams, 1948) that alcoholism is a progressive, irreversible disease characterized above all by loss of control over drinking during periods of alcohol consumption and omnipresent craving for alcohol during periods of sobriety. This belief - that even a sip of alcohol by a sober alcoholic invariably leads to loss of control of drinking - lent important credence to the philosophy of Alcoholics Anonymous that abstinence be the only goal of its efforts.

It is not within the purview of this review to evaluate the legitimacy of abstinence as the sole treatment goal for alcoholism or the validity of recent reports that controlled drinking might be a more appropriate goal for some alcoholics. Another chapter in this book (Miller, Chapter 18) deals with both issues, as do several recent reviews in the alcoholism literature (e.g., Briddell & Nathan, in press; Miller, in press; Nathan, in press; Nathan & Briddell, in press). What is appropriate to review here, however, are recent behavioral data that reflect on the continued viability of the concepts of craving and loss of control, both essential elements of the abstinence model of alcoholism treatment.

Earliest behavioral challenges to the widespread assumption that craving and loss of control are invariable accompaniments of chronic alcoholism were demonstrations that one drink -- or several -- do not always precipitate uncontrollable craving and loss of control over drinking (Cutter, Schwab, & Nathan, 1970; Gottheil, Crawford, & Cornelison, 1973; Marlatt, Demming, & Reid, 1973; McNamee, Mello, & Mendelson, 1968; Merry, 1966; Williams, 1970). Giving both obvious and disguised alcohol to alcoholics under a variety of experimental laboratory conditions, these researchers noted that alcoholics did not report systematic changes in their desire to drink or in their actual drinking behavior itself following either the recognized or unrecognized introduction of alcohol. Further support for this challenge to the universality of craving and loss of control came, in addition, from demonstrations by Nathan, Mendelson, and Mello, all of whom reported that even in ad lib drinking situations alcoholics rarely drink all the alcohol available to them, especially during the latter stages of a prolonged drinking episode. Similar conclusions were drawn by the Baltimore City Hospitals group, which found that chronic alcoholic volunteers will choose to drink moderately, in the face of large quantities of available beverage alcohol, in order to reside in enriched rather than impoverished ward environments (Cohen, Liebson, Faillace, & Allen, 1971) or to spend time with other alcoholics rather than alone (Griffiths, Bigelow, & Liebson, 1974). Other investigators (e.g., Davies, 1962; Pattison, 1968; Pattison, Headley, Gleser, & Gottschalk, 1968) have also reported that substantial numbers of chronic alcoholics return voluntarily to moderate, controlled levels of drinking in the absence of specific therapeutic efforts to this end.

Despite these data and the increasing numbers of clinical researchers who have reported success in training chronic alcoholics to become controlled drinkers, Alcoholics Anonymous continues to hold to the view that craving and loss of control do exist to play important roles in the maintenance of chronic alcoholism. In view of the experience, commitment to treatment, and integrity the A.A. movement brings to the field, one cannot dismiss its continued adherence to this position out of hand. One must also acknowledge that some experienced behavioral scientists continue to hold to the same position. Chief among them is Arnold Ludwig who, in a variety of recent theoretical position papers and research reports (Ludwig & Stark, 1974; Ludwig & Wikler, 1974; Ludwig, Wikler, & Stark, 1974), claims support for the existence of craving as well as belief in its central role in the etiology and maintenance of alcoholism. Ludwig's own words describe most accurately his view of the role of craving in alcoholism:

> Craving for alcohol is hypothesized to represent the cognitive correlate of a subclinical alcohol withdrawal syndrome. The more severe the prior withdrawal experiences, the greater the predisposition to the conditioned withdrawal symptoms, with subsequent desire (craving) for relief through drinking. Craving can be aroused either by interoceptive cues, e.g., ingested alcohol stimulating cerebral neuronal receptors, or exteroceptive cues, environmental situations associated with prior heavy drinking or with the psychological and physical effects of prior withdrawal experiences. Craving...is a necessary but not sufficient condition for relapse or loss of control; the cognitive labels used to define the feeling, the mood and the physical setting will determine whether craving will be consciously perceived and expressed in drinking..." (Ludwig & Wikler, 1974, Abstract)

A complementary study which varied both alcohol dosage and the environmental properties of the experimental drinking situation (Ludwig, Wikler, & Stark, 1974) confirmed this hypothesis by finding that both craving and alcohol acquisition were functions of "appropriate interoceptive and exteroceptive cues."

One cannot help but be swayed by the overwhelming mass of recent behavioral evidence against the view that craving and loss of control are invariable accompaniments of alcoholism. At the same time, it is clearly possible that craving is a factor in the decision of some alcoholics, enmeshed in certain specific environmental situations, to resume drinking. Involuntary loss of control, by contrast, appears to have been effectively dismissed by these data as a major factor in the behavior of most chronic alcoholics.

BEHAVIORAL DETERMINANTS OF DRINKING

This section will review the results of behavioral studies of variables which behavioral researchers have concluded are centrally involved in the decision of chronic alcoholics to resume drinking after a period of sobriety, to continue drinking in the face of compelling factors against continuation, or to increase levels of consumption in the midst of a prolonged period of consumption.

SOCIAL INTERACTION FACTORS. In one of the earliest studies of drinking patterns as a function of social interaction, Mendelson, Mello, and Solomon (1968) brought four alcoholics who had known and drunk with each other to a laboratory whose central feature was a common alcohol reservoir. Any subject could add alcohol to the reservoir at any time by successfully operating an amusement park driving simulator. And any subject, whether or not he had helped fill the reservoir, could withdraw alcohol from it at any time. The drinking phase of the study lasted 30 days. As anticipated, each of the three subjects who remained in the study (a fourth was discharged after he became physically assaultive to fellow subjects and staff) quickly adopted roles in the group like those they had filled outside the laboratory (one man became group leader and provider, another the manipulator and taker, the third the freeloader). The special characteristics of this group drinking setting precipitated differences in drinking patterns and social interaction from those observed in earlier studies by these investigators. Specifically, the drinking behavior of the group leader was found to have a direct and immediate influence on the drinking behavior of the other two group members. In subsequent group drinking studies by the same research group, Weiner, Tamerin, Steinglass, and Mendelson (1971) and Steinglass, Weiner, and Mendelson, (1971) examined the drinking behavior dynamics and interpersonal behavior of an alcoholic father and an alcoholic son and two pairs of alcoholic brothers before, during, and after periods of experimentally-induced intoxication. In the first study, profound changes in interpersonal behavior between father and son were catalyzed by alcohol. Periodically, this behavior led to sudden increases in interpersonal stress in both father and son, followed immediately by a reduction in drinking by both. Mello (1972) observes that this kind of change in drinking following stress accords with prior observations of experimental drinking in other settings with other subjects. Essentially the same sequence of events transpired with the alcoholic brother pairs.

In another simulated "bottle-gang" study undertaken by one of Nathan's students (Goldman et al., 1973), four chronic alcoholic subjects living together on an experimental ward were required to make group decisions about drinking every two hours 16 hours a day. Five such daily decision sessions resulted in drinking decisions that were binding for all group members; the other three decision sessions were for the purpose of making individual drinking decisions. Results were that group decision-making significantly reduced the amount of drinking by all individuals in the group during the two-hour drinking periods that followed the decision sessions; when individual drinking decisions were permitted, however, significantly more drinking took place. Goldman and his colleagues concluded from these data that drinking groups existing outside laboratory settings might well have the capacity to modulate drinking by group members, although groups containing members all of whom were united in their desire to drink excessive quantities of alcohol might have less of an effect in this regard than those containing one or more members wishing to drink moderately.

Chief among other behavioral investigators who have examined the effects on drinking of social interaction factors are Bigelow, Griffiths and their colleagues at the Baltimore City Hospitals. As we noted above, these investigators believe that one of the most frequent accompaniments of drinking by alcoholics is an increase in their socialization levels. The other side of this coin is their observation that the presence or absence of opportunity for socialization has as important an impact on concurrent drinking behavior. Two studies of this phenomenon from this laboratory will be reviewed here.

In the first of these (Bigelow, Liebson, & Griffiths, 1974), eight male alcoholic inpatient volunteers were given access to a daily alcohol ration that ranged from 12 to 24 ounces of 95-proof ethanol in orange juice. The ration could be gotten on request between 7 a.m. and 11 p.m. During the 5-10 day baseline phase of this study, subjects had free access to all ward areas and could request and consume their beverages on a non-contingent basis. Following baseline, during which subjects consumed 93.4% of available alcohol, a contingent isolation phase was initiated, during which subjects were required to sit in a isolation booth for 10 to 15 minutes immediately after receiving each drink. Average consumption of available alcohol during contingent isolation fell to 45.6%; in other words, contingent isolation suppressed drinking. When baseline conditions were reintroduced, drinking rate returned to 90.4% of available alcohol. In a subsequent study, Griffiths, Bigelow, and Liebson (1974a) gave six additional alcoholic subjects daily access to 17 ounces of 95-proof ethanol in orange joice, provided that at least 40 minutes elapsed between their one-ounce drinks. During baseline, the 40-minute interval could be spent with the other subjects anywhere on the ward; subjects drank about 80% of available alcohol on these days. During the next phase of the study, however, when the 40-minute interval had to be spent in social isolation, drinking was suppressed in most subjects.

This brief section completes our review of behavioral research on the interaction of alcohol and socialization. We concluded above that while alcohol appears to facilitate socialization in most alcoholics, it clearly inhibits it in some. From research reviewed here, we now conclude that social interaction facilitates alcohol consumption in most alcoholics and has little or no effect on others. The significance of these data for a behavioral view of the etiology of the disorder seems clear. Above all else it seems certain that the reciprocal reinforcement value alcohol and social interaction have for each other might well account for much of the marked resistance of the disorder to remediation.

INTERPERSONAL ANXIETY AND SOCIAL STRESS. The tension-reduction hypothesis of alcoholism, still the most influential behavioral theory of alcoholism, posits that alcoholics drink above all to escape or avoid conditioned anxiety generated by social stress. The widespread acceptance of this theory has induced many behavioral researchers to concentrate their research efforts on attempts first to induce and assess interpersonal anxiety and social stress and then to measure their impact on alcohol ingestion. But study of relationships between anxiety and stress and alcohol consumption is also important beyond its direct relevance to the tension-reduction model of alcoholism. It is important because of the conflict between results of empirical studies of drinking by alcoholics which suggest that alcoholics become more anxious and depressed during periods of prolonged drinking and the widespread belief by many (e.g., Isbell, Fraser, Wikler, Belleville, & Eisenman, 1955; Zwerling, 1959) that alcoholics drink to reduce prevailing high levels of anxiety.

The study by Allman, Taylor, and Nathan (1972) was the first behavioral exploration of relationships between experimentally-imposed stress and alcohol consumption, mood, and psychopathology. Three chronic alcoholic inpatients participated in the 32-day study. The study was divided into a four-day predrinking period, during which subjects as a group earned reinforcement points for later purchase of beverage alcohol, a 20-day drinking period, during which subjects continued to earn reinforcement points which they could spend for alcohol, and an eight-day postdrinking, withdrawal period. The 20-day drinking period was further divided into alternating four-day periods of no stress and stress and concurrent two-day periods of socialization and isolation. Stress was imposed by telling subjects at the beginning of each of the stress periods that their operant work had deteriorated and that, at the rate the group was earning points, they would shortly be unable to continue drinking. This stress message was designed to convince subjects that one of them was slacking off, a possibility none of the three could test out because operant work was performed at operant consoles in each subject's room.

The stress manipulation suppressed drinking during periods of interpersonal isolation and facilitated drinking during periods of socialization, a finding at variance with the belief that stress consistently reduces drinking. To this end, the authors of the report on the study observed that "the effect of stress on drinking behavior..might be considered a function of at least the following: (1) whether the subject is a 'stress responder' to begin with; (2) whether the stress is interpersonal or environmental; and (3) whether it is imposed in the context of social or isolated drinking." (Allman et al., 1972, pp. 677-678).

Miller, Hersen, Eisler, and Hilsman (1974) completed a subsequent study that compared the effects of social stress on operant drinking by eight male alcoholics and eight matched social drinkers. Drinking rate was quantified by requiring subjects to work at an operant console for ten minutes after the induction of stress to earn points to purchase beverage alcohol. The stress manipulation involved confronting all subjects with a set of simulated interpersonal encounters, each requiring an assertive response. On giving an assertive response to the final encounter, a subject was informed that he had given poor assertive responses and that, as a consequence, it was clear that "you let people boss you around." Although both groups of subjects demonstrated the same degree of autonomic arousal in the face of the stress and emitted the same number of operant responses for alcohol following imposition of a non-stress, control condition, the alcoholic subjects emitted significantly more operant responses for alcohol following the stress induction than the social drinkers. Miller and his colleagues do not take these results to mean that alcoholics have a lower tolerance for social stress than nonalcoholics but that they have learned to respond to stressful situations inappropriately, by consuming alcohol, rather than adaptively, by being appropriately assertive. This interesting hypothesis remains speculative in the absence of data to confirm it.

Marlatt and his colleagues, first at the University of Wisconsin, then at the University of Washington, have completed a series of studies examining the role of stress and related factors on alcohol consumption. In the first of these studies, Higgins and Marlatt (1973) assigned alcoholics and nonalcoholics to high or low threat conditions prior to participation in Marlatt's taste-rating task (described previously as an analogue measure of consumption).

"High-threat" subjects were told they would receive a painful electric shock during the taste rating task "to excite your sense of touch because then we can carefully control the amount of stimulation that you get." "Low-threat" subjects believed that they would be given a very low level of stimulation, sufficient to achieve the desired effect on taste. The taste test, which required subjects to compare three alcoholic beverages along a variety of taste dimensions, served as an unobtrusive measure of alcohol consumption following the stress/anxiety manipulation. At its conclusion, after no subjects actually received shock, all were told they had been placed in a non-shock, control condition.

Threat of shock in this study failed to have an impact on subsequent drinking by either alcoholic or nonalcoholic subjects. The only experimental variable which did affect drinking behavior was identity of subjects: overall, alcoholics in both high-and low-threat groups drank significantly more than nonalcoholics during the taste test. In a later overview of these results, Marlatt (in press) concludes that "at least in this context, arousal of fear of physical pain did not seem to increase consumption in the taste-rating task."

On the assumption that fear of electric shock may not be relevant to alcohol consumption because alcohol does not lessen shock-induced pain, Higgins and Marlatt (in press) explored the effects on drinking of social anxiety, a stress factor of more obvious relevance to alcohol consumption. For this purpose, heavy social drinker male college students were divided into high and low "evaluation threat" groups. High evaluation threat subjects were told that they were to take part in a second study following the taste rating task, which was the one for which they were first recruited. In this later study, they were told, they would interact with female peers who would rate them along selected dimensions of personal attractiveness. Low evaluation threat subjects were also told they would participate in a group experiment following the taste task but they were not told they would be evaluated by others. Unlike the first Higgins and Marlatt study (1973), this stress manipulation did alter drinking behavior. High evaluation threat subjects drank almost twice as much wine during the taste-rating task as low evaluation threat subjects, a difference significant beyond the .005 level. These findings, like the results of the study by Allman and his colleagues, suggest that threat of interpersonal evaluation can have an impact on alcohol consumption; the two studies taken together also suggest that alcoholics are not alone in their susceptibility to this influence process.

In a continuing effort to make these experimental analogue studies more true to real-life drinking and actual stress, Marlatt, Kosturn, and Lang (1974) designed a study permitting some experimental subjects the opportunity to retaliate against a critical evaluator. Two of three groups of subjects in this study were deliberately insulted by the experimenters' confederate before they participated in the wine-tasting task. The third group was not so insulted. Of the two groups which received stress-inducing critical evaluations, one was permitted to retaliate against the confederate by delivering a fixed number of painful electric shocks to him in a standard teacher-learner paradigm; the other insulted group was not given this opportunity to retaliate. Results indicated, as predicted, that the "insult-only" group consumed the most beverage alcohol during the taste task and the "insult-retaliation" group the least, a difference significant beyond the .01 level.

Despite the results of the latter two of these studies, however, Marlatt (in press) concludes that the tension-reduction model of alcohol consumption does not receive overwhelming support from the bulk of the experimental literature, a conclusion with which we agree. That is, the results of the studies by Marlatt, Allman, and Miller which favor the model, when weighed against the mass of negative data in the area, seem more like isolated findings deriving from special stress conditions (e.g., isolated stress, interpersonal stress, retaliative stress) than from conditions which play important tension-inducing roles in the alcoholic's real life beyond the laboratory.

"SET" AND SOCIAL INFLUENCE. Gottheil and his colleagues recently tested the possibility that social reinforcement of a specific set toward drinking could influence the drinking behavior of some of their FIDD research/treatment subjects (Alterman, Gottheil, Skoloda, & Grasberger, 1974). For this purpose, 44 male alcoholic patients in the FIDD program were divided into two groups. The first (drinking set) group was given the set during FIDD's initial, week-long pre-drinking phase that patients would benefit most from the program by drinking moderately during the forthcoming drinking period. Drinking, these patients were told, would permit them to observe the effects of a few drinks on their behavior, gain understanding of the circumstances within which they drank, and test their control over drinking. The second (abstinence set) group was told that being able to refuse drinks and to explore and gain support for alternate behaviors to drinking would be most therapeutic. Both sets were instituted by frequent positive reinforcement for the one or the other during regular group meetings held prior to the initiation of drinking. At the same time, public commitments to abstinence by members of the abstinence set group and to drinking by members of the drinking set group were elicited. Fifteen of 24 of the former patients but only 9 of 20 of the latter patients gave such commitments. This difference in willingness to make a commitment about drinking was significant beyond the .02 level.

Results of this study were as follows: While 13 of 20 patients in the drinking set group drank at some time during the program, only 8 of 24 abstinence set group members drank, a difference significant beyond the .02 level. On comparing these drinking rates to baseline FIDD drinking data, the authors concluded that the abstinence set had induced significantly more abstinence than the drinking set had induced drinking. Further, although public commitment to the drinking set had no apparent effect on subsequent drinking by patients in the drinking set group, public commitment to abstinence was associated with subsequent adherence to abstinence by all but one of the 15 patients in the abstinence set group. In other words, while arbitrary assignment to the abstinence set (and the social influence surrounding it) influenced subsequent drinking behavior, public commitment to that set had an even stronger effect on drinking.

Marlatt, with one of his students, recently completed a study exploring the impact of another social influence factor on analogue drinking (Caudill & Marlatt, in press).

Male heavy social drinker college students participated in the 3 x 2 factorial study. The first social influence factor studied was alcohol modeling condition during the taste-rating task. Three modeling conditions, heavy consumption model, light consumption model, and no model, were employed in this regard. Thus, a third of the subjects observed a confederate drinking very heavily (approximately 700 ml wine in 15 minutes) during a parallel taste-rating test in the same room. A third saw him drink lightly (about 100 ml in 15 minutes), and a third completed the taste-rating task with no one else in the room. The study's second factor required subjects to engage in brief social interaction in a waiting-room prior to the taste-rating task with another confederate who was either warm and supportive or cold and aloof.

Results of the study were: (a) while subjects rated the warm confederate as more likeable, warmer, and friendlier than the cold confederate, warm or cold pre-drinking social interaction failed to have an impact on subsequent drinking rates; (b) By contrast, the modeling condition factor had an effect significant beyond the .001 level. Subjects exposed to the high-consumption model consumed significantly more wine than subjects in either the low-consumption modeling condition or the no model control group; subjects in the latter two groups did not consume significantly different amounts of wine.

Beyond the intriguing heuristic opportunities this research model offers the alcohol researcher -- exploration of the impact on drinking of a wide variety of modeled alcohol-related or non-alcohol-related behaviors, assessment of variables which influence a positive modeling effect, consideration of the therapeutic significance of the modeling paradigm as a component of multimodal behavior therapy for alcoholism--this study also provides initial (and tentative) confirmation for the long-held view that alcoholics as children may in fact have modeled heavy parental drinking behavior. While but an initial pilot study that must be vastly expanded and replicated, this deceptively simple and straightforward study nonetheless explores an area of inestimable import to alcohol researchers.

BEHAVIORAL AND MOTIVATIONAL PATTERNS OF ALCOHOLICS: AN OVERALL ASSESSMENT

Behavioral research on the topography, concomitants, and determinants of alcohol consumption to this time has much to recommend it to researchers with other perspectives on alcoholism. Methods developed and employed by behavioral researchers for these purposes have proven to be, in large part, more reliable and objective and as sensitive as earlier methods with the same goals. These procedures have also enabled confirmation of relationships between a variety of social and setting variables and alcohol consumption previously only suspected or assumed. Delineation of the precise nature of those relationships has been most helpful. And when behavioral researchers have disconfirmed other presumed relationships between environmental factors and consumption, that research has also been of importance, if only to impel non-behavioral investigators to redouble their efforts to sharpen their analytic tools to confirm what the behaviorists failed to confirm. Another strength of the behavioral approach to these issues has been its constant thrust to give experimental findings therapeutic significance, as when data on the topography of drinking serve as baseline data for behavioral efforts to modify excessive or uncontrolled drinking.

However, energetic development of behavioral approaches to alcoholism has also revealed problems with the approach. To begin with, while the analogue measures of drinking behavioral researchers have used bear some doubtless relationship outside the laboratory, the precise nature of that relationship remains uncertain. As a result, behavioral researchers do not know at this point whether the operant measures developed by Nathan, Mello, and Mendelson are more like real drinking than Marlatt's or Miller's taste-rating tasks, or whether, for that matter, either is superior to the ad lib measures other researchers have employed. Behavioral research on alcoholism has also confined itself almost entirely to the observables of the disorder. It is easy enough to observe the amount and kind of alcohol alcoholics consume in the laboratory as well as how they consume it; it is more difficult to identify and measure the complex of environmental, interpersonal, and psychological variables associated with that consumption. The imaginativeness which behavioral researchers have brought, albeit belatedly, to the latter effort is impressive, although the areas of potential import they have not yet explored, including complex functions like cognitions and social influence, is still sobering. But if there be any real doubt about the readiness of behavioral researchers to rush in where angels fear to tread, one can refer, for example, to work by Briddell, Wilson, and Lawson currently underway at the Alcohol Behavior Research Laboratory, Rutgers University, tracing relationships among alcohol ingestion, sexual arousal, and expectancy in both men and women. That the science of human behavior is, at long last, prepared to support such important research bodes well for the future.

The authors of this chapter are convinced that the limited purview which has characterized basic behavioral research into the topography, concomitants, and determinants of alcoholism to this time will expand even further as time passes. Certainly the ingenuity and creativity of the behavioral effort thus far holds that promise for the future.

ACKNOWLEDGMENT

Preparation of this chapter was aided by NIAAA Grant AA 00259-06 to Peter E. Nathan. The authors also wish to acknowledge the important role in the preparation of this manuscript played by Barbara Honig.

REFERENCES

Allman, L.R., Taylor, H.A., & Nathan, P.E. Group drinking during stress: Effects on drinking behavior, affect and psychopathology. *American Journal of Psychiatry*, 1972, *129*, 669-678.

Alterman, A.I., Gottheil, E., Skoloda, T.E., & Grasberger, J.C. Social modification of drinking in alcoholics. *Quarterly Journal of Studies on Alcohol*, 1974, *35*, 917-924.

Bennett, R.M., Buss, A., & Carpenter, J.A. Alcohol and human physical aggression. *Quarterly Journal of Studies on Alcohol*, 1969, *30*, 870-876.

Bigelow, G. *Experimental analysis of human drug self-administration.* Paper presented at the meeting of the Eastern Psychological Association, May 1973.

Bigelow, G., Liebson, I., & Griffiths, R.R. Alcoholic drinking: Suppression by a behavioral time-out procedure. *Behaviour Research and Therapy*, 1974, *12*, 107-115.

Boyatzis, R.E. The effect of alcohol consumption on the aggressive behavior of men. *Quarterly Journal of Studies on Alcohol*, 1974, *35*, 959-972.

Briddell, D.W., & Nathan, P.E. Behavior assessment and modification with alcoholics: Current status and future trends. In M. Hersen, R.M. Eisler, & P.M. Miller (Eds.), *Progress in behavior modification*(Vol.2). New York: Academic Press, in press.

Buss, A. *The psychology of aggression*. New York: John Wiley & Sons, 1961.

Carpenter, J., & Armenti, N. Some effects of ethanol on human sexual and aggressive behavior. In B. Kissin & H. Begleiter (Eds.), *The biology of alcohol* (Vol. 2). New York: Plenum Press, 1972.

Caudill, B.D., & Marlatt, G.A. Modeling influences in social drinking: An experimental analogue. *Journal of Consulting and Clinical Psychology*, in press.

Cohen, M., Liebson, I.A., Faillace, L.A., & Allen, R.P. Moderate drinking by chronic alcoholics. *Journal of Nervous and Mental disease*, 1971, *153*, 434-444.

Cutter, H.S.G., Schwab, E.L., Jr. & Nathan, P.E. Effects of alcohol on its utility for alcoholics. *Quarterly Journal of Studies on Alcohol*, 1970, *30*, 369-378.

Davies, D.L. Normal drinking by recovered alcohol addicts. *Quarterly Journal of Studies on Alcohol*, 1962, *23*, 94-104.

Docter, R.F., & Bernal, M.E. Immediate and prolonged psychophysiological effects of sustained alcohol intake in alcoholics. *Quarterly Journal of Studies on Alcohol*, 1964, *25*, 438-450.

Goldman, M.S., Taylor, H.A., Carruth, M.L., & Nathan, P.E. Effects of group decision-making on group drinking by alcoholics. *Quarterly Journal of Studies on Alcohol*, 1973, *34*, 807-822.

Gottheil, E., Corbett, L.O., Grasberger, J.C., & Cornelison, F.S., Jr. Fixed interval drinking decisions. I. A research and treatment model. *Quarterly Journal of Studies on Alcohol*, 1972, *33*, 311-324.

Gottheil, E., Crawford, H., & Cornelison, F.S. The alcoholic's ability to resist available alcohol. *Diseases of the Nervous System*, 1973, *34*, 80-84.

Gottheil, E., Murphy, B.F., Skoloda, T.E., & Corbett, L.O. Fixed interval drinking decisions. II. Drinking and discomfort in 25 alcoholics. *Quarterly Journal of Studies on Alcohol*, 1972, *33*, 325-340.

Gottschalk, L., & Gleser, G. *The measurement of psychological states through the content analysis of verbal behavior.* Berkeley: University of California Press, 1969.

Griffiths, R., Bigelow, G., & Liebson, I. Assessment of effects of ethanol self-administration on social interactions in alcoholics. *Psychopharmacologia*, 1974, *38*, 105-110. (a)

Griffiths, R., Bigelow, G., & Liebson, I. Suppression of ethanol self-administration in alcoholics by contingent time-out from social interactions. *Behaviour Research and Therapy*, 1974, *12*, 327-334. (b)

Hartocollis, P. Drunkenness and suggestion: An experiment with intravenous alcohol. *Quarterly Journal of Studies on Alcohol*, 1962, *23*, 376-389.

Higgins, R.L., & Marlatt, G.A. The effects of anxiety arousal upon the consumption of alcohol by alcoholics and social drinkers. *Journal of Consulting and Clinical Psychology*, 1973, *41*, 426-433.

Higgins, R.L., & Marlatt, G.A. Fear of interpersonal evaluation as a determinant of alcohol consumption in male social drinkers. *Journal of Abnormal Psychology*, in press.

Isbell, H., Fraser, H., Wikler, A., Belleville, R., & Eisenman, A. An experimental study of the etiology of "rum fits" and delirium tremens. *Quarterly Journal of Studies on Alcohol*, 1955, *16*, 1-16.

Jellinek, E.M. *The disease concept of alcoholism.* New Haven: Hillhouse Press, 1960.

Kalin, R., McCelland, D.C., & Kahn, M. The effects of male social drinking on fantasy. *Journal of Personality and Social Psychology*, 1965, *1*, 441-452.

Kessler, M., & Gomberg, C. Observations of barroom drinking: Methodology and preliminary results. *Quarterly Journal of Studies on Alcohol*, 1974, *35*, 1392-1396.

Lang, A.R., Goeckner, D.J., Adesso, V.J., & Marlatt, G.A. The effects of alcohol on aggression in male social drinkers. *Journal of Abnormal Psychology*, in press.

Ludwig, A.M., & Stark, L.H. Alcohol craving: Subjective and situational aspects. *Quarterly Journal of Studies on Alcohol*, 1974, *35*, 899-905.

Ludwig, A.M., & Wikler, A. "Craving" and relapse to drink. *Quarterly Journal of Studies on Alcohol*, 1974, *35*, 108-130.

Ludwig, A.M., Wikler, A., & Stark, L.H. The first drink: Psychobiological aspects of craving. *Archives of General Psychiatry*, 1974, *30*, 539-547.

Marlatt, G.A. Alcohol, stress, and cognitive control. In C.D. Spielberger & I.G. Sarason (Eds.), *Stress and anxiety* (Vol.3). New York: Hemisphere Publishing Co., in press.

Marlatt, G.A., Demming, B., & Reid, J.B. Loss of control drinking in alcoholics. An experimental analogue. *Journal of Abnormal Psychology*, 1973, *81*, 233-241.

Marlatt, G.A., Kosturn, C.F., & Lang, A.R. *Provocation to anger and opportunity for retaliation as determinants of alcohol consumption in social drinkers*. Paper presented at the meeting of the Western Psychological Association, April 1974.

Martorano, R.D. Mood and social perception in four alcoholics: Effects of alcohol consumption and assertive training. *Quarterly Journal of Studies on Alcohol*, 1974, *35*, 445-457.

McNamee, H.B., Mello, N.K., & Mendelson, J.H. Experimental analysis of drinking patterns of alcoholics. Concurrent psychiatric observations. *American Journal of Psychiatry*, 1968, *124*, 1063-1069.

Mello, N.K. Behavioral studies of alcoholism. In B. Kissin & H. Begleiter (Eds.), *The biology of alcoholism*. New York: Plenum Press, 1972.

Mello, N.K., McNamee, H.B., & Mendelson, J.H. Drinking patterns of chronic alcoholics: Gambling and motiviation for alcohol. In J.O. Cole (Ed.), *Clinical research in alcoholism*. Washington, D.C.: American Psychiatric Association, 1968.

Mello, N.K., & Mendelson, J.H. The effects of prolonged alcohol ingestion on the eating, drinking, and smoking patterns of chronic alcoholics. In W.A. Hunt (Ed.), *Learning mechanisms in smoking*. Chicago: Aldine Press, 1970.

Mello, N.K., & Mendelson, J.H. A quantitative analysis of drinking patterns in alcoholics. *Archives of General Psychiatry*, 1971, *6*, 527-539.

Mello, N.K., & Mendelson, J.H. Drinking patterns during work-contingent and noncontingent alcohol acquisition. *Psychosomatic Medicine*, 1972, *34*, 139-164.

Mendelson, J.H. (Ed.) Experimentally induced chronic intoxication and withdrawal in alcoholics. *Quarterly Journal of Studies on Alcohol*, 1964, *Suppl. No. 2*, 1-29.

Mendelson, J.H., Mello, N.K., & Solomon, P. Small group drinking behavior: An experimental study of chronic alcoholics. In A. Wikler (Ed.), *The addictive states*. Baltimore: Williams & Wilkins (Vol.46, Res. Publ. Assoc. Nerv. Ment. Dis.), 1968.

Merry, J. The "loss of control" myth. *Lancet*, 1966, *1*, 1267-1268.

Miller, P.M. *Behavioral treatment of alcoholism*. New York: Pergamon Press, in press.

Miller, P.M., Hersen, M., Eisler, R.M., & Hilsman, G. Effects of social stress on operant drinking of alcoholics and social drinkers. *Behaviour Research and Therapy*, 1974, *12*, 67-72.

Nathan, P.E. Alcoholism. In H. Leitenberg (Ed.), *Handbook of behavior modification and behavior therapy*. Englewood Cliffs, N.J.: Prentice-Hall, in press.

Nathan, P.E., & Briddell, D.W. Behavioral assessment and treatment of alcoholism. In B. Kissin & H. Begleiter (Eds.), *The biology of alcoholism* (Vol. 5). New York: Plenum Press, in press.

Nathan, P.E., Goldman, M.S., Lisman, S.A., & Taylor, H.A. Alcohol and alcoholics: A behavioral approach. *Transactions of the New York Academy of Sciences*, 1972, *34*, 602-627.

Nathan, P.E. & O'Brien, J.S. An experimental analysis of the behavior of alcoholics and nonalcoholics during prolonged experimental drinking: A necessary precursor of behavior therapy? *Behavior Therapy*, 1971, *2*, 455-476.

Nathan, P.E., O'Brien, J.S., & Lowenstein, L.M. Operant studies of chronic alcoholism: Interaction of alcohol and alcoholics. In M.K. Roach, W.M. McIsaac, & P.J. Creaven (Eds.), *Biological aspects of alcohol*. Austin: University of Texas Press, 1971.

Nathan, P.E., Titler, N.A., Lowenstein, L.M., Solomon, P., & Rossi, A.M. Behavioral analysis of chronic alcoholism. *Archives of General Psychiatry*, 1970, *22*, 419-430.

Nathan, P.E., Zare, N.C., Ferneau, E.W., & Lowenstein, L.M. Effects of congener differences in alcoholic beverages on the behavior of alcoholics. *Quarterly Journal of Studies on Alcohol*, 1970, *Suppl. No. 5*, 87-100.

Pattison, E.M. A critique of abstinence criteria in the treatment of alcoholism. *International Journal of Social Psychiatry*, 1968, *14*, 268-276.

Pattison, E.M., Headley, E.B., Gleser, G.C., & Gottschalk, L.A. Abstinence and normal drinking: An assessment of changes in drinking patterns in alcoholics after treatment. *Quarterly Journal of Studies on Alcohol*, 1968, *29*, 610-633.

Reid, J.B. Workshop at Conference on Behavioral Approaches to Alcoholism and Drug Dependencies. University of Washington, 1975.

Schaefer, H.H., Sobell, M.B., & Mills, K.C. Baseline drinking behavior in alcoholics and social drinkers: Kinds of drinks and sip magnitude. *Behaviour Research and Therapy*, 1971, *9*, 23-27.

Shuntich, R., & Taylor, S. The effects of alcohol on human physical aggression. *Journal of Experimental Research in Personality*, 1972, *6*, 34-38.

Skoloda, T.E., Alterman, A.I., Cornelison, F.S., & Gottheil, E. Treatment outcome in a drinking-decisions program. *Journal of Studies on Alcohol*, 1975, *36*, 365-380.

Smith, R., Parker, E., & Noble, E. Alcohol and affect in dyadic social interaction. *Psychosomatic Medicine*, 1975, *37*, 25-40.

Sobell, M.B., Schaefer, H.H., & Mills, K.C. Differences in baseline drinking behavior between alcoholics and normal drinkers. *Behaviour Research and Therapy*, 1972,*10*, 257-267.

Steffen, J.J., Nathan, P.E., & Taylor, H.A. Tension-reducing effects of alcohol: Further evidence and some methodological considerations. *Journal of Abnormal Psychology*, 1974, *83*, 542-547.

Steinglass, P., Weiner, S., & Mendelson, J.H. A systems approach to alcoholism: A model and its clinical application. *Archives of General Psychiatry*, 1971, *24*, 401-422.

Takala, M., Pinkanen, J.A., & Markanen, T. *The effects of distilled and brewed beverages. A physiological, neurological, and psychological study*. Helsinki: The Finnish Foundation for Alcohol Studies, 1957.

Talland, G.A., & Kasschau, R. Practice and alcohol effects on motor skill and attention: A supplementary report on an experiment in chronic intoxication and withdrawal. *Quarterly Journal of Studies on Alcohol*, 1965, *26*, 393-401.

Talland, G.A., Mendelson, J.H., & Ryack, P. Tests of motor skills. In J.H. Mendelson (Ed.), Experimentally induced chronic intoxication and withdrawal in alcoholics. *Quarterly Journal of Studies on Alcohol*, 1964, *Suppl. No. 2*, 53-73.

Taylor, S., & Gammon, C. The effects of type and dose of alcohol on human aggression. *Journal of Personality and Social Psychology*, 1975, *32*, 169-175.

Thornton, C.C., Alterman, A.I., Skoloda, T.E., & Gottheil, E. Drinking and sccializing in "introverted" and "extraverted" alcoholics. Paper presented at the National Council on Alcoholism convention, April 1975.

Tracey, D.A., & Nathan, P.E. Behavioral analysis of chronic alcoholism in four women. *Journal of Consulting and Clinical Psychology*, in press.

Vannicelli, M. Mood and self-perception of alcoholics when sober and intoxicated. *Quarterly Journal of Studies on Alcohol*, 1972, *33*, 341-357.

Weiner, S., Tamerin, J.S., Steinglass, P., & Mendelson, J.H. Familial patterns in chronic alcoholism: A study of a father and son during experimental intoxication. *American Journal of Psychiatry*, 1971, *127*, 1646-1658.

Williams, R.J. Alcoholics and metabolism. *Scientific American*, 1948, *179*, 50-53.

Williams, T.K. *The ethanol-induced loss of control concept in alcoholism*. Doctoral dissertation. Western Michigan University, 1970.

Zwerling, I. Psychiatric findings in an interdisciplinary study of forty-six alcoholic patients. *Quarterly Journal of Studies on Alcohol*, 1959, *20*, 543-554.

CHAPTER 14

EPIDEMIOLOGICAL AND SOCIAL FACTORS ASSOCIATED WITH DRINKING PROBLEMS

Don Cahalan
Ira H. Cisin

Although the key word in the title of this book is "alcoholism," it is difficult, if not impossible, to find a definition of alcoholism that is sufficiently operational to use in any precise description of the factors associated with it in real life. For reasons given below, we find we can deal only with drinking problems -- always specifying which problem or problems -- rather than alcoholism as a viable entity.

It is no accident that issues surrounding the definition of alcoholism and its etiology have become charged with emotionalism and misunderstanding among representatives of the various disciplines or territorial enclaves in this field. Some of these problems of definition are discussed elsewhere in this book, by Davies, Tarter, Nathan, and others, and hence will not be dealt with in any detail here. It is essential, however, in order to understand the workings of epidemiological

Ralph E. Tarter and A. Arthur Sugerman (eds.), Alcoholism

ISBN: 0-201-08146-6
ISBN: 0-201-08145-8 (pbk.)

and social factors related to drinking behavior, briefly to discuss how problems of definition and perceptions of alcoholism have very real consequences on the research questions one would pose as being crucial in this field, as well as in issues of policy on how alcoholism is to be treated, prevented, or minimized.

DIFFERENCES IN PERSPECTIVES AMONG VARIOUS INTERESTED GROUPS

Confusion and misunderstanding over definitions of alcoholism and their implications have been inevitable, considering the widely divergent interests of the various disciplines or action groups in this field. In fact, as Christie and Bruun (1969) have observed, a good deal of the lack of precision in definitions is highly functional because vagueness and "fat words" in relation to alcoholism help to smooth over the inevitable conflicts of interests and values. For alcoholism is unique in its serving as a focal point for widely divergent philosophies and specialization of interests, being perceived variously as a disease, a bad habit or moral problem, or a problem rooted in dislocations in society (Siegler, Osmund, & Newell, 1968). Because drinking is so prevalent in society and because the effects of alcohol long have been both eagerly sought by so many and abhorred by so many, it is little wonder that beverage alcohol and its attendant problems when overused have become the focus of conflict among the various interest groups that have evolved since prehistoric times to define and to cope with human problems.

Like the blind men whose elephant assumed different shapes depending upon what part of it they groped at, various disciplines and action groups perceive alcoholism differently, depending upon their training and self-interest. Perhaps these differences in perceptions would be merely academic in consequence were it not that the various differences are directly related to wide differences in emphasis in etiology and particularly in treatment and prevention efforts.

Some clinical practitioners' experiences have led them to see alcoholism as a relatively hopeless condition (Robinson & Podnos, 1966). If the physician sees as patients primarily the more advanced alcoholics, he will tend to be pessimistic as to prognosis, treating the more obvious physical damage as best he can and releasing the detoxified patient as soon as he is ambulatory. Since many physicians are far too busy with a steady stream of patients to concentrate upon the aftercare of the alcoholic, and since specializing in treating alcoholics can give one's practice a bad name, it is small wonder the average physician cannot be expected to do much to contribute to the full recovery of the chronic alcoholic. The general practitioner's or internist's general role is to provide emergency care, and we should not expect him to do much more for the alcoholic.

Thus many physicians perceive alcoholism as a progressive and well-nigh incurable disease because of the types of alcoholics who come or are brought to their doors, and because the medical profession has very high prestige in our society, this perception of alcoholism has been widely adopted by the rest of society.

Perception of alcoholism as a rather far-advanced and debilitating disease is reinforced by Alcoholics Anonymous, who found a generation ago that the positioning of alcoholism as a disease helped dramatically both in getting the alcoholic decent treatment as being ill rather than merely weak-willed and in reinforcing the alcoholic's determination to abstain altogether from alcohol in order to avoid the consequences of an allergy or a physiological deficiency like diabetes. The physician and A.A. tend to enjoy a mutually useful relationship. The physician ordinarily does not know what to advise the alcoholic patient to do in the way of long-term rehabilitation that would be better than joining A.A., which has had an excellent record in helping probably many more alcoholics than any other single agency. Also, A.A. benefits through sharing the prestige of the medical profession in according to the alcoholic the modicum of hope and human self-esteem that he needs in order to try to improve his condition.

Despite the helpful association between the medical profession and A.A. in providing emergency treatment and after-care for advanced alcoholics, however, neither the average physician nor the average A.A. adherent has sufficient motivation or resources to emphasize the importance of preventive or early-identification efforts to reduce the number of persons graduating yearly into full-blown alcoholism. Part of the reason for this is that both the physician and the A.A. member are so preoccupied with the job of coping with the alcoholic's immediate problems that they have little time or resources to work on long-term prevention. Also, the medical tendency toward Aristotelian either/or differential diagnosis of individuals as either clearly alcoholic or nonalcoholic fits very neatly with the A.A. ideology of "once an alcoholic, always an alcoholic."

Psychiatrists or clinical psychologists are unable to

do much for the average chronic alcoholic because they have neither the time nor resources to provide individual therapy. Thus many of them find it convenient to turn over much of the increasingly popular group therapy treatments to A.A. members and staff social workers, who rarely have sufficient resources to do an adequate job of follow-up support for the alcoholic on an outpatient basis. In any case, the medically and morally-oriented concentration upon the individual as the locus of the problem on the part of psychiatrists and clinical psychologists de-emphasizes the importance of early preventive efforts, which tend to stress environmental factors with which the clinician is not ordinarily knowledgeable or equipped to cope.

To summarize: we see a community of interest on the part of many groups to put a heavy emphasis upon alcoholism as a chronic, progressive disease. These include (for reasons stated above) many general practitioners, psychiatrists, clinical psychologists, and social welfare program planners.

Also, the administrators responsible for allocation of resources are under so many fiscal pressures from competitive social or welfare programs that they seldom can do even an adequate job of providing emergency care for critically ill or intoxicated chronic alcoholics, much less having the hardihood to put more of the public's tax dollars into preventive or early-identification programs. Thus, prevention always gets short shrift because it is harder to justify long-term prevention efforts than short-term treatment efforts even though it is obvious from the available research that heavy drinking behavior which might have been prevented at an early age almost certainly will turn into chronic alcohol problems if unchecked for twenty years: the weight of the evidence is that chronic alcoholics are made, not born.

DIFFERENCES IN CLINICAL AND GENERAL-POPULATION RESEARCH PERSPECTIVES

Relatively few well-controlled longitudinal studies of clinically-defined alcoholics are available for comparison with recent general-population studies of changes in drinking behavior and problems over time (for clinical studies, see especially Emrick, 1975; and Schuckit & Cahalan, in press; and for general-population studies, see Cahalan, 1970; Cahalan & Roizen, 1974; Cahalan & Room, 1974; Clark & Cahalen, 1973). This difference is inevitable in view of the fact that the clinically-defined alcoholic is more likely to be the one who finally shows up at (or is brought to) the clinic because he has exhausted all other resources. The clinical alcoholic is demonstrably more likely to have accumulated fewer assets and more health and social liabilities than the noninstitutionalized heavy drinker who is still at large in the general population. Thus it is inevitable that the clinician's experience with alcoholics will give him a different perspective from that of the behavioral scientist who conducts surveys of the general population (Bacon, 1962; Cisin, 1963). The clinician tends to see society's failures and to see them repeatedly if they are chronic alcoholics; he does not see those who solve their problems without ever showing up in clinics. The selective process that determines who will show up in clinics almost inevitably leads to a perception of the alcoholic as being possessed of a rather distinct disease syndrome in which the sufferer has a host of physical and mental symptoms.

The alcohol studies of the behavioral scientists also have their limitations. While general-population sampling studies of drinking behavior and alcohol-related problems can provide rather accurate estimates of the incidence and prevalence of various alcohol-related behavior, and while the behavioral scientist dealing with large samples has available a greater range of multivariate techniques than the clinician in assessing the correlates of drinking behavior, the general-population survey is often lacking in depth and in certain types of detailed information (e.g., an interviewer cannot conduct a thorough physical examination in conjunction with a household survey). There is a general need for studies in which the skills and resources of the clinician are combined with those of the survey specialist, in which both general-population and clinic samples are interviewed, and in which detailed medical histories are gathered. Until such studies are conducted, it will be very difficult to determine the differences between clinic alcoholics and heavy drinkers in the general population: are the clinic alcoholics largely self-selected by factors which might have little relation to consumption of alcohol? Are the motivations of the two groups toward self-improvement the same or different? To what extent does the non-clinic heavy drinker possess more effective social and economic supports? Parallel studies of clinic alcoholics and non-clinic problem drinkers are vitally needed in order to give us insights into improvements in treatment and prevention programs so that we can get away from the largely hopeless revolving-door experience that results from our society's sobering up the chronic alcoholic and turning him loose within a couple of days without being able to do much to insure that he will not return to the clinic again and again.

We believe that some common ground can be negotiated between epidemiologists and other behavioral scientists in bringing about research programs that are integrated with clinical observations because the epidemiologist (whose charter consists of dealing with the incidence, distribution, and control of disease within populations) enjoys at least an uneasy acceptance by both the clinical and the social-scientist camps. We have seen at first hand violent disagreements between classical disease-oriented epidemiologists and sociologists about issues of prevention of alcoholism, in which a few epidemiologists say that the only viable approach to prevention is to reinstitute prohibition (in the same fashion as preventing cholera by taking the handle off the Broad Street pump) and that the social scientists are either mollycoddling liberals or are unduly influenced by the liquor industry when they protest that prohibition has not worked. However, epidemiologists can share common ground with other behavioral scientists on at least a limited range of studies in which the classical skills and perspectives of the epidemiologist are most at home, such as in studies of relative mortality rates in longitudinal surveys of heavy drinkers and others, in which behavior and attitudes at one time are related to later outcomes (Room & Day, 1974). The following discussions of findings from surveys of drinking practices and drinking problems illustrate the usefulness of many epidemiological concepts in relation to drinking behavior, especially as concerns longitudinal studies in which the temporal sequences of various phenomena are analyzed in a search for possible causal relationships.

SUMMARY OF GENERAL-POPULATION STUDIES OF DRINKING BEHAVIOR AND DRINKING PROBLEMS

The program of community and national sampling surveys that we are now completing has had three general phases: first, an emphasis upon description of drinking practices and related attitudes (Cahalan, Cisin, & Crossley, 1969; Cisin, 1963; Knupfer, Fink, Clark, & Goffman, 1963); second, a concentration upon description of specific problems related to drinking (Cahalan, 1970; Cahalan & Room, 1974; Clark, 1966; and Knupfer, 1967); and finally, analysis of longitudinal data on drinking behavior, attitudes, and problems as measured by two or more interviews with the same individuals conducted over a span of a number of years (Cahalan & Roizen, 1974; Clark & Cahalan, 1973).[1]

The findings of these studies are summarized below. All of these community and national surveys have been conducted with strictly controlled probability (scientifically randomized) samplings of the general population aged 21 and older, attaining high completion rates, thus permitting (within the limits of sampling error) projection of the findings against the total population from which the samples

---

[1] These studies, which have been supported by grants from the National Institute of Alcohol Abuse and Alcoholism and its predecessors, were begun in 1959 in the California State Department of Public Health under the direction of Wendell Lipscomb, Ira H. Cisin, and Genevieve Knupfer, were continued through parallel national and community studies directed by Cisin and Knupfer at The George Washington University and the State Department of Public Health, respectively, and are being completed under the direction of Don Cahalan and the staff of the Social Research Group, School of Public Health, University of California, Berkeley.

were drawn.

DRINKING BEHAVIOR AND RELATED PUBLIC ATTITUDES

The findings of our early national surveys, as well as those of other writers (Bacon, 1962; Gusfield, 1962; Keller, 1971) and other reporters of survey findings (Haberman & Sheinberg, 1969; Mulford & Miller, 1961; and especially Harris & Associates, 1971) are very consistent in reflecting the conflict in values between groups--and even within individuals--concerning drinking. Much ambivalence and confusion has been found by various writers concerning whether alcoholism is an illness or a moral or social problem, whether alcohol does more harm than good, and what might be done to reduce alcohol problems. The 1971 Harris & Associates survey also found that a large proportion of U.S. adults were very poorly informed about the effects of alcohol and how to cope with overdoses. The general state of ill-informed knowledge and ambivalent attitudes about drinking in our national surveys (reported below) are completely congruent with our national heritage of the classical clash between the Protestant ethic and modern-day shifts toward a hedonistic ethic.

Our first national survey found that most adults (68%) drank at least once a year--77% of the males and 60% of the females (Cahalan, Cisin, & Crossley, 1969). Of the total adults 12% were classified as heavy drinkers in terms of a rather arbitrary definition (ranging from those who drank three or more times per day, to those who drank only two or three times a month but usually consumed five or more drinks per occasion). While this 1964-1965 survey found the adult population quite evenly divided between the 47% who did not drink as often as once a month and the 54% who drank once a month or more, there is later evidence that the proportion of drinkers is increasing (Cahalan & Cisin, in press). More recent surveys by Harris also indicate that drinking is on the increase in recent years, particularly on the part of women and young persons. As with the surveys of others, our national surveys have shown vastly different patterns of drinking among various sub-groups: among those who drink at all, the highest proportion of heavy drinkers was found among men in their 40's, those of lower social status, those living in larger cities and in the Middle Atlantic, New England, and Pacific regions, and those of Irish or British or Latin American backgrounds (see Figure 1). However, the groups with the highest proportions drinking at least occasionally were not found necessarily to be those with the highest proportions of heavy drinkers, e.g., while Jews and Episcopalians had the highest proportions of drinkers of any religious groups, they also had extremely low rates of heavy or problem drinkers among those who drank.

Abstainers (those drinking not at all or less often than once a year) were found more likely than others to be older persons, of below-average income, from the South or rural areas, of native-born parentage, and from conservative or fundamentalist Protestant denominations.

As to attitudes toward drinking, even though at-least-occasional drinking was found to be the norm, and while relatively few (9%) of all drinkers said they worried at all about their own drinking, a strong ambivalence toward alcohol is reflected in the finding that 75% of all respondents (and a majority of even male heavy drinkers) said they thought "drinking does more harm than good." Alcohol appeared to be

Most Likely to be Drinkers:	Among Drinkers, Most Likely to be Heavy Drinkers:
Men under 45 years	Men aged 45-49
Men and women of higher social status	Those of lower social status
Professional, business, and other white collar workers	Operatives; service workers
College graduates	Men who completed high school but not college
Single men	Single, divorced, or separated men and women
Residents of the Middle Atlantic, New England, East North Central, and Pacific areas	Residents of Middle Atlantic, New England, and Pacific areas
Residents of surburban cities, towns	Residents of largest cities
Those whose fathers were born in Ireland or Italy (age-adjusted findings)	Fathers were born in Ireland, Latin America, the Caribbean, or the United Kingdom (age-adjusted)
Jews, Episcopalians	Protestants of no specific denomination, Catholics, those without religious affiliation

Figure 1. Summary of National Survey of 2,746 Adults, 1964-65

a greater threat to those of lower economic and social status, perhaps because those of lower status are generally more vulnerable than others.

The cooperation and interest of respondents in this first national probability sample on drinking practices lent encouragement for us to proceed with more intensive inquiries into the details of people's drinking problems. The results of this next series of studies are summarized below.

NATIONAL SURVEYS OF DRINKING PROBLEMS

At this writing, we have completed four nationwide surveys on the prevalence of specific drinking problems. The first was a follow-up in 1967 of a subsample of 1,359 of the respondents in the 1964-65 survey of drinking practices described above; the findings have been reported in Cahalan (1970). The second survey on drinking problems was conducted in 1969 with a sample of 978 men in the high-risk group, aged 21-59, and was reported on in detail in Cahalan and Room (1974). In the third national study of drinking problems 725 from the special sample of young men obtained in the second survey were reinterviewed in 1973 in order to measure changes in drinking behavior and problems over a four-year span; the preliminary results of this study are reported in Cahalan and Roizen (1974). An additional national follow-up study was conducted in 1974 among 900 men and women who were initially interviewed in the 1964-65 survey and again in the 1967 survey; the data from this three-wave study have not as yet been reported. Here we will summarize the single-time measures of drinking problems from 1967 and 1969 surveys, leaving the measures of changes in drinking behavior and problems to be discussed in a later section of this chapter.

All these studies of drinking problems consistently emphasize that what is being measured is the prevalence of specific types of problems (or potential problems) associated with the use of alcohol rather than variants of alcoholism, however defined. We followed Plaut's (1967) definition, "Problem drinking is a *repetitive use of beverage alcohol causing physical, psychological, or social harm to the drinker or to others*" (pp. 37-38), which is consistent with Knupfer's (1967) more general definition that "a problem--any problem--connected fairly closely with drinking constitutes a drinking problem" (p.974).

The national drinking-problem surveys we have conducted have been patterned rather closely after the 1964 San Francisco survey conducted by Knupfer and her colleagues (Clark, 1966; Knupfer, 1967), with whom we have collaborated closely over many years. As with Knupfer's 1964 survey, our national surveys of drinking problems have taken into account the following two factors in scoring survey responses into one or more of a dozen specific types of problems or potential problems: (a) the severity of problems in terms of the frequency and degree to which the problem is applicable (e.g., the number of times the respondent has had trouble with police over his drinking); and (b) the currency of each problem (or potential problem) in terms of whether it has occurred during the last three years or prior to that time.

The types of problems or potential problems in the 1967 national survey are as follows:

1. *Frequent intoxication*: a high score on this potential problem is attained by drinking a maximum of five

or more drinks at least once a week; or eight or more on one of the most recent two drinking occasions and twice during the last year; or currently getting high or tight at least once a week.

2. *Binge drinking*: this potential problem is defined in this analysis as being intoxicated for at least several days at a time or for two days on more than one occasion.

3. *Symptomatic drinking*: this potential problem refers to signs of Jellinek's "Gamma alcoholism" (1960, p.37), consisting of signs of physical dependence and loss of control (e.g., drinking to get rid of a hangover, having difficulty in stopping drinking, having blackouts or lapses of memory, skipping meals while on drinking bouts, drinking very rapidly for quicker effect, or sneaking drinks). Positive responses on three or more of seven items are required to qualify respondents for a high score.

4. *Psychological dependence*: this potential problem includes drinking to relieve depression or nervousness or to escape from problems of everyday living. A high score is attained if one rated at least one of five psychological effects of alcohol as being "very helpful" or "very important," plus two others as "fairly helpful" or "fairly important."

5. *Problems with spouse or relatives*: includes the spouse's leaving or threatening to leave the respondent or being concerned over his drinking, or the spouse's or relative's asking the respondent to cut down on his drinking, or the respondent's judging his drinking as having had a harmful effect on his home life. (Respondents are rated as having higher scores on this problem if the spouse is reported as angry or threatening to leave over the respondent's drinking, or any two of the following: spouse expressed concern, spouse

or relative said respondent should cut down, or respondent rated drinking as harmful to his marriage or home life).

6. *Problems with friends or neighbors*: a high score includes two or more of the following: friends indicated respondent should cut down on drinking, neighbors so indicated, or respondent felt his drinking had had a harmful effect on his friendships and social life.

7. *Job problems*: a high score consists of any one of the following: having lost a job or nearly lost one because of drinking, having people at work suggest he cut down on drinking, or rating drinking as harmful to one's work and employment opportunities.

8. *Problems with law, police, accidents*: a high score consists of having had trouble with the police over driving after drinking or over other drinking, or having had his drinking contribute to a personal-injury accident.

9. *Health*: a high score is based on reporting both that drinking had been harmful to the respondent's health and that a physician had advised him to cut down.

10. *Financial problems*: a high score is applicable when the respondent perceived his drinking as having had a harmful effect on his finances and also when he felt he was spending too much money on drinking.

11. *Belligerence associated with drinking*: (feeling aggressive or cross after drinking, or getting into a fight or heated argument): This was included as a potential problem in order later to test the hypothesis that belligerence may often be followed by later increase in interpersonal problems.

Table 1 presents a summary of the prevalence of each of the above types of actual or potential problems in terms of occurrence during the last three years. At the

TABLE 1

Prevalence of Drinking-Related Problems Over Three Years, by Sex
(1967 survey - in percentages)

Type of Problem	MEN (N = 751) Extent of Problem			WOMEN (N = 608) Extent of Problem		
	None	Moderate[a]	High	None	Moderate[a]	High
1. Index of frequent intoxication[b]	83	3	14	97	1	2
2. Binge drinking	97	-	3	100	-	*
3. Symptomatic drinking[c]	84	8	8	93	4	3
4. Psychological dependence	61	31	8	85	12	3
5. Problems with current spouse or relatives	84	8	8	96	3	1
6. Problems with friends or neighbors	93	5	2	97	3	*
7. Job problems	94	3	3	98	2	1
8. Problems with police or accidents	99	-	1	99	-	1
9. Health[d]	88	6	6	93	4	4
10. Financial problems	91	6	3	98	2	1
11. Belligerence associated with drinking	88	8	4	93	5	3
Current Overall Problems Score, combining results for the 11 specific problems, (High score: 7+ of a maximum of 58)	57	28	15	79	17	4

Note. From Table 1, Cahalan, 1970.

a Moderate: less than High (for definitions, see Cahalan, 1970, Chapter II).

b Components: frequency and amount-per-occasion, and frequency of getting high or tight.

c Positive responses to such items as difficulty stopping drinking, blackouts, sneaking drinks.

d Physician told respondent to cut down drinking.

* Less than .5%.

bottom of the table appears a Current Overall Problems Score, in which each type of problem is given equal weight for health, financial, and belligerence problems (which were given a lesser weight not because they are unimportant but because we had limited information on them). A high overall current problems score of seven or more points could be attained only by having problems in two or more areas, of which one would be rated as being in severe form; or problems in three or more areas, of which at least two were at least moderate in severity; moderate to severe problems in five or more areas; or slight problems in seven or more areas. (For details of scoring, see Cahalan, 1970, Chapter III.)

The most frequent specific problems for men shown in Table 1 were frequent intoxication, symptomatic drinking, psychological dependence, and problems with one's spouse or relatives. The only problem among women which attained a level as high as 4% was health problems. With an arbitrarily selected cutting point, 15% of the men and 4% of the women, or 9% of the total, were classified as achieving a high current problems score.

Although the selection of an arbitrary cutting point is essential in this kind of research for the study of relationships and for simplicity of communication, examples of the misuse and misinterpretation of such cutting points are legion. In this particular case, the arbitrarily selected cutting point was used in official governmental reports as the basis for estimating the proportion of *alcoholics* in the adult population as 9,000,000 (Keller, 1971), even though we made clear (Cahalan, 1970), that the proportion to be considered *problem drinkers* is entirely dependent upon where one cuts the continuum of scores. Table 1 clearly shows that depending on the cutting point, one can picture the adult population as having a high rate of problem drinking (since 43% of the men, 21% of the women, and 31% of the total reported having had some degree of one or more of the problems during the preceding 3 years) or as having a relatively low rate (almost 6 out of 10 of the men and 8 out of 10 of the women reported having none of the actual or potential problems at any time during the last 3 years.) Other cutting points obviously would give different impressions of the prevalence of problems.

Many respondents have more than one problem: except for those who reported alcohol-related health problems, a majority of those with any given problem had one or more of the 10 other actual or potential drinking problems. For example, problems with friends and neighbors in most instances were accompanied by frequent intoxication, symptomatic drinking, or problems with spouse or friends; in other words, by the time that friends or neighbors are driven to showing an individual they disapprove of his drinking, the person usually will have accumulated problems in several other areas of his life.

DRINKING PROBLEMS AMONG MEN 21-59. When we combine the data from the 1967 and 1969 surveys to yield a larger total of 1,561 men in this high-risk group, we see (Table 2) that all of these types of drinking problems are most prevalent among the men in the youngest age group, and that the percentage with a high Current Overall Problems Score among men aged 21-24 is almost twice as high (40%) as it is for any of the older men.

TABLE 2

Higher Severity Level for Specific Current Problems by Eight Age Groups (combined 1967-69 surveys)

	21-24 (147) %	25-29 (204) %	30-34 (186) %	35-39 (216) %	40-44 (226) %	45-49 (201) %	50-54 (199) %	55-59 (182) %	Total (1561) %
1. Heavy intake	7	7	5	7	6	3	5	6	6
2. Binge drinking	10	3	3	3	1	2	4	2	3
3. Psychological dependence	5	4	4	4	4	5	4	3	4
4. Loss of control	12	5	4	5	7	5	4	4	6
5. Symptomatic drinking	26	11	8	7	6	10	9	3	9
6. Belligerence	15	12	10	8	7	8	6	2	8
7. Problems with wife	19	17	15	10	9	9	11	6	12
8. Problems with friends or neighbors	15	5	7	5	4	4	6	4	6
9. Problems on job	10	4	3	5	5	5	6	2	5
10. Police problems	10	4	2	2	2	2	4	1	3
11. Health or injuries from drinking	8	4	5	6	4	6	8	6	6
12. Finances	11	4	6	4	3	2	4	3	4
13. Current Overall Problems Score 7+	40	22	20	21	17	17	17	11	20

Note. [a]From Table 7, Cahalan and Room, 1974. As noted therein, scorings of problems differed slightly from those in Table 1.

This pronounced age trend, showing heavy rates of drinking problems among the younger men and relatively smaller rates among the older men, is borne out by separate studies conducted within the Army and Navy under the direction of the present authors (Cahalan & Cisin, 1975, Cahalan, Cisin, Gardner, & Smith, 1972). As shown in Table 3, the younger enlisted men had dramatically higher levels of problems than the older enlisted men; the same trend was true among male Army officers. In this analysis, the summary statistic is a High Consequence Score based on interpersonal, health, or financial problems of some severity which were measured comparably in all the studies (see Cahalan & Room, 1974, for details of scoring).

These findings by age groups provide interesting perspectives in addition to the revelation that the highest rate of problem drinking is among men under 25 years of age instead of in the fortyish age group in which the average clinical alcoholic is found. Findings from longitudinal studies (Cahalan & Roizen, 1974) indicate a great turnover or change in problem-drinking status over time. This is evidenced by the finding that only two-thirds of the men aged 21-59 who report ever having had a problem of any severity also report having had a current problem (during the last three years) (Cahalan & Room, 1974). The initial study on drinking problems also found that a substantial proportion changed their problem drinking status over a three-year period (Cahalan, 1970). The same findings have emerged from our more detailed latest studies on changes in drinking practices, reported below. Such findings cast serious doubt on the usefulness of the characterization of drinking careers in terms of a relatively irreversible progressive deterioration

TABLE 3

Current Problem Drinkers (High Consequences Score for Last Three Years)[a] by Age

	Civilians 1969 Surv.		Naval Officers		Army Officers		Naval Enlisted		Army Enlisted	
	(n)	%	*(n)*	%	*(n)*	%	*(n)*	%	*(n)*	%
Age Group:										
17-20	-	-	(3)	#	(6)	#	(788)	46	(1007)	53
21-24	(130)	34	(368)	16	(709)	21	(1167)	43	(1942)	42
25-29	(117)	17	(1095)	18	(1048)	16	(624)	32	(898)	37
30-34	(122)	19	(733)	18	(832)	19	(523)	30	(625)	30
35-39	(124)	15	(686)	19	(681)	16	(457)	29	(573)	26
40-44	(133)	18	(569)	21	(408)	14	(116)	24	(316)	25
45-49	(114)	13	(230)	22	(130)	12	(31)	10	(81)	20
50-Up	(238)	16	(73)	8	(130)	12	(6)	#	(43)	7

Note. Sources: Cahalan and Cisin, Note 5, Navy report, tables as indicated.
Cahalan, Cisin, Gardiner, and Smith, Note 6, ICI Army Report, tables as indicated.
Civilian 1969 National 3 survey, conducted by Social Research Group. (Unlike Tables 2 and 4-7, data here exclude the 1967 results because the 1969 survey is more comparable in time to the 1972 and 1974 Army and Navy surveys.)

[a]High Consequences Score: interpersonal, health or financial problems of some severity (see Cahalan and Room, 1974, Chapter 4).

#Too few interviews for reliable percentages.

since it will be shown that a large proportion of those who show relatively severe signs of drinking problems at one point in time will be found several years later to show a material remission of such problems. These age-trend findings, in addition to the retrospective reports of heavy drinkers about their early drinking behavior revealed in our first national survey (Cahalan, Cisin, & Crossley, 1969), clearly indicate that many of the problem drinkers in their forties formed their drinking and drinking-problem habits 20 or more years earlier.

SOCIO-ECONOMIC STATUS. It was noted earlier that persons of lower status have a higher proportion of abstainers than among those of higher status. It was also found that those of lower status who do drink tend to be heavier drinkers than other persons (Cahalan, Cisin, & Crossley, 1969, Table 3). Consistent with this, a larger share of those of lower status also tend to have drinking problems, particularly interpersonal problems related to their drinking. As shown in Table 4, which presents findings on men aged 21-59 in terms of a five-category typology of drinking problems, it is found that those of lowest status have a higher absolute rate of drinking problems. Further, if one inspects the relationship between Consequences of Drinking and Heavy or Binge Drinking, it is seen that the poor have a relatively higher ratio of consequences in relation to the heaviness of their drinking. In other words, more of the poor than of the well-to-do get into difficulty over their drinking, whether or not they drink heavily.

TABLE 4

Current Problems Typology for Four Social Position Groups, Men Aged 21-59 (Combined 1967 and 1969 surveys - in percentages)

	(n)	Non-drinker[a]	Drank, no problems[b]	Potential problems only[c]	Heavy intake or binge: No consequences[d]	High Consequences Score 3+[e]
Lowest Social Position	(281)	19	22	19	14	26
Lower Middle	(411)	17	38	19	10	17
Upper Middle	(401)	14	39	24	15	8
Highest Social Position	(468)	11	47	22	11	9
Total	(1561)	15	38	21	12	14

Note. From Cahalan and Room, 1974, Table.

[a]Non-drinkers: did not drink during last three years.

[b]Drank, no problem: has been a drinker within the last three years, but not in any of the above groups.

[c]Potential problems only: not in the above groups, but a problem of at least minimal severity in any problem area.

[d]Intake or binge: not in above, but at least minimal severity intake or binge problems.

[e]High Consequences Score of 3+: tangible consequences, i.e., social consequences, health, or injury problems associated with drinking, or financial problems.

"WETTER" AND "DRYER" REGIONS. That cultural traditions continue to have considerable impact on drinking behavior is seen by comparing (Table 5) areas of the country rated as "Dryer" (in terms of past voting or public opinion poll results concerning prohibition) with "Wetter" areas. Although there is little difference between the two kinds of areas in the proportion of men aged 21 to 59 showing High Consequences of their drinking, the dryer areas as a whole showed a significantly higher proportion of nondrinkers and a significantly lower proportion with heavy intake but no consequences, when compared with the wetter areas. One implication of these findings is that efforts toward minimizing drinking problems might be more efficient if they took into account the cultural traditions in each region: it appears unlikely that any single national prevention program will fit all regions.

ETHNORELIGIOUS GROUPINGS. Table 6 shows that most Jewish men aged 21-59 drink at least some, but few drink heavily or get into trouble over their drinking; that most Catholics and liberal Protestants drink and that an above-average proportion get into difficulty over their drinking; and that conservative Protestants (from denominations favoring complete abstinence) show a rather high proportion of abstainers but also a relatively high rate of consequences relative to the rates of Heavy Intake or Binge Drinking.

These findings are congruent with the connections between religious affiliations and use of alcohol as summarized by Skolnick (1958) from a number of earlier studies and case histories. The implication of all of these findings may be that instead of trying to de-emphasize ethnic and religious-

TABLE 5

Current Problems Typology[a] by Region, Men aged 21-59
(Combined 1967 and 1969 surveys -- in percentages)

	(*n*)	Non-drinker	Drank, no problems	Potential problems only	Heavy intake or binge: No consequences	High Consequences Score
Dryer Regions						
South Atlantic	(156)	28	30	19	12	12
East South Central	(113)	29	30	16	5	20
West South Central	(188)	23	40	17	5	14
West North Central	(134)	10	47	17	12	14
Mountain	(61)	21	33	26	3	16
Total	(652)	22	37	18	8	15
Wetter Regions						
New England	(89)	7	43	33	11	7
Middle Atlantic	(288)	7	39	20	19	15
East North Central	(353)	13	41	22	13	12
Pacific	(179)	10	32	27	14	16
Total	(909)	10	39	23	15	13

Note. From Cahalan and Room, 1974, Table 17.

[a]Defined in Table 4 footnote.

TABLE 6

Current Problems Typology by Ethnoreligious Categories
(Combined 1967-69 surveys - percentages, for men aged 21-59)

Ethnoreligious Category	(*n*)	Non-drinker	Drank, no problems	Potential problems only	Heavy intake or Binge: No consequences	High Consequence Score
British						
Catholic	(34)	12	35	27	18	9
Liberal Protestant	(48)	13	31	38	8	10
Conservative Prot.	(204)	20	39	22	3	16
Irish						
Catholic	(77)	4	33	27	16	21
Conservative Prot.	(74)	27	46	15	3	10
German						
Catholic	(76)	7	40	21	22	11
Liberal Protestant	(86)	12	47	24	9	8
Conservative Prot.	(120)	22	42	21	7	9
Italian						
Catholic	(64)	5	52	14	23	6
Latin American						
Catholic	(42)	10	10	21	17	43
Jewish	(40)	8	60	25	5	3
Negro						
Conservative Prot.	(97)	18	23	16	13	31
Eastern European						
Catholic	(71)	6	38	21	21	14
Other ethnicity						
Catholic	(114)	7	42	26	11	13
Liberal Protestant	(56)	5	43	18	23	11
Conservative Prot.	(158)	34	35	15	8	8

Note: Categories with small *n*'s are omitted from this table. Ethnicity is defined by religion for Jews, by race for Negroes, and by country most ancestors come from for the remainder.

affiliation differences in drinking behavior--as is traditional among those imbued with the "melting pot" philosophy--there may be considerable benefits to be derived from studying these differences more intensively to see what we can learn from them. For example, it is entirely possible that if we make more detailed studies of how most American Jews manage to avoid drinking problems even though they tend to live in larger cities where the aggregate rates of drinking problems are rather high, we will know more about how to set up more effective programs to inculcate moderate drinking habits and attitudes among the U.S. population as a whole.

MULTIVARIATE ANALYSIS OF CORRELATES OF DRINKING PROBLEMS. Table 7 presents a condensation of a number of detailed analyses in Cahalan and Room (1972). This analysis shows that drinking attitudes and environments are highly correlated with high drinking-problem scores. None of a number of psychologically oriented personality scales among the 51 variables tested showed a very high relationship with drinking problems--an observation consistent with the earlier findings of Syme (1957), Armstrong (1958), and Rosen (1960) that the problem drinker does not represent a unique personality type.

It may be argued that attitudes toward alcohol may be as much the effect of prior heavy drinking as the "cause" of later heavy drinking. However, the earlier two-stage study in the same series (Cahalan, 1970) found that very favorable attitudes toward drinking were found to precede drinking problems more often than drinking problems preceded favorable attitudes toward drinking. Our conclusion is that

TABLE 7

Multiple Correlation of 51 Variables Against Combined Problems Score of 7+ (1967 and 1969 surveys--1,561 men aged 21-59)

Step No.	Cumulative Multiple Correlation	Partial Correlation	Simple Correlation (Pearson *r*)
1. Drinking by significant others	.26	.15	.26
2. Tolerance of deviance	.33	.13	.22
3. Own attitude toward drinking	.37	.18	.26
4. Index of social position	.41	.11	.16
5. Negro	.42	.09	.15
6. Non-helpfulness-of-others	.43	.06	.16

Note. The cumulative multiple correlation for 51 variables (including demographic and intervening variables) was .47, or 22% of the total variance in problem drinking (from Cahalan & Room, 1972, Table 9).

while certain personality variables (such as under-control and low self-esteem) may contribute to drinking problems, if the person's attitudes toward alcohol are very favorable and there exists an environment permissive toward heavy drinking, the environmental and attitudinal influences are of paramount importance in determining which of today's heavy drinking young people will be the problem drinkers of tomorrow. One obvious inplication is that individual psychotherapy may not be very effective in cases of problem drinking if no effort is made to change the person's environmental situation.

CHANGES IN DRINKING-PROBLEM STATUS OVER SEVERAL YEARS

As discussed earlier, clinical observations of alcoholics have contributed to a relatively pessimistic outlook on the likelihood of expecting much change in drinking behavior on the part of those who have become heavy drinkers to the extent that they repeatedly get into trouble over their drinking. However, as we have emphasized, clinical alcoholics may not be at all similar to heavy drinkers in the general public because the clinics tend to inherit those who have failed to find help through other resources. What is obviously needed is intensive study of the extent of change in drinking problems on the part of a random sample of the nonclinical public.

While the earlier national and community surveys in this series of studies on drinking behavior brought to light considerable evidence on a retrospective basis as to frequent changes in drinking behavior on the part of a large proportion of people (Cahalan et al., 1969), and later surveys yielded much evidence in the same direction (Cahalan, 1970; Cahalan & Room, 1974), but still on a largely retrospective basis, it was not until 1973 that detailed evidence was available on changes in drinking behavior and problems as measured by two surveys of the same probability samples of individuals when the surveys were three or four years apart.

A SAN FRANCISCO PROBABILITY SAMPLE OF 615 MALES AGED 21-59 initially interviewed in 1967 and reinterviewed in 1972 made it possible to measure detailed changes in drinking practices and problems over a four-year period. Table 8 shows the extent of changes within four years on the part of those who had specified problems (or potential problems) at Time 1 As discussed earlier, the traditional expectation concerning alcoholism is that alcoholics will accumulate increasing numbers of problems, with the later symptoms of progressive alcoholism not being thought of replacing early symptoms but merely adding to problems already existing (Room, 1970). However, the findings are at variance with the conventional expectation in that there does not appear to be much snowballing of problems in more and more areas of the person's life with the passage of time.

The first two columns of Table 8 below bear upon the snowballing hypothesis of the disease model of alcoholism. It will be seen that for each problem at Time 1, the proportion who no longer have the identical problem at Time 2 is generally quite high, ranging from 50 to 96 percent. However, the last column of Table 8 shows that drinkers with drinking problems at Time 1 tend to have some type of problem at Time 2, although not necessarily the same problem; and the

TABLE 8

Drinking Problems at Time 1 (1967) by Selected Outcomes at Time 2 (1972)
(San Francisco white men aged 21-59 in 1967, in percentages)

Time 1 problems or potential problems	(*n*)	Remission of problem by Time 2	Heavy intake at Time 2	Binge drinking at Time 2	One or more drinking problems at Time 2[a]
Binge drinking	(29)	59	48	41	55
Symptomatic drinking	(21)	51	62	38	76
Psychological dependence	(42)	50	48	14	48
Loss of control	(18)	78	67	17	78
Police problems	(13)	77	23	38	61
Job problems	(24	96	37	21	50
Problems with relatives or friends	(23)	61	56	35	70
Accidents	(10)	80	50	20	50
Financial problems	(98)	63	42	13	50
Problems with wife	(25)	52	52	20	64

Note. From Clark and Cahalan, 1973, Table 4.

[a]Problems here include only the following current (Time 2) problems: police problems, job problems, spouse problems, other interpersonal problems, accidents, and financial problems.

second and third columns show that those with problems at Time 1 tend to continue to have high rates of heavy or binge drinking as of Time 2. It appears appropriate to conclude from this study that continuity of specific problems over time is low, but that continued involvement in some alcohol problems is very likely for those with drinking problems at Time 1. Thus the progressive disease concept of problem drinking is open to considerable question. However, the fact that those who have drinking problems at one time tend to have drinking problems of varying character at a subsequent time may imply that situational factors probably loom large in determining whether the individual will tend to continue to get into trouble.

A NATIONAL PROBABILITY SAMPLE MEASURING CHANGE was conducted as part of this same series, with 725 men aged 21-59 being first interviewed in 1969 and again four years later, in 1973. Table 9 (derived from Cahalan & Roizen, 1974) bears out the findings of the San Francisco change study as regards finding a high turnover or change in drinking problems even though the data are presented in a different type of analysis. Here it is seen that about as many shifted into, or out of, a drinking-problem status as stayed in the same drinking-problem status. To illustrate: at the 3+ problems level the change-ratio is a high .72 while the correlation of problem-status for the two measurements is a relatively low .36. The same tendency toward high turnover appears in all of these measures of change, as well as in the measures of individual problems (not shown here).

Our longitudinal studies are still undergoing intensive

TABLE 9

Turnover in Summary Drinking Problems Scales
Nationwide sample, 725 men aged 21-59 in 1967, reinterviewed in 1972

	% Turnover Proportions				Turnover Statistics	
High Problems Level	"No/No"	"No/Yes"	"Yes/No"	"Yes/Yes"	*r*	Change Ratio
1+ Drinking Problems	59	9	13	20	.49	.53
3+ Drinking Problems	82	6	7	5	.36	.72
Social Consequences Summary Scale[a]	82	6	6	6	.40	.69
Tangible Consequences Summary Scale[b]	77	7	8	9	.48	.61
Problematic Intake Summary Scale	81	7	6	7	.45	.65
Subjective Problems Summary Scale[c]	82	7	7	4	.29	.77

Note. Headings: "No/No": proportion reporting problem neither at Time 1 nor Time 2
"No/Yes": proportion reporting problem at Time 2 but at Time 1
"Yes/No": proportion reporting
"Yes/Yes": proportion reporting problem at both Time 1 and Time 2
r: Pearson product-moment correlation coefficient
Change-ratio: proportion of $\frac{\text{"No/Yes"} + \text{"Yes/No"}}{\text{"No/Yes"} + \text{"Yes/No"} + \text{"Yes/Yes"}}$

[a]Social Consequences: alcohol related problems with spouse or relatives, friends, neighbors; job problems; problems with police, or accidents.

[b]Tangible Consequences: social consequences plus health and financial problems.

Subjective Problems: summary score combining psychological dependence, loss of control, and symptomatic drinking scales.

analysis of the correlates of change in drinking problems. However, from the preliminary analyses cited above it is obvious that the "symptom" or "prodromal" status of specific drinking problems as predictors of later problems has been considerably overrated, since our general-population change data suggest that an early warning measure based on such symptoms will yield a substantial number of false positives who will never come to clinical attention and also will yield a substantial number of false negatives who will newly report problems at a later time. The high rates of turnover in specific drinking problems implies that specific circumstances and life events may have important effects on drinking behavior and problems, and we are now conducting an intensive study of the impact of events on changes in drinking behavior, to be reported upon in the near future.

IMPLICATIONS OF THESE SURVEYS FOR PREVENTION OR MINIMIZATION

Measurement of the effectiveness of programs to minimize drinking problems is a difficult task, at best, for many reasons: difficulty in isolating the effects of specific prevention campaigns from other influences, difficulty in obtaining financing and moral support for a lengthy experimental prevention program, and difficulty in obtaining agreement among official agencies and voluntary agencies in deciding what is to be prevented or minimized and how the program is to be carried out. In order to have any lasting effects in a general atmosphere that is rather permissive toward heavy drinking and in which the attractiveness of drinking is continuously reinforced through massive advertising expenditures, campaigns to minimize drinking problems would have to entail intensive efforts over a lengthy period of time. Since the funding cycle for legislatures is usually only one or two years at best, and since legislators' perseverance in funding of alcohol programs tends to be short-lived--as most grantsmen in the alcohol field will testify--there usually is only a relatively small amount of money available for longer-term prevention programs. The great bulk of alcohol funding goes for treatment and support of alcoholics in hospitals, clinics, and other institutions, leaving very little public funding for prevention programs. In fact, many persons who are a part of the alcoholic-treatment interest group--whether hospital or halfway house administrators, medical and other clinical personnel actively engaged in treating alcoholics, or many of the recovering alcoholics themselves--may perceive prevention programs as competing for funds with their own favorite treatment programs.

Indeed, for one reason or another we fail to see that there have been any serious efforts toward prevention of alcohol problems since the repeal of Prohibition.

Prohibition did work rather well, after a fashion, in preventing many alcohol problems, particularly cirrhosis (Terris, 1967). However, Prohibition is a dramatic example of a relatively draconian experiment that few would like to repeat because of the disadvantages of interfering with the right to drink on the part of the vast majority of non-problem drinkers, as well as the atmosphere of lawlessness and cynicism that Prohibition brought about. In fact, it is highly possible that because of our bad experiences with national Prohibition, we are highly resistant to any kind of preventive measure which might result in inconvenience or increased costs of alcoholic beverages.

In the 1971 Harris Poll, only 17% of those surveyed would like to see a return to Prohibition. In our own national surveys, substantial proportions of interviewees say that they enjoy drinking, would miss it if they had to give it up, and that they "enjoy getting drunk once in a while." One-fifth of a national sample of men aged 21-59 reported that they had driven an automobile under the influence of alcohol at some time within the last year, and 16% of this same sample said they got high or tight an average of once a month or more often.

The 1971 Harris national survey revealed a generally ambivalent and guilt-laden attitude toward drinking. On the one hand, 73% agreed that, "A mature and healthy person is his own best judge of what and where to drink," and 70% agreed that, "A little social drinking makes people friendlier, and often releases their inhibitions so that they feel more relaxed and open." On the other hand, 39% answered, "Never," when asked what was a safe and proper age for a young man to begin drinking. While a majority agreed with the statement that, "It is all right to drink moderately on a regular basis as long as a person eats properly," a majority of those with opinions disagreed with the statement, "With the pressures of life today, a drink or two in the evening is a real benefit." The report also found that a large proportion of this national sample were poorly-informed on the effects of alcohol, tending to minimize the hazards of, for example, drinking before driving.

The unwillingness of the general public to support measures which would be inconvenient or more expensive is illustrated in Table 10, which summarizes the public support accorded to various specific measures for controlling

TABLE 10

Proportions Believing Governments *Should* Do More on Specified Prevention and Treatment Measures (*California statewide survey*)

Measures that might be taken	Results by Sex: Men (442) %	Women (582) %	Total (1024) %
(*n*)	(442)	(582)	(1024)
Offering treatment for people who want help with their drinking problems	89	92	90
Being tougher with people who drive while drunk	85	91	88
Making it very expensive for heavy drinkers to get auto liability insurance	69	83	76
Requiring all new cars to have a device to keep the care from starting if the driver is intoxicated	61	72	67
Providing more recreation for people that doesn't involve drinking	61	72	66
Making arrangements to have the police take people home if they have had too much to drink to be able to drive	63	66	65
Being tougher on people who walk or sit around drunk in public	49	59	54
Requiring people with serious drinking problems to be treated for alcoholism, whether they want the treatment or not	50	53	51
Closing bars earlier	34	48	41
Making drinking mre expensive by increasing alcohol taxes	32	45	38
Rationing alcohol so that everybody could buy only a modest amount each month	14	24	19
Prohibiting the sale of all alcoholic beverages	6	11	8

Note. From Cahalan, Roizen, and Room, in press.

drinking problems in a statewide California survey conducted for us by the Field organization in 1974 under the auspices of the California Office of Alcohol Program Management (Cahalan, Roizen, & Room, in press). The survey found that while the vast majority would be tougher on drunken drivers (88%), relatively fewer would cut down on the hours during which bars were open (41%), or would increase alcohol taxes in the interest of decreasing consumption (38%).

Even the experts find it hard to agree upon the details of what they would consider to be principal points in a prevention program that would be effective in minimizing alcohol problems and still be humane. In an international conference held in Berkeley in December, 1974 under the auspices of the University of California School of Public Health and the sponsorship of the California Office of Program Management, a dozen or more social scientists and program administrators specializing in the field of prevention came up with a mixed set of opinions--much like the opinions of the California laymen cited above. While the experts generally agreed that public school programs to inculcate moderation in drinking would be--like chicken soup--unlikely to do any harm and might do some good, and that secondary prevention efforts through early casefinding and rehabilitation of those not too far gone in alcoholism should be intensified, there was strong disagreement by at least a few recognized experts on whether increases in alcohol taxes for the purpose of holding consumption in check would be either effective or advisable.

Experts generally agree that prevention efforts in the form of early education are probably a good thing; and in any event, since all states have mandated some form of alcohol education, it would be well to have realistic and emotionally healthy alcohol education programs rather than old-fashioned, traditional scare tactics about the evils of drink. While we do not obviously advocate that children be taught how to drink, we do think that they should know that most people in our society do drink and that most of those who drink do so without apparent harmful consequences. Since most young people are exposed to drinking in any case, perhaps we can teach about drinking as we do about swimming or driving, by emphasizing how to avoid the dangers. However, no matter what kind of early education on alcohol is adopted, we should beware lest we fall into the temptation of passing the buck about alcohol education to the formal school system, which is the "dumping ground" for all the things which we are unwilling or unqualified to teach our own children in the home or in other informal social environments.

The "values clarification" approach to alcohol education is increasingly popular these days, particularly among the teachers and school administrators who find that they must move into the general moral vacuum left by the abdication of responsibilities on the part of the many parents who for one reason or another fail to transmit responsible drinking attitudes to their children. While the values clarification approach can be an excellent one in acquainting the young person with community norms where such norms are relatively clear and consistent, the approach can lead to increased ambivalence and confusion if the norms of the community and of the youthful peer group are at cross-purposes.

MEDIA CAMPAIGNS to inculcate moderate drinking habits have been popularized in recent years, largely through the leadership of Morris Chafetz, recent Director of the National Institute on Alcohol Abuse and Alcoholism. The NIAAA has had its own campaigns of television shorts and radio announcements, which have been augmented to some extent by occasional announcements by alcohol marketing organizations promoting moderation and by NIAAA-sponsored media campaigns put on by such organizations as the Junior Chamber of Commerce. While such media campaigns may not do much harm and may do some good through sensitizing more people to alcohol-related problems, it is naive to expect that such short-lived campaigns can accomplish much in the way of changing deep-seated attitudes and behavior concerning drinking. Alcohol program administrators who put faith in the effectiveness of media campaigns often fail to see the difference between switching consumer purchasing from one branded product to another, and asking people to give up long-established dependence upon alcohol as a means of achieving euphoria or of escaping boredom or other problems. Unless media campaigns are linked to people-to-people programs to follow through on bringing about the general public's commitment to moderation, they will be of little consequence--particularly since media campaigns have to compete against the "live-it-up" appeal of much alcohol advertising.

In the light of the climate of attitudes and practices concerning alcohol that has prevailed in the U.S. for many generations, we believe it is very unlikely that much will be done toward effective minimization of alcohol problems until (or unless) there springs up a genuine social movement toward moderation that enlists the energies and hopes of large numbers of people at the grass-roots level. The prohibitionist movement was indeed such a genuine social movement that gained the energetic support of many millions of Americans and sustained itself over many generations, presumably because the movement filled a perceived need. While we are emphatically not advocating the rekindling of the prohibitionist movement--both because of the apparent unworkability of Prohibition and because of the class divisiveness which Gusfield (1962) has described so well--we feel that only a large-scale social movement could provide the grass-roots person-to-person evangelizing that will be needed to crystallize the social norms within which moderate drinking behavior will be informally enforced on a peer-pressure basis.

That such a social movement toward moderation might become possible is hinted at by at least two indicators. One is that an overwhelmingly high proportion of Americans pay at least lip service to the concept of moderation in drinking, and high proportions feel guilty or uneasy about their own or others' heavy drinking. Another indicator of the possibility of stimulating the growth of a social movement toward moderation is the existence of several ethnocultural groups in the U.S. with a quite consistent recent history of moderation in the use of alcohol--particularly among such groups as the Jews and the Chinese, most of whom drink, but among whom relatively few develop problems because of their drinking. We strongly suspect that study of such groups would reveal that moderation is directly related to parental and peer-group example at home and in other social situations, inculcated at a very early age.

It might take us many years to bring about an atmosphere of moderation; but we will never get there until we begin real attempts toward setting an example of moderation, rather than self-indulgently feeling that drinking problems can be solved by such band-aids as sloganeering television commercials and radio announcements.

IMPLICATION OF DRINKING SURVEYS FOR TREATMENT OF DRINKING PROBLEMS

The importance of early case-finding in treating persons with drinking problems is demonstrated in many ways in the many surveys on drinking behavior which we and others have conducted during the past decade. For the first time, these surveys have made it abundantly clear that the average person with alcohol-related problems worked up to his problem-drinker status through many years of heavy drinking. The popular press to the contrary , we know of no "instant alcoholics". It should be only too clear to any observant person that anyone in his family or among his friends who repeatedly drinks more than is appropriate for the occasion is heading for trouble, be he sixteen or sixty. However, because of a combination of guilt about our own present or past drinking, unwillingness to appear to be a "dry" or a busybody, or the belief that alcoholics are born and not made, few of us are motivated to exert social influence toward appropriate drinking behavior. Even those who are so motivated generally do not know how to go about it effectively, yet gracefully. Accordingly, we urge that much attention be focused upon the process of influencing those around us toward moderate drinking.

The treatment of those labeled as secondary or tertiary alcoholics should be reexamined on the basis of what we have learned from surveys about drinking behavior and attitudes on the part of the general (noninstitutionalized) population. In these surveys we have found that favorable attitudes toward heavy drinking and drunkenness are very prevalent, particularly among young, urban men. Even despite the considerable ambivalence toward alcohol on the part of the average heavy or problem drinker, we have found that the problem drinker tends to be preoccupied with alcohol and what it will do for him. In fact, repeatedly we have found that favorable attitudes or values about alcohol are the best single predictor or correlate of drinking problems--far more closely correlated than stress factors or personality attributes. In fact, Americans tend to be so immersed in their own cultural hangups about alcohol and alcoholism that many will say, "Of course, it is obvious that people who drink heavily will have favorable attitudes toward heavy drinking; but that doesn't prove anything." We do not accept this "Of course..." response: we contend that it is even more obvious that the attitudes and values of the person with drinking problems will have to be changed in order to affect his drinking behavior in the long run.

The implications of attitudes and values for treatment are seen in many ways when one looks at some of the statistics regarding alcoholic clinics. If one considers "no-shows"--those who fail to follow through on treatment after having been induced to make an initial visit or telephone call to a clinic--one clearly sees that at least half of those who make an initial contact with a clinic fail to follow through with any treatment, no matter what the inducements. How else can one explain the magnitude of this "no-show" group except in terms of attitudes and values--that they are "voting with their feet" by turning to resumption of drinking rather than toward treatment because they are unwilling to give up or reduce their drinking? While much research remains to be done on the motivations of the "no-show" as compared to the motivations of the person who goes through treatment, it is possible to guess that basic values concerning alcohol lie at the root of failure to accept treatment.

Additional evidence that attitudes about alcohol are basic to avoiding alcohol problems can be drawn from the recent Stanford Research Institute study on the presumed effectiveness of federally-funded alcoholism treatment centers (Ruggels, Armor, Polich, Mothershead, & Stephen, 1975). This ambitious study found that *if* the client stayed in treatment as long as six months, the chances of his showing improvement were approximately 70%, no matter what specific treatment modalities were employed. However, it is a big *if*, because one must first get the client to accept treatment. In the SRI study fully 24% of the eligible clients are contacts only never really entering treatment, and an additional 45% either never go beyond the "pre-intake" stage or drop out before 30 days (Ruggels et al., 1975). In any case, both the research and the rates of improvement will be facilitated in the future if more attention is paid to the lessons learned from Morris Chafetz' (1970) clinical experiment of a decade ago, in which he raised the level of retention in treatment and reduced recidivism through an intensive program of identification of alcoholics among the patients of an emergency hospital clinic, coupled with vigorous efforts to induce the patient to accept treatment for alcoholism, followed up by solicitious inquiries about his health over a period of time.

Our survey findings are consistent with the characteristics of the revolving-door type of problem drinker or alcoholic (Wiseman, 1970) even though we studied the general adult population and not the institutionalized population. Given a person's membership in an ethnic or cultural subgroup with a history of permissiveness and encouragement of intoxication, a history of childhood neglect, the development of a high valuation of alcohol as a means of solving one's problems, and finally the development of personality characteristics consistent with using alcohol to escape (such as low self-esteen and low motivation to seek longer-term rather than shorter-term gratifications), one has indeed a fine recipe for creating the revolving-door alcoholic.

In closing, the findings in our surveys have for years called for more effective action in longer-term follow-up in restoring and reinforcing appropriate economic and social supports for the person with recurrent drinking problems. Our society must not seek cheap and easy shortcuts in assisting in rebuilding the self-esteem and interpersonal mutual-support systems to which the problem drinker has devoted so many years of neglect. It will neither be easy nor inexpensive to devise a system of measures to minimize the development of drinking problems in the first place. However, it seems obvious to us that the integration of realistic preventive measures and of longer-term treatment and rehabilitation of chronic problem drinkers will turn out to be far cheaper and more humane, in the long run, than the patchwork of programs that now prevail throughout the United States.

REFERENCES

Armstrong, J.D. The search for the alcoholic personality. *Annals of the American Academy of Political and Social Science*, 1958, *315*, 40-47.

Bacon, S.D. Alcohol and complex society. In D.J. Pittman & C.R. Snyder (Eds.), *Society, culture, and drinking patterns*, New York: John Wiley & Sons, 1962.

Cahalan, D. *Problem drinkers*. San Francisco: Jossey-Bass, 1970.

Cahalan, D., & Cisin, I.H. Drinking behavior and drinking problems in the United States. In H. Begleiter & B. Kissin (Eds.), *Social Biology*, Vol. 4, *The Biology of Alcoholism*. New York: Plenum Publishing Corp. (in press).

Cahalan, D. & Cisin, I.H. *Final report on a service-wide survey of attitudes and behavior of naval personnel concerning alcohol and problem drinking*, Washington, D.C.: Bureau of Social Science Research, 1975.

Cahalan, D., Cisin, I.H., & Crossley, H.M. American drinking practices: A national study of drinking behavior and attitudes. New Brunswick, N.J.: Rutgers Center of Alcohol Studies, 1969. (Monograph No. 6)

Cahalan, D., Cisin, I.H., Gardner, G.L., & Smith, G.C. *Drinking practices and problems in the U.S. Army, 1972*, (Report No. 73-6). Arlington, Va.: Information Concepts Incorporated, December 1972.

Cahalan, D., & Roizen, R. *Changes in drinking problems in a national sample of men*. Paper presented at a meeting of the Alcohol and Drug Problems Association, San Francisco, December 1974.

Cahalan, D., Roizen, R., & Room, R. Alcohol problems and their prevention: Public attitudes in California. In R. Room & S. Sheffield (Eds.), *The Prevention of alcohol problems*. Sacramento: California State Office of Alcohol Program Management (in press).

Cahalan, D., & Room, R. Problem drinking among American men aged 21-59. *American Journal of Public Health*, 1972, *62*, 1473-1482.

Cahalan, D., & Room, R. *Problem drinking among American men.* New Brunswick, N.J.: Rutgers Center of Alcohol Studies, 1974.

Chafetz, M., Blane, H.T., & Hill, M.J. *Frontiers of alcoholism.* New York: Science House, 1970.

Christie, N., & Bruun, K. Alcohol problems: The conceptual framework. In M. Keller & T.G. Coffey (Eds.), *Proceedings of the 28th International Congress on Alcohol and Alcoholism,* (Vol. 2). New Haven: Hillhouse Press, 1969.

Cisin, I.H. Community studies of drinking behavior. *Annals of New York Academy of Science,* 1963, *107,* 607-612.

Clark, W. Operational definitions of drinking problems and associated prevalence rates. *Quarterly Journal of Studies on Alcohol,* 1966, *27,* 648-668.

Clark, W., & Cahalan, D. *Changes in problem drinking over a four-year span.* Paper presented at annual meeting of the American Public Health Association, San Francisco, November 1973.

Emrick, C. A review of psychologically oriented treatment of alcoholism. *Journal of Studies on Alcohol,* 1975, *36,* 88-108.

Gusfield, J.R. Status conflict and the changing ideologies of the American temperance movement. In D.J. Pittman & C.R. Snyder (Eds.), *Society, culture, and drinking patterns.* New York: John Wiley & Sons, 1962.

Haberman, P.W., & Sheinberg, J. Public attitudes toward alcoholism as an illness. *American Journal of Public Health,* 1969, *59,* 1209-1216.

Harris, L., & Associates, Inc. *American attitudes toward alcohol and alcoholics.* (Study No. 2138) A survey of public opinion prepared for the National Institute on Alcohol Abuse and Alcoholism. New York: Louis Harris & Associates, Inc., 1971.

Jellinek, E.M. *The disease concept of alcoholism.* New Haven: Hillhouse Press, 1960.

Keller, M. (Ed.), *Alcohol and health: New knowledge,* Second special report to the U.S. Congress (DHEW Publication No. (ADM) 75-212). Washington, D.C.: U.S. Government Printing Office, 1974.

Knupfer, G. The epidemiology of problem drinking. *American Journal of Public Health,* 1967, *57*, 973-986.

Knupfer, G., Fink, R., Clark, W., & Goffman, A. *Factors related to amount of drinking in an urban community.* Drinking practices study (Report No. 6). Berkeley: State of California, Department of Public Health, 1963.

Mulford, H.A., & Miller, D.E. Public definitions of the alcoholic. *Quarterly Journal of Studies on Alcohol*, 1961, *22*, 312-320.

Plaut, T.F. *Alcohol problems : A report to the nation by the Cooperative Commission on the Study of Alcoholism.* New York: Oxford University Press, 1967.

Robinson, L.H., & Podnos, B. Resistance of psychiatrists in treatment of alcoholism. *Journal of Nervous and Mental Disease*, 1966, *143*, 220-225.

Room, R. *Assumptions and implications of disease concepts of alcoholism.* Paper presented at the 29th International Congress on Alcoholism and Drug Dependence, Sydney, Australia, February 1970.

Room, R., & Day, N. Alcohol and mortality. In M. Keller (Ed.), *Alcohol and health*: *New knowledge,* Second special report to the U.S. Congress (DHEW Publication No. (ADM) 75-212) Washington, D.C.: U.S. Government Printing Office, 1974.

Rosen, A.C. A comparative study of alcoholic and psychiatric patients with MMPI. *Quarterly Journal of Studies on Alcohol,* 1960, *21*, 253-266.

Ruggels, W.L., Armor, D.J., Polich, M., Mothershead, A., & Stephen, M. *A follow-up study of clients at selected alcoholism treatment centers funded by NIAAA.* Final Report. SRI Project URU-3124. Menlo Park, Calif: Stanford Research Instititue, May 1975.

Schuckit, M.A., & Cahalan, D. Evaluation of alcohol treatment programs. In W.J. Filstead, J.J. Rossi, & M. Keller (Eds.), *Alcohol, new thinking and new directions.* Cambridge: Ballinger, in press.

Siegler, M., Osmond, H., & Newell, S. Models of alcoholism. *Quarterly Journal of Studies on Alcohol*, 1968, *29*, 571-591.

Skolnick, J. Religious affiliation and drinking behavior. *Quarterly Journal of Studies on Alcohol*, 1958, *19*, 452-470.

Syme, L. Personality characteristics of the alcoholic. *Quarterly Journal of Studies on Alcohol*, 1957, *18*, 288-301.

Terris, M.A. Epidemiology of cirrhosis of the liver: National mortality data. *American Journal of Public Health*, 1967, *57*, 2076-2088.

Wiseman, J. *Stations of the lost*. Englewood Cliffs, N.J.: Prentice-Hall, 1970.

CHAPTER 15

CULTURE AND ALCOHOLISM

Richard Stivers

"Culture" and "alcoholism" are on the one hand words and concepts and on the other hand their referents in objective reality. This recognition only adds to the obvious difficulty in specifying any relationship between culture and alcoholism. As Chapter 2 has already indicated, historically speaking, there exist many and varied definitions of alcoholism. In the same vein Williams (1966) has indicated historical changes in the concept of culture from the end of the eighteenth century through the middle of the twentieth century, while Schneider and Bonjean (1973) have illustrated important differences in the meaning of the concept among social scientists.

Alcoholism, as Jellinek (1962) noted, is a cultural definition and as such varies between cultures. Furthermore, alcoholism as a cultural definition functions as a cultural control, as both a theory of behavior and an institutional

---

Ralph E. Tarter and A. Arthur Sugerman (eds.), Alcoholism

ISBN: 0-201-08146-6
ISBN: 0-201-08145-8 (pbk.)

mandate to alter this behavior. Alcoholism as a cultural concept may be broadly or narrowly defined and widely or selectively enforced.

But culture can be concurrently for and against alcoholism. Culture can directly hasten the advent of alcoholism by attaching a spiritual value to and regarding as sacred both consumer goods and techniques of escape which involve the loss of self. In contradictory fashion a society might broadly define alcoholism, wage a propaganda campaign against it, and employ a large number of helping professionals to treat alcoholism while simultaneously promoting the unrestricted use of consumer goods, defining the goal of life as individual happiness, and encouraging people to lose themselves in their activities, whether work or leisure.

Through its contradictory demands culture can also create anxiety escape from which is sought in alcohol. For example, Horney (1937) has pointed out that our inherited Christian tradition in the Western world is at odds with the social and cultural demands of competition and technology. While the religious tradition stresses brotherly love and humility, secular ideologies of success and power contradict this, notwithstanding the vain attempts to reconcile the two. Just as important, too, given the erosion of this Christian tradition, are the contradictions between secular culture and social organization. In a word, all that culture promotes, social reality restricts.

Thus culture can influence the prevalence and extent of alcoholism in at least three ways: (a) in the quasi-tautological sense that alcoholism as definition can be broadly or narrowly defined and widely or selectively enforced; (b) in the attribution of immense spiritual value to consumer goods, such as alcohol, and to escapism, the loss of self; and (c) in the creation of anxiety through its contradictory demands. In cases one and two culture is a controlling force--against alcoholism in the first, and in favor of alcoholism in the second. In the third case culture is an agent of strain.

ANOMIE AND ALIENATION

The sociological questions of control and strain have often been dealt with through two seminal concepts: anomie and alienation. Originally these concepts contained a criticism of western civilization in nineteenth century Europe (Horton, 1964). Only later were they transformed into their present sterile and totally abstract form.

The concept of anomie is most identified with the writing of the great French sociologist, Emile Durkheim (1897/1951). Strictly speaking, anomie referred to the breakdown of Judaic-Christian morality in industrial Europe. One of the major factors Durkheim associated with this "normlessness" was the stimulation of unrestricted and insatiable ambition by the new industrial order. While he criticized the lusting after success, he did so less from the vantage point of the individual who could never realize his ambitions and more from the perspective of the need for order in society. Hence, anomie proved an essentially conservative critique of modernization by its primary emphasis on the failure of moral control in industrial society. If competition was the fuel of the industrial engine, individual ambition had to be titillated to overcome the initial inertia. And where insatiable ambition lay, so Durkheim reasoned, there also was a breakdown of moral order, at least by traditional standards.

Although anomie was seen lurking behind high rates of many forms of deviant behavior, Durkheim never related it to rates of alcoholism (Snyder, 1964). Not one to leave problems unsolved, Durkheim (1897/1951) proffered several ways in which a new morality could be institutionalized, one of which involved transforming each occupation into a profession with its own code of ethics.

The concept of alienation derives from the earlier writings of Karl Marx (1964). Here the concern is with man's growing dehumanization under capitalism. Because Marx defined man as a species who could realize his true nature only when free to work, i.e., to develop his innate talents and abilities, he argued that capitalism had dehumanized and enslaved the proletariat. The worker's labor, his talents and their fruits, belonged to the capitalist who paid the worker the minimum necessary for the survival of the worker and his family, appropriating the value of the remainder of the worker's production for his profits. However, the essential point was not the rate of exploitation but rather the fact that the worker's labor had been made the condition for him to survive. Estranged labor had reversed man's free relationship to his labor so that, as Marx (1964) powerfully expressed it, man's labor had become "a mere means to his existence."

Alienation is to be understood in a threefold sense: (a) alienation from labor, (b) alienation from the products of one's labor, and (c) alienation from others. Estranged labor was ultimately responsible for all three types of alienation. The concept of alienation was revolutionary, because it suggested that man's alienation would be abolished only under worldwide communism. Alienation was a concept of the larger society but one written from the individual's perspective, while anomie was a concept about the larger society written from society's point of view.

Over the years the concepts of alienation and anomie became more abstract and vague as the larger sociohistorical contexts of these formerly critical concepts were dropped. Alienation came to mean almost any discontent of the individual whether it be his powerlessness, his isolation, or the meaninglessness of his life (Seeman, 1961). Anomie became equated with normlessness whether of the group, community, or society.

In actuality neither the concept of anomie (Snyder, 1964) nor alienation has appeared very often in the literature on alcoholism. However, their abstract equivalents, the lack of control (anomie) and strain (alienation), are frequently invoked.

In a review of the literature on anomie and drinking, Snyder (1964) claimed that only two research efforts had been directed toward exploring that relationship. One was completed near the turn of the century, and it was more interested in Durkheim's related concept of egoism than in anomie. The other (Jessor, Graves, Hanson, & Jessor, 1968) used the concept less in its original sense and more in its principal revised sense. Merton (1957) also spoke of normative breakdown, but his concept differed most from Durkheim's on the question of ambition. For Merton the key issue was not unlimited and unreachable ambition but the lack of opportunities for many to realize even limited ambitions because of their location in the social structure.

Jessor et al. (1968) found some empirical evidence to support a theoretical relationship between anomie (defined on three levels of sociocultural organization) and deviant drinking behavior. In no way, however, could much of this drinking be seen as alcoholic. Furthermore, they reached a tentative conclusion that both cultural control and access to the legitimate opportunity structure were less important than social control as variables in predicting deviant drinking behavior (Jessor et al., 1968).

Frederick Engels (1845/1958), Marx's collaborator, and the neo-Marxist, Willem Bonger (1916/1969), discussed alcoholism from a Marxist perspective. Yet neither was couching their arguments primarily in terms of the concept of alienation. Both regarded alcoholism as a problem of capitalist societies, especially of their egoistic tendencies. Capitalism forced all to become selfish, but it especially brutalized those on the lower strata of society. Alcoholism was the result of alienation only in the most general sense of the term.

Neither alienation nor anomie has fared well in macro-level research. Yet related concepts have been frequently employed. Anxiety, often regarded as a type of strain or alienation, commonly appears in the literature. As Snyder (1964) has sagely noted, the concept of anomie is implicit in any explanation of alcoholism formulated in terms of social organization. That is, if weak social organization is related to a high incidence of alcoholism, does it not follow that weak cultural control or anomie would be related as well? Do not the social and cultural systems vary directly? There appears to be the implicit moral assumption in some cross-cultural research that no socially and culturally well organized society would encourage drunkenness. But even those studies which both admit and prove that drunkenness can be a ritual in highly integrated societies are quick to draw a distinction between drunkenness and alcoholism. This suggests that while a highly organized culture might prescribe drunkenness, it would never promote alcoholism.

CROSS-CULTURAL STUDIES OF DRINKING

There have been six comparative studies of drinking behavior which have drawn a large enough sample to qualify as being truly cross-cultural. The smallest sample included 44 cultures. All of the studies focused on primitive societies and were conducted between 1943 and 1972. It should be noted that none of these studies dealt with alcoholism per se but rather with drinking patterns, some of which sanctioned drunkenness.

The first of these is the now classic "The Functions of Alcohol in Primitive Societies: A Cross-Cultural Study" by Donald Horton. Although Horton (1943) spoke of the "inseparability of psychologic and cultural variables," he seemed to neglect culture at least in its holistic sense in explaining insobriety. Certainly he did mention acculturation as a source of anxiety (Horton, 1943) but it received scant attention by comparison with other variables.

His two most important propositions were that "the strength of the drinking response in any society tends to vary directly with the level of anxiety in that society" and that "the strength of the drinking response tends to vary inversely with the strength of the counteranxiety elicited by painful experiences during and after drinking" (Horton, 1943, p. 230).

Horton (1943) identifed three major causes of anxiety: (a) level of subsistence economy, (b) subsistence hazards, and

(c) acculturation. Thus, the more primitive a society's economy, the more subsistence hazards it suffers; and the more intense the acculturation it undergoes, the more anxiety that society will experience, and ultimately the greater will be the degree of its insobriety.

With respect to the second proposition, Horton (1943) specified four sources of pain capable of producing counter-anxiety: (a) real dangers, (b) social punishment for impaired functioning, (c) social punishment for sexual behavior, and (d) social punishment for aggressive behavior.

Horton's (1943) research generally supported his first proposition about anxiety. The research provided no direct test of the second proposition, and the indirect tests only tentatively validated the hypothesis that counteranxiety brought about by apprehensiveness over social punishment for sexual behavior inhibited insobriety.

Of special import are two of Horton's ideas. The first was the discovery that many cultures were ambivalent about drunkenness; that is, they approved of it under special circumstances but disapproved of its consequences. Second, Horton treated acculturation as a source of anxiety or strain and not as a failure of control.

Not satisfied with the above conclusions about anxiety and insobriety, Peter Field (1962) restudied the same 56 societies Horton had included in his sample. He discovered a direct relationship between degree of formal social organization and sobriety. Corporate or formal social organization purportedly exercised greater control over the individual than personal or informal organization. Formally organized societies tended "to have a high degree of lineal social solidarity, and to have interpersonal relationships structured along hierarchical or respect lines" (Field, 1962, p. 72). This prevented, Field hypothesized, fighting and drunkenness at social festivities.

Field's assumptions about human nature and social order were that man, left to himself, is inclined toward evil, e.g., fighting and drinking, and that no society, correctly organized, would deliberately foster drunkenness, an offense against natural law.

Although Field omitted culture as a factor in his theory, he did suggest that the variable he found related to drunkenness, loose social organization, was similar to Durkheim's concept of anomie (Snyder, 1964). The common idea is that of control, the difference being whether social or cultural control is more important.

The next study, and undoubtedly the most intriguing, was Samual Klausner's "Sacred and Profane Meanings of Blood and Alcohol." His data were collected from material in the Human Relations Area Files. Klausner attempted to test the hypothesis attributed to Robert Bales (1959) and Charles Snyder (1958) of an inverse relation between drinking at religious rituals and heavy drinking at secular festivities. This is sometimes referred to as the cultural consistency hypothesis, which means that the "use of alcohol generalizes along lines of common meaning" (Klausner, 1964, p. 33). Hence the meaning of sacred acts transfers to their performance in profane settings.

Blood was taken to be a symbolic equivalent to alcohol in primitive societies. Both blood and alcohol have been important symbolic components of religious rituals. Klausner (1964) found the greatest linkage between religious ritual and heavy secular drinking to be in the case of sacrifice.

If sacrifice is in part an attempt to expel evil, sacrificial drinking is of the same ilk. This meaning is generalized, then, to the secular situation.

The sacredness of blood, and by extension alcohol, in a society was indicated by the strength of its menstrual taboo. The idea of the relative sacredness of blood and alcohol was the key to the reformulation of the Bales-Snyder hypothesis: "where blood is considered holy, as indicated by the existence of a severe menstrual taboo, blood will tend not to be used secularly; nor will alcohol, its symbolic equivalent, tend to be drunk heavily in purely secular situations" (Klausner, 1964, p. 39). His data offered partial support for this idea.

Of great interest is Klausner's assumption about man's inherent need to deal with the problem of evil through ritualistic sacrifice. Therefore, the fewer religious rituals man provides the more secular ones he must develop. Hence, if alcohol is not considered very sacred, and its meaning is diminished in religious rituals, its use in secular settings should be ritualistic. As to why secular ritual drinking might be heavy, Klausner (1964) mentions anxiety. Presumably, religious ritual can better allay anxiety thus making drunkenness unnecessary.

His hypothesis still leaves unclear why alcohol should be used heavily in secular rituals in societies which do not hold alcohol to be very sacred. Also, what about heavy alcohol use in religious rituals? It would seem that Klausner needed to inquire deeper into the precise cultural meanings of alcohol use beyond the superficial indicators demanded by extensive cross-cultural research. Despite these criticisms, his hypothesis has provided a springboard for ideas developed later in this chapter.

A 1965 study of 138 primitive societies represents one of the most ambitious efforts at cross-cultural research on drinking. Bacon, Barry, and Child (1965) discovered that drunkenness was positively correlated with the punishment or deprivation of dependency needs in all stages of the life cycle and with cultural pressures toward individual achievement and self-reliance. When culture placed great pressure on individuals to be independent, competitive, and self-reliant and did not allow for the satisfaction of dependency needs, drunkenness was most frequent.

Furthermore, they discovered that culturally integrated drinking in highly organized societies was not related to the frequency or infrequency of drunkenness (Bacon, et al., 1965). These two sets of variables proved independent. This is in general agreement with much anthropological research and casts serious doubts on the lack of control (whether cultural or social) hypotheses about drunkenness.

Finally it was noted that the above two findings, the former on dependency needs and the latter on culturally integrated drinking, were not mutually exclusive (Bacon, et al., 1965). Thus control or its absence are not the only factors related to drinking. Drunkenness then can be rewarding to those with frustrated dependency needs, especially in cultures which approve of drunkenness. Thus culture concurrently approves of drunkenness in its drinking rites and provokes it through the anxiety generated in the overemphasis on individual independence and in the punishment of dependency needs.

The final two studies are closely related; indeed the second is a spin-off of the first. Dissatisfied with the previously cited studies, largely because they failed to establish empirical links between culture and personality leaving their interpretations of the data highly tenuous, McClelland, Davis, Wanner, and Kalin (1972) attempted to circumvent this problem by examining folktales in primitive societies with respect to psychological attitudes including those about drinking. Folktales then were to provide this essential empirical link between culture and personality.

Discovering that "cultures which do not institutionally stress maleness are the ones that drink," McClelland et al. (1972, p. 63) argue that this indicates that unstructured societies with low male solidarity do not provide organized support for the male individual to mediate the conflict between achievement and obedience (McClelland et al., 1972). Moreover, the response systems of achievement and obedience are more polarized in the unstructured societies (McClelland et al., 1972). Given this conflict and the content of the imagery and themes in folktales in unstructured societies, McClelland et al. (1972) conclude that the male individual solves his problem of achievement versus obedience by becoming powerful in a "primitive, non-instrumental, impulsive way," that is, through drunkenness (p. 72).

Eric Wanner, who was an associate in the above study, later revised what had come to be known as the "magical potency" theory. Reanalyzing differences between sober and drunken societies, Wanner (1972) identified two syndromes: (a) a society which forces its male members to be assertive but simultaneously provides no institutional means for the attainment of manhood, and (b) a society which promotes loyalty and cooperation in lieu of individual assertiveness. The former society was most drunken since its members used alcohol to meet impulsive power needs to manipulate others.

All of these massive cross-cultural studies suffer

from a similar weakness which is inherent in the very nature of their strength. The weakness is their superficiality and abstractness, and the strength is their extensive sampling. As Bunzel (1940) observed years ago, the meaning of alcohol use can only be ascertained when one has studied an entire culture in an holistic fashion. This would mitigate against large-scale cross-cultural studies until the time came that each culture included had previously and satisfactorily been studied in depth. To discover finally that drunkenness is related to anxiety, or to frustrated dependency needs, or to impulsive power needs, or to faulty social organization is not only too simplistic but also too abstract. Such findings readily assume that anxiety, dependency, and impulsive power mean the same and are handled the same across cultures. This idea is clearly contradicted by some of the more in-depth cultural studies of alcohol.

At the same time, however, we think that these studies (with the exception of Field's) are correct--at least about modern technological societies and only here in a highly qualified way. Indeed, one has the impression that in several of these studies the researchers have read the problems of modern societies into primitive societies.

CULTURAL ATTITUDES TOWARD ALCOHOL AND DRINKING

Anthropological studies of cultural attitudes toward alcohol indicate a full range of meaning: (a) from sacred to profane and (b) from "essential and blessed" to "destructive and dispensable" (Mandelbaum, 1965, pp. 281-282). To complicate the picture, societies possess differing degrees of consciousness about their real attitudes (Mandelbaum, 1965).

Among the attempts to delineate the logical possibilities of cultural attitudes toward drinking, three stand out. Bales (1959) identified four basic drinking attitudes: abstinence, ritual, convivial, and utilitarian. The first attitude prohibits the use of alcohol. The second, the ritualistic attitude, is fundamentally a religious attitude demanding the use of alcohol in the ritual. Usually the drinking is a sacred act symbolizing communion with a deity, The third attitude, the convivial, is largely a secular attitude in which drinking symbolizes solidarity. The solidarity predates the drinking, albeit the drinking may enhance the emotional cohesion of the group. The fourth attitude, the utilitarian, views drinking as a means to individual gratification. Although it may occur in a group context, it is often solitary drinking whereby the individual uses the group as a shield for his own purposes.

Of the four cultural attitudes toward drinking, Bales (1959), thought the utilitarian to be most related to alcohol addiction. It was, of course, not a sufficient explanation, but when it occurred concurrent with "dynamic" or stress factors, the probability of alcoholism increased in that society. He also regarded the ritual attitude as the one least likely to lead to alcoholism, arguing that where alcohol was an integral and pervasive part of religious ritual, its abuse was inhibited.

Bales' hypothesis about utilitarian drinking encouraging alcohol addiction and ritual drinking preventing it was confirmed, he thought, by his empirical study of Irish-American and Jewish-American drinking. Irish-Americans with an extremely high rate of alcoholism among ethnic groups and Jewish-Americans with the lowest rate represented polar types. He proceeded to typify the Irish pattern as convivial-utilitarian, actually more utilitarian than convivial, and the Jewish pattern as ritualistic.

Jellinek (1965) combined Bales' categories of ritual and convivial drinking into what he called the symbolic functions of drinking and contrasted it with the utility function. Therefore, what ritualistic and convivial drinking had in common was that this drinking was community oriented and symbolic with respect to religious communion, in the former, and in the latter with respect to social solidarity. The utility function, by way of contrast, is best exemplified in egotistical drinking; that is, drinking with almost exclusively personal objectives.

However, the two functions are intimately related in several ways. For the individual drinker, even if he is participating in ceremonial drinking, the utility function may become more important the more he drinks. Secondly, over time within the same culture the utility function may become predominant even without the symbolic meaning of drinking being changed (Jellinek, 1965). This has occurred in the modern era because of improved techniques of production and preservation of alcoholic beverages as well as the individualization of the sources of anxiety. Finally, the two functions can virtually merge under certain conditons, as when solidarity is to be achieved through drinking rather than its being an expression of solidarity.

Speaking to this last point Fallding (1964) took into account situations where community only occurs with and after drinking. Although he eventually identified four types of drinking, Fallding (1964) maintained that only two of the four would be positively institutionalized in a society.

The first type, ornamental, community-symbolic drinking, presupposes a community with a high level of integration or mutual trust. Here Fallding (1964), too, rejects Bales' distinction between ritual and convivial drinking, preferring to treat them together since both are ceremonial and symbolic. The crucial point is the high level of preexisting community.

The second type, facilitation drinking, occurs in a less integrated and less trusting society as an effort to recover whatever integration and trust is lacking (Fallding, 1964). This category acknowledges Jellinek's observation about the occasional interrelationship of symbolic and utility functions. Yet Fallding (1964) qualifies his argument in acknowledging that there can be movement back and forth between ornamental, community-symbolic drinking and facilitation drinking. Furthermore, ornamental drinking may involve rites of drunkenness without, however, leading to alcoholism (Fallding, 1964).

The previous three writers all shared in common a concern with the symbolic, religious, ritualistic side of cultural attitudes toward drinking. The other side is the moral. Both are intimately related.

Larsen and Abu-Laban (1968), taking a lead from the earlier work of Mizruchi and Perrucci (1962), identified three types of drinking norms: proscriptive, prescriptive, and nonscriptive. Proscriptive norms prohibit drinking of all kinds. Prescriptive norms positively encourage drinking except heavy drinking. Nonscriptive norms neither prohibit drinking, nor do they specify what drinking conduct is permitted (Larsen and Abu-Laban, 1968). Nonscriptive norms are really the absence of norms, or anomie.

In a study designed to discover which type of drinking

norm was most frequently related to serious drinking behavior, it was discovered to be the nonscriptive norm (Larsen and Abu-Laban, 1968). However, the definition of drinking norms and the research design precluded an adequate test of the full range of drinking norms. That is to say, prescriptive norms were always moderate norms because in the authors' words, "deviation from the prescriptive norms is defined only by heavy drinking" (Larsen and Abu-Laban, 1968, p. 441). There was an implicit assumption that no group would prescribe drunkenness.

There are several important studies which point to the shortcomings of the previously cited typologies of cultural attitudes toward drinking. The collective research of Heath (1962), Klausner (1964), Nida (1959), and Sayres (1956), among others, has indicated that ritual drinking may be either religious, secular, or both, that the religious ritual drinking may be drunken or not, that the secular ritual drinking may be drunken or not, and that religious and secular drinking patterns may prove independent of one another. The cultural consistency hypothesis, or more specifically the Bales-Snyder hypothesis, that religious ritual drinking inhibits secular drunkenness would not appear to be confirmed.

Jellinek's distinction between symbolic and utility functions seemed inadequate by his own admission where the drinking appeared to be both simultaneously. Especially revealing are Nida's (1959) observations about drunkenness serving as a vehicle for the attainment of religious ecstasy in highly integrated societies. Thus, religion in its Dionysian forms cultivates individual and collective ecstasy. Here religion itself becomes utilitarian for man's purposes. Sensual and quasi-mystical experiences are the end of religious practices.

Even Fallding's admirable attempt to distinguish between drinking that symbolizes preexisting community (ornamental, community-symbolic) and that which simulates community (facilitation) does not cover all contingencies. Lemert (1956) for one, and almost furtively it would appear, pointed out that culture need not be morally consistent. Drunkenness then can be seen as an "institutionalized pattern operating in a relatively autonomous way and only tenuously related to the other aspects of culture" (Lemert, 1956, p. 313). Drunkenness could be permitted, yes even demanded for some, as a means of protecting something valued even more highly. Lemert's remarks were qualified as based on impressions from his own research. However, some recent research of my own casts more light on Lemert's point.

But first we need to be more precise about what we mean by culture. Culture is ultimately dependent upon faith in some dominant symbol. Without faith there can be no authority, only the exercise of power (Rieff, 1968). Every culture makes a set of moral demands upon those who fall under its purview. This morality is of course related to the dominant faith. Rieff (1968) has described the two major functions of all cultures:

> (a) to organize the moral demands men make upon themselves into a system of symbols that make men intelligible and trustworthy to each other, thus rendering also the world intelligible and trustworthy; (b) to organize the expressive remissions by which men release themselves, in some degree, from the strain of conforming to the controlling symbolic, internalized variant readings of culture that constitute individual character. The process by which a culture changes at its profoundest level may be traced in the shifting balance of controls and

> releases which constitute a system of moral demands. (pp. 232-233)

From this it follows that drunkenness could be a cultural control or cultural remission. Lemert's previous remarks about drunkenness institutionalized in a way only tenuously related to the larger culture, we take to mean a cultural remission. But the institutionalized drunkenness is only superficially unrelated to the larger culture because it is actually supportive of it even as it appears as a way around it. This distinction also allows the symbolic and moral aspects of cultural attitudes to be combined, something previous typologies had neglected.

Take for instance the hard drinking of the Irish in Ireland versus that of the Irish in America in the late nineteenth century through the early twentieth century. In my study (Stivers, 1976) I defined the Irish drinking as culturally remissive and that of Irish-Americans as a direct cultural control. The difference between the two is not small.

In the latter half of the nineteenth century a pattern of late age at marriage, low marriage rate, and single inheritance gradually became institutionalized in Ireland. Concomitantly, Irish Catholicism became both devotional and puritanical. The puritanism was both cause and effect of the need to keep in check a large number of unmarried men and women, many of whom would never marry. These individuals, if they bore children, were a direct threat to a single inheritance farm economy, and given the already extant religious beliefs, puritanism was inevitable. Hard drinking for men was a cultural remission as a way of circumventing puritanism. By defining manhood in terms of hard drinking, sexual standards were preserved. Next to sexual indiscretion hard drinking and even drunkenness was a minor failing--it was a "good man's fault." Institutionalized ritual hard drinking was an admission that a culturally remitted way around puritanism had to be provided for men or they would be driven to more serious offenses. Yet the ability to hold one's own, to drink a great amount without appearing intoxicated, was a standard. In this way hard drinking would not appear to be against the sin of drunkenness.

Among Irish-Americans, on the other hand, hard drinking became a direct cultural control in that it assumed a religious quality. In the new religion of Irish-American nationalism, whatever set Irish-Americans apart from other ethnic groups became sacred. The previous religious restraints about drunkenness in Ireland failed, for now the Irish-Americans had two religions--Catholicism for the private sphere and Irish nationalism for the public sphere. Ultimately then, the more one drank the more Irish one became. It was this setting of hard drinking as a direct cultural control that was more rife for alcoholism than was culturally remitted hard drinking. As an open-ended religious practice, hard drinking could readily turn into alcoholism when the necessary stress factors were present.

Irish-American "religious drinking" appears similar in many ways to the religious rituals of drunkenness in primitive societies. There are some important differences, however. For instance, the Irish-American community was much less integral than its primitive counterpart. Then too the Irish drinking was individualistic and that among primitives collectivistic. Hard drinking or drunkenness as a religious rite is most dangerous in an individualistic society especially if the level of anxiety is very great.

The dialectically related concepts of cultural control

and cultural remission can contribute much to the study of drinking patterns, even that of alcoholism in modern culture.

MODERN CULTURE AND ALCOHOLISM

It may appear in this section that I am doing exactly what I criticized others for having done earlier, that is, talking about too many cultures in a superficial and abstract manner. Actually, however, American culture and other Western cultures have been studied in great depth and are becoming increasingly similar (Horkheimer, 1974a). Likewise, modern culture has become abstract. Given that modern technological societies are exactly the same in their infrastructures--technique--and even similar in the commonplaces (Ellul, 1968) which underlie their obvious ideological differences, it seems safe to speak about "modern culture."

Modern technological societies are perhaps best understood in terms of their most pervasive phenomenon--technique. Several writers (Ellul, 1964; Habermas, 1970; Horkheimer, 1947/1974) seem largely in agreement on this point. Technique is the "*totality of methods rationally arrived at and having absolute efficiency* (for a given stage of development) in *every* field of human activity" (Ellul, 1964, xxv). The end of technique is efficiency and order.

Men have always employed techniques, but in the past they were always able to integrate them into civilization. Today the reverse is true--technique dominates civilization and man himself. Historically the conjunction of technique and the political state were the most important factors in the development of a technical civilization (Ellul, 1964). The state became dependent upon technique to fulfill its obligations while the diffusion of and continued advancement of technique were contingent upon the finances and power of a highly developed state.

Technique has become most menacing for man in the area of human techniques (Ellul, 1964). Psychological techniques such as education, vocational guidance, and propaganda act upon men as objects to manipulate them and conform them to their environment. But whether one is the object of technique or the subject (we all are both), the results are far-reaching and devastating.

Technique implies an absence in man--an absence of spontaneity, reflection, and criticism (Ellul, 1964). When the single most efficient method is learned, when all one has to do is to "plug it in" and the desired results are accomplished, and when techniques dominate our relationships with each other, the outcome is Dale Carnegie and human engineering courses, behavior modification, extroverted personality types, and role-playing. But perhaps the greatest handicap is the dissociation between thought and action which technique effects. As action becomes dominated by the routine and mechanization of technique, thought turns to daydreams, fantasy, and any escape from the maddening repetition. Therefore, unconscious forces come to control us to a much larger extent than ever before. The repression technique exerts on man's ecstatic energy leads to irrational outbursts of unparalleled intensity (Ellul, 1964).

Cultural contradictions are a major force in the creation of anxiety. Because real contradictions are unbearable, man is compelled to seek their resolution. Yet faced with *cultural* contradictions, the individual is usually outmatched in his efforts. Horney (1937) briefly sketched three major contradictions:

> (a) between competition and success on the one hand, and brotherly love and humility on the other; (b) between the stimulation of our needs and our factual frustrations in satisfying them; (c) between the alleged freedom of the individual and all his factual limitations. (pp. 288-289)

There are many others as Horney noted, such as the idolization of peace and the omnipresent threat or state of war (Ellul, 1969a).

To be more precise some of these are cultural conflicts and others are conflicts between culture and social reality. Horney's first conflict is between a Christian morality stressing the private virtues, especially charity, or a similar humanistic ideology and a collectivistic technological morality which demands success, efficiency, and the normal (Ellul, 1969b). The latter two contradictions are between a therapeutic culture which stresses freedom and consumerism and a social reality which is neither free nor satisfying, either because some are prevented from realizing these artificially created needs or because even when they are realized they prove empty.

Much of modern culture concerns itself with channeling man's unbridled instincts, frustrations, and anxieties into safe, nonrevolutionary movements. Rieff (1968) calls our modern culture a therapeutic culture, one that makes it moral demands through cultural remissions which are to superficial glance permissions. Hence the commonplace assertion that ours is a permissive society overlooks the fact that what seems to be permitted is really demanded!

However, "permissive" appears a more apt description because the illusion of freedom, e.g., the freedom to consume, is rampant. As Ellul (1964, p. 424) has observed technique "transforms culture into luxury," or in other words "culture fuses with entertainment" (Horkheimer & Adorno, 1944/1972, p. 143). The propaganda of advertising creates needs and turns us all into consumers (Ellul, 1969a). We have a choice about whether to consume one brand or another, one color, shape, size, or another; but increasingly we have no choice about whether to be consumers or not.

In the face of such profound contradictions, anxieties, and frustrations, men feel accused and guilty and seek escape (Ellul, 1969a). The long-standing ideology of happiness and all the new religions encourage this escape. The cultural admonitions to "get away from it all," to take in entertainment that is billed as "escapist fare," and "T.G.I.F." are the inverse recognition that man has no choice but to escape.

The new religions are the cults, therapies, political parties, and social movements which so abound today. Religion is the institutionalization of what man values spiritually and regards as sacred. For several centuries technology and politics have served as the sacred for man. It was believed that politics could achieve a utopia, and technology the individual's well-being. Thus the myths of progress and happiness became widespread. Nevertheless, technique, while making man happy superficially, has generated great tension and anxiety.

Still it is technique, the cause of so much anxiety, which itself satisfied man's mystical tendencies (Ellul, 1964). Mysticism is a means of being possessed, of achieving communion, of losing oneself. The dissociation of thought and action in technique involves a loss of self.

William James (1902) observed that drunkenness was a

mystical experience which had a genuine religious dimension to it. Aldous Huxley (1965, p. 69) once pointed out that both Marx who was utopian and Freud who was anti-utopian regarded religion as the opium of the people, but that in the utopian society of *Brave New World* "opium was the religion of the people." In this sense alcoholics are religious fanatics who take to an extreme the moral demands of a therapeutic culture to excape. The alcoholic creates an artificial community of one, satisfies the mystical need to lose the self in total communion. Therefore, the alcoholic not only suffers anxiety to an extreme degree but also pursues a culturally remitted escape, a religion, to an extreme.

Alcoholism, both definition and behavior, is a crisis in the development of a technological society. Until man's ecstatic energies and his need to revolt have been perfectly expressed through technique, irrational and self-defeating behavior such as alcoholism will continue unabated. This behavior is a sign of man's revolt against a too ordered, pacified society. But each revolt brings new definitions and therapies.

Alcoholism as cultural definition is often regarded as an illness. The concepts of illness, maladjustment, social problems, and deviant behavior are the modern counterparts to those of sin and immorality. Both the former and latter are concepts of evil. The concept of illness when applied to moral, political, and social behavior is an expression of a technological morality which demands the normal, the successful, and the efficient. This morality deals exclusively with means; the end tends to disappear as the distinction between end and means is blurred. The real problem with the alcoholic from the point of view of this morality is that he is inefficient on the job and, secondarily, a failure at home. In short he is a real problem and an embarrassment to a technical system. Thus the alcoholic's illness is an illness of the system as well. Alcoholics "screw up the works" and the company loses time and money. Hence the alcoholism becomes business and industry's problem. It is not surprising then to find alcoholism broadly defined and widely applied. The more alcoholic behavior increases or becomes visible, the greater the need to enforce the definition; likewise, the more therapeutic culture becomes, the broader the definition of alcoholism will become.

In summary, modern culture influences alcoholism in at least the following three ways: (a) as a cultural definition of evil in terms of illness and inefficiency, alcoholism will be more broadly defined and will be more widely applied as the efficiency needs of modern technological societies increase; (b) by attaching spiritual value to and regarding as sacred consumer goods and services, pleasure, and escapism, modern culture cultivates alcoholic ecstasy; and (c) through its internal contradictions and contradictions with social reality, modern culture generates anxiety, escape from which is sought in alcoholism. Dialectically then anxiety (c) creates a need to escape which in turn is reflected in an ideology of escape/therapy (b) both of which lead to a broad therapeutic definition of alcoholism (a).

Both alcoholism and its treatment are therapies; the former from the individual alcoholic's perspective, the latter from society's view. Alcoholism as a therapy is unacceptable precisely because it is inefficient. The need to be taken care of (escape) and the need to care for (therapy) are intimately related. In modern culture the advocacy of therapy for others is the unconscious reflection of one's own need to escape. And both are the result of anxiety and the repression of technique. Widespread alcoholism, both behavior and definition, a fairly recent phenomenon of the past two centuries, is a by-product of modern technological society and its therapeutic culture.

REFERENCES

Bacon, M.K., Barry, H., III, & Child, I.L. A cross-cultural study of drinking: II. Relations to other features of culture. *Quarterly Journal of Studies on Alcohol*, 1965, *Suppl. No. 3*, 29-48.

Bales, R.F. Cultural differences in rates of alcoholism. In G. McCarthy (Ed.), *Drinking and intoxication*. Glencoe, Ill.: The Free Press, 1959. (Reprinted from *Quarterly Journal of Studies on Alcohol*, 1946, *6*, 480-499)

Bonger, W. *Criminality and economic conditions*. Bloomington, Ind.: Indiana University Press, 1969. (Originally published, 1916.)

Bunzel, R. The role of alcoholism in two Central American cultures. *Psychiatry*, 1940, *3*, 361-387.

Durkheim, E. [*Suicide*] (J.A. Spaulding & G. Simpson, Trans.) New York: The Free Press, 1951. (Originally published, 1897).

Ellul, J. [*The technological society*] (J. Wilkinson, Trans.). New York: Knopf, 1964.

Ellul, J. [*A critique of the new commonplaces*] (H. Weaver, Trans.). New York: Knopf, 1968.

Ellul, J. [*Propaganda*] (K. Kellen & J. Lerner, Trans.). New York: Knopf, 1969. (a)

Ellul, J. [*Technological morality*] In C.E. Hopkin (Trans.), *To will and to do*. Philadelphia: Pilgrim Press, 1969. (b)

Engels, F. [*The condition of the working class in England*] (W.O. Henderson & W.H. Chaloner, Trans.). New York: Macmillan, 1958. (Originally published, 1845.)

Fallding, H. The source and burden of civilization illustrated in the use of alcohol. *Quarterly Journal of Studies on Alcohol*, 1964, *25*, 714-724.

Field, P. A new cross-cultural study of drunkenness. In D.J. Pittman & R. Snyder (Eds.), *Society, culture, and drinking patterns*. New York: John Wiley & Sons, 1962.

Habermas, J. [*Technology and science as 'ideology.*] In J.J. Shapiro (Ed. and Trans.), *Toward a rational society*. Boston: Beacon Press, 1971.

Heath, D. Drinking patterns of the Bolivian camba. In D.J. Pittman & R. Snyder (Eds.), *Society, culture, and drinking patterns*. New York: John Wiley & Sons, 1962. (Reprinted from *Quarterly Journal of Studies on Alcohol*, 1958, *19*.)

Horkheimer, M. *Critique of instrumental reason* (M.J. O'Connell, Trans.). New York: Seabury, 1974. (a)

Horkheimer, M. *Eclipse of reason*. New York: Seabury, 1974. (Originally published, 1947.) (b)

Horkheimer, M., & Adorno, W. [*The culture industry: Enlightenment as mass deception.*] In J. Cumming (Trans.), *Dialectic of enlightenment*. New York: Herder & Herder, 1972. (Originally published, 1947)

Horney, K. *The neurotic personality of our time*. New York: Norton, 1937.

Horton, D. The functions of alcohol in primitive societies: A cross-cultural study. *Quarterly Journal of Studies on Alcohol*, 1943, *4*, 199-320.

Horton, J. The dehumanization of anomie and alienation: A problem in the ideology of sociology. *British Journal of Sociology*, 1964, *15*, 283-300.

Huxley, A. *Brave new world revisited*. New York: Perennial Library, 1965.

James, W. *The varieties of religious experience*. New York: The Modern Library, 1902.

Jellinek, E.M. Cultural differences in the meaning of alcoholism. In J. Pittman & R. Snyder (Eds.), *Society, culture, and drinking patterns*. New York: John Wiley & Sons, 1962. (Reprinted from *World Health*, 1957, *10*).

Jellinek, E.M. The symbolism of drinking: A culture-historical approach. Substudy 3-2 & Y-65, Toronto: Addiction Research Foundation, 1965. (Mimeographed)

Jessor, R., Graves, T.D., Hanson, R.C., & Jessor, L. *Society, personality and deviant behavior*. New York: Holt, Rinehart & Winston, 1968.

Klausner, S. Sacred and profane meanings of blood and alcohol. *The Journal of Social Psychology*, 1964, *64*, 27-43.

Larsen, D.E., & Abu-Laban, B. Norm qualities and deviant drinking behavior. *Social Problems*, 1968, *15*, 441-450.

Lemert, E. Alcoholism and the sociocultural situation. *Quarterly Journal of Studies on Alcohol*, 1956, *17*, 306-317.

Mandelbaum, D. Alcohol and culture. *Current Anthropology*, 1965, *6*, 281-293.

Marx, K. [*The economic and philosophic manuscripts of 1844*] (M. Milligan, Trans.). New York: International Publishers, 1964.

McClelland, D., Davis, W., Wanner, E., & Kalin, E. A cross-cultural study of folk-tale content and drinking. In D.C. McClelland, N. Davis, R. Kalin, & E. Wanner (Eds.), *The drinking man*. New York: The Free Press, 1972, (Reprinted from *Sociometry*, 1966, *29*.)

Merton, R.K. *Social theory and social structure*. New York: The Free Press, 1957.

Mizruchi, E., & Perrucci, R. Norm qualities and differential effects of deviant behavior: An exploratory analysis. *American Sociological Review*, 1962, *27*, 391-399.

Nida, E.A. Drunkenness in indigenous religious rites. *Practical Anthropology*, 1959, *6*, 20-23.

Rieff, P. *The triumph of the therapeutic*. New York: Harper Torchbooks, 1968.

Sayres, W.C. Ritual drinking, ethnic status and inebriety in rural Colombia. *Quarterly Journal of Studies on Alcohol*, 1956, *17*, 53-62.

Schneider, L., & Bonjean, C. (Eds.). *The idea of culture in the social sciences*. New York: Cambridge University Press, 1973.

Seeman, M. On the meaning of alienation. *American Sociological Review*, 1961, *26*, 753-758.

Snyder, C.R. *Alcohol and the Jews*. Glencoe, Ill.: The Free Press, 1958.

Snyder, C. Inebriety, alcoholism, and anomie. In M. Clinard (Ed.), *Anomie and deviant behavior.* New York: The Free Press, 1964.

Stivers, R. *A hair of the dog: Irish drinking and American stereotype.* University Park, Pa.: Penn State Press, 1976.

Wanner, E. Power and inhibition: A revision of the magical potency theory. In D.C. McClelland, N. Davis, R. Kalin, & E. Wanner, *The drinking man.* New York: The Free Press, 1972.

Williams, R. *Culture and society, 1780-1950.* New York: Harper & Row, 1966.

CHAPTER 16

THE FEMALE ALCOHOLIC

Edith S. Gomberg

The fact that more women are drinking in 1975 than before and that there has been a steady rise in the percentage since World War II is a fact of life (Alcohol & Health, 1971; Gomberg, 1974). What this means is that there are fewer abstainers among women, and that the social mores have changed in the direction of more permissiveness, and that the trend is toward less differentiation of the sexes in acceptable social comportment. This does not mean that we are moving toward unisex, nor does it mean that all these changes make people happier. The increase in percentage of American women who drink like the percentage of young women with children who work outside the home is part of social change over time.

Although the right to drink might carry with it the right to intoxication, the facts are quite unclear. We have come a long way from the temperance movement, primarily a

Ralph E. Tarter and A. Arthur Sugerman (eds.), Alcoholism

ISBN: 0-201-08146-6
ISBN: 0-201-08145-8 (pbk.)

women's movement, which sought to protect women from the consequences of male alcoholism. The present women's movement seeks economic and social equality, and this may include equal rights to intoxication. One item in an Attitudes Toward Women scale states, "Intoxication among women is worse than intoxication among men," (Spence & Helmreich, 1972, p. 19). Agreement with this statement is a "conservative" attitude; disagreement is an expression of a "liberal" attitude. Yet we have no indication that social attitudes have changed much since the reports of more intolerance of female intoxication by Lawrence and Maxwell in 1962 and by Knupfer in 1964. Knupfer's viewpoint, that the double standard for intoxication was probably related to anxiety about women's sexual behavior and alcohol-induced impairment in sensitivity seem apt and relevant today. In spite of social change, there are still deep feelings over the sexual acting out of women and unresponsiveness to the needs of spouse and children. It would be useful to know if attitudes toward female intoxication have indeed become more "liberal." Among college students, a shift over 20 years has changed the percentage of male students who drink from 77% to 80%, but the percentage of female students who drink has gone from 61% to 73% (Hanson, 1974; Straus & Bacon, 1953). Does this mean that college students look upon intoxication of female students more permissively than they did 20 years ago? We don't know.

However, women engaging in social drinking may involve as little as one occasion a year, e.g.,a family gathering. Instead of speaking of the increase in the percentage of American women who drink perhaps we should be speaking of the shrinking percentage of women abstainers. Lowered percentages of abstainers seem to relate to relaxation of religious and social taboos and to changes in social standards of acceptable female behavior. For some, that is a sign of the decline of our civilization.

MALE:FEMALE ALCOHOLISM RATIOS

Are alcoholism rates for women going up? Some authors relate rising rates of female alcoholism to female emancipation but that makes two assumptions: first, that rates are rising; and second, that the increased rates are caused somehow by new freedoms. The evidence of rising rates is ambiguous. The picture is confused for several reasons: (a) male:female ratios vary widely depending on whether the source of the ratio is a report from private physicians, Alcoholics Anonymous, clinics, courts, or state hospitals; (b) increases in the statistics of female alcoholism could mean increases not in rate but in the number of those willing to come for help; (c) we may be influenced by the number of prominent women who are willing to be publicly visible as former alcoholics; and (d) we may be influenced by public statements made by public figures but largely undocumented.

There has been concern about female overindulgence in alcohol since earliest times, and we may find evidence of this concern in ancient Roman law. Concern was expressed in the post-World War II period and in 1947, Jellinek was writing against the assertion that, "the ratio of male to female inebriates is becoming lower and lower" (p. 21) and commenting that, "Female alcoholism is by no means 'a sign of the times'" (p. 41).

The evidence of rising rates is ambiguous as we look

at different treatment settings. In a survey of physicians in private practice (Jones & Helrich, 1972), more than a third report that women make up half or more of their problem drinking patients. The 1974 survey of the membership of Alcoholics Anonymous (Norris, 1974) shows women alcoholics constitute 31% of those who have joined A.A. in the last three years.

Based on the Jellinek formula, ratios were estimated in the past to be approximately 5.5:1 (Lisansky, 1957). Ten years ago, a state hospital which serves a high income suburban area close to New York City reported 3:1 ratio of male to female admissions for alcoholism (Oltman & Friedman, 1965), but a recent study of a rural midwestern state hospital turned up a male to female admission rate of 11:1 (Hoffmann & Noem, in press). Apparently, ratios vary by region, as well as by treatment setting.

To complicate matters further, there are quite different ratios depending on the criterion of alcoholism used. Edwards, Hensman, and Peto (1972) point this up very effectively in comparing male:female ratios in the United Kingdom, based on different drinking problems. If "drunkenness arrests" are used for comparison, the male to female ration is 14:1[1]; if mental hospital admissions for alcoholism are used, 5:1; if deaths from liver cirrhosis, approximately 1:1.

However, it does seem likely that the ratio of female alcoholism has gone up in recent years. If a larger percentage of women drink, then presumably a larger percentage of women

[1]Edwards, Hensman, & Peto present numbers for England, Wales and Scotland which I have averaged.

who might be vulnerable to alcoholism are exposed. Groups which have traditionally had very low rates of alcoholism, e.g. the Jews, also change over time; one study of 62 hospitalized alcoholic women includes 8% who are Jewish (Browne-Mayers, Hamilton, Seelye, & Sillman, 1975). There are population trends which indicate an increasingly higher percentage of persons over 65, and the life expectancy of women is greater. A recent British study of alcohol problems among elderly psychiatric and geriatric patients shows women outnumbering men (Rosin & Glatt, 1971). And, finally, surveys which seek to identify persons with drinking problems in the general population often show male to female ratios other than 5.5:1. One such survey in Louisiana (Rutledge, Carroll, & Perkins, 1974) reports a 4:1 ratio and the authors suggest that,

> since fellow workers constitute the social groups with which persons tend to drink most frequently, the escalated movement of women into the labor force may expose them to drinking behavior more frequently. (p. 109)

This 4:1 ratio is consistent with the national survey findings of Cahalan, Cisin, and Crossley (1969): heavy drinkers constitute 21% of the male sample and 5% of the female.

It is not necessary to see this as a sign of the decadence of our times, but it does appear that the rate of female alcoholism has risen over the last two decades. It is really an academic question in one sense: whether the rate has risen or not, we do not have adequate treatment facilities for those women who come for help.

THE DEVELOPMENT OF ALCOHOLISM AMONG WOMEN

The organization of the research literature into physiological, psychological, and social factors is based on a view of alcoholism that

physiological predisposing factors	+	psychological predisposing factors	+	social predisposing factors

add up to a high potential for alcoholism. While none of these factors is unique to alcoholic persons, the *combination* makes for high risk, and in adult life, the stresses which are inevitable, may trigger problem drinking.

This formula seems to apply to many groups of women alcoholics but not to all. There are women who are into problem drinking in their teens and others who have no problem until their 50's. There are women in state hospitals and prisons with long histories of socioeconomic and emotional deprivation, and there are well-to-do women in private hospitals. One formula will hardly cover all. The research literature tends to be about women alcoholics in their 30's and 40's, usually middle class, usually white.

PHYSIOLOGICAL FACTORS. Related to problem drinking in women are a number of physiological variables: the menstrual cycle and premenstrual tensions, gynecological-obstetrical problems, the fetal alcohol syndrome, menopause, and the medical complications of alcoholism.

The menstrual cycle and premenstrual tensions: Jones (1975) has demonstrated that female subjects with the same amount of alcohol attain a significantly higher blood alcohol level during the premenstrual phase than at other times in the cycle. This suggests some support for a relationship between premenstrual tension and female alcoholism.

Belfer, Shader, Carroll and Harmatz (1971) studied this relationship and report that the majority of their sample of 34 alcoholic women did indeed relate their drinking to their menstrual cycle. But Driscoll and Barr (1972) in their study of drug dependent and alcoholic women report,

> Other studies associating mood changes to women's menstrual cycles, particularly the premenstrual period, were not supported by the analyzed data. Only one alcoholic woman (sample of 100) offered such information spontaneously. (p. 18)

Support for a stress viewpoint, i.e. that emotional response and conflict rather than premenstrual tension per se may trigger problem drinking, comes from a historical comparison. Studying women hospitalized at different times in the same private hospital, Browne-Mayers et al. (1975) note that 80% of women alcoholic patients in 1933 (Wall, 1937) and 23% of patients in 1972 reported dysmenorrhea. There are behaviors, e.g., fainting, blushing, menstrual complaint, i.e., largely learned "feminine" responses which vary over time. One need not deny the very real discomforts of the premenstrual period for some women, but its use as rationalization and defense to account for alcohol problems should be understood. Premenstrual tension, while organic in origin, seems to be a reminder of tensions and conflicts about being female.

Gynecological-obstetrical problems: A relatively high incidence of infertility problems, miscarriages, and hysterectomies seem to occur among alcoholic women. Kinsey

(1966) stated that his sample of state hospital alcoholic women frequently associated the onset of alcoholism with "physiological disorders of some type." These disorders, however, included homosexuality, menopause, and frigidity, the last reported by 74%. Infertility was reported by 28% of Kinsey's subjects. Wilsnack's (1973) comparison of the gynecological-obstetrical difficulties of alcoholic women and a control group included infertility, miscarriages, hysterectomy, difficult birth, and difficulties in conceiving and carrying to term. The difference between the two groups is significant: of the alcoholic women, 78% report problems, and of the controls, 35%.

Whether the high incidence of gynecological-obstetrical problems acts as precipitant for a vulnerable woman, or whether it is a consequence is unclear. The age distribution we find in most facilities suggests the former; although there are many young women alcoholics, most are likely to be at or near the end of their childbearing period when they seek help. Of course it is more complicated than that; the women, when they come at age 40, may have been alcoholic for years, including their childbearing years. Nor, considering the very high incidence of alcoholism in the families of alcoholic women, can we rule out a possible genetic component which might contribute to an alcoholism-proneness and possibly to gynecological-obstetrical problems.

Fetal alcohol syndrome: There has been much interest in the effects of various drugs on pregnant women and the fetuses, triggered partly by concern over the effects of drugs prescribed during pregnancy and partly by concern over the apparent addiction-withdrawal behavior of infants born to addict mothers.

An early study of alcohol effects described the *fetal alcohol syndrome*: a pattern of craniofacial, limb, and cardiovascular defects associated with maternal alcoholism (Jones, Smith, Ulleland, & Streissguth, 1973), and a second study reported abnormalities suggestive of the syndrome in 32%, a perinatal mortality of 17%, and mental deficiency in 44% (Jones, Smith, Streissguth, & Myrianthopoulos, 1974). A recent paper (Streissguth, 1975) reports evidence of significantly lower intelligence in the children of chronic alcoholic mothers compared with controls and the presence of severe fetal alcohol syndrome signs in 8 out of 12 offspring studied. Streissguth does list several caveats: (a) the possible relationship between social class, alcoholism, and intellectual deficit, (b) the fact that some children of alcoholic mothers showed no intellectual defect, and (c) the fact that the subjects did manifest "complications secondary to alcoholism."

It has been pointed out (Warner & Rosett, 1975) that the idea of defective children produced by maternal alcoholism is many centuries old, and that it was, within recent times, set aside in favor of explanations that emphasize poor home environments and poor nutrition.

Other research has been reported. In a study of 200 women from a prenatal care clinic, mean age 23.6 (Rosett, 1975), it was found that 14 of the women were classified as "heavy drinkers," but of these 11 reduced their alcohol intake during pregnancy. Most of these heavy drinking women were also heavy smokers and had inadequate diets during the pregnancy.

No one will argue with the high probability of negative effects on the fetus of heavy drug/alcohol intake by the mother.

It does seem important to clarify the role of (a) heavy smoking and poor diet, (b) social class differences in health, prenatal care, etc., (c) the presence of medical complications of continued heavy drinking, (d) possible diagnoses other than alcoholism in the mothers, e.g., mental retardation, and to distinguish between heavy and problem drinkers who continue drinking heavily throughout a pregnancy and those who stop.

Menopause: It has been suggested that a relationship exists between menopause and susceptibility of the liver to the toxic effects of alcohol (Wilkinson, Santamaria, & Rankin, 1969). The prevalence of cirrhosis, it was noted, increases slightly with age among men alcoholics but increases markedly with women alcoholics in the age range 40 to 60 years old. Research on the "empty nest", depressed behavior of middle-aged women might be relevant.

Medical complications: There do appear to be sex differences in the incidence and mortality from cirrhosis among alcoholics (Pequignot, 1974; Spain, 1945; Tokuhata, Digon, & Ramaswamy, 1971). Comparative study of sex differences in the various medical complications of alcoholism is needed.

PSYCHOLOGICAL FACTORS. There has been a proliferation of reviews which emphasize psychological studies (Beckman, 1975; Gomberg, 1974; Lindbeck, 1972; Schuckit, 1972). The research literature not only presents conflicting findings, but analysis of psychological factors relating problem drinking to early learning or to recent learning is rare although the psychodynamic approach clearly emphasizes the former, and learning theory emphasizes the latter. There are some factors, however, which are reported frequently in the research literature:

1. Early life experiences which may include alcoholism or mental illness in the family, loss of a parent, and other stresses which seem to result in difficulty in forming interdependent relationships. This difficulty in turn produces isolation and loneliness.

2. Many potential problem drinkers develop attitudes toward feminine sex roles which are described as "hyperfemininity" or "overidentification," a very high valuation of wife-mother-homemaker role.

3. Parallel to this, there tends to be overt social behavior which is passive-submissive and a good deal of covert resentment and anger.

4. Tolerance for frustration, delay, disappointment seems inadequate; impulse control is inadequate.

We believe that there is a sequence of events and response which makes for a high degree of vulnerability or proneness to alcoholism. Early life experience has made for an adolescence characterized by isolation, difficulty in accepting healthy dependency relationships, depressed feelings, and unpredictable impulsivity (Jones, 1971). In this upheaval the vulnerable young woman turns toward love and marriage with its promise of happiness, expectations which cannot possibly be fulfilled[2]. Frustration in marriage, a

---

[2]The relationship between expectations of need satisfaction and alcohol use is explored in a study of college women: the lower the expectation the greater the recourse to alcohol (Jessor, Carman, & Grossman, 1968).

low degree of frustration tolerance and of impulse control make a combination which leads to trouble. Alcohol appears as a kind of magic substance which dims the sharpness of conflict, and the multiple reinforcements of alcohol for this woman become apparent: drinking is pretty much subject to one's own control; alcohol is available; it permits one to express hostility toward others and self-contempt, too; it is escape, fantasies of feminine happiness, a balm for psychic pain.

How might this relate to the clinical picture of an alcoholic woman entering a facility? It is important to realize that by the time most women seek help, there is a history of problem drinking with its inevitable shifts over time, but there is also a compounding because of the effects, social and physical, of drinking. The distaste and rejection of people in her world, including "helpers", i.e., husbands, physicians, family and friends, counselors, etc. has compounded the distrust.

Some of the women who come for help have done well with their lives and their responsibilities up to a recent point, and perhaps we should make a distinction between essential and reactive female alcoholism. What seem most relevant to rehabilitation are past effectiveness and present style of coping, precipitating stresses and frustrations which seem to have triggered the problem drinking, and the consequences -- no small task to sort out.

Isolation: The theme of loneliness and isolation goes back to early work (e.g., Curran, 1937). In recent work, the theme is recurrent. Garrett & Bahr (1973) conclude about women on skid row:

> Homeless women do not participate in the drinking institutions of skid row in the same way as men, and their drinking activities...are considerably less group oriented than those of men...homeless women alcoholics may very well be the most isolated and disaffiliated residents of skid row (p. 1240).

Or about women in a working class tavern, described by LeMasters (1975):

> There are a few women who frequent the tavern who obviously 'have a drinking problem'...One of these women...would appear at the Oasis several times a week and drink beer until she could scarcely walk. She was not accepted by the other women at the tavern and was also avoided by most of the men.
>
> Several other women who might be labeled 'alcoholics'...made their appearance at the Oasis at various times and disappeared. These were fringe members and not accepted by the regular customers. (p. 152)

Loneliness and isolation may occur as somewhat different phenomena in lower-income and higher-income women. Fort (1949) suggested that women in the "higher social classes" were more protected against public disgrace but more punished within the family. Class difference is one line of research; another is age difference: the study of isolation and affiliative behavior of women alcoholics under 30 and older women alcoholics or those with long histories of problem drinking and those who have recently and reactively developed a drinking problem.

Sex role problems: This issue is discussed in most of the recent reviews. In essence, findings seem to be that at least on a conscious, articulated level, women alcoholics often emphasize and value traditional female role activity, but data and clinical observations suggest that there are intense conflicts. It seems remarkable that similar findings are available about male alcoholics (Jones, 1968; McCord & McCord, 1960). The McCords speak, in fact, of "a facade of intense masculinity." Certainly conflict over being a woman or a man and the ambiguity in current social definitions of sex role are universally experienced. But one is struck with this mirror image finding in the two sexes: both men and women who become alcoholic as adults show overemphasis on and overidentification with the masculine/feminine role as adolescents.

Anger: Inadequate handling of one's aggressive feelings does seem to be a strong component of alcoholism-proneness for both men and women. There are leads in some early reports which seem worth following: the intensity, overtness, and direction of aggression seems to vary with prognosis and to shift among treated alcoholics, both male and female (Lisansky, 1967).

Frustration tolerance: Jones' reports of longitudinal research (1968, 1971) permit some comparison of problem drinkers of both sexes and, interestingly: "There are 10 characteristics which the problem drinkers of both sexes have in common. These are in the area of unstable, unpredictable impulsivity." (p. 68)

SOCIAL FACTORS. One of the consistencies of the research literature is the very large percentage of women alcoholics who have an alcoholic "significant other" while growing up or in adult life. But research in this area is minimal.

How about the influence of peer groups in adolescence, among young and older adults? We know that the social contagion of alcoholism goes from husband to wife significantly more frequently than it goes in the other direction (the same is true of addiction to narcotics), but what about peer patterns? There is a sizeable percentage of women in the labor force: what are the drinking patterns of women factory workers, office workers, executives? One recent survey (Rutledge et al., 1974) shows "fellow workers" to be the group with whom their respondents drank most frequently. The popular image of the woman alcoholic is of a suburban housewife, but there are indications that problem drinking rates are at least as high for women who work outside the home (Gomberg, 1975).

We may assume that there are differences in female alcoholism rates and patterns in different ethnic, racial, and religious groups. Social class differences are probably significant. Tamerin, Neumann, and Marshall (1971), describing upper-class alcoholism, write:

> In a lower-class woman this amount of drinking would not be considered socially acceptable, and would be observed, or regarded as deviant earlier. Certainly a welfare mother's drinking would come to the attention of a supervising caseworker in a relatively short period of time.

To date, however, it would seem that the most significant social determinants of female alcoholism lie within the family. For women, the likelihood that there will be an alcoholic model within the family is far greater for those who become alcoholic than for those who do not and greater than for men who do.

DRINKING BEHAVIOR AND PATTERNS OF WOMEN ALCOHOLICS

There are consistent findings that women in general start to manifest problem drinking at a later age than men, that they come for treatment with shorter histories, and that they more often cite a specific stress or traumatic event as precipitant to problem drinking. It is probably true that there is more heterogeneity and variability among women alcoholics than among men although when they show up for detoxification after years of drinking, the "sameness in secondary behaviors, i.e., reactions to excessive drinking" (Lisansky, 1960) make for homogeneity. We know that women tend to be solitary drinkers much more often than are men, but this seems related to customary social roles (particularly as housewives) and to greater disapproval of public drinking. We know that women alcoholics tend to use drugs other than alcohol more frequently than men alcoholics, but that again is related to findings about women's drug use in the general population (Alcohol and Other Drug Use and Abuse in the State of Michigan, 1975; Differential Drug Use Within the New York State Labor Force, 1971).

We would like to know more about different groups; about the drinking behavior of women prisoner alcoholics, Lesbian women alcoholics, adolescent problem drinkers, and so on. We need more information about black female alcoholism. A higher percentage of black women than white are abstainers, and a higher percentage of those who drink are heavy drinkers (Cahalan et al., 1969). Black women alcoholics begin alcohol use at an earlier age than white women alcoholics although the ages are the same for the use of other drugs (Driscoll

& Barr, 1972). Black women heavy drinkers, compared with black women moderate drinkers, are less apt to be regular churchgoers and less often have Southern rural backgrounds. They are also more likely to have a heavy drinker at home, to drink for reasons of "personal escape," and to drink in public places than moderate female drinkers (Sterne & Pittman, 1972).

A recent report compares hospitalized samples of men and women alcoholics, black and white, and finds men reporting significantly earlier onset, more daily and morning drinking, more bender drinking, and more delirium tremens and blackouts (Rimmer, Pitts, Reich, & Winokur, 1971). Studies have consistently reported more suicide attempts by women than by men alcoholics; the rate of suicide is significantly higher among alcoholics than it is in the general population, and the pattern of more women attempters and more male completed suicides is the same among alcoholics as it is in the population at large.

Reports are also consistent that alcoholic women are far more likely to be drinking with spouse or male companion than are alcoholic men with wife or girl friend (e.g., Wanberg & Knapp, 1970). Study of the husbands of alcoholic women has just begun (Busch, Kormendy, & Feuerlein, 1973; Rimmer, 1974). A recent article ("Equal Opportunity for Lushes," 1974) notes that an analysis of women's magazines from 1967 to 1971 yielded 24 articles on alcoholism in all of which the alcoholic was a woman. It comments:

> Five of the 13 wives of alcoholics were represented as nagging contributors to their husbands' conditions. In only four stories were they seen as supportive of their husbands' recoveries. The husbands of alcoholics, on the other hand, were labeled sympathetic and helpful in six of the 10 cases.

Lindbeck (1972) notes that, "the nonalcoholic spouse of the alcoholic woman is more likely to be regarded as a deprived person who receives more sympathy than censure" (p. 575). That makes for an interesting contrast with the literature on the wives of alcoholic men. Lindbeck also notes the wide variety of responses from husbands of alcoholic women: denial, protectiveness, bewilderment, anger; the alcoholic woman's husband "uses denial more extensively than his female counterpart."

It seems pretty evident that the pattern of consequences related to drinking will differ for men and for women. Men are more likely to come for help under job pressure. Women alcoholics are better able to conceal their alcoholism, but difficulties in marriage and divorce are more common in marriages where the woman is a problem drinker. It is a clinical observation often made that women come more frequently by themselves to a facility. Arrests and hospitalizations are reported more frequently by men alcoholics (Edwards, et al., 1972; Lisansky, 1957; Rimmer et al., 1971). Comparison of the sexes on the medical consequences of alcoholism merits study.

From the research literature (and from common sense knowledge of social roles) the generalization can be made that men seem to feel the consequences of their alcoholism more frequently in the work situation; women within the family. Men have more of the legal consequences, i.e., arrests, but this varies among women depending upon social class.

ARE MEN AND WOMEN ALCOHOLICS THE SAME OR DIFFERENT?

We have come quite a distance. A generation ago, women alcoholics were described as "much more abnormal" (Karpman, 1948). Now there are many who argue that there are, "no really obvious clinical differences" (Lester, 1975). If we look at the question, there appear to be several different components:

1. The presenting clinical picture: what the therapist sees and what the patient reports of his/her drinking and other behaviors.

2. The past history including disruptions and frustrations, the reasons for drinking, the factors that precipitate one into alcoholism, the factors that drive one to seek help.

3. Deviance from the norms established by society as to what is acceptable behavior for men and for women.

4. Prognosis for recovery, response to treatment and resistances.

From the feminists comes a demand for "'equal' treatment for women...defined as the same kinds of facilities" (Kammeier, 1975). But is this a demand for equal resources or for identical therapies? Do we rehabilitate as though the sex of the patient was irrelevant? Should women patients have women therapists? Is it possible to gather data about alcoholism that are not biased by cultural definitions of acceptable masculine and female behaviors?

Clinically, the caretakers, those who detoxify, deal with inpatient problems, work with the alcoholic patient, and struggle with the family, feel that male and female alcoholism present no really obvious clinical differences. For rehabilitators, differences are overridden by the realistic problems of patient care. The abuse of alcohol and the goal of effective coping without dependence on alcohol is the same for both sexes. But there are differences: definition of adjustment and goals of therapy may vary; there is, for example, some evidence that reconstituting the family, the emotional support system, may be more significant for alcoholic women than for their male counterparts. Societal attitudes toward men and women alcoholics are not the same; stigma and rejection are greater for women. Loneliness and isolation characterize many alcoholics of both sexes, but it seems to be more widespread and deeper among women.

CLINICAL PICTURE. Those who cope with alcoholic emergencies and rehabilitation emphasize the sameness. When we look at research data about patterns of alcohol abuse and effects, a mixed conclusion emerges. Where an attempt has been made to compare men and women alcoholics on psychological tests, the results are inconclusive. Using the MMPI, Zelen, Fox, Gould, and Olson (1966) report no significant differences, while Mogar, Wilson, and Helm (1970) report different profiles for men and women alcoholics. Curlee (1970) found "quite similar" patterns; Goss and Morosko (1970) found differences, and Jansen and Hoffmann (1973) found that, "the similarities between the two sexes clearly outnumber the differences." Although clinically it is observed that women alcoholics seem harder on themselves than men alcoholics, a test of self-esteem (Clarke, 1974) showed no significant sex difference. In a treatment setting, men and women patients report almost identical perceptions of significant daily events (Kammeier,

Lucero, & Anderson, 1973).

The question of psychiatric diagnosis is relevant although here one runs into the difficulty of criteria used for diagnosis and whether they are the same for men and women (e.g., in diagnosing depression). Comparing women alcoholics and drug addicts, Driscoll and Barr (1972) report an approximately equal percentage of personality disorder, primary passive-aggressive personality, but the two groups differ in the frequency of depressive neurosis, more common among the alcoholic women. There are few comparisons of men and women alcoholics in diagnosis, but Mogar et al (1970) report five distinct MMPI types among female alcoholics: normal, depressive, hysterical, psychopathic, and passive-aggressive, and four types among the men: passive-aggressive, depressive compulsive, schizoid prepsychotic, and passive dependent. Hoffmann and Jackson (1974) used the Differential Personality Inventory and report male subjects scoring significantly higher in character disorder and women alcoholics significantly higher in neuroticism scales. This may be a fruitful line of inquiry if neurotic and impulse disorder behavior can be defined and measured in a meaningful way for both sexes.

PAST HISTORY. Generally, women more frequently report an early history of family disruption by death, divorce, alcoholism, or psychiatric disorder. These comparisons do not seem very meaningful because an early history of family disruption is found frequently in other disorders and frequently among individuals who show no deviant behavior at all. How are we to answer the question as to whether emotional deprivation is the same experience for a male and a female child?

Comparisons seem more meaningful if we confine ourselves to recent events, i.e., the development of problem drinking, the consequences, and the reason for coming for help. If we take reasons for drinking, a recent study (Edwards et al., 1973) suggests that motivation is the same ("ataractic" reasons) and also different in that social pressure to drink is a more significant motivator for women. Kielholz (1970) reports, as do many others, that the reasons for problem drinking differ among men and women alcoholics. If one asks alcoholics what precipitated their drinking, we know that women more frequently cite a specific traumatic event, and this may be a greater vulnerability to stress, more defensiveness, or the simple truth.

The percentage of women alcoholics who are separated or divorced from their husbands is higher than the male percentage. Cause-effect may work two ways here: problem drinking may lead the husband to break up the marriage more often than nonalcoholic wives break up their marriages. It may also be true that marital breakup leads to problem drinking more often among women than among men.

If we look at patterns of drinking, women begin somewhat later and show up at facilities with shorter alcoholic histories; this, of course, will not apply to adolescents and very young women, but it does appear that among very young alcoholics, the stages of alcoholism are shortened and telescoped anyway. What, where, and with whom one drinks differs for the sexes: women do less drinking in public places, drink more often alone, drink with spouse or family member more frequently. Women alcoholics tend to use drug substances other than alcohol more often than men alcoholics (also true of female/male comparison in the general population, at least with reference to drugs like minor tranquilizers and barbiturates). The consequences of alcoholism are different. Among heroin addicts, too, there is clear indication of more social disapproval and punishment for the female addict (Maglin, 1974). Clinicians report that there is more guilt and more self-condemnation among women patients, and this may be a reflection of different social response. Reasons for coming to a facility differ, and the usual description is that women come more frequently because of marital disruption, men because of job problems. How this varies with social class, and how it will change as more women enter the labor force is suggested by a report of Sjolund (1971) of admissions to a state hospital in which 33% of the women reported job loss because of drinking, and 53% had arrest records.

DEVIANCE FROM NORMATIVE BEHAVIOR. Since alcoholism among women is more disapproved than alcoholism among men, the reasoning seems to be that the female alcoholic must be an individual more deviant from female norms than male alcoholics from male norms. The trend of evidence is that alcoholic women do indeed deviate more from feminine normative behavior than alcoholic men from male normative behavior. Jones' (1971) comparison of behavior ratings shows:

> Ratings for men who were problem drinkers differed at significant levels from other drinkers on 41 of 100 traits. For women, there were 62 such differences in ratings

> suggesting that women who drink excessively are more unlike the normal drinkers of their sex than are male problem drinkers unlike other men who drink. (p. 68)

A recent psychological test study found female inpatient alcoholics differing from a normative sample more than male inpatients from a male normative sample (Nowicki & Hopper, 1974), and a prevalance study in Canada, using an alcoholic consumption method, notes that "female alcoholics deviate more drastically from the drinking norms than do male alcoholics" (deLint & Schmidt, 1973).

Does this consistent finding that alcoholic women differ more from female normative behavior than alcoholic men from male normative behavior mean that "their alcoholism is of a more serious nature" (deLint & Schmidt, 1973)? Are they a more disturbed group? It seems reasonable to me that we may accept the idea of greater deviance without necessarily accepting the idea of "sicker." First, we may safely assume that greater deviance elicits more social punishment, and such punishment is already interwoven in the clinical picture of the alcoholic woman. The societal and self condemnation result in "depressive, self-negating, distrustful tendencies" seen more in alcoholic women than men (Jones, 1971). Breaking away from the normative restrictions on one's sex is not necessarily maladaptive, pathological, or "sick".

PROGNOSIS AND RESPONSE TO THERAPY. The issue of prognosis and outcome is clouded by conflicting reports, some reporting women patients as more improved (Fox & Smith, 1959; Hoffmann, 1975; Kattan, Horwitz, Caballero, Cordua, & Marambio, 1973) or as equally improved compared with men in treatment (Davies,

Shepherd, & Myers, 1956). Some studies report better outcome with male patients (Pemberton, 1967). Bateman and Petersen (1972) report different prognostic indicators for men and women alcoholics, with only age and full time employeemnt significant as indicators for both sexes.

Suppose that rather than better or worse prognosis, we assume that patterns of response to treatment will differ. Years ago, Karpman (1948) noted that "it is hard to keep (women) in treatment," but can we assume that dropping out at first try will mean the same for men and women? Curlee (1970) reported that women alcoholic patients had "been in and out of therapy repeatedly" more than men. But Fitzgerald, Pasewark, and Clark (1971) report from a four year follow-up study:

> Our results suggest that a higher dropout rate among women can be anticipated during their first treatment attempt. However, this dropout rate does not appear to have the same significance as in men. While in men, noncompletion on first admission is a rough predictor of noncompletion in a second treatment attempt, for women this predictor cannot be used as effectively. Many of the women who are good prospects for later treatment efforts drop out of the program during their first try. (p. 642)

We are suggesting that patterns of response to treatment and prognostic indicators do differ in the two sexes and that this may be a useful research direction. At the same time, factors such as intactness of the family, employment, social competence, and presence of supportive persons are undoubtedly relevent to both sexes although possibly of different weightings.

TREATMENT CONSIDERATIONS

Are men and women alcoholics the same or different, and are their treatment needs the same? They are the same, and they are different; abuse of alcohol is an overriding commonality, and clinicians who must deal with medical consequences and rehabilitation issues are likely to emphasize the samenesses. But men's and women's lives are different; they diverge sharply at adolescence, and it is true that the patterns of vulnerability, alcohol usage, and consequences show more differences than similarities.

Does this mean separate treatment facilities or women therapists for women clients? This question cannot be answered objectively--it is a matter of opinion, and it is my opinion that while some all-female residential units and all-female therapy groups should be available, segregation of therapy by sex seems unnecessary.

Can we not have men and women alcoholics using a clinic or hospital in which rehabilitating persons recognize the special needs of men and women? What are some of the special needs of women? First, recognition of the heavier social disapproval and the wariness with which women often approach a treatment situation. Second, a concern in detoxification and hospital units not only with the restoration of health but with aid in the restoration of one's appearance. Third, understanding the fact that alcoholic women will come often with few marketable skills and in greater need of vocational help and training than men clients. Fourth, emphasis and insistence on conjoint therapy, conjoint with husband or lover, parent, or anyone else who will be part of the rehabilitating social environment. If there is no supportive family structure left, the woman will need help and training in the business of living and coping on her own. Fifth, recognition of the difference between alcoholic men and women relating to concern about the children. Most alcoholic women are deeply concerned about their children, and help with the children's problems is essential. The children of alcoholics, male or female, tend to be troubled persons with a high risk for alcoholism.

Although the evidence is not equally good for all facets of this description, what does seem to hold up with time and a variety of clinical and research reports is this: the alcoholism prone woman begins significantly often with an early history of deprivation, of trouble in early family life in the form of death, desertion, psychiatric disorder, or alcoholism among relatives. She develops into an isolated, distrustful adolescent, fearful of dependence, rather pessimistic and depressed, often unpredictably impulsive and inadequate in frustration tolerance and defense mechanisms for coping with stress. The facade she presents is one of intense femininity, an overidentification with the traditional female role. It is striking that conflict over dependence and over the issue of traditional sex role should be characteristic of both men and women alcoholics.

When marriages falter, when childrearing or a job brings its inevitable strains, alcohol soothes. When difficulties relating to female physiological or obstetrical problems arise, alcohol soothes. Along with the dependency on alcohol comes use of other drug substances, often prescribed. The alcoholic woman will drink alone or, if her husband collaborates, with him, but the family knows, the neighborhood knows, and she in turn knows their view of her. Some women go on self-destructively to the ruin of health and family life; others reach an ultimatum point in their lives, and sometimes the ultimatum is from within. When she appears at a facility, she will have a shorter alcoholic history than her male counterpart, less difficulty with the law but more family rejection.

We need information and sex comparisons on the patterns of response to therapy, on the development of medical complications of alcoholism, on related psychiatric diagnoses, and the differential social and familial repercussions of alcoholism. We need comparisons between women who choose different drugs of dependence and between alcoholic women and those who express their conflicts in other symptomatic behaviors. We need to study alcoholic women who are young, middle-aged, and old; who are black or belong to other minority groups; respectables and women in prison; and alcoholic women who are poor, working class, middle class, and wealthy.

REFERENCES

Alcohol and health: First special report to the U.S. Congress. (DHEW Publication No. (HSM) 72-9099). Washington, D.C.: U.S. Government Printing Office, 1971.

Alcohol and other drug use and abuse in the State of Michigan: *Summary report*. Lansing, Michigan: Office of Substance Abuse Services, Department of Public Health, 1975.

Bateman, N.I., & Petersen, D.M. Factors related to outcome of treatment for hospitalized white male and female alcoholics. *Journal of Drug Issues*, 1972, *2*, 66-74.

Beckman, L.J. Women alcoholics: A review of social and psychological studies. *Journal of Studies on Alcohol*, 1975, *36*, 797-824.

Belfer, M.L., Shader, R.I., Carroll, M., & Harmatz, J.S. Alcoholism in women. *Archives of General Psychiatry*, 1971, *25*, 540-544.

Browne-Mayers, A.N., Hamilton, F.J., Seelye, E.E., & Sillman, L. *Psychosocial study of hospitalized middle class alcoholic women in the U.S.* Unpublished manuscript, Bloomingdale Hospital, White Plains, N.Y., 1975.

Busch, H., Kormendy, E., & Feuerlein, W. Partners of female alcoholics. *British Journal of Addiction*, 1973, *68*, 179-184.

Cahalan, D., Cisin, I.H., & Crossley, H.M. *American drinking practices: A national study of drinking behavior and attitudes*. New Brunswick, N.J.: Rutgers Center of Alcohol Studies, 1969, (Monograph No.6).

Clarke, S.K. Self esteem among men and women alcoholics. *Journal of Studies on Alcohol*, 1974, *35*, 1380-1381.

Curlee, J. A comparison of male and female patients at an alcoholic treatment center. *The Journal of Psychology*, 1970, *74*, 239-247.

Curran, F.J. Personality studies in alcoholic women. *Journal of Nervous and Mental Disease*, 1937, *86*, 645-667.

Davies, D.L., Shepherd, M., & Myers, E. The two-years' prognosis of 50 alcohol addicts after treatment in hospital. *Quarterly Journal of Studies on Alcohol*, 1956, *17*, 485-502.

de Lint, J., & Schmidt W. *Alcoholism prevalence in male and female population : A brief note*. Substudy No. 545, Toronto: Addiction Research Foundation, 1973.

Differential drug use within the New York State labor force. Supplement to *An assessment of drug use within the general population*, New York Narcotic Addiction Control Commission, 1971.

Driscoll, G.Z., & Barr, H.L. Comparative study of drug dependent and alcoholic women. *Proceedings of the 23rd Annual Meeting of the Alcohol and Drug Problems Association of North America*, Atlanta, Georgia, 1972.

Edwards, G., Hensman, C., & Peto, J. Drinking in a London suburb. III. Comparisons of drinking troubles among men and women. *Quarterly Journal of Studies on Alcohol*, 1972, *Suppl. 6*, 120-128.

Edwards, G., Hensman, C., & Peto, J. A comparison of male and female motivation for drinking. *International Journal of Addictions*, 1973, *8*, 577-587.

Equal opportunity for lushes. *Human Behavior*, May 1974, p. 42.

Fitzgerald, B.J., Pasewark, R.A., & Clark, R. Four-year follow-up of alcoholics treated at a rural state hospital. *Quarterly Journal of Studies on Alcohol*, 1971, *32*, 636-642.

Fort, T.W. *A preliminary study of social factors in the alcoholism of women*. Master's thesis, Texas Christian University, 1949.

Fox, V., & Smith, M.A. Evaluation of a chemopsychotherapeutic program for the rehabilitation of alcoholics: Observations over a two-year period. *Quarterly Journal of Studies on Alcohol*, 1959, *20*, 767-780.

Garrett, G.R., & Bahr, H.M. Women on skid row. *Quarterly Journal of Studies on Alcohol*, 1973, *34*, 1228-1243.

Gomberg, E.S. Etiology of alcoholism. *Journal of Consulting and Clinical Psychology*, 1968, *32*, 18-20.

Gomberg, E.S. Women and alcoholism. In V. Franks & V. Burtle (Eds.), *Women in Therapy*. New York: Brunner/Mazel, 1974.

Gomberg, E.S. *Alcoholism and women: State of the knowledge today*. Paper presented at the meeting of the National Council on Alcoholism, Milwaukee, April 1975.

Gomberg, E.S. Alcoholism in women. In H. Kissin & H. Begleiter (Eds.), *The biology of alcoholism*(Vol. 4) New York: Plenum Press, in press.

Goss, A., & Morosko, T.E. Relation between a dimension of internal-external control and the MMPI with an alcoholic population. *Journal of Consulting and Clinical Psychology*, 1970, *34*, 189-192.

Hanson, D.J. Drinking attitudes and behaviors among college students. *Alcohol and Drug Education*, 1974, *19*, 6-14.

Hoffmann, H., & Jackson, D.N. Differential personality inventory for male and female alcoholics. *Psychological Reports*, 1974, *34*, 21-22.

Hoffmann, H., & Noem, A.A. Sex differences in a state hospital population of alcoholics on admission and treatment variables. *Psychological Reports* (in press).

Hoffmann, H. Personal communication, April 28, 1975.

Jansen, D.G., & Hoffman, H. Demographic and MMPI characteristics of male and female state hospital alcoholic patients. *Psychological Reports*, 1973, *33*, 561-562.

Jellinek, E.M. Recent trends in alcoholism and in alcohol consumption. *Quarterly Journal of Studies on Alcohol*, 1947, *8*, 1-42.

Jessor, R., Carman, R.S., & Grossman, P.H. Expectations of need satisfaction and drinking patterns of college students. *Quarterly Journal of Studies on Alcohol*, 1968, *29*, 101-116.

Jones, B.M. Alcohol and women: Intoxication levels and memory impairment as related to the menstrual cycle. *Alcohol Technical Reports*, 1975, *4*, 1-11. Oklahoma State Department of Mental Health Division on Alcoholism.

Jones, K.L., Smith, D.W., Streissguth, A.P., & Myrianthopoulos, N.C. Outcome in offspring of chronic alcoholic women. *Lancet*, 1974, 1076-1078.

Jones, K.L., Smith, D.W., Ulleland, C.N., & Streissguth, P. Pattern of malformation in offspring of chronic alcoholic mothers. *Lancet*, 1973, 1267-1271.

Jones, M.C. Personality correlates and antecedents of drinking patterns in adult males. *Journal of Consulting and Clinical Psychology*, 1968, *32*, 2-12.

Jones, M.C. Personality antecedents and correlates of drinking patterns in women. *Journal of Consulting and Clinical Psychology*, 1971, *36*, 61-69.

Jones, R.W., & Helrich, A.R. Treatment of alcoholism by physicians in private practice, a national survey. *Quarterly Journal of Studies on Alcohol*, 1972, *33*, 117-131.

Kammeier, S.M.L. Alcoholism and women. *The Catholic Woman*, May-June 1975, p. 14.

Kammeier, S.M.L., Lucero, R.J., & Anderson, D.J. Events of crucial importance during alcoholism treatment, as reported by patients. *Quarterly Journal of Studies on Alcohol*, 1973, *34*, 1172-1179.

Karpman, B. *The alcoholic woman*. Washington, D.C.: Linacre Press, 1948.

Kattan, L., Horwitz, J., Caballero, E., Cordua, M., & Marambio, C. [Evaluation of results of alcoholism treatment in women: Indicators of prognostic value]. *Acta Psiquiátry Psicologia América Latin*, 1973, *19*, 265-279. (*Quarterly Journal of Studies on Alcohol*, 1974, *35*, Abstract No. 679).

Kielholz, P. Alcohol and depression. *British Journal of Addiction*, 1970, *65*, 187-193.

Kinsey, B. *The female alcoholic: A social psychological study*. Springfield, Ill.: Charles C Thomas, 1966.

Knupfer, G. *Female drinking patterns*. Paper presented at the 15th Annual Meeting of the North American Association of Alcoholism Programs, Washington, D.C., September 1964.

Lawrence, J.J., & Maxwell, M.A. Drinking and socioeconomic status. In D.J. Pittman & C.R. Snyder (Eds.), *Society, culture and drinking patterns*. New York: John Wiley & Sons, 1962.

LeMasters, E.E. *Blue-collar aristocrats*. Madison: University of Wisconsin Press, 1975.

Lester, B.K. Alcoholism and women. *Alcohol Technical Reports*, 1975, *4*, 1-3. Oklahoma State Department of Mental Health Division on Alcoholism.

Lindbeck, V. The woman alcoholic: A review of the literature. *International Journal of Addictions*, 1972, *7*, 567-580.

Lisansky, E.S. Alcoholism in women: Social and psychological concomitants. *Quarterly Journal of Studies on Alcohol*, 1957, *18*, 588-623.

Lisansky, E.S. The etiology of alcoholism: The role of psychological predispostion. *Quarterly Journal of Studies on Alcohol*, 1960, *21*, 314-343.

Lisansky, E.S. Clinical research in alcoholism and the use of psychological tests: A reevaluation. In R. Fox (Ed.) *Alcoholism: Behavioral research, therapeutic approaches*. New York: Springer, 1967.

Maglin, A. Sex role differences in heroin addiction. *Social Casework*, 1974, *55*, 160-167.

McCord, W., & McCord, J. *Origins of alcoholism*, Stanford University Press, 1960.

Mogar, R.F., Wilson, W.M., & Helm, S.T. Personality subtypes of male and female alcholic patients. *International Journal of the Addictions*, 1970, *5*, 99-113.

Norris, J.L. *A.A.'s 1974 membership survey*. Paper read at the North American Congress on Alcohol and Drug Problems, San Francisco, December 18, 1974.

Nowicki, S., & Hopper, A.E. Locus of control correlates in an alcoholic population. *Journal of Consulting and Clinical Psychology*, 1974, *42*, 735-740.

Oltman, J.E., & Friedman, S. Trends in admissions to a state hospital, 1942-1964. *Archives of General Psychiatry*, 1965, *13*, 544-551.

Pemberton, D.A. A comparison of the outcome of treatment in female and male alcoholics. *British Journal of Psychiatry*, 1967, *113*, 367-373.

Pequignot, G. [Nutritional problems of industrial society]. *Vie medicale au Canada françois*, 1974, *3*, 216-225. (*Quarterly Journal of Studies on Alcohol*, 1974, *35*, Abstract No. 742).

Rimmer, J. Psychiatric illness in husbands of alcoholics. *Quarterly Journal of Studies on Alcohol*, 1974, *35*, 281-283.

Rimmer, J., Pitts, F.N. Jr., Reich, T., & Winokur, G. Alcoholism. II. Sex, socioeconomic status, and race in two hospitalized samples. *Quarterly Journal of Studies on Alcohol*, 1971, *32*, 942-952.

Rosett, H.L. *A pilot prospective study of the fetal alcohol syndrome at the Boston City Hospital*: I. *Maternal drinking*. Paper presented at the meeting of the National Council on Alcoholism, Milwaukee, April 1975.

Rosin, A.J., & Glatt, M.M. Alcohol excess in the elderly. *Quarterly Journal of Studies on Alcohol*, 1971, *32*, 53-59.

Rutledge, C.C., Carroll, G.B., & Perkins, R.A. *A socio-epidemiological study of alcoholism in East Baton Rouge Parish*. Baton Rouge: Alcohol and Drug Abuse Section, Division of Mental Health, Louisiana Health and Social and Rehabilitation Services Administration, and the School of Social Welfare, Louisiana State University, 1974.

Schuckit, M. The alcoholic woman: A literature review. *Psychiatry in Medicine*, 1972, *3*, 37-43.

Sjolund, G.C. Women's Alcoholic Rehabilitation Unit utilization in demographic data. *Maryland State Medical Journal*, 1971, *20*, 42-45.

Spain, D.M. Portal cirrhosis of the liver. A review of 250 necropsies with reference to sex differences. *American Journal of Clinical Pathology*, 1945, *15*, 215-218.

Spence, J.T., & Helmreich, R. The attitudes toward women scale: An objective instrument to measure attitudes toward the rights and roles of women in contemporary society. *Journal Supplement Abstract Service*, 1972, *2*, 66.

Sterne, M., & Pittman, D.J. *Drinking patterns in the ghetto* (Vol. 1 & 2). St. Louis: Social Science Institute, Washington University, 1972.

Straus, R., & Bacon, S.D. *Drinking in college*. New Haven: Yale University Press, 1953.

Streissguth, A.P. *Psychological handicaps in children with fetal alcohol syndrome*. Paper presented at the annual meeting of the National Council on Alcoholism, Milwaukee, April 27-29, 1975.

Tamerin, J.S., Neumann, C.P., & Marshall, M.H. The upper-class alcoholic: A syndrome in itself? *Psychosomatics*, 1971, *12*, 200-204.

Tokuhata, G.K., Digon, E., & Ramaswamy, K. Alcohol sales and socioeconomic factors related to cirrhosis of the liver mortality in Pennsylvania. *HSMHA Health Reports*, 1971, *86*, 253-264.

Wall, J.H. A study of alcoholism in women. *American Journal of Psychiatry*, 1937, *93*, 943-952.

Wanberg, K.W., & Knapp, J. Differences in drinking symptoms and behavior of men and women alcoholics. *British Journal of Addictions*, 1970, *64*, 347-355.

Warner, R.H., & Rosett, H.L. The effect of drinking on offspring: An historical survey of the American and British literature. *Journal of Studies on Alcohol*, 1975, *36*, 1395-1420.

Wilkinson, P., Santamaria, J.N., & Rankin, J.G. Epidemiology of alcoholic cirrhosis. *Australas. Annals of Medicine*, 1969, *18*, 222-226.

Wilsnack, S.C. Sex-role identity in female alcoholism. *Journal of Abnormal Psychology*, 1973, *82*, 253-261.

Zelen, S.L., Fox, J., Gould, E., & Olson, R.W. Sex-contingent differences between male and female alcoholics. *Journal of Clinical Psychology*, 1966, *22*, 160-165.

Part III

Treatment Approaches

CHAPTER 17

PSYCHOTHERAPY: INTEGRATION OF INDIVIDUAL AND GROUP METHODS

Douglas H. Fehr

The treatment of alcoholism makes heavy demands on psychotherapists and allied health professionals. By the time the alcoholic seeks treatment, his personal, social, and financial resources are frequently all but exhausted, and even then, he accepts help only reluctantly. His rehabilitation is expensive, time consuming, and, all too often, unsuccessful. Because the alcoholic represents such a difficult treatment task, most agencies utilize a multifaceted approach, involving a number of treatment specialists and modalities while relying heavily on psychotherapy as their therapeutic mainstay.

The alcoholic is widely viewed as a poor treatment risk who makes only limited use of therapeutic efforts on his behalf (Hartocollis, 1964; Szasz, 1966), and there is no doubt that it is frustrating to the psychotherapist who

Ralph E. Tarter and A. Arthur Sugerman (eds.), Alcoholism

ISBN: 0-201-08146-6
ISBN: 0-201-08145-8 (pbk.)

sees techniques that work well with, for example, neurotics, frequently fail with alcoholics. Despite rather discouraging results, however, health professionals continue to rely on psychotherapy in one form or another as a primary treatment tool, although they have had to set rather modest goals for a vast majority of those treated since few alcoholics continue treatment long enough to make substantial changes in their overall functioning.

In working concurrently for the past five years at an alcohol treatment program and a university hospital outpatient clinic, this writer has observed that many of the more conventional, "nondirective" psychotherapeutic methods were not as effective with alcoholic as with nonalcoholic patients. Specific treatment problems encountered in his work with alcoholics necessitated some modifications of psychotherapeutic methods typically utilized in the treatment of neurotic outpatients. The culmination of these modifications is an approach which combines individual and group psychotherapy methods within the context of a group setting. Before considering this approach in detail, some of the problems encountered with alcoholics will be discussed.

PASSIVITY OF THE ALCOHOLIC

In working with the alcoholic, the psychotherapist is faced with the difficult task of how to conduct psychotherapy with a passive participant who often enters treatment reluctantly, and even then only because of outside pressure. Many alcoholics have little sincere desire to stop drinking, seeking only medical relief from withdrawal symptoms or a place to be detoxified. Consent to undergo treatment is accompanied by the expectation of quick relief either from a short stay in the hospital or a limited number of outpatient meetings. The belief among many psychotherapists that alcoholics have poor motivation for treatment has led many psychotherapists to exclude alcoholics from their practices, choosing instead to work with more personally satisfying patients. The alcoholics' passivity simply overwhelms many psychotherapists, especially within the individual treatment setting.

That the alcoholic is passive-dependent seems obvious. In fact, this is so much the case that many investigators merely mention it in passing and without elaboration. Passivity, more than any other characteristic, is seen as the hallmark of the alcoholic. This conclusion is aptly expressed in a statement by Blane (1968):

> No-one is certain that there is one personality trait that serves as the central organizing factor among most alcoholics. However, one observer after another has implicated conflict over dependency wishes in one form or another. Details of formulations vary and language differs, but dependency and inner struggles with it form the background of much of what has been said about the alcoholic. (p.33)

The alcoholic's passivity is reflected in the expectation with which he approaches treatment; he expects the psychotherapist or agency to assume the major responsibility in stopping his drinking. Schiff and Schiff (1971) discuss the difficulties involved in treating patients where passive behaviors are significantly present. The major treatment hurdle is that these passive patients discount that they have any problems. When they do recognize the existence of problems, they often fail to see their significance. Frequently, even when they do recognize their significance, "it doesn't matter because the problems can't be solved anyway." That is, they discount the solvability of their difficulties, leaving no hope for anything better in their lives.

The alcoholic is rarely able to recognize the real reasons for his drinking. Many do not even see their excessive alcohol consumption per se as a significant problem and deny difficulties that seem blatantly obvious to the observer. Many patients appear quite oblivious to consequences of their particular life styles and fail to comprehend, for example, the seriousness of the physical problems as well as the drastic social consequences that accompany continued alcohol consumption. It is said that alcoholics just do not want to stop drinking. It seems more accurate to state that many alcoholics do not realize the possibility of another type of lifestyle. For them, alcoholism is really the only "career" they have known.

In contrast with the above, neurotic patients frequently have identified their major difficulties by the time they seek the services of a psychotherapist. They are concerned about their marriage, other significant relationships, and/or other aspects of themselves. These patients seem to have hope that their problems can be solved as suggested by the very fact that many are self-referrals. With such patients the psychotherapist functions much like a "consultant". The patient does much of the therapeutic work on his own, frequently between therapy sessions. The psychotherapist listens, guides, and in general, attempts to limit his input to a few carefully selected interventions. In fact, he is most likely to err in the direction of too much intervention. With alcoholics, in contrast, the therapeutic error is more likely to be made in the direction of too little intervention. The more nondirective or inactive the therapist, the less effective he is likely to be. More conventional type psychotherapies simply do not have much impact on the passive alcoholic patient.

The passive-dependent behavior of the alcoholic thus poses serious psychotherapeutic problems, and conventional methods are frequently inadequate. In particular, the demands placed on the psychotherapist who treats alcoholics in an outpatient setting are so overwhelming that treatment is often doomed from the start. Those who have continued to work with alcoholics have had to modify substantially many of their psychotherapeutic methods to counter this pervasive passivity. Additionally, the psychotherapist is forced to modify his expectation that the patient is motivated to undergo treatment.

GROUP PSYCHOTHERAPY WITH ALCOHOLICS

Alcoholics in group therapy tend to support each other's passivity. Valuable group time is expended in overcoming this pervasive group resistance to any substantive therapeutic movement. It is, of course, not unexpected that alcoholics would reinforce each other's avoidance behaviors. This cohesiveness is in part due to the homogeneous symptom of the group members. The group rallies around the subject of alcoholism, its causes and cures, endlessly debates the merits of Alcoholics Anonymous, and covers many issues, typically extraneous to the task at hand. New topics introduced for group discussion are generally circumstantial, being offered only to aid the group in avoiding significant issues. Group members focus on themselves and each other as alcoholics rather than persons, thereby limiting the amount of genuine interaction possible among themselves. As such, there is relatively little in these early exchanges between group members that can be considered therapeutically productive.

Group therapy is generally more effective when the members are capable of comparable levels of participation in the group. All patients should be able to comprehend the significance of the major interactions within the group and, ideally, the more subtle meanings as well. As the group moves to a more intensive and sophisticated level of functioning, hopefully no patients are left behind. With alcohol groups, this level of group functioning is rarely attained and, if so, only after a considerable number of meetings. This is in part due to the fact that alcoholics are highly variable in their response to psychotherapeutic intervention. Patients in group therapy progress at widely varying rates with some patients making rapid therapeutic progress right from the onset of treatment, while others require much time before they even begin to make use of the group. What is effective intervention for one patient frequently leads to little or no change for another. Reconstructive type therapy is helpful to some patients, whereas others need primarily supportive therapy. Frequently, there are a few patients who "carry the group," the rest making substantially less progress often because they need considerably more individual psychotherapy. Patients also vary in psychological awareness, intellectual functioning, social competence level, and various other factors which influence the effectiveness of psychotherapeutic interventions.

This diversity in response to treatment intervention represents a major stumbling block in alcohol therapy groups which depend on the group members to be the primary change-agents for each other. Many such patients either are not capable of this or take an inordinate length of time to become so. Those requiring a considerable amount of individual psychotherapy literally have to be taught how to be effective group participants which, as outlined in the next section, can be accomplished in a *diagnostic-teaching phase* of psychotherapy. This prefacing of the conventional treatment phase with a diagnostic-teaching phase seems essential in the view of this writer in the effective treatment of this disorder.

INDIVIDUAL PSYCHOTHERAPY WITHIN THE GROUP SETTING

In this section, individual psychotherapy procedures in a group setting as utilized in the present approach are discussed. In a following section consideration will be given to the combined use of individual and group procedures in the group treatment setting. Individual psychotherapy is utilized most extensively in the initial phases of treatment, with group psychotherapy procedures introduced as the members become more sophisticated in their ability to be change-agents for themselves and each other. To clarify the manner in which some essential terms will be used, I offer the following definitions: In *group psychotherapy*, therapeutic exchanges take place between the psychotherapist and the various group members, or directly between the patients in the group. The psychotherapist attends to the interactions of the individual group members and to group process as a whole. In contrast, in *individual psychotherapy* within a group setting, the exchanges are primarily, and at times solely, between the psychotherapist and a *single patient*. There is little or no interaction between the psychotherapist and other group members or between the group members themselves. Rather, the psychotherapist systematically does individual therapy with one patient at a time.

The seating arrangement for individual psychotherapy within the group setting is presented in Figure 1. It is

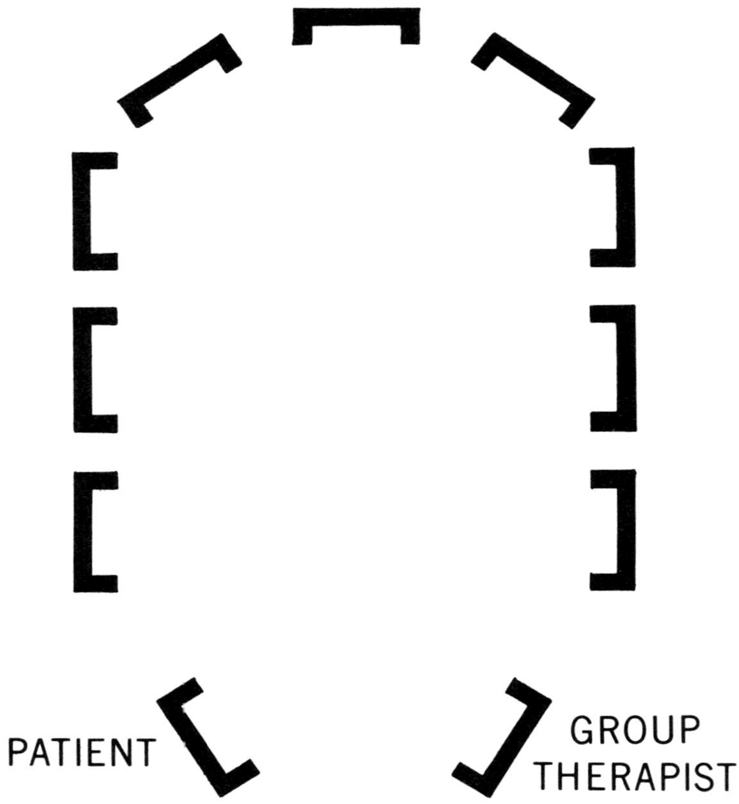

Figure 1 GROUP THERAPY SEATING DIAGRAM

similar in most respects to other group settings except for the two chairs at the front of the group which are for the therapist and the particular patient working in individual therapy. These chairs are positioned so that the occupants may look and talk directly to each other, or they may face and speak directly to other members in the group. This seating arrangement allows the therapist and patient flexibility for talking directly to each other or other members of the group. The proximity of the chairs also enables therapist and patient to more easily speak to each other. This arrangement is similar to the "working chair" or "hot seat" concept employed in those approaches where therapeutic exchanges are primarily between the therapist and patient.

In this psychotherapy setting patients are in the working chair for time periods varying from a few minutes to usually no more than twenty minutes. The time spent with each patient in a given session varies, depending primarily on the needs of the particular patient. Insofar as possible, individual sessions are relatively brief so as to enable more patients to participate within a given therapy session. The psychotherapist takes primary responsibility for treatment in this initial phase of therapy maintaining a highly active position contrasted to the previously discussed "consultant role". Indeed, the essence of the approach is active therapeutic intervention by the psychotherapist working intensely with each individual patient.

The patient assumes relatively little treatment responsibility at this time. A minimum level of participation might consist of answering questions, providing information, and paying attention. Because underlying problems are so difficult for the alcoholic patient to identify, it is necessary for the psychotherapist to take the lead in identifying them. The psychotherapist explores what these problems are, their significance in the patient's life and suggests changes that the patient might make if he chose to do so. To ask the patient to be primarily responsible for doing this is rarely productive as alcoholics are seldom able to state the real reasons for their drinking behavior. The psychotherapist must find a way to respond to each patient's way of discounting his problems, the significance of his problems, and their solvability (Schiff & Schiff, 1971). To counter the discount, the psychotherapist repeatedly brings to the patient's attention certain realities that he, the patient, would rather avoid. The psychotherapist offers his opinion as to the seriousness of the situation since it is essential for the patient to accept the fact that he has significant problems in addition to his major symptom. His genuine acceptance of these problems, however vague his understanding of them, is the first indication of positive therapeutic movement.

During these initial phases of individual group treatment, occasional exchanges between group members occur which, while accepted, are not encouraged. If they are relevant and brief, the psychotherapist accepts them without comment. If, however, the intervening patient's statements interrupt or detract from the ongoing therapeutic work, the psychotherapist steps in. His task is to stop the patient's interruption, rather than explore or interpret the patient's behavior. The manner in which the therapist accomplishes this varies with each patient. One way is to ask a relevant question about that patient who is already in the working chair. This is usually enough to redirect the group's focus.

A more direct way is to simply stop the interruption with an explanation to the patient and group.

There are times when a group member interrupts the patient in the working chair and continues talking despite the psychotherapist's efforts. When this happens, this patient is asked to come up to the working chair and continue his "interruption." The psychotherapist explores the meaning of the interruption, typically leading to a short therapy session with that person. This procedure interrupts the work of the patient who is already in the working chair but generally presents no real problem since the therapist can return to that patient.

Occasionally a group member interrupts not to detract but because another patient's individual work has stimulated some thoughts about his own life. This sharing may entail only a few brief comments or expression of feelings and does not substantially interrupt the therapy of the person in the working chair. If, however, the patient wishes to share more than a few comments, he comes up to the working chair and continues. Typically occurring after a given patient has finished his individual work, this therapeutic maneuver has been referred to as "coat-tailing" by some psychotherapists.

The next section of this chapter discusses the combination of individual diagnostic-teaching methods and group psychotherapy procedures. Before moving on, however, I want to mention one other psychotherapeutic issue (anxiety level) involved in the diagnostic-teaching phase of treatment and offer a brief example to illustrate how psychotherapeutic interventions vary with the specific patient, his defenses, and anxiety levels.

With each patient, an optimal level of anxiety is

necessary to maximize treatment impact. The group therapist diagnoses moment to moment the individual patient's stress level, and therapeutic interventions are gauged accordingly. If anxiety is too low or too high, the patient may terminate treatment. Some patients immediately return to drinking if they become too anxious; others have an initial high level of anxiety only to terminate abruptly if it is alleviated too quickly. The optimal level depends on a number of patient and treatment variables, one of the most important being the amount of support available to the patient, i.e., in an inpatient setting, support would likely be greater than in an outpatient clinic.

Individual patient's treatment needs are different, and therapeutic interventions vary accordingly. Patients are aware that each is treated uniquely and generally accept this. An example of this differential treatment is the way the psychotherapist deals with highly defended patients, many of whom remain resistant to change despite multiple therapeutic interventions. Some of these patients are most effectively worked with initially by consistently confronting denials and rationalizations. The therapist repeatedly cuts across undue verbiage and directs the patient to concentrate on what is therapeutically significant. In contrast, there are patients who rely heavily on the same defenses of denial and rationalization, but for whom therapeutic handling must be extremely gentle. The therapist works closely with the patient, focusing on concrete specific daily living problems rather than confronting defensive behavior. Therapy goals for such patients are usually limited, as the therapist reaches an early decision that reconstructive therapy would be not only extremely difficult but unrealistic as well.

COMBINED INDIVIDUAL AND GROUP THERAPY

The shift from the sole usage of *individual psychotherapy* sessions within the group setting to the addition of *group psychotherapy* procedures as well occurs only after each patient has had a number of individual sessions in the working chair. At this point, patients have identified problems and have begun to work on them, and the psychotherapist can begin to permit interaction between group members. The point at which the psychotherapist begins to make use of group psychotherapy procedures has to do with the issue of diagnosis vs. treatment. That is, in the early stages of the group, the therapeutic focus is primarily one of diagnosis. The therapist knows, of course, that the official diagnosis is one of alcoholism, but frequently neither he nor the patient know much more than this. Individual psychotherapy is a most effective procedure in these early stages of treatment specifically to allow psychotherapist and patient to identify the patient's problems and their significance in his life. Individual psychotherapy is most effective in diagnosis precisely because the psychotherapist obviously has greater psychodiagnostic skill than either the patient or patients collectively. Much valuable group therapy time is expended in alcohol groups where the therapist does not take such an active therapeutic stance but rather relies heavily on group process and interactions. In the early stages, then, the primary goal is one of diagnosis; only after the patient had identified problems and become concerned about them, can treatment "officially" begin.

As the task shifts to a greater emphasis on treatment as opposed to diagnosis, group psychotherapy techniques are introduced into the treatment plan. Now, patients begin to face the task, often reluctantly, of making changes within themselves and their life situations. Individual psychotherapy continues to be utilized by the therapist and is now combined with group therapy procedures. It is only in the early stages of treatment that there is a fairly clear distinction between diagnosis and treatment. This distinction is, of course, somewhat artificial and only a matter of emphasis inasmuch as both diagnosis and therapy are constantly overlapping and interacting processes. It is, however, a useful distinction for determining when individual or group procedures are most effectively applied.

Individual psychotherapy in the working chair continues in the second and primarily treatment (as opposed to diagnostic) phase with an increase in utilization of group therapy procedures occurring gradually. The therapist has already spent considerable time with each patient. Through these individual sessions and by watching others in the working chair, patients have gradually learned to be more effective group participants. They begin to make spontaneous comments following individual sessions in the working chair. Initially, these comments are made directly to the therapist about the person in the chair and only later directly to that person. Group member comments increase as they see what is relevant and are willing to risk making direct statements. The next phase involves more exchanges directly between the various group members. Thus, for example, members may expand on a topic that has arisen during a patient's individual session.

By the time the group reaches the point where members spontaneously interact, the quality of group functioning has changed dramatically. Group members are now more psychologically sophisticated; they recognize each other's denials and rationalizations and are less cautious about confronting each other. Patients model after the therapist whom they have seen repeatedly confront and provide feedback in individual sessions; they share thoughts and opinions and even on occasion directly express feelings towards each other. The honest sharing of positive and negative feelings between group members now leads to more authentic relationships between some members.

The group as a whole moves progressively to a more mature level of functioning. It is at this time that the very powerful effects of the group members' interaction and overall group therapy processes are most evident. Group members are now capable of being therapeutically helpful to each other and group interaction is not only desirable but essential for confronting the passivity and avoidance behaviors of group members.

Once the group attains this level of functioning, it more closely approximates group therapy with neurotics. As such, more conventional psychotherapy procedures can be utilized, and the therapist is able to take a less active therapeutic stance. He openly encourages group members to assume more of the treatment responsibility. At the same time, as the amount of interaction between group members increases, however, the therapist still engages in considerable individual therapy work. He now has more flexibility in the use of both individual and group procedures and is more able to individualize treatment for each patient, taking into account the varying capacities of group members. Some patients profit more by interacting with members; others need considerable individual work often throughout the whole course of treatment. Flexibility in the use of both individual and group procedures becomes more evident with increasing group maturity. Because of his awareness of the patient's reality, the psychotherapist has been a change-agent from the onset of the group; only after a period of training do the group members become similarly effective.

In this mature stage of group process, it is important to stress that the psychotherapist exercise considerable sensitivity in choosing between his own interventions and those of group members. When an individual member or the group as a whole are capable of being their own change-agents, he encourages them to do so. He is careful not to do the therapeutic work that the individual or group is capable of doing on their own, lest he err in the direction of too much intervention. Nonetheless, he continues to take a highly active therapeutic stance where appropriate.

SUMMARY

The treatment of alcoholism presents to the psychotherapist a number of problems with which the more conventional "nondirective" psychotherapeutic methods deal inadequately. Specifically, the psychotherapeutic task is a difficult one because alcoholic patients tend to assume a passive stance with regard to their drinking problems as well as other concomitant life problems. Therapeutic intervention typically meets with much resistance. To counter this passivity, the psychotherapist is forced to modify his methods by assuming a more active, intervening, psychotherapeutic position.

The approach presented in this chapter combines individual and group psychotherapy methods within the group setting. In the early stages of treatment, the psychotherapist works individually with each patient, specifically excluding interaction among members of the group. This is a *diagnostic-teaching* phase of treatment wherein the patient explores those problems that contribute to and are associated with his excessive alcohol consumption. In this process, he also learns how to be an effective change-agent for himself and other group members. Thus, in the early stages of treatment, the group therapy time is utilized more efficiently in *individual diagnostic* work with each patient by the psychotherapist.

Conventional group psychotherapy procedures, where the emphasis is on the interaction between group members, are not employed during the early phases of treatment because of their relative ineffectiveness with this passive patient population. Such group procedures are, however, introduced into the treatment plan as the members progressively mature in their ability to function within the group. This approach leads to more efficient treatment by specifically excluding matters extraneous to the therapeutic task while enhancing consistent individual and group development.

ACKNOWLEDGEMENTS

This chapter was written while I was on the staff at the Veterans Administration Hospital in Oklahoma City. I am grateful to colleagues on the Alcohol Treatment Units for their suggestions and support. I wish to thank Del Vanderpool for reviewing the chapter and suggesting some important revisions. I am especially indebted to Grace Gavin for her invaluable assistance in the preparation and editing of this manuscript.

REFERENCES

Blane, H.T. *The personality of the alcoholic: Guises of dependency*. New York: Harper & Roe, 1968.

Hartocollis, P. Some phenomenological aspects of the alcoholic condition. *Psychiatry*, 1964, *27*, 345-348.

Schiff, A., & Schiff, J.L. Passivity. *Transactional Analysis Journal*, 1971, *1*, 71-77.

Szasz, T.S. Alcoholism: A socio-ethical perspective. *Western Medicine*, 1966, *7*, 15-21.

CHAPTER 18

A COMPREHENSIVE BEHAVIORAL APPROACH TO THE TREATMENT OF ALCOHOLISM

Peter M. Miller

Historically, the treatment of alcoholism has been characterized by a variety of fads based upon the current popularity of a particular theoretical orientation. These fads involve the widespread application of a specific treatment modality (e.g., LSD, sensitivity training, transactional analysis) with claims that finally a viable alcoholism treatment has been found. Unfortunately, experimental efforts to evaluate the effects of these treatment strategies (apart from short-term attention-placebo effects apparently related to the enthusiasm of the therapist) have been few and in most cases non-existent.

Over the past several decades, behavior therapists have also been guilty of this faddism in the form of aversion therapy. The rationale for this simple conditioning approach is related to the fact that it is based upon well founded

Ralph E. Tarter and A. Arthur Sugerman (eds.), Alcoholism

ISBN: 0-201-08146-6
ISBN: 0-201-08145-8 (pbk.)

principles of learning developed through animal experimentation. Hersen, Eisler, and Miller (1975) note that early behaviorists "assumed that the principles of reinforcement governing the modification of simple motor responses of animals in a highly controlled laboratory setting could be applied directly to clinical disorders in humans" (p.9). Numerous investigators as early as 1929 reported clinical success rates ranging from 23% to 96% using either electrical (Blake, 1965; Kantorovich, 1929), chemical (Lemere & Voegtlin, 1950), or verbal (Anant, 1967; Cautela, 1966) aversion with chronic alcoholics. The efficacy of these treatments has only recently been challenged by direct controlled experimentation. For example, Hallam, Rachman, and Falkowski (1971) and Miller, Hersen, Eisler, and Hemphill (1973) concluded that the clinical success of electrical aversion therapy appears more related to general therapeutic factors (e.g., expectancy, social reinforcement by the therapist, demand characteristics of the situation) rather then conditioning per se. There appears to be a recent awareness on the part of behavior therapists that this rather naive approach to a complex clinical problem such as alcoholism is unwarranted. At best it may be a useful approach with patients who already possess adequate adjustment skills (Pattison, in press). Contemporary behavioral approaches to alcoholism are much more comprehensive in nature. Insistence on continuous monitoring of therapeutic progress is providing a much firmer base for current behavioral strategies.

Although empiricism is stressed, behavior therapists tend to view alcohol abuse within a social-learning model. Within this model, alcohol abuse is

> viewed as a socially acquired, learned behavior pattern maintained by numerous

> antecedent cues and consequent reinforcers that may be of a psychological, sociological, or physiological nature. Such factors as reduction in anxiety, increased social recognition and peer approval, enhanced ability to exhibit more varied spontaneous social behavior, or the avoidance of physiological withdrawal symptoms may maintain substance abuse (Miller & Eisler, in press).

Therapeutic goals within this framwork include (a) a detailed assessment of the specific antecedent and consequent events related to the excessive use of alcohol, (b) the use of social-learning treatment procedures to teach social skills that can serve as alternatives to abusive drinking, (c) the rearrangement of consequences for both excessive drinking and sobriety within the community environment, and (d) the short and long term evaluation of the effects of the intervention program using objective measurement procedures.

The alcoholism literature describing and researching these aspects of behavioral treatment is growing rapidly. Since this literature has been presented in detail and critically evaluated elsewhere (Franks, 1958, 1963, 1966, 1970; Hamburg, 1975; Miller, 1973; Miller, in press), the present chapter will represent an attempt to present the framework of a comprehensive treatment program for alcoholics based upon this literature.

ASSESSMENT OF THE PROBLEM

Behavior therapists consider a detailed behavioral assessment of the alcoholic as a necessary precursor to treatment. The purpose of this assessment is to provide a detailed picture of the functional relationships between abusive drinking and various cognitive, emotional, social, environmental, and physiological events associated with it. In addition, the extent and nature of the individual's drinking patterns must be objectively assessed without relying solely on self-reports. These initial or "baseline" assessments not only provide a basis for the establishment of a therapeutic plan but also help to establish criteria for the evaluation of that plan both during and after intervention.

In assessing alcoholic drinking behavior the therapist must use all of the sources of data at his disposal. These sources frequently consist of self-reports, reports based on observations by significant others, and direct observations by the therapist. In addition, behavior patterns which correlate with abusive drinking are evaluated. These might include number of hospitalizations or arrests for alcohol related problems. Self-reports of drinking by the alcoholic are the most easily obtainable source of data. However, due to the possibility of distortion, forgetfulness, or misrepresentation, the reliability of this information must be established. This can be accomplished by obtaining either continuous or periodic reports of the alcoholic's drinking from relatives, friends, or employers. The usefulness of self and other reported information is enhanced when the reporters are provided with a simple quantitative method for monitoring drinking behavior. L.C. Sobell and M.B. Sobell (1973) have devised an Alcohol Intake Sheet which is useful in this regard. This sheet is kept by the client or other and includes space for the date, specific type of drink, per cent of alcohol content in the drink, time the drink was ordered or prepared, number of sips per drink, amount of the drink consumed, and the situation in which drinking occurred. Specific data such as these promote discussions regarding antecedent conditions which serve to elicit abusive drinking. Behavior therapists help to ensure that these sheets are completed by frequent social reinforcement (i.e., praise and recognition) for the behavior. Care must be taken not to censure clients for reporting abusive drinking episodes since such reactions frequently lead to an avoidance of future confrontations by presenting only favorable reports.

Drinking behavior can also be assessed more directly and quantitatively through operant measures, taste test measures, ad lib drinking in simulated natural environments, and breath/alcohol assessments. The first three of these measures are analogues which are administered within the treatment facility. During the operant analogue measure, alcohol is made contingent upon the performance of a simple motor response such as lever pressing. Motivation for alcohol is quantified in terms of the number of lever presses to obtain alcohol which is delivered automatically by the operant apparatus. The system is often designed so that the more lever presses, the more alcohol is obtained. Treatment effects are easily evaluated on the basis of reductions in the number of lever presses. Cohen, Liebson, and Faillace (1971) and Miller, Hersen, Eisler, and Hemphill (1973) have demonstrated the sensitivity of this measure to therapeutic intervention. In addition, Miller, Hersen, Eisler, and Elkin (1973) have used this measure to assess alcoholics' motivation to participate in and benefit from a comprehensive behavioral treatment program. It appears that this operant measure may have predictive significance for treatment such that those who respond less on this measure respond better to treatment.

The "taste test" measure (Marlatt, Demming, & Reid, 1973; Miller & Hersen, 1972) is similar but more surreptitious. This measure is presented to the alcoholic under the guise of a taste rating task. He or she is then required to taste and rate various alcoholic and nonalcoholic beverages on such dimensions as sweet-sour or weak-strong. After completion of the task, the total amount of alcohol consumed serves as the drinking measure. Attitudes toward alcohol can be assessed by using a semantic differential rating scale and by scoring the evaluative dimension. This assessment procedure can be administered before and after treatment, or periodically, as a probe measure, throughout treatment.

A more naturalistic assessment procedure involves observations of the client's drinking in a simulated natural environment. Schaefer, Sobell, and Mills (1971) and Mills, Sobell, and Schaefer (1971) described the use of a cocktail lounge setting within a hospital dayroom. Subjects could order a variety of alcoholic beverages while observers both in the bar and via closed circuit television rated their drinking behavior. Miller, Becker, Foy, and Wooten (1975) utilized a living room setting and videotaped drinking in a similar manner. These measures have the advantage of allowing for a more comprehensive assessment not only of alcohol consumption per se but also the components (e.g., amount of sip, rate of drinking, potency of drinks) of the drinking process. In addition, the alcoholic's drinking in a wide range of situations (e.g., alone or with others) can be assessed. This procedure is especially relevant when controlled, social drinking, as opposed to complete abstinence, is the ultimate goal of treatment.

A more global measure is the assessment of blood/alcohol

levels via breath samples. Breath samples can be easily acquired randomly on an outpatient basis. Miller (1975) and Miller, Hersen, Eisler, and Watts (1974) successfully demonstrated the use of this procedure in evaluating the effects of contingency management of skid row alcoholics.

In addition to drinking behavior, the alcoholic's functioning in other important areas of life must be assessed prior to, during, and after treatment. This assessment is accomplished for two reasons. First, chronic abusive drinking frequently leads to marital, social, emotional, or occupational problems which must be resolved along with the drinking problem. Alterations in these stressful circumstances ensures a greater chance of long term therapeutic success. Voegtlin and Broz (1949), McCance and McCance (1969), and Lunde and Vogler (1970) have demonstrated a significant relationship between satisfactory social, emotional, and occupational functioning and therapeutic success in alcoholism treatment, regardless of the type of therapy used. Second, social-emotional problems can serve as precipitating events for excessive drinking and thus serve to maintain its occurrence. Accumulation of a detailed functional analysis of the social, emotional, cognitive, environmental, and physiological antecedents and consequences of drinking serves to delineate which factors or combination of factors must be modified. Treatment is then geared toward altering either the event itself (e.g., modifying the positive social consequences of drinking) or the individual's response to the event (e.g. teaching the individual to respond more assertively in anger provoking situations).

Antecedents and consequences of excessive drinking are frequently complex and varied. It is seldom the case that one factor, such as anxiety, by itself is the sole precipitating event for drinking. Recent research evidence (Cappell & Herman, 1972) has questioned this single factor notion which has been most often cited in reference to the tension reduction hypothesis. Individual alcoholics, however, are likely to attribute their drinking to single global factors such as anxiety or depression. In terms of behavioral treatment, a more descriptive assessment is necessary. For example, in the past, individual A may have initiated heavy drinking in response to the following set of circumstances occurring together: (a) an argument with his wife, (b) a critical remark by his boss, (c) feeling hurt and angry, (d) being encouraged by a friend to "have one drink to make you feel better." Specification of these antecedents enables the alcoholic to become attuned to events that lead to his drinking. In addition, treatment can be easily geared toward teaching new responses to "arguments with his wife" or "critical remarks" whereas the modification of general anxiety or "a poor self concept" can be less clearly defined.

The assessment of these areas of functioning can be evaluated in a variety of ways including self-reports, reports from significant others, and direct observations. Behavior therapists prefer direct observational information since it can be quantified, is objective, and its reliability can be readily established. Typically, social-emotional functioning is described in terms of excessive behaviors (e.g., high frequency of self-related conversation when with others) and deficit behaviors (e.g., inability to express personal rights and feelings). These can then be easily quantified and modified.

Direct observations of the alcoholic's social-emotional

functioning have been greatly enhanced by the use of closed circuit television systems. Eisler, Hersen, and Agras (1973) have described a videotaping procedure to assess interpersonal behavior. Through this system various verbal (number of positive comments) and non-verbal (smiling, eye contact) behaviors can be rated quantitatively from videotapes of marital or peer interactions.

On the basis of these assessment procedures two major therapeutic goals are established: (a) to teach the alcoholic behavior patterns that can serve as alternatives to alcohol abuse (specific alternatives vary from individual to individual and depend on the results of the initial assessment), and (b) to alter consequences of drinking behavior via family, friends, and employers (this strategy follows an operant conditioning approach in which certain systematic consequences -- extinction or social punishment -- lead to decreases in the problem behavior).

ALTERNATIVES TO ALCOHOL ABUSE

The range of possible alternatives to alcohol abuse is varied and depends, to a great extent, on the nature of the situations that precipitate drinking. Behaviors in which alcoholics are frequently deficient include social, self-management, relaxation, vocational, and recreational skills. With some alcoholics controlled social drinking is thought of as an alternative skill.

Social skills have generally been thought of in terms of assertiveness. Assertiveness is the ability to express both positive (e.g., complimentary remarks, statements of agreement) and negative (e.g., difference of opinion, statements of anger or dissatisfaction) feelings and remarks (Eisler et al., 1973). Social skills, however, are actually more complex than this, and research into their components has only recently been initiated. One important aspect of these skills includes the ability to initiate and maintain mutually satisfying personal relationships. Deficits in this ability may be particularly important with respect to an alcoholic whose drinking is precipitated by loneliness and boredom. Nathan and O'Brien (1971) have demonstrated that social isolation can serve as a powerful cue for excessive drinking in some alcoholics.

Behavior therapists, however, have focused mainly on teaching alcoholics (a) assertive skills and (b) marital interaction skills. Skills training is accomplished via a social learning model using a variety of procedures such as videotape feedback, instructions, modeling, behavioral rehearsal, and verbal reinforcement. Eisler, Miller, Hersen, and Alford (1974) illustrated the use of these techniques when they evaluated the effects of assertion training not only on an alcoholic's drinking but also on his marital relationship. The patient was a 52-year-old chronic alcoholic who typically handled conflicts, particularly with his wife, in a passive-avoidant manner. Using instructions, modeling by the therapist, videotape feedback, and behavioral rehearsal the patient was taught to behave more assertively in role-played marital encounters. A female therapist enacted the part of the patient's wife. Pre and post videotapes of marital interactions between the patient and his real wife indicated a marked change in his behavior toward her. On objective measures which were rated retrospectively from the tapes, he tended to look directly at her, speak more, be more direct, and offer constructive suggestions for marital improvement. The patient's drinking was also assessed via breath samples, collected randomly, during each of six weeks before and six weeks after treatment. Assertion training resulted in a marked decrease in mean blood/alcohol levels from .08% prior to treatment to .02% after treatment.

Assertion training has also been used to teach alcoholics how to refuse drinks when under social pressure. Foy, Miller, Eisler, and O'Toole (1975) have developed a procedure to teach the components of drink refusal. These components include: (a) eye contact, (b) affect, (c) requesting a change in the other person's behavior (e.g., "Please don't ask me again, I've quit drinking permanently"), (d) offering an alternative (e.g.,"No, I won't have a beer, but why don't we get a cup of coffee"), and (e) changing the subject. Role played scenes are enacted in which the alcoholic is pressured to take a drink with such arguments as,"Come on, one beer won't hurt you!" "What kind of a man are you?"; "If you were really my friend you'd have a drink with me!"; "It'll make you feel better!" Using videotaped modeling of appropriate responses together with instructions and feedback during practice sessions, alcoholics gradually learn to respond to these situations. Clients report a feeling of increased self esteem when they are able to successfully handle their "drinking buddies."

Muscular relaxation has also been taught as an alternative to drinking with alcoholics whose alcohol abuse is precipitated by anxiety. As an adjunct to aversion therapy, Blake (1967) reported that relaxation training resulted in a significantly higher rate of abstinence (46%) when compared to aversion therapy alone (23%). Steffen (1974) found that, with four chronic alcoholics, relaxation training resulted in decreased blood/alcohol levels, lower muscle tension levels, and less subjective anxiety. Kraft (1969) and Kraft and Al-Issa (1967) have utilized relaxation training as part of the more traditionally utilized systematic desensitization. In this procedure anxiety producing stituations associated with abusive drinking are repeatedly associated imaginally with relaxation. The authors report a number of case studies in which this procedure was used successfully in the treatment of alcoholism.

Self control or self-management skills have been used successfully as alternatives to overeating, chronic cigarette smoking, and other habit disorders. However, their use with alcoholics has been limited. This is probably due to the fact that this skills training approach is relatively new, and all possible alternatives have not as yet been investigated with alcoholics. Self-management skills consist of responses that the alcoholic himself makes which decrease the probability of drinking. They include self-monitoring, rearranging stimuli that precipitate drinking, or rearranging consequences of heavy drinking. In one of the few reported uses of this procedure with alcoholics, Miller (in press) describes self-management skills training in the context of a case study. The client was a 49-year-old salesman whose abusive drinking was limited to highly specific situations. These situations related to his business and included (a) being alone in a motel room when on a business trip and (b) being in a restaurant with a customer who is encouraging him to have a drink before dinner. Drinking in these situations resulted in binges lasting from a few days to two weeks. As a self-control program the client agreed to (a) arrange his business trips so that he would not have extended periods of time in motels, (b) arrange to excuse himself from business cocktail parties, (c) order a coke or coffee prior to dinner in a restaurant, and (d) learn (with the assistance of the therapist) to use prepared verbal statements when others encouraged him to take a drink. Relaxation was also taught, and the client was instructed to use it in a self-control manner whenever tension built up over a desire to drink. Using these rather simple procedures, the client has remained completely abstinent for one year.

Occupational and recreational skills are often extremely important as alternatives to drinking. In their community reinforcement approach to alcoholism, Hunt and Azrin (1973) developed specific ways to teach these skills. Probably the most basic occupational skill deficit for alcoholics involves finding a job opportunity and then successfully undergoing the job interview. Hunt and Azrin instructed their patients to prepare a resumé of their past experience, call friends and relatives for job leads, call the major factories and plants in the area, place an ad in the local newspaper, rehearse job interviews, and place applications for jobs that are available. Job interviews were practiced through role playing, and clients were provided with as much assistance as possible in regard to typing resumés, transportation to work, etc. Miller, Stanford, and Hemphill (1974) have used a similar procedure, placing much emphasis on rehearsing interviews through role playing. These investigators noted that the alcoholic's passive manner, his inability to "sell" his assets to potential employers, and his inability to answer difficult interview questions (e.g., "Why haven't you been working for the past two months?") were significant liabilities in job interviewing situations. Clients role played such interviews with a job counselor and were taught (through modeling, performance feedback, and behavioral rehearsal) more successful modes of handling an interview. Clients were taught to be positive about their abilities (e.g., "I'm certain that I can do this job if you'll give me the opportunity"), to honestly answer questions about their drinking (e.g., "Yes I have had a drinking problem in the past, but I have quit for good"), and to offer "behavioral proof" of his contention that he is serious about changing his drinking pattern (e.g., "I'll agree to take my Antabuse tablet in front of you everyday when I come to work").

Hunt and Azrin (1974) also stressed the development of social-recreational behavior patterns. The therapists created a social club for clients which was actually a former tavern! This club organized spare time activities such as parties, picnics, fish fries, bingo games, movies, and dances. Alcoholic beverages were strictly forbidden from these activities, and members who had been drinking prior to an activity or who brought alcohol with them were told to leave.

Another alternative behavior pattern is physical exercise. Although this has not been extensively used, Gary and Guthrie (1972) reported improvement in alcoholics' self-esteem, sleeping patterns, and cardiovascular functioning as a function of a daily jogging program.

One possible alternative to the abusive drinking of some alcoholics is the development of controlled, social drinking skills. There appears to be enough clinical (Lemere, 1953; Pattison, 1968: Selzer & Holloway, 1957;

Shea, 1954) and experimental (Lovibond & Caddy, 1970; Sobell & Sobell 1973b) evidence to support controlled drinking as an alternative goal to abstinence. At this point, however, it is not clear which individuals would be most likely to benefit from controlled drinking versus abstinence as a treatment goal. It may be that younger, less chronic alcoholics who have a history of social drinking would benefit most from a controlled drinking program. Certainly, regimes designed to teach the controlled use of alcohol are significant in terms of alcoholism prevention programs, for example, DWI projects (driving while intoxicated).

A number of clinical researchers have developed procedures to teach controlled drinking skills to alcoholics. Lovibond and Caddy (1970) taught alcoholics to discriminate their own blood/alcohol levels and then use this information to maintain moderate drinking. During discrimination training the client was instructed to drink alcohol mixed in fruit juice and then to periodically judge his blood/alcohol level on the basis of subjective feelings (e.g., numbness). Breathalyzer assessments were accumulated and the client was provided with feedback on the accuracy of his judgments. During conditioning sessions electric shocks were delivered to the client when his blood/alcohol level reached .065% or higher. Conditioning sessions were held on six to twelve different occasions. Alcoholics were taught to discriminate their blood/alcohol levels within + or - .01%. Results on 28 alcoholics undergoing this procedure indicated that 21 were maintaining controlled drinking patterns at follow-up contacts ranging from 16 to 60 weeks.

Sobell and Sobell (1973b) have presented the most comprehensive evaluation of a controlled drinking treatment procedure. Their behavioral approach was very comprehensive and included behavioral self-analysis, self-management training, social skills training, videotaped feedback of behavior, a programmed failure experience, and aversion conditioning to teach controlled drinking skills. In an experimental bar situation, subjects received electric shocks if they (a) ordered a straight as opposed to a mixed drink, (b) took a sip larger than 1/6 of the total volume of the beverage, (c) ordered a drink within 20 minutes of one previously ordered, and (d) ordered a total of more than 3 drinks. As treatment progressed, the clients could avoid all shocks by drinking in a controlled fashion. With groups of state hospital alcoholics, controlled drinking subjects actually performed better than subjects whose goal was abstinence on a number of drinking and social adjustment follow-up measures over a two year period of time. It was found that 78.90% of controlled drinking subjects were functioning well more than 80% of all follow-up days as compared to 53.87% of the abstinence subjects. Regardless of the goal, groups receiving behavior therapy were functioning significantly better at follow-up intervals than groups receiving traditional hospital care.

Finally, Miller, Becker, Foy, and Wooten (1975) found that simply instructing alcoholics in the components of controlled drinking led to moderation of drinking behavior within treatment sessions. It was also found that modification of one drinking component in the controlled drinking direction (i.e., taking smaller sips) frequently led to more "alcoholic" drinking in another component (i.e., drinking at a faster rate). The authors noted that such negative reciprocity among drinking components must be taken into account in treatment geared toward teaching controlled, social drinking.

ALTERING CONSEQUENCES

It has been demonstrated that reinforcing consequences of excessive drinking behavior actually helps to maintain its occurrence. Thus, increased attention from relatives and friends, even though it might be negative attention, may actually exacerbate the alcoholic's problems. On the other hand, alcoholics are frequently "saved" from naturally occurring negative consequences of their heavy drinking (e.g., being arrested and incarcerated) by well intentioned relatives and friends. Behavioral strategies attempt to schedule social-environmental consequences so that the alcoholic receives maximum rewards.for abstinence or moderate drinking and maximum punishment or withdrawal of rewards for excessive drinking. Miller (in press) notes that this approach involves the following elements:

1. Removal of reinforcers for abusive drinking.
2. Systematic, frequent, and varied social punishment for abusive drinking.
3. Reinforcement of behaviors incompatible with excessive drinking.
4. Rearrangement of environmental cues which set the occasion for abusive drinking.

Thus, while drinking is being suppressed, more appropriate behaviors are being reinforced. This helps to ensure that the alternative behavior patterns that the alcoholic learns in treatment (e.g., assertiveness) are maintained, over time, in the natural environment.

Probably the most basic method of altering consequences is through a token economy program with alcoholics in either inpatient or halfway house settings. In a token economy system patients are "paid off" (via points, credit slips, tokens) for appropriate, adaptive behaviors such as promptness, active participation in group therapy, or appropriate assertiveness. Credits are lost for inappropriate or counter-therapeutic activities such as physical abuse of another patient, voluntary social isolation, or drinking on the ward. These credits are then exchanged for hospital reinforcers such as ward privileges, passes, or more desirable living accommodations. The purpose of the token economy is threefold: (a) to teach the alcoholic the relationship between his or her behavior and its social-environmental consequences, (b) to foster more adaptive coping behaviors that can serve as alternatives to alcohol abuse, and (c) to provide a structured therapeutic environment to assist in ward management and in the smooth implementation of each patient's therapeutic plan.

Narrol (1967) was one of the first to report the use of this procedure with alcoholics. His goal was to increase activities of hospitalized alcoholics by paying them 100 points per hour for work assignments. As with money in the real world, patients were expected to use these points to purchase hospital room and board, clothing, maintenance, etc. Patients even paid for treatment with these points. Patients on this program averaged 8 hours of work per day compared to 4 hours a day for patients in a control group. The goal was to foster responsible occupational behaviors which would generalize to the natural environment after hospital discharge. Miller, Stanford, and Hemphill (1974) and Rozynko, Flint, Hammer, Swift, Kline, and King (1971) utilized a token economy more broadly in alcoholism treatment programs. Each group of investigators reinforced a wide range of personal-social and vocational activities.

In order to emphasize the influence of social pressure on an alcoholic's behavior, Cohen, Liebson, and Faillace (1971) used a group fine token economy. Under these conditions, whenever a patient was fined for inappropriate behavior, all other patients on the ward were fined a similar amount. This procedure resulted in a reduction of major ward infractions by 25%.

Although not within a token economy framework, Cohen, Liebson, & Faillace (1971) demonstrated the effects of altering consequences on drinking behavior per se. They initially allowed an inpatient alcoholic access to up to 24 ounces of ethanol daily. In an attempt to decrease alcohol consumption, if the patient drank five ounces of ethanol or less on a particular day, he was placed in an "enriched" ward environment complete with television, telephone, etc. Drinking above this level resulted in loss of all privileges for the rest of the day. When these contingencies were being applied (for as long as 5 successive weeks) the subject drank in moderation on all but two days. Drinking returned to immoderate levels when these contingencies were removed. Similar results have been reported in subsequent studies by Bigelow, Liebson, and Griffiths, (1973), Cohen, Liebson, Faillace, and Speers, (1971) and Liebson, Bigelow, and Flamer (1973) using a variety of reinforcers.

Once the alcoholic is an outpatient, more naturalistic reinforcers for his behavior must be used. This almost always requires the cooperation of friends, relatives, or employers. These significant others are trained to provide maximum social-emotional support and reinforcement for both sobriety and newly acquired coping skills. Simultaneously, they are taught to withdraw such reinforcement when the patient demonstrates heavy drinking or inappropriate behavior. These consequences are scheduled within a group setting in which the alcoholic, the significant other, and the therapist meet.

A good example of rearranging social reinforcers has been reported by Sulzer (1965). In this study peer companionship was made contingent upon total abstinence from alcholic beverages. It was arranged so that the client and his friends would meet periodically for a "drink." If the client ordered an alcoholic beverage at this meeting, his friends immediately left his presence. If he ordered a nonalcoholic beverage, they sat with him and conversed in a friendly manner. This set of circumstances is practically opposite from the traditional way in which many peers of alcoholics, or even social drinkers, respond to nonalcoholic drinking (particularly at a drinking event such as a cocktail party).

Most contingency management on an outpatient basis is scheduled through the use of behavioral contracts. These consist of signed written agreements between the alcoholic and others in his environment and specify the exact consequences which will accrue contingent upon his or her behavior. These contracts have the additional advantage of being reciprocal in that contingencies are also placed on the behavior of the significant others.

Miller (1972) reported the use of such a contract between a heavy drinker and his wife. The mutually agreed upon goal of treatment was moderate drinking (i.e., not more than three 1½ ounce alcoholic beverages either straight or mixed). The contract specified that the husband was to limit his daily drinking to three drinks maximum in the presence of his wife. Drinking more than this amount or in any other situation (as detected by reports from others or observations of intoxication) resulted in a $20 fine payable to his wife and immediate withdrawal of all social contact with the wife for the rest of the day. Moderate drinking resulted in increased attention and affection by the wife. The contract also specified that the wife was to refrain from all alcohol related nagging. Nagging resulted in her having to pay $20 to her husband and withdrawal of all attention from the husband for the rest of the day. Daily records of drinking were kept by both marital partners. Although a great deal of variability was noted early in the contracting period, the client's drinking decreased to the acceptable limits and stabilized there within three weeks. A six-month follow-up revealed improved marital adjustment and maintenance of a moderate drinking level.

In a similar case, Miller and Hersen (in press) combined the use of social skills training and behavioral contracting in the treatment of a 49-year-old alcoholic and his wife. Via videotaped sessions of marital interactions, modeling, feedback, and behavior rehearsal were used to teach the couple to (a) increase their ability to express themselves more directly and to solve problems more effectively, (b) increase positive verbal and nonverbal interactions, (c) decrease alcohol related discussions, (d) use positive social skills to modify each other's behavior. Concomitantly, mini-contracts were written at the end of each weekly treatment session. These were designed to expand and generalize behavior changes to the natural environment.

The contracts specified one or two behavioral goals that each partner would strive to achieve each week. In one contract, the wife agreed to refrain from mentioning her husband's past or possible future drinking. If she was successful at accomplishing this, her husband agreed to take her out to dinner, to a movie, for a drive, or shopping on three occasions. This reinforcer was utilized since the wife expressed a desire to engage in more frequent mutual outings with her husband. The agreement was binding on each partner only if the other partner fulfilled his or her part of the arrangement. Terms of the contract were renewable at the beginning of each day. The emphasis of treatment was placed on the couples's learning to negotiate and implement their own contracts based on problems as they arose. At nine months follow-up the husband had maintained complete abstinence and the couple's relationship had markedly improved.

Contracts can also be negotiated between the alcoholic and his or her employer. Such contracts might include the alcoholic's willingness to take Antabuse in the presence of his employer in return for the opportunity to work each day or possibly a small monetary bonus at the end of each week.

EVALUATION AND FOLLOW-UP

Objective, systematic evaluation of therapeutic progress is one of the major components of behavior therapy programs. This evaluation is closely tied into the initial assessment procedures. Thus, the alcoholic's behavior patterns both before and after treatment can be compared. In this way, each individual's progress is a function of changes in his own behavior after treatment rather than as a function of arbitrary standards of treatment success (e.g., total abstinence for one year). In fact, these arbitrary standards often do not reflect the full impact of the treatment program. For example, in past evaluations of many behavioral and non-behavioral treatment programs, only one major criterion of success or failure was established, namely, total abstinence for a specified period of time. Patients who did not stay totally abstinent for that time (e.g., one year) were classified as treatment failures. The fact that the individual's total life functioning had greatly improved, even though he had become intoxicated 4 to 5 times during the year, goes unnoticed. This would appear to be an illogical evaluation system which is not reflective of the vast array of changes which can occur or of the periodic ups and downs which occur in every individual's life (whether he is an alcoholic or not).

One of the best behavioral evaluation systems has been devised and implemented by Sobell and Sobell (1973a). In evaluating a comprehensive behavior therapy treatment program, they collected follow-up data for each patient on (a) number of days intoxicated (consumption of 10 ounces of alcohol or more), (b) number of controlled drinking days (consumption of 6 ounces of alcohol or less), (c) number of abstinent days, (d) number of abstinent days resulting from hospital or jail incarceration, (e) vocational status, (f) use of therapeutic supports (such as Alcoholics Anonymous), and (g) residential stability. One of the most important aspects of the evaluation procedure was that all information was verified by a number of sources other than the patient himself (e.g., friends, relatives, employers, courts, hospitals, Welfare

Department).

A complete follow-up evaluation should consist of information on the following dimensions: alcohol use, social-emotional functicning, vocational and/or educational functioning, and medical status. A sample treatment evaluation system follows:

1. ALCOHOL USE

a. *Self-reports*: Detailed data on self-monitoring of alcohol use should be accumulated. Daily or weekly checklist forms as to the use of alcohol should be filled out by patients and should be collected at 3,6,9 and 12-month follow-up intervals. Reliability of this information should be obtained via similar checklist forms filled out by friends or relatives.

b. *Breathalyzer assessments*: Blood/alcohol levels should be assessed via randomly administered breathalyzer tests. A number of random samples can be obtained at 3,6,9 and 12-month follow-up assessments.

c. *Arrest and hospitalization data*: Information on the exact number of alcohol related arrests and number of hospitalizations for alcohol related problems should be obtained through self-reports of clients. These reports can be validated via periodic contacts with local hospitals and law enforcement agencies. In this regard Sobell and Sobell (in press) have reported that the validity of alcoholics' reports of life history information (e.g., number of alcohol related arrests) is surprisingly high.

2. SOCIAL-EMOTIONAL ADJUSTMENT

a. *Self-reports*: Patients should be requested to keep daily or weekly entries in "behavioral diaries." Emphasis should be placed on information related to number and types of social contacts, events precipitating episodes of emotional stress, and specific responses to problem situations. Data should be accumulated weekly during treatment and at 3,6,9 and 12-month intervals at follow-up. Periodic contacts with significant others should be used to corroborate this information.

b. *Inventories*: Behavioral observations of the client's social and leisure time activities by relatives can be assessed by such inventories as the Katz Adjustment Scale (Katz & Lyerly, 1963), administered every three months during follow-up.

c. *Videotaped Interactions*: At 3-month intervals a standardized interpersonal and/or marital interaction between the client and a peer and/or spouse should be videotaped. The specific nature of the situations may include a simulated interaction involving such problems as refusing drinks under social pressure, solving a marital problem more efficiently, or expressing anger more appropriately. Videotapes can then be rated on a number of verbal (e.g., frequency of self-reference statements) and non-verbal (e.g., eye contact) components.

3. VOCATIONAL AND/OR EDUCATION FUNCTIONING

a. *Self-reports*: Weekly self-reports of attempts to find employment, number of days worked per week, or number of days attended school should be obtained.

b. *Check stubs*: To corroborate self-report data, paycheck stubs should be collected on a weekly or monthly basis.

c. *Grade reports*: Reports from schools or training facilities should be obtained periodically.

4. MEDICAL STATUS

a. *Self-reports*: At 3-month intervals reports from the client on medical complaints and physician visits should be obtained.

b. *Medical Examination*: General medical examinations including liver function studies should be obtained 2 to 3 times during follow-up period.

CONDLUSIONS AND FUTURE TRENDS

The major thrust of this paper has been to illustrate the variety of behavioral treatment strategies that are currently being used with alcoholics. Behavior therapy with alcoholics has developed from a rather simplistic conditioning approach to a much more sophisticated and comprehensive treatment system. This development has been fostered by the growing number of behavioral clinicians becoming involved in alcoholism together with the research and evaluation methods that behaviorists are bringing with them into the field. The systematic assessment and evaluation upon which behavior therapy is based has added much to our knowledge of the efficacy of both behavioral and non-behavioral alcoholism treatment approaches.

Behavior therapy with alcoholics is still developing and expanding. Current treatment trends emphasize (a) teaching alcoholics a wide range of more efficient coping skills and (b) rearranging social-environmental consequences of drinking in order to decrease its occurrence. Behavior therapists have developed a number of specific treatment strategies to accomplish these goals on a short-term basis.

Longer term evaluative studies are needed, however, with more attention focused not only on the initiation of new behavior patterns but also on their continued maintenance.

Eventually, specific behavioral treatment packages for different subgroups of alcoholics must be developed. For example, while intervention programs aimed at skid row alcoholics might emphasize the alteration of basic environmental reinforcers (e.g., providing clothing or meals contingent upon lowered blood/alcohol levels), such an approach would be inappropriate for younger, more affluent alcoholics. The eventual goal would be to match up patient characteristics with specific treatment strategies to predict the most parsimonious (in terms of time, money, and personnel) and most efficacious treatment for each individual alcoholic.

Finally, behavior therapy with alcoholics has become associated with the goal of controlled, social drinking. Although behavioral researchers are evaluating this treatment goal they are aware of the care that must be taken in espousing this approach prematurely (i.e. before sufficient research evidence demonstrates its efficacy). However, as scientists, behaviorists cannot ignore the growing body of data indicating that controlled, social drinking may be a viable alternative for some alcoholics.

REFERENCES

Anant, S.S. A note on the treatment of alcoholics by a verbal aversion technique. *Canadian Psychologist*, 1967, *8*, 19-22.

Blake, B.G. The application of behavior therapy to the treatment of alcoholism. *Behavior Research and Therapy*, 1965, *3*, 75-85.

Blake, B.G. A follow-up of alcoholics treated by behavior therapy. *Behaviour Research and Therapy*, 1967, *5*, 89-84.

Bigelow, G., Liebson, I., & Griffiths, R. Experimental analysis of alcoholic drinking. Paper presented at the American Psychological Association, Montreal, 1973.

Cappell, H., & Herman, C.P. Alcohol and tension reduction: A review. *Quarterly Journal of Studies on Alcohol*, 1972, *33*, 33-64.

Cautela, J.R. Treatment of compulsive behavior by covert sensitization. *Psychological Record*, 1966, *16*, 33-41.

Cohen, M., Liebson, I., & Faillace, L.A. The role of reinforcement contingencies in chronic alcoholism: An experimental analysis of one case. *Behaviour Research and Therapy*, 1971, *9*, 375-379.

Cohen, M., Liebson, I., Faillace, L., & Speers, W. Alcoholism: Controlled drinking and incentives for abstinence. *Psychological Reports*, 1971, *28*, 575-580.

Eisler, R.M., Hersen, M., & Agras, W.S. Videotape: A method for the controlled observation of nonverbal interpersonal behavior. *Behavior Therapy*, 1973, *4*, 420-425.

Eisler, R.M., Miller, P.M., Hersen, M., & Alford, H. Effects of assertive training on marital interaction. *Archives of General Psychiatry*, 1974, *30*, 643-649.

Foy, D., Miller, P.M., Eisler, R.M., & O'Toole, D. Teaching alcoholics to refuse drinks. Unpublished manuscript. University of Mississippi Medical Center, 1975.

Franks, C.M. Alcohol, alcoholism, and conditioning: A review of the literature and some theoretical considerations. *Journal of Mental Science*, 1958, *104*, 14-33.

Franks, C.M. Behavior therapy, the principles of conditioning and the treatment of the alcoholic. *Quarterly Journal of Studies on Alcohol*, 1963, *24*, 511-529.

Franks, C.M. Conditioning and conditioned aversion therapies in the treatment of the alcoholic. *International Journal of the Addictions*, 1966, *1*, 61-98.

Franks, C.M. Alcoholism. In C.G. Costello (Ed.), *Symptoms of psychopathology: A handbook*. New York: John Wiley & Sons, 1970.

Gary, V., & Guthrie, D. The effect of jogging on physical fitness and self-concept in hospitalized alcoholics. *Quarterly Journal of Studies on Alcohol*, 1972, *33*, 1073-1078.

Hallam, R., Rachman, S., & Falkowski, W. Subjective, attitudinal and physiological effects of electrical aversion therapy. *Behaviour Research and Therapy*, 1972, *10*, 1-13.

Hamburg, S. Behavior therapy in alcoholism: A critical review of broad spectrum approaches. *Quarterly Journal of Studies on Alcohol*, 1975, *36*, 69-87.

Hersen, M., Eisler, R.M., & Miller, P.M. Historical perspectives in behavior modification: Introductory comments. In M. Hersen, R.M. Eisler, & P.M. Miller (Eds.), *Progress in Behavior modification*. New York: Academic Press, 1975.

Hunt, G.A., & Azrin, N.H. A community reinforcement appraoch to alcoholism. *Behaviour Research and Therapy*, 1973, *11*, 91-104.

Kantorovich, N.V. [An attempt at associative-reflex therapy in alcoholism]. *Novaye Refleksologii i Nervonoy Fiziologii, Sistemy*, 1929, *3*, 436-447. Cited by Razran, G.H.S. Conditioned withdrawal responses with shock as the conditioning stimulus in adult human subjects. *Psychological Bulletin*, 1934, *31*, 111-143

Katz, M.M., & Lyerly, S.B. Methods for measuring adjustment and social behaviors in the community: I. Rationale, description, discriminatory validity, and scale development. *Psychological Reports*, 1963, *13*, 503-535.

Kraft, T. Alcoholism treated by systematic desensitization: A follow-up of eight cases. *Journal of the Royal College of General Practice*, 1969, *18*, 336-340.

Kraft, T., & Al-Issa, I. Alcoholism treated by desensitization: A case study. *Behaviour Research and Therapy*, 1967, *5*, 69-70.

Lemere, F. What happens to alcoholics. *American Journal of Psychiatry*, 1953, *104*, 674-676.

Lemere, F., & Voegtlin, W.L. An evaluation of the aversion treatment of alcoholism. *Quarterly Journal of Studies on Alcohol*, 1950, *4*, 199-204.

Liebson, I., Bigelow, G., & Flamer, R. Alcoholism among methadone patients. A specific treatment method. *American Journal of Psychiatry*, 1973, *130*, 483-485.

Lovibond, S.H., & Caddy, G. Discriminated aversive control in the moderation of alcoholics' drinking behavior. *Behavior Therapy*, 1970, *1*, 437-444.

Lunde, S.E., & Vogler, R.E. Generalization of results in studies of aversion conditioning with alcoholics. *Behaviour Research and Therapy*, 1970, *8*, 313-314.

Marlatt, G.A., Demming, B., & Reid, J.B. Loss of control drinking in alcoholics: An experimental analogue. *Journal of Abnormal Psychology*, 1973, *81*, 233-241.

McCance, C., & McCance, P.F. Alcoholism in North-East Scotland: Its treatment and outcome. *British Journal of Psychiatry*, 1969, *115*, 189-198.

Miller, P.M. The use of behavioral contracting in the treatment of alcoholism: A case study. *Behavior Therapy*, 1972, *3*, 592-596.

Miller, P.M. Behavioral treatment of drug addiction: A review. *International Journal of the Addictions*, 1973, *8*, 511-519.

Miller, P.M. A behavioral intervention program for chronic public drunkenness offenders. *Archives of General Psychiatry*, 1975, *32*, 915-918.

Miller, P.M. *Behavioral treatment of alcoholism*. New York: Pergamon Press, in press.

Miller, P.M., Becker, J.V., Foy, D.W., & Wooten, L.S. Instructional control of the components of alcoholic drinking behavior. Unpublished manuscript. University of Mississippi Medical Center, 1975.

Miller, P.M., & Eisler, R.M. Alcohol and drug abuse. In W.E. Craighead, A.E. Kazdin, & M.J. Mahoney (Eds.), *Behavior modifications: Principles, issues, and applications*. Boston: Houghton Mifflin, in press.

Miller, P.M., & Hersen, M. Quantitative changes in alcohol consumption as a function of electrical aversive conditioning. *Journal of Clinical Psychology*, 1972, *28*, 590-593.

Miller, P.M., & Hersen, M. Modification of marital interaction patterns between an alcoholic and his wife. In J.D. Krumboltz & C.E. Thoresen (Eds.), *Counseling methods*. New York: Holt, Rinehart, & Winston, in press.

Miller, P.M., Hersen, M., Eisler, R.M., & Elkin, T.E. A retrospective analysis of alcohol consumption-laboratory tasks as related to therapeutic outcome. *Behaviour Research and Therapy*, 1974, *12*, 73-76.

Miller, P.M., Hersen, M., Eisler, R.M., & Hemphill, D.P. Electrical aversion therapy with alcoholics: An analogue study. *Behaviour Research and Therapy*, 1973, *11*, 491-497.

Miller, P.M., Hersen, M., Eisler, R.M., & Watts, J.G. Contingent reinforcement of lowered blood/alcohol levels in an outpatient chronic alcoholic. *Behaviour Research and Therapy*, 1974, *12*, 261-263.

Miller, P.M., Stanford, A.G., & Hemphill, D.P. A social-learning approach to alcoholism treatment. *Social Casework*, 1974, *55*, 279-284.

Mills, K.C., Sobell, M.B., & Schaefer, H.H. Training social drinking as an alternative to abstinence for alcoholics, *Behavior Therapy*, 1971, *2*, 18-27.

Narrol, H.G. Experimental application of reinforcement principles to the analysis and treatment of hospitalized alcoholics. *Quarterly Journal of Studies on Alcohol*, 1967, *28*, 105-115.

Nathan, P.E., & O'Brien, J.S. An experimental analysis of the behavior of alcoholics and non-alcoholics during prolonged experimental drinking. *Behavior Therapy*, 1971, *2*, 455-476.

Pattison, E.M. A conceptual approach to alcoholism treatment goals. *Addictive Behavior*, in press.

Rozynko, V.V., Flint, G.A., Hammer, C.E., Swift, K.D., Kline, J.A., & King, R.M. An operant behavior modification program for alcoholics. Paper presented at the Western Psychological Association, April 1971.

Schaefer, H.H., Sobell, M.B., & Mills, K.C. Baseline drinking behaviors in alcoholics and social drinkers: Kinds of sips and sip magnitude. *Behaviour Research and Therapy*, 1971, *9*, 23-27.

Selzer, M.L., & Holloway, W.H. A follow-up of alcoholics committed to a state hospital. *Quarterly Journal of Studies on Alcohol*, 1957, *18*, 98-120.

Shea, J.E. Psychoanalytic therapy and alcoholism. *Quarterly Journal of Studies on Alcohol*, 1954, *15*, 595-605.

Sobell, L.C., & Sobell, M.B. A self-feedback technique to monitor drinking behavior in alcoholics. *Behaviour Research and Therapy*, 1973, *11*, 237-238.

Sobell, L.C., & Sobell, M.B. Self-reports by alcoholics. *Journal of Nervous and Mental Disease*, in press.

Sobell, M.B., & Sobell, L.C. Alcoholics treated by individualized behavior therapy: One year treatment outcome. *Behaviour Research and Therapy*, 1973, *11*, 599-618. (a)

Sobell, M.B., & Sobell, L.C. Individualized behavior therapy for alcoholics. *Behavior Therapy*, 1973, *4*, 49-72. (b)

Steffen, J.J. Electromyographically induced relaxation in the treatment of chronic alcohol abuse. *Journal of Consulting and Clinical Psychology*, 1974, *43*, 275.

Sulzer, E.S. Behavior modification in adult psychiatric patients. In L.P. Ullman & L. Krasner (Eds.), *Case studies in behavior modification*. New York: Holt, Rinehart, & Winston, 1965.

Voegtlin, W.L., & Broz, W.R. The conditioned reflex treatment of chronic alcoholism: X. An analysis of 3,125 admissions over a period of ten and a half years. *Annals of Internal Medicine*, 1949, *30*, 580-597.

CHAPTER 19

PHARMACOLOGICAL THERAPY

Jonathan A. Cole

Ralph S. Ryback

It is impossible to speak of a single drug therapy for the disease alcoholism. Much of the diversity in the literature on clinical psychopharmacology of chronic alcoholism results from the fact that drugs are used in a variety of ways for a variety of purposes. Some are alleged or hoped to alter motivation. Others are used to relieve tension or depression associated with alcohol abuse or to make the patient violently ill if he drinks, while still others are used as pharmacological aversive stimuli in conditioning therapy. Most commonly, drugs are used and studied to treat the withdrawal symptoms encountered during detoxification, and drugs are generally judged essential in the prevention and/or treatment of delirium tremens. Some areas, such as the chronic organic brain syndromes secondary to chronic alcoholism, seem unreasonably neglected as targets for innovative drug therapies.

Ralph E. Tarter and A. Arthur Sugerman (eds.), Alcoholism

ISBN: 0-201-08146-6
ISBN: 0-201-08145-8 (pbk.)

In general, the available clinical drug literature in alcoholism is plagued with defects in the design and execution of studies. Many studies are poorly controlled. Nevertheless, the authors of this chapter feel a good deal more sanguine than some recent reviewers of the literature (Mottin, 1973; Viamontes, 1972), who take the position that despite glowing uncontrolled clinical reports no drug therapy of alcoholism is ever much better than placebo.

The organization of the present chapter is broadly by treatment setting and phase of illness, considering specialized treatments as subsections. The general drug therapy of non-alcoholic psychiatric disorders will not be discussed in any detail; the interested reader is referred to Hollister's (1973) book on this subject or to the relevant chapters in the 1975 edition of Freedman, Kaplan, and Sadock's *Comprehensive Textbook of Psychiatry*.

ALCOHOL WITHDRAWAL

Ingestion of alcohol in large amounts for prolonged periods leads to clear physical dependence and a range of withdrawal symptoms which emerge when the patient stops drinking voluntarily or involuntarily. Agitation, dysphoria, tremulousness, nausea, and some confusion are common symptoms of alcohol withdrawal, generally considered etiologically as effects of central nervous system (CNS) excitation occurring as a rebound from alcohol-caused CNS depression. When the physical dependence is more intense and prolonged, or when the patient may be biologically more vulnerable, withdrawal-related epileptic seizures (rum fits) or progression to marked confusion, panic, and disorientation (delirium tremens or D.T.'s) can occur. Generally, the convulsions are not a major problem and can easily be handled pharmacologically. Delirium tremens, however, is a more serious problem and is not uncommonly fatal.

The early detection of alcohol withdrawal is vital to the prevention of delirium tremens. Unless signs and symptoms of withdrawal are recognized at their onset and followed by sensitive, yet aggressive treatment, more serious withdrawal symptoms or delirium tremens may well ensue. The symptoms and signs of withdrawal may range from clinically mild to moderately severe. However, although "moderately severe" may be professionally considered "non lethal" and therefore acceptable to the therapist, it is important to realize that from the patient's perspective, symptoms judged by a clinician to be mild may be viewed by the patient as very severe. Such symptoms and signs can occur as early as 24-36 hours following cessation of steady alcohol ingestion.

The signs and symptoms of withdrawal, delirium tremens, and the intermediate phase are as follows:

1. WITHDRAWAL

Symptoms: Nervousness, anxiety, agitation, sleeplessness, restlessness, tremulousness, nausea, vomiting, sweats, and (less frequently) itching.

Signs: Tremor, rapid pulse, sweating, mild fever, elevated blood pressure.

A patient may have any or all of the above. It should be noted, in addition, that signs of agitation will always be expressed in context, i.e., in accordance with the patient's basic personality and therefore differing in outward manifestation from patient to patient.

2. DELIRIUM TREMENS

Symptoms: Any or all of the above plus delirium (disorientation), confusion, hallucinations, extreme agitation, and fever (usually higher and more frequent than in withdrawal, i.e., 104-105°). Hallucinations per se are an equivocal symptom since they can also occur in alcoholic hallucinosis without disorientation.

3. INTERMEDIATE SYNDROMES

Symptoms: Agitation without delirium, hallucinations without autonomic signs, confusion without severe illness, or any of a number of syndromes not clearly classifiable as either distinctly withdrawal or delirium tremens.

Thus, the recognition of patient signs and symptoms can help determine which phase is being experienced and then what course of treatment is most desirable.

In connection with this, it is important to note that any such recognition requires careful patient observation both while the patient is alone and also during his interactions with others. For, although some symptoms may be obvious when viewed in one situation, they may be totally absent in another. For example, hallucination may be obvious when observing the patient from a distance but may not be recognizable while talking with him. Conversely, talking with a patient may reveal extreme inner agitation and anxiety, but when viewed from a distance or in the absence of conversation, the patient may appear to be calm.

Because early detection of withdrawal is crucial, common first signs should be stressed so that they are most carefully watched for. Therefore, hostile or paranoid behavior (e.g., refusal of injections, desire to leave the hospital, etc.) may be the first indication that withdrawal is beginning. Sleeplessness, though not uncommon in the hospital, may also be a first sign. A rising pulse (remember to check it) or increasing restlessness are often first signs. Tremor and shakiness (though relatively unreliable due to their absence in the young or gross exaggeration in the elderly) can, nonetheless, be important indicators of possible withdrawal.

The majority of the available controlled drug trials concern themselves with the treatment of general withdrawal symptoms in in-patient detoxification programs. Few studies, however, make any serious effort to use discrete criteria (e.g., Victor & Adams, 1953) for differentiating alcohol withdrawal from delirium tremens, incipient or manifest.

In considering the available literature, it is interesting to consider the role of "standard therapy" as a force in clinical settings. It is obviously helpful for programs treating large numbers of alcoholic patients requiring detoxification to set up a standard set of medical orders to be followed in almost all cases. This simplifies life for the medical and nursing personnel and is essential if free-standing nurse-run detoxification facilities are to become as widely used as is now the case in Massachusetts. In their favor is also the argument that patients on a standard regimen generally respond in ways familiar to ward staff. Therefore, patients showing atypical responses (severe agitation or marked sedation) are immediately singled out as requiring special evaluation, something which might not occur so readily if each patient were having his drug therapy juggled uniquely by a variety of physicians (Kissin & Gross, 1968). As an example of such a standard regimen, the orders used at McLean's Alcoholism Treatment Center are presented in Table 1. Although we believe our program to be rational and effective, we will attempt to avoid the ethnocentricity of some detoxification programs by not claiming that our approach is the standard approach that all should follow. We once heard an angry member of the audience bitterly attack Kaim after a presentation of his excellent multicenter study of drug therapies in detoxification for not using the standard treatment of alcohol withdrawal, phenobarbital! There is even a Scandanavian study in which the standard treatment for delirium tremens was electroconvulsive therapy (Giacobini & Salum, 1961). And some units have used paraldehyde for years with alleged excellent results (Kissin & Gross, 1968).

TREATMENT OF ALCOHOL WITHDRAWAL

WERNICKE'S SYNDROME. For this there is a simple drug treatment: on admission thiamine 100 mg given intramuscularly if the patient's cooperation or ability to hold down oral medication is in doubt. This approach is worthwhile as a ward against incipient Wernicke's syndrome even though eye muscle weakness or paralysis is not seen. Given Victor's (Victor, Adams, & Collins, 1972) and Ryback's (1971) defense of the position that Wernicke's syndrome and Korsakoff's psychosis are parts of a single clinical syndrome, it is worthwhile to give thiamine routinely in the hope of averting serious organic brain damage even if the evidence of thiamine's efficacy in the Korsakoff's end of the spectrum is less clear

TABLE 1

McLean Hospital

Sheet 1 of 2

PHYSICIANS MEDICATION ORDER SHEET

In all instances physicians should write their orders. Stat orders only are given by phone and these require the physician's signature within twenty-four hours.

PATIENT'S NAME ______________________ WARD ______________

DATE OR TIME ORDERED	ORDER	Signature of H.N. or Chg. N. copying standing order. Initial of nurse carrying out stat orders.

1. Chlordiazepoxide

   (a) 50 mg. p.o. q.i.d. days 1 & 2
   (b) 50 mg. p.o. t.i.d. day 3
   (c) 25 mg. p.o. q.i.d. day 4
   (d) 25 mg. p.o. b.i.d. day 5
   (e) 25 mg. p.o. h.s. day 6

2. Chlordiazepoxide

   (a) 50 mg. p.o. or IM stat.
   (b) 25 mg. or 50 mg. IM or p.o. prn. q. 4 hr. x 7 days.

3. Thiamine 100 mg. IM or p.o. on admission and then 50 mg. p.o. qd x 31 days

4. Diphenylhydantoin 100 mg. p.o. stat then 100 mg. p.o. q.i.d. x2 d., t.i.d. x 2 d., b.i.d. x2 d., qd x2 d., then D/C. (Patients with a history of seizures and/or poor historian).

5. Diazepam 5 mg. IV stat for seizure by MD.

6. Multivitamins tab I p.o. b.i.d., x6 days, then tab I p.o. qd.

7. Dalmane 30 mg. p.o. tab. h.s. prn. for sleep. MR x1. x 7 days.

8. Kaopectate 30 cc. p.o. after each BM for diarrhea.

9. Riopan 30 cc. p.o. q 2-4 hrs., prn.

10. Tylenol, tabs 2, p.o. for headache prn. q. 4 hr.

11. MOM 30 cc. p.o. h.s. prn for constipation.

12. Coricidin 5cc. p.o. prn q. 4 hr. for cough.

TABLE 1

McLean Hospital — Sheet 2 of 2

PHYSICIANS ORDER SHEET

In all instances physicians should write their orders. Emergency orders only are given by phone and these require the physician's signature as soon as possible.

PATIENTS NAME________________ WARD____ ATC________

DATE OR TIME ORDERED	ORDER	Signature of H.N. or Chg. N. copying standing order, Initial of nurse carrying out stat orders.
	Admit to Hall	
	PERSONNEL: Therapist/Resident: Social Worker: Patient Coordinator:	
	DIET: As tolerated: clear liquids x 1-2 meals if condition unstable: then regular house diet.	
	OBSERVATIONS: Checks q. 30 minutes. Vital signs q.i.d. x 3 days.	
	PRIVILEGES: Restrict to hall for first 24 hours for orientation & detoxification @ CND. Then group on & off grounds.	
	MANAGEMENT: Notify DOC if: 1) pulse is 120 or greater, especially if after third day. 2) temp. is 100 orally, or 101 rectally, or greater. 3) antacid, Tylenol, or Coricidin is given 2 or more times in a 12 hr. period. 4) chlordiazepoxide is given in excessive doses.	
	TESTS: 1) Physical examination 2) EKG 3) Chest x'ray 4) Routine urinalysis 5) CBC 6) VDRL 7) SMA - 12 8) Prothrombin Time 9) Australian Antigen	

than the vitamin's rapid restorative action in typical Wernicke's syndrome.

CONVULSIONS. The use of diphenylhydantoin[1] (or other anticonvulsants) to prevent grand mal seizures also has a documented place in the therapy of alcohol withdrawal. Despite Rothstein's (1973) study showing diphenylhydantoin to be no more effective than chlordiazepoxide alone in preventing seizures during detoxification, the more recent study by Sampliner and Iber (1974) is compelling. It shows that diphenylhydantoin added to chlordiazepoxide is clearly useful in preventing seizures during detoxification in alcoholics who have a history of previous seizures of any sort, even unrelated to prior episodes of alcohol withdrawal. Within the first 48 hours, 11 of 70 such patients on placebo and chlordiazepoxide had a seizure; none occurred in the comparison group receiving 300 mg of diphenylhydantoin per day as well as chlordiazepoxide. Sampliner and Iber note that seisures are very rare (4 out of 2,200 admissions) in patients without a history of seizures, making anticonvulsant therapy in such patients unnecessary. One wonders at the absence of any contribution of chlordiazepoxide's anticonvulsant properties to these results (Greenblatt & Shader, 1974).

FLUID BALANCE. An aspect of the management of alcohol detoxification on the borderland of pharmacotherapy is the

---

[1]See glossary of drugs mentioned at end of chapter.

problem of hydration and electrolyte balance. Some programs give intravenous fluids to detoxifying patients almost routinely. On the other hand, the McLean program has been running for over 3 years and has treated over 500 patients without any use of parenteral fluids except in rare patients with severe vomiting or fever. It is our understanding that other programs for alcoholic detoxification in Boston (the Cambridge Hospital and the Lemuel Shattuck Hospital) also use intravenous fluids very sparingly. Two recent papers support this general position: Beard's study finding that 29 of 30 alcoholics were overhydrated on admission (Beard, 1968), while Bolsano (1970) shows that a fluid restriction program can be successfully used in alcohol withdrawal.

WITHDRAWAL SYMPTOMS. The standard and largest controlled study of drug treatments during apparently uncomplicated alcohol withdrawal was completed by the V.A. (Kaim, Klett, & Rothfeld, 1969) on 537 patients, comparing chlordiazepoxide, chlorpromazine, hydroxyzine, thiamine, and placebo. Overall about 5% of the patients developed convulsions or delirium tremens. Chlordiazepoxide was clearly the best treatment (with D.T.'s and convulsion rates of 1% each), with the other treatments being no different from placebo. With regard to subjective efficacy, all treatments were generally equivalent with most patients greatly improved within 48 hours.

This study nicely fits current pharmacological preconceptions. Sedative drugs (e.g., paraldehyde, benzodiazepines, such as chlordiazepoxide, barbiturates, even alcohol) ought to show pharmacological cross-tolerance with alcohol. The task, pharmacologically viewed, in alcohol detoxificiation ought to be one of replacing alcohol with a comparable sedative drug which can then be smoothly withdrawn. If this were clearly the only and best way to treat alcohol withdrawal, life would be relatively simple. Unfortunately a number of articles document the utility of drugs, such as phenothiazines, haloperidol, and the autonomic sedative, hydroxyzine, in alcohol withdrawal. None of these agents show cross-tolerance to alcohol and would, therefore, be predicted to fail in protecting alcoholics from delirium tremens and "rum fits". The phenothiazines, particularly promazine and chlorpromazine, lower the convulsive threshold in experimental animals and man (Jarvik, 1965). On the other hand, these drugs are good antiemetics; they may be symptomatically useful in alcoholics showing nausea and vomiting and are generally useful in reducing anxiety, tension, and agitation. Many physicians use phenothiazines routinely in treating alcohol withdrawal, perhaps for the above reasons, and also because such drugs are free of euphoria and induce neither physiological nor psychological dependence of the type found with alcohol, barbiturates or, to a lesser extent, the benzodiazepines.

Alcoholics being detoxified may prefer the effects of a drug like paraldehyde to those of a clear noneuphoriant like promazine and might tend to more frequent recrudescences of abstinence symptoms with paraldehyde, the shorter acting drug. One study (Hart, 1961) clearly states the preference of nursing staffs for the less troublesome promazine patients as opposed to more cantankerous paraldehyde patients. That the difference may be duration of action or freedom from spells of excited intoxication is suggested by another study in which diazepam was not only generally superior to paraldehyde (Thompson, Johnson, & Maddrey, 1975) but in which paraldehyde patients bit the medical staff twice, got sheet burns and one tore out his brachial plexus! It should be noted that, in this study, the paraldehyde was administered by rectum, a procedure with ominous psychodynamic implications!

Other programs have used paraldehyde exclusively for years with evident satisfaction (Kissin & Gross, 1968), suggesting perhaps that many agents are safe and valuable if the staff is familiar with them and knows how to use them with finesse.

To return to the published evidence from controlled or comparative studies, it is unfortunately true that almost any conclusion is supported by at least one study: promazine is more effective than paraldehyde (Hart, 1961); promazine is better at 48 hours than paraldehyde in relief of subjective symptoms in ordinary withdrawal (but more dangerous in treatment failure) (Thomas & Freedman, 1964); a paraldehyde-chloral hydrate combination is more effective than promazine, alcohol infusions, or chlordiazepoxide (Golbert, Sanz, Rose, & Leitshuh, 1967); paraldehyde is more effective than low dose (250 mg daily) chlorpromazine (Friedhoff & Zitrin, 1959); chlordiazepoxide is superior to promazine and placebo (Sereny & Kalant, 1965); though promazine is as effective as chlordiazepoxide the first day only, promazine and chlordiazepoxide are both no better than placebo (Schwartz, Schmidt, & Stern, 1968); both chlordiazepoxide and promazine are superior to diazepam (Chambers & Schultz, 1964); chlordiazepoxide is superior to placebo (Kissen, 1965); and chlordiazepoxide is equivalent to placebo, but both are superior to nicotinamide adenine dinucleotide (NAD) (Hekimian, Friedhoff, & Alpert, 1966).

The situation is not improved by the tendency of more recent studies examining newer neuroleptic drugs in alcohol withdrawal to compare them with other drugs of the same class or placebo but not to benzodiazepines. Thus chlorpromazine has been shown to be equivalent to mesoridazine (Frost, 1973); haloperidol is more effective than placebo (Greenberg & Rosenfeld, 1969); and haloperidol is more effective than mesoridazine and hydroxyzine, an autonomic sedative antihistamine (Palestine, 1973).

DELIRIUM TREMENS. The whole matter is further complicated by a second large scale V.A. collaborative study of patients with overt delirium tremens (Kaim & Klett, 1972) in which chlordiazepoxide, paraldehyde, pentobarbital, and perphenazine (a neuroleptic) were compared in groups of about 50 patients per treatment. All treatments resulted in cessation of delirium in 74-80 hours with no significant differences between any of the treatments being observed. There was a trend toward slightly better qualitative outcome with paraldehyde and chlordiazepoxide. These treatments resulted in only one failure each as against three failures each for perphenazine and pentobarbital.

If one reviews the seriously adverse outcomes in the various studies, promazine consistently shows more deaths, convulsions, and emerging deliria (Chambers & Schultz, 1964; Golbert et al., 1967; Schwartz et al., 1968; Sereny & Kalant, 1965; Thomas & Freedman, 1964). One study, in fact, showed a statistically significant increased mortality in patients with overt delirium tremens on promazine as compared to paraldehyde. All in all, it can be strongly stated that promazine, despite some efficacy in mild withdrawal, is a dangerous drug when used in delirium tremens or even in heterogeneous alcohol withdrawal syndromes. Unfortunately it is less clear that other antipsychotic drugs share this disadvantage. On the available evidence, both perphenazine (Kaim & Klett, 1972) and haloperidol (Palestine, 1973) look reasonably safe and effective in delirium tremens.

There is also a pinch of disquieting material suggesting that cardiovascular effects of thioridazine (Sydney, 1973) may be a problem in alcohol withdrawal. It is unclear whether other neuroleptics might have similar effects. Hydroxyzine and mesoridazine have been observed to be related to undesirable electrocardiographic changes during detoxification treatment (Palestine, 1973) but no clinical cardiovascular toxicity was observed.

Weighing all this, most authorities come out in favor of sedative-hypnotic drugs such as diazepam or chlordiazepoxide as more rational in terms of their pharmacological effects and as the most suitable agents for the treatment of alcohol withdrawal syndrome, and most favor them for delirium tremens (Greenblatt & Shader, 1974; Hollister, 1973). Our reservations on this subject are recorded below. A recent survey of alcoholism treatment programs reveals a general trend for such programs to shift from reliance on promazine or paraldehyde to one of the benzodiazepines (Favazza & Martin, 1974). These drugs, as long acting alcohol-like drugs, qualify rationally for a place similar to that occupied by methadone in opiate withdrawal.

Local experience suggests that benzodiazepines are *not* effective once full blown delirium tremens with fever, tachycardia, and hyperventilation occurs. This is a theoretically defensible position; it has long been known that sedative drugs relieve alcohol-barbiturate type withdrawal symptoms effectively only *before* the patient goes into delirium tremens. It could follow that delirium tremens is a different process not relieved by sedative drugs and that, at least for the hyperthermic and agitation aspects of the syndrome, an antipsychotic drug with its known hypothermic effects could be more effective. If one assumed that the Kaim study (Kaim & Klett, 1972) included both patients going into delirium tremens and those already in delirium tremens and that chlordiazepoxide would be more effective for the former and the antipsychotic, perphenazine, for the latter, their equivocal findings might become more comprehensible.

Our clinical experience, plus that of Dr. William Clark at the Cambridge Hospital in Cambridge, suggests that chlorpromazine (25 mg initially with repeat doses of 50 to 100 mg intramuscularly in a half hour if agitation and fever do not respond) is more useful than chlordiazepoxide in febrile-agitated, delirious alcoholics.

If paraldehyde were to be really superior to chlordiazepoxide in severe delirium tremens, one can only suggest that its rapid action as a sedative-hypnotic is responsible. The recently documented marked delay in action for intramuscular chlordiazepoxide and diazepam (far slower than when the drugs are given orally) (Greenblatt & Shader, 1974) could also account for some unsatisfactoriness of these drugs in the emergency management of acute delirium.

Any way you view it, delirium tremens is a medical emergency requiring careful and constant nursing care and frequent medical backup. Major dangers besides hyperthemia are self-destructive behavior (suicide, panic-induced jumping from windows, etc.) or respiratory arrest secondary to hyperventilation. The newer nurse-run simple detoxification units should not attempt to handle delirium tremens; it requires the medical and technical resources of a hospital.

OUTPATIENT DETOXIFICATION

Many clinicians have for a number of years detoxified their private alcoholic patients as outpatients for a variety of reasons including the social stigma of hospitalization, press of time or work demands of the patient, inability to afford inpatient services, or the lack of any real clinical necessity for hospitalization. It is quite obvious that thousands of alcoholics or heavy drinkers detoxify themselves daily without medical intervention. In its mildest form the hangover dealt with by a Bloody Mary may be a simple example of self-treatment of withdrawal symptoms.

Outpatient detoxification should be viewed as one form of entry into a comprehensive treatment program. Continuation of treatment as an outpatient was found by Gerard and Saenger (1966) to be predictably related to three variables, namely: (a) the patient received medications: (b) the patient was immediately involved in peer group activities, and (c) family and significant others were quickly involved in rehabilitation. It is quite clear that medication to reduce the withdrawal symptoms, though symptomatically desirable, also serves as a lure to ensure frequent contact with the patient; his or her return every 12 or 24 hours to the treatment program for medication provides the opportunity for the development of supportive human relationships which form the basis of longer term treatment.

Recently, Feldman, Pattison, and Sabell (1975) have reported on their experience with 564 alcoholics treated as outpatients; they found "outpatient detoxification can be successfully conducted without undue morbidity or mortality." They found that only 47% of their patients required detoxification, and only 19% of these required inpatient care. Of all those who required detoxification, only 36 (17%) were recidivists. One hundred and eight (50%) of those detoxified on an outpatient basis continued in treatment. The mortality rate for the total sample was zero! Though only 50% continued into the rehabilitation program, the cost of this type of program for those it can reach (i.e., approximately $20/day) suggests that its cost-benefit ratio should lead to its increasing utilization.

Successful outpatient detoxification almost always requires voluntary involvement (i.e., patient should sign a voluntary consent for treatment), involvement of significant others (i.e., family members or friends), and residence within reasonable driving time of the program so that daily or more frequent attendance at the clinic or office is possible in the early phases of the treatment regime.

High blood alcohol levels in and of themselves are not a criteria for medical detoxification. Nevertheless, a patient seen in the office with a blood alcohol content (BAC) greater than .10% should be held and observed (e.g., sequential BAC's with a breathalyzer) until his BAC drops below .10%. Any patient with clinically mild to moderate withdrawal symptoms who does not have other significant medical problems and who is not dehydrated from vomiting or sweating can be detoxified as an outpatient. Patients with significant medical or psychiatric problems and severe withdrawal symptoms (e.g., marked elevation in blood pressure, temperature, atypical symptoms, etc.) or any patient in delirium tremens should be hospitalized.

Though there has been considerable discussion in the literature about the pros and cons of various medications in alcohol withdrawal, chlordiazepoxide is probably the medication of choice in outpatient detoxification. Chlordiazepoxide should only be prescribed for withdrawal from alcohol. It and other minor tranquilizers should never be prescribed for longer periods as a tranquilizer or antianxiety drug since they are often abused by an alcoholic patient in a manner similar to alcohol. Many A.A. members complain about physicians who make them drunk with pills. It is not reasonable treatment to switch the addiction to minor tranquilizers which the doctor controls and dispenses.

There are certain conditions which should ideally be fulfilled before initiating outpatient detoxification. The patient must agree to return the next day. Also, a mild or moderate withdrawal should be anticipated (e.g., no history of previous severe withdrawal symptoms). Finally, the patient should not be going out alone. Should unforeseen events occur, he or she must have a family member or reliable friend to return him or her to the hospital or detoxification center, or to dispense medication.

The following guidelines can help avoid crisis situations. The patient and his relative or friend should be told to come back at the first sign of any problem, but particularly the beginning of hallucinations or disorientation, seizures, or bleeding. Detoxification should not begin without first obtaining medical approval. The patient's take-home medication should be no more than one 25 mg chlordiazepoxide tablet each 4 hours or 6 tablets for 24 hours. Ideally, patients should return at shorter intervals if possible and therefore would receive less medication to take home. In any case, the patient should never be given more than a one-day supply. The nurse in charge can dispense up to 100 mg intramuscularly of chlordiazepoxide once initially if a thorough evaluation of the patient's signs and symptoms indicate that need.

NOVEL DRUG TREATMENTS OF ALCOHOL WITHDRAWAL

The best-studied new drug for the treatment of alcohol withdrawal is chlormethiazole (Heminevrin) (Gershon, 1967), which chemically resembles the thiazole portion of the thiamine molecule. It is a short-acting sedative which can be given either as an intravenous injection in 0.8% solution or in 300 mg tablets. It is usually given at frequent intervals titrating patients into a light sleep. In Hollister's open study (Hollister, Prusmack, & Lipscomb, 1972) it was an acceptable treatment with doses of about 4 to 6 grams a day being required in the first days of hospitalization. Glatt (1966) has found chlormethiazole to be significantly superior to placebo in overall improvement during alcoholic withdrawal (but all patients also received an anticonvulsant, diphenylhydantoin (Glatt, George, & Frisch, 1966). A Swiss study has shown chlormethiazole to be somewhat superior to chlordiazepoxide in the treatment of delirium tremens (Benuzzi & Muller, 1967). In general, this drug appears to be a short-acting, low-potency sedative with obscure virtues in the treatment of alcohol withdrawal. Only if the Swiss data were confirmed in a larger multi-center study, would one be tempted to substitute a short-acting sedative for a longer-acting one in alcohol withdrawal.

Two other treatments have been the subject of recent reports. One concerns the use of magnesium sulfate to reverse hypomagnesemia in alcohol withdrawal (Victor, 1973). Another concerns the use of fructose (1,000 mg of 20% fructose followed by 500 mg of 40% fructose within 6 hours) to speed recovery from delirium tremens with alleged success in 21 patients (Dalton & Duncan, 1970). The drug was given because of its ability to speed alcohol metabolism. Why such an action should help in delirium tremens is unclear.

SYMPTOMATIC DRUG THERAPY AFTER DETOXIFICATION

It has long been assumed that alcoholics probably drink because they are anxious, tense, irritable, depressed, or otherwise dysphoric, an assumption that may, of course, be incorrect (Cappell & Herman, 1972). Ryback (1974) suggests in a recent article that many alcoholics describe the effects of alcohol as numbing or detaching rather than as pleasurable: "I'm just as depressed, but I don't care anymore when I'm drunk," suggesting that alcohol may be more of a psychic aspirin than a "fun trip." It is also possible that chronic alcoholics are in some way biologically dependent on a sedative drug, alcohol, in the same way that heroin addicts are dependent on an opiate. If the latter hypothesis is correct, a long-acting sedative drug, perhaps chlordiazepoxide or diazepam might provide the benign sedative that would be less toxic and more regulatable than alcohol. If dysphoria causes drinking, then antidepressants or antianxiety drugs ought to be clinically useful.

The available controlled studies of antianxiety and antidepressant drug efficacy, though limited, are helpful in resolving these issues. An excellent pair of studies by Shaffer, Yeganah, Foxwell, and Kurland (1968), carried out with alcoholic patients in a state hospital for one month after detoxification, find that patients on chlordiazepoxide are less anxious than patients on placebo as judged by psychiatric interview. Nursing staff, however, observe the placebo patients to be the more improved. Chlordiazepoxide patients rate themselves as more friendly. They also engage in illicit drinking more frequently than do placebo patients. In addition, these patients show more impairment than placebo patients on some measures of cognitive functioning. In the one comparable subacute inpatient study by Gallant, Bishop, Guerero-Figueroa, Selby, and Phillips (1969), diazepam was only slightly (insignificantly) better than placebo and inferior to doxepin at one week. Of the 24 diazepam patients 5 claimed, at the end of the study, to "feel better than ever before!"

Several studies of chlordiazepoxide have been carried out in outpatients. Bowman and Thimann (1966) find it (and oxazepam and promazine) better than placebo in a study with an unusually low dropout rate in all treatment groups. Rosenberg (1974) finds that chlordiazepoxide promotes clinic attendance in a city hospital outpatient department more effectively than no drug or vitamin therapy. Both chlordiazepoxide and disulfiram cause a marked reduction in anxiety and depression relative to the other two therapies. Mooney, Ditman, and Cohen (1961) find chlordiazepoxide and, in a later study in the same program, diazepam (Ditman, 1966) more effective than placebo in promoting continuing clinic attendance. The whole series of studies of other drugs done by this group under Ditman (1966) have been most disappointing on even this measure. Thioridazine, trifluoperazine, imipramine, diethylpropion (an anorexigenic drug), tybamate, and meprobamate have all been shown to be relatively ineffective with only trifluoperazine surprisingly causing an increase in physical energy while yet decreasing mental alertness. Generally, these studies showed return-to-clinic rates of 44% at one week, 23% at 2 weeks, and 5.6% at 6 weeks! On chlordiazepoxide these rates change to 71%, 56%, and 20%. Interestingly, in Mooney's study (1961), a drug-placebo difference was found in the skid row subsample only after the first week and in the better integrated subsample from the second week on. A British study (Bliding, 1973) has shown oxazepam to be superior to both chlorprothixene, a neuroleptic thioxanthene, and to placebo in a three week study. Chlorprothixene was also superior to placebo. A Swedish study (Malmgren, 1967) also finds chlordiazepoxide to be more effective than placebo in reducing dysphoria and agitation in a three week, three treatment, multiple cross-over study. The third treatment, dixyrazine (a chemical hybrid between promazine and hydroxyzine), was preferred by the patients to chlordiazepoxide to a significant degree.

There is less data on the utility of antidepressants in alcoholism. Kissin and Gross (1968) have had some success with a chlordiazepoxide-imipramine combination as being better than either of its components and have had no success with amitryptiline or isocarboxazide, other antidepressants, or with sedatives such as chlordiazepoxide, meprobamate, or emyclamate. Butterworth and Watts (1971) found doxepin to be superior to diazepam on doctor's ratings but not on patient self-ratings. As noted above, Ditman (1966) had been unimpressed by imipramine and diethylpropion, a mild stimulant. Again Shaffer, Freinek, Wolf, Foxwell, and Kurland (1964) have done an interesting study in hospitalized alcoholics, using nialamide, a monoamine oxidase inhibitor (not notable for its efficacy in depression) (Cole & Davis, 1975). Nialamide is not generally superior to placebo on symptom measures but is superior to placebo in the extent of improvement that patients show on the Raven's Progressive Matrices and the Trail Making Test (measures of intellectual performance). Kissin, Platz, & Su (1970), in a very complicated study comparing treatment modalities in chronic alcoholism, judge drug therapy (mainly the chlordiazepoxide-imipramine combination), to be most suited to socially intact, but psychologically unsophisticated, alcoholic outpatients.

Studies of neuroleptics are generally even less promising and have been reviewed, en passant, above. One study, not noted previously, found thiothixene and thioridazine to be no different from placebo (Turek, Ota, Brown, Massari, & Kurland, 1973).

From the above information it is possible to infer that neither antidepressants nor antianxiety agents have, to date, shown dramatic success in improving either the dysphoria or the clinic attendance of chronic alcoholics. Chlordiazepoxide, the best studied drug, is better than placebo in symptom reduction but at some risk of impaired psychological functioning and return to drinking. The benefits may be more obvious to the patient than to other observers. The degree of benefit, such as it is, is not enough to make chlordiazepoxide a reliable or useful long-term therapy. Our clinical and theoretical positions both reinforce the presumption that sedative antianxiety agents like the benzodiazepines resemble alcohol too closely and are likely to produce a "pill drunk" or to reactivate binge drinking by creating a psychological state similar to that experienced by alcoholics in the early stages of a binge. The antidepressants do not look much more promising. One estimate of the role of such therapies in clinic treatment was made by Rosenberg (1974) who observed that only 2.3% of the variability in outcome in his study was attributable to drug therapies (chlordiazepoxide, disulfiram, vitamins, and placebo) while 11.2% of the variance was attributable to the legal coercion imposed on some of his patients.

More recent developments in this area include studies of propranolol (a beta-adrenergic blocking drug)used to attempt to block adrenergic aspects of alcohol withdrawal (Carlsson & Johansson, 1971; Gardos, 1975) or of alcohol intoxication per se (Mendelson, Rossi, Bernstein, & Kuehnle, 1974). The drug does have some ameliorative influence on tension and depression, as against placebo, in the first 8 days in hospital. However, it clearly does not influence acute alcohol effects in volunteer normal subjects. The drug has some antianxiety actions in neurotic outpatients (Wheatley, 1969).

More intriguing is the study carried out by Kline (1974) and associates at the V.A. Hospital in Togus, Maine, of a 48 weeks comparison of lithium carbonate and placebo in patients having both chronic alcoholism and nonpsychotic depression as inpatients. Although 59% of the original 73 failed to take study medication, a comparison of the 16 remaining lithium patients with the 14 remaining placebo patients shows that lithium patients were significantly less likely to have disabling drinking episodes (25%) as compared to placebo patients (64%). The lithium patients who relapsed in this way had fewer such episodes than did relapsed placebo patients. Both groups were improved on self-ratings of depression at 48 weeks. The number of drinking episodes per year were unchanged by placebo therapy. Lithium therapy caused a 75% reduction in episodes in its first year as compared with the patient's experience in the preceding year. The same finding was obtained for the 18 patients who had been on lithium for 2 years. Patients' lithium levels were maintained around 0.8 m Eq./liter. This approach looks promising and deserves further study.

As a final caveat, the clinician should not make the error implicit in much of the clinical drug study literature on alcoholism, that of assuming that all alcoholics are homogeneous and can respond to a single drug therapy. This is relatively true only during detoxification. Otherwise, there are schizophrenic alcoholics who urgently need antipsychotics, severe depressives with alcoholism who deserve trials on antidepressants, and emotionally unstable poly-drug abusers who may best be handled by careful avoidance of all drug therapies. Each patient must be evaluated individually; the average results derived from controlled trials in a large heterogeneous group of presumed alcoholics in a clinical facility totally unfamiliar to the reader must, in most instances, be viewed as suggestions about possible drug therapies, not as definitive recommendations to be applied indiscriminately to all alcoholics within reach.

DRUGS WHICH INTERFERE WITH ALCOHOL CONSUMPTION

DISULFIRAM. Disulfiram, at an adequate level in the body, will interact with ingested alcohol to induce the following symptoms in this general order: flushing, sweating, palpitations, dyspnea, hyperventilation, tachycardia, hypotension, nausea, and vomiting. These events are usually followed by drowsiness with complete recovery generally prevailing after sleep.[1] These reactions are presumably dose dependent, but the minimal amounts of either agent needed to produce the adverse reaction are unclear in the literature. Presumably 250 mg of disulfiram a day, perhaps less, is enough; as little as 7 ml of ethyl alcohol can produce the reaction. Since disulfiram is fat soluble and long acting, patients may still react for as long as seven days after they stop taking disulfiram.

Our experience at McLean Hospital is that 125 mg of disulfiram a day in the a.m. is a satisfactory, relatively trouble-free initial and maintenance level for patients weighing under 170 lbs. Patients on this dose who start to drink report typical disulfiram-alcohol reactions of moderate intensity which are aversive without being catastrophic.

Disulfiram probably acts by blocking the metabolism of alcohol, inhibiting the further oxidation of acetaldehyde. The drug also inhibits the conversion of dopamine to norepinephrine by blocking the enzyme dopamine-ß-hydroxylase. This

---

[1] It was discovered by mistake. Two Danish scientists took the drug themselves to assess its safety as a vermifuge. While on disulfiram, they went to a cocktail party with disastrous results. They inferred, correctly, that the drug might be useful in preventing alcohol consumption.

second action may explain the paradox that acetaldehyde alone causes a rise in blood pressure. The alcohol-disulfiram interaction may have the opposite (hypotensive) effect because of disulfiram's interference with the synthesis of norepinephrine, a biogenic amine active in elevating blood pressure (Ritchie, 1965). Side effects of the drug, other than the alcohol reaction, include fatigue, lethargy, a metallic taste, impotence, and, rarely, toxic psychosis, perhaps secondary to increased brain dopamine.

Although two good psychologically and psychiatrically oriented reviews exist (Lundwell & Baeckeland, 1971; Mottin, 1973), and although disulfiram has been used in alcoholism for almost 30 years, there is no good compilation of the frequency or severity of the various possible side effects at various maintenance dosage levels. These range from 1 gram to 125 mg per day. Rumor suggests that some alcoholics manage to drink and take disulfiram. In fact, this old drug has almost never been exposed to double blind controlled clinical trial. One Russian study, showing no difference between disulfiram and placebo, is described in Mottin's review. Wallerstein's 1957 study compared disulfiram with conditioned reflex therapy, hypnotherapy, and a control group. After two years 53% of the disulfiram patients were doing well as against about 30% of the patients in the other three treatment groups. Hoff (1953), in a large comparative study, found alcoholic clinic patients who were willing and medically able to take disulfiram did better than patients who refused the drug. The fact that a third group, patients willing to take disulfiram but denied it for medical reasons, did as well as the group who actually received it, makes one suspect that the drug is only a test of motivation. An interesting study by Gallant and his associates (Gallant, Bishop, Faulkner, Simpson, Cooper, Lathrop, Brisolara & Bossetta, 1968) compared court enforced disulfiram therapy with court enforced group psychotherapy and a voluntary program (court referral without enforcement). They found no treatment differences. However, they suggest that the study patients were too ill to understand clearly the court's actions and believe an inpatient detoxification phase prior to court assignment to the various treatments might have led to a more valuable study. Over the years a shift has occurred in the practice of disulfiram therapy. Originally, all patients were given a test dose of alcohol early in their disulfiram therapy to acquaint them with the full unpleasantness of the alcohol reaction. This practice has now almost completely stopped. It is unfortunate that the contribution, if any, of this aversive experience to the patient's future abstinence has never been adequately studied.

Recently, Rosenberg's group (Gerrein, Rosenberg, & Manohar, 1973) has taken a lead from methadone maintenance and compared disulfiram therapy given on two schedules--once a week administration by a nurse and twice a week administration by a nurse--with the patients being expected to dose themselves the rest of the time. This was compared to non-disulfiram programs involving once or twice weekly clinic visits. Interestingly, the biweekly disulfiram group did very well in terms of clinic attendance (55% at 6 weeks as opposed to about 25% for the other groups). In addition, 40% of the biweekly disulfiram patients remained abstinent for 8 weeks as opposed to about 10% in the other treatment groups (including once a week disulfiram). A more recent study (Rosenberg, 1974) compared this successful regimen with chlordiazepoxide, vitamins, and no drug. The results were slightly less favorable, but disulfiram was still superior to either vitamin or no drug treatment and equal to chlordiazepoxide. In this study, disulfiram (which is said to cause depression as a side effect) actually acted to decrease depression and anxiety. Patients who continued to return to the clinic for up to 26 weeks tended to be sober as a group; disulfiram's sobriety rate of 85% was a bit higher than the 75% for the other treatment groups.

Lundwell and Baeckeland (1971), in their review, observe that successful disulfiram patients tend to be older, more socially stable, more highly motivated, better able to form dependent relationships, less depressed, and less likely to have blackouts or sociopathic traits. The problem, of course, is that these same traits may be associated with a better prognosis in chronic alcoholism in the absence of disulfiram.

Despite the limited evidence favoring disulfiram therapy, it seems to have an assured place in the outpatient therapy of chronic alcoholics. The position in favor of its use can be stated as follows: disulfiram is not a cure but affords the patient with a sincere desire to stop drinking support in avoiding an impulsive drink. The rationale for its use is that the patient knows that he has to avoid alcohol at least three days after taking disulfiram or he will experience some or all of the previously mentioned symptoms. In this way, the patient's self-control is increased. He also allows himself an interval of sobriety, with regular use of disulfiram, in which to learn to deal with his life without alcohol. Moreover, taking disulfiram is something positive the patient is doing to help himself. This self-imposed treatment can increase the patient's self-esteem and encourages his family and friends to regain confidence in him. Many patients also see disulfiram as a "good friend" which they take each morning with their orange juice. This "friend" sees that they stay out of trouble as any good friend would.

Patients on disulfiram should avoid disguised forms of alcohol, such as cold alcohol-laden sauces, fermented vinegar, and certain cough syrups. Absorption of alcohol through skin is minimal and, consequently, after-shave lotions are not contraindicated at the disulfiram dosages previously suggested. Gourmets need not become disheartened as Julia Child, "The French Chef" (1974), has suggested the substitution of "chicken broth, fish stock, and beef stock in fish or meat dishes and orange juice or cider in desserts, along with appropriate spices and herbs in meat dishes and cloves, cinnamon, cardomon, etc., in sweet dishes" for wine. Finally, well-cooked dishes will evaporate off all the alcohol during preparation.

Disulfiram should not be given to organically confused, psychotic, severely depressed, or suicidal patients. The confused or psychotic patient may inadvertently drink alcohol for a variety of reasons (e.g., memory deficits, voices telling him to), while the severely depressed or suicidal individual may use disulfiram in an attempt to kill himself (Jacobsen, 1952). Accordingly, because of the latter, as well as the necessary responsibility for daily or bi-weekly self-administration, the patients chosen for this therapy have to have a reasonably sound personality structure. Of course, "an alcoholic who becomes determined to desert his sobriety will simply stop taking the pills for a few days until he is safe, or he may even start drinking right through the disulfiram, accepting the frightful resulting symptoms as a kind of punishment in advance for his break, with authorization to go on drinking thereafter with impunity" (Solomon, 1966). Finally many patients are resistant to taking disulfiram, particularly men. They see the drug as taking away the opportunity to "do it on their own" and in that sense undermining their masculinity. In term "crutch" is often used, suggesting that their having to take disulfiram infers that they are crippled or at best unreliable. More suspicious patients are concerned that the drug will control them or place them under the physician's control. Education is directed at helping the patients recognize that disulfiram will support their own self-control as the result of their own decision to take it. Low doses (125 to 250 mg a day) are usually clinically useful and avoid almost all side effects other than occasional transient skin rashes, dizziness, headache, or gastric irritability. Most doctors feel disulfiram is contraindicated during pregnancy because of possible danger to the fetus, and in patients with psychosis, and even heart disease (due to its β-hydroxylase inhibiting properties); (Kissin & Gross, 1968). Moreover, if a patient is taking diphenylhydantoin, the dose must be decreased or toxicity may result since disulfiram slows its metabolism.

It is, however, always possible that, in the social context described, a placebo which was believed by both parties to be disulfiram would do as well. It is unclear to what extent actual disulfiram-alcohol reactions play a significant role in the long-term success of disulfiram in some patients.

DISULFIRAM IMPLANTS. A long acting disulfiram implant which may possibly last as long as six months has been developed and is in clinical trial. The most positive and only comparative published study (Whyte & O'Brien, 1974) compares outcome in 22 "implanted" male alcoholics with 23 "matched controls," apparently not randomly assigned to nonimplant therapy. The treatment group averaged 5.4 months until their first drink as opposed to 1.9 months in the comparison group. In terms of the implant itself, the eight tablets formed a sore, inflamed nodule which was uncomfortable for the first week; the operation was done under local anesthetic; no implants were rejected in the series. Local infection or rejection of the tablets occurred in 13 out of 70 implants in the series described by Malcolm and Madden (1973). These patients were, as a group, significantly longer abstinent than had been the case at any time in the two years prior to implantation. Nine patients drank and had a reaction in the first six months after implantation, but only four of these reactions, were judged typical of disulfiram-alcohol reaction and twelve of the 46 patients increased their use of sedatives.

In a South African study of 19 patients (Obholzer, 1974) over half the implants were complicated by infection. Four out of six patients began drinking within seven months of the implant, and only two experienced the expected adverse reaction. There is more extensive data in the Polish literature, which is summarized in the above article.

In summation, it is still too early to assess the ability of disulfiram implants to actually induce reliable alcohol reactions for any fixed duration of time. If they do, it is unclear whether they will be of use in other than specially selected and motivated patients. The potential medico-legal problems attached to the use of this agent are bothersome.

CITRATED CALCIUM CYANAMIDE. The literature on this shorter acting disulfiram-like drug is well reviewed by Mottin (1973). Its alcohol reactions are usually considered to be generally milder than those occurring with disulfiram, and the alcohol effect is no greater two hours after a single dose than two hours after the seventh of seven daily 100 mg doses (Lader, 1966). In the only comparative study (Levy, Livingston, & Collins, 1967, calcium carbimide (the generic name) was compared to disulfiram. During alcohol challenges in patients, abnormal electrocardiograms were less common when on carbimide (4 of 19) than on disulfiram (3 of 7). Seven of the 19 calcium carbimide patients did well as against an unknown number (less than 5) of the 11 disulfiram patients. It appears that the carbimide patients were local alcoholics; whereas, disulfiram was given to patients likely to leave the area. Hence conclusions about the real relative efficacy of the two drugs cannot be drawn. The drug is marketed in England and Canada but not in the United States.

METRONIDAZOLE. This drug, marketed for use in Trichomonas infections, achieved a certain notoriety after Taylor (1964) reported that males taking the drug reported a distaste for alcohol and a reduction in drinking. This led to a surprising number of studies (9 controlled) which have been well reviewed by Mottin (1973). Although three studies were positive, most were depressingly negative or showed only a small subsample of patients with the metronidazole effect -- i.e., alcohol tastes different, alcohol is disliked, intoxication occurs on lesser amounts. All in all, the effects were generally small or nonexistent. Thus, the ability of the drug to actually produce disulfiram-like effects when combined with alcohol is dubious, with Gelder and Edwards study (1968) testing this most directly. Unfortunately, the positive placebo-controlled studies were in obscure languages and not available to the present reviewers. In an interesting side study, Wilson, O'Brien, and MacAirt (1973) showed that metronidazole at 800 mg a day (but not at 600 mg) was able to raise taste thresholds for alcohol for both aversive and pleasurable (e.g., sweet) thresholds. (800 mg is higher than the daily dose 500-750 mg used in most controlled studies).

The intriguing aspect of the metronidazole story is that this weak drug has inspired such a range of investigative activity while disulfiram has remained almost unstudied by identical controlled trial methodology.

DRUGS AS AVERSIVE STIMULI

There is modest literature on the aversion conditioning treatment of chronic alcoholism, which is well reviewed by Costello (1969) and less clearly reviewed by Mottin (1973). The general principle, of course, is to associate a highly unpleasant stimulus (the unconditioned stimulus--UCS) with an alcoholic beverage (the conditioned stimulus--CS). This is usually done in a Pavlovian rather than an operant conditioning paradigm in the hope that the unpleasant effects will be associated with the alcohol and lead the patient to avoid, or be upset by, alcohol in the future. In past decades, drugs causing vomiting were generally used--emetine or apomorphine. Here there was a problem in timing since, ideally, the UCS and CS should be placed only seconds apart for maximal effect. A complex emetine regimen has been used clinically for years at the Schick-Shadel Hospital in Seattle and is well detailed by Costello (1969). No controlled studies of its efficacy are available although Lemere of Schick-Shadel Hospital reports excellent results (60% abstinent for at least one year). One wonders whether going to a hospital for enforced vomiting may not imply strong motivation to stop drinking and whether being able to afford a private sanatorium may not be associated with above average social stability. Both are predictors of good outcome in alcoholism independent of the specific treatment used.

In an effort to develop even more drastic and closely timed aversive stimuli, succinylcholine and other drugs which cause total, brief paralysis of all muscles (as well as severe anxiety) have been tried. Here, a pair of controlled studies have been done. In both studies, patients not receiving both the UCS and the CS have done about as well as patients receiving the full pairing of stimuli.

Overall, the results of these therapies are not impressive. Neither approach is free from danger. One hopes that other nonpharmacological behavioral methods using more active operant procedures with provision for positive reinforcing alternative behavioral outlets would be more useful.

PSYCHOTOMIMETIC DRUGS

Early reports from hospitals in Saskatchewan, Palo Alto, and Spring Grove, Maryland, led to a presumption that the administration of lysergic acid diethylamide (LSD) in a context of psychotherapy resulted in remarkable changes in drinking behavior of a favorable sort (Cole & Katz, 1964). The Josiah Macy, Jr., Foundation Conference on "The Use of LSD in Psychotherapy" (Abramson, 1960) documents the flavor of that exciting and controversial time.

The early claims have now been tested in at least five well-designed controlled trials. In the most elaborate of these, Ludwig and Levine, who earlier had found short-term favorable effects of LSD therapy in institutionalized drug addicts, compared hypnodelic therapy (an LSD experience guided by hypnosis), psychedelic therapy (LSD and psychotherapy during the experience), LSD without psychiatric intervention and, as a no-treatment control, an equivalent period of quiet solitary contemplation of personal problems by the patient. Throughout a year of detailed and successful follow-up studies of the 44 patients in each treatment group, no differences were found on any of a range of drinking, social adjustment, or subjective state measures between any of the four groups of chronic alcoholics (Ludwig, Levine, Stark, & Lazar, 1969). Half the patients were randomly placed on disulfiram. This also had no effect on any of the measures used.

Hollister, Shelton, and Krieger (1969) compared 600 micrograms LSD with 60 milligrams dextroamphetamine in 72 alcoholics. The experience was intended as a several hour period of self-examination. At two months the LSD group was somewhat better off, but at six months the drinking and social status of the two groups were identical.

Johnson (1970) compared about 550 micrograms LSD intravenously with psychiatric psychodynamic interviewing; a similar period after LSD with attention from a nurse; a psychiatric interview after intravenous administration of sodium amobarbital and methamphentamine; and routine care. There were approximately 25 patients per treatment group. After one year, there were no differences in outcome between the four groups.

Smart, Storm, Baker, and Solursh (1966) compared 800 micrograms with 60 milligrams of ephedrine and a no-drug session control group (10 subjects per group). Interviews with the drug patients emphasized dynamic insight. The two drug groups showed improvements in abstinence over the 6 month period (34% and 32%) while the no-drug group showed 20% improvement. Overall, no significant differences were found between groups on any of several outcome measures.

Only the Spring Grove group recorded favorable results, but failed to use a placebo or no treatment control. In comparing high dose LSD with low dose LSD or comparing patients who had or failed to have intense transcendental LSD experiences independent of dose (Pahnke, Kurland, Unger, Savage, & Grof, 1970), they observed somewhat better social and drinking behaviors after one year in the high dose and the intense peak experience groups. However, this treatment program involved 12-15 hours of counseling prior to the LSD experience, an eight-hour elaborately programmed LSD experience with constant presence of a therapist plus extensive counseling after the session to consolidate and digest insights and experience.

In sum, LSD therapy for alcoholism is generally ineffective and, at best, is only partially effective even when elaborate, intensive, and expensive psychotherapy is interwoven into the experience. Other hallucinogens have been studied in preliminary trials in alcoholism with little in the way of substantial findings worthy of detailed review (Denson & Sydiaha, 1970; Grof, Soskin, Richards, & Kurland, 1973; Simonopoulos, Pinto, Babikow, Kurland, & Savage, 1970).

CONDLUSIONS

The available clinical literature assessing drug therapies in various phases of alcoholism has its limitations and is often either inconclusive or controversial. Nevertheless, some general assertions are possible:

1. In the treatment of withdrawal symptoms chlordiazepoxide (and probably other benzodiazepines) is safe and effective and can abort or avert delirium tremens.

2. Promazine, in patients with severe withdrawal symptoms or delirium tremens, is contraindicated. It appears to increase the occurrence of full delirium tremens and has been associated with a higher death rate than any other treatment studied

3. No antianxiety or antidepressant drug (or lithium carbonate) has been shown to offer any clear advantage over placebo in the treatment of detoxified alcoholics in the community. The one available study on lithium carbonate in alcoholics with associated depression is promising and deserves replication.

4. Although disulfiram is widely used and popular with both doctors and patients and probably is useful in selected patients, studies comparing it with placebo or no drug treatment generally show it to have little or no overall clinical value. Nevertheless, it appears to have a firm place in the therapy of chronic alcoholism. The newer variants, calcium carbimide and metronidazole, are equally ineffective and lack

the virtue of wide clinical exposure. Disulfiram implants also seem to offer no advantage over oral medication and may not, in fact, really provide their promised chronic anti-alcohol effect.

5. Aversion techniques -- using either emetics or paralyzing agents -- appear crude and unvalidated and may merely be tests of motivation.

6. LSD and related psychotomimetics used as adjuncts to psychotherapy of alcoholics have been well studied and are generally without any prolonged effect on drinking behavior.

COMMON PROPRIETARY NAMES OF DRUGS MENTIONED

amitriptyline hydrochloride	Elavil (U.S.),Tryptizol (U.K.) Laroxyl (U.K.)
chlordiazepoxide hydrochloride	Librium
chlorpromazine hydrochloride	Thorazine (U.S.),Largactil (U.K.)
chlorprothixene	Taractan
citrated calcium carbimide (cyanamide)	Abstem (U.K.)
diazepam	Valium
diethylpropion hydrochloride	Tenuate (U.S. & U.K.), Apisate (U.K.)
diphenylhydantoin, sodium	Dilantin (U.S.), Epanutin (U.K.)
disulfiram	Antabuse
dixyrazine	Esucos (Belgium), not marketed in U.S.
emylcamate	Nuncital (Sweden) not at present marketed in U.S. or U.K.
haloperidol	Haldol (U.S. & U.K.) Serenace (U.K.)
hydroxyzine hydrochloride	Atarax
hydroxyzine pamoate	Vistaril

imipramine hydrochloride	Tofranil, Presamine, Imavate
isocarboxazid	Marplan
lithium carbonate	Eskalith, Lithane, Lithonate (U.S.), Camcolit (U.K.)
meprobamate	Equanil, Miltown
mesoridazine	Serentil
metronidazole	Flagyl
nialamide	Niamid
oxazepam	Serax (U.S.),Serenid-d (U.K.)
pentobarbital	Nembutal
perphenazine	Trilafon (U.S.),Fentazin (U.K.)
promazine hydrochloride	Sparine
propranolol hydrochloride	Inderal
succinylcholine chloride	Anectine (U.S. & U.K.) Scoline (U.K.)
thioridazine hydrochloride	Mellaril (U.S.), Melleril (U.K.)
trifluoperazine hydrochloride	Stelazine
tybamate	Tybatran

GLOSSARY OF ABBREVIATIONS IN TABLES

b.i.d.	twice a day
d.	day
D/C	discontinue
h.s.	at bedtime
IM	intramuscularly
IV	intravenously
MOM	milk of magnesia
MRx1	may be repeated once
p.o.	orally
prn.	whenever needed
q	every
q.d.	once a day
q.i.d.	four times a day
stat.	immediately
tab	tablet
tid	three times a day

REFERENCES

Abramson, H.A. (Ed.). *The use of LSD in psychotherapy.* New York: Josiah Macy, Jr. Foundation, 1960.

Beard, D. Fluid and electrolyte balance during acute withdrawal in chronic alcoholic patients. *Journal of the American Medical Association*, 1968, *204*, 135-139.

Benuzzi, P., & Muller, C. Three methods of treatment for delirium tremens - comparative study. *Schweizerische Medizinische Wochenschrift*, 1967, *97*, 1283-1289.

Bliding, A. Efficacy of antianxiety drug therapy in alcohol post-intoxication symptoms: A double-blind study of chlorprothixen, oxazepam, and placebo. *British Journal of Psychiatry*, 1973, *122*, 465-468.

Bolsano, N.A. Fluid restriction and the management of acute alcohol withdrawal. *Surgery*, 1970, *68*, 283-286.

Bowman, E.H., & Thimann, J. Treatment of alcoholism in the subacute stage: A study of three active agents. *Diseases of the Nervous System*, 1966, *27*, 342-346.

Butterworth, A.T., & Watts, R.D. Treatment of hospitalized alcoholics with doxepin and diazepam. *Quarterly Journal of Studies on Alcohol*, 1971, *32*, 78-81.

Cappell, H., & Herman, C.P. Alcohol and tension reduction: A review. *Quarterly Journal of Studies on Alcohol*, 1972, *33*, 33-64.

Carlsson, C., & Johansson, T. The psychological effects of propranolol in the abstinence phase of chronic alcoholics. *British Journal of Psychiatry*, 1971, *119*, 605-606.

Chambers, J.F., & Schultz, J.D. Double blind study of three drugs in the treatment of acute alcoholic states. *Quarterly Journal of Studies on Alcohol*, 1964, *25*, 10-18.

Child, J. Personal communication, 1974.

Cole, J.O., & Davis, J. Antipsychotic, antidepressant, and antianxiety drugs. In A. Freedman, H. Kaplan, & B. Sadock (Eds.), *Comprehensive textbook of psychiatry* (Vol. 2). Baltimore: Williams & Wilkins, 1975.

Cole, J.O., & Katz, M. The psychotomimetic drugs, an overview. *Journal of the American Medical Association*, 1964, *187*, 758-761.

Costello, C.G. An evaluation of aversion and LSD therapy in the treatment of alcoholism. *Canadian Psychiatric Association Journal*, 1969, *14*, 31-41.

Dalton, S., & Duncan, D.W. The effects of fructose in the management of delirium tremens. *The Medical Journal of Australia*, 1970, *1*, 659-661.

Denson, R., & Sydiaha, D. A controlled study of LSD treatment in alcoholism and neurosis. *British Journal of Psychiatry*, 1970, *116*, 443-445.

Ditman, K.S. Review and evaluation of current drug therapies in alcoholism. *Psychosomatic Medicine*, 1966, *28*, 248-258.

Favazza, A.R., & Martin P. Chemotherapy of delirium tremens: A survey of physicians' preferences. *American Journal of Psychiatry*, 1974, *131*, 1031-1033.

Feldman, D.J., Pattison, M., & Sabell, L.C. Outpatient alcoholic detoxification: Initial findings on 564 patients. *American Journal of Psychiatry*, 1975, *132*, 407-412.

Freedman, A., Kaplan, B., & Sadock, I. *Comprehensive textbook of psychiatry*. Baltimore: Williams & Wilkins, 1975.

Friedhoff, A., & Zitrin, A. A comparison of the effects of paraldehyde and chlorpromazine in delirium tremens. *New York Journal of Medicine*, 1959, *59*, 1060-1065.

Frost, I.B. Mesoridazine and chlorpromazine in the treatment of alcohol withdrawal syndrome. *Canadian Psychiatric Association Journal*, 1973, *18*, 385-387.

Gallant, D.M., Bishop, M.P., Faulkner, M.A., Simpson, L., Cooper, A., Lathrop, D., Brisolara, A.M., & Bossetta, J.R. A comparative evaluation of compulsory (group therapy and/or antabuse) and voluntary treatment of the chronic alcoholic municipal court offender. *Psychosomatics*, 1968, *9*, 306-310.

Gallant, D.M., Bishop, M.P., Guerero-Figueroa, R., Selby, M., & Phillips, R. Doxepin versus diazepam: A controlled evaluation in 100 chronic alcoholic patients. *The Journal of Clinical Pharmacology*, 1969, *9*, 57-65.

Gardos, G. Personal communication.

Gelder, M.G., & Edwards, G. Metronidazole in the treatment of alcohol addiction: A controlled trial. *British Journal of Psychiatry*, 1968, *114*, 473-475.

Gerard, D.L., & Saenger, G. *The outpatient treatment of alcoholism.* Toronto: University of Toronto Press, 1966.

Gerrein, J.R., Rosenberg, C.M., & Manohar, V. Disulfiram maintainance in outpatient treatment of alcoholism. *Archives of General Psychiatry*, 1973, *28*, 798-807.

Gershon, S. A review of the use of a thiazole derivative (Heminevrin) in delirium tremens and allied conditions. In J.O. Cole (Ed.), *Clinical research in alcoholism*, Psychiatric Research Report No. 24, Washington, D.C.: American Psychiatric Association, 1967.

Giacobini, E., & Salum, I. Treatment of delirium tremens. *Acta Psychiatrica Scandinavica*, 1961, *37*, 198-208.

Glatt, M.M. Controlled trials of non-barbiturate hypnotics and tranquillizers with special reference to their use in alcoholics. *Psychiatric Neurology*, 1966, *152*, 28-42.

Glatt, M.M., George, H.R., & Frisch, E.P. Evaluation of chlormethiazole in treatment for alcohol withdrawal syndrome: Results of a controlled trial. *Acta Psychiatrica Scandinavica*, 1966, *42*(Suppl.), 121-137.

Golbert, R.M., Sanz, C.J., Rose, H.D., & Leitschuh, T.H. Comparative evaluation of treatments of alcohol withdrawal syndromes. *Journal of the American Medical Association*, 1967, *201*, 99-102.

Greenberg, L.A., & Rosenfeld, J.E. Haloperidol in the treatment of acute alcoholism. *Psychosomatics*, 1969, *10*, 172-175.

Greenblatt, D., & Shader, R. *Benzodiazepines in clinical practice.* New York: Raven Press, 1974.

Grof, S., Soskin, R.A., Richards, W.A., & Kurland, A.A. DPT as an adjunct in psychotherapy of alcoholics. *International Pharmacopsychiatry*, 1973, *8*, 104-115.

Hart, W.T. A comparison of promazine and paraldehyde in 175 cases of alcohol withdrawal. *American Journal of Psychiatry*, 1961, *118*, 323-327.

Hekimian, L.J., Friedhoff, A.J., & Alpert, M. Treatment of acute brain syndrome from alcohol with nicotinamide adenine dinucleotide and chlordiazepoxide. *Quarterly Journal of Studies on Alcohol*, 1966, *27*, 214-220.

Hoff, E.C., & McKeown, C.E. An evaluation of the use of tetraethylthiuram disulfide in the treatment of 560 cases of alcohol addiction. *American Journal of Psychiatry*, 1953, *109*, 670-673.

Hollister, L. *Clinical use of psychiatric drugs*. Springfield: Charles C Thomas, 1973.

Hollister, L.E., Prusmack, J.J., & Lipscomb, W. Treatment of acute alcohol withdrawal with chlormethiazole (Heminevrin). *Diseases of the Nervous System*, 1972, *33*, 247-250.

Hollister, L.E, Shelton, J., & Krieger, G. A controlled comparison of lysergic acid diethylamide (LSD) and dextroamphetamine in alcoholics. *American Journal of Psychiatry*, 1969, *125*, 1352-1357.

Jacobson, E. Deaths of alcoholic patients treated with disulfiram in Denmark. *Quarterly Journal of Studies on Alcohol*, 1952, *13*, 16-18.

Jarvik, M.E. Drugs used in the treatment of psychiatric disorders. In L. Goodman & A. Gilman (Eds.), *The pharmacological basis of therapeutics*. New York: Mac Millan, 1965.

Johnson, F.G. A comparison of short-term treatment effects of intravenous sodium amytal-methedrine and LSD in the alcoholic. *Canadian Psychiatric Association Journal*, 1970, *15*, 493-497.

Kaim, S.C., & Klett, C.J. Treatment of delirium tremens: A comparative evaluation of four drugs. *Quarterly Journal of Studies on Alcohol*, 1972, *33*, 1065-1072.

Kaim, S.C., Klett, C.J., & Rothfeld, B. Treatment of the acute alcohol withdrawal state: A comparison of four drugs. *American Journal of Psychiatry*, 1969, *125*, 1640-1646.

Kissen, M.D. Management of psychomotor agitation in acute alcoholism. *Diseases of the Nervous System*, 1965, *26*, 364-368.

Kissin, B., & Gross, M.M. Drug therapy in alcoholism. *American Journal of Psychiatry*, 1968, *125*, 69-79.

Kissin, B., Platz, A., & Su, W.H. Social and psychological factors in the treatment of chronic alcoholism. *Journal of Psychiatric Research*, 1970, *8*, 13-27.

Kline, N.S., Wren, J.C., Cooper, T.B., Varga, E., & Canal, O. Evaluation of lithium therapy in chronic and periodic alcoholism. *American Journal of the Medical Sciences*, 1974, *268*, 15-22.

Lader, M.H. Alcohol reactions after single and multiple doses of calcium cyanamide. *Quarterly Journal of Studies on Alcohol*, 1966, *28*, 468-475.

Levy, M., Livingstone, B.L., & Collins, D.M. A clinical comparison of disulfiram and calcium carbimide. *American Journal of Psychiatry*, 1967, *123*, 1018-1022.

Ludwig, A., Levine, J., Stark, L., & Lazar, R. A clinical study of LSD treatment in alcoholism. *American Journal of Psychiatry*, 1969, *126*, 97-107.

Lundwell, L., & Baekeland, F. Disulfiram treatment of alcoholism. *Journal of Nervous and Mental Disease*, 1971, *153*, 381-394.

Malcolm, M.T., & Madden, J.S. The use of disulfiram implantation in alcoholism. *British Journal of Psychiatry*, 1973, *123*, 41-45.

Malmgren, G. Comparative investigation of the effects of dixyrazine, placebo, and chlordiazepoxide on alcoholics during hospital care. *Acta Neurologica Belgica*, 1967, *67*, (Suppl.), 65-75.

Mendelson, J.H., Rossi, M., Bernstein, J.G., & Kuehnle, J. Propranolol and behavior of alcohol addicts after acute alcohol ingestion. *Clinical Pharmacology and Therapeutics*, 1974, *15*, 571-578.

Mooney, H.G., Ditman, K.S., & Cohen, S. Chlordiazepoxide in the treatment of alcoholics. *Diseases of the Nervous System*, 1961, *7* (Suppl. to No. 2), 44-51.

Mottin, J.L. Drug induced attenuation of alcohol consumption. *Quarterly Journal of Studies on Alcohol*, 1973, *34*, 444-472.

Obholzer, A.M. A follow-up study of nineteen alcoholic patients treated by means of tetraethyl-thiuram disulfide (antabuse) implants. *British Journal of the Addictions*, 1974, *69*, 19-23.

Pahnke, W.N., Kurland, A.A., Unger, S., Savage, C., & Grof, S. The experimental use of psychedelic (LSD) psychotherapy. *Journal of the American Medical Association*, 1970, *212*, 1856-1863.

Palestine, M.L. Drug treatment of the alcohol withdrawal syndrome and delirium tremens. *Quarterly Journal of Studies on Alcohol*, 1973, *34*, 185-193.

Ritchie, J.M. The aliphatic alcohols. In L. Goodman, & A. Gilman (Eds.), *The pharmacological basis of therapeutics*. New York: MacMillan, 1965.

Rosenberg, C.M. Drug maintainance in the outpatient treatment of chronic alcoholism. *Archives of General Psychiatry*, 1974, *30*, 373-380.

Rothstein, E. Prevention of alcohol withdrawal seizures: The roles of diphenylhydantoin and chlordiazepoxide. *American Journal of Psychiatry*, 1973, *130*, 1381-1382.

Ryback, R.S. The continuum and specificity of the effects of alcohol on memory: A review. *Quarterly Journal of Studies on Alcohol*, 1971, *32*, 995-1016.

Ryback, R.S. Psychological aspects of alcohol and alcoholism. *Massachusetts Journal of Mental Health*, 1974, *5*, 19-44.

Sampliner, R., & Iber, F.L. Diphenylhydantoin control of alcohol withdrawal seizures: Results of a controlled study. *Journal of the American Medical Association*, 1974, *230*, 1430-1432.

Schwartz, L., Schmidt, H., & Stern, J.A. A double-blind trial of the efficacy of promazine in the treatment of alcohol withdrawal syndrome. *Diseases of the Nervous System*, 1968, *29*, 173-177.

Sereny, G., & Kalant, H. Comparative clinical evaluation of chlordiazepoxide and promazine in treatment of alcohol-withdrawal syndrome. *British Medical Journal*, 1965, *1*, 92-97.

Shaffer, J.W., Freinek, W.R., Wolf, S., Foxwell, N.H., & Kurland, A.A. Replication of a study of nialamide in the treatment of convalescing alcoholics with emphasis on prediction of response. *Current Therapeutic Research*, 1964, *6*, 521-531.

Shaffer, J.W., Yeganeh, M.L., Foxwell, N.H., & Kurland, A.A. A comparison of the effects of prazepam, chlordiazepoxide, and placebo in the short-term treatment of convalescing alcoholics. *The Journal of Clinical Pharmacology*, 1968, *8*, 392-399.

Simonopoulos, A.M., Pinto, A., Babikow, P.W., Kurland, A.A., & Savage, C. Psychotomimetic properties and therapeutic potentials of dexadrol on convalescing alcoholics. *Diseases of the Nervous System*, 1970, *31*, 203-207.

Smart, R.G., Storm, T., Baker, E.F.W., & Solursh, L. A controlled study of lysergide in the treatment of alcoholism. *Quarterly Journal of Studies on Alcohol*, 1966, *27*, 469-482.

Solomon, P. Psychiatric treatment of the alcoholic patient. *International Psychiatry Clinics*, 1966, *3*, 159-188.

Sydney, M.A. Ventricular arrhythmias associated with the use of thioridazine hydrochloride in alcohol withdrawal. *British Medical Journal*, 1973, *4*, 467.

Taylor, J.A.T. Metronidazole, a new agent for combined somatic and psychic therapy of alcoholism. *Bulletin of the Los Angeles Neurological Society*, 1964, *29*, 158-162.

Thomas, D.W., & Freedman, D.X. Treatment of the alcohol withdrawal syndrome: A comparison of promazine and paraldehyde. *Journal of the American Medical Association*, 1964, *188*, 316-318.

Thompson, W.L., Johnson, A.D., & Maddrey, W.L. Diazepam and paraldehyde for treatment of severe delirium tremens: A controlled trial. *Annals of Internal Medicine*, 1975, *82*, 175-180.

Turek, I.S., Ota, K., Brown, C., Massari, F., & Kurland, A.A. Tiotixene and thioridazine in alcoholism treatment. *Quarterly Journal of Studies on Alcohol*, 1973, *34*, 853-859.

Viamontes, J.A. Review of drug effectiveness in the treatment of alcoholism. *American Journal of Psychiatry*, 1972, *128*, 570-571.

Victor, M. The role of hypomagnesemia and respiratory alkalosis in the genesis of alcohol-withdrawal symptoms. *Annals of the New York Academy of Sciences*, 1973, *215*, 235-248.

Victor, M., & Adams, R. Effects of alcohol on the nervous system. *Proceedings of the Association for Research in Nervous and Mental Diseases*, 1953, *32*, 526-576.

Victor, M., Adams, R., & Collins, G. *The Wernicke-Korsakoff syndrome*. Philadelphia: F.A. Davis Co., 1972.

Wallerstein, R.S. Comparative study of treatment methods for chronic alcoholism: The alcoholism research project at Winter V.A. Hospital. *American Journal of Psychiatry*, 1956, *113*, 228-233.

Wheatley, D. Comparative effects of propranolol and chlordiazepoxide in anxiety states. *British Journal of Psychiatry*, 1969, *115*, 1411-1412.

Whyte, C.R., & O'Brien, P.M.J. Disulfiram implant: A controlled trial. *British Journal of Psychiatry*, 1974, *124*, 42-44.

Wilson, C.W.M., O'Brien, C., & MacAirt, J.G. The effect of metronidazole on the human taste threshold to alcohol. *British Journal of the Addictions*, 1973, *68*, 99-110.

CHAPTER 20

ALCOHOLICS ANONYMOUS AND OTHER SELF-HELP GROUPS

John L. Norris

> Alcoholics Anonymous is a fellowship of men and women who share their experience, strength, and hope with each other that they solve their common problem and help others recover from alcoholism.
>
> The only requirement for membership is a desire to stop drinking. There are no dues or fees for A.A. membership; we are self-supporting through our own contributions. A.A. is not allied with any sect, denomination, politics, organization, or institution; does not wish to engage in any controversy, neither endorses nor opposes any causes. Our primary purpose is to stay sober and help other alcoholics to achieve sobriety.

This is the description of Alcoholics Anonymous which is read at the beginning of many meetings of A.A. throughout the world. For anyone who wishes to understand and work with Alcoholics Anonymous this description warrants study. A.A. is

Ralph E. Tarter and A. Arthur Sugerman (eds.), Alcoholism

ISBN: 0-201-08146-6
ISBN: 0-201-08145-8 (pbk.)

the sort of warm, close fellowship that comes from sharing a common problem, in depth, in a helping relationship, without thought of reward, financial or otherwise, except the reward of staying sober oneself.

"The only requirement for membership is a desire to stop drinking." Race, religion, class, income, education -- none of the usual distinctions between people are considered. Even when there is dependence on or addiction to another chemical, so long as there is a desire to stop drinking a person can belong.

"There are no dues or fees for A.A. membership, but we are self-supporting through our own contributions." The "hat" is passed at most meetings to defray the cost of meeting places, but it is often suggested that only members should contribute.

A.A. avoids any entangling alliances, sometimes, it seems to some people, to an unreasonable degree. Individual A.A. members cooperate with and join other organizations as individuals and/or as recovered alcoholics but not as A.A. members. One of the reasons for this distinction is to reinforce the principle of self-support so that no other organization will be able to use the A.A. name in soliciting contributions. It is especially important that this be understood by those who are responsible for programs in treatment facilities, as it has been the source of considerable misunderstanding in the past.

Alcoholics Anonymous is almost always mentioned in articles about alcoholism as one of the treatment resources, as it should be, for until people began to recover in A.A. almost everyone equated the word "alcoholic" with the hopeless derelict. Until quite recently there was little professional treatment available and no enthusiasm for what there was. That the picture has changed is due largely to the demonstration that alcoholic people do recover in considerable numbers for long periods of time, especially when professionals and A.A. work together. The dedicated work of many of those who have recovered has also helped greatly in promoting programs in government, industry, and elsewhere throughout society.

THE A.A. PROGRAM

There is a minimum of formal organization, no power of punishment or exclusion in A.A., and the only authority is shared experience. The program is expressed in three sets of principles which developed over the years as experience indicated the need. The Twelve Steps came first as a program for personal recovery. The Twelve Traditions, principles for relationships between groups, came second and the Twelve Concepts, principles for personal and group relations within the movement, were developed last.

THE TWELVE STEPS. The Twelve Steps, first printed in *Alcoholics Anonymous* (1939), and further explained in *Twelve Steps and Twelve Traditions* (1953), are introduced with this most significant sentence: "Here are the steps we took, which are suggested as a program of recovery."

Step One - We admitted we were powerless over alcohol -- that our lives had become unmanageable.

Step Two - Came to believe that a Power greater than ourselves could restore us to sanity.

Step Three - Made a decision to turn our will and our lives over to the care of God as we understood Him.

Step Four - Made a searching and fearless moral inventory of ourselves.

Step Five - Admitted to God, to ourselves, and to another human being, the exact nature of our wrongs.

Step Six - Were entirely ready to have God remove all these defects of character.

Step Seven - Humbly asked Him to remove our shortcomings.

Step Eight - Made a list of all persons we had harmed, and became willing to make amends to them all.

Step Nine - Made direct amends to such people wherever possible, except when to do so would injure them or others.

Step Ten - Continued to take personal inventory and when we were wrong promptly admitted it.

Step Eleven - Sought through prayer and meditation to improve our conscious contact with God as we understood Him, praying only for knowledge of His will for us and the power to carry that out.

Step Twelve - Having had a spiritual awakening as the result of these steps, we tried to carry this message to alcoholics, and to practice these principles in all our affairs.

When first written, the chapter in which the steps were introduced was directed to the alcoholic; that is, "You were wrong - you must - you should." After much discussion, this was changed to read, "We were wrong -- we must -- we should." We realize the importance of this change when we become aware of the two qualities most characteristic of the drinking alcoholic: defiant individuality and grandiosity. Authority is resented. As Margaret Bean (1975) writes

> A.A. at present is trying to accommodate new trends and individual variability... This leads to member's claiming that the steps are merely suggestions and then in the same meeting discussing explicit requirements concerning each step, implying that there is a single correct interpretation and a single path to recovery." (p.10)
> There is great emphasis throughout the fellowship on "sharing experience" and avoiding the parent-child, teacher-pupil, physician-patient relationship.

Step One -"We admitted we were powerless over alcohol--that our lives had become unmanageable." Bill W., co-founder of A.A., often emphasized in letters, in articles in the A.A. magazine, *The Grapevine*, and in conversations the importance of "deflation at depth." Tiebout (1949), in "The Act of Surrender in the Therapeutic Process," analyzes the mechanism of surrender --of admitting "we were powerless over alcohol -- that our lives had become unmanageable." In another paper, "Surrender Versus Compliance in Therapy," Tiebout (1951) points out that taking the first step may be a process. Many new members, especially when they are attending A.A. meetings as a result of pressure from employer, friends, family, clergyman, social worker, or physician are compliant but tense and unhappy for awhile. Many, after weeks or months of attending meetings, become aware of a change in feeling, often expressed as, "I'm free," or "I've stopped fighting." A change in physical appearance at this time is often noticeable. Some, after a few meetings, stay away, returning to drinking, and return to A.A. weeks or years later. Members will say of these people, "They weren't ready," or "They haven't suffered enough." Jellinek (1960) suggested three aspects of admission-- admission to self, admission to someone else, and collapse of alibis.

Many studies have demonstrated the importance of this recognition or admission as a turning point in recovery. (Bailey & Leach, 1965; Brook, 1962; Maxwell, 1954; Trice, 1957 a & b). It is significant that drinking is not mentioned as such, that alcohol is mentioned only in the First Step, and by implication in the Twelfth Step.

In *Step Two* help is offered. "Came to believe that a Power greater than ourselves could restore us to sanity." The absence of any definition or description of the Power greater than ourselves is significant. For many, perhaps most, of those first coming to A.A. any implication that this Power is a supernatural being would be rejected out of hand. For many the group or the fellowship as a whole is that Power, at first at least. Some remain atheists or agnostics.

Step Three - "Made a decision to turn our will and our lives over to the care of God as we understood Him." This is evidence of ego deflation; not the ego which psychiatrists wish to strengthen, but the "omnipotent ego" which Tiebout mentions. This turning over of self direction is akin perhaps to the acceptance of a regimen prescribed by a physician for a disease. The decision is made to accept reality, to stop trying to run things, and to let the "Power greater than ourselves" take over. As we have said earlier, this Power could be the group, or the wisdom and experience of a sponsor. "God as we understand Him" - there is no attempt to impose a theological concept.

Step Four - "Made a searching and fearless moral inventory of ourselves." It is often urged that this be done in writing. A.A. is a program of action.

Step Five - "Admitted to God, to ourselves, and to another human being the exact nature of our wrongs." "We'd have to have outside help if we were surely to know and admit the truth about ourselves--the help of God and another human being. Until we actually sit down and talk aloud about what we have so long hidden, our willingness to clean house is still largely theoretical."

Step Six - "We're entirely ready to have God remove all these defects of character." "Delay is dangerous, and rebellion may be fatal. This is the exact point at which we abandon limited objectives, and move toward God's will for us."

Step Seven - "Humbly asked Him to remove our shortcomings." "The Seventh Step is where we make the change in our attitude which permits us, with humility as our guide, to move out from ourselves toward others and toward God."

Step Eight - "Made a list of all persons we had harmed, and became willing to make amends to them all." "Having carefully surveyed this whole area of human relations, and having decided exactly what personality traits in us injured and disturbed others, we can now commence to ransack memory for the people to whom we have given offense. To put a finger on the near-by and most deeply damaged ones shouldn't be hard to do. Then, as year by year we walk back through our lives as far as memory will reach, we shall be bound to construct a long list of people who have, to some extent or other, been affected. We should, of course, ponder and weigh each instance carefully. We shall want to hold ourselves to the course of admitting the things we have done, meanwhile forgiving the wrongs done us, real or fancied. We should avoid extreme judgments, both of ourselves and of others involved. We must not exaggerate our defects or theirs. A quiet, objective view will be our steadfast aim. Whenever our pencil falters, we can fortify and cheer ourselves by remembering what A.A. experience in this step has meant to others. It is the beginning of the end of isolation from our fellows and from God."

Step Nine - "Made direct amends to such people wherever possible, except when to do so would injure them or others." We cannot buy our own piece of mind at the expense of others.

Step Ten - "Continued to take personal inventory and when we were wrong promptly admitted it." "The wise have always known that no one can make much of his life until self-searching becomes a regular habit, until he is able to admit and accept what he finds, and until he patiently and persistently tries to correct what is wrong."

Step Eleven - "Sought through prayer and meditation to improve our conscious contact with God as we understand Him, praying only for knowledge of His will for us and the power to carry that out." "Perhaps one of the greatest rewards of meditation and prayer is the sense of belonging that comes to us. We no longer live in a completely hostile world. We are no longer lost and frightened and purposeless. The moment we catch even a glimpse of God's will, is the moment we begin to see truth, justice, and love as the real and eternal things in life."

Step Twelve - "Having had a spiritual awakening as the result of these steps, we tried to carry this message to alcoholics, and to practice these principles in all our affairs." That some sort of personality change takes place in A.A. members is common experience and has been observed and recorded by many who have studied and written about A.A.. Helping others has been emphasized as a necessary part of recovery by other similar movements: the Washingtonian movement, Catch-my-Pal, Oxford groups, and Father Mathew's, among others. "The joy of living is the theme of A.A.'s Twelfth Step, and action is its key word. Here we turn outward toward our fellow alcoholics who are still in distress. Here we experience the kind of giving that asks no rewards. Here we begin to practice all Twelve Steps of the program in our daily lives so that we and those about us may find emotional sobriety. When the Twelfth Step is seen in its full implication, it is really talking about the kind of love that has no price tag on it."

MEETINGS

There are two types of meetings: open and closed. To the open meetings anyone is welcome. There are usually one or two A.A. members who will tell their own stories, "How I was then, and how I am now." To the closed meetings only members are welcome since the discussions are more intimate, frequently dealing with personal problems and the meaning of some of the steps or traditions in the lives of those present. Since most people who are not members attend only the open meetings, they miss observing the growth that occurs in the interaction of the small discussion groups, and may develop a biased view of the fellowship. Considerable A.A. activity goes on apart from formal meetings: luncheons, dinners, all sorts of informal social contacts. Most members frequently visit or telephone the members with whom they have become most intimate. The usual comment of a sponsor to a new member is, "Call me anytime, day or night, if you need to talk." Although there are special interest groups, young people's groups, women's groups, and others, this trend has been resisted since, "the only requirement for membership is the desire to stop drinking."

After attending many meetings in and around Boston in the early 1970's Bean (1975) wrote:

> Many of these people are likeable, and their stories fascinate me. It is easy to stereotype and pigeonhole them, but very hard to convey the quality of each one's private pain. While there was often a good deal of hilarity at A.A. meetings, there was also something serious.
>
> These people had had a reckoning with themselves. Each one had "bottomed out." No one admits, to himself or anyone else, that he is an alcoholic if he is not. Most of them fought against that name and that stigma long after the evidence for it was overwhelming. While they have no corner on the market for human misery, they have more personal experience of degradation than most people; and although they felt helplessly out of control when they were drinking, they knew that they were debased by their own hand and could easily be again.
>
> One by one they came to A.A.. Some left, to come back later. They come back, night after night lest they become complacent, lest they forget. They come back to remember what they have been and celebrate what they have become. A.A. gives these people something that is precious to them, for without A.A. many of them would still be destroying themselves with drink. (p.21)

THE PLACE OF A.A. IN RECOVERY CAREER

It is often said by A.A. members that the problem is not so much getting sober as in staying sober and learning to cope comfortably with life. ("Learning to Handle Sobriety," 1975.) To quote Bean (1975) again:

> A.A. improves the chance of successful recovery by providing evidence of success and inspiring hope. It also provides tools and treatment techniques for all the determinants of alcoholism, except the medical treatment of withdrawal complications and the internalization of controls." (p.32)

Referral to and/or involvement of A.A. is suggested usually after active medical treatment is well under way but may be effective at any stage in the development of the disease. The degree and duration of involvement will depend on the severity of the social, physical, and personal damage. Once the diagnosis is made and the patient persuaded that alcohol is the problem, contact with A.A. will be useful, even while the patient is under active medical care. This may take some persuasion as the stereotype of A.A. which is prevalent today is rejected by many. The therapists must be knowledgeable and enthusiastic about A.A. themselves. Insincerity here is fatal.

The April 1945 issue of *A.A. Grapevine* included a 36-item questionnaire under the caption "Big Light Can Be Shed on Alcoholism if A.A.'s Fill This in and Return to *The Grapevine*."(p.1) The answers to this questionnaire were part of the data used by E.M. Jellinek to develop his "Profile of the Alcoholic." In *The Disease Concept of*

Alcoholism (1960) he says, "American ideas about alcoholism were created by A.A.'s in their own image." Since his profile was originally published, other patterns have been identified and the term "alcoholisms" has come to be used. More recently we have come to understand that the rebuilding of the physical, social, economic, and personal structure of the patient is usually a long process called "the recovery career" and may require support from a variety of community resources in which A.A., Al-Anon, and Alateen should always be considered. An article by Glatt (1958), entitled "Group Therapy in Alcoholism", included what is known as the "Valley Chart" which portrays the development of the disease and the recovery. Both processes are about the same length. In a recent personal communication Glatt pointed out that early recognition, confrontation, and referral can short-circuit the more serious aspects of both the disease and recovery. Early identification may be made in the employment situation as problems develop at work, by social workers and/or clergy involved with disturbed families, by police and the courts (especially relating to traffic violations), and by physicians if they are aware of the early behavioral manifestations and take histories of their patients with these factors in mind. Jellinek also said, "The most challenging problem we face in the field of alcoholism is to bring about the collapse of the alibi structure before it would happen in the natural course of events." In some treatment centers A.A. meetings are held in the hospital, and attendance is required as soon as the patients are able to attend. At St. Bernard's Hospital in London, where Glatt is consultant psychiatrist, this is the procedure during the 12 weeks of inpatient treatment.

The more usual procedure has been to make attendance

at meetings voluntary, outside the hospital, with transportation to and from the meetings provided either by the institution or by members of the A.A. group. Where treatment is being given on an outpatient basis, meetings may be held in the institution, with attendance at other meetings recommended.

In February 1975 this author received a letter from a member of A.A. (who at the time was a second-year medical student), in which he described an experience at the school he was attending. All members of the first-year class were urged to become acquainted with an A.A. member and attend some A.A. meetings with this person. Three members of that medical class have since become members of A.A.. Few therapists would identify these physicians-in-training as alcoholic people; yet they recognized in themselves enough of the reactions to alcohol which they heard described at the meetings to identify themselves as alcoholics. Similar programs exist in two other medical schools in the United States.

THE TWELVE TRADITIONS

As more people of all sorts from varied cultures and backgrounds became involved in A.A., problems developed and it became obvious that guidelines were needed for the interrelationships of groups. In 1946 these guidelines, written by Bill W. and known as traditions were published as a series of 12 articles in *The Grapevine*, headed "Our A.A. Experience has Taught Us That." At the movement's first international convention in Cleveland, Ohio in 1950 the traditions were officially adopted.

1. Our common welfare should come first; personal recovery depends upon A.A. unity. Each member of Alcoholics Anonymous is but a small part of a great whole. A.A. must continue to live or most of us will surely die. Hence our common welfare comes first. But individual welfare follows close afterward.

2. For our group purpose there is but one ultimate authority - a loving God as He may express Himself in our group conscience. Our leaders are but trusted servants; they do not govern.

3. The only requirement for A.A. membership is a desire to stop drinking. Our membership ought to include all who suffer alcoholism. Hence we may refuse none who wish to recover. Nor ought A.A. membership ever depend on money or conformity. Any two or three alcoholics gathered together for sobriety may call themselves an A.A. group.

4. Each group should be autonomous except in matters affecting other grups or A.A. as a whole. A letter to Bill W. from his first secretary says:

> One of the biggest things you ever did for the solid growth of A.A. in my opinion was to set up a policy of non-interference in the development of individual groups. You set up a policy of suggestion, not direction, with which I agreed all the way and which I always followed. An individual or a group can resent and argue an order or direction but how much can you resent a suggestion which carried the intimation that possibly they might come up with a better answer if they work it out themselves. If a group wrote us a description of a problem in their midst and asked for an answer, we would usually describe what another group had done in similar circumstances, or suggest possibilities, and put the problem squarely back in their laps. In other words, as each individual is responsible for his own sobriety, so is each group.

5. Each group has but one primary purpose - to carry its message to the alcoholic who still suffers.

6. An A.A. group ought never endorse, finance, or lend the A.A. name to any related facility or outside enterprise, lest problems of money, property, and prestige divert us from our primary purpose.

7. Every A.A. group ought to be fully self-supporting, declining outside contributions. No contributions or legacies from nonmembers are accepted at the General Service Office in New York City, and no more than $300 per year from any one member, and for only one year after death.

8. Alcoholics Anonymous should remain forever nonprofessional, but our service centers may employ special workers. Many A.A. members are working today as counselors in alcoholism treatment centers, and this is creating some confusion and misunderstanding. The recommendation commonly made to A.A. members is that they do not take a job in a treatment center unless they have training in counseling other than and in addition to their A.A. membership, so that their salary is justified apart from their A.A. membership. This policy has been suggested to administrators of treatment facilities.

9. A.A., as such, ought never be organized; but we may create service boards or committees directly responsible to those they serve...The small group may elect its secretary, the large group its rotating committee, and the groups of a large metropolitan area their central committee which often employs a full-time secretary. The trustees of the Alcoholic Foundation (now General Service Board) are in effect our General Service Committee. They are the custodians of A.A. tradition and the receivers of voluntary A.A. contributions

by which they maintain A.A. General Headquarters and our General Secretary in New York. They are authorized by the groups to handle our overall public relations and they guarantee the integrity of our principal publication, *The A.A. Grapevine.* All such representatives are to be guided by the spirit of service, for true leaders in A.A. are but trusted and experienced servants of the whole. They derive no real authority from their titles. Universal respect is the key to their usefulness....A.A. has to function, but at the same time it must avoid those dangers of great wealth, prestige, and entrenched power which necessarily tempt other societies. Though Tradition Nine at first sight seems to deal with a purely practical matter, in its actual operation, it discloses a society without organization, animated only by the spirit of service -- a true fellowship.

10. Alcoholics Anonymous has no opinion on outside issues; hence the A.A. name ought never be drawn into public controversy....All history affords us the spectacle of striving nations and groups finally torn asunder because they were designed for, or tempted into, controversy. Others fell apart because of sheer self-righteousness while trying to enforce upon the rest of mankind some millennium of their own specification.

11. Our public relations policy is based on attraction rather than promotion; we need always maintain personal anonymity at the level of press, radio, and films.

12. Anonymity is the spiritual foundation of all our traditions, ever reminding us to place principles before personalities.

Bill W., in his last message to the fellowship at a dinner honoring his 36th anniversary in A.A., October 10, 1970, said:

> If I were asked which of the blessings I felt was most responsible for our growth as a fellowship and most vital to our continuity, I would say the Concept of Anonymity. Anonymity has two attributes essential to our individual and collective survival, the spiritual and the practical. On the spiritual level, anonymity demands the greatest discipline of which we are capable; on the practical level anonymity has brought protection for the newcomer, respect and support of the world outside, and security from those of us who would use A.A. for sick and selfish purposes.

Since the beginning there has been a minimum of competition for prestige, recognition, or position. Rotation is practiced throughout the fellowship. In many groups the secretary serves for six months and then is replaced (the secretary plans the meeting agenda, selects speakers, is the contact person for communication with other groups and with the General Service Office in New York). Delegates to the General Service Conference in New York serve for two years. A.A. member trustees serve four years and may not serve longer.

Considering the number of people involved, "anonymity breaks" (reports in the media where full names or pictures appear) have been surprisingly few. Reporters, writers, TV program planners have been most considerate in giving up one of their chief stocks in trade: people in situations. I am sure that many of the "breaks" are unintentional and due to misunderstanding.

ORGANIZATION

The Alcoholic Foundation was established in May 1938

in New York City as a "trusteeship for A.A." with a Board of Trustees that was made up of a majority of non-alcoholics. Initially the Board met each month in New York. From the beginning, the office in New York, now known as the General Service Office, has been the major communications center of A.A..

A publishing company now known as A.A. World Services Inc., a wholly owned subsidiary of the Foundation, was formed to publish *Alcoholics Anonymous*. In 1944 *The A.A. Grapevine* began publishing as a separate entity, also wholly owned, with its own volunteer board of directors. In order to understand the structure of A.A., we must remember that "each group is autonomous" and that there is no government in the usual sense of the term. But in order for unity, strength, and continuity to develop, there must be a structure; a center of activity, communication, and leadership.

For many years A.A. leadership was provided by its two founders and the General Service Board. The founders were in touch with the fellowship and with the board and provided the link between the A.A. groups and their General Service Board and Service Office. With the realization that one day the two founders would no longer be able to provide this vital link, the concept of an ongoing structure which could fill this need was developed. This structure is known in the A.A. fellowship as the Conference Plan -- a plan by which the A.A. groups assume full and permanent responsibility for the conduct of the fellowship's most vital affairs.

The basic premise in this plan is that the final responsibility and ultimate authority for A.A. World Services would reside in the collective conscience of the entire fellowship. The practical means through which this is accomplished is the annual General Service Conference which meets in New York City and is made up of 91 delegates from the United States and Canada: the members of the Board of Trustees, the directors of the two Corporate Boards, and the staffs of the General Service and *A.A. Grapevine* offices.

The General Service Conference was first held in 1951 and has been held annually ever since. It has grown as A.A. has grown and thus more delegates have been added. In an effort to hold the Conference to a manageable size, 91 Conference areas are divided into districts that are made up of 6 - 15 groups, served by a District Committee Member. Each local group in North America elects a General Service Representative. District Committee meetings, made up of the District Committee Member and the General Service Representatives from the groups in his district, usually meet monthly. Assembly meetings comprising all General Service Representatives, District Committee Members and Area Committee Officers are held quarterly. At an assembly meeting one delegate, is elected to represent all groups in an area at the General Service Conference. The District Committee Members serve as assistants to the delegate, helping him to carry his message to all of the groups in his area. Thus the link between the A.A. groups and their General Service Board and General Service Office is established and maintained, and the General Service Conference becomes, as nearly as possible, the voice of A.A..

The Board of Trustees, now known as The General Service Board, is made up of 21 members. Seven are non-alcoholic people: three physicians, a sociologist, a penologist, a Canadian government official, and a banker. Fourteen are members of A.A., four from the Metropolitan New York region who can attend meetings of the A.A. World Service Board of Directors. The General Service Board meets quarterly. The A.A. World Service Board, and the *A.A. Grapevine* Board, both consisting of nine members, each meet monthly to discuss the usual problems relating to the publishing business plus their relationship to the fellowship of A.A.. The democratic structure of A.A. is outlined in the Twelve Concepts.

THE CONCEPTS

1. The final responsibility and the ultimate authority for A.A. World Services should always reside in the collective conscience of our whole fellowship.

2. When, in 1955, the A.A. groups confirmed the permanent charter for their General Service Conference, they thereby delegated to the Conference complete authority for the active maintenance of our world services and thereby made the Conference -- excepting for any change in the Twelve Traditions or in Article 12 of the Conference Charter -- the actual voice and the effective conscience for our whole Society.

3. As a traditional means of creating and maintaining a clearly defined working relation between the groups, the Conference, the A.A. General Service Board and its several service corporations, staffs, committees and executives, and of thus insuring their effective leadership, it is here suggested that we endow each of these elements of world service with a traditional "Right of Decision."

4. Throughout our Conference structure, we ought to maintain at all responsible levels a traditional "Right of Participation," taking care that each classification or group

of our world servants shall be allowed a voting representation in reasonable proportion to the responsibility that each must discharge.

5. Throughout our world service structure, a traditional "Right of Appeal" ought to prevail, thus assuring us that minority opinion will be heard and that petitions for the redress of personal grievances will be carefully considered.

6. On behalf of A.A. as a whole, our General Service Conference has the principal responsibility for the maintenance of our world services, and it traditionally has the final decision respecting large matters of general policy and finance. But the Conference also recognizes that the chief initiative and the active responsibility in most of these matters should be exercised primarily by the Trustee members of the Conference when they act among themselves as the General Service Board of Alcoholics Anonymous.

7. The Conference recognizes that the Charter and the By-laws of the General Service Board are legal instruments: that the Trustees are thereby fully empowered to manage and conduct all of the world service affairs of Alcoholics Anonymous. It is further understood that the Conference Charter itself is not a legal document: that it relies instead upon the force of tradition and the power of the A.A. purse for its final effectiveness.

8. The Trustees of the General Service Board act in two primary capacities: (a) With respect to the larger matters of over-all policy and finance, they are the principal planners and administrators. They and their primary committees directly manage these affairs. (b) But with respect to our separately incorporated and constantly active services, the

relation of the Trustees is mainly that of full stock ownership and of custodial oversight which they exercise through their ability to elect all directors of these entities.

9. Good service leaders, together with sound and appropriate methods of choosing them, are at all levels indispensable for our future functioning and safety. The primary world service leadership once exercised by the founders of A.A. must necessarily be assumed by the Trustees of the General Service Board of Alcoholics Anonymous.

10. Every service responsibility should be matched by an equal service authority -- the scope of such authority to be always well defined whether by tradition, by resolution, by specific job description or by appropriate charters and bylaws.

11. While the Trustees hold final responsibility for A.A.'s world service administration, they should always have the assistance of the best possible standing committees, corporate service directors, executives, staffs and consultants. Therefore the composition of these underlying committees and service boards, the personal qualifications of their members, the manner of their induction into service, the systems of their rotation, the way in which they are related to each other, the special rights and duties of our executives, staffs and consultants, together with a proper basis for the financial compensation of these special workers, will always be matters for serious care and concern.

12. General Warranties of the Conference in all its proceedings, the General Service Conference shall observe the spirit of the A.A. Tradition, taking great care that the Conference never becomes the seat of perilous wealth or power; that sufficient operating funds, plus an ample reserve, be

its prudent financial principle; that none of the Conference Members shall ever be placed in a position of unqualified authority over any of the others: that all important decisions be reached by discussion vote and whenever possible, by substantial unanimity; that no Conference action ever be personally punitive or an incitement to public controversy; that though the Conference may act for the service of Alcoholics Anonymous, it shall never perform any acts of government; and that, like the Society of Alcoholics Anonymous which it serves, the Conference itself will always remain democratic in thought and action.

COMMITTEES

Committees of the General Service Board are usually paired with a Conference committee. They meet together only at Conference. Board committees meet quarterly at the time of the General Service Board Meeting.

The Policy Committee, the largest of all the committees, discusses matters of general concern. Frequently a person widely known in the alcoholism field is invited to join the discussion. All trustees, staff secretaries, World Service and *Grapevine* Board members, and regular volunteers are invited.

The Literature Committee develops new pamphlets, and reviews existing books and pamphlets for revision or discontinuance.

The Public Information Committee meets each month to review and act on anonymity breaks; prepares material for distribution to the media, to the membership, and to the

Public Information Committees of State or regional committees; and prepares exhibits for professional meetings. A policy statement approved by the General Service Conference in 1956 says: "In all public relationships, A.A.'s sole objective is to help the still suffering alcoholic. We believe that our experience should be made available freely to all who express sincere interest."

The Committee on Relations with the Professional Community prepares guidelines for professional organization, treatment facilities, and members, suggesting ways of working together and quoting experiences of individuals and groups. *A.A. Cooperation in Alcoholism Agencies and Facilities, On Court Programs, For Members Employed in the Alcoholism Field, On Industry Programs*, are several such pamphlets.

The Institutions Committee explores the needs of correctional institutions and hospitals and communicates with the administrations of many of these institutions so that working relationships may be developed or improved.

Other committees are *Finance* and *Nominating*.

LITERATURE

The A.A. Grapevine, published each month since June 1944, is the A.A. story written mostly by A.A. members, but with frequent comments about A.A. and alcoholism by physicians, psychiatrists, clergy, sociologists, and others. As of June 1, 1975 it had a circulation of more than 82.000. It contains a wealth of anecdotal material, comments about a particular aspect of life experience, suggestions for topics to be discussed at a meeting, letters to the editor, a section "About Alcoholism" containing abstracts of news articles from journals and newspapers, and a calendar of large A.A. meetings in North America. A quotation from a brochure describes the magazine:

> The early A.A.'s carried the message of hope for alcoholics from person to person until there were about 100 of them participating in a miracle - the regeneration of chronic drinkers for whom medicine and society could up to this time, offer little. A.A.'s Big Book *Alcoholics Anonymous*, was a Twelfth Step call by those pioneers - on the world! And so it was.

Early correspondence reveals much of the thinking and discussion that went into the final writing of *Alcoholics Anonymous* (1939). As Bill W. wrote in *A.A. Comes of Age* (1957) describing some of the discussions leading up to the title, *Alcoholics Anonymous*, "This was everybody's book ... I had been mostly the umpire of the discussions that created it."

Following publication of an article about A.A. by Jack Alexander in *The Saturday Evening Post* (1941) orders for the book came to the tiny office on Vesey Street in New York City from all over the world. Groups often started where a copy of the book was owned and read. Seamen have carried the book with them and started groups in ports. Individuals, isolated from centers where there was an A.A. group, from sheep herders "out back" in Australia to public figures who feared exposure, have read the book. Many of these people keep in contact with other members through a correspondence "round robin." Some circulate tapes rather than letters.

Alcoholics Anonymous Comes of Age - A Brief History of A.A. (1957) is Bill W.'s report of the events which he considered significant during the years 1934-57.

Twelve Steps and Twelve Traditions (1953), an interpretation of the steps and traditions, was requested by many members beginning soon after the Convention in Cleveland in 1950.

The A.A. Way of Life (1967), a book of daily readings pertinent to the problems of alcoholic people; two booklets, *Came to Believe* and *Staying Sober,* and forty-six Pamphlets, designed to meet particular problems, (e.g., *The Alcoholic Wife; A.A. and the Medical Profession; A Clergyman asks about A.A.*) complete the A.A. literature. When a new pamphlet is suggested, the literature committee of the General Service Conference considers the suggestion and makes a recommendation to the Conference. If the Conference disapproves, the idea is dropped. If the Conference approves, the suggestion is referred to the trustees' Literature Committee which will discuss the idea and, if they think it feasible, will select as author a volunteer or professional writer who is a member of A.A.. Often there are people known to some of the staff at the General Service Office whose personal experience is pertinent to the problem at hand. These stories are brought together for consideration by the writer of the new pamphlet. Most of the pamphlets contain pertinent personal-experience stories. At each meeting of the literature committee, progress is discussed and completed writing criticized. When the pamphlet is complete or nearly so, each member of the committee studies it and comments. The comments are considered by the author and these ideas are included in the final writing. Then the members of the Conference Committee on Literature review the final product and recommend approval by the Conference, if no further changes are suggested. Like the steps and traditions and the books, most of the literature records the experience of several people.

HISTORY

Soon after it became reasonably certain that the fellowship was a significant innovation in the long history of mankind's problems with alcohol, the two founders of Alcoholics Anonymous became anxious that its origins and development be documented. In the archives room at the General Service Office in New York City are most of the letters between the founders. Bill W. wrote many personal letters to early members and associates, and these have been preserved. Minutes of the meetings of the Alcoholic Foundation record much of the growth in organizational maturity from its first meeting on April 11, 1938, through the change of its name to The General Service Board, to the present. A paragraph from the minutes of the first meeting (1938) is interesting:

> Mr. Amos asked Mr. W. to recount the work to date. The following report was made: In the Eastern section, 41 alcoholics recovered. Six alcoholics in the questionable class. Twelve alcoholics upon whom a great deal of time has been spent, but so difficult that the cases are classed as practically hopeless. There are ten alcoholics who have recovered, but who are out of touch with the group. There are at present over 25 prospects.

Bill W.'s list of "Landmarks in A.A. History" in *A.A. Comes of Age* (1957) is a personal record of his own recovery and of the development of the fellowship. Subsequent landmarks have been listed in *The A.A. Grapevine.* Some of the landmarks are:

May 1935: Dr. Bob and Bill W. met in Akron and started A.A.

Nov. 1937: Dr. Bob and Bill W. met in Akron and reported 40 people were sober in A.A.

Feb. 1938: John D. Rockefeller gave $5,000 and refused to give more. "Money and property will spoil it."

May 1938: Alcoholic Foundation was established. The writing of *Alcoholics Anonymous* was begun.

April 1939: *Alcoholics Anonymous* was published.

June 1950: the first International Convention of A.A. held in Cleveland, Ohio and the Twelve Traditions were adopted.

April 1951: the first conference of delegates from all over North America was held in New York City. This was suggested in an article written by Bill W. and Dr. Bob in the December 1950 issue of the *A.A. Grapevine.* This conference for North America has been held each year since.

October 1951: the American Public Health Association gave its Lasker Award to A.A., "In recognition of its unique and highly successful approach to that age-old public health and social problem - alcoholism. (*A.A. Comes of Age*, 1957)

June 1953: *Twelve Steps and Twelve Traditions* an interpretation by Bill W., was published. To date more than 500,000 copies have been sold.

July 1955: the 20th Anniversary Convention was held in St. Louis. The organizational structure of the fellowship was presented and accepted.

July 1960: the 25th Anniversary Convention was held in Toronto; 10,000+ were registered. The pledge, "When anyone, anywhere, reaches out for help, I want the hand of A.A. always to be there and for that, I am responsible," was adopted.

1966: Ratio of nonalcoholics to alcoholics on the Board of Trustees changed. Nonalcoholics had been in the majority since the board was formed. In 1966 this was changed so that there are now 14 A.A.'s and 7 "civilians."

October 1969: the First World Service meeting was held in New York City. Twelve countries which had developed central headquarters were represented.

July 1970: 35th Anniversary Convention was held in Miami, Florida; over 11,000 people were registered.

January 1971: Bill W.'s death.

April 1973: Distribution of the book *Alcoholics Anonymous* reached 1,000,000. The one millionth copy was presented to the President of the United States.

October 1974: The Third World Service Conference was held in London; 17 countries were represented.

July 1975: 40th Anniversary Convention was held in Denver, Colorado; over 19,000 were registered.

WORLDWIDE GROWTH

Almost immediately after publication of the article about A.A. in *The Saturday Evening Post*, groups were formed in other parts of the world; at first in countries where English is the primary language, later in French Canada where *Alcoholics Anonymous* was translated into French, and then through direct personal contact between friends or relatives into other countries. The first member in Finland was brought into A.A. through correspondence with a friend who was living in California. There are now more than 2,000 members in Finland. The first member in Norway became a member after his brother who had joined in New York City sold his business and went back to Norway to help his brother whom he knew was in trouble with alcohol. Seamen have started groups in ports all over the world. Members in the United States and Canadian armed services have carried the message wherever they have been.

Alcoholics Anonymous has been translated into eight languages, French, Spanish, Portuguese, German, Finnish, Norwegian, Swedish, and Afrikaans. Pamphlets and parts of the book have also been translated into many other languages and dialects. For instance, there are three dialects in Bombay, India in which some of the pamphlets are printed.

Groups from 95 countries are registered at the General Service Office in New York City, and listed in the World Directory which is published biannually. Membership figures can be no more than estimates. We believe the figure of 896,700 active members to be conservative. This does not include those who have recovered in A.A. and are no longer attending meetings.

DISTRIBUTION OF GROUPS AS OF JANUARY 1, 1975

Reported	Groups
U.S.	14,448
Canada	2,427
Overseas	6,088
Hospitals	1,046
Prisons	1,021
	25,030

Since 1957 the estimated average active membership reported to the General Service Office in autonomous A.A. groups in North America has varied between 16.7 and 19.1. Growth has been most rapid in Canada, going from about 600 per million population in 1950 to 1225 in 1970. In the United States in 1950 there were 601 active members per million population; in 1970 there were 820. In Australia in 1950 there were 70 active members per million population; in 1970 there were 427. In the British Isles in 1950 there were 9 active members per million population; in 1970 there were 126.

The General Service Board has made three attempts to evaluate the effectiveness of A.A. by asking those attending an A.A. meeting to fill out a questionnaire, the first in 1968, the second in 1971, and the last in 1974. There was no attempt in any of the three surveys to promote attendance at meetings or to reach any who had moved or were no longer attending meetings. In these surveys delegates to the General Service Conference of that year were asked to distribute questionnaires over a two-week period to a percentage of the groups in the area from which they came, 5% in 1968, 1% in 1971, and 3% in 1974. Members were asked to fill out only one questionnaire in case they happened to attend two groups where the forms were distributed. The 1974 questionnaire is identical with the questionnaires for 1968 and 1971 except that five questions were added in 1974 asking about present employment; membership in one A.A. group; treatment by professionals; anonymity with family, friends, physicians, clergy, etc.; quality of present life as compared to life while drinking.

The three surveys covered U.S. and Canadian groups only. Thus they do not reflect world-wide A.A. membership.

Nor did they reach the alcoholics who have become sober in A.A. but who no longer belong to groups or attend meetings. Membership of U.S. and Canadian groups in 1968 was estimated at 170,153 and the size of the survey sample was 11,355. In 1971 there were an estimated 210,492 members of which the survey sampled only 7,194. The census for 1974 is not yet completed, but we now have about 285,000 members. The survey sample was 13,467, the largest yet.

It is necessary to note that this procedure does not provide a completely random sample of the membership. Nor was any control exercised centrally. Packages of questionnaires were sent to all area delegates, and they in turn selected groups in their areas to receive the questionnaires and instructions. Nevertheless, there is strong reason to believe that the results, properly interpreted, are representative of all U.S. and Canadian groups and their members. This is because: first, the samples are quite large, and second, the results of the three surveys taken over a period of six years are remarkably stable. This in spite of the fact that the selection of groups was done independently and by different individuals for each of the surveys. Finally, almost half the people responding to our 1974 questionnaire had not come to A.A. by 1968, which makes the stability of the results even more significant. One exception has to be noted at the outset. The samples are clearly biased towards members who make a practice of attending meetings. However, it is possible to correct the data to remove this bias. Moreover, the results themselves show that other factors such as age and length of sobriety do not have a strong influence on the tendency to attend meetings.

Some of the questions deal with matters of significance

primarily to A.A.'s, such as anonymity. However, others serve to characterize the A.A. population of sober alcoholics and to measure the effectiveness of the A.A. process. I will turn now to some of the factors which are of general interest. During the discussion of these factors as measured in three different surveys, we will repeatedly observe the stability of the distributions.

FREQUENCY OF ATTENDANCE AT MEETINGS

Approximately half of those surveyed attend meetings three or more times a week and more than 40% once or twice a week. Even though respondents are apt to be A.A. members who go to comparatively more meetings than the general A.A. population, it is possible to adjust the data to determine meeting attendance for the A.A. population as a whole. Once this is done, we then calculated that only 25% of our group members attended three or more meetings a week, while 64% go once or twice a week, and 11% go to fewer than one meeting a week.

SEX OF RESPONDENTS

The percentage of women in our sample steps up from 22% in 1968, to 26% in 1971, to 28% in 1974. We believe this trend to be significant particularly since a subdivision of our sample - those who have come to A.A. in the last three years - shows the percentage of women to be 31%.

AGE

The age distribution over the six-year study period shows no discernable trend either with regard to the young (30 and under) or older (over 50) segments of our sample. The 30 and under group ranges from 7% to 6% to 7¼% over the three surveys; the 31 to 50 group decreased from 57% to 55%, and the 51 plus age group increased from 34% to 36½%.

We have also taken a statistical look at those who have come to A.A. in the past three years, and conclude from this group that the overall age distribution of our A.A. membership is not changing.

SOURCE OF REFERRAL

In the survey we asked for the two most important factors in bringing the respondents to A.A.. The four most frequently mentioned were:

1. An A.A. member - 55% down to 51% over the three surveys.
2. The family - about 35%.
3. The doctor - 15%.
4. The media - 11-12%.

While these factors also seem remarkably stable, there is a decline between 1968 and 1974 of from 55% to 51% in the number that named an A.A. member. And if we look at the subgroup of our 1974 sample - those who came to A.A. in the last three years - we see evidence that the trend is continuing. Another interesting result of this subgroup is that 11% cited a counseling agency as opposed to 9% in 1968.

In a separate question we asked the respondents to indicate whether medical, psychological, or spiritual counseling, other than A.A. was of importance in their coming to A.A.. Approximately 30% replied in the affirmative. Many also said that they felt such services to be important in their recovery after they joined A.A.. These results are very heartening as indicators of growth in mutual understanding and consequent improvement in the effectiveness of all of us in helping people in their continuing recovery.

SOBRIETY

Sobriety is the primary goal of A.A.. As a result of these surveys we are now able to develop additional quantitive information regarding sobriety, to supplement our earlier findings. In all three surveys, approximately 40% of the survey sample had been sober less than one year, 35% one to five years, and the remaining 25% sober from five to more than twenty years.

Many of those who were part of the populations surveyed in 1968-71 are also part of the 1974 survey. This permits us to make checks on consistency. Second, members with long sobriety attend fewer meetings per week than those who are newer. Thus, though they represent a proportionately greater part of the A.A. population as a whole, they were less likely to be present at a meeting to fill out a survey questionnaire. Taking these and other factors into account and recognizing that the following numerical results will be approximations, we can discuss what happens to a typical survey respondent as time goes on.

Analysis of the data shows that 35% of the people sober less than a year in the fellowship will not drink and will remain in the fellowship during the succeeding year. Of the 65% remaining, most will drink and either remain in the fellowship or leave the fellowship. A breakdown suggests that most of these remain in A.A. to try again, and only 5% to 10% of the total leave A.A.. Of the people sober between 1 and 5 years, about 79% will not drink and will remain in the fellowship. The remaining 21% will go one of three ways: (a) they will become inactive in the fellowship and remain sober; (b) they will leave the fellowship and resume drinking; (c) they will drink and start over again in A.A.. Of the people sober more than five years, about 91% will not drink and will remain in the fellowship. The remaining 9% may go several ways, with sober death now an appreciable additional alternative to the three cited above.

In spite of the rather sweeping assumptions and averages upon which these calculations are based, we believe that they provide some useful quantitative information. In particular, the three phases in the sobriety process of our members, while only an approximation to the more complex reality, do seem to correspond with our intuitive ideas:

1. It is difficult to make it to the first anniversary.
2. Having succeeded, there are still perils the alcoholic faces in the next few years.
3. Most of those who maintain five sober years with A.A. seem to remain permanently sober in the fellowship.

About 92% of those surveyed also cited an improvement in the overall quality of their lives. Breaking down the survey sample by occupation, we found 38% of our members to be in the executive/professional/technical category. Blue collar and office clerical account for another 32%. About 11% said they were housewives.

Finally, we asked the members about anonymity at the level of family, friends, doctors, and co-workers. Anonymity at the public level is at the heart of the A.A. program, and at the private level is offered to all who desire it for personal reasons. We found that most A.A. members have not hesitated to reveal their A.A. membership to those around them. This self-disclosure helps to make the nature and effectiveness of the A.A. program known to other still-drinking alcoholics. However, anonymity at the public level remains the spiritual foundation of the program and a cornerstone of members' sobriety.

OTHER SELF-HELP ORGANIZATIONS

Al-Anon, the companion organization to A.A., but entirely separate, is made up of family members, usually the marriage partners of alcoholic people. Where one or more members of a family are in serious trouble because of their use of alcohol, the whole family is involved since others in the family may also have emotional problems with which they need help. The program is patterned closely after the A.A. program, with the Steps and Traditions covering almost identical areas of experience. Many members of Al-Anon will say that they started going to meetings to learn how to get their partner to stop drinking and later discovered their own needs and inadequacies. As they learn how to cope with their own emotional problems, as they stop dancing to their drinking partner's tune, as they stop denying the problem to their neighbors and friends, stop protecting the alcoholic from the natural consequences of what he does while drinking, frequently the alcoholic will then begin to do something about his or her alcoholism.

Al-Anon began officially in 1964, although there had been a good deal of informal activity for more than ten years. It is growing rapidly now with more than 10,000 groups, world-wide. The Al-Anon literature includes 60 pamphlets, a monthly bulletin, and six books, *Living with an Alcoholic, The Dilemma of the Alcoholic Marriage, One Day at a Time in Al-Anon, Al-Anon's Favorite Forum Editorials, Alateen-Hope for Children of Alcoholics.*

The organization is similar to A.A. with groups, regions, delegates, and an Annual Conference of Delegates.

Alateen, usually sponsored by Al-Anon, is made up of the children and young people in families where one or both parents are alcoholic.

Many other self-help groups have patterned themselves after A.A., some of them using almost identical steps and traditions. Permission to reprint all or part of the Steps and Traditions and pamphlets has been granted to 38 outside organizations. When the request is made to use A.A. ideas in another program, the suggestion is made that they be put in their own words. To our knowledge 43 different organizations have been formed which have used many or all of the ideas and principles of A.A.. Those with which we are most familiar are:

1. Al-Anon Family
2. Alateen
3. Emotions Anonymous
4. Emotional Health Anonymous

5. Gamblers Anonymous National
6. Gam-Anon National Service Office
7. Nar-Anon Family Groups
8. Narcotics Anonymous World Service Office
9. Neurotics Anonymous International Liason Inc.
10. Overeaters Anonymous World Service Office
11. Parents Anonymous
12. Recovery, Inc.
13. Schizophrenics Anonymous

HOW TO WORK WITH A.A.

The sine qua non for working with A.A., and with most alcoholics, in my opinion, is to attend A.A. meetings, including closed meetings; for it is here that the real story of alcoholism as it is experienced surfaces. It is here that experiences with sedatives, tranquilizers, and the other mood-changing chemicals are discussed, as many of these people have become dependent on or addicted to more than one drug. The denial mechanism, the alibi structure, and the manipulative skills of the alcoholic are so strong that rarely do physicians and other therapists get beneath the surface. Intimate acquaintance with several A.A. members is very helpful in the selection of one who will be congenial with a patient whom the therapist refers for A.A. contact. A.A. is listed in most telephone directories. Dates, times, and places of meetings are readily available. A.A. members are more than willing to call for a patient at his home. I have found it useful to make an appointment at my office where the three of us could talk briefly. Continuing contact with the patient is important as an interface between therapist and A.A.. Problems requiring professional help may surface after a time in A.A., so it is important that the contact be maintained after referral. Analysis of the results of the 1974 survey showed that many A.A. members have found this helpful. Books and pamphlets and copies of the *A.A. Grapevine* give both therapist and the patient understanding of A.A. and the disease. They are an important supplement to meetings and personal contact.

After the medical emergency and the serious medical complications are under control the patient faces the need to rebuild his personal relationships with family, friends, employers, fellow workers, as well as his own self-respect which, as a result of his loss of control, has been lost. Introduction to an A.A. member during active medical treatment will help prepare the patient for his return to life. Treatment and/or introduction of the family to Al-Anon and Alateen may modify the hostile environment to which the patient will return unless the family has help. The recovery of both the alcoholic and the family may take months or even years so that continuing active membership is advisable until the whole family has returned to normal. Many remain active, attending meetings regularly so long as they live, finding in the fellowship their most rewarding social contacts.

The primary physician should be sufficiently familiar with all community resources in order to make the optimal referral, and to be able to act as interface between the various treatment modalities.

REFERENCES

Alcoholics Anonymous. New York: A.A. World Services, Inc. 1939.

Alcoholics Anonymous comes of age - A brief history of A.A. New York: A.A. World Services, Inc., 1957.

Alexander, Jack. Alcoholics Anonymous. *The Saturday Evening Post*, March 1, 1941. (Reprinted as The Jack Alexander article about A.A. New York: A.A. World Services, Inc.

Bailey, M.B., & Leach, B. Alcoholics Anonymous, pathway to recovery. A study of 1,058 members of the A.A. fellowship in New York City. New York: National Council on Alcoholism, 1965.

Bean, M. Alcoholics Anonymous I. *Psychiatric Annals*, 1975, *5*(2), 7-61.

Brook, R.R. Personality correlates associated with differential success of affiliation with Alcoholics Anonymous (Doctoral dissertation, University of Colorado, 1962). University Microfilms No. 62-6262.

Glatt, M.J. Group therapy in alcoholism. *British Journal of Addiction*, 1958, *54*, 133-150.

Hock, R. Personal communication, November 1955.

Jellinek, E.M. *The disease concept of alcoholism.* New Haven: Hillhouse Press, 1960.

Learning to handle sobriety. *The A.A. Grapevine*, March, 1975.

Maxwell, M.A. Factors affecting an alcoholic's willingness to seek help. *Northwest Science*, 1954, *28*, 116.

Minutes of first meeting of Alcoholic Foundation, 1938.

Questionnaire. *The A.A. Grapevine*, April 1945.

Tiebout, H.M. The act of surrender in the therapeutic process. *Quarterly Journal of Studies on Alcohol*, 1949, *10*, 48-58.

Tiebout, H.M. Surrender versus compliance in therapy. *Quarterly Journal of Studies on Alcohol*, 1953, *14*, 58-68.

Trice, H.M. Social factors in association with A.A. *Journal of Criminal Law, Criminology, and Police Science*, 1957, *48*, 378. (a)

Trice, H.M. A study of the process of affiliation with Alcoholics Anonymous. *Quarterly Journal of Studies on Alcohol*, 1957, *18*, 39-54. (b)

Twelve Steps and Twelve Traditions, New York: A.A. World Services, Inc., 1953.

W., Bill, & Dr. Bob. Your third legacy. *The A.A. Grapevine*, December 1950.

CHAPTER 21

COMMUNITY PROGRAMS FOR THE TREATMENT OF ALCOHOLICS

George P. Dominick

The preparation and writing of this chapter on community programs for the treatment of alcoholics evoked the same hopes, frustrations, and needs that W.C. Fields felt about his roses. He loved roses and must have known the time, nurture, and patience that had to precede the joy experienced in the blooming of a rose. But he was once observed standing in front of a particular rose saying, "Bloom damn you, bloom!"

A great deal of time and money, pain and pleasure, sweat and tears, as well as failure and success have gone into the establishment, development, and continuation of community programs in our time, yet they never seem to come into full bloom. Why can't we make it bloom? Why can't we lay out all the pieces and put them together to do the job we know should be done?

Despite the urgency expressed by W.C. Fields, he was

Ralph E. Tarter and A. Arthur Sugerman (eds.), Alcoholism

ISBN: 0-201-08146-6
ISBN: 0-201-08145-8 (pbk.)

a person who knew how to back off, smile, and take another look. By taking a look at community programs we may learn, and by putting our knowledge together differently, we may come up with better answers.

TYPES OF PROBLEMS ARISING FROM ALCOHOL USE

Anthropologists have found few communities that have not used alcohol in some social setting (Child, 1965; Gilliam, 1951). "By the time ancient man was carving his earliest historical reports, these beverages were long known, accepted, and often prized foods, as magic fluids and as medicines" (Leake & Silverman, 1966). In cultural studies of the function of alcohol in primitive societies Horton (1943) found a wide variation in the use of alcohol beverages. For some groups they fulfilled a communal function, bringing people together, helping them relate to one another. Horton mentions that moderate drinking was relatively rare, and drinking to excess was characteristic of primitive peoples.

Four types of problems arising from the use of alcohol have been distinguished.

1. Direct problems are those that show evidence of physical and social damage to the user.

2. Accompaniment problems are those in which the use creates other problems of major concern such as crime, family disorganization, highway deaths, and poverty.

3. Problems of response to direct problems and accompaniment problems are the kinds of measures individuals and groups take in hopes of alleviating, controlling, or

preventing conditions which lead to direct and accompaniment problems. Examples of this are the prohibitionist movement and the continuing "wet," "dry" controversy.

4. Intellectual problems are those issues arising out of exploring certain aspects of the alcohol problem leading to basic and applied research. These give rise to theories of metabolism, etiology of alcoholism, and interdisciplinary approaches to treatment.

From these four points a listing of problems caused by alcohol use could be formulated, and depending upon how they were organized, we could review how various community groups and organizations have attempted to deal with them. In fact the voluminous mass of literature in the field does exactly that. It tells largely how such problems have been attacked but little about results.

Some of the literature, even from early times, has focused on or hinted at the "people" dimension of alcohol problems. I think particularly of Jellinek's *Disease Concept of Alcoholism* and the Alpha, Beta, Gamma, etc. classification (Jellinek, 1960). Seldon Bacon in written material and lecture has been talking about the "alcoholisms" for a long time.

Nevertheless, for many years community programs have been designed to meet the needs of what can be called a single-line growth profile of an alcoholic. This profile describes the slow beginning of a social drinker gradually developing into the early, middle, and late stages of alcoholism, entering into recovery at some stage, perhaps having slips. This is the profile most people apply to all alcoholics.

Material offered by Dr. Bacon at Rutger's Summer School

of Alcohol Studies, 1975, challenges us to think in terms of groupings of alcoholics with profiles reflecting differences in time span and age and varying courses of recovery and recidivism. In other words a more accurate profile is multifaceted, and both the development of and recovery from the illness must be considered with a great deal more knowledge of the interaction of the patient with his or her social reality.

Broadening this idea to the larger drug scene, Treffent (1971) makes the point that programs must reflect some study of the people who use the substance and some analysis of the stimulus to which they are responding. He refers to the American fairy tale in which we are taught: "happiness is what you do, happiness is things, and happiness is mental health." Given this, people become "joiners," "protesters," "seekers," "losers," and some emerge as "recreational users," those who use drugs as a rational choice for recreational purposes.

Until recently community programs largely responded to alcoholism as it was initially conceptualized -- as a single-line or longitudinal phenomenon. The knowledge gained from operating programs for youth, blacks, government and industrial workers, American Indians, women, drinking criminal drivers, public inebriates, and older people may help in the development of more effective community programs meeting the problems of certain groups of alcoholics.

Community programs are developing at a rapid pace and there is a need to define what they encompass. Community programs are here understood to be programs providing services to persons without respect to creed, color, the ability to pay, or choice of a physician or staff, which are supported and carried out by federal, state, county or local groups.

EIGHT FUNDAMENTAL ASSUMPTIONS - A PHILOSOPHY OF TREATMENT

For several years this author was a member of a multidisciplinary team which traveled to several designated county health centers in Georgia participating in the training and consultation work necessary for the establishment of community alcoholism treatment programs (Methvin, 1969). The team was composed of persons representing administration, nursing, social work, psychiatry, and chaplaincy, all of whom had many years experience in clinical work with alcoholics. The unique quality of this team was that all members held similar fundamental assumptions concerning the disease of alcoholism and had a basic philosophy concerning the treatment approach.

Since those early days a great many more local community clinics have been established, and the one recurring need that is voiced over and over again is the need for a philosophy of treatment around which staff can organize their services. A philosophy is a set of principles or beliefs which comes from knowledge and experience of a given subject. A philosophy will always reflect the present state of understanding of the subject and therefore is always subject to change and revision.

Basic assumptions in a philosophy of treatment really involve what one thinks alcoholism is. "Some Views on the Nature of Alcoholism" (Keller, 1969) presented Mark Keller's personal formulation of what alcoholism is not, and some of what it is. A later formulation (Keller, 1975) states more of what he conceptualizes alcoholism to be.

People involved in community programs cannot wait for someone else to come up with the definitive answer concerning what alcoholism is before they move forward. Any group of treatment persons working together must take time to hammer out some philosophy, some basic assumption upon which they agree.

The following basic assumptions have come from years of working with patients and staff and through reading others' experiences in treatment. I present them as a beginning philosophy which in turn will influence and determine programs of treatment.

ALCOHOLISM MUST BE CONCEPTUALIZED IN HOLISTIC TERMS. Experience and observation show that persons who have developed advanced conditions of alcoholism indicate they are physically, emotionally, socially, and spiritually affected.

Alcoholism causes certain diagnosible physical conditions that have been recently summarized in "Criteria for the Diagnosis of Alcoholism," by the National Council on Alcoholism (1972). The individual builds a tolerance to the chemical, and certain withdrawal symptoms develop when the intake is cut off abruptly. There are recognizable organ effects regardless of whatever other diagnosis can be made.

The psychological dimension of alcoholism is seen in the long established, skillfully learned habit the alcoholic develops of medicating himself. A life style is developed by which the individual has one answer for every condition he or she encounters - that is alcohol - a drink. If it's hot, it cools him off; if it's cold, it warms him up; if he's down it lifts him up; if he is high, it relaxes him and calms him down. The core of his feeling life centers around the presence or absence of the availability of alcohol.

The social dimension of alcoholism is recognized by the change in self perception of the alcoholic. When alcoholism is well developed, friends and significant others and frequently the victim himself see him as a "drinking problem," rather than as a person who has problems and feelings like other people. There is a pseudo identity, the drinking problem, that replaces former individuality and personhood. Frequently the person or others will refer to him or her as "just a drunk." This conveys a depersonalized concept of self. It represents an erosion of self worth and individuality.

The spiritual dimension of alcoholism is seen in the shift in what the person feels is worth living for. What becomes worthwhile is what can be taken or experienced now -- immediately. Goals to be attained by working a little longer figure less and less in the individual's plan. "I want what I want, when I want it," becomes the measuring stick for achievement. This essentially is a breakdown or erosion of a value system and is part of the spiritual change which takes place. In a deeper vein the alcoholic finds it more and more difficult to articulate what he or she considers worth living or dying for. Living and dying require a larger measure of commitment than the alcoholic can muster on his own. Taking another drink -- the slip -- represents the suspension of making serious or far reaching commitments.

This holistic concept means that treatment has to be geared to approach persons on these four dimensions of involvement: the physical, psychological, social, and spiritual.

TREATMENT REQUIRES A MULTIDISCIPLINARY APPROACH. The multidisciplinary concept of treatment is an old perspective. As Keller (1975) points out there is a real need for a working model of the integration of the many disciplines now in the treatment picture.

Treatment situations often bring together the psychiatrist, internist, psychologist, social worker, clergyman, nurse, alcoholism counselor, vocational rehabilitation counselor, judge, court, and probation officer, but very often they "do their thing" in isolation and in competition with one another. In many alcoholism clinics the actual operation pits the medical men and women against the counseling men and women. Team approaches are talked about, and the expertise of various medical and behavior science skills are recognized as needed, but the services do not become integrated. It need not be that way (Fox, 1970).

Multidisciplinary integration is to some extent successful in a model with which the author is working in an inpatient treatment setting in the Georgia Mental Health Institute, Atlanta, Georgia. This structure will be discussed in the section of this chapter dealing with inpatient care. The staff is divided into five teams. A doctor is on a particular team as are the psychiatrist, psychologist, many nurses, a chaplain, etc. These disciplined people function on the team as persons first and assume the added role of patient treatment coordinators working as enablers and managers of the patients' entire treatment plan. The role of the physician, for example, will change outside of the team when he functions as a physician doing the physical examination and managing the detoxification regime.

Another aspect of the team function which contributes

to integration is that the authority for making decisions about patients is focused in the team. With the authority for discharge located in the team,what then happens to the legal and official authority of physicians in the inpatient hospital organization? The physicians' legal rights are respected at all times, but the working relationship is such that all people working with a given patient are heard and respected. Differences are discussed until they are resolved.

ALCOHOLISM IS A CHRONIC AND TREATABLE ILLNESS. More evidence than not supports the fact that alcoholism is not only a long lasting illness but also recurring. The use of the word "chronic" means that this illness has acute phases but is nevertheless present in remission. Perhaps alcoholism fits best alongside other chronic illnesses such as diabetes, heart disease, stomach ulcers, emphysema, and hypertension, with of course obvious differences.

The current debate concerning controlled drinking versus abstinence for identified alcoholics puts in question some aspects of the chronicity of alcoholism. *Drinkwatchers*, a newly formed organization, national in scope, is offering a philosophy and program of moderation in all things and respect for the individual's right to control his or her own life. *Drinkwatchers'* monthly mailings from P.O. Box 179, Haverstraw, New York, 10927 explain their purpose and methods.

A second assumption is that alcoholism is treatable. Though we do not yet know the complexities that bring it about, a significant number of people recover from the damage it causes.

THE NATURE OF ALCOHOLISM IS THAT IT IS INTERPERSONAL. Most people who work with alcoholics come to know rather early that alcoholics make many, frequently impossible, demands upon others. They create crisis situations and put others under a great deal of stress. An alcoholic husband repeatedly asks his wife to accept his broken promises and drunkenness, and if she doesn't he will say, "You don't really love me." Some alcoholics seem to live from one crisis to another. Treatment people frequently encounter this in the late phone call from a wife who is at the end of her rope and says, "I can't stand it any longer. I'm going to leave him;" or from the alcoholic who calls while drinking and threatens suicide. One clear characteristic in all this is the unusual capacity of the alcoholic to put all those around him under stress, and to involve them in a variety of ways. Why this is true is not easy to explain, but the very fact that it happens defines the nature of the illness as an interpersonal one.

The alcoholic externalizes the process of relationships which has formed his way of responding to other people (his illness) by involving his family, friends, employers, and helping people in his illness. He insists on relating to those around him in the same manner which others have related to him in the past. He also insists on their relating to him in the same manner in which he has learned to relate to others.

The story of the man at the Pool of Bethesda (John 5: 1-18) illustrates this kind of illness. The man's basic type of relationship was that which he tried with Jesus -- the one of dependency. He complained that he was helpless and no one would help him. If one is helpless and no one else will take over, then he has no responsibility in the matter and can stay ill for thirty-eight years or forever. The interpersonal nature of the illness also is apparent in the process of recovery. Significant others usually have to be involved in making some changes in the pattern of their living in the recovery process. Studies of family members (Jackson, 1954), both in the occurrence of the illness and recovery, show alcoholism to be like other chronic illnesses.

SOBRIETY AND PERSONAL GROWTH. A treatment philosophy must at least clarify whether or not the operating goal is sobriety, and if it is sobriety, whether anything else is expected, such as personal growth. Immediate and long term goals are a part of any philosophy. If stabilization is a beginning goal, what is understood by that? Is it defined as freedom from chemicals as well as improved behavior, such as being able to form a meaningful relationship with a staff member?

A community program in Baltimore offered some alcoholics a clean, safe, comfortable place to live with dignity. Sobriety was not a condition of his or her being able to live in that particular place. Help in terms of counseling and education about the illness was offered, but sobriety was not a condition of its use. A consensus on these issues is necessary.

LOVE, JUSTICE, AND COMPASSION. I am indebted to Jody Kellerman through some of his writings and conversations for this part of the philosophy. A necessary operating principle for treatment persons to understand and accept is a genuine concept of love. What does this mean on the part of a treatment worker? Love does not mean acting or behaving in such a manner as to spare the alcoholic the pain of his drinking. Love does mean allowing the alcoholic to experience the consequences of his own behavior.

If the family bears the pain of the alcoholic's drinking and also the pain of the consequences of the drinking, there is no justice. Love is destroyed, at least at the human level, when there is no justice. Compassion is suffering with a person, but it is not taking that person's suffering on yourself. The only way love can be kept operating toward the alcoholic is by learning not to suffer when drinking is going on and by refusing to undo the consequences of drinking (Kellerman, 1972).

This item of philosophy presents a community program with hard, sometimes impossible alternatives. No one can or will refuse emergency medical service on the basis of its being loving to allow the patient to suffer the consequences of his own behavior. However, after the clearing of the mind and body one can begin to relate on the basis of this principle. The use of this principle has more hope in it for the alcoholic than the usual God-like, omnipotent posture in which rescue is the goal.

ALCOHOLICS NEED AN INDENTIFIABLE STAFF AND PROGRAM. Judging by the alcoholic's own testimony and by the success rate of Alcoholics Anonymous, peer group identity seems to be a powerful factor in patients' seeking treatment and attaining a certain degree of recovery. To be able to identify with other alcoholics and relate to a constant staff person is important. This allows a dynamic to develop which expresses support on one hand and confrontation on the other, enabling the alcoholic to begin to recognize reality. Staff who work with alcoholics also develop a concern, a spirit, a commitment to the alcoholic that is not often found in general areas of mental health but has been found to be of a healing nature.

Special disabilities have largely been treated by specialists. This way service is usually more efficient, evaluations of treatment needs are more thorough, and therefore, decisions are facilitated. The treatment process -- usually a group effort -- seems to function at a more intense level.

What about mixing drug and alcohol patients? The movement to mix alcohol and drug patients is evidenced by the merging of drug and alcohol state agencies. The treatment of drug addicts and alcohol addicts is considered by some not only feasible but beneficial (Barr, Rosen, & Antes, 1973). The Eight Basic Assumptions can be the beginning of a working treatment philosophy.

ORGANIZATIONAL CONSIDERATIONS OF COMMUNITY PROGRAMS

In *Alcohol Problems - A Report to the Nation*, Plaut (1967) reports on an extensive survey of community treatment facilities. The chapter on "Current Alcoholism Treatment Services" describes the narrow, limited, uneven, haphazard fashion in which the alcoholic is treated. In Chapter 4 the author presents a list of proposals. (a) All services should provide services to problem drinkers on an equal basis with other clients. (b) All opportunities for the establishment, expansion, and improvement of services should be utilized. (c) Additional personnel and funds should be provided to ensure appropriate services by all agencies. (d) Assistance for medical care should be made available. (c) Intermediate (or transitional) facilities should be available as part of all community treatment programs. (f) A variety of treatment programs and settings should be used. (g) Community mental health programs should provide care and treatment. (h) The case-finding and referral functions of all helping agencies should be strengthened. (i) Agencies should improve their recording and record keeping systems. (j) Medical and hospital care should be covered by insurance. (k) Industry and unions should develop policies for detection, referral, and treatment. (l) Organizational mechanisms should be developed and personnel assigned to insure coordination of various treatment programs. (m) Additional research should be undertaken in key settings. (n) Long-term support should be provided to special research centers. (o) A Federal grant program should be established to expand research and communication of research findings. (p) Training programs of all helping professions should include attention to drinking problems. (q) Federal grants should be provided for persons seeking training and for professional schools.

Many of these proposals have since been implemented on the federal, state, and local level. Material on programs from individual state agencies shows there has been phenomenal growth in the number of community alcoholism treatment clinics providing a range of services not previously available. Also, the number of schools of alcohol studies and persons being trained increased tremendously. In Georgia, for example, five years ago there were about 11 well established and functioning community clinics and one or two state hospital based programs. Today there are 34 community clinics and all nine regional hospitals have 24-hour, seven-day a week alcoholism services.

The Federal Government has given impetus to this growth

by establishing the National Institute of Alcohol Abuse and Alcoholism (NIAAA) with the leadership of many committed state directors. Voluntary groups and individual, state, and local government agencies have also worked closely together to achieve successes.

Goals and objectives of treatment and prevention are outlined in *Guide to the Community Control of Alcoholism* (Cross, 1968). There are sections on resources and existing services and on the roles of judicial, law enforcement, and social service and health care agencies. Problems of staff and financing are discussed.

A more recent publication (*Developing Community Services for Alcoholics - Some Beginning Principles*, 1974) provides a helpful common frame of reference for concerned citizens, administrators, and professionals to use in planning for alcohol services, some of which have been started by state alcoholism agencies. The Williamsburg workshop which resulted in publication of this document brought together 36 persons representing the professions of medicine, psychiatry, psychology, nursing, social work, and health administration, as well as public and private agencies concerned with alcoholism. First, the two broad areas to be considered were delineated: (a) community planning and (b) inter-agency or administrative planning.

COMMUNITY PLANNING. Community planning includes cooperation with existing health and welfare services. Community must be defined also in terms of the area to be considered. For some it is a neighborhood; for others a town, a catchment area of counties, or a state or region. In order to begin planning, two decisions must be made: (a) who are all the people responsible for the health needs, and (b) what is the appropriate level at which planning must occur? Planning must be thought of as a continuing affair, not a one shot deal.

Every community has its own unique characteristics which certainly affect any suggested procedure, but at the risk of too much generalization, certain areas suggested from the Williamsburg Workshop seem helpful and have proven to be practical.

Developing a feeling of concern. If this is not present, it must be kindled. In most communities there are usually many shared concerns but some are not brought into focus. Community leaders, consumers, and present agencies perhaps represent the latent concern for better services to alcoholics. At any rate sparks have to be fanned, candles have to be lit.

Assembling a group of planners. These will have to be educated. Experience has taught most of us that myths and prejudices are hidden stumbling blocks to establishing or improving services for alcoholics. Myths and prejudices exist as firmly if not more firmly in professionals of all kinds and will always be encountered.

Surveying needs. It is seldom possible to obtain reliable figures on needs in a local community. In our time, however, it is generally conceded by national and regional figures that the needs of the alcoholic population are more like the hidden part of an iceberg, that is, 80% to 90% more than is visible.

Compiling resources. Existing resources and the areas in which they are most successful must be listed. Resources enumerated without some idea of their attitude and success with alcoholics will not be very helpful to planning.

Financing planning activities. This may be a consideration in persuading people to plan effectively.

Formulating goals of the community service. Describing what a community group wants to do will inevitably involve arriving at some consensus of its philosophy for treatment of alcoholics. It will also require consideration of what is most needed and what constitutes comprehensive care. An example of the task is the 26-county catchment area where this author directs the inpatient hospital service. After two years of working together, patient and alcoholism coordinators, who are members also of mental health centers, are just beginning to formulate a philosophy, a mission statement, and goals and objectives.

Establishing priorities. The scope of providing comprehensive services to alcoholics is admittedly huge and so any planning group should establish priorities and work through them.

Financing services. There is never enough money to do all that needs to be done, and it is probably safe to say there never will be. Planning groups today need to explore various federal and state funding mechanisms for services to alcoholics.

INTRA-AGENCY OR ADMINISTRATIVE PLANNING. The problems encountered at the level of administrative planning are those of power needs and politics. Communities, organizations, and agencies have their power structures, and it is vain to think that community planning for alcoholics will not be affected. Somehow the cause and concern for service to people must be kept in focus with the realization that power needs of persons and politics will have to be considered.

Intra planning means changes that are necessary when an agency, such as a general hospital, considers admitting alcoholics for detoxification when the policy of the board of the hospital is not to admit alcoholics. Consultation, education, and attitude changes may be essential aspects of overall organizational considerations.

The larger goal of community planning is to form some viable organization to deliver the desired alcoholism services. Beigel (1973) offers four approaches.

The governmental approach. Either a state or local government assumes the primary responsibility for the organization and administration of alcohol services.

The single community agency approach. A single community-based agency with previous experience in the field of alcoholism services assumes the primary responsibility.

The consortium model approach. Multiple agencies, jointly interested in the development of a comprehensive community-based alcoholism program, employ an organizational pattern in which no single agency has the primary organizing responsibility or primary administrative responsibility over the other agencies but instead join together in an equal partnership and establish a board which is independent from the operation of any specific agency.

The for profit approach. An established, private, profit-making corporation, not a public, community-based agency, assumes the initiative and responsibility for the organization and delivery of comprehensive alcoholism services to a target population.

Regardless of which administrative approach is chosen, there are certain substantive issues which transcend any and all of these organizational approaches. If these issues are ignored, the group involved in the planning of comprehensive alcoholism services will undermine its own ability to successfully implement the chosen organizational approach. The issues are: (a) community boards, (b) traditional versus non-traditional approaches to the delivery of alcoholism services, (c) pre-program planning, (d) continuity of care, and (e) funding (Beigel, 1973). Where these key issues are not kept in clear focus and good working order programs fail. In many programs community boards are token boards; traditional and non-traditional approaches are not integrated; pre-program planning is not completed; continuity of care is sporadic; and funding is not diversified.

One final word needs to be written about community organization. There is more to community planning than manipulating systems; there is more to coordination of resources than writing policies and procedure; there is more to formulating community service goals than collecting data on death rates and crash victims.

What is missing is the same ingredient that is a key to the recovery of many alcoholics: the dimension of one or more committed, understanding, caring persons (Davies, Shepherd, & Myers, 1956; Kendell & Stanton, 1966). Where state or local programs function well and offer services that continue to grow and expand, there are extraordinarily committed people leading them. This dimension makes the difference in community planning as well as in the delivery of services. The missing ingredient in the patients' re-integration process (Mulford, 1970) is empathetic understanding. The missing ingredient in community programs is empathetic understanding on the part of decision-making authorities.

COMPONENTS OF COMPREHENSIVE SERVICES

Spurred by the action of such organizations as Alcohol and Drug Programs of America, by federal and state agencies, and by legislation, most every state today is providing more services and better care for the alcoholic.

One of the key words in alcohol services today is *comprehensive*. This means that there should be available a range of services from emergency care to care that allows a person to become increasingly self-sustaining and personally responsible. Every training experience, every workshop is concerned with the components of comprehensive services. *Developing Community Services for Alcoholics* (1974), published by the National Institute of Alcohol Abuse and Alcoholism (NIAAA), devotes a section to this. In addition to direct service to the sick patient, financial assistance, employment and training services, legal, housing, social and recreational services are also offered. Even consultation and educational services are included. Many of these services are needed by other people also and therefore usually already exist for use by the alcoholic.

It seems possible to limit this discussion to the more specialized services to alcoholics and to use as a reference the components developed and published by the Joint Commission on Accreditation of Hospitals (*Accreditation Manual*, 1974). The manual defines areas of care, sets standards of eligibility for accreditation, and aims to insure a quality of care for all facilities in a community serving alcoholics.

Although accreditation procedures differentiate between required and optional components, the full range of services needed by the alcoholic in his recovery will be discussed here. These services, available through a network in the community, fulfill the criteria for adequate and quality treatment offered to patients with other illnesses. I will discuss, therefore, in some detail all of these components and refer you to the manual for further details.

MANAGEMENT SUPPORT SERVICES. The family caught up in the crisis of an alcoholic's drinking episode first thinks of getting the loved one to a "place" -- to some center or building where there are caretakers who can give immediate evaluation and care appropriate to the patient's condition.

Seldom does the family think of a governing authority that gives legal and medical responsibility to do what they need to do to the sick patient. Few family members consider for long the other elements that are included in management and support services to maintain and continue a quality of service. Such issues as the legal rights of a patient, the kind of environment that has to be maintained, the fiscal management, the planning and personal aspects of care are all behind the delivery of services. Other aspects of support services important for good care include the orderly management of patients' records, medication control, dietetic services, referral of patients to other services, and a continuing need to evaluate what is being done and to research new methods.

For example, just one facet of management concerning services to the alcoholic is financing treatment. Patients cover the costs of meeting most illnesses today through insurance. Only recently, however, has alcoholism treatment been covered by insurance. There remain many problems to be worked out in that area of management. Insurance coverage for alcoholism treatment has been a high priority in the National Institute of Alcohol Abuse and Alcoholism for many years. The insurance industry has made it very clear to NIAAA that they need assurance that alcoholism treatment program costs and procedures are responsibly managed and that benefits for such treatment are actuarially sound. The pressure due to funding of services has forced and will continue to require close evaluation of the cost/benefit ratio.

A summary article in *Alcohol Health and Research World*, Spring 1975) describes how NIAAA and the insurance industry are working together to answer some of the questions. Together they have:

1. Effected the establishment of standards and procedures for the accreditation of alcoholism treatment programs by the Joint Commission on Accreditation of Hospitals. The standards were developed by the Joint Commission under a contract from NIAAA.

2. Established model standards for certification/licensure of alcoholism counselors by appropriate state certification boards and licensing authorities.

3. Prepared a model health insurance alcoholism benefits package and continued to refine cost analysis and cost schedule data.

4. Awarded incentive contracts to several pilot outpatient treatment centers operated by profitmaking organizations, with contractors' fees determined by the level of third-party payments they are able to generate.

5. Held management training programs for the staff of projects funded by NIAAA.

6. Established a model cost accounting system for alcoholism facilities, including a fiscal assistance manual.

7. Initiated a financial management training program for the staff of alcoholism treatment facilities, emphasizing accounting requirements of health insurance carriers.

8. Funded a study of current and planned state legislative and regulatory activities in health insurance coverage for alcoholism.

Management and support services can make or break direct services and require trained people. Treatment through administration is not a new idea, but it is sometimes not well performed.

EMERGENCY CARE SYSTEM. An emergency care system is defined as a system that "shall provide for 24-hour availability of the following services to all persons and their families with problems related to alcohol use and abuse: (a) immediate medical evaluation and care, (b) supervision of persons by properly trained staff until they are no longer incapacitated by the effects of alcohol, (c) evaluation of medical, psychological, and social needs, leading to the development of a plan for continuing care, (d) effective transportation services."

This component involves immediate screening, medical evaluation, and referral or acceptance of patients. One of the most useful and basic aids formulated for physicians, but usable for any profession, is the material offered in the *Criteria for the Diagnosis of Alcoholism* (Criteria Committee,

National Council of Alcoholism, 1972). Here major and minor criteria are catalogued in tables weighted for easy application in the process of diagnosis. Most centers accomplish screening and evaluation in some triage team where nurses and assistants, with the backup of a physician, function effecttively. Twenty-four hour, seven-day a week service with the availability of ambulance or driver and emergency hospital room contacts are all necessary for immediate use and referral.

Acceptance of patients is usually to a 24-hour in-bed facility with trained nurses and assistants to carry out the physician's orders for medication and supervision of patients until the acute effects of alcohol have subsided. Delirium tremens, hallucinations, and some degree of disorientation can be handled also. An important aspect of emergency care is detoxification. A thorough discussion and presentation of specific detoxification services is presented in the proceedings of a seminar held by NIAAA in March of 1972. (*Proceedings on Alcohol Emergency Care Service*, 1972.)

This conference unanimously opposed the term "detoxification service" because it usually conveyed the idea that such a service was an end in itself and nothing further was needed. The paper on "Recommendations for Detoxification Services" (Fox, 1972) presents a flow chart illustrating the scope of emergency services. In addition, it recommends that 40 hospital beds for detoxification and comprehensive medical care for 200,000 population be provided. It advises that "sprinkling" alcoholics among people with other problems means that the caretakers will continue to ignore their alcohol problems. The traditional medical or psychiatric models of staffing are not efficient. A higher concentration of medical services is needed in the early detoxification process, but even at this stage staff disciplines can be fused so that nurses, doctors, and even psychiatrists can service patients in groups and interact as patient coordinators. This model has the advantage of enabling a doctor be a doctor using his medical skills and also to be a "human being" and use his humanity skills. It also calls for attention to an outreach function.

In emergency services, as in other services offered, it is important to develop a team function. Subgrouping by disciplines to deliver a single service is a natural phenomenon. Grouping for the purpose of delivery of a single service, and delivering the service as a team, is different phenomenon. This is not to ignore the fact that people are different, and each can meet some of the patient's needs. If there is on the staff a high degree of agreement as to a core philosophy the staff will function more as a team and will make more of an impact on the patient.

Emergency care services, of which detoxification is a part, present different considerations if you are treating a mixed population of alcohol and drug abusers. A thorough consideration of this problem is presented by Ottenberg (1972) who emphasizes the role of the director and his or her attitude.

The special concerns of emergency services, including detoxification, were abruptly brought to many community treatment programs when a landmark court decision was made in 1966. For approximately 350 years intoxication in the United States had been handled under criminal law (Grad, 1973). The decisions of the courts ended the practice of primitive incarceration of the alcoholic and provided appropriate statutory framework for treatment and rehabilitation of the alcoholic. A Uniform Alcoholism and Intoxication Treatment Act was drafted by the National Conference of Commissioners on Uniform State Laws and approved and recommended for enactment in all states at their annual conference in Vail, Colorado, in August 1971 (*Alcohol and Health*). Many states passed such laws which meant persons publicly intoxicated would be offered help by either being taken to an evaluation and treatment center or home, or in some cases, to jail for 12-24 hours if there were no suitable treatment facility. More than 30 states have passed different versions of the Uniform Intoxication Act. Some states such as Maryland, Minnesota, Massachusetts, and others have specially funded programs.

Some states have passed the legislation but have made little change in what happens to the drunk person. A paper presented by Bradley (1972) gives an acount of what happened when Washington, D.C. adopted its own Uniform Alcoholism Act in 1968.

In a severely overloaded and at times understaffed treatment center, positive findings were reported. The findings and conclusions of the evaluation of this project are summarized: (a) the study demonstrated that a public health service for the emergency care of simple intoxication is feasible as an alternative to criminal procedures or hospitalization; (b) it demonstrated that the present staffing pattern and procedures are efficient and economical from a financial and management standpoint in handling a large number of inebriates who have no medical complications; (c) it demonstrated that public inebriates will accept a medically oriented program for withdrawal from intoxication. Since admission was open to both self-referred and agency-referred inebriates, the center reached a broader group of problem drinkers than if it had been restricted to those brought in by the police; (d) it demonstrated that the center is effective in referring alcoholic patients for long-term inpatient rehabilitation treatment; (e) it demonstrated that alcoholics are manageable at a detoxification center. For further reading on the advantages of detoxification instead of jail and a description of programs already in operation, the reader is referred to Siegal (1973).

The segment of the population that this act most clearly affects is the chronic skid row person, estimated to be from 3% to 5% of the alcoholic population. This group is the most visible and the most difficult to help. Serving these persons should be part of the planning concept of comprehensive services. Due to the attention received in the courts, this group has tended to be given separate and specialized treatment. It is, however, one among many identifiable groups of persons suffering from alcohol abuse and needs to be incorporated into the total treatment concept.

Of special interest have been current programs offering social setting detoxification or non-medical emergency care service. The emphasis is placed on a quiet, positive atmosphere without drugs or medical intervention in the detoxification process. Much of the model and rationale was developed at the Addiction Research Foundation (ARF) of Toronto, Canada in 1969. The rationale seems to be based on a philosophy of care which is sensitive to life style, crisis orientation, and the genuine need for identity of the alcoholic. The approach does not mean to indicate that medical examination or medical attention is not needed.

As described by O'Briant (1974) and also by H.V.

Peterson, his associate, the program emerges as follows. The center with which Dr. O'Briant is now working, in Stockton, California, has as its objectives to: (a) develop a social setting detoxification center for alcoholic persons; (b) develop a facility which will serve as a starting point for referral to recovery programs and community resources; (c) establish a model of treatment without some of the problems inherent in traditional medical and judicial approaches to the alcoholic person; (d) demonstrate the model of treatment to the community, service agencies, professional groups, and to other communities; (d) demonstrate that this model of treatment can provide detoxification at a lower cost than the established detoxification methods.

The facility at Stockton is a firehouse remodeled into a modest home setting where the atmosphere is intimate and quiet. Several rooms open off a reception office. A 20-bed dormitory is provided. The staff works with 25 people at a time, purposely keeping the number small. There are no physicians, nurses, or medical personnel on the staff, but there is a hospital medical backup to which patients are transferred immediately if medical complications develop. An estimated 5% of 6,000 patients served in the first two years have needed medical intervention. Seizure rates are reported to be lower than in medical facilities.

Each person is given a clean bed and assured that someone will stay with him until he feels better; meals and showers are provided. When the person is ready, a counselor evaluates him for physical recovery at the center and referral is then made to other community agencies, including the San Joaquin County health agencies. Counselors are recovered alcoholics; no medications are used. Counselors function as information sources, encouraging the person to be responsible for his own recovery. Clients are sent out into the community to make their own contacts, but if there are medical problems they are assisted with appointments at outpatient clinics.

Some statistics of the two-year operation are interesting. Admission rates for first and second year have been very similar -- 2,999 and 2,968 respectively. The average admission rate is 248 a month. Sixty-six percent were admitted once or twice, 19% three to five times, and 14% more than five times during the first year. These rates are less than recidivism rates in more traditional centers for public inebriates.

The majority of clients were in the 30-50 year-old age group; average age 39.2 years. Slightly over one third were single, more than two-fifths were separated or divorced and less than 10% were married. The trend over the two-year period in length of stay has been for a lessening of short stays -- those under 24 hours -- an increase in the number of stays over 24 hours -- and an increase in the number of stays over 48 hours. There has been a decrease in police referrals and an increase in community agency referrals.

Dr. O'Briant states several guidelines for persons working with this model: (a) social setting detoxification programs must have hospital affiliation; (b) special training for staff in recognizing withdrawal symptoms and stages, knowledge of community resources, and an understanding attitude are essential; (d) referral is the primary goal and each person must be apprised of community resources; (e) multiple admissions are expected, but chronic repeaters will not form the majority of clients.

The Toronto program and the Stockton experience, in Dr. O'Briant's opinion, suggest that 95% of alcoholics can be detoxified without medical intervention, and referrals can be made to other community resources.

INPATIENT CARE. The inpatient care component is defined in the *Accreditation Manual* as providing "24-hour supervised care under the direction of a physician in a hospital or other suitably equipped medical setting designated for the diagnosis and/or treatment of medical and/or psychiatric illness derived from or associated with alcohol abuse and/or alcoholism."

Alcoholism and alcohol abuse can and usually do mask many medical problems and psychiatric conditions. The debate still continues concerning the symptomatic nature of alcoholism. This author's position, as stated in the section on Basic Assumptions, is that alcoholism has its own set of criteria but at the same time can cover other diagnosable mental and physical conditions. Adequate service requires readily available medical persons, especially internists and psychiatrists. Criteria for admission to an inpatient service are helpful, but their usefulness is easily influenced by the attitudes and prejudices of those using them. Someone knowledgeable in alcoholism and sufficiently in touch with his or her own alcohol attitude must be available for consultation and decision making.

Inpatient treatment care can vary in length from 24 hours to 30 or more days, and at present there is little conclusive evaluation or research to settle the question of an optimal length of time for inpatient services leading to a dependable length of recovery.

Inpatient care frequently offers one of the first ways of beginning a treatment relationship. A family interview on admission of the patient should not be lost or neglected. Group therapy offered to the family member at least once, and possibly regularly, and preferably as soon as possible after the patient has been admitted is helpful in beginning the process of involvement with family. Written information giving local community resources and encouraging the family to contact them while the patient is in the hospital is also helpful. Everything should be done to change to some degree the situation to which the patient will eventually return. Another dimension of care to the alcoholic which involves the family should be considered here. Kellerman (1974) points out that it is through the family that the alcoholic frequntly becomes involved in treatment. In addition, the family, spouse, and children desperately need help themselves.

There are many kinds of inpatient care programs across the country, too numerous to summarize. The program with which this author is identified can serve as a model illustrating an inpatient care system operating with a multidisciplinary staff in which the designed structure carries some of the weight created by the demanding job of serving an average of 100 alcohol and drug patients a month.

The inpatient alcohol and drug service of the Georgia Mental Health Institute, Atlanta, Georgia, is assigned two cottages of 58 beds each to service a total population of 700,000 people. A receiving-admissions team, part of the entire Georgia mental health admissions process, screens alcohol and drug patients as well as all other prospective patients (psychiatric) for treatment.

The staffing pattern of inpatient service is as follows: One program director (non-medical), two physicians, one psychiatrist (half time), 30 nursing personnel (staff nurses, licensed practical nurses, mental health technicians, and psychiatric assistants), one psychologist, two social workers, one social work technician, one clinical chaplain, one clinic counselor, one vocational rehabilitation counselor, and secretaries and clerks.

The 26-county catchment area from which we receive patients comprises 23 counties of a rural mountainous North Georgia area and three urban and suburban counties. At the unit level we accept patients who are screened and determined in need of inpatient care by community workers and/or the admissions-receiving team. Ninety-five percent require detoxification. Specific reasons for admission include: (a) medical and psychiatric conditions associated with the middle and late stages of alcoholism; (b) the patient's inability to interrupt a drinking episode or cycle; (c) separation of the drinking person from his immediate environment while clinic personnel work with the family; (d) evaluation of mental and physical conditions brought on by the complication of drugs and alcohol; and (e) preventative intervention (brief hospitalization not available in the local community for patients who are about to resume drinking or have just begun a drinking episode).

The entire staff of both cottages is divided into five teams. We mixed persons so there would be staff representing all shifts and different disciplines, including a physician and a psychiatrist on each team. Patients, as they are admitted, are assigned by the admitting person to one of the five teams. Within the first 24 hours, each patient is assigned an individual treatment coordinator who is also a team member and who becomes, as it were, the manager of the patient's treatment program.

Each team has a leader who is responsible for supervising staff members and for convening four meetings a week. Authority for the formulation of a problem list and treatment plan, and decisions relative to the individual's management (such as passes, discharge date, family involvement, etc.) rests with the team members (staff and patients). Team meetings are devoted to "getting with the patient" -- surfacing needs, focusing on the reality of the patient's drinking behavior, and making any decisions requested by the patient. The treatment coordinator is the patient's individual enabler, coordinator, and communicator, if necessary, but is not to be a "prime therapist." The treatment coordinator bears the responsibility of much of the necessary paper work -- data base, problem list, treatment plan, specific discharge appointments, and discharge summary.

In our concept of crisis intervention, detoxification is understood to be an integral part of a treatment process that begins the same hour as admission. Most patients are on their feet the second day, attending education and motivation classes that are held twice a day in addition to their team meetings. A variety of lectures, films, and tapes are used by individual staff members in classes which promote discussion and interaction for learning purposes. We also developed breakfast orientation sessions three days a week during which a staff member explains the entire program to all patients.

Relationships between an inpatient center and local community centers are vital. In a system where the inpatient service is recognized and used as one of a number of treatment alternatives, it becomes quickly apparent that close communication must be established and maintained with the local health center which either referred the patient or should know of the patient's presence. It is important to establish contact with the patient quickly but equally important to develop a means of communication with the local community. This has been accomplished by working out with our four geographical area centers the assignment of liaison workers -- patient advocates -- who meet with staff and patients weekly, beginning a personal contact to nudge the patient toward available outpatient groups and counseling.

The concept and practical application of the program is far from being solely either a medical or detoxification unit. The alcoholic or drug addictive person in acute stages first receives medical attention. At the same time he is encouraged while he is suffering to look at his destructive life style and the fantasies he holds on to surrounding it. He needs to look at his reversal of values and at the denial, guilt, rationalization, and projection, which take the place of reality. Our treatment concept came out of the understanding that unless we tried, while the person was collapsed, to infringe upon his denial system, we would fail to motivate him to further community treatment resources in the developing local clinics.

Major problems encountered with the inpatient program and the area geographical centers were as follows: (a) broadening of the role of disciplined trained persons such as physicians, nurses, social workers, vocational rehabilitation counselors, attendants, and technicians to offer more than their disciplines trained them to do; (b) divergency of levels of understanding on the part of staff for acutely sick and chronic alcoholics; (c) the difficulty in maintaining a treatment program that offers more than medical care; (d) the "feeding" of staff so they can offer understanding, patience, and hope when serving an average of 100 patients a month; (e) keeping competition among staff out in the open; (f) criteria on which decisions for admission are made by the geographical area centers; (g) meaningful involvement of alcohol and drug coordinators in the inpatient alcohol service, especially concerning conflicts around admissions and discharges; (h) the limited but developing community alcoholism services to which the patient has to return.

We have learned a number of things in working with this program. A structure of groups with staff involvement helps to support the patient in treatment so that staff members do not have to carry all the weight. Removing the dichotomy of "medical" versus "counseling" allows staff to be involved more fully with patients. The broadened role makes the work more interesting and the staff becomes more willing. Development of understanding has progressed through regular weekly in-service training. In addition, a structure that provides weekly group supervision for all staff personnel is felt to be a must.

One answer to maintaining a treatment program beyond medical care in a short-term stay is to establish regular shifts for nursing personnel, maintaining a continuity of patient-staff involvement. This, together with a twice-daily review of all patient admissions, planned discharges, and changes that occur through the team meetings, helps us maintain our treatment emphasis.

Staff "feeding" is accomplished by team leaders

planning trips to community centers, surveying local resources, and encouraging experimentation by offering special interest groups. A weekly luncheon to which staff bring their special dishes helps. A personnel committee, made up of staff members, which makes promotions and fills vacancies also serves to "make it worth while."

A special weekly gathering of all full-time staff, chaired by an outside consultant, where staff concerns and conflicts can be voiced, functions to surface competitive struggles and begin some resolutions.

Problems surrounding admissions and discharge are not so much a matter of clear criteria as they are attitudes of various decision-making people in the community as well as in the inpatient service. Changing attitudes and minimizing conflicts involve sitting down face to face and discussing problems. We of the inpatient service invited the Alcohol and Drug Program Coordinators in the four geographical area centers to participate in weekly executive meetings. This was an opportunity to work on policies and procedures about inappropriate admissions, premature referrals of patients to the community, patients leaving against medical advice, re-admission requests by severely chronic patients, and many other problems. These meetings established valuable communication lines, developed continuous understanding of the program and program changes, and gave the geographical areas a voice in policy making.

The care of the alcoholic felon is an area of special concern involving inpatient care in the alcoholism field today. My own interest comes from eight years of service in the federal prison system and new programs that are being tried in jails in different parts of the country. In the

1950's before research was done, the estimated percentage of crimes in which alcohol played a part was 50%. In Pavloff's (1974) opinion, in 50% of murders alcohol abuse is involved.

Following a seminar in the fall of 1973, jointly sponsored by NIAAA, the Law Enforcement Assistance Administration, and the Federal Bureau of Prisons, a strong appeal was made for alcohol programs to be offered to persons in prisons.

INTERMEDIATE CARE. In the *Accreditation Manual*, the intermediate care component is defined as designed to "facilitate the rehabilitation of the alcoholic person by placing him in an organized therapeutic environment in which he may receive diagnostic services, counseling, vocational rehabilitation, and/or work therapy while benefiting from the support which a full or partial residential setting can provide."

The implications of the intermediate care system are that there be a flow of services and several types of programs available. The term "transitional services" is sometimes used interchangeably with "intermediate." Halfway houses, quarterway houses, nursing homes, foster family placement, small group homes, and partial hospitalization can all be included under this topic.

It is commonly recognized that all of these services are in great demand by alcoholic treatment organizations and there is a decided weakness in our care system at this point. The Association of Halfway Houses, through NIAAA assistance, contracted on July 1, 1973 to "study and determine problems encountered in growth, financing, standards for operations, and relationships with community resources as it pertains to halfway house alcoholism programs in the 50 states, District of Columbia and Puerto Rico.: The resultant report published by the Association summarizes the findings and gives guidelines, standards and an operational philosophy for halfway house programs. (Status Report, 1974.) This document along with other helpful material from the Association is extremely useful in working with communities in establishing such facilties.

Many communities have developed different and complementary alternatives for meeting the alcoholics' needs. Families are frequently not receptive to having the alcoholic at home; some alcoholics have no homes, and some need a bridge between accepting the full responsibility of living in the world and the protective care of hospitalization.

OUTPATIENT CARE. The outpatient care component is defined as "designed to provide a variety of diagnostic and primary treatment services on both a scheduled basis and non-scheduled basis in a nonresidential setting to alcoholic persons and their families whose physical and emotional status allows them to function in their usual environment." Outpatient care provides direct services for detoxification and medical treatment, and also should perform a major coordinating role with the alcoholic and his family. Outpatient detoxification (Feldman, Pattison, Graham, & Sobell, 1975) is being used widely and has been judged to be cost effective and useful in the majority of cases.

Most outpatient services provide screening, evaluation, medical detoxification, and individual and group therapy as well as occupational and recreational activities. Job training with vocational rehabilitation, emotional support to patient and families, and use of A.A., Al-Anon, and Alateen are indispensable offerings in an outpatient service. Without a doubt the success or failure of outpatient services to the alcoholic rests with the ability of the director and staff to coordinate those services and provide them when needed with an attitude of care and concern.

Since outpatient alcoholism services are more often situated where the patient lives and works, strong emphasis should be placed on counseling the family of the alcoholic participating in treatment. Offering services to the significant other persons in the alcoholic's life can eventuate in bringing treatment to the alcoholic. Reality is more apparent; action is more often forced if the significant other persons can be educated, informed, and supported to remove themselves from the dependency role and to withdraw their protective stance. Children are especially vulnerable to parents' drunkenness (Cureton, 1973) and react with stress and utilize fewer coping activities (Rouse, Waller, & Ewing, 1973). They need to be considered in planning to provide services.

OUTREACH. The outreach component is defined as a program "to facilitate identification of persons and their families who have problems related to the use of alcohol, to facilitate procurement of alcohol services, and to alert all public and private human service agencies who serve the same target population to the importance of early identification and easy access to the service delivery system."

In state alcoholism plans and programs one of the words most consistently used is "outreach," more often cited as a need rather than a reality. Material on special projects, such as American Indians, youth, the older alcoholic, and occupational programs stresses the great need for outreach. Projects operating to bring help to alcoholics in major cities attest to the fact that when alcoholism services are offered close to home or work, people will avail themselves of those services. As a component of comprehensive services it does appear that staff objectives and a plan with some clear methods of personnel utilization in the outreach service is necessary.

Two areas of community programs really test the ability of communities to reach out and offer services. They are (a) young people and alcohol, and (b) older people with drinking problem. Let us consider first the youth. Preliminary results of a national survey conducted by NIAAA early in 1974 indicated that 93% of boys and 87% of girls in their senior year of high school had experimented with alcohol, and more than 50% of the nation's seventh graders had tried drinking at least once during the previous year (*Alcohol Health and Research World*, Summer 1975). Alcohol use is on the increase among youth (*Drug Use in America*, 1973). One clearcut example of the growing problem is the increased number of persons under 18 who have been arrested for alcohol related offenses. Between 1960 and 1973 arrests increased 135%. Arrests for driving while intoxicated increased more than 400% (*Uniform Crime Report*, 1973).

The statistics alert us to the problem, and there are programs that are reaching out to intervene and prevent the problem. *Alcohol Health and Research World* has reviewed a number of these which cover areas such as pilot projects in prevention, the use of older counselors in decisionmaking, and treatment programs for youth already addicted. Prevention efforts are primarily aimed at promoting responsible decisionmaking about the use of alcohol. The family is viewed by many authorities as most effective in influencing decisions of young people. The concept of drinking in moderation should be aimed at parents who can set standards. In an inner-city neighborhood of Philadelphia one program pays college students to tutor high school students in academic subjects and at the same time explain decisionmaking about the responsible use of alcohol (*Alcohol Health and Research World*, Spring 1974).

The NIAAA-funded Youth Values Program (YVP) focuses on fourth, fifth, and sixth graders and their families. College-aged counselors are trained to work with youngsters. The YVP concept assumes that attitudes toward alcohol are related to a person's value system, decisionmaking skills, and self esteem. Alcohol education is also either, incorporated into science curricula or offered as a special educational unit.

A number of youth treatment centers are already operating. Alcoholics Anonymous has groups now entirely of adolescents; four such groups are in California. The Cabrini Center in New York City is another group for treatment of young people between 12 and 18 years of age with their parents' consent. There is an emphasis on family involvement in counseling. Another ambitious youth treatment center is funded by NIAAA in Santa Fe, New Mexico (La Fe Youth Hostel). The residential program for youth in Duluth, Minnesota, administered by the State Department of Mental Health also conducts extensive alcohol educational and outreach programs in the public school system.

Another area in the outreach phase of community programs is that of the older problem drinker. Only recently has the older problem drinker come to the attention of people in the alcohol field. Now, however, courses such as the one taught by E. Polly Williams at Rutgers School of Alcohol Studies, include such groups. *The First Special Report to the U.S. Congress on Alcohol and Health* gave figures that indicated drinking and heavy drinking declined with age in both men and women. A very low percentage of heavy drinkers was found among older people (Cahalan, Cisin, & Crossley, 1969). Work at the Rutgers School of Alcohol Studies (Carruth, Williams, Mysock, & Boudreaux, 1973) was also addressed to a two-year study of problem drinkers among older persons.

This population group includes the older persons who have been alcoholic for 20, 30, 40, or 50 years and the older persons who have recently started using alcohol because of grief, loneliness and depression, retirement, and lowered income. Rosin and Glatt (1971) found these elements very important. It has been found that families are very reluctant to identify grandfather or mother as alcoholic. Because of shame or guilt, families tend to protect and cover up until they can no longer do so. Reports and discussions with people in the field who work with older problem drinkers indicate that existing services are not geared in attitude or structure to adequately serve the older person.

Alcohol World reports on the Queens Nursing Home and Treatment Center in Minneapolis, Minnesota. They have purposely prepared, trained, and planned to serve this aspect of older persons and have trained alcoholism counselors for the program. Their referrals are from state, veteran and local hospitals. They serve persons with long alcoholism histories who have felt hopeless for a long time.

The program calls for the patient to assume maintenance chores and to participate in craft activities. The goal is interaction with others. The control of personal items, such as money, and the clarity of expectations serve to give structure and support to each person. Each patient has a counselor. A daily routine is followed with individual and group counseling, activities, housekeeping chores, etc.; and passes are not allowed for 60 days. Treatment lasts three to six months. Contact after discharge is felt to be vital. An alumni group is operating, and alumni are welcome to return. In an encouraging article Zimberg (1974) agrees with others that older problem drinkers can recover and that they do respond, particularly if there is follow-up by a counselor.

Another outreach component of community programs concerns industry and government services for alcoholics. For years we have heard of the tremendous cost of alcoholism to industry in our country. In 1947 Consolidated Edison began a policy of trying to rehabilitate the alcoholic employee rather than firing him. Since then over 300 companies have instituted programs and policies. Assisted by NIAAA, states have employed professionals to work with both industry and government to develop policies and help implement programs for troubled employees. It is very difficult to find out how effective many of the individual programs are. Much work has been done on profiles of alcoholic employees (Cahalan, 1970; Roman & Trice, 1967). The foreman's role in identification and encouragement in treatment is found to be crucial (Roman & Trice, 1973).

Any discussion of the outreach aspect of treatment for alcoholics must address itself to the long ignored and poorly met needs of the American Indians. The number one problem of the American Indian is alcoholism. Most sources date this from the time Europeans came in contact with the Indians (Dailey, 1968; MacAndrew & Edgerton, 1969; Winkler, 1968). Some studies seriously question whether the Indians' level of drinking constitutes alcoholism. A review of this material and the questions pertaining to data collection and interpretation has been summarized by Levy and Kunitz (1973).

Approximately 100 projects for Indians have been funded by NIAAA, about 50% through the Office of Economic Opportunity. Funding was purposely limited to three years to stimulate efforts toward ending paternalism and toward planning, developing, and implementing programs operated by the Indians themselves. In many cases state alcoholism agencies share in the funding, and programs become a joint affair. The states of Arizona, Colorado, Montana, Oregon, and South Dakota established Indian Commissions while other states, such as Kansas, Oklahoma, and Texas, established regional organizations.

A later development, funded by NIAAA, was the formation of the American Indian Commission on Alcoholism and Drug Abuse (AICADA), based in Denver, Colorado, which provides a broad range of technical assistance to Indian alcoholism treatment programs. Besides money, NIAAA also provides organizational, fiscal, administrative, and evaluative help.

One of the early studies, described at the First Annual Conference of NIAAA, was on drinking among the Papago Indians in Tucson, Arizona (Waddell, 1971). Treatment programs were established on reservations 30 miles outside of Tucson. A key part of this program consists of bringing the program to the people -- outreach. Five alcoholism counselors, recovered alcoholics trained in intervention, move through 72 villages. Programs include education and information sessions and offer one-to-one counseling and follow-up.

At the Fourth Annual Conference of NIAAA in 1974 a panel of Indian students fielded questions concerning alcohol and Indians. They represented the first boarding school in the nation -- the Chemawa Indian School near Salem, Oregon -- to have an alcohol education program on campus. The school has an enrollment of 500 students and offers four years of high school education. The education center has a director and a staff of counselor and student volunteers who do education outreach as well as on-campus teaching. The school has alcohol abusers among its student body. Through the center, it provided detoxification services as well as educational services to 200 students in a seven-month period in 1973. The main emphasis of this program, which reaches out to 11 reservations, is prevention and intervention through education.

AFTERCARE. The aftercare component is defined as the attempt "to provide care to patients who have progressed sufficiently through emergency, inpatient, intermediate, and/or outpatient services to a point in their recovery where they will benefit from a level of continued contact which will support and increase the gains made to date in a treatment process."

Aftercare in the treatment of alcoholics is considered so important that the Accreditation Manual for Alcoholism Programs (JCAH) has made it a required part of eligibility criteria. Most people in this field have known for years that the alcoholic doesn't have a chance at maintaining his sobriety after a period of emergency or inpatient care if he does not work at some form of aftercare. The key word is "linkage."

To effectively help a patient ally himself with an ongoing treatment activity sometimes means referring the person back to his community. Liaison persons from local treatment clinics meet regularly in an inpatient service with patients from their geographical area. Patients become acquainted with the workers face to face. They begin to discuss their problems. In our treatment facility we have found an increased number of patients following up with treatment when they have established a meaningful relationship while an inpatient. For the patient it means work. He or she must attend some kind of peer group or individual ongoing treatment as regularly and as certainly as he does his employment. For some persons it will be his "work" in the initial stages of recovery.

Arranging aftercare involves a great deal more than making a verbal referral to go to a certain place. For a referral to succeed, three elements are necessary. First, the patient must make some meaningful identification with at least one person during the initial phase of his treatment. This may be on an outpatient or an inpatient basis. Secondly, that identity must be transferred to another person or program in an effort to seek more extended help. The third element is proper timing of the referral and the attitude of the person making it. Too early a referral is regarded as rejection -- too abrupt a cutoff is also considered rejection. A patient usually gives many clues concerning his feelings and will alert a sensitive counselor to the quality of the process.

The six components discussed in this section, when implemented in a network of services, will provide the needed care system in community programs.

EDUCATION AND TRAINING -- GROWTH AND SURVIVAL

I was privileged in April 1966 to participate, as one of 15 representatives from 11 facilities visited by the Joint Information Service, in finalizing their report assessing treatment programs for alcoholics in the United States (Glasscote, Plaut, Hammersley, O'Neill, Chafetz, & Cummings, 1967). This report covered 43 facilities surveyed first by means of a questionnaire and then by visitation. It was found that not one single alcoholism facility provided a full range of services to all applicants. This was published soon after another study which also called the nation's attention to the limited services available to alcoholics (Plaut, 1967).

Since these two reports there has been a great increase in services for alcoholics through community programs. All states have produced plans which can be secured from the individual state alcoholism authorities outlining the goals and direction of alcohol planning and also summarizing services now being rendered. The crucial result is that focus on treatment has overshadowed the critical requirements for qualified manpower to staff new facilities (Mitnick, 1974).

To discuss the areas more related to community programs I would like to cover the following: (a) alcoholism preventors; (b) community gatekeepers; (c) service oriented gatekeepers; and (d) service deliverers.

ALCOHOLISM PREVENTORS. Some aspects of prevention were suggested in the component of outreach discussed in the previous section. The peer approach to prevention in which an inner-city neighborhood in Philadelphia has college students as models for high school students is one. Pilot projects under NIAAA in Harlem and East Harlem support an experimental program in which peers select 14 to 18-year-olds from their own group and, after training, develop and teach their own curriculum on alcohol. A similar peer group alcohol education is supported by the Texas Commission on Alcoholism and is implemented through the Southwest Allied Youth Organization in Dallas, Texas.

These are specific programs for specific areas, but alcohol prevention also takes place in home, church, and school when the roots of personal and family living are strengthened. The clergyman calling to make men whole and the ministry of reconciliation constitute a fundamental effort in the area of prevention. The school teacher who genuinely accepts and cares for a little toddler makes a significant contribution to prevention. Honest and straight-shooting youth leaders who help young men and women to break through their incipient shellls of isolation and to know the value of sharing their feelings with others contribute to prevention. Warm, accepting groups in civic and service clubs can provide a constructive alternative to the alcoholic's flight into the bliss of the bottle.

For all the dangers of simplification the principle is clear; a person either learns constructive ways of handling the stresses of life, or he is tempted to learn destructive escape techniques. Alcoholism is one such escape technique. People learn these constructive alternatives from others -- family, teachers, minister, friends.

COMMUNITY GATEKEEPERS. There is a group of community gatekeepers defined by Pittman as policymaking gatekeepers which include "state and local government officials such as legislators, city and county council members; municipal, county, and state judges and other court officers such as parole and probation directors; upper-echelon law enforcement personnel such as police chiefs; industrial leaders such as directors of personnel for large corporations; union leaders; lay board members of health and welfare councils, Community Chests and United Funds, and newspaper, magazine, television and radio personnel" (Pittman & Sterne, 1965). These people can support existing programs and be instrumental in beginning programs if they are educated to the subject.

SERVICE ORIENTED GATEKEEPERS. This is another phrase coined by Pittman. There is a large number of persons in every community who provide an entrance into the community alcoholism treatment system. These are clergymen, family physicians, law enforcement officers, social workers, nurses, teachers, attorneys, bartenders, pharmacists, Al-Anon, Alcoholics Anonymous, and local councils on alcoholism. It is important that these people be trained, receiving professionally oriented guidelines so referrals can be helpful.

The writer was the chief training director of such a project for clergymen under a NIMH grant from 1964 to 1969 at the Georgian Clinic in Atlanta, Georgia (Pilot Project for Clinical Training of Clergymen in the Field of Alcoholism, 1969). Of 1,360 clergymen exposed in primarily the clinical setting of alcoholism treatment and peer group seminar learning, most returned to their parishes and church duties and functioned as key community alcoholism gatekeepers.

SERVICE DELIVERERS. In spite of treatment demands overshadowing training, there are more training opportunities offered to train persons to deliver alcohol services than ever before. It is also true, I believe, that the success of treatment depends upon the effectiveness of alcoholism personnel (Mitnick, 1974).

The debate on the role of the professionals and the need for them in alcoholism treatment is very alive. Beyond the role of the professional is also the question of the role of the paraprofessional (Staub & Kent, 1973), and beyond that there is the question of whether training helps or hinders the counselor (Carkhuff & Berenson, 1967). These questions pose others: is specialized training needed? What qualities should a trained counselor have? What is training, and what is orientation?

Studies have been made indicating that therapists contribute not only to the improvement of the patient but also sometimes to the reverse (Traux & Carkhuff, 1967). Counselors with certain traits or characteristics make up a core of qualities that contribute to their effectiveness as counselors (Carkhuff & Berenson, 1967). High functioning therapeutic personalities exhibit the following characteristics and are more effective when the client is also exhibiting high rather than low functioning (Wolf, 1972): empathy, respect, genuineness, concreteness, confrontation, self-disclosure, immediacy, warmth, potency, self-actualization. There is also some indication that training can interfere with and even reduce high functioning in these qualities (Carkhuff & Berenson, 1967).

This kind of information is being used in training. Counselors need practical and didactic training, such as how to assess the amount of impairment caused by alcoholism, the formulation of treatment goals and objectives, how to manage a patient in a crisis, and referral and termination issues. Training, however, that does not offer a substantial amount of clinical experience and does not deal with the trainee's own attitude and feeling about alcoholics is not effective. It is my experience that persons who plan to be involved with alcoholics should be in a clinical setting long enough -- six months at least -- and consistently enough to have to deal emotionally with rapid regrouping of defenses such as denial and projection and to live through the broken promises encountered with several admissions of the same persons. Adequate training should also include group experience in which the trainee himself is in a group of an experiential nature.

The history of most alcoholism staffs is that they never achieve integration and have difficulty keeping people long enough to accumulate experience as a group. Many factors of an attitudinal nature and organizational nature are involved (Gottheil, 1975). A number of factors keep recurring which contribute to lack of interest and workers' discouragement. In one inpatient service program with which I am familiar, there were 28 readmitted persons out of 105 admissions in one month. The 28 people have a tendency to seem like 100. The reasons for this exaggeration result from the realization that many patients are not interested in themselves and their treatment. They readily deny there is anything wrong with them although they have to hang onto the wall to come in and say that they are all right. They look and act like our concept of skid row alcoholics though they are not on skid row. Despite the persistent presentations of writers on this concept (Blane, Overton, & Chavetz, 1963; Wolf, Chafetz, Blane, & Hill, 1965) problems still persist. Actually fairly good responses with current treatment methods have been achieved.

Although attitudinal stumbling blocks seem more persistent, organizational factors are as insurmountable. Gottheil (1975) describes three areas of organizational concern: (a) fragmentary and disconnected services; (b) lack of transitional resources; and (c) outcome criterial and conflicting objectives.

Several of the ways we have chosen to work with these problems include: (a) the use of an outside consultant for an intensive one or two-day workshop involving all segments of the staff; (b) an ongoing staff group led by an outside consultant in which it is appropriate to discuss interpersonal working problems; (c) a weekly or bi-weekly gathering of staff; and (d) a daily staff report which deals with patient and non-patient happenings. Growth and survival are the two words that epitomize education and training. They require constant work which means frequent contact for the kinds of experiences mentioned above.

REFERENCES

Accreditation manual for alcoholism programs. Chicago: Joint Commission of Accreditation of Hospitals, 1974.

Alcohol Health and Research World. Rockville, Maryland: National Clearinghouse for Alcohol Information.

Alcohol and health: First special report to the U.S. Congress. (DHEW Publication No. (HSM 72-9099). Washington, D.C.: U.S. Governmant Printing Office, 1971.

Barr, H.L., Rosen, A., & Antes, D.E. *Two year follow-up study of 724 drug and alcohol addicts treated together in an abstinence therapeutic community*. Unpublished paper presented at the Fifth Annual Methadone Conference, Washington, D.C. March 1973. National Association for Prevention of Addiction to Narcotics.

Beigel, A. *Organizational approaches to the delivery of "comprehensive" community-based alcoholism services*. Paper presented at the Third Annual Alcoholism Conference of the National Institute of Alcohol Abuse and Alcoholism. Washington, D.C., June 1973.

Blane, H.T., Overton, W.F., & Chafetz, M.E. Social factors in diagnosis of alcoholism. I. Characteristics of the patient. *Quarterly Journal of Studies on Alcoholism*, 1963, *24*, 640-643.

Bradley, D.S. Recommendations for alcohol detoxification services. In G.G. Pavloff (Ed.), *Proceedings*: *Seminar on alcoholism emergency care services*. DHEW Publication No. (HSM) 73-9024. Washington, D.C.: U.S. Government Printing Office, 1972.

Cahalan, D. *Problem drinkers*: *A national survey*. San Francisco: Jossey-Bass Inc., 1970.

Cahalan, D., Cisin, I.H., & Crossley, H.M. *American drinking practices*: *A national study of drinking behavior and attitudes*. New Brunswick, N.J.: Rutgers Center of Alcohol Studies, 1969. (Monograph No. 6.)

Carkuff, R.R., & Berenson, B.G. *Beyond counseling and therapy*. New York: Holt, Rinehart & Winston, Inc., 1967.

Carruth, B., Williams, E., Mysock, P., & Boudreaux, L. Community care providers and the older problem drinker. In *Selected papers, 24th Annual Meeting of the Alcohol and Drug Problems Association of North America*. Washington, D.C., 1973.

Child, I.L. A cross-cultural study of drinking. I. Descriptive measurements of drinking customs. *Quarterly Journal of Studies on Alcohol*, 1965, *Suppl. 3*, 1-28.

Criteria Committee, National Council on Alcoholism. Criteria for the diagnosis of alcoholism. *American Journal of Psychiatry*, 1972, *129*, 127-135.

Cross, J. *Guide to community control of alcoholism.* New York: American Public Health Association, 1968.

Cureton, L.W. Police records for drunkenness and behavior problems of their children. *Proceedings of the First Annual Alcoholism Conference of National Institute of Alcohol Abuse and Alcoholism*, 1973.

Dailey, R.C. The role of alcohol among North American Indian tribes as reported in the Jesuit Relations. *Anthropologica*, 1968, *10*, 45-57.

Davies, D.L., Shepherd, M., & Myers, E. The two-years' prognosis of 50 alcohol addicts after treatment in hospital. *Quarterly Journal of Studies on Alcoholism*, 1956, *17*, 485-502.

Developing community services for alcoholics: some beginning principles. National Institute of Alcohol Abuse and Alcoholism, (DHEW Publication No. (ADM) 74-77). Washington, D.C.: U.S. Government Printing Office, 1974.

Drug use in America: Problems in perspective. Second report of The National Commission on Marijuana and Drug Abuse. Washington, D.C.: U.S. Government Printing Office, 1973.

Feldman, D.J., Pattison, E.M., Sobell, L.C., Graham, T., & Sobell, M.B. Outpatient alcohol detoxification: Initial findings on 564 patients. *American Journal of Psychiatry*, 1975, *132*, 407-412.

Fox, V. *The best prime therapist for an alcoholic is an interdisciplinary team.* Paper presented at the 29th International Congress on Alcoholism and Drug Dependence, Melbourne, Australia, February 1970.

Fox, V. Recommendations for detoxification services. In G.G. Pavloff (Ed.) *Proceedings: Seminar on alcoholism emergency care service.* (DHEW Publication No. (HSM) 73-9024). Washington, D.C.: U.S. Government Printing Office, 1972.

Gilliam, J. *The culture of security.* New Orleans: Tulane University, Middle American Research Institute, 1951.

Glasscote, R.A., Plaut, T.F.A., Hammersley, D.W., O'Neill, F.J., Chafetz, M.E., & Cummings, F. *Treatment of alcoholism: A study of programs and problems.* Washington, D.C.: The Joint Information Service of the American Psychiatric Association and the National Association of Mental Health, 1967.

Gottheil, E. Poor morale in treatment personnel. *Alcohol Health and Research World*, Spring 1975.

Grad, F.P. Legal aspects of alcoholism. In Bourne, P.G., & Fox, R. (Ed.), *Alcoholism: Progress in research and treatment*. New York: Academic Press, 1973.

Guidelines for planning and developing state and community alcohol safety programs. (U.S. Department of Transportation Publication No. DOT, Hs, 800-955). Washington, D.C.: U.S. Government Printing Office, 1973.

Horton, D. The functions of alcohol in primitive societies: A cross-cultural study. *Quarterly Journal of Studies on Alcohol*, 1943, *4*, 199-320.

Jackson, J.K. The adjustment of the family to the crisis of alcoholism. *Quarterly Journal of Studies on Alcoholism*, 1954, *15*, 562-586.

Jellinek, E.M. *The disease concept of alcoholism*. New Haven: Hillhouse Press, 1960.

Keller, M. *Some views on the nature of alcoholism.* Presented at the 15th International Institute on Prevention and Treatment of Alcoholism, Budapest, Hungary, June 1969. Pamphlet).

Keller, M. Multidisciplinary perspectives on alcoholism and the need for integration: An historical and prospective note. *Journal of Studies on Alcohol*, 1975, *36*, 133-147.

Kellermann, J.L. *A guide for the family of the alcoholic.* New York: Al-Anon Family Group Headquarters, 1972. Also available from Kemper Insurance Group, Long Grove, Ill.

Kellerman, J.L. Focus on the family. *Alcohol Health and Research World*, Fall 1974.

Kendell, R.E., & Stanton, M.D. The fate of untreated alcoholics. *Quarterly Journal of Studies on Alcohol*, 1966, *27*, 30-41.

Leake, C.D., & Silverman, M. *Alcoholic beverages in clinical medicine*. Chicago: Year Book Medical Publisher, Inc. 1966.

Levy, J.E., & Kunitz, S.J. Indian drinking: Problem of data collection and interpretation. *Proceedings of the First Annual Alcoholism Conference of the National Institute on Alcohol Abuse and Alcoholism*, 1973.

MacAndrew, C., & Edgerton, R.B. *Drunken comportment: A social explanation.* Chicago: Aldine, 1969.

Methvin, C.B. *Demonstration of community services for alcoholics.* Demonstration Project No. MH 49 343-03-69. Atlanta: Georgia Department of Public Health, 1969.

Mitnick, L. The problem in perspective. *Alcohol Health and Research World*, Spring 1974.

Mulford, H.A. Metting the problem of alcohol abuse: A testable action plan for Iowa. *Selected Papers, 21st Annual Meeting,NAAAP,*, San Antonio, Texas, 1970.

O'Briant, R.G. *New look in non-medical care for the public inebriate.* Paper presented at the Fourth Annual Alcoholism Conference, NIAAA, Washington, D.C., June 1974.

Ottenberg, D.J. Detoxification in a community alcoholism treatment program. In G.G. Pavloff (Ed.), *Proceedings: Seminar on alcoholism emergency care services.* (DHEW Publication No. (HSM) 73-9024. Washington, D.C.: U.S. Government Printing Office, 1972.

Pavloff, G.G. The alcoholic felon. *Alcohol Health and Research World*, Fall 1974.

Pilot project for clinical training of clergymen in the field of alcoholism. National Institute of Mental Health Demonstration Project, MH 8589. 1964-1969.

Pittman, D.J., & Snyder, C.R. *Society, culture, and drinking problems.* New York: John Wiley & Sons, 1962.

Pittman, D.J., & Sterne, M.W. *Alcoholism: Community agency attitudes and their impact on treatment services.* Washington, D.C.: U.S. Public Health Service Publication No. 1723, 1965.

Plaut, T.F.A. *Alcohol problems: A report to the nation by the Cooperative Commission on the Study of Alcoholism.* New York: Oxford University Press, 1967.

Proceedings on Alcohol Emergency Care Service, NIAAA, (DHEW publication No. (HSM) 73-9024). Washington, D.C.: U.S. Government Printing Office, 1972.

Roman, P.M., & Trice, H.M. *Schizophrenia and the poor*. Ithaca: New York State School of Industrial and Labor Relations, 1967.

Roman, P.M., & Trice, H.M. Alcoholism and the worker. In P.G. Bourne & R. Fox (Eds.), *Alcoholism: Progress in research and treatment*.. New York: Academic Press, 1973.

Rosin, J., & Glatt, M.M. Alcohol excess in the elderly. *Quarterly Journal of Studies on Alcohol*, 1971, *32*, 53-59.

Rouse, B.I., Waller, P., & Ewing, J. *Adolescents' stress level, coping activities and fathers' drinking behavior*. 81st Annual Meeting of American Psychological Association, Montreal, 1973.

Siegal, H.H. *Alcohol detoxification programs: Treatment instead of jail*. Springfield, Ill.: Charles C Thomas, 1973.

Status Report. St. Paul, Minn.: Association of Halfway Houses, 1974.

Staub, G., & Kent. L.M. *Paraprofessionals in the treatment of alcoholism: A new profession*. Springfield, Ill.: Charles C Thomas, 1973.

Treffent, D.A. Is it in drugs or in people? *Rehabilitation Record*, March-April 1971.

Traux, C.G., & Carkhuff, R.R. *Toward effective counseling and psychology: Training and practice*. Chicago: Alcine Publishing Co., 1967.

Uniform crime report for the United States - 1973. Issued by Clarence M. Kelley, Director, F.B.I., Washington, D.C.: U.S. Government Printing Office, 1974.

Waddell, J.O. "Drink friend!" - social context of convivial drinking and drunkenness among Papago Indians in an urban setting. *Proceedings of the First Annual Conference of the National Institute of Alcohol Abuse and Alcoholism*. 1971.

Winkler, A.M. Drinking on the American frontier. *Quarterly Journal of Studies on Alcohol*, 1968, *29*, 413-445.

Wolf, I., Chafetz, M.E., Blane, H.T., & Hill, M.J. Some factors in diagnosis of alcoholism. II. Attitudes of physicians. *Quarterly Journal of Studies on Alcohol*, 1965, *26*, 72-79.

Wolf, S. Counseling for better or worse. *Selected papers, 23rd Annual Meeting of the Alcohol and Drug Problems Association of North America.* Washington, D.C., 1972.

Zimberg, S. The elderly alcoholic. *Gerontologist*, 1974, *14*, 221-224.

CHAPTER 22

FAMILY THERAPY

Donald E. Meeks

> Whether a particular pathology is conceived to inhere in an individual or in a situation determines the locus and mode of the intended interventions. (Lennard & Berstein, 1969, p.3)

Traditionally, therapists have assumed alcohol problems to reside primarily in the body, mind, or behavior of the drinker. As a consequence, therapy has been directed primarily toward the individual. In recent years with the more rigorous application of social science concepts to socio-behavioral therapies, those assumptions have been challenged. A contemporary view of alcohol problems requires consideration of interacting biological, intrapersonal, and social systems. Given such a comprehensive view, differential assessment will indicate the required directions and modes of intervention.

While intervention in certain broader social systems (e.g., economic or political) may lie outside the purview of

Ralph E. Tarter and A. Arthur Sugerman (eds.), Alcoholism

ISBN: 0-201-08146-6
ISBN: 0-201-08145-8 (pbk.)

therapy, therapists increasingly conceive intervention in other relevant social systems (e.g., family, industrial, and judicial) as integral to their helping functions. Drinking may indicate stress or dysfunction in a social system, may be secondary to dysfunction in a social system, or may lead to dysfunction in a social system. In this framework, some alcohol problems may reside as much in social structures and processes as in people.

A consideration of extrinsic factors broadens our therapeutic focus to include other significant individuals and groups. This chapter views the family as a small social system. It is concerned with those situations where family dysfunction plays a significant role in alcohol proglems. A family therapy perspective requires that interpersonal transactions rather than disease or psychopathology become the primary reference points for the behavior under study: the family as a whole becomes the unit of therapy. To facilitate recovery, to consolidate gains made in therapy with the drinking member, and to minimize the risks of a drinking relapse, not only the drinker but the entire family system must be helped to change.

THEORETICAL FRAMEWORK

The theoretical underpinnings of family therapy can be traced to Kurt Goldstein (1939) and other organismic theorists influenced by the Gestalt movement. Goldstein observed that individual behaviors could best be understood as manifestations of the total organic environment in which the behaviors take place.

> The laws of the whole govern the functioning of the differentiated parts of the whole. Consequently, it is necessary to discover the laws by which the whole organism functions in order to understand the functioning of any member component. (Goldstein, 1939)

Theories underpinning work with families and other groups were strongly influenced by these tenets. Polsky (1963) applied organismic concepts and the structural-functional theories of Parsons (1953) to group therapy. This model posited that group organization should be treated as an independent variable, not solely determined by the properties of its individual units. In therapy, the group is viewed as a means rather than a context for changing individuals. If the group remains unchanged, it may militate against changes in an individual member. In applying these concepts to family therapy, Haley (1962) contends that "changes in the individual can occur only if the family system changes, and resistance to change in the individual centers in the influence of the family as a group."

The influence of role interaction in affective (emotional) and instrumental (goal-oriented) family activities is further explicated by the concept of equilibrium. Equilibrium refers to the tendency of a social system to achieve a balance among the various forces operating within and upon it (Chin, 1969). Equilibrium may be described as the permissible range of variations (e.g. behaviors) that may occur within a system without loss of its identity and organization (Lennard & Berstein, 1969). Behavior that markedly deviates from patterned role expectations may be perceived as threatening and disruptive to the established order. To avoid disruption, the family may act to force deviant behavior back in the direction of its core values.

The idea of the family as a role-governing, rule-enforcing system with the capability to induce or maintain pathology was first advanced in studies of the families of schizophrenics (Jackson, 1960; Lidz, Cornelius, Fleck, & Terry, 1957; Wynne, 1958). The concept of family resistance to changes in equilibrium was further elaborated in the work of Haley (1962). Equilibrating mechanisms in a family may be employed to support "healthy" behavior or to create and support "sick" behavior. Behavior that is functional for the group may be dysfunctional in the view of outside observers. For some families, sobriety may be functional for the system. For others, continued drinking may be functional. It is axiomatic that rigidity in a family system may run counter to therapeutic aims in work with alcoholics.

FAMILIES OF ALCOHOLICS

Developments in work with the families of alcoholics run parallel to developments in other problem areas with a sociobehavioral component. Literature dating back to the mid-nineteenth and early 20th century reflects a moralistic view. Alcoholics were regarded as villains and families as victims. Approaches to assistance typecast the drinker as character defective and, thus, incorrigible. Helping efforts were geared toward other members of the family, usually wives and children (Bailey, 1963).

With the advent of psychoanalytic concepts, the drinker came to be regarded as a victim - of his unconscious. Attributing his drinking to unconscious drives and motivations required a similar attribution to the spouse. This perspective is best illustrated by Whalen's (1953) characterization of the prototypes of wives of alcoholics: viz., Suffering Susan, Controlling Catherine, Wavering Winifred, and Punitive Polly. It was widely accepted (and still is by some) that the wives of alcoholics were women whose unconscious led them to require martyrdom, to have a need to control others, to vacillate weakly in the face of opposing drives, or to be hostile toward men.

Long before the advent of system theory, Knight (1937) and Chassell (1938) stressed the importance of understanding the total family in order to understand individual drinking behavior. In intervening years, clinicians have reported that in some families the well-being of other family members seems to be dependent upon the alcoholic member's continued drinking; in others, the nondrinking member began to decompensate as the drinking member got better; that spouses often sought to sabotage treatment; and that drinking relapses frequently were influenced by the re-entry of a recovered alcoholic into a family that had not changed (Bailey, 1968).

Jackson's three-year study (1954) reported seven stages in the adjustment of the family to alcoholism: attempts to deny the problem, attempts to eliminate the problem, disorganization, attempts to reorganize in spite of the problem, efforts to escape the problem, reorganization of part of the family, and recovery and reorganization of the whole family. To the extent that these adjustments reflect efforts to avoid family disruption and disorganization, they are adaptable to a systems approach as will be illustrated later.

Since the late 1960's, more of the literature has been

rooted in interpersonal concepts and "theories". In *Games Alcoholics Play*, Steiner (1971) employs transactional analysis to describe interpersonal transactions. Two of the three alcoholic games, "Drunk and Proud" and "Lush," revolve around the mutual perceptions and interdependent actions of the husband-wife dyad. Treatment is directed toward role interactions involving parent, adult, and child ego states. Gorad (1971) examined the interaction of alcoholic husbands and their wives under experimental conditions. He found the communication of alcoholics to be characterized by responsibility-avoidance messages in their interaction. The reverse was true in the communication styles of wives. He also found the couple unable to cooperate as a unit for mutual benefit.

Hanson, Shanks, and Sheldon (1968) found alcoholic husbands to be less open and revealing about themselves and their feelings than their wives. Steinglass, Winer, and Mendels (1971) examined interactional patterns of paired family members with a previous history as drinking companions, (i.e., father and son, brothers). The drinking took place in a controlled ward environment. Drinking interaction was found to be governed by rules clearly related to the "drinking system." Changes in role interaction were charted by observing these familial dyads during pre-drinking, drinking, and post-drinking stages. Each stage had a distinctive set of rules governing role performance. Behavior could better be understood in relation to the system governing role performance at a given time than by understanding the personalities involved. Rae and Drewery (1972) in their study of marital patterns found male alcoholic subjects to be more "feminine" than male controls, confused about their sociosexual roles, and more conflicted about needs for dependence and independence.

It is fair to say that these findings are not always directly applicable to interpersonally-oriented work with the families of alcoholics. It is, nonetheless, useful to consider games, impoverished communication, avoidance of responsibility, inability to cooperate in goal-oriented activity, patterned behavior in drinking systems, confusion in sociosexual roles, and dependence-independence conflicts as partial formulations relative to role interaction. For the clinician more importance may be attached to the actual practice of family therapy. The next section contains some practical guides for family therapy with families of alcoholics with reference to the relevant literature.

FAMILY THERAPY WITH THE FAMILIES OF ALCOHOLICS

Work with families of alcoholics has been undertaken in four primary formats: marital counseling, marital or couples groups, counseling with the nondrinking spouse and children, and conjoint family therapy. Marital counseling is focused on the interaction of the marital couple (Bailey, 1968). Marital or couples groups bring together a number of alcoholics and their spouses (Cadogan, 1973). In some settings, efforts are made to work with other family members, exclusive of the drinking member who will not engage in therapy (Cork, 1969). Conjoint family therapy generally involves the parents, children, and sometimes others forming a common household. While the focus of this chapter is on conjoint family therapy, modalities should be employed to fit specific situations and problems.

Studies of family therapy, in general, are rare and are marked by the absence of a unifying model which would permit replication or accurate comparison of findings. The Group for the Advancement of Psychiatry (GAP) found that only three percent of family therapists surveyed were involved in research (Olson, 1970). Research into family therapy with the families of alcoholics is virtually nonexistent. Cheek and Mendelson (1973) designed a program using behavior modification techniques to modify "destructive interaction" of couples with an alcoholic member. Esser (1970) directed his intervention toward the family system of the alcoholic, including children where possible. Likewise, Meeks and Kelly (1970) studied family therapy with the families of recovering alcoholics. That investigation also attempted, with little success, to involve children. None of these studies employed controls. The following guide to work with families of alcoholics is drawn from these reports and others based on clinical experience.

THE INTERVENTIVE PROCESS

IDENTIFIED PATIENT EFFECTS. Alcoholism involves not only the interaction of a person with an environment but the interaction of a person with a drug. It may be necessary for the drinker to undergo some form of treatment for the drinking before family therapy can proceed effectively. Little light is shed in the literature about efforts to work with entire families at, or near, the beginning of treatment. If the drinking member is involved in a separate therapeutic process, he or she is reinforced in the "identified patient" or "identified problem-bearer" role. Subsequent efforts to shift the focus to the family as the unit of treatment may be difficult. One promising approach to reduce "identified patient" effects is to see the spouse and other family members separately, gradually shifting the focus from the drinking and the drinker to family interaction. This may pave the way for eventually bringing the whole family together with a transactional system focus (Meeks & Kelly, 1970). The family therapist aims to help the family focus on all contributions to family interaction and problems, including the drinking.

THERAPIST ORIENTATION. The conceptual orientation of the therapist is critical. A traditional orientation to *intra-personal* approaches makes difficult the quantum leap to a focus on transactional systems. A transactional systems approach, not to be confused with transactional analysis, deals with the here-and-now process of family interrelationships. In a "Family Systems Approach to Alcoholism," Bowan (1974) observes that the focus in on *what* happened, *how* it happened, and *when* and *where* it happened, insofar as observations are made on fact. It carefully avoids man's automatic preoccupation with *why* it happened. In that context, the therapist is concerned with reciprocal actions, reactions, ways of relating, communicating, and meeting needs in a given family.

> The family system operates in such a way that any change in one member has an impact on the whole family. Within the transactional framework, the focus is on the process of the family as a system. As a result, the family is ideally treated conjointly during most or all of the therapy sessions. (Olson, 1970, p. 509)

CONTRACT. Whatever preparation has preceded, initial attention must be given to clarify why the entire family is being seen in therapy. This may best be done in the context of developing a "contract" describing the mutual expectations of therapist and family members. In that setting, residual "identified patient" effects, "scapegoating," and other perceptions and processes may be readily identified. The establishment of a contract, from the standpoint of the therapist is at once a diagnostic step and a process through which the family is helped to conceptualize issues in a transactional system framework. As well, the contract establishes shared expectations about the frequency of therapy sessions, processes to be employed, expectations about the attendance of family members, and the goals of therapy. Embodying assessment, the contract culminates in a plan for action. It should be perceived as binding on therapist and family members but open to renegotiation. Goal setting should avoid a narrow focus on drinking behavior. A range of problems (e.g., parenting, managing finances, employement, sexual adjustment) may rank high in importance. A useful device is the goal-scaling technique advanced by Kiresuk (1968) which provides a framework for listing and measuring goal-attainment.

FAMILIES OF MALE AND FEMALE ALCOHOLICS. In a previous paper (Meeks & Kelly, 1970) we have described the relative difficulties observed in reducing "identified patient" effects with male and female alcoholic members. Alcoholic wives seemed (a) more inclined to accept and reinforce the "identified patient" role, and (b) nondrinking wives seemed better able to shift the focus away from their drinking husbands to to family transactions. While these findings offer fertile grounds for speculation, they have yet to be confirmed by a controlled study. We may be remiss in the uncritical application of models derived from studies involving male alcoholics in our work with families of female alcoholics.

EQUILIBRIUM. It is important to individualize families and the transactional patterns that characterize their interaction. The therapist, in effect, becomes a student of a given family's normative rules, affective and instrumental roles, verbal and non-verbal communication, and ways of dealing with pressures from within the family and from outside. Taken together these observations provide a picture of that family's equilibrium. Not only are these interactional patterns observed by the therapist; they should be the subject of ongoing feedback by the therapist as well. The goal of the process is itself a process whereby family members improve their ability to observe family behaviors, provide feedback, and improve techniques of problem prevention and problem-solving. Family therapy is posited on the belief that feedback - collective inputs to a system -- can be error-correcting. Feedback may come from outside (e.g., a therapist) or from family members. With some families it is useful to teach them the theory being employed so that cognitive as well as affective mechanisms can be brought into play.

THERAPIST STYLE. Ford and Urban (1963) describe two distinct approaches to family therapy, *conducting* and *reacting*. Conductors are more active in organizing, orchestrating, leading.

Reactors are less controlling, letting the interaction develop with less structure and control. Clinical observations, unverified by systematic study, suggest the efficacy of a more active approach (i.e., conducting) with the families of alcoholics because:

1. The therapeutic process is often characterized by ambivalence, denial, and avoidance.
2. Concrete goals established early in the process seem to be associated with successful outcomes in therapy.
3. "Identified patient" effects may be more difficult to overcome with families of alcoholics when a passive approach is employed.

As will be discussed later, the active penetration of the denial conspiracy must take into account the family functions served by the denial. Because acceptance of the problem requires fundamental shifts in the established equilibrium, resistance can be anticipated. Where resistance to giving up the denial is encountered, the active therapist will help the family to explore the implications of problem acceptance and its potential for threat. In this way an early abortion of therapy may be averted.

COMMUNICATION AND RULES. Family rules can be understood by observing the communication implicit in all patterns of family interaction. With the inclusion of nonverbal communication, communication may be regarded as synonymous with interaction. Ways of relating contain messages patterned by shared role expectations or rules. Each family has rules about (a) self-expression, (b) what members expect of other members, and (c) how members are expected to relate outside the family (Satir, 1971). Some rules are clear and explicit. Others may not be in conscious awareness. The therapist can help the family understand their own rules and the effects of these rules on transactions and individual behavior.

Family members can be helped to become critical spectators of their own "games" and to interrupt them, using the therapist as a role model. Communication patterns may also be made more vivid by using videotapes of family interviews as a means of feedback. Particular attention may be given to how individuality and differences are expressed and reacted to and how decisions are made.

Understanding these patterns helps the therapist and the family to discern rules for manifesting self, validating one's uniqueness to others, validating individuality, making decisions, acknowledging the presence of differences and reacting to and using differentness as a vehicle for growth (Satir, 1970).

STAGES OF FAMILY ADJUSTMENT: CLINICAL IMPLICATIONS. Jackson's (1954) seven stages of family adjustment to alcoholism provide a sequential framework for considering clinical implications at various stages in the progression of the problem. In the initial phase, the drinker may be joined by the wife and older children in a virtual conspiracy to deny the problem or its severity. The family may approximate a closed system in its inability to observe and report reality or to accept feedback from anyone inside or outside the system. This is a misguided effort to avoid the threat of family disintegration. It is unlikely that help from a therapist will be sought at this stage. Early intervention requires that helping persons at key contact points actively intervene to change communication in the system as clues to the drinking problem are detected.

In the face of absences from work, relationship problems, the drain of family finances, and repeated drinking episodes, the nondrinking spouse may be the first to abandon the denial. This may produce a marital "schism" as husband and wife begin to perceive reality differently. The children may be forced to take sides. As the family rules undergo transition, a period of anomie (i.e., "normlessness") may prevail. The now desperate spouse may seek magical solutions from a helping agency. While magical solutions do not exist, help can be given to the spouse and children. This help may focus on assistance in objectifying the situation and considering the options available for adjustment and getting the drinking member into treatment.

Eventually the drinking member may be excluded from the "healthier" aspects of role interaction. The tendency of the system toward organization may lead to a reorganization of the rest of the family under the leadership of the nondrinking spouse. It is here, before therapy begins, that the drinker is first cast in the "identified problem" or "scapegoat" role. Once this new equilibrium is established, resistance to changing it will often create problems as the recovering alcoholic seeks to resume his or her relinquished status and associated roles.

It is sometimes difficult to conceive family adjustment to sobriety as a difficult stage. It is a stage when the equilibrium established around the drinking behavior must shift to accommodate the drinker's reentry into functional role interaction; when trust, eroded by a multitude of drinking episodes, must be restored; when other family members must relinquish new, sometimes satisfying roles against the hope that, this time sobriety will be sustained; when patterns of meeting emotional needs must be altered; when the projection of all family problems onto the drinker are no longer reasonable. Often it is the expectation of the family that when the drinking stops, all other problems will disappear. In fact, relationships may become worse as other deep-seated problems are unmasked and can no longer be attributed to the drinking (Cohen, 1966).

The family purposes served by the drinker's being assigned or assuming the scapegoat role are no long fulfilled. By providing a focal point for the projection of family discord, the scapegoat provides a channel for problem avoidance. By bringing the rest of the family together in opposition to the drinker, to protect the drinker or themselves or to maintain a sense of order and stability, the scapegoat performs a "binder" role. The closeness established in this way must be relinquished with sobriety and the reentry of the drinking member. It is in this context that the therapist and family must consider resistance to changes in the drinker both in terms of what the family may gain and what it may be giving up. The stage of recovery, far from being a time when family therapy is less needed, may be a time when work with the whole family is critical.

It was stated earlier that the goals of the family therapy process are to improve communication, problem-prevention, and problem-solving. Desirably, the active role of the therapist early in the process will give way to more active contributions by family members. The ultimate goal is to enable family members to learn techniques of communication, as well as techniques of dealing with real and potential problems that can be used in the real world outside of therapy.

SUMMARY

The application of communication, role, and general system theory to family therapy has opened up new avenues for study and treatment. The family is conceived as a small social system with properties different from the sum of its parts. Changing a family member in isolation from the family system may be ineffectual. To consolidate gains made in the individual treatment of the drinker and to minimize the risk of relapse, the family system must be helped to change. As a change-agent, the family therapist focuses on communication and other transactions of the family rather than on changing only individual members. Research into interpersonal transactions in families of alcoholics is increasing in scope and rigor. As yet, few of the studies are sufficiently rigorous to permit replication or generalizability. Clinical reports suggest the efficacy of working with entire families in which a member has a drinking problem.

REFERENCES

Bailey, M.B. (Ed.), *Alcoholism and family casework.* New York: Community Council of Greater New York, 1968.

Bailey, M.B. The family agency's role in treating the wife of an alcoholic. *Social Casework,* 1963, *44*(5), 273-279.

Bowan, M. A family systems approach to alcoholism. *Addictions,* 1974, *21,* 28-40.

Cadogan, D.A. Marital group therapy in the treatment of alcoholism. *Quarterly Journal of Studies on Alcohol,* 1973, *34,* 1187-1194.

Chassel, J. Family constellation in the etiology of essential alcoholism. *Psychiatry*, 1938, *1*, 473-503.

Cheek, F.E., & Mendelson, M. Developing behavior modification programs with emphasis on self-control. *Hospital and Community Psychiatry*, 1973, *24*, 410-416.

Chin, R. The utility of system models and developmental models for practitioners. In B. Bennis, D. Benne, & R. Chin, (Eds.), *The planning of change*. New York: Holt, Rinehart & Winston, Inc., 1969.

Cohen, P. *A new approach to the treatment of male alcoholics and their families*. Unpublished manuscript, 1966. (Available from the Family Service Association of the Cincinnati Area).

Cork, M.R. *The forgotten children*. Toronto: Addiction Research Foundation, 1969.

Esser, P. Conjoint family therapy with alcoholics - A new approach. *British Journal of Addictions*, 1970, *64*, 275-286.

Ford, D. & Urban, H. *Systems of psychotherapy*. New York: John Wiley & Sons, 1963.

Goldstein, K. *The organism*. New York: American Book Co., 1939.

Gorad, S. Communication styles and interaction of alcoholics and their wives. *Family Process*, 1971, *32*, 475-489.

Haley, J. Whither family therapy. *Family Process*, 1962, *1*, 69-100.

Hanson, R., Shanks, R., & Sheldon, R. Patterns of communication in alcoholic married couples. *Psychiatric Quarterly*, 1968, *42*, 538-547.

Jackson, D.D. (Ed.), *The etiology of schizophrenia*. New York: Basic Books, 1960.

Jackson, J.K. The adjustment of the family to the crisis of alcoholism. *Quarterly Journal of Studies on Alcohol*, 1954, *15*, 562-586.

Kiresuk, T.J., & Sherman, R.E. Goal-attainment scaling: A general method for evaluating community mental health programs. *Community Mental Health Journal*, 1968, *4*, 443-453.

Knight, R. The dynamics and treatment of chronic alcohol addiction. *Bulletin of the Menninger Clinic*, 1937, *1*, 233-250.

Lennard, H.L., & Berstein, A. Clinical sociology: A new focus. *Patterns of human interaction.* San Francisco: Jossey Bass, Inc., 1969.

Lidz, T., Cornelius, S., Fleck, S., & Terry, D. Schism and skew in the families of schizophrenics. *American Journal of Psychiatry*, 1957, *64*, 241-248.

Meeks, D., & Kelly, C. Family therapy with the families of recovering alcoholics. *Quarterly Journal of Studies on Alcohol*, 1970, *31*, 399-413.

Olson, D.H. Marital and family therapy: Integrative review and critique. *Journal of Marriage and the Family*, 1970, *32*, 501-538.

Parsons, T., Bales, R.E., & Shils, E. Phase movement in relation to motivation, symbol formation and role structure. *Working papers in the theory of action.* Glencoe, Illinois: The Free Press, 1953.

Polsky, H.W. *Structural-functional theory: Guideline to group work.* Paper presented at the meeting of the Group Work Section, National Association of Social Workers, New York City, March, 1963.

Rae, J., & Drewery, J. Interpersonal patterns in alcoholic marriages. *British Journal of Psychiatry*, 1972, *120*, 615-621.

Satir, U. The family as a treatment unit. In J. Haley (Ed.), *Changing families*. New York: Grune & Stratton, 1971.

Steiner, C. *Games alcoholics play*. New York: Grove Press, 1971.

Steinglass, P., Winer, S., & Mendelson, J. A systems approach to alcoholism: A model and its clinical application. *Archives of General Psychiatry*, 1971, *24*, 201-408.

Whalen, T. Wives of alcoholics: Four types observed in a Family Service Agency. *Quarterly Journal of Studies on Alcohol*, 1953, *14*, 632-641.

Wynne, L.C. Pseudo-mutuality in families of schizophrenics. *Psychiatry*, 1958, *21*, 205-220.

INDEX

Addison-Wesley Publishing Company, Inc.
Advanced Book Program
Reading, Massachusetts